THE WHOLE GOLF CATALOG

THE WHOLE GOLF CATALOG

*YOUR GUIDE TO ALL THE
IMPORTANT SOURCES, RESOURCES, AND
SERVICES IN THE WORLD OF GOLF*

Edited by LARRY SHEEHAN

NEW YORK **ATHENEUM** *1979*

LIBRARY OF CONGRESS CATALOGING IN PUBLICATION DATA
Main entry under title:
The Whole golf catalog.

1. Golf.   I. Sheehan, Larry.
GV965.W614 1979   796.352   78-20351
ISBN 0-689-10979-2

Designed by Helen Barrow
FIRST EDITION

Contents

Instruction

BEST-SELLING INSTRUCTION BOOKS OF ALL TIME
CONSENSUS ON THE GOLF SWING
CONSENSUS ON SWING FAULTS AND CURES
PSYCHOLOGICAL MATERIALS
INSTRUCTION BOOKS FOR THE WOMAN GOLFER
INSTRUCTION BOOKS FOR THE LEFTHANDER
GOLF SCHOOLS
GOLF INSTRUCTION FILMS
SOME LEADING U.S. GOLF INSTRUCTORS

BEST-SELLING INSTRUCTION BOOKS OF ALL TIME

To paraphrase Henry Cotton on the subject of the golf swing, estimating golf-book sales is an art, not a science. What follows is a first attempt to list the instruction books that have sold the most copies over the years. According to an impressive bibliography developed by Joseph S. F. Murdoch, over 450 golf-instruction books have appeared and spread their wisdom since the appearance in 1857 of *The Golfer's Manual* by "A Keen Hand." I have not seen all of these, and of those I have seen, I have been able to obtain reliable sales figures on relatively few. On the other hand, I have had the benefit of informed guesswork by various writers, edtiors, and publishers as to what books may have managed to or definitely did sell in volume in their day, and these have lent some credibility to what follows. I am more certain of my facts and figures on those books published since World War II than those which came out before it. For the postwar period, I have had to arbitrarily DQ any books that appear to have sold less than 100,000 copies—no matter how worthy they otherwise may have been in style or content. Indeed, I have no figures on the early books. I have limited my gropings primarily to books published in the U.S., with the exception of the three 19th-century classics that lead off this how-to hit parade.

1887

THE ART OF GOLF by Sir Walter Simpson. 186 pages, Edinburgh: David Douglas.

Ernest Jones, Bernard Darwin, Henry Cotton, and Ben Crenshaw, among others, have placed great store by this pioneering work. Written with genuine literary flourish and wit, it may deserve nomination as a best-seller, at least in relation to the total golfing population in those golden wood-shafted days. It did make a second printing. Simpson was a firm believer in permitting individualization of the swing to fit the player—an idea that perhaps pulls the rug out from under the premise on which much subsequent golf instruction was based.

1890

GOLF, Horace Hutchinson, ed. 463 pages, London: Badminton Library.

This was one in a collection of guides to sports and hobbies created expressly for the English Gentleman—something akin to a *Time-Life* series, only funded by a duke. Hutchinson was a good player as well as an expert writer and editor: he won the British Amateur two years running (1886 and 1887).

HUNTING TIGERS IS EASIER

Of all the games in which the soul of the Anglo-Saxon delights, there is perhaps none which is a severer test of that mysterious quality called "nerve" than the game of golf. It is a game in which a very great deal is apt to depend upon a single stroke—indeed, upon each single stroke throughout the round—and it is at the same time a game which calls for delicately-measured strokes, and, consequently, for steadiness and control of hand.

"I cannot understand at all," a famous tiger-slayer was once heard to exclaim, in desperation. "I have shot tigers in India, knowing that my life depended upon the steadiness of my aim, and could swear that the ball would go true through the heart; but here is a wretched little putt, a foot and a half long, and I miss it of very nervousness!"

—from *Golf*

1896

THE GAME OF GOLF by Willie Park, Jr. 227 pages, London: Longmans, Green.

Another milestone—the first book to publish the secrets of a pro: "How I won the 1887 and 1889 British Opens."

FIG. 24.—A GOOD TEE   FIG. 25.—A BAD TEE

An early "correct-incorrect" golf illustration, from <u>The Game of Golf</u>.

1901

PRACTICAL GOLF by Walter J. Travis. 266 pages, N.Y.: Harper.

Several editions appeared.

1905

THE COMPLETE GOLFER by Harry Vardon. 283 pages, N.Y.: McLure, Phillips.

This Vardon masterwork was reprinted 20 times or so. A later book, *How to Play Golf,* also performed well.

VARDON EXPLAINS HIS GRIP

Now comes the all-important consideration of the grip. This is another matter in which the practice of golfers differs greatly, and upon which there has been much controversy. My grip is one of my own invention. It differs materially from most others, and if I am asked to offer any excuse for it, I shall say that I adopted it only after a careful trial of all the other grips of which I had ever heard, that in theory and practice I find it admirable—more so than any other—and that in my opinion it has contributed materially to the attainment of such skill as I possess. My contention is that this grip of mine is sounder in theory and easier in practice, tends to make a better stroke and to secure a straighter ball, and that players who adopt it from the beginning will stand a much better chance of driving well at an early stage than if they went in for the old-fashioned two-V. My grip is an overlapping, but not an interlocking one. Modifications of it are used by many fine players, and it is coming into more general practice as its merits are understood and appreciated. I use it for all my strokes, and it is only when putting that I vary it in the least, and then the change is so slight as to be scarcely noticeable.

It will be seen at once that I do not grasp the club across the palm of either hand. The club being taken in the left hand first, the shaft passes from the knuckle joint of the first finger across the ball of the second. The left thumb lies straight down the shaft—that is to say, it is just to the right of the centre of the shaft. But the following are the significant features of the grip. The right hand is brought up so high that the palm of it covers over the left thumb, leaving very little of the latter to be seen. The first and second fingers of the right hand just reach round to the thumb of the left, and the third finger completes the overlapping process, so that the club is held in the grip as if it were in a vise. The little finger of the right hand rides on the first finger of the left. The great advantage of this grip is that both hands feel and act like one, and if, even while sitting in his chair, a player who has never tried it before will take a stick in his hands in the manner I have described, he must at once be convinced that there is a great deal in what I say for it, although, of course, if he has been accustomed to the two V's, the success of my grip cannot be guaranteed at the first trial. It needs some time to become thoroughly happy with it.

—from The Complete Golfer

1930

BOBBY JONES ON GOLF by Robert T. Jones, Jr. 112 pages, N.Y.: Metropolitan Fiction.

I am guessing that this paperback, which sold for 50¢ and, in a later edition, for $1.00, may have ridden the crest of Jones' Grand Slam achievement to substan-tial sales. Jones' good autobiographical work, *Down the Fairway*, had appeared three years earlier with critical if not great commercial success. Jones' real impact as an instructor for the masses came not in books but through a widely syndicated newspaper column (which Charles Price edited down to *Bobby Jones on Golf* for Doubleday in 1966) and a film series, produced by Warner Bros.

1932

A NEW WAY TO BETTER GOLF by Alex J. Morrison. 187 pages, N.Y.: Simon & Schuster.

By the time of its seventh printing, this book had sold 43,700 copies, and the knowledgeable golf editor Ross Goodner assures me that it eventually went into a 40th printing. Part of this success stemmed from the publisher's aggressive ad campaign, which featured many "testimonials," and to the author's own promotions—Morrison appeared on stage and in music halls with a "golf act." He also had many illustrious pupils, including Babe Ruth, Henry Ford, Douglas Fairbanks, and Charlie Chaplin, none of whose names he hesitated to drop in his book. Actually, hardly any show-business shines through his writing style, which is solemn, methodical, and at times rather overbearing. Morrison breaks down the swing into eight stages and explains each stage, using precise anatomical and mechanical references. Among other things, he believes golf is a "left-sided" game, and he advocates the interlocking grip.

POINTING THE CHIN

Unless the chin is pointed back of the ball before the start of the backswing, there is little chance of keeping it independent of the body action. If the chin is allowed to turn with the body, you immediately lose the only certain means of sensing and controlling the various positions and movements of the swing.

You cannot keep your chin pointed properly by observing the timeworn golfing precepts, "Keep your head down," and "Keep your eye on the ball." But the converse is true. Keeping your eye on the ball and your head in the proper position will follow of themselves if the chin is held in position. Actually to hold the head still throughout the swing is a physical impossibility, and the effort to do so results only in shutting off the principle source of muscular control. Also, you can stare at the ball till you're pop-eyed, and still fail to sense properly the movements of your body during the swing.

So important and so necessary to a successful swing is the pointing of the chin that, once the correct starting position is assumed, it is relatively easy to hit a successful shot with the eyes shut—if only the chin is kept properly pointed. *I have done this scores of times and it has been hailed as a marvelous feat. The only marvelous thing about it is that I have trained myself to resist the tendency to let my chin follow the clubhead in its path toward the ball.*

Pointing the chin has both a physiological and psychological effect. It is the most important single item in the correct swing, but it is not, of course, all there is to the swing. It would be too much to expect that merely pointing your chin properly would permit you to take your mind entirely off your stroke, and still make it correctly. It would be too much, too, to expect the pointing of the chin to bring the proper set of muscles into play automatically. But pointing your chin will relieve you from the necessity of "concentrating" upon too many details of your stroke; it will insure the correct use and control of your body once you have learned the proper positions and proper order of movement.

In other words, you must learn the swing—all of it. But once you have caught the feel and by practice have made the correct movements your own, you need only assume the correct starting position and pointing your chin will take care of the rest.

While aiming the chin, the body should be kept in motion because action is a sure means of avoiding tension. If you permit yourself to "get set" or tighten up at this point you will surely ruin your swing.

—from *A New Way to Better Golf*

1937

SWINGING INTO GOLF by Ernest Jones and Innes Brown. 150 pages, N.Y.: Whittlesey House.

This book went through at least four printings in its first year of publication, but may well have failed to sell the minimum required for this best-seller section. It is included because a later version of the same man's theories very likely did make our imaginary "chart," at least in conjunction with the first version, and also for the fact that Jones has had (and continues to have) a large following. Jones was a budding world-rank player, but during action in France in World War I, he lost his right leg below the knee and had to abandon hopes for a playing career in favor of a life of teaching. His rapid adjustment to his physical handicap—he resumed shooting par within four months—actually confirmed an earlier belief of his that the effective golf swing is a one-piece action based on control of the clubhead through the hands and fingers. He built his successful career as a teaching professional in Great Britain and the United States upon this insight. As the book shows, he devised numerous means for getting his pupils to swing instead of hit.

SETTING UP "RELAXED"

Avoid any effort at digging the feet into the ground, as if to engage in a weight-lifting contest or a tug of war. Such a procedure sets up a feeling of tenseness in the legs, which will be communicated to other parts of the body; this is distinctly hostile to the easy freedom needed for launching a swinging action. Aim at acquiring the easy freedom that accompanies a simple physical exercise, such, for instance, as one feels on the dance floor just at the instant of picking up the timing of the music to start dancing.

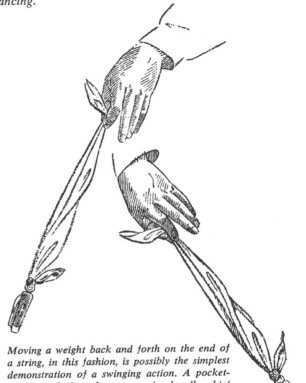

Moving a weight back and forth on the end of a string, in this fashion, is possibly the simplest demonstration of a swinging action. A pocket-knife attached to the corner of a handkerchief serves the same purpose. Since the handkerchief is flexible, it cannot transmit power through leverage.

There is no scale of measurement to determine the necessary distance between the two feet, but roughly the width of the stance should be about that of the shoulders. Too wide a stance will restrict the action of the body, while placing the feet too closely together restricts the base of action and tends to disturb balance. Ordinarily the toes should be pointed so as to form an angle of approximately 45 degrees. From time to time one hears of some well-known player who has discovered special merit in standing with the toe pointed slightly inward. This may serve some purpose, but it is not clear to me what it is.

As to the distance one should stand from the ball, clearly the length of the club chosen for the stroke must be a factor. But in any case it is important to bear in mind that the position of the feet is to be determined by first placing the club head in position back of the ball and then adjusting the position, never by taking a position and then adjusting the swing to fit.

It has been suggested above that a slight bend at the waist is necessary to permit the player to take a starting position for the stroke. The prevailing error is toward bending over too much. The body ought to be kept reasonably erect, and, once the position is established, it should be maintained throughout the swing. Straightening up or bending lower cannot but destroy the effectiveness of the stroke.

The keynote to a smoothly timed stroke is a feeling of relaxation and freedom from tenseness. If there is tenseness either in the hands and arms or in the legs, it will absolutely forestall a swinging action at the start. This prompts me to say a few words about waggling, or the preliminary movement of the club head back and forth over the ball. A few movements of this kind are helpful. They allow the body to relax, and help to provide a feel of the club head. But excessive waggling may become a habit, and an objectionable one. In such a case the practice is probably more harmful than helpful.

—from *Swinging into Golf*

1946

ON LEARNING GOLF by Percy Boomer. 258 pages, N.Y.: Alfred A. Knopf.

Boomer died in 1949, after a long and successful career as professional at the *très chic* Saint-Cloud Club near Paris, and later at Sunningdale in England. He is credited with originating a good deal of the common parlance in golf instruction today—terms such as "turn in a barrel"—and with articulating the need for developing the "feel" of a good swing in a pupil instead of making the poor fellow grasp your pet swing-theory before all else. He comes across here as a good-humored, clear-thinking teacher who as he proceeds seems always to have the student's likely questions, worries, and reactions in mind. He relies on numerous examples from his own lesson tee to clarify or dramatize his points. He insists on his title throughout—that this book is not on the science of golf, but about *learning* the game. The book went through at least nine printings in a 20-year span.

THE FEELING OF "IN-TO-OUT"

From the first time we see golf played to the first time we take a club in our hands, we have instinctively formed a false conception of the movement. We visualize the club head going up and over our shoulder and down onto the ball. You need only take any neophyte to see how he immediately takes the club up and down. His conviction that this is the correct movement is strengthened by the fact that he sees the ball soaring into the air and concludes that

it must have been hit with an upward *motion. So to make matters worse, he brings his hands into play to assist the up-down-up movement—and is fully equipped for a career of scooping.*

Now here are two devastatingly false impressions, and it is astonishing how long in many golfers' lives they remain. We must not try to lift either the club head or the ball, and we shall never be good golfers until we can feel that we pull the club head along as we swing, along not up and down.

Let us put this in another way. If I were to ask you to:

(1) Drive a wedge under a door
         and
(2) Drive a nail into the floor

—you would visualize two entirely different directions of hammer-head travel. Driving the wedge under the door is the direction we must feel at golf. The force must go along through the length of the wedge, along through the length of the ball.

With this in mind, it becomes clear that in swinging, the weight of the club head should be brought along from behind the ball, not from above it. This is what we call the wide swing, wide not *high: a wide sweep that brings the club head in from behind the back of the ball . . .*

Now another impression we get which impedes progress is that the club shaft goes up and above the right shoulder. In fact it does this not by arm or hand movement, but by the wrists being broken at the top of the swing. Consequently you must not try to get your club up by lifting it with your arms; you must feel at the top of the swing that your club and left arm are in a straight line and are waist high. *Please ponder over this until you see its practical implications. You can try it out anywhere without a club and you will find that, if you are standing well up and your body is braced and you have the straight-left-arm-waist-high feeling referred to above, you will* not be able *to hit in a downward direction, but you will* be able to *swing the club head along through the ball—with power from feet and legs.*

—from *On Learning Golf*

1946

WINNING GOLF by Byron Nelson. 187 pages, N.Y.: A. S. Barnes.

Nelson and great golf were synonomous at the time this book came out; the previous year, he had won 19 of the 30 PGA tournaments he entered, 11 of them in a row, and had averaged only 68.33 strokes per round. No great surprise, then, that his first book would appear briefly on the general-trade best-seller list. Tommy Armour's 1953 book has been the only other golf book to have risen to such heights.

UNIFORMITY OF SWING

Before getting into the mechanics of the golf swing we should give attention to an important consideration— "Uniformity of Swing."

Many golfers add unnecessary complexity to the game by feeling that they must use a different swing for each club in the bag. This is incorrect.

Actually there is a slight variation in swing from club to club, but, *you should* not *make a conscious effort to swing one club differently than another. The natural variation is caused by the different positions in which you must stand to hit the ball for the great variety of lies encountered on any course, and the range of shaft lengths and clubhead angles.*

For instance, in using a driver you stand the farthest from the ball because the club shaft is longer, the clubhead at a flatter angle to the shaft, and the ball is teed up. As you use shorter clubs, move closer to the ball, and play the ball more off the center of your stance. In doing this, you automatically take a more upright and shorter swing. There is no other reason, under normal conditions, for changing your swing from shot to shot.

I am completely unaware of making any attempt to swing one club differently than another.

—from *Winning Golf*

1947

THE NINE BAD SHOTS OF GOLF (AND WHAT TO DO ABOUT THEM) by Jim Dante and Leo Diegel, with Len Elliott. 189 pages, N.Y.: Whittlesey House.

This problem-and-solution treatment with the magic of a number in the title sold nearly 200,000 copies in one paperback edition alone.

THE NINE BAD SHOTS AND WHAT CAUSES THEM

SLICING: *Hitting with an open face, usually from the outside in*

HOOKING: *Hitting with a shut face*

TOPPING: *Hitting with a lifted head, a sway to the right, or hitting with a raised arc*

SMOTHERING: *Hitting with club face hooded*

PULLING: *Hitting from the outside in with a shut face*

PUSHING: *Hitting with an open face while the club is still moving from the inside out*

SKYING: *Hitting with a chopping downswing, usually with a sway to the left or with the club face turned over*

SCLAFFING: *Hitting with too much weight on the right foot*

SHANKING: *Hitting with little or no pivot, very loose wrists, and with an exaggerated outside-in swing*

—from *The Nine Bad Shots of Golf*

1948

POWER GOLF by Ben Hogan. 166 pages, N.Y.: A. S. Barnes.

This may be the number one all-time best-seller. Sales in English language only: 178,000 hardbound and 3,230,000 mass-market paperback. Contains black and white sequence photos of Hogan's driver, long-iron, and short-iron swing.

1950

HOW TO HIT A GOLF BALL by Sam Snead. 74 pages, $1.00, Garden City, N.Y.: Doubleday.

A primer-style instruction paperback that sold 300,-000 copies and is still on the stands.

THE TEE SHOT

Use whichever stance is best adapted to your build and game, but don't employ an extremely open or closed stance for the tee shot. Many championship golfers have used the square stance, while others have used the slightly open or closed stance with great success.

The swing should be a relaxed motion. Don't try to "kill" the ball to obtain extra distance. The longest drives from the tee result from free moving, coordinated swings.

Because I have somewhat long arms, I use an upright swing on the tee shot, but this will depend upon the physical characteristics of the individual golfer. A person with short arms and a deep chest will naturally feel freer using a flatter swing.

The chief difference between the upright and the flat swings is that in the latter the body is required to turn more fully than in the former.

Balance and relaxation are important in the drive. Sole the club behind the ball, then step into a position that feels comfortable for you. In most cases, this position will be one which places the weight equally upon each foot. The toes should be pointed slightly outward because this is the normal stance for most of us.

If you are standing too close or too far from the ball, your position will feel awkward and off-balance. I use practically a square stance for driving. That is, a line along my toes is almost parallel to the intended line of flight.

—from *How to Hit a Golf Ball*

1952

SWING THE CLUBHEAD by Ernest Jones and David Eisenberg. 126 pages, N.Y.: Dodd, Mead.

This is a more doggedly "how-to" work than the 1937 Jones book, with fewer of the charming, essaylike detours into "what-about" that characterize the earlier volume, and therefore perhaps more readily accessible to the modern, bottom-line-minded American golfer. But the message is no different: "Your hands are everything in this business of playing good golf easily." The book was in its fifth printing five years from publication date, and widely reprinted and reported on.

TIMING AND RHYTHM

There are critics who insist that everyone knows you have to swing the clubhead, but that you must do much more than swing, if you wish to play good golf. I disagree. You need only learn to swing the clubhead so that it will strike the ball the most forceful and most accurate blow possible with the power at your command. The rest will take care of itself.

You create maximum force by developing clubhead speed in swinging. But you cannot force a swing. Unfortunately, too many people think they can force the power with which they strike the clubhead against the ball. That is not so. A swing is a definite motion. You, to get maximum force, must get all the power you can into that motion, but without disturbing it, without forcing it from the arc of the swing. You must swing with authority.

Perfect swinging is perfect rhythm. I shall repeat that over and over again. A stroke to make the ball travel a few inches, takes the same measure of time as one to make it go 200 yards, if the same club is used.

A pupil recently described his sensation after watching Sam Snead play a round of golf. He was perplexed, because watching had failed to give him a single pointer which could help his own game.

The pupil was paying Snead a high compliment. He is one of the most beautiful swingers the game ever developed. Snead gets tremendous speed into the clubhead, the result of the steady, smooth application of power through swinging. There is no waste of power, no counteraction which produces contortions that might be mistakenly identified as the keynote of success in the stroke.

Had my pupil watched Snead correctly he would have learned something. He should have watched the action of Snead's hands when going through the swinging motion. If you have the opportunity, watch those hands. Watch the clubhead. Notice the smooth rhythm with which it picks up speed from the moment it is started back until the ball has been struck.

A characteristic of centrifugal application of power— i.e. swinging—is its apparent effortlessness. There is no strain, as in levering. A giant wheel spun at the rate of 1,000 or 2,000 revolutions per minute, gives no hint of the terrific power driving it because it is applied evenly and smoothly.

But if there is a flaw in the construction of the wheel, it will fly apart under the force developed. Parts will be thrown a great distance, with much damage resulting. The power driving a perfectly functioning wheel is ever present, but the rhythm of its application does not readily suggest force, as measured by the results obtained.

It is the same in golf. The smoother and more rhythmic the swing, the less you are likely to suspect the range of the power when watching its application by an expert.

—from *Swing the Clubhead*

1953

HOW TO PLAY YOUR BEST GOLF ALL THE TIME by Tommy Armour, illustrated by Lealand Gustafson. 152 pages, N.Y.: Simon & Schuster.

Armour (with the uncredited aid of Herb Graffis) lays down the law quickly and jauntily: Use whippier shafts and a strongish grip, close your stance on wood shots, and keep more weight on the front foot for irons. And above all, in the book's most celebrated phrase, "Let the left arm and hand act as a guide and whack the hell out of the ball with the right hand." Indispensable points on key positions and actions have been printed in red—just as all the words of Christ are treated in certain "Bible Belt" editions of the New Testament. The book sold 250,000 copies in its first year and was on the trade-nonfiction best-seller list for a spell—a rare thing for a golf title. At last count, 400,000 hardbound copies had been sold. The book continues to sell at the rate of about 10,000 a year without promotion by the publisher.

USE THE RIGHT KNEE FOR CORRECT FOOTWORK

In simplifying footwork, I'll give you one simple little tip that probably will greatly improve the hitting portion of your swing. The tip is to have the right knee come in fast at the right time.

Perhaps you'll think that this tip is out of order at this place, but everything else is secondary to hitting the ball, and if that right knee comes in fast at the right time, you'll hit the ball pretty well. The body, arms, and hands will coordinate with the knee action more than you realize is possible.

There's so much said that really isn't too important about the backswing. I've seen some backswings that, because of individual physical characteristics, didn't look ideally orthodox, but those backswings had two features performed perfectly. The footwork was right, and the head was kept steady.

If you're an older golfer, you'll remember how the critics used to say Bob Jones' swing was faulty because he had quite a loop at the top. You also may recall that Hagen's sway was declared by those specious critics as being a violent offense against classic form.

But all those critics missed the point, and that was that the foot action of Jones and Hagen always got them into position to hit superb shots. The situation hasn't changed a bit today; good footwork is what makes the great golfers stand up.

You hear and read a great deal that probably confuses you about "hitting against the straight left side," and about having the hips in a line somewhat facing the hole as the ball is hit.

If I wanted to be maliciously and deliberately confusing, I could write a long book about just those two details, but it wouldn't be understood, applied, or of any value whatsoever to any more than possibly fifty golfers in the whole world.

To boil down all that such a book would mean, practically, to the other millions of golfers, I'll say that the key to hitting against the straight left side and having the body facing as it should at impact is the action of the right knee.

When the right knee comes in toward the direction you're hitting, your right heel comes off the ground, and you're pushing the body around into perfect position for hitting. Your left side is bound to straighten up as your left knee straightens.

But, if you keep your right heel on the ground, it is physically impossible to get your right knee to play its proper part in the swing. Therefore, your entire right side—the right shoulder and the right hip—can't get into position for hitting.

—from *How to Play Your Best Golf All the Time*

1957

*FIVE LESSONS: THE MODERN FUNDAMEN-
TALS OF GOLF* by Ben Hogan, with Herbert
Warren Wind; illustrated by Anthony Ravielli.
127 pages, N.Y.: A. S. Barnes.

The reader feels that he is in the presence of the Golfing Oracle with this one, because it is so deftly organized, economically written, and superbly illustrated. Beyond that, there is a certainty of tone here that unmistakably reflects the character of the Master Shotmaker, and brooks no argument unless you happen to be a pupil who is very sullen or very bold indeed. Collaborator Herb Wind wrote elsewhere: "No one in our time has contributed half as much as Hogan to analyzing and understanding the mechanics of the golf swing, and while he will, of course, be best remembered as an almost peerless champion, he will also go down in history as one of the game's great pathfinders." Total sold to date: 262,000 hardbound, 740,000 paperback.

BACKSWING—ORDER OF BATTLE

The waggle gives the golfer a running start. It blends right into the swing. For all general points and purposes, the backswing is simply an extension of the way the golfer takes the club back on the waggle. The club follows that same path and it is swung back at the speed the waggle has regulated. There is, however, one significant difference between the waggle and the backswing which must be made

crystal-clear. During the waggle, the shoulders do not turn. On the actual swing, they do, right from the beginning of the backswing. The backswing is, in fact, initiated by the almost simultaneous movement of the hands, arms and shoulders. Introducing the shoulders does not alter the pattern you set up in the waggle. By turning your shoulders on your actual backswing, you simply increase the arc of your waggle.

Throughout these lessons we have placed special emphasis on the fact that the golf swing is, in principle, a continuous chain of actions. Like the component parts of the engine of an automobile, the component parts of the swing fuse together and work together in a purposeful sequence. As each component performs its part of the operation, it sets up the proper operation of the other components with which it is connected. I bring this up at this particular point, for if a golfer clearly grasps the interrelationship of the hands, arms, shoulders and hips, he will play good golf— he can't help but play good golf.

On the backswing, the order of movement goes like this: hands, arms, shoulders, hips. (*On the downswing the order is just reversed: hips, shoulders, arms, hands.*) *On the backswing, the hands, arms, and shoulders start to move almost simultaneously.* Actually, the hands start the clubhead back a split second before the arms start back. And the arms begin their movement a split second before the shoulders begin to turn. As a golfer acquires feel and rhythm through practice, the hands, arms, and shoulders will instinctively tie in on this split-second schedule. *The main point for the novice is to know that they do start back so closely together that their action is unified.*

On the backswing the shoulders are always ahead of the hips as they turn. The shoulders start turning immediately. The hips do not. Just before your hands reach hip level, the shoulders, as they turn, automatically start pulling the hips around. As the hips begin to turn, they pull the left leg in to the right.

—from *Five Lessons*

1962

FOUR MAGIC MOVES TO WINNING GOLF by
Joe Dante, with Len Elliott; illustrated by William
Canfield. 218 pages, N.Y.: McGraw-Hill.

After starting out with a few kind words for all predecessors ("The golf swing has been heavily overlaid with a sludge of fallacy, misunderstanding, faulty theory, myth and just plain ignorance"), the authors get down to business and in an admirably detailed and systematic manner, expose the swing as seen by Joe Dante, a noted New Jersey professional for many years and son of Jim Dante (author of the best-selling *The Nine Bad Shots of Golf*). The "magic moves" of the title are (1) early wrist break on the backswing, (2) a "purposeful shoulder turn" at the top, (3) lateral hip slide starting down, and (4) hitting through with the hands. The book sold over 100,000 copies in its Cornerstone paperback edition alone.

LATERAL HIP ACTION

We cannot emphasize too strongly that the movement of the hips must be lateral *and not a turning motion. When the hips are moved laterally to the left from the top of the swing, they carry the weight (which has been mostly on the right leg) along. They get it on the left leg where it must be if we are to hit the ball with anything but a weak slap.*

That is the first reason we must move the hips laterally. The second reason is that, since we are twisted and wound up tightly at the top, any turning movement of our hips turns our shoulders too. It turns our right shoulder around high and toward the ball. Hence, when we bring the club down, we have to bring it from the outside in.

The hips will turn if they are moved laterally, but they are very liable not to move laterally if they are merely turned. You can prove this to yourself by standing up and moving your hips to the left as far as they will go. As they near the limit of extension, they will turn and you cannot stop them. At the top of the swing, of course, the hips are turned somewhat to the right, maybe 45 degrees, and as you move them laterally they will quickly begin to turn back to the left. The trick is get them going to the left, laterally, before they turn too much. If you ask how much is too much, you become hopelessly involved. You might as well ask how many angels can dance on the head of a pin. You don't have to worry about that. Just be sure you get the hips going laterally and that you don't try to turn them.

A third reason for the lateral slide of the hips is that this is the movement which starts the club down toward the ball, by causing the shoulders to rock slightly as they turn. That movement of the hips—and nothing else—provides the first impetus for the downswing.

It might help you to visualize this action if you think of the spine as being the axis of the swing. Now think of the axis as being a T-square, with the shank as the spine and the crosspiece the shoulders. The end of the shank reaches down to the pelvis or hips. As we address the ball this T-square is, for purposes of the comparison, vertical. On the backswing the hips move slightly to the right, causing the crosspiece to tilt slightly to the left, as it turns, of course, with the turning shoulders. On the downswing (and here is the critical point), the low end of the shank (the hips) is moved sharply to the left. This causes an immediate and definite tilting of the crosspiece to the right— and that is what starts the shoulders, arms, and club moving down toward the ball. This will be true so long as the whole swinging system is twisted tight, so that a movement against the twist in any one part moves all the other parts. Make no mistake about it, the hips are what move the shoulders and club and start the downswing.

—from *Four Magic Moves to Winning Golf*

1964

55 WAYS TO LOWER YOUR GOLF SCORE by Jack Nicklaus, illustrated by Francis Golden. 125 pages, $8.95, N.Y.: Simon & Schuster.

Short, well-illustrated tips based on a series appearing originally in *Sports Illustrated*. This is the pudgy Jack on his way to the top, not the svelte Jack of *Golf My Way,* who has already gotten there. Sold 125,000 copies.

1968

GOLFER'S BIBLE by Frank Kenyon Allen and Tom LoPresti, Dale Mead, and Barbara Romack. 159 pages, $1.95, Garden City, N.Y.: Doubleday.

Has sold over 250,000 copies, paperback.

1970

THE SQUARE TO SQUARE GOLF SWING by Dick Aultman, illustrated by Anthony Ravielli. 127 pages, *Golf Digest,* N.Y., distributor: Simon & Schuster.

This "model method for the modern player" stirred some excitement when it first came out, and people are still either swearing by it or at it. The method is based on the idea of pulling the clubhead into the ball with the left hand, arm, and side dominant, as opposed to the older, Jones-style technique of throwing the club on the downswing largely with the right side. The artwork is ingenious; because of the complexity of the subject, it needed to be. Copies sold in U.S.: 68,000 hardbound; 100,000 paperback (Bantam).

PROPER GRIP PRESSURE

The other goals we seek to encourage through proper gripping—swinging on a relatively upright plane, keeping the clubface from fanning open, sustaining clubhead speed and avoiding slippage of the club—are largely dependent on grip pressure, rather than on the positioning of the hands.

Teachers of the Method advocate that grip pressure be emphasized in the last three fingers of the left hand. Pressure with the thumb and forefinger of the left hand, and all fingers of the right hand, should be only firm enough to avoid any slippage.

Gripping the club primarily in the last three fingers of the left hand, immediately begins to put your left side in control, by activating the muscles on the underside of your left forearm. With these muscles in charge, the normal tendency is to start the clubhead straight back from the ball with the clubface continuing to look down the target line. Starting the clubhead straight back puts the swing on a properly upright plane and also precludes fanning open the clubface. Thus, grip pressure in the last three fingers of the left hand directly influences plane and clubface alignment during the swing.

CHECKPOINT. If you are properly emphasizing pressure in the last three fingers of your left hand, you should experience a bunching of muscles on the underside of your left forearm, just below the elbow, when you grip with the clubhead resting on the ground. Too much pressure with the thumb and forefinger will reduce this bunching and increase tension in the forearm's upper side.

Too much pressure in the grip of the right hand will cause your right arm and shoulder muscles to tighten. Such tightening greatly restricts your ability to make a full shoulder turn on a sufficiently upright plane. Right-hand pressure also causes the right side to take over on the backswing. This causes a premature lifting of the clubhead, which shortens and flattens your swing. Your left side, with the last three fingers of your left hand dominating your grip, should be responsible for moving the clubhead back and up on the backswing.

—from *The Square to Square Golf Swing*

1971

THE TOUCH SYSTEM FOR BETTER GOLF by Bob Toski, with Dick Aultman; illustrated by Stan Drake. 128 pages, *Golf Digest.*

This book, which helped launch Toski into superstar teaching status, has sold 135,000 copies to date (including 40,000 Bantam paperbacks). It is all about the "feel" of a good golf swing, rather than mechanics, and abounds in images and analogies. Toski believes that virtually all the top pros play primarily by feel and that ordinary mortals, once they have their fundamentals in place, must do the same thing in order to produce a dependable, repeating swing.

OVERALL SWING SENSATIONS

Nobody ever hit the ball on their backswing. Yet, many golfers take the club back so fast that it seems like they're trying to do just that. It's no wonder they lose control of the club. Then, on the downswing, they lose a great deal of clubhead speed simply because they must burn up so much energy trying to regain club control.

Others swing back too methodically, then slash at the ball with their arms because they feel they must do something to make the club move faster. They never get much clubhead speed because they don't use their legs. Whatever speed they do generate is wasted before impact because they use their hands too soon.

A good mental image for these golfers is that of an automobile stuck in mud or snow. Recall how you'd try to "rock" the car out. You would put it in "reverse" and slowly roll the wheels up the back edge of the rut. Then you'd put it in forward gear and slowly—to avoid spin-

ning the wheels—accelerate. You'd keep doing this, slowly taking the car back and up until it's in position to gradually accelerate forward. Back slow, then gradually faster forward. Picture this in your mind. Sense how it would feel inside the car. Imagine the same movement back and forward when you swing the golf club.

Or think of yourself as a rubber band. A rubber band is like your muscles. It can stretch and contract.

If you stretch the rubber band too far, it will break. It loses its tension. If you stretch your muscles too far during your backswing, something will collapse to relax the tension. You may loosen your grip; or your left arm may bend; or your left wrist may bow inward; or your body may sway. Something has to give sooner or later.

If you stretch a rubber band fully, and then let go, you get a powerful "snap." This is what happens during your downswing if you retain your left side's stretching, if you keep your left arm extended, and if your right arm and wrist stay bent or cocked until near impact . . .

But if you stretch a rubber band between your hands and then move your hands back together, relaxing the tension, it won't snap. That's what happens when your right shoulder and right hand take over on your downswing. You release your stretch too soon, before impact. No snap.

—from *The Touch System*

1974

GOLF MY WAY by Jack Nicklaus, with Ken Bowden; illustrated by Jim McQueen. 264 pages, $9.95, N.Y.: Simon & Schuster.

Some 220,000 copies of *Golf My Way* have been sold thus far—not counting sales in the various foreign languages in which the book has also been produced. Nicklaus covers in great detail all aspects of his shotmaking and his thinking about technique, usually lucidly and sometimes with a light touch that reflects his attitude that golf should be first and foremost a *game*, not a course in engineering. The artwork is lavish. Nicklaus believes you should adopt a method that makes the most of your particular physical strengths—in his case, the legs and back. He also stresses body-and-leg action over hand-and-arm movement.

TAKEAWAY

I believe you cannot start the golf club back too slowly, provided you swing it back rather than take it away from the ball. I said in a previous book that the ideal swing start is a "terribly forced, ridiculously slow movement of the club away from the ball." I still feel that way. The harder I want to swing, the slower I try to start back. But on every shot I endeavor to swing the club into motion very deliberately, very positively, only just fast enough to avoid jerkiness. Obviously the motion speeds up as my

These are ideal, acceptable, and worst top-of-the-swing clubface positions. I play best when I am what I believe to be "square": left hand, wrist, and forearm forming a straight line, and thus setting the clubface midway between horizontal and vertical. I can usually play fairly decently from an "open" position, caused by a slight concave kink in my left wrist angling the clubface closer to vertical than horizontal. When a convex arching of my wrist at the top "closes" the clubface so that it looks too far skyward, I'm liable to be all over the park, and sometimes beyond it.

backswing develops, but the slower I can keep it those first few feet of the takeaway the better I'll play.

Reasons? Primarily three. First, the slower you start back, the better your chance of moving the clubhead on a particular line, and thus the better your chance of establishing the particular arc and plane you desire. Second, the slower you start back, the easier it is to coordinate or unify the movements of the feet, legs, hips, hands, arms, and shoulders; the better your chance of starting back in "one piece." Third, the slower you start back—while still swinging the club, mind you—the smoother the over-all tempo you'll establish. Let's take a closer look at these factors.

Many golfers get confused about the line along which the club should start back, particularly when they have been made conscious of "hitting from the inside." (In pro-ams you see a lot of golfers almost wiping out their right ankle, they whip the club back so sharply "inside." The

inevitable result is that, in trying to get back on line coming down, they throw the club "outside.")

If you've stayed with me thus far in this book, you must know that I start the club back neither "inside" nor "outside," but straight along a backward extension of the line on which I want the ball to take off. *Another way to put this would be to say I start the club straight back along a line parallel to my shoulders.*

If I am intending to fade the ball, my shoulders will be aligned left of target. My start-back line will then, of course, actually be a little outside the direct ball-to-target line. Conversely, if I am endeavoring to draw the ball, my shoulders will be aligned a little right of target. My start-back line will then be a little inside the direct ball-to-target line. *The point is that in each case my start-back line* matches my shoulder alignment at address—not the ball-to-target line. Only if I were trying to hit the ball straight would the start-back line and the direct ball-to-target line coincide.

I may be laboring this point, but it has to be stressed if we are going to eradicate the many confusions that exist about the club's correct start-back path. What the golfer has to clearly understand is that "straight back" and "straight through" must relate to his direction of aim, *not to his direct ball-target line, unless he's trying to hit the shot dead straight.*

—from *Golf My Way*

1977

JACK NICKLAUS' LESSON TEE by Jack Nicklaus, with Ken Bowden; ill. by Jim McQueen. 157 pages, $9.95, *Golf Digest*.

Based on the *Golf Digest* series, full color throughout (amazing considering the low price of this book by today's standards), and broken down into the following categories: full-swing fundamentals, critical swing-factors, cures for common problems, short game, special shotmaking techniques, trouble shots, and strategy. Copies sold through the end of 1978 (English language only): 130,000.

FURTHER READING

None of the books listed below were best-sellers, but they would be of interest to anyone who dares to muse further on the subject of fancies and fashions in golf technique over the years.

THE METHODS OF GOLF'S MASTERS by Dick Aultman and Ken Bowden. 1975, 191 pages, $12.95, N.Y.: Coward, McCann & Geohegan.

How the great players went at the game, including their characteristic swing styles and attitudes:

HARRY VARDON—The Master Mold
WALTER HAGEN—"Three of 'Those' and One of 'Them' Count Four"
GENE SARAZEN—Hitting It Hard for Fifty Years
BOBBY JONES—Never Tinker with Talent
HENRY COTTON—The Supreme "Hands" Player
BYRON NELSON—The Birth of the Modern Method
SAM SNEAD—A Swing for All Ages
BEN HOGAN—"There is Always Something Left to Improve"
BOBBY LOCKE—Benign Imperturbability—and the Hottest Putter in History
CARY MIDDLECOFF—Play Away When Ready, When Ready, When Ready, When . . .
PETER THOMSON—"A Light, Tender, Sensitive Touch Is Worth a Ton of Brawn"
ARNOLD PALMER—A Matter of the Mind
BILLY CASPER—"Play Safe and Play Within Yourself"
GARY PLAYER—To Be the Greatest, You Need an Edge
LEE TREVINO—Five Wrongs Add Up to One Immaculate Right
JACK NICKLAUS—The Most and the Best

DICTIONARY OF GOLF by Ken Adwick. 1974, 200 pages, N.Y.: Drake.

This lexicon to instructional terms by noted British professional Adwick allows you to flip pages and quickly find out what they are talking about when they say you are hitting from the top or rolling your hands or smothering all your shots.

THE SEARCH FOR THE PERFECT GOLF SWING by Alastair Cochran and John Stobbs. 1968, 242 pages, London: Heinemann.

A team of British scientists, with the guidance of the authors, examines every conceivable measurable facet of the swing. The definitive report on the technical side of the game—and an effective squelcher of some old saws about playing technique.

THE AMERICAN GOLFER, Charles Price, ed. 1964, 241 pages, $9.95, N.Y.: Random House.

This anthology of the best writings to appear in *American Golfer* magazine from 1920 to 1935 includes numerous instructional pieces by the great players and teachers of that era. Sample contents: "How to Look at the Ball," by Jock Hutchinson; "How is Your Slice?" by Jim Barnes; "The Six-Inch Golf Course (Between Your Ears)," by Eddie Loos; "Getting Distance on the Drive," by Ted Ray; "My Angle of Putting," by Walter Hagen; and "Think Before You Putt," by Walter Travers. Also, a half-dozen pieces on technique and match-play by Bob Jones.

ESQUIRE'S WORLD OF GOLF by Herb Graffis, illustrated by Lealand Gustafson. 1961, 240 pages, N.Y.: Trident Press.

This volume in effect picks up where the Price anthology leaves off, except that instead of reprinting the best golf articles from *Esquire* from the early 1930s into the 1950s (a period when the magazine ranked golf among its must topics for regular coverage), Graffis has weighed and synthesized those various contributions, and done so ably and interestingly. In the instructional section, which occupies the first two-thirds of the book, he reports the viewpoints on technique and style of top players—including Jones, Hagen, Farrell, Harmon, Snead, Middlecoff, Sarazen, Armour, Demaret and Penna—and of highly successful teachers—including Alex Morrison, Frank Walsh, Eddie Loos, and Joe Novak.

THE SEARCH FOR THE PERFECT TEACHING METHOD by Gary Wiren.

Reprint of an article appearing originally in *Professional Golfer* that spells out the "laws, principles, and preferences" that govern every golf swing. Write to National Golf Foundation, 200 N. Castlewood Drive, North Palm Beach, FL 33408.

CONSENSUS ON THE GOLF SWING

The following material, excerpted from the National Golf Foundation's recent publication *Golf Lessons,* comes as close as any material available to summing up the prevailing orthodoxy in the golf profession with regard to grip, stance, and swing. It was produced in association with NGF educational consultants and represents the latest techniques advocated by experienced golf instructors. (A copy of the entire 48-page softbound book is available for $2.50 from the NGF, 200 Castlewood Drive, North Palm Beach, FL 33408.)

The Grip

(1) Extend your left hand (back of hand facing the target) and place it on the grip of the club below the cap. As you sole the clubhead make certain the clubface is squarely aligned with your target.

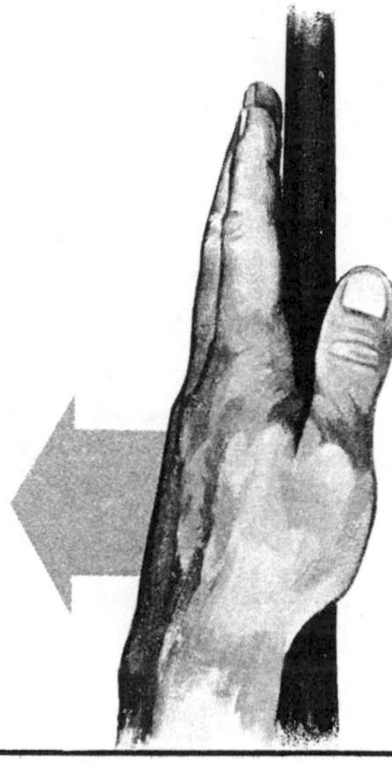

Fig. 27

• Back of left hand toward the target.

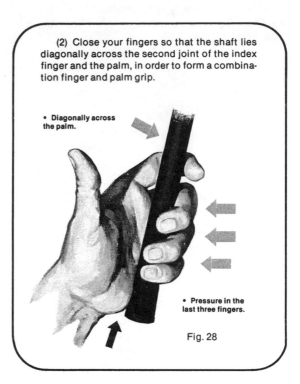

(2) Close your fingers so that the shaft lies diagonally across the second joint of the index finger and the palm, in order to form a combination finger and palm grip.

• Diagonally across the palm.

• Pressure in the last three fingers.

Fig. 28

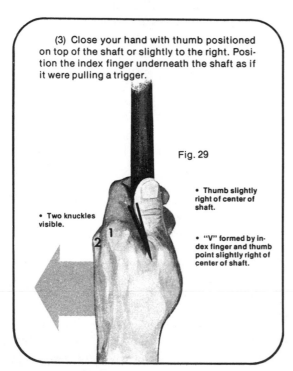

(3) Close your hand with thumb positioned on top of the shaft or slightly to the right. Position the index finger underneath the shaft as if it were pulling a trigger.

Fig. 29

• Two knuckles visible.

• Thumb slightly right of center of shaft.

• "V" formed by index finger and thumb point slightly right of center of shaft.

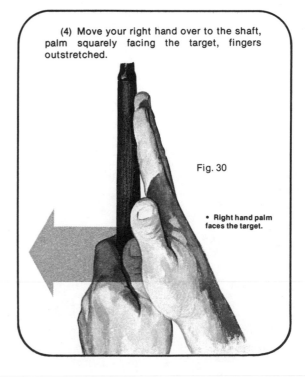

(4) Move your right hand over to the shaft, palm squarely facing the target, fingers outstretched.

Fig. 30

• Right hand palm faces the target.

(5) Close your fingers around the shaft so that the little finger will touch the index finger of the left hand. The palm will rest slightly to the right of the shaft and then will cover the left thumb. This is called the **natural** grip (Fig. 31). In the **overlapping** grip (Fig. 32) used by the majority of professionals, the little finger of your right hand will overlap the index finger of your left, thus placing your hands closer together. In the **interlocking** grip (Fig. 33), the little finger of the right hand interlocks the index finger of the left, removing the left forefinger from the shaft.

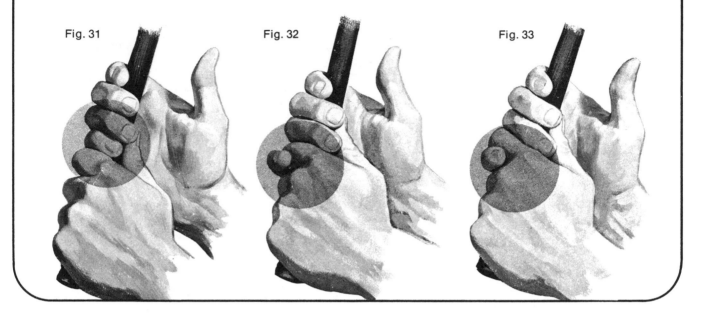

Fig. 31   Fig. 32   Fig. 33

Whichever grip you use, keep your hands firmly together, though not rigid, and properly aligned with the clubface.

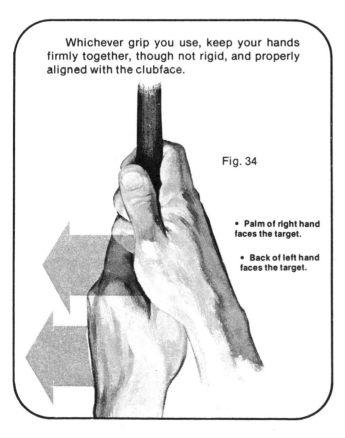

Fig. 34

- Palm of right hand faces the target.

- Back of left hand faces the target.

Pictured below is a **left**-hander's **overlapping** grip showing proper hand placement.

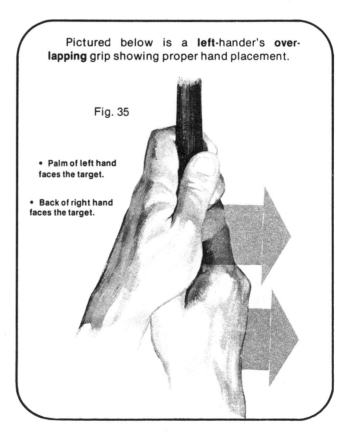

Fig. 35

- Palm of left hand faces the target.

- Back of right hand faces the target.

The Address Routine

Take your stance in relation to your target. Start by imagining a straight line through the ball to the target (**target line**) and a perpendicular line from the ball to your feet (**ball line**). Place the club behind the ball so that its face is "square" to the intended line of flight (target line). As a guide use the diagram below (Fig. 36 or Fig. 37) to build your stance.

For your full swing, separate your feet approximately shoulder width apart. A stance that is too wide will restrict proper body motion; one too narrow will result in a loss of balance. Complete your set-up position by extending your arms, keeping your back straight, bending at the hips,

and then flexing the knees slightly. Your body has now a balanced "ready" position (Fig. 38 or Fig. 39).

In Fig. 40, an overhead view of a golfer in the set-up position, note the **aiming llines** on the clubface.

Fig. 36

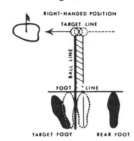

Fig. 37

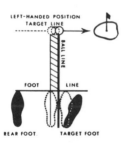

Start with your feet together as indicated by the dotted lines. Move the target foot a short distance away from the ball line *toward* the target (moving along the **foot line** which is parallel to the target line) and turn the toes slightly outward, as shown by the solid footprint. Then move your rear foot along this same foot line a greater distance from the ball line *away from* the target. These moves will automatically position the ball forward of center and form a "square stance".

SET-UP POSITION

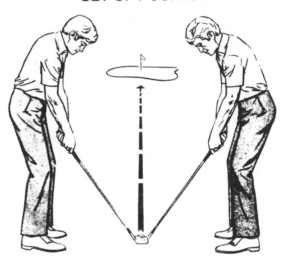

Fig. 38
RIGHT-HANDED
PLAYERS

Fig. 39
LEFT-HANDED
PLAYERS

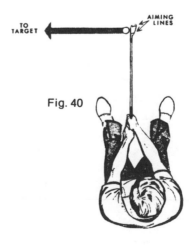

Fig. 40

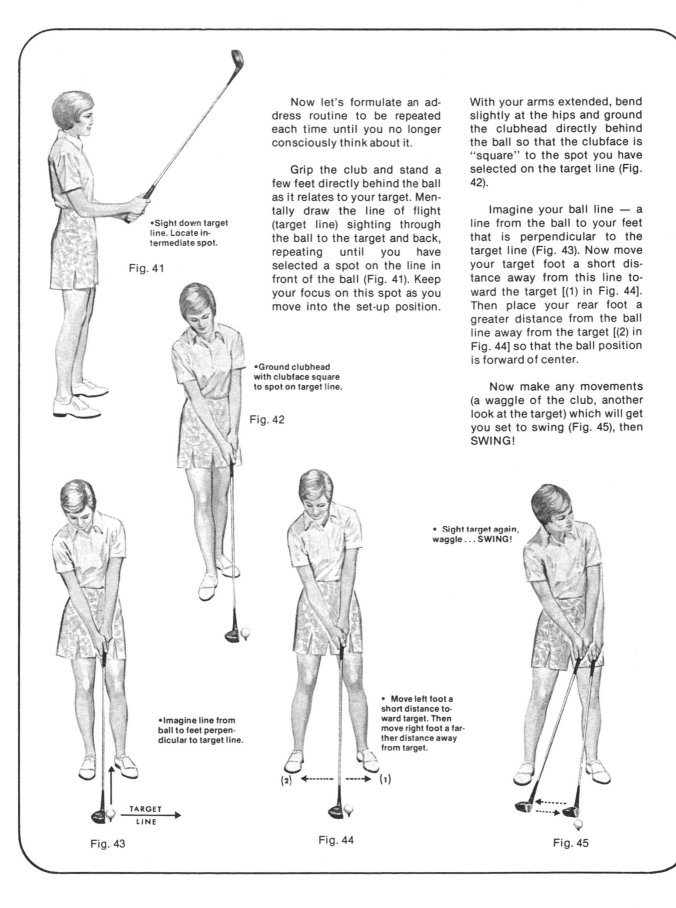

• Sight down target line. Locate intermediate spot.

Fig. 41

Now let's formulate an address routine to be repeated each time until you no longer consciously think about it.

Grip the club and stand a few feet directly behind the ball as it relates to your target. Mentally draw the line of flight (target line) sighting through the ball to the target and back, repeating until you have selected a spot on the line in front of the ball (Fig. 41). Keep your focus on this spot as you move into the set-up position.

With your arms extended, bend slightly at the hips and ground the clubhead directly behind the ball so that the clubface is "square" to the spot you have selected on the target line (Fig. 42).

Imagine your ball line — a line from the ball to your feet that is perpendicular to the target line (Fig. 43). Now move your target foot a short distance away from this line toward the target [(1) in Fig. 44]. Then place your rear foot a greater distance from the ball line away from the target [(2) in Fig. 44] so that the ball position is forward of center.

Now make any movements (a waggle of the club, another look at the target) which will get you set to swing (Fig. 45), then SWING!

• Ground clubhead with clubface square to spot on target line.

Fig. 42

• Imagine line from ball to feet perpendicular to target line.

TARGET LINE

Fig. 43

• Move left foot a short distance toward target. Then move right foot a farther distance away from target.

(2) ← - - - → (1)

Fig. 44

• Sight target again, waggle . . . SWING!

Fig. 45

The Swing

Think of the swing as a whole movement with these characteristics: (1) a repeatable rhythmic pattern (Figs. 46 and 47) . . . (2) a plane for your hands and arms to follow (Fig. 48) . . .

Fig. 46

Fig. 47

Fig. 48

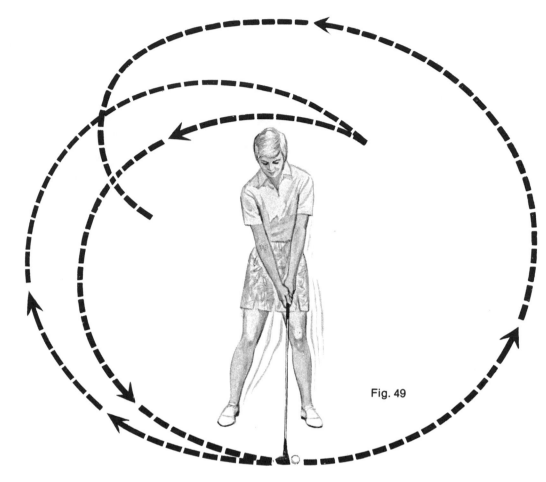

Fig. 49

Fig. 50

(3) a constant arc (Fig. 49) . . . (4) and a definite sequential flow of body movement around the swing center, or "hub" — that point just above your sternum (Fig. 50).

These characteristics must be interdependent to accomplish their purpose, and together depend upon the integrating forces of balance and timing for proper execution.

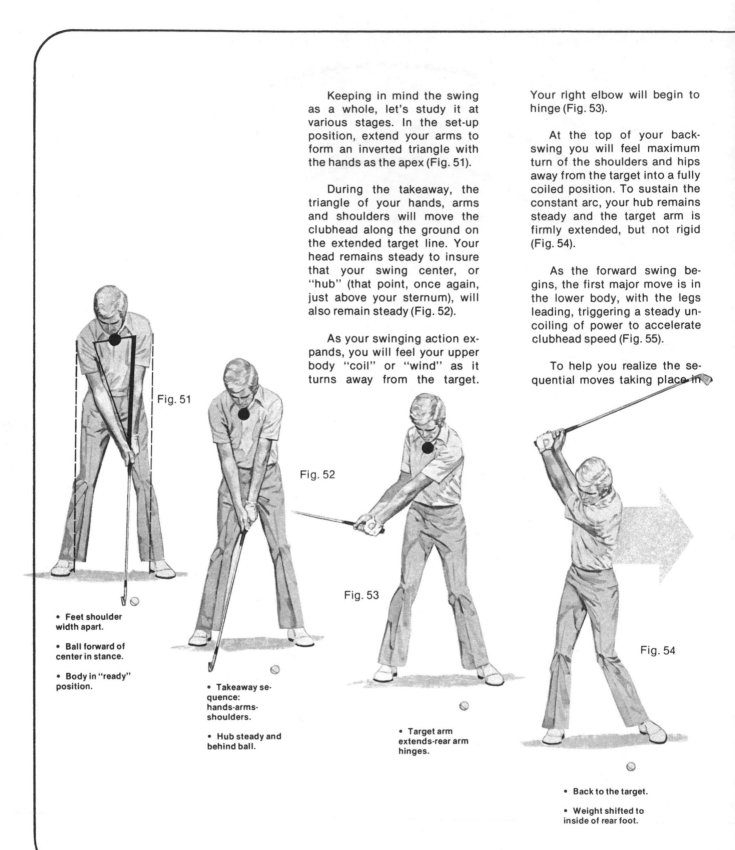

Keeping in mind the swing as a whole, let's study it at various stages. In the set-up position, extend your arms to form an inverted triangle with the hands as the apex (Fig. 51).

During the takeaway, the triangle of your hands, arms and shoulders will move the clubhead along the ground on the extended target line. Your head remains steady to insure that your swing center, or "hub" (that point, once again, just above your sternum), will also remain steady (Fig. 52).

As your swinging action expands, you will feel your upper body "coil" or "wind" as it turns away from the target.

Your right elbow will begin to hinge (Fig. 53).

At the top of your backswing you will feel maximum turn of the shoulders and hips away from the target into a fully coiled position. To sustain the constant arc, your hub remains steady and the target arm is firmly extended, but not rigid (Fig. 54).

As the forward swing begins, the first major move is in the lower body, with the legs leading, triggering a steady uncoiling of power to accelerate clubhead speed (Fig. 55).

To help you realize the sequential moves taking place in

Fig. 51

Fig. 52

Fig. 53

Fig. 54

- Feet shoulder width apart.

- Ball forward of center in stance.

- Body in "ready" position.

- Takeaway sequence: hands-arms-shoulders.

- Hub steady and behind ball.

- Target arm extends-rear arm hinges.

- Back to the target.

- Weight shifted to inside of rear foot.

the swing, note the position of the club, arms and hands in relation to the hips (Figs. 55 and 56).

At the moment of impact you want to feel all body movement and energy directed toward the target (Fig. 56). Your hips will have begun to turn, and by Fig. 57 are well out of the way, allowing the arms and hands to swing freely, fully extending the clubhead out toward the target. Think of swinging **through** the ball not **to** the ball.

In the follow through strive to maintain full extension of both arms until the diminishing momentum of clubhead speed

carries them to a natural resting position.

At the completion of your swing, your shoulders and hips will have completed their rotation, shifting the majority of your weight to the target foot and forcing a natural lift of the rear heel from the ground. Your arms and hands should finish high (Fig. 58).

Think of the foregoing stages as one continuous movement governed by balance and timing that will maneuver the clubhead into position to strike the ball squarely and at its greatest speed.

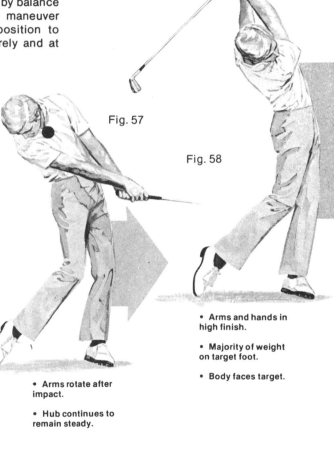

Fig. 55

Fig. 56

Fig. 57

Fig. 58

• Arms and hands in high finish.

• Majority of weight on target foot.

• Body faces target.

• Arms rotate after impact.

• Hub continues to remain steady.

• Weight shifted to target side.

• Hands and arms produce "square" clubface at impact.

• Hub remains steady behind the ball.

• Clubhead at maximum speed.

• Legs drive laterally toward target.

• Arms follow.

• Hands delay.

CONSENSUS ON SWING FAULTS AND CURES

These charts are from the *Golf Instructor's Guide* of the National Golf Foundation. Though addressed specifically to instructors, the charts are of interest to all golfers because they represent the collective wisdom of today's teaching establishment on the subject of golfing errors and their correction. Dozens of leading PGA and LPGA golf professionals, golf coaches, and golf instructors in schools and colleges throughout the country contributed to the project. (A copy of the complete 104-page softbound book is available for $4.00 from the NGF, 200 Castlewood Drive, North Palm Beach, FL 33408.)

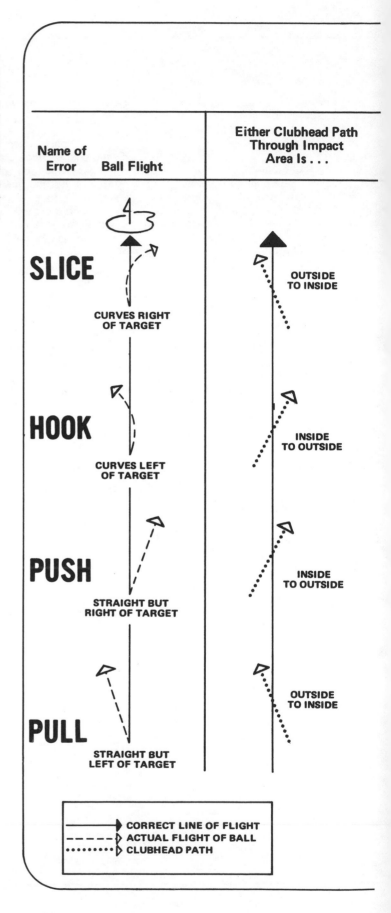

ERROR IDENTIFICATION CHART

. . . And Clubface Position In Relation To Clubhead Path At Impact Is:	OR	Clubhead Path Through Impact Area Is . . .	. . . But Clubface Position In Relation To Club-Head Path At Impact Is . . .

OPEN

CLOSED

SQUARE

SQUARE

STRAIGHT (CORRECT)

STRAIGHT (CORRECT)

OPEN

CLOSED

NAME OF ERROR	POINT OF CONTACT WITH CLUBHEAD
WHIFFED	none
TOPPED	lower half of clubface or sole
TOED	toe
HEELED	heel
FAT	ground behind ball
SHANKED	hosel or neck

ERROR CORRECTION CHART

Stage	Common Error	Illustration	Usual Shot Result	Suggested Correction
			NOTE: Factors of club length and presence of concurrent errors may cause some deviation from result indicated.	NOTE: Directions refer to the right-handed golfer.
Address Position NOTE: A great number of errors originate in the address position and takeaway stages. Special effort should be taken by the instructor to detect these errors and help the student become proficient in these initial phases of the swing.	Right (rear) hand positioned too far under shaft.	 Fig. 22	Hook Pull "Smothered" (topped action with extreme overspin - ball fails to leave ground.)	1. Regrip club placing palm of right (rear) hand facing target. Refer to **Golf Lessons**, p. 6. 2. Practice correct grip with visual guidance from NGF Film Loop, Unit 1.
	Right (rear) hand positioned too far over top of shaft.	 Fig. 23	Slice Lack of power	Same as above.
	Body aligned to left of target. Open stance.	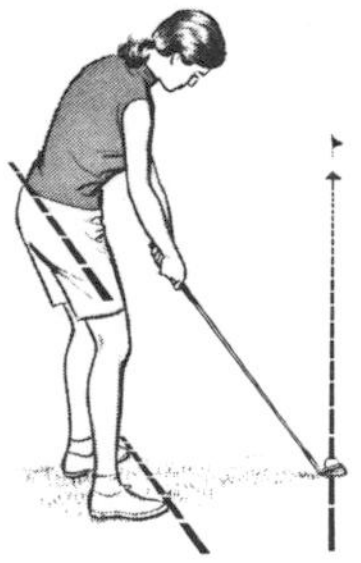 Fig. 24	Slice	1. Draw "H" diagram using clubs or chalk to show proper target line, foot line and ball line relationship. Refer to **Golf Lessons**, p. 8. 2. Study stance diagram and address position shown in NGF Film Loop 1. 3. Encourage pupil to recheck alignment with target each time by rotating head only. (Lifting shoulders tends to weaken sense of alignment and widen the "sight channel".)
	Body aligned to right of target. Closed stance.	 Fig. 25	Hook	Same as above.

Stage	Common Error	Illustration	Usual Shot Result	Suggested Correction
	Open clubface	See chart on p. 47.	Slice	1. Place clubface at right angles to target line. Place tee or other mark on target line a few feet in front of ball. Align clubface with marker. 2. Check hand positions and grip pressure.
	Closed clubface	See chart on p. 47.	Hook	Same as above.
	Lack of hip and knee flexion and/or hyper-extension of wrists. Tension through legs, shoulders, arms.	 Fig. 26	Whiffed Topped Toed Fat	1. Four-step procedure: Stand erect with pelvic tilt increased; flex knees slightly and lean forward from hips; let arms hang naturally from shoulders; grip club, keeping right arm relaxed. 2. "Knees easy"; "bounce" lightly to reduce tension. 3. To correct wrist position recheck grip and lie of clubhead. **Note correct address position shown with ghosted lines in Figure 30.**
	Stance too wide (restricts proper body tilt and turn during swing).	 WIDTH OF SHOULDERS Fig. 27	Slice	Reposition feet with inner borders shoulder distance apart. Ghosted lines indicate correct placement in Fig. 27 .
	Stance too narrow (encourages loss of balance during swing)	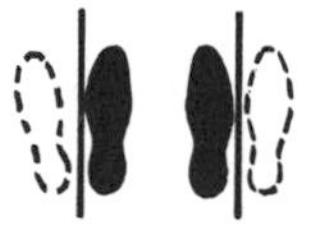 Fig. 28	Inconsistent pattern	Same as above. Stress placement of weight along inner borders of feet. Ghosted lines show correct placement in Fig. 28.
	Failure to place left (target) side of body in dominant position. A. Right side set up too strong.	 Fig. 29	Slice Pull	1. Relax right elbow; drop right shoulder. Right side should feel "soft" and underneath the left. Note correct position indicated by ghosted lines in Fig. 29. 2. Instructor or buddy inserts clubshaft between arms at elbow level; shaft should pass over right arm and under left elbow.

Stage	Common Error	Illustration	Usual Shot Result	Suggested Correction
		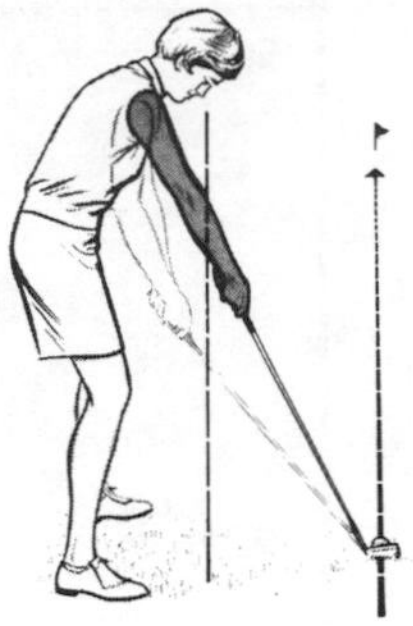 Fig. 30		Note in Fig. 30 how correction (ghosted lines) positions hands **inside** the eye plumbline. Visual checks made of students should reveal hands positioned **on or inside** this line.
	B. Left (target) side collapsed.	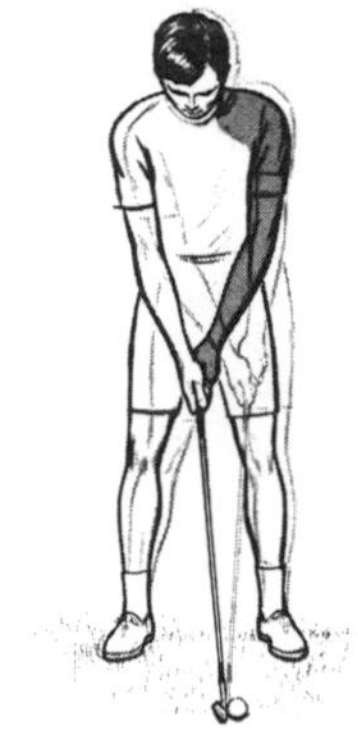 Fig. 31	Whiffed Topped Fat Lack of power	1. Straighten left (target) arm; feel arm as a firm extension of clubshaft. 2. Draw left shoulder up toward ear. Feel left side set up higher and firmer than right. **Note correct position indicated by ghost lines in Fig. 31.** 3. Strengthen left side dominance through use of FIRM, TAUT, CONTROL EXERCISE, **Golf Lessons**, p. 26.
Takeaway	Lifting club ("picking up" action, done primarily with right hand.)	 Fig. 32	Slice Pull	1. Encourage low, extended takeaway by initiating move with left side pushing clubhead away from ball. Instructor faces pupil; places a clubshaft against that of pupil's at point below the middle of pupil's shaft in a manner that will resist pupil's takeaway. During takeaway attempts, resistive forces will travel up pupil's left side, making him sensitive to its proper dominant role. 2. Place a tee or extra ball 4"-6" behind ball in line with target; Have pupil "brush the extra ball out of the way" during takeaway. **Corrected position indicated by ghosted lines and dotted arrow in Fig. 32.**

Stage	Common Error	Illustration	Usual Shot Result	Suggested Correction
	Pronation of left hand	 Fig. 33	Inconsistent pattern: slice, hook, push, pull.	1. Emphasize keeping back of left hand "facing target" during takeaway. 2. Maintain pressure in last three fingers of left hand during takeaway.
	Club moving back too far inside direction line.	 Fig. 34 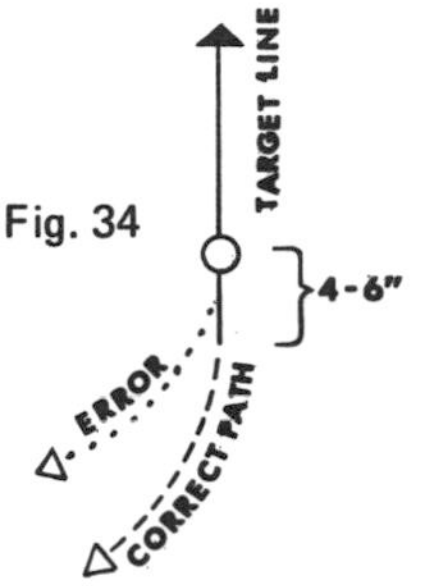	Hook Topped	1. Push clubhead away from body rather than around body. See correction 2 under "Lifting club". 2. Emphasize use of left hand and importance of keeping back of hand "facing target" during takeaway.
	Swaying of head and body (lateral weight shift).	 Fig. 35	Inconsistent pattern Lack of power	1. Emphasize feet controls. 2. As a practice technique only, toe inward with right foot. 3. Use HEAD CONTROL EXERCISE, p. 8 or HEAD-WALL EXERCISE, **Golf Lessons**, p. 24. 4. Stress stretch of left side muscles during takeaway. 5. "Glue" dominant eye to ball and hold there during back-swing.
	Sliding hips to right	See lower half of Fig. 35	Inconsistent pattern Lack of power	Corrections 1 and 2 under preceding error.
	Raising body		Fat Whiffed Inconsistent pattern	1. HEAD-CONTROL EXERCISE p. 8 or HEAD-WALL EXER-CISE, **Golf Lessons**, p. 24. 2. Stress maintaining golf posture throughout backswing.

Stage	Common Error	Illustration	Usual Shot Result	Suggested Correction
Top of Backswing	Lack of upper body tilt and shoulder turn. (swinging with arms only.)	Fig. 36	Slice Pull Topped Lack of power	3. Develop proper shoulder turn with TOWEL EXERCISE, **Golf Lessons,** p. 25 and CANE EXERCISE, **Golf Lessons,** p. 24. 1. Teacher manipulation of pupil's shoulders. Work left shoulder down under chin. Upper back should face target. (Visual cue for pupil: left shoulder points behind ball at top of backswing). 2. TOWEL EXERCISE, **Golf Lessons,** p. 25. 3. CANE EXERCISE, **Golf Lessons,** p. 24. 4. Study NGF Film Loop 2. Follow with swing practice. **Note correct position indicated by ghosted lines in Fig. 36.**
	Loosened grip (Fig. 37-A) (Common visual cue: club drops below horizontal)	Fig. 37-A Sideview Fig. 37	Slice Pull	1. Stress firmness of left hand grip with pressure in last three fingers. 2. Check grip pressure at address for extreme looseness or tension. Adjust accordingly. 3. Develop left hand strength through conditioning with hand dynamometer or isometric exercise for grip described on p. 12. **Corrected position shown by ghosted lines in Fig. 37.**
	Bent left arm (lacks full extension)	Fig. 38	Fat Topped Whiffed Inconsistent pattern	1. Set up firm extension of left arm at address. Feel as though left arm were "in a cast". 2. Develop awareness of left side dominance and stretch during takeaway. Sustain stretch throughout coiling motion to top of backswing. 3. Check degree of hip and knee flexion at address. Adjust accordingly.

Stage	Common Error	Illustration	Usual Shot Result	Suggested Correction
	Tension in legs ("locked knees") and lack of responsive foot action.	See Lower half of Fig. 26.	Whiffed Topped	**Correct position noted by ghosted lines in Fig. 38.** 1. Recheck address position for correct posture, weight distribution. Maintain posture throughout swing. 2. Develop sensitivity to swinging movement and responsive foot action with PARTNER SWING EXERCISE, p. 9.
	Open clubface	 Fig. 39	Slice	1. Recheck address and takeaway positions. Make needed correction from those suggested for these stages. 2. Teacher manipulation of hand position at top, so that hand-forearm relationship is straight. (Note angle line indicating error in adjacent illustration). 3. Have pupil memorize feel of correct hand position at top. Practice reaching this position with right side facing a mirror. Check each time for straight hand-forearm relationship as observed from the side view. **Refer to correct position in Golf Lessons,** p. 40.
	Closed clubface	 Fig. 40	Hook Pull	See corrections for "Open clubface" above.
Downswing	Initiated with hands and/or arms (loss of arm-shaft angle, often referred to as "Casting")	 Fig. 41	Slice Pull Fat Loss of power	1. Initiate downswing with major weight shift through **lower body** toward target. (Note dotted arrows in Fig. 41). Use PARTNER SWING EXERCISE adaptation described in item 2 under Swing Manipulation, p. 49. 2. Offer resistance to pupil's club at top of backswing, forcing pupil to lead downswing with lower body.

Stage	Common Error	Illustration	Usual Shot Result	Suggested Correction
				3. Trigger thoughts to initiate downswing: "Plant left heel on ground" . . . "Drive knees toward target!"
				4. Check for left side dominance in previous stages. Develop where weak through appropriate exercises.
				5. Avoid any conscious move of hands. Concentration on lower body move and left side pulling force will retain wrist cock automatically.
				Ghost lines and dotted arrows indicate correct downswing motion in Fig. 41.
	NOTE: Research indicates that due to the speed of the swing, no conscious influence on the club is possible beyond this point. Error correction, therefore, should focus on the foregoing stages. Faulty position and motion observed during the following stages are the result of earlier errors.			
Impact	Lack of clubhead speed (despite proper mechanics of performance).		Lack of power	1. Develop pupil's sensitivity to rhythmic qualities of swing . . . the relative tempo between backswing and forward swing. Verbal cues to induce acceleration through the ball: "B-a-c-k and **Through!**" . . . "S-t-r-e-t-c-h and **Spring!**"
				2. Practice swings using teaching aid which exaggerates the "swooshing" sound of acceleration. See implement with three plastic balls in place of clubhead shown on p. 60.
				3. Question pupil to identify source of inhibited swing. Cultivate attitude of aggressive determination to accelerate clubhead "down the fairway toward the target!" Exaggerate drive through lower body. Project mind off the ball and out to target . . . "Give clubhead the freedom to 'chase' the ball"!

Stage	Common Error	Illustration	Usual Shot Result	Suggested Correction
	Left side collapsed; right side dominant	Fig. 42	Pull Topped Lack of power	1. Develop left side dominance in address position, takeaway and at top of backswing. 2. See correction 1 for hands-initiated downswing error. 3. Use FIRM, TAUT, CONTROL EXERCISE, **Golf Lessons,** p. 26 to develop left side leader-ship and pulling action. **Note correct impact position shown by ghosted lines in Fig. 42.**
	Lateral moving of head toward target.	Fig. 43	Push Extreme low flight	1. HEAD CONTROL EXERCISE, p. 8. 2. Check for correct shoulder turn and lower body action. Instill mental image of body revolving around a steady head, as the arm of a compass encircles its anchor point. **Note correct head position shown by ghosted lines in Fig. 43.**
Follow Through	Failure to allow club to swing out toward target.	Fig. 44	Slice Loss of distance and accuracy	1. Place tee or other small object 12" in front of ball on target line. Retain object in peripheral vision during swing with thought of brushing object with clubhead after striking ball. **Correct extension noted by ghost lines in Fig. 44.** 2. "Finish with hands high"
	Lack of body turn toward target.			1. Allow force of swing to turn head and body naturally toward target. Belt buckle should face target.

Stage	Common Error	Illustration	Usual Shot Result	Suggested Correction
Finish	Weight remains on right foot; loss of balance	Fig. 45	Slice Topped	1. Develop lower body weight shift at start of downswing. See corrections suggested for arms-hands-initiated downswing error. 2. Strengthen projection of mind toward target. **Proper finish appears as ghosted position in Fig. 45.**
Total Swing	Jerky, tense, unrhythmic pattern		Inconsistency	1. Have student observe a relaxed, rhythmic swing; then swing to a rhythmic cue such as "B-a-c-k and through!" . . . "S-l-o-w and Smooth!" 2. Swing to music or tune which has beat of the golf swing rhythm. Selections of 3/4 or 6/8 time often can provide the desired beat. 3. Adjust elements of student's address position which build tension. 4. Have student dangle club with thumb and forefinger of left hand. Allow clubhead to swing freely in pendular motion, noticing feeling of clubhead weight. Continue until cultivated sensitivity can be incorporated into golf swing. 5. Remove concentration from ball itself and project mind down the fairway. Convince student that ball is merely going to "get caught in the path of the swing". The importance of the ball is secondary to that of the swing.

PSYCHOLOGICAL MATERIALS

Here is a mixed bag of some of the books, cassette tapes, and other programs that attempt to illuminate that dark side of golf where many top players and teachers believe 80 to 90 percent of the battle is waged, anyway. Good technique-type instruction books (including some that appear on the above best-seller list) also pay their respects to the mental side of the game. In a comprehensive survey of psychological materials on golf, some of the "technique" books would deserve mention—and indeed, many would perhaps emerge with a higher ranking, for style and common sense, than some of those in the sampling below.

BOOKS

THE NEW GOLF MIND by Dr. Gary Wiren and Dr. Richard Coop, with Larry Sheehan. 1978, 160 pages, $8.95, *Golf Digest,* N.Y. distributor: Simon & Schuster.

This book builds its argument upon the relatively recent discovery of the fact that the human brain consists of two hemispheres of "gray matter," each with its own way of thinking and its own special functions in relation to motor-skill performance. The authors present and attempt to solve mental/emotional/psychological problems in golf caused by faulty use either of the "Analyzer" side of the brain (responsible for analysis of playing conditions, preshot routine, club selection, hole strategy, target alignment, and attention to details such as lie of ball and grain of greens) or the "Integrator" side (responsible for visualizing ball

An illustration from The New Golf Mind.

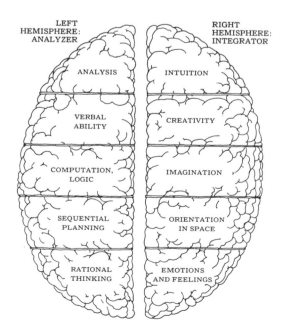

THE TWO-SIDED BRAIN: GENERAL FUNCTIONS

flight, estimating distance on short shots, imagination on trouble shots, and feel, touch, and tempo).

THE INNER ATHLETE: MIND PLUS MUSCLE FOR WINNING by Robert Nideffer. 1979, paperback, $4.95, N.Y.: Crowell.

Dr. Nideffer, a clinical psychologist at the University of Rochester, effectively analyzes the various nonphysical factors that contribute to or detract from performance in athletes at the highest levels of competition in all sports. He assesses various self-management techniques being tried by many athletes today, including the martial arts, meditation, biofeedback, autogenics (a relaxation technique), and hypnosis. He concludes that many of these procedures, properly applied, can help athletes raise or lower their tension level; broaden or narrow their focus of attention; improve their concentration; facilitate memory; reduce fears and variability in performance; stop choking; and increase learning speed, endurance, self-confidence, self-awareness, and enjoyment.

THE PSYCHIC SIDE OF SPORTS by Michael Murphy and Rhea A. White. 1978; cloth $10.95, paperback $5.95; 227 pages, Reading, Mass.: Addison-Wesley.

This book represents the efforts of six years of sifting through some 4,500 case histories of unusual psychic events in dozens of sports, ranging from body-building to skydiving, and encompassing martial arts, team sports, and individual sports—including golf. Most of the experiences reported here happened to top practitioners of the various sports, but the authors suggest that ordinary folk may also partake of the mystical sensations, altered perceptions, and extraordinary feats that make up what they term "the spiritual underground in sports." A proposed training regimen suitable for any sport makes use of such techniques as meditation, biofeedback, mental practice, "inner seeing" (a heightened form of visualization), sensory awareness, and the harnessing of previously untapped energy sources. In the plethora of examples cited in this book, one occasionally loses sight of the forest for the trees, but emphasis throughout is on those enriching aspects of sport other than achievement, self-improvement, and competitiveness. Such appreciation might well help the golfer unnecessarily uptight about his or her game to get back to fully enjoying a day out on the course.

SLOW-MOTION GOLF

If slowed perception is a feature of exceptional performance in sport, then most athletes would naturally want to induce this altered perception of time. A number of athletes, especially golfers, have recognized the im-

portance of slow motion and have deliberately tried to swing more slowly in the interest of achieving more power. Bobby Jones is said to have felt it was not possible to swing a golf club too slowly. This advice is given by many golfers. Dick Aultman reports that during the start of his downswing, Jack Nicklaus' hands move more slowly during the last part of his backswing. This is even more significant when one considers that his is one of the slowest backswings on the golf tour. Aultman cites a British scientist, Dr. David Williams, who has concluded "that, all things being equal, the more leisurely the hands and arms start down, the greater the clubhead speed at impact."

Several golfers carry this advice a step further and advocate slowing down the pace throughout the entire round. Among them are Bruce Devlin, Henry Ransom, Sam Snead, and Jane Blalock. For example, Larry Dennis reports, "[Tom] Weiskopf credits last summer's [1973] startling streak of five victories and a bunch of near misses to a decelerated pace on the golf course." But some golfers carry it still one step further and suggest getting ready for a tournament by moving slowly even when they are off the course.

Cary Middlecoff tells a story about a fellow pro, George Knudson, who held the lead going into the final round of a tournament. Knudson was driving Middlecoff and another pro, Fred Hawkins, to the golf course at the rate of about 16 miles per hour. When urged by his impatient passengers to hurry it up, Knudson, says Middlecoff: ". . . just looked . . . through those dark glasses and said, 'Man, this is my way to cool it. I started thinking this way last night.' " Knudson shot a 65 that day and won the tournament.

It is exciting to consider that even though the passage of time has not actually slowed down, nevertheless the fact that it feels as if it has apparently enables the athlete to accomplish more, just as he would if in fact he did have more time, more amplitude.

—from *The Psychic Side of Sports*

SPORTS PSYCHING by Thomas Tutko and Umberto Tosi. 1976, 229 pages, $6.95, Los Angeles: J. P. Tarcher; Hawthorn Books, distributor.

Sports psychology is right up there with veterinary medicine as an acceptable line of work these days, and Dr. Tutko, cofounder (with Dr. Bruce Ogilvie) of the Institute of Athletic Motivation at San Jose State University, is one of its most famous practitioners. In this book he hammers out a complete mental approach suitable for all sports. He knows his golf and makes fairly frequent and always pertinent references to it. "Sports Psyching" techniques discussed include "getting loose," "breathing easy," "staying on the ball," "mental rehearsal," and "body rehearsal." Also included is a test the reader can take to detemine his or her "sports

emotional-reaction profile"; it measures desire, assertiveness, sensitivity, tension control, confidence, personal accountability, and self-discipline.

GETTING YOURSELF COMPLETELY INTO THE ACTION

The pre-game warm-up routine can take anywhere from three minutes to 20 minutes, depending on how much time you have to devote to it. It can be done while you're sitting on the bench, waiting to get on the court, before you take your practice shots or do your rallying or whatever your usual warm-up is. Here's how it works:

1. "GETTING LOOSE." Briefly tense your legs, buttocks and thighs, stomach, back and neck, arms and shoulders, jaw, face, and eye muscles, holding each muscle briefly and telling it, Let go.

2. "BREATHING EASY." Do two or three "Breathing Easy" exercises—inhaling, holding your breath while counting to four, then slowly exhaling while saying to yourself, Easy . . . easy . . . easy . . . easy.

3. "STAYING ON THE BALL." Look at the ball, basketball rim, bowling pins, or whatever you've made your object of concentration, and say to yourself, Ball . . . ball, or whatever word you've been using. Do this for about a minute.

4. MENTAL REHEARSAL. Close your eyes and in your mind picture the upcoming plays you will have to make, visualizing their successful accomplishment in slow motion. Obviously, you can't anticipate every play, but you can mentally rehearse the fundamental moves. For example, in tennis you can mentally rehearse the serve, then the several kinds of strokes you have to employ in rallying the possible return. In baseball you can rehearse the act of hitting, of how you will handle the various kinds of pitches likely to come at you.

5. BODY REHEARSAL. This can be done when you take the field or court and do your usual physical warm-ups. Shadow-box the moves, first with eyes closed, then with eyes open, one set in slow motion, one at normal speed.

You are now ready to commence play.

—from *Sports Psyching*

THE MISSING LINKS by David C. Morley, M.D. 1976, 235 pages, $8.95, N.Y.: Atheneum/SMI. Tempo paperback, $1.95.

Greenwich, Conn., psychiatrist Morley tries to cover the mental and emotional waterfront in this tome, and in some places he succeeds quite well, notably in his chapters "Nine Holes with a Shrink on Your Shoulder," "How a Top Teacher Would Like Your Mind to Work," and "Ten Questions Most Golfers Need Answering." Elsewhere, the analytical habit occasionally gets the better of him, as when he spends 15 pages describing anxiety in all its forms, and only one paragraph on how to get rid of it. Much food for thought, nonetheless.

BALL OBSESSION

We have mentioned before that the immobility of the golf ball creates a problem of concentration, in that it is much easier to pay attention to a moving object than to a stationary one. However, the ball's immobility is not entirely a negative force, in that obviously the ball isn't going to move until it is hit, which means that the golfer doesn't have to concern himself about its position. Indeed, once he has developed a vivid image of the path of the club head, he should theoretically be able to make perfect contact with the ball even when blindfolded. And, indeed, all the great golf teachers and many of the touring professionals can easily do this, which proves that, whether they are aware of it or not, all golfers have the capability of almost obliterating the ball from their vision. The subtle paradox is that, although the good golfer seems to be gazing fixedly at the ball his mind is actually occupied with other things. Primarily, in my researches, these other things prove to be the club head's position and the muscular feel and tempo of the swing.

I firmly believe that the infamous putting disaster known as the "yips" is a clear manifestation of a person being mesmerized by the ball. The ball, through its hypnotic effect, causes the muscles of the hands and arms to congeal and jerk in an unsightly spasm that destroys any chance of a decent stroke. If the golfer could sometime make himself mentally ignore the ball by concentrating instead entirely on the speed and direction of the putter's head, his "yipping" days would, I believe, quickly be over.

—from *The Missing Links*

POWERS OF MIND by Adam Smith. 1976, paperback, 419 pages, $1.95, N.Y.: Ballantine Books.

George Plimpton-style, Adam Smith checks out personally virtually every significant mind-trip fad of the past decade—est, Zen, Arica, LSD, biofeedback, rolfing, Sufism, transcendental meditation, yoga, *I Ching*, and others. No golf, but good perspective on some of the mental techniques being test-piloted with increasing frequency these days in golf and in sports generally. Extensive notes and bibliography, too.

THE HANDBOOK OF INNER SPORTS by James Zabriskie. 1976, paperback, 173 pages, $1.95, N.Y.: Kensington Publishing Corp.

This book is in the nature of a ruminative essay on sport, with which the author was obsessed as a youth, and its role in Life. The author then develops a set of recommendations for playing the game similar to Gallwey's "inner tennis" approach.

THE INNER GAME OF TENNIS by W. Timothy Gallwey. 1974, 141 pages, $7.95, N.Y.: Random House.

This, the self-help book *par excellence* of our Aquarian Age, sold over 300,000 copies and is still selling. Gallwey's inner-game techniques, derived from Zen and yoga and theoretically applicable to all sports, include "quieting the mind," "increasing awareness," "letting go," and "trusting the body." The book stresses attitudes and outlook rather than technique and practice, and predictably, met resistance in the tennis-teaching establishment when it first appeared. (Gladys M. Heldman, writing in *World Tennis,* unkindly lumped the Gallwey approach with ". . . Moonism, Buddhism, and all the other 'isms' that ex-book salesmen, deadbeats, dingbats, and religious nuts are attempting to sell to the public.") Various learning problems are usefully depicted throughout the book through the presentation of imaginary dialogues between "Self 1" and "Self 2." For Gallwey, Self 1 represents the judgmental and critical aspect of mind/personality. Self 2 is a kind of noble savage lurking within all of us, who could perform tasks of coordination and skill quite ably if only Self 1 stayed off his back. Gallwey has already translated his theories into a book for skiers and is at work on *The Inner Game of Golf* (tentatively scheduled to appear in late 1979). For information on this latter project, contact Inner Golf, P.O. Box 4206, Malibu, CA 90265.

SELF 1 AND SELF 2

Now we are ready for the first major postulate of the Inner Game: within each player the kind of relationship that exists between Self 1 and Self 2 is the prime factor in determining one's ability to translate his knowledge of technique into effective action. In other words, the key to better tennis—or better anything—lies in improving the relationship between the conscious teller, Self 1, and the unconscious, automatic doer, Self 2.

Imagine that instead of being parts of the same person, Self 1 (teller) and Self 2 (doer) are two separate persons. How would you characterize their relationship after witnessing the following conversation between them? The player on the court is trying to make a stroke improvement. "Okay, dammit, keep your stupid wrist firm," he orders. Then as ball after ball comes over the net, Self 1 reminds Self 2, "Keep it firm. Keep it firm. Keep it firm!" Monotonous? Think how Self 2 must feel. It seems as though Self 1 doesn't think Self 2 hears well, or has a short memory, or is stupid. The truth is, of course, that Self 2, which includes the unconscious mind and nervous system, hears everything, never forgets anything, and is anything but stupid. After hitting the ball firmly once, he knows forever which muscles to contract to do it again. That's his nature.

And what's going on during the hit itself? If you look closely at the face of the player, you will see that his cheek muscles are tightening and his lips are pursed in effort and attempted concentration. But face muscles aren't required to hit the backhand, nor do they help concentration. Who's initiating that effort? Self 1, of course. But why? He's supposed to be the teller, not the doer, but it seems he doesn't really trust 2 to do the job or else he wouldn't have to do all the work himself. This is the nub of the problem: Self 1 does not trust Self 2, even though the unconscious, automatic self is extremely competent.

Back to our player. His muscles tense in over-effort, contact is made with the ball, there is a slight flick of the wrist, and the ball hits the back fence. "You bum, you'll never learn how to hit a backhand," Self 1 complains. By thinking too much and trying too hard, Self 1 has produced tension and muscle conflict in the body. He is responsible for the error, but he heaps the blame on Self 2 and then, by condemning it further, undermines his own confidence in Self 2. As a result the stroke grows worse and frustration builds.

Getting it together mentally in tennis involves the learning of several internal skills: 1) learning to program your computer (Self 2) with images rather than instructing yourself with words; 2) learning to "trust thyself" (Self 2) to do what you (Self 1) ask of it. This means letting Self 2 hit the ball; and 3) learning to see "nonjudgmentally"— that is, to see what is happening rather than merely noticing how well or how badly it is happening. This overcomes "trying too hard." All these skills are subsidiary to the master skill, without which nothing of value is ever achieved: the art of concentration.

—from *The Inner Game of Tennis*

GOLF IN THE KINGDOM by Michael Murphy.
1972, 205 pages, $7.95, N.Y.: Viking Press.

Murphy's novel-like work manages to get the elusive Scots golfing soul on paper, principally in the characters of Shivas Irons, the philosopher/pro, and Seamus MacDuff, author of an unpublished tract called *The Logarithms of the Just.* But it is the likable young American narrator of the story, a searcher after truth in golf and life, who for us makes sense out of the various on-course mystical experiences and in-pub recondite references. The book is "psychological" in that it continually explores the possibilities in the role of the mind in golf, and feelingly reports on the game's spiritual dimension.

THE TERRIBLE AGE OF SHANK

One starry night during the war Shivas rediscovered the zodiac. The "true zodiac" he called it, since it bore little resemblance to the one your ordinary astrologer refers to. He did not see it all that night, in fact there was still a constellation missing when I met him fifteen years later. But during his lonely nighttime vigils he looked up there and eventually put most of it in place.

It had thirteen signs. An extra one was needed, he said, to fit the stars to our new age. As in other spheres science was badly out of touch here. We were passing now from the age of Shank to the age of MacDuff; he had named the governing constellation of the coming age after his teacher. Reading round the heavenly circle, the signs went like this: Burningbush (where Aries had been), the first sign of spring, then Porky Oliver, Morris and Morris (after Tommy, Jr., and Old Tom), Vardon, Jones, Slice, one unnamed, Hook, Disappearing Hole, Swilcan Burn (after a famous golf hazard), Hogan, MacDuff, and Shank. These were the configurations marking his "milky fairway." He had been born, I believe, on the cusp between Hogan and MacDuff, hence his enormous regard for them both.

The most interesting sign as far as I am concerned was "Disappearing Hole." I thought about it after I saw the movie 2001: A Space Odyssey, for it was something like the stargate through which the astronaut plunged toward his shattering transformation. Apparently it was the sign Shivas peered into first during his nocturnal meditations, at least when it was in the sky. For all I know, he was looking for it that night on the window ledge. He related it to the mystery of the hole in golf, our willingness—our passion even—to humble ourselves to that tiny opening after ranging "far and wide across the green world." Stargate and golf hole, two symbols of Man's crossing through. I wish I could make it out on a clear night. But I have trouble with all the signs he showed me, even though he took great pains to point them out.

It was good to hear that we were passing out of the terrible age of Shank. The past centuries, like the dreadful golf shot after which they were named, were the very worst in civilization's troubled history; we could look forward now to an age of "true gravity" and the apotheosis of his teacher's vision. Hook and Slice had been other bad eras in the world's unfoldment. The Age of Jones had been a good one.

If my memory is correct, he said I had several planets in Swilcan Burn—though my birthdate fell on the cusp between Slice and the unnamed sign. He could tell just by looking at me that the planets were there, and this meant that I was always in danger of ending in the final hazard. Though he pronounced upon the fact with great solemnity and conviction, I have never been able to remember what the "final hazard" was.

I asked him why he didn't name that last sign, seeing that he could always change it later if it didn't seem right. But he shook his head decisively and said that every sign made itself known "when he was ready." Naming a constellation "was nae little thing."

—from *Golf in the Kingdom*

ZEN IN THE ART OF ARCHERY by Eugene Herrigel. 1971, 109 pages, $1.95, N.Y.: Random House.

A German scholar travels to Japan to learn how to shoot a bow and arrow from a Zen master, and in the course of his experience he learns how to learn. Some readers will readily see the applicability to golf of the experience ("For this is what the art of archery means: a profound and far-reaching contest of the archer with himself") and appreciate the concentration problems exposed here. The book is something of an underground classic and a precursor of *Golf in the Kingdom* and *The Inner Game of Tennis*. It originally appeared in 1953.

HOW TO KEEP YOUR TEMPER ON THE GOLF COURSE by Tommy Bolt, as told to C. W. Griffith. 1969, 145 pages, $3.95, N.Y.: David McKay.

Though this is basically a lighthearted approach to solving temper tantrums and related mental/emotional problems on the course, Bolt offers much solid—sometimes familiar—advice and cites freely from his and other pros' careers to show how one can lose strokes, matches, or tournaments by not doing so. Bolt explains in passing why his thorny reputation was not entirely deserved. The only clubs he throws in the book are aimed at today's too-long courses—and at lateral water hazards of every epoch.

BOLT'S LAWS

I. *On Temper: One bad shot deserves another.*

II. *Also on Temper: Anger destroys both concentration and coordination and that compounds the anger and it's one helluva mess.*

III. *On Beating Yourself: The mind messes up more shots than the body. So watch it!*

IV. *On Learning the Game: First of all learn how you are supposed to hit the ball, then get out and start hitting until you come up with a logical swing. Then and only then if you hit a bad shot, cuss—but softly, or you can end up with laryngitis.*

V. *On Putting and Chipping: Nobody can putt better than he can, but everybody can putt worse than he can.*

VI. *On Look-Ups: Don't get sore if your head gets into the act now and then—after all, it wants to play, too.*
—from *How to Keep Your Temper on the Golf Course*

MIND OVER GOLF by Tom Nieporte and Don A. Sauers. 1968, 112 pages, Garden City, N.Y.: Doubleday.

Subtitled "What 50 Top Pros Can Teach You About the Mysterious Mental Side of Golf," this book is based mainly on results of a short questionnaire circulated among a number of professionals, including 30 who were regulars on the PGA tour at the time. The best chapters reveal the numerous tricks of visualization and self-hypnosis used by various pros. The most predictable and least interesting parts dwell on pros' ratings of nebulous though obviously important factors such as confidence, concentration, practice, etc. One question somewhat surprisingly reveals that half the pros surveyed approved of the use of tranquilizers on the circuit. Another shows that 80 percent of the players actually resort to saying prayers on the golf course during tournaments—so *that's* their secret! Nieporte is a rare bird—a highly successful club pro who managed to win big in the past in occasional ventures on tour. But for some reason, he keeps his personal experience of mental/emotional/psychological factors almost completely out of this treatment.

VISUALIZATION IN PUTTING

The most commonly mentioned trick was the imaginary line method. . . . Billy Casper and our two former U.S. Open champions were among several pros who told us that they use it.

Several variations on this also were mentioned. Bob Benning, of the Plainfield Country Club in New Jersey, said that he tried to visualize both the line and the sight of the ball dropping into the cup. Two other pros said that they first visualize the line and then pick out two spots along that line and try to roll the ball over the spots. One of the pros was quite explicit about where these spots should be. He said that one should be near the hole, or at the point where the ball will start to break, and that the other should be a few inches in front of the ball—a spot over which the ball must travel to arrive at the more distant spot.

Our favorite suggestion of this type came from Tom Strafaci, the same pro who likes to aim at the sky when faced with a narrow fairway. He told us that he visualizes "a canal to the hole." If that doesn't get the ball into the cup, nothing will.

Al Geiberger likes to feel that he is "stroking the ball with the back of the putter, rather than with the leading edge." Bob Crowley, on the other hand, concentrates on tapping the back of the ball.

Two others focus their attention on the writing on the ball. Bob Goalby likes the number of the ball to be in the same place on every putt. And one of our anonymous experts lines up the name on the ball with the line to the hole.

Dewitt Weaver, Jr. of Cairo, Georgia, and Vince Sullivan of Metuchen, New Jersey, concentrate on the hole; Dewitt on a small spot in the hole, rather than on the whole

hole, and Vince on the back of the cup—"the white rim, rather than the hole itself."

Tom Weiskopf keeps his head still and concentrates on hitting the ball "as solidly as possible." This is similar to the popular idea of concentrating on "tapping" the ball, rather than "pushing" it.

One of our pros said simply, "I believe that the ball is going into the hole!"

One of the old golfer's tales which has been subjected to severe questioning by our experts is that famous phrase, "Never up, never in." This time, we'll present the arguments and let you decide.

This debate may be older than the one raging around the "blank mind" theory. The first written discussion of it that we could find appeared in a book called The Brain and Golf, written by C. W. Bailey in 1923.

Mr. Bailey was a believer. He said, "When we are short with the approach putt we have an annoying sense of failure and a suggestion of a continuance of it; but on the other hand, if we putt boldly, even if the ball runs past the hole, the shot appears to be a more meritorious performance and gives us confidence for the return putt." Where have we heard the word "confidence" before?

We didn't take an actual vote on the "never up, never in" issue, but we feel confident (there we go again) that the majority of today's professionals preach this gospel.

And yet—Paul Runyan, the putting expert's expert (he gives lessons to the best), has said that this is a wise theory only at distances of less than ten or twelve feet. On longer putts he recommends going for an imaginary one-foot circle.

—from Mind Over Golf

GOLFMANSHIP by Stephen Potter. 1968, 177 pages, N.Y.: McGraw-Hill.

The humorist who gave us Gamesmanship and One-upmanship here fixes his mad gaze upon the gambits, ploys, counter-ploys, and parries involved in the game of golf. His knowledge of the complexities of the game and of the convoluted relationships of the people competing at it is vast. The text clearly applies to the U.S. golfer, although most examples are British and from time to time slightly opaque to the American reader. The book may be usefully consulted as a kind of golf-psychology treatise, hence the inclusion of it here rather than under "Good Reading."

ON THE FIRST TEE

Many golfers have been frightened all their lives of the first tee. This is precisely the kind of situation where, difficult as it is, gamesmanship can be of some help.

What is the predominant feeling as we wait on this tee? It is fear. How can we counteract—gain advantage? Quite often on this tee there are tall youths waiting to drive off. As they take practice swings, the earth trembles, the air sings, with the speed of their club-heads through that vast arc. You will feel inclined to take no practice swing at all because you know your swing may either make no sound whatever or merely hit the ground a puny 'bonk' and stop there.

One is waiting on the tee before driving. A pause. A bit of a hold up. Two couples to play before you. Before being caught up in the game, one's mind is a confusion of golf and non-golf thoughts, fag ends of anxieties, attempts to remember the time you drove beyond the bunker at the 7th last Saturday and what it was you did right mixed up with an attempt to work out why Senator Kodex drifted away from you at the party, and what possessed you to make a sort of financial boast to Jean? Here on this haunted square of turf, when the golfer is at his most vulnerable, the gamesman should be at his most alert. Yet too often he lets the opportunity slip.

A few suggestions. If opponent starts to talk about golf, walk five paces away and stare in the opposite direction. Make him feel as if he were talking in church.

Usually, in our lot, there was silence while the half-dozen or so waited. Tickler used this fact to make tastelessly timed introductions.

"Let's see, do you know Major Cornpetter?" he would say. "This is 'Tootles' Austin," he would go on, using a little-known nickname, which Austin hated. Later Tickler would be heard whispering that Austin was "shy."

The worst thing that Tickler did was to choose the wrong time to tell a funny story, and if there is a worst time, it is on the first tee.

"I've told you the story about Spears on the 1st tee at Moujins," he would begin.

"Yes," Cornpetter would say.

"About the little man with a limp in front?" Tickler would go on, laughing as if the whole world was laughing with him. "Who turned out to be Field-Marshal Lord Methuen," said Cornpetter, in a dead voice. But Tickler simply doubled up at this reminder.

There are ways of increasing first tee tension, or reversing it. Young Cornpetter knew that his father the Major disapproved of his longish hair. He would, when playing against his father and waiting to play before strangers, take out a pocket comb . . .

In foursome play Ackminster, who was a bit of an all-rounder, used to say to his opponents: "Let's see, which of you is the first string?" This is a phrase from rackets, and it is accepted that rackets is a more esoteric game than golf.

But my model for first tee behavior has always been G. Paine. He is simple, he is quiet. He stands a little apart. He takes no practice swings with driver. Calling for a number 6, he holds it in his left hand and makes a gentle stroking motion grazing the turf. Nothing more.

—from Golfmanship

IT'S THE DAMNED BALL! by Ike S. Handy. 1966, 150 pages, Chicago: Twentieth Century Press.

A layman's look at the game by a lawyer who took it up at age 38 and became a scratch golfer shortly thereafter. Much interesting speculation and advice here, but one is somewhat troubled to discover that the author tries out every one of his theories on his wife first.

ANXIETY

One of the strongest contributing factors to making an error in the mechanics of the swing is the inability to control the nervousness or anxiety to get to the ball and, having reached it, to begin preparations for the next shot, waggling or swinging the club, or where playing under winter rules or the ball is on the putting green, preparing a good lie or cleaning up the line of putt, cleaning the ball, squatting and sighting the line, etc., sometimes surreptitiously feeling the grain of the grass, with occasionally a glance at the player who is making a shot, more often not. This, of course, refers to the usual golf game, not to tournament play where the rules are more or less observed. The unconscious nervousness of the player who indulges in these habits will continue into his swing and is fatal to it, whereas if he could control this unconscious anxiety he could approach his ball with calmness and deliberation and concentrate more completely and more readily on his swing. I have often forecast a missed shot from observation of this one fact.

The successful cooperation of both the conscious and subconscious demands not only that the subconscious should be allowed to take fairly complete charge of as large a portion of the labor as it can efficiently direct, but that it should do so under a favorable oversight by the conscious mind, not a nervous, or intimidating, or vacillating or too conscious one.

Again I say, the only way this can be accomplished is to completely employ the conscious mind with the mechanics of the swing. It must not dwell upon the result of the shot; nor must it cause any hurrying of the stroke for other reasons.

Many of the bad shots of golf are caused only by the anxiety or nervousness of the player. In most instances it is the rapidly executed swing which causes the shanked or topped shot brought about by the player thinking of the result and being on needles and pins to get the ball on its way. He is the antithesis of calmness and deliberation and under these circumstances the subconscious is not acting under a favorable oversight but the conscious mind is furnishing a nervous or excited influence instead of concerning itself strictly with the method and timing of making the swing. While there are ten bad shots in golf, if you attribute to each a specific designation, there are only three *types. They are classified as nervous, intimidating and*

vacillating; that is, those terms describe the state of the conscious mind which undertakes to supervise the stroke; the same terms used by Dr. Jastrow, who was not referring particularly to golf. Under the "intimidating" classification come those shots where the player, even though calm and deliberate and not acting under the "nervous" influence, carries in his mind the thought that he is not using the right club or that he will hit the ball too far or not far enough or into a troublesome position to right or left. And under the "vacillating" head are those where the player allows his conscious mind to wander to some one or more of the millions of things irrelevant to making the stroke, resulting in a careless shot. This is my own bête noir. *I hope you will not be so afflicted; that you are one of those who can truthfully say, "nothing bothers me." But I am bound to add that if you are a good golf player you can't.*

—from *It's the Damned Ball!*

THE MYSTERY OF GOLF by Arnold Haultain. 1965, N.Y.: Serendipity Press.

This fascinating book by a Canadian essayist first appeared in a private edition of 400 copies in 1908, then again two years later in a regular edition. Reports Herbert Warren Wind (who wrote the foreword to the 1965 edition): "It got around fairly well because Haultain had a good mind—he was an avant-gardist in matters of psychology and knew a good deal about anatomy and philosophy—and he had two other things going for him: he obviously knew golf (and its history) fairly well, and he knew the game first-hand. As a result, his book, which probed the magnetism of golf and its other psychological aspects in a deeper way than had been done up to that time (and, I might add, since), got to be quite well known."

ARNOLD PALMER: MY GAME AND YOURS by Arnold Palmer. 1963, 158 pages, N.Y.: Simon & Schuster.

The bulk of this book is devoted to mental aspects, or "How to play golf from the shoulders up." Much sensible advice enlivened with accounts of some of the ups and downs in Arnie's own game, collected under such headings as "Developing a Winning Frame of Mind," "Relaxation and Concentration," "How to Reach Inside Yourself When in Trouble," "The Mental Approach to the First Three Holes," "The Mental Approach to the Last Three Holes," and "How to Talk Yourself Into Better Putting."

THE SECOND NINE

There is another hazard during the final holes of a golf round, not so much for us professionals as for the amateur, and especially for the amateur who doesn't play often. To a man who has been sitting at a desk all week, who hasn't walked any farther than from his front door to the bus stop and back again in the evening, a round of golf can be pretty tiring. Many weekend players come up to those last three holes feeling a little beat. Their legs are tired; their hands are starting to hurt; their shoulders are getting stiff.

The tendency, when you feel like this, is to try too hard. You know you're tired, you're not as strong as you were on the first nine; so you feel you have to put an extra effort into hitting the ball. You think you have to wind up a little more, take a longer backswing, press for some kind of hidden reserve of physical strength that will make up for your fatigue. But when you're tired, your legs can't move as fast as usual. You can't get the same kind of body action. Trying too hard can only result in overswinging and getting off-balance, so now you miss your shots. Your game goes all to pieces, and what started out as a good round winds up a fiasco.

The secret of living with fatigue on the golf course is not to try harder, but to settle for hitting the ball with a little less than your maximum strength. This is the time to take a shorter backswing, not a longer one. The swing has to become more *compact, not* less *compact. You have to play now as if you were ten years older, because fatigue has actually made your muscles ten years older for the time being. Your drives can't possibly be as long as they were earlier in the day. You're going to have to use a 5-iron, maybe even a 4-, where on the first nine you were using a 6-. The pros do this all the time when they feel tired. I've done it hundreds of times. You should try it too.*

—from *My Game and Yours*

THE EDUCATION OF A GOLFER by Sam Snead, with Al Stump. 1962, 248 pages, N.Y.: Simon & Schuster.

With its wonderful dialogue, West Virginia wit, and tall tales of the burgeoning tour of the postwar era, this book not only captures Sam Snead's flavorful character and career, but also delivers a series of informal lectures on psyching yourself up and your competitor out.

THE "HOW'S-YOUR-LOVE-LIFE?" PLOY

Don't ever depend on the rules to protect you: it's dog-eat-dog out there, and I've known few big winners who, consciously or unconsciously, wouldn't rattle the other man any little way they could.

Frankly, I've never gotten over stage fright out there in front of the people, which makes you vulnerable to the smart tricks. Every man's chest has a heart in it, and that thing goes thump, thump, thump—*and never stops doing it when other folks are standing around, judging you.*

After I'd put some age on me, along came a young star who thought he'd upset old Sam and make a headline—and the way he chose to do it was by using the needle.

We were teeing off at Charleston, West Virginia, a course he was more familiar with than I was, and as I placed my ball he spoke up with, "Now watch it, Sam, over to the right. There's woods and a big drop-off there and you can get into real trouble if you hit in there."

This sort of strategy I cut my teeth on—warning a man of something so strongly that it'll prey on his mind to the point of creating an almost magnetic pull when you swing the club. Talk of trouble can draw you straight to trouble.

This youngster needed to be given a lesson for trying such an old gimmick on me. As it happened, he was thirty years old and still a bachelor, the reason being, as everyone said, that he was still tied to his mother's apron strings. And such talk bothered him.

After driving safely to the left, I waited until he stepped up to hit, then remarked, "Billy, when did you say you got married?"

With that he put his ball right into those woods. He lost, 8 and 7.

—from *The Education of a Golfer*

THE WINNING TOUCH IN GOLF by Peter G. Cranford, Ph.D. 1961, 171 pages, Englewood Cliffs, N.J.: Prentice-Hall.

A lot of common-sense golf advice and no unnecessary psychological jargon in this book, based on the author's experience as a golfer (a 70s shooter for many years, reports Cary Middlecoff in his foreword, as well as a practicing psychologist and teacher) and his perception of the experiences of teaching pros and touring pros. Chapters are labeled "Secrets," and the author invariably enumerates his reasons and solutions for problems. The trouble with common sense applied across the board in golf is that some of it can sound pretty obvious. (To control temper tantrums, says Dr. Cranford, "you must practice continuous self-control.") This is too bad because the author is consistently mindful of the potential instructional value in the areas he explores and some of his "chapter-secrets" are provocative and genuinely helpful.

LONGER DRIVES AND HOW TO GET THEM

Very often, the biggest factor preventing a person from obtaining maximum power is his psychological attitude. If this attitude is not a proper one, he puts an artificial limit on his distance. Since there is a good correlation between one's distance and one's over-all play, he thus also places an artificial limit on his scoring averages.

The first requirement for obtaining greater length is an understanding of the fact that very few golfers attain their maximum effective distance, and that it is not likely that the reader has. Some day we shall have a test that will indicate the maximum distance for each golfer, but until that time we must believe that there is a good bit of dif-

ference between how far we do hit and how far we could hit the ball.

The second requirement for greater length is an understanding of the theory of golfing power. *The mechanics of generating power have been so well described in other sources that it would be inappropriate to deal with it in detail here. However, it is psychologically helpful if we understand the theory of the power swing.*

Power becomes cumulative in the correct golf swing—somewhat as it does in a four-stage rocket. In the rocket, the first speed is generated by the burning of the lower end of the rocket. When the rocket is making all the speed it can with this energy, the second stage adds its burst of speed. Then the third stage adds its power. Finally, the fourth stage (in the golf swing, the hands) capitalizes on all the other speeds and adds its own.

It is obvious that no single application of power can do the cumulative job of all four, and it is also obvious that if the stages of the rocket go off in the wrong order, speed must be lost. The part of psychology in this is rather small, but that small bit is important. You must have a proper image of how the power is theoretically applied before you can get out of yourself all that is within you. The greatest single cause of the loss of power is the lack of a proper image of golfing mechanics. "Hitting hard" is not enough. A small golfer who applies his power correctly can out-drive a larger one who does not.

The third requirement for distance is exercise of the will to hit. *Many golfers do not obtain the distance they should because they do not hit the ball as hard as they can. Somewhere along the way they found a method of hitting the ball more squarely by hitting it easily. This produced the common golfing delusion that you can hit a ball just as far by hitting it easily as you can by hitting it hard. Those who have made this "discovery" or have picked it up on hearsay are convinced that they cannot hit it hard and squarely. They lose the will to hit hard. This becomes a habit, difficult to overcome.*

—from *The Winning Touch in Golf*

HOW YOU CAN PLAY BETTER GOLF USING SELF-HYPNOSIS by Jack Heise. 1961, 125 pages, $2.00, North Hollywood, Calif.: Wilshire Book Co.

Jargon-free introduction to the subject of hypnosis, with plenty of relevant quotes from golfers and teachers.

BETTER GOLF THROUGH MENTAL PICTURES

The secret of good golf is the employment of the visual image or mental picture.

There are two mental pictures used to improve golf. One is the visual image of the swing; the other is the flight of the ball.

You must get into your mind a clear picture of what your clubs and body ought to do during a stroke. Picture your favorite pro making a perfect swing. You will notice its main characteristics are power, rhythm, and balance. Once you have it fixed firmly in your mind, try to model your own swing after it. Instead of seeing the professional make the swing, picture yourself doing it. Make it so real in your mind that you actually feel the swing of the club and see the flight of the ball.

Horton Smith, who collected 33 titles during his career, suggests: "Try to develop a mental picture of the ideal swing, whether it be that of a single player, or a composite of the features of several. I visualize a composite of such players as Chick Evans, Walter Hagen, and Bobby Jones and try to blend them into a personalized swing of my own."

Lloyd Mangrum, in his book, Golf . . . A New Approach, *reveals how he deliberately tried to copy the swing of Sam Snead, the short game of Johnny Revolta, and the putting style of Horton Smith.*

Don't be afraid of following this advice just because someone has told you that every golfer swings differently. It isn't true! Bob Toski, known as "Mighty Mouse," stands 5'8" and weighs 127 pounds. Yet, he has the same basic movements in his golf swing as does George Bayer, former University of Washington football star tackle, who has a powerful 6'5½" frame and 260 pounds of solid muscle. He is one of the mightiest hitters in the game, once belting a tee shot seven yards past the flag on a 435-yard hole. What may appear to be a difference in swing is only individual peculiarities and temperament.

By using visual imagery, you see yourself in the champion's place. You are actually making the swing of the professional in your mental movie. It is this transference of identity that produces the subconscious feel. It is formed in your conscious mind by a combination of messages received from your senses.

—from *Better Golf Through Self-Hypnosis*

CASSETTES

GOLF MED-A-TAPE. 1977, 1-hour cassette, 16-page instruction manual, $12.50.
The "Med-A-Tape" Co.
P.O. Box 3477
Walnut Creek, CA 94598

On the theory that "poor play comes mainly from tension and lapses in concentration," Side 1 drills the listener in standard progressive-relaxation techniques and proposes a methodical approach to setting up for each shot to help minimize anxiety and sharpen focus. Side 2 talks you through the full swing and (somewhat less successfully) the putting stroke, the idea being to use visualization powers to acquire a subconscious feel

for a good golf swing. The voice on tape (that of a professional hypnotist) is suitably lulling and suggestive. The accompanying manual claims one to two weeks of repetitive listening will produce tangible improvement in your golf game. Most intriguing suggestion: Imagine a good shot several times in a row "at the speed of a dream" and you'll instill the mental picture firmly in your own swing.

SUBCONSCIOUS GOLF. 1977, four 30-minute cassette tapes, 16-page instruction manual, $39.95 (also available in 8-track and on records).
Mindgame Enterprises, Inc.
J. C. Whitted and Associates
1650 W. Alameda, Suite 100
Tempe, AZ 85282

These tapes record a lecture on psychological factors in golf given frequently by Ed Grant, a self-taught golfer who majored in psychology at the University of Arizona and later caddied on the pro tour for three years. Grant conceptualizes a three-part mind consisting of a conscious, subconscious, and creative subconscious processes and offers a number of tools for making use of these various processes more effectively in golf, mainly through the mechanisms of self-talk and self-image-formation. The tapes are more descriptive than prescriptive but there are specific tips on nervousness, confidence, visualization, concentration, and slumps. Grant is a bit free-and-easy with some psychological concepts and terms and would probably provoke the wrath of academicians who didn't realize he is only trying to get us around the course in fewer strokes.

GOLF POWER. Two cassette tapes and booklet, $31.50.
Golf Power
Box 8719
Denver, CO 80201

Alex Merklingar, the creator of these tapes designed to help the golfer use energies more effectively, discussed his ideas in *Golf* magazine a couple of years ago. He summed up his approach to shotmaking as a four-step process: Visualize, Stabilize, Energize, Execute. An educational psychologist who is also a low-handicap golfer listened to these tapes and reported: ". . . overly simplistic . . . made statements that are rather naive and would be very difficult to substantiate . . . ranged into the metaphysical realm at times . . . the deliberately created background noises proved distracting to me rather than relaxing or reinforcing, as they claim."

POWER ZONE GOLF. Two cassette tapes and booklet, $29.95.
Power Zone/The Stress Clinic
122 Glen St.
Snohomish, WA 98290

Not seen. Based on a method developed by stress management specialist Hoyt Griffith. "Enables you to form perfect guide patterns for game control directly in the nervous system before you tee off."

HYPNOSIS/SELF-HYPNOSIS PROGRAMS FOR GOLFERS

According to *Golf* magazine Instruction Editor Desmond Tolhurst, the programs listed below offer a chance at improved golf through hypnosis techniques.

American Golf Seminars
2255 Camino Del Rio South
San Diego, CA 92108
(Dean Reinmuth, director)

Golf-O-Genics
102 Ruby Circle
Brandon, FL 33511
(Dean Refram and Art Burgoyne, directors)

Nassau Hypnosis Golf Program
Nassau Pain and Stress Center
Nassau Professional Building/222 Station Plaza North
Mineola, NY 11501

INSTRUCTION BOOKS FOR THE WOMAN GOLFER

INSIDE GOLF FOR WOMEN by Patty Berg, with Marsh Schiewe. 1977, 86 pages, $4.95, Chicago: Contemporary Books.
Good basic instruction in well-illustrated (b/w pho-

tos of Patty) paperback format. Especially suitable for the older woman golfer.

A NATURAL WAY TO GOLF POWER by Judy Rankin, with Michael Aronstein; illustrated by Dom Lupo. 1976, 126 pages, $8.95, N.Y.: Harper & Row. 1977, Cornerstone Library paperback, $2.95.

A sophisticated instruction guide geared to the woman golfer who already has learned the fundamentals of the game. It may be especially suitable for ambitious junior golfers and all women who are thinking of making golf their career. A few chapters are devoted to how Rankin herself learned to play, her amateur golfing days and her life on the LPGA Tour.

THE COMPLETE WOMAN GOLFER by Vivien Saunders. 1975, £5.95, 144 pages, Stanley Paul, London.

Clear, common-sense instruction by a former British playing pro who also has had a great deal of practical experience on the lesson tee. She interprets the golf swing expressly for women, in a way beginners can understand, yet with enough sophistication and perceptiveness that the advanced player will also benefit from reading. Excellent b/w photos throughout this large format book.

GIVE IT A SWISH

Now you have reached the stage where you can put the swing together sufficiently well to get the ball airborne from this grassy type of lie, just brushing the grass on which it sits and letting the loft of the club send the ball into the air. From here we want to build up length. Hitting the ball a long way is usually fairly natural for a man; in fact most men try to hit the ball too hard. For women, however, the major handicap even into the single figure handicap range is just not being able to hit the ball far enough. It is true that amongst world class players the very longest hitters tend to be big and powerful, but to become a long hitter, certainly by club standards, muscle and strength are not required. It is far more a question of achieving the right knack—almost a throwing action or flick of the wrists.

For the professional golfer this flick of the wrists is so natural, just as in throwing a ball, that he or she is unconscious of it. In fact, because the professional is more concerned with accuracy as a rule than with distance, the natural flick of the wrists almost has to be curbed. But not so with the average woman golfer and beginner. With these players, the hands and wrists need most definite training. To develop this knack of a flick of the wrists one needs a strange combination of firmness and looseness in the muscles; one wants firm, perfect control with the hands and yet looseness in the wrists and arms to permit them to

travel at speed. Try this experiment. Without holding a club, stiffen up your left arm and swing it in front of you. Now relax it and feel the difference as it swings. The first feels strong, but it is with the second that all the speed can be felt. So the first hurdle is to develop this idea of relaxation and speed, not force.

—from *The Complete Woman Golfer*

GOLF: A NATURAL COURSE FOR WOMEN by Sandra Haynie. 1975, 208 pages, $8.95, N.Y.: Atheneum.

In the first chapter, Haynie steers her reader into feeling confident as a woman golfer and tells her why and how to avoid the inferiority complex about playing the game that so many women have suffered from. Instruction covers the main problems beginners encounter and a few faced by more-experienced golfers. Each chapter concludes with a useful summary of the points most important to remember.

THE NEW GOLF FOR WOMEN edited by John Coyne. 1973, 223 pages, $9.95, N.Y.: Doubleday. A Rutledge Book.

Eight top women golf professionals explain the techniques and attitudes that made them winners. Excellent b/w photos clarify the instruction. The book concludes with an interesting simulated golf clinic in which the questions of typical woman golfers are answered by the pros.

PLAY GOLF THE WRIGHT WAY by Mickey Wright, with Joan Flynn Dreyspool. 1962, 96 pages, N.Y.: Doubleday.

This is a "How-I-do-it" book mainly for the more advanced golfer by one of the most exciting woman players in the history of the game. Numerous b/w illustrations depict the classic Wright swing. Chapters on stroke-saving and the psychology of putting are especially valuable.

INSTRUCTION BOOKS FOR THE LEFTHANDER

THE LEFT-HANDERS GOLF BOOK by Earl Stewart, Jr., and Dr. Harry E. Gunn. 1976, 166 pages, $5.95, Matteson, IL: Greatlakes Living Press.

LEFTHANDED GOLF by Bob Charles, with Roger Ganem. 1965, 127 pages, $4.95, Englewood Cliffs, N.J.: Prentice-Hall.

A Golf Digest School in full swing at Palmetto Dunes, Hilton Head Island.

GOLF SCHOOLS

If your game is a shambles and you're going to take a golf vacation anyway, why not spend a little more money and treat yourself to a golf-school experience? In the hothouse atmosphere of concentrated practice and play, under the watchful eyes of some of the most innovative and dynamic teachers in the business, and with your own motivation to improve perhaps keener than ever now that you've written the check to cover it all—you are likely to shave your handicap by at least a stroke or two.

The brief descriptions below are based on information supplied by the golf schools listed. Contact individual schools for the latest information on schedules, sites, and fees. Most schools have brochures or other prepared material that they gladly mail out to interested golfers.

BERTHOLY METHOD GOLF SCHOOLS
Foxfire Golf & Country Club
P.O. Box 711
Pinehurst, NC 28374
(919) 295-5555

SITE: Foxfire Golf & Country Club.

NUMBER OF SCHOOLS: About 10 one-week schools, March–October.

SAMPLE FEES: $795 per person, double occupancy. Includes 7 days, 6 nights, 3 meals a day, all golf, taxes, tips, and 5 days' instruction.

INSTRUCTORS: *Paul Bertholy,* director, has personally taught over 65,000 golfers in the past 40 years; assisted by *Steve Goldsmith,* PGA professional, *Christl Pastore,* LPGA professional, and *Doug Ferreri,* PGA apprentice.

PROGRAM: Rather than emphasize the proper way to launch the club into the golf ball, Bertholy believes in feeding the ingredients of a fine swing into the body's muscle-memory. A student at the school teaches his muscles the various components of a sound swing by initially using a weighted swing pipe and a program of isometric and isotonic exercises. The idea is to hold the club in various cardinal positions until the muscles respond without conscious direction from the brain.

THE COOL SCHOOL AT SAPPHIRE VALLEY

Sapphire Valley Resort
Star Route 70, Box 80
Sapphire Valley, NC 28774
(704) 743-3441

YEAR ESTABLISHED: 1977.
SITE: Sapphire Valley.
NUMBER OF SCHOOLS: About 8–10 schools, half in the spring and half in the fall.
SAMPLE FEES: $675, double occupancy. Includes 6 days, 5 nights, 3 meals a day, unlimited greens fees and use of electric carts, club storage and cleaning, practice facilities, golf movies nightly, cocktail party, golf tournament and awards dinner, taxes and gratuities. Nonplaying spouse pays $260.
INSTRUCTORS: *Louise Suggs,* a member of the LPGA Hall of Fame and the first woman to be elected to the Georgia Athletic Hall of Fame; *Lionel Hebert,* winner of many PGA tour events, including the PGA Championship; *Henry Lindner,* longtime golf professional, lecturer on golf instruction, twice awarded Horton Smith Award for contribution to fellow professionals. (A guest instructor participates at each school in addition to the above.)
PROGRAM: Size of classes is kept small, enabling student to obtain personalized attention.

Former PGA champ Lionel Hebert helps pupil get a grip on her game during a Cool School session.

CONCORD HOTEL GOLF SCHOOL

Kiamesha Lake, N.Y. 12751
(212) 244-3500
(914) 794-4000

YEAR ESTABLISHED: 1977.
SITE: Concord Hotel. 45 holes including the "Monster" course.
NUMBER OF SCHOOLS: About 10 adult 6-day schools planned from June through August.
SAMPLE FEES: $650 per person, double occupancy. Includes 6 days, 5 nights, 3 meals a day, free practice balls, club storage, greens and golf car fees, cocktail party and awards dinner. Nonplaying spouse pays $275.
INSTRUCTORS: *Hubie Smith,* director, has 20 years' teaching experience; a former PGA Golf Professional of the Year, he directed the golf school at Pinehurst prior to coming to the Concord. Other Class A PGA professionals assist. Touring pros *Larry Ziegler* and *Miller Barber* are also a part of the teaching staff.
PROGRAM: Some clinics, but most of the time is spent in working with each student on improving his or her game, in lessons on the practice tee or on the course. Videotape replay used.

SHIRLEY ENGLEHORN SCHOOL OF GOLF

c/o Gil Enterprises, Inc.
2252 Caminito Preciosa Sur
La Jolla, CA 92037

YEAR ESTABLISHED: 1979.
SITE: Whispering Palms Lodge and Country Club, Rancho Santa Fe, Calif.
NUMBER OF SCHOOLS: 3 tentatively scheduled for first year.
SAMPLE FEES: $1,000 per person, single occupancy. Includes 6 days, 5 nights, all meals, airport/hotel transfers, unlimited greens fees, 5 days' instruction, golf cart, videotaping, practice balls, club cleaning, storage, taxes and gratuities, cocktail parties and fashion show. Special rates for accompanying husbands or for students sharing accommodations.
INSTRUCTORS: *Shirley Englehorn,* director, a former top amateur and touring pro; *Shirley Spork,* a past president of Western Teaching Division of LPGA and featured instructor at many college and university workshops; *Diane Keppen,* Class A member of LPGA and former California State golf coach; *Barbara Crawford,* Class A LPGA teaching professional and executive director of Mind and Body Science Foundation; *Micki MacDonald,* a member of LPGA Teaching Division and teaching professional at Mission Viejo Country Club.
PROGRAM: The school's program is specifically designed for women who want to develop a sound, con-

sistent, confident swing and a mental approach to the game that ensures relaxed enjoyment on the course. Beginners are not encouraged to participate; however, high handicappers are welcome and should benefit dramatically. Instruction groups will be formed by handicap. While there is time set aside for fun and relaxation, golf will occupy most of the daylight hours and some evenings as well. A ratio of 1 teacher to each 5 or 6 pupils maximizes corrective instruction on an individual basis.

GOLF DIGEST INSTRUCTION SCHOOLS
495 Westport Avenue
Norwalk, CT 06856
(800) 243-6121 (toll-free)
(203) 847-5811 (Connecticut)

YEAR ESTABLISHED: 1971.
SITES: Various sites, including Tucson, Ariz. National Golf Club; Carmel Valley, Calif. Country Club; La Romana/Casa DeCampo, Dominican Republic; Boca West Club and Resort, Boca Raton, Fla.; Cypress Gardens-Grenelefe Golf Resort, Cypress Gardens, Fla.; The Cloister, Sea Island, Ga.; Pinehurst Country Club, Pinehurst, N.C.; Palmetto Dunes Resort; Hilton Head, S.C.
NUMBER OF SCHOOLS: 30–40 schools a year; some special sessions, such as 1-week school for low handicappers (15 and under) only, playing school, 3-day "commuter" school, school for juniors.
SAMPLE FEES: $1300 per person, double occupancy. Includes 6 days, 6 nights, all meals, 5 days of instruction, greens fees, golf car, practice balls, club cleaning, storage, transportation to and from airport, and cocktail parties. Nonplaying spouse pays $425.
INSTRUCTORS: Head instructors are *Bob Toski,* formerly a leading money-winner on tour, the author of several successful instruction books, and a commentator on golf telecasts; *Jim Flick,* one of nation's most sought-after teaching professionals; *Davis Love,* winner of 14 pro events, now at Sea Island (Ga.) Golf Club; and *Peter Kostis,* a teaching associate of Flick's and Toski's for several years. Other instructors include *Dick Aultman,* golf analyst, teacher, and author; *John Elliott,* former tour player; *Jim Ferree,* former tour player, Westmoreland Country Club, Export, Pa.; *Hank Johnson,* North River Yacht Club, Tuscaloosa, Ala.; *Len Kennett,* Los Verdes (Ga.) Golf Club; *Jack Lumpkin,* Cherokee Country Club, Dunwoody, Ga.; *Jack Silvey,* Skyline Country Club, Tucson, Ariz.; *Sam Snead,* the all-time great whose insights have helped guide the *Golf Digest* Professional Panel for many years; and *Bob Spence,* Kemper Lakes, Long Grove, Ill., a former tour player.
PROGRAM: Each day's program is designed to maxi-

mize individual instruction. Each group of participants is broken down into smaller groups within handicap ranges, so that while one group is on the practice tee, another might be on the putting green, another in the practice bunker, and so on. Teaching aids used include a permanent, personal notebook of instruction in which key points are to be recorded each day; a written progress-report record; a videotape analysis of each pupil's swing; sequence photos of the swing (marked by teachers to point out strengths and weaknesses); drills to make the swing more effective; and correct set-up photos of each pupil to take home for future reference.

GREAT LAKES GOLF SCHOOL
Heights-Rockefeller Building
2483 Lee Boulevard
Cleveland Heights, OH 44118
(216) 932-3900

SITE: Lehigh Acres (Fla.) Golf Club.
NUMBER OF SCHOOLS: Four 7-day golf schools planned January–February.
SAMPLE FEES: $1250 per person, man and wife. Includes 7 days, 7 nights, all meals, cocktail parties, all greens fees, practice balls, golf carts, club storage, all instruction, tax, pro-am tournament, and final analysis of your progress.
INSTRUCTORS: *Bill Spiccia, Ed Preisler,* and *Hank Meiers.* Assisted by *Bob Bourne,* Beechmont Country Club; *Dominic Antenucci,* Alliance Country Club; *Charles Wood,* Mayfield Country Club; *Charles Stock,* Acacia Country Club; *Mike Limback,* Tanglewood Country Club; *Rod Johnston,* Oakwood Club; *Joe Haase,* Pine Ridge Country Club; *Joe Flogge,* Edgewood Country Club; *Randy Padavick,* Acacia Country Club.
PROGRAM: Personal instruction; each day packed full of classes (no more than 6 students per pro) and play, with high and low handicappers grouped accordingly. Analysis by video camera, swing groove, backboard showing head movement, and rapid-sequence photos.

HARDER HALL GOLF SCHOOL
Sebring, FL 33870
(800) 237-2491 (toll-free)
(813) 385-0151

YEAR ESTABLISHED: 1973.
SITE: Harder Hall.
NUMBER OF SCHOOLS: Adult schools run weekly, December–April (teenage golf camp in the summer).
SAMPLE FEES: $679 per person, double occupancy. Includes 7 days, 7 nights, 3 meals daily, 3 cocktail parties, dancing and entertainment nightly, daily playing lessons, unlimited golf, instant-replay TV and

graph-check camera, practice balls, golf cart, gratuities, and transportation.

INSTRUCTORS: *Ben Roman,* Harder Hall professional for 25 years, plus 12 additional teaching pros.

PROGRAM: Ben Roman is at the school each day and gives all students a swing analysis. One professional is assigned to each 4 students for daily instruction on the practice tee and the golf course.

PAUL HARNEY GOLF ACADEMY
74 Club Valley Drive
East Falmouth, MA 02536
(617) 563-3454

YEAR ESTABLISHED: 1971.

SITE: Paul Harney Golf Club, North Falmouth, Mass.

NUMBER OF SCHOOLS: About 25 three-day golf schools from June through October, including sessions for women only, men only, and couples only.

SAMPLE FEES: $185 for 4 days, 3 nights, per person, double occupancy. Includes lessons, golf cart, continental breakfast each day, sequence pictures of swing along with comments and analysis by Paul Harney. Single occupancy, $210. Day school with lessons and cart for three days, $150 per person.

INSTRUCTORS: *Paul Harney,* winner of 7 PGA tournaments and 1974 PGA Pro of the Year, assisted by staff.

PROGRAM: Geared to beginners as well as advanced players. Instruction based on individual needs. Lessons in the morning cover all aspects of the game; each afternoon is spent playing on course with an instructor.

JOHN JACOBS GOLF SCHOOLS
104 Wilmot Road, Suite 170
Deerfield, IL 60015
(800) 323-1338 (toll-free)
(312) 948-0450

YEAR ESTABLISHED: 1978.

SITES: Various sites, including Tucson (Ariz.) National Golf Club; Lake Buena Vista (Fla.) Golf Club; Sea Brook Island, Charleston, S.C.; Playboy Resort and Country Club, Lake Geneva, Wisconsin.

NUMBER OF SCHOOLS: 6 schools planned, February–July.

SAMPLE FEES: 3-day schools for $550. Includes unlimited use of practice balls, all instruction fees, club cleaning and storage, shoe cleaning, continental breakfast and lunch daily, greens fees and cart fees, all taxes and gratuities, and tape recording to keep of your personal instruction.

INSTRUCTORS: Director *John Jacobs* has taught all over the world for the past 30 years and coached European stars such as Tony Jacklin, Peter Oosterhuis, and Severiano Ballesteros; also, the author of several golf-instruction books and a leading golf commentator for British television. Other instructors: *Bert Buehler,* 28-year pro, heads teaching program at Olympic Club, San Francisco; *Shelby Futch,* former head professional at Twin Orchard Country Club, Chicago, served several years on Illinois PGA executive and educational committees; *Jim Hardy,* turned pro in 1966 and played the tour regularly until 1974, then became head pro at the Exmoor (Ill.) Country Club.

PROGRAM: Sessions of intense concentrated instruction, designed to explore and improve every aspect of game. Emphasis is on individual improvement regardless of level of play. Students learn ballistics of golf and how they as individuals can achieve a method that enables them to produce a correct, repeating swing.

OBITZ & FARLEY
SWING'S THE THING GOLF SCHOOLS
Box 200
Shawnee-on-Delaware, PA 18356
(717) 421-6666

SITES: Various sites, including Cathedral Canyon Country Club, Palm Springs, Calif.; Whispering Palms Country Club, Rancho Santa Fe, Calif.; Innisbrook Resort, Tarpon Springs, Fla.; Pinehurst (N.C.) Hotel and Country Club; Shawnee Inn and Country Club, Shawnee-on-Delaware, Pa.

NUMBER OF SCHOOLS: 6 adult 6-day schools planned February–July.

SAMPLE FEES: $1000 per person, double occupancy. Includes accommodations at first-class resorts, all meals, cocktail parties, all tax and gratuities, greens fees, golf cars, unlimited practice balls, sequence pictures of your swing, instruction, and an autographed

Harry Obitz and Dick Farley go two on one during one of their Swing's the Thing schools.

copy of Obitz and Farley's book, *Six Days to Better Golf*. Nonstudent guest pays $495.

INSTRUCTORS: *Harry Obitz* and *Dick Farley,* long-time teaching team, assisted by *Mil Radler* and *Rick McCord.*

PROGRAM: "Mass production isn't our style," say Obitz and Farley, who have a year-round schedule of corporate golf schools and private teaching. Maximum of 24 students in each of the 6 schools.

PINE NEEDLES GOLFARIS

P.O. Box 88
Southern Pines, NC 28387
(919) 692-7111

YEAR ESTABLISHED: 1969.
SITE: Pine Needles Lodge & Country Club.
NUMBER OF SCHOOLS: About a half-dozen schools or "golfaris" per year in varying lengths and formats: families, couples only, women only, and youth.
SAMPLE FEES: Adult/Family 7-day golfaris at $350 per person, double occupancy. Includes accommodations, all meals, greens fees, golf carts, range balls, gratuities and tax, all instruction, golf films, videotape analysis of all participants, tournaments, prizes and fun.
INSTRUCTORS: Head instructor is *Peggy Kirk Bell,* a former touring pro and LPGA Teacher of the Year award-winner; assisted by *Wiffi Smith, DeDe Owens, Jimmy Nichols, Bob Zydonik, Scott Trethaway,* and *Lee Kosten.*
PROGRAM: Concentrated golf instruction mixed with films and lectures, daily tournaments and prizes. Warren and Peggy Kirk Bell have been running a small, personalized resort for over 25 years, and their "golfaris" reflect the same atmosphere.

GOLF SCHOOL FOR SENIORS

P.O. Box 9199
Canton, OH 44711
(216) 453-4350

YEAR ESTABLISHED: 1970.
SITE: Kings Inn Country Club, Sun City Center, Fla.
NUMBER OF SCHOOLS: 18 one-week schools, December–April; 4 one-week schools, October–November.
SAMPLE FEES: $800 per person, double occupancy. Includes 8 days, 7 nights, breakfast and dinner, all greens fees, playing lessons, personalized instruction, club storage, golf cars, practice balls, cocktail parties, pro-am tournament and prizes, sequence picture, instructional movies, and color TV with stop action and instant replay.
INSTRUCTORS: *Ben Sutton,* director; assisted by *Denny Lyons,* Niagara Falls Country Club, Lewiston, N.Y.; *Bill Costello* and *Bill Richardson,* Thousand

Island Golf Club, Alexandria Bay, N.Y.; *Harry Offutt,* Green Hill Yacht & Country Club, Salisbury, Md.; *Neal Doyle,* Peach Valley Country Club, Spartansburg, S.C.; *Don Murphy,* Texarkana (Ark.) Country Club; *Dick Lawrence; Henry S. Castillo; John Faeriari,* Spruce Needles Golf Club, Timmons, Ontario, Canada; *Fred Dobbins,* Sun City (Fla.) Golf Club. *Toby Lyons,* Niagara Falls Country Club; *Mike Dudley,* Coldstream Country Club, Cincinnati, Oh.; *Penny Zavichas,* 1973 LPGA Teacher of the Year; *Mary Lena Faulk,* The Broadmoor, Colorado Springs, Colo.; *Joyce Ann Jackson,* former LPGA touring pro; *Kathy Welch,* former LPGA touring pro; *Sue Tubman,* 13 years' teaching experience and LPGA tour player; *Linda Craft,* LPGA tour player over 5 years, with 12 years' teaching experience; *Carla Glasgow,* 12 years' teaching experience and professional at Piping Rock Country Club, Long Island, N.Y.
PROGRAM: Personalized instruction on the practice tee, as well as on the 2 courses, from 15 experienced PGA and LPGA teaching professionals. Teaching aids used include color TV with stop action and instant reply, and a sequence camera.

TENNESSEE PGA/MASON RUDOLPH SCHOOL OF GOLF

P.O. Box 50574
Nashville, TN 37205
(615) 833-9689

YEAR ESTABLISHED: 1977.
SITE: Henry Horton State Park, Chapel Hill, Tenn.
NUMBER OF SCHOOLS: One adult 4-day school in spring; also several junior schools in summer.
SAMPLE FEES: Adult school costs $395 per person, double occupancy. Includes four nights, all meals, greens fees, unlimited practice balls, golf carts, all instruction, club storage, and gift package.
INSTRUCTORS: *Mason Rudolph,* 18-year tour player, is at the school full-time, assisted by other top Tennessee club-professionals.
PROGRAM: Golfers are divided into groups according to handicaps. Emphasis is placed on transferring knowledge from the practice tee to the golf course. A videotape stop-action TV camera is used for swing analysis.

STRATTON GOLF ACADEMY

Stratton Mountain, VT 05155
(800) 451-4261

YEAR ESTABLISHED: 1979.
SITE: Stratton Mountain Golf Club, a par-72, 6,516-yard course and a 22-acre "training center" consisting of 3 practice tees, 2 target greens, a chipping green, and a putting green.

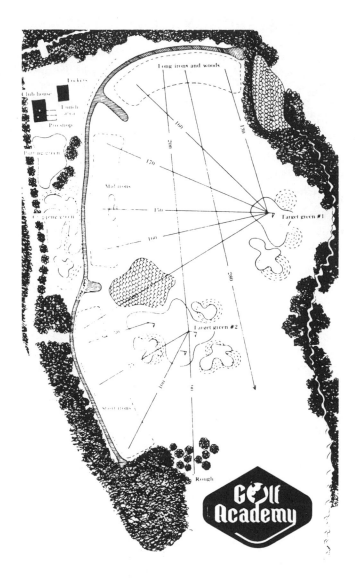

NUMBER OF SCHOOLS: 5-day and weekend sessions, mid-June through mid-September.

INSTRUCTORS: Staff of PGA and LPGA pros led by *Bill Cullum.*

PROGRAM: Participants are divided into beginner, intermediate, and advanced. Stress is on swing fundamentals and learning to concentrate. Videotaping and sequence-photo analysis included.

VISION-DYNAMICS GOLF SCHOOLS
  263 Ocean Avenue
  Laguna Beach, CA 92651

YEAR ESTABLISHED: 1979.

SITE: Princeville, Hawaii.

NUMBER OF SCHOOLS: Five 5-day sessions (tentative schedule for first year).

INSTRUCTORS: Include touring pros *Jim Colbert* and *Jim Simons;* noted teacher *Jim Ballard.*

PROGRAM: Based on optometrist Bill Harrison's system for visualization and concentration.

GOLF SCHOOLS FOR YOUNGSTERS

Reprinted with permission from the May, 1979 issue of *Golf Digest.* © 1979, Golf Digest, Inc.

Most schools offer 1-week sessions and range in cost from $100 to $600 per week.

SCHOOL, ADDRESS	PARTICULARS
Arnold Palmer Golf Academy, 9000 Bay Hill Blvd., Orlando, Fla. 32811.	Boys only, 11–17. Play 27-hole Bay Hill Cse. Arnie appears. Resort. Golf director, Dick Tiddy.
Boyne Ntl. Golf Academy, P.O. Box 6R, Boyne Falls, Mich. 49713.	Coed, 10–18. Play Boyne Mtn., Boyne Highland cses. 5 pros. Resort.
Billy Casper's California Golf Camp (San Diego), 8245 Ronson Rd., San Diego, Calif. 92111.	Coed, 10–18. Range, play area courses. Billy appears. Dorms. 10 on teaching staff.
Cedar River Club Junior Golf Camp, Indian Lake, N.Y. 12842.	Boys, 11–17. Play regulation course; range. Cottages on course.
Chase Golf Camp, P.O. Box 1446, Manchester, Mass. 01944.	Coed, 11–17. Play regulation course in Bethlehem, N.H. Pro instruction.
Crimson Tide Sports Academy, Box K, University of Alabama, Ala. 35486.	Coed, 11–18. Play at univ. cse. Coach Conrad Rehling. College dorms.
Frank Cronin Golf Camp, University of Maryland, College Park, Md. 20740.	Coed, 10–18. Play univ. cse.; range. Frank Cronin, director. Day camp only.
Duke Univ. Youth Golf Camp, Duke G. Cse., Durham, N.C. 27706.	Ages 11–18. Play at univ. cse. Coach Rod Myers. Dorms.
Ferris State College Golf Camp, Big Rapids, Mich. 49307.	Coed, 10–17. Play college course; range. Ron English, director. Dorms.
Florida PGA Junior Golf Academy, 4381 Sanderling Cir-E, Quail Ridge 725, Boynton Beach, Fla. 33436.	Coed, 10–17. Play Mission Inn resort cse., Howey-in-the-Hills, Fla. Resort.
Golf Academy of the Southwest, 3811 Country Lane, Conroe, Texas 77302.	Coed, 13–17. Play Waterwood Ntl. Cse. West Hilzer, director. Resort.
Golf Digest Schools for Juniors, 495 Westport Ave., Norwalk, Conn. 06856.	Coed, 11–17. 1st two Boyne Highlands, Mich.; 3rd and 6th Univ. Alabama; 4th and 5th Furman Univ.
E. Harvie Ward Golf Academy, Box 711, Pinehurst, N.C. 28374.	Coed, 9–17. Play Foxfire cse., Pinehurst. Condos, resort facilities.
Harder Hall Golf & Tennis Camps, Harder Hall, Sebring, Fla. 33870.	Coed, 11–17. Play regulation cse.; range. Doug Ford, Jr., director. Resort.
Metropolitan PGA Jr. Golf School, Box 268, Wykagyl Station, New Rochelle, N.Y. 10804.	Coed, 17 and under. Regulation cse., trip to Westchester Classic. Day camp only.

SCHOOL, ADDRESS	PARTICULARS
NEPGA Junior Golf Camp, Radisson-Ferncroft Bldg., 50 Village Dr., Danvers, Mass. 01923.	Boys, 12–16. 36-hole cse.; range. Ken Campbell, director. YMCA camp.
North Carolina, Univ. of Golf Camp, Box 2675. Chapel Hill, N.C. 27514.	Coed, 10–18. Play Finley G.C. Dorms. Devon Brouse, director.
North Texas Golf Academy, 2815 Valley View Lane, Suite 214, Dallas, Texas 75234.	Boys (1st and 3rd sessions), coed (2nd session). Play univ. cse. James McAfee, director. Dorms.
Peggy Kirk Bell Youth Golfari, Pine Needles Lodges & C.C., Box 88, So. Pines, N.C. 28387.	Coed, 10–18. Play at Pine Needles. Pro instruction. Resort facilities.
Pinehurst School of Golf, P.O. Box 4000, Pinehurst, N.C. 28374.	11–17. Boys only, except coed 7/8 session. Play 5 cses. Lou Miller, director. Resort.
Princeton Hills Golf Academy, 700 Park Ave., Suite 303, Plainfield, N.J. 07060.	Coed, 11–18. Play Lawrenceville school cse. Video. Dorms.
PGA Ntl. Academy of Golf for Juniors, Box 12458, Lake Park, Fla. 33403.	Coed, 12–17. Intermediate-advanced players. At Boca West resort. Tour pros visit.
Silver Sands Jr. Golf Academy, 1809 S. Shore Dr., Delavan, Wis. 53115.	Boys only, 10–17. Play 4 18-hole cses. Wayne Rolfs, director; resort.
Soaring Eagles Golf Camp, Elmira College, Elmira, N.Y. 14901.	Coed, 9–17. 18-hole cse. Paul Cornelius, director. College dorms.
Tennessee Golf Academy, Box 50574, Nashville, Tenn. 37205.	Boys only, 11–17. Play Fall Creek cse., Pikeville, Tenn. PGA conducts. Lodge.
Tennessee PGA Jr. Competition School, P.O. Box 50574, Nashville, Tenn. 37205.	Boys only, 14–18, handicaps 8 or less. Play H. Horton Resort Park cse. Resort lodging. PGA conducts.
Texas A&M Golf School, Texas A&M University, College Station, Tex. 77843.	Boys only, 13–16. Play univ. cse. Coach Bob Ellis. Dorms.
Whispering Pines Golf School, Whispering Pines, N.C. 28389.	Boys only, 10–17. Play 3 18-hole cses. Avery Beck, pro. Resort facilities.
West Coast Golf Academy, 1430 Parsons Ave., Campbell, Calif. 95008.	Coed, 9–18. Regulation cse. Jack Guio, director, pro.
Youth on Tour, 5478 River Rd., Salem, Ore. 97302.	Boys only, 13–17. In Oak Brook, Ill. to coincide with Western Open.

GOLF INSTRUCTION FILMS

Here is a sampling of films available for sale or rent from distributors. A complete, 18-page listing of films available may be obtained from National Golf Foundation, 200 Castlewood Drive, North Palm Beach, FL 33408.

FILM COMM INC.
  103 West Grand Avenue
  Chicago, IL 60610

National Golf Foundation Instruction Series (1975). Rent: Two-day—Unit I, II (Part 1 or Part 2), IV, V, VI—$15; Unit III—$10.

I. *Golf—A Special Kind of Joy* (16 minutes). The joy and challenge of golf—understanding its equipment—applying principles of club-loft and length in playing a golf hole—your most valuable equipment, your golf swing, etc.

II. *How to Build a Golf Swing* (two 17-minute reels). Conditioning mind and body to understand the swinging movements based upon six major concepts: flow of power, rhythm, steady center, plane, arc, direction.

III. *The Short-Approach Shots* (10 minutes). Establishing the need for greater control of direction as you near the green—identifying golf's short-approach shots: the pitch and the chip—their flight and roll factors for greenside accuracy—identifying the short-approach swing as an adaptation of the basic swing.

IV. *The Special Challenge Shots* (15 minutes). Overview of golf's architectural beauty, harboring the challenges that test a player's skill—learning how to answer each challenge by predicting the natural forces of weather.

V. *Putting—Golf's End Game* (13 minutes). The geometric factors of putting, its demand for "exactness" calling for the ultimate in control of direction and distance, etc.

VI. *Courtesy on the Course* (18 minutes). Depicts a positive presentation of etiquette procedures as they occur during the normal sequence of play.

Keep 'em in the Fairway (1958, 38 minutes). Created by *Life* magazine and the PGA, under the supervision of the PGA Teaching Committee, features Bobby Jones in conversation with Horton Smith about golf and the great strides in golf teaching over the past 40 years. Highlights the five golf fundamentals that the PGA believes essential to every good golf swing. Split-screen techniques show these fundamentals in simple fashion.

Million Dollar Golf Lesson (27 minutes). Rent—$25. Filmed at Firestone Country Club. Features 12 former PGA champions and Paul Hahn, demonstrating every shot in golf, with every club in the bag. Introduced by Chris Schenkel, moderated by Chick Harbert.

NCAA FILM SERVICE
P.O. Box 1906
Shawnee Mission, KS 66222

Winning Golf (35 minutes). Cosponsored by Mac-Gregor and Dupont, under the technical supervision of Bob Kepler, Ohio State golf coach. Included in illustrating the proper golf form as taught by Kepler are two of his former NCAA champions, Tom Nieporte (1951) and Jack Nicklaus (1961). In addition, two-time NCAA champion Dick Crawford of Houston illustrates do's and don't's.

UNIVERSITY OF WISCONSIN—EXTENSION
Bureau of Audio-Visual Instruction
1327 University Avenue
P.O. Box 2093
Madison, WI 53701

Golf by Tommy Armour (30 minutes). Rent—$5.00. Armour demonstrates the fundamentals.

U.S. GOLF ASSOCIATION
Golf House
Far Hills, NJ 07931
(201) 234-2300

How I Play Golf by Robert T. Jones, Jr. (10 min. each; rent—$15 each). Among the rarest golf films ever made: 17 classic shorts of Bobby Jones instruction in which an astonishing cast of Hollywood celebrities took part. Completely unrehearsed and often ad-libbed, these serials include scenes such as W. C. Fields lazily juggling golf balls. For several months in 1931 and 1933, Bobby Jones was a familiar and popular figure in Hollywood, where he filmed these reels on the fundamentals of golf with such stars as James Cagney, Edward G. Robinson, Loretta Young, Walter Huston, Richard Barthelmess, Joan Blondell, Douglas Fairbanks, Jr., and Richard Arlen. The graphic techniques featured an early version of what we now call "stop action." Jones served not only as the model but as the writer and narrator.

SOME LEADING U.S. GOLF INSTRUCTORS

The following golf professionals have been invited to demonstrate the art of teaching at various workshops organized by the PGA over the past five years.

Paul Bertholy
Foxfire Golf &
   Country Club
Pinehurst, NC

Johnny Bulla
res., Phoenix, AZ

Jack Burke
Champions Golf Club
Houston, TX

Joe Dante
Rockaway River
   Country Club
Denville, NJ

Dick Farley
Shawnee Inn
Shawnee-on-Delaware, PA

Dow Finsterwald
The Broadmoor
Colorado Springs, CO

Jim Flick
res., Cincinnati, OH

Chick Harbert
Ocean Reef
   Country Club
Key Largo, FL

Davis Love
The Cloister
Sea Island, GA

Gene Mason
Black Butte (OR) Ranch

Al Mengert
Oakland Hills Country Club
Birmingham, MI

Eddie Merrins
Bel-Air Country Club
Los Angeles, CA

Cary Middlecoff
res., Lost Tree Village, FL

Harvey Penick
Austin Country Club
Austin, TX

Conrad Rehling
U. of Alabama Golf Club
University, AL

Paul Runyan
Green Gables Country Club
Denver, CO

Irv Schloss
res., Dunedin, FL

Bill Strausbaugh
Columbia Country Club
Chevy Chase, MD

Manuel de la Torre
Milwaukee (WI)
   Country Club

Bob Toski
res., Boca West, FL

Gary Wiren
PGA Headquarters
Lake Park, FL

The following professionals have received the Teacher of the Year award given annually by the Ladies Professional Golf Association.

Gloria Armstrong
C/o LPGA
New York, NY

Goldie Bateson
Golf Arena
West Allis, WI

Peggy Kirk Bell
Pine Needles Lodge
Southern Pines, NC

Marge Burns
Golf Acres
N. Myrtle Beach, SC

Vonnie Colby

Mary Dagraedt
Miami Dade College
Miami, FL

Helen Dettweiler
Thunderbird Country Club
Rancho Mirage, CA

Sally Dodge
Lake Chabot Golf Club
Oakland, CA

Shirley Englehorn
Desert Island Country Club
Rancho Mirage, CA

Gloria Fecht
Bermuda Dunes
    Country Club
Palm Desert, CA

Ellen Griffin
University of North Carolina
Chapel Hill, NC

Carol Johnson
National Golf Foundation
North Palm Beach, FL

Ann Casey Johnstone
Stephens College
    Country Club
Columbia, MO

DeDe Owens
Pine Needles Lodge
Southern Pines, NC

Jackie Pung
La Costa Country Club
Carlsbad, CA

Jeannette Rector
Penasquintos Golf Club
Escondido, CA

Lee Spencer
Austin, TX

Shirley Spork
Tamarisk Country Club
Rancho Mirage, CA

JoAnne Winter
Coronado Golf Club
Scottsdale, AZ

Penny Zavichas
Pueblo, CO

The following are winners of the annual Joe Graffis Award, given by the National Golf Foundation to an individual who has demonstrated outstanding service to the educational advancement of golf.

Patty Berg
LPGA tour great
res., Fort Myers, FL

Les Bolstad
PGA Golf Coach
University of Minnesota

Ellen Griffin
University of North Carolina
Chapel Hill, NC

Opal Hill
LPGA Player/Teacher
res., Kansas City, MO

Shirley Spork
Tamarisk Country Club
Rancho Mirage, CA

Bill Strausbaugh
Columbia Country Club
Chevy Chase, MD

Gary Wiren
PGA Headquarters
Lake Park, FL

The following golf professionals have been recognized by the National Golf Foundation as highly qualified instructors and serve on the NGF area consultant staff.

Jim Bailey
Adams Country Golf Club
Brighton, CO

Luca Barbato
Acadian Hills Country Club
Lafayette, LA

Goldie Bateson
Golf Arena
West Allis, WI

Marge Burns
Golf Acres
North Myrtle Beach, SC

John Carroll
Wilderness Country Club
Naples, FL

Gordon J. H. Crossman
Borck Golfland
St. Catharines, Ontario, Canada

Brown Cullen
Hunting Creek Golf Club
Prospect, KY

Mrs. Andrea (Andy) C. Fischer
Sugar Valley Country Club
Bellbrook, OH

Jim Flick

Dorothy Germain
The Farm
Randelman, NC

Jack P. Henrich
Elma Meadows Golf Club
Elma, NY

Max Hines
Clinton Country Club
Clinton, IA

Hank Johnson, Jr.
North River Yacht and
    Country Club
Tuscaloosa, AL

Pat Lange
Ironwood Golf Club
Golden, CO

Bill Madonna
Bill Madonna School of Golf
Clearwater, FL

Alex McNeil
International Town &
    Country Club
Fairfax, VA

Lou Miller
Pinehurst Country Club
Pinehurst, NC

DeDe Owens
Pine Needles Lodge
Southern Pines, NC

Joey Rey
Whispering Palms Lodge &
    Country Club
Rancho Santa Fe, CA

Mike Reynolds
Dorado Beach Hotel
Dorado Beach, Puerto Rico

Mrs. Jackie Riggs
Lake Hefner Golf Club
Oklahoma City, OK

Shirley Spork
Tamarisk Country Club
Rancho Mirage, CA

Bill Strausbaugh
Columbia Country Club
Chevy Chase, MD

George Valentine
Brookside Park & Recreation Dept.
Ashland, OH

Nancy Wilbert
Bill Madonna School of Golf
Clearwater, FL

Dr. Betty Jane Wills
Renton Driving Range
Seattle, WA

JoAnne Winter
Coronado Golf Club
Scottsdale, AZ

Equipment

GOLF EQUIPMENT GUIDE

The following material on *Men's Clubs, Women's Clubs,* and *Guide to Clubfitting* is reprinted with permission of *Golf Magazine,* March 1979. © 1979 by Times Mirror Magazines, Inc.

MEN'S CLUBS

KEY (W) Woods (I) Irons SHAFT TYPES ● (S) Steel (LS) Lightweight steel (ST) Stainless steel (G) Graphite (TM) Titanium (UCV) UCV-304 chrome-vanadium steel (B) Bionize FLEXES ● (L) Ladies (A) Flexible (R) Regular (T), (S) Stiff (X) Extra stiff CLUBHEADS ● (L) Laminated (P) Persimmon (IC) Investment cast (F) Forged (R&LH) Right and Left-Handed ● Prices are suggested retail for steel-shafted clubs unless otherwise indicated. Hogan Shaft Flex Equivalents: 1-L; 2-A; 3-R; 4-S; 5-X.

COMPANY	MODEL	FEATURES	SHAFT TYPE	FLEX	CLUB HEAD	PRICE (4 WOODS 9 IRONS)
Action/T.M.I	Slot-back (I)	Heel & toe weighted	S,LS	All Flexes	IC	$216
	Low-profile (I)	Low c of g, cavity back	S,LS	All Flexes	IC	$216
	Tour Model (I)	Classic blade, sole weighted	S,LS	All Flexes	IC	$216
	(W)	Horizontal face weighting	S,LS	All Flexes	L	$184
					P	$220
Acushnet	Titleist Lite 100 (W)	12° loft driver	LS	L,A,R,S	L	$154
	(I)	Variable back weighting	LS	L,A,R,S	IC	$279
	Titleist Accu-Flo (W)	12° loft driver	S	L,A,R,S	L	$154
	(I)	Modified low profile	S	L,A,R,S	IC	$315
	Titleist Accu-Flo Plus (W)	3-piece, perimeter weighted	S	L,A,R,S	IC	$183
	Titleist Tour Model (W)	10.5° loft driver	S	R,S	L	$154
	(W)	Same as above	S	R,S	P	$183
	(I)	Traditional lines	S	R,S	F	$292.50
American Golf	Pro Cast (I)		LS	All Flexes	IC	$350
	(W)		LS	All Flexes	P	$200
	Libertine (I)		LS UCV-304	All Flexes	IC	$380
	(W)	1-7 available	LS, UCV-304	All Flexes	P	$215
American Precision	American (I)	Heel & toe weighted	S,LS	R,S,X	IC	$355.50
	(W)	4-way weighting	S,ST,G,	R,S,X	L	$208
	American G-F (I)	Shaft in hosel	S,ST,G,	R,S,X	IC	$387
Jerry Barber	X22 (I)	Cavity back	Any	All Flexes	IC	$315
	Goldentouch #7 (I)	Low profile	S	All Flexes	IC	$315
	Left-handed (W)	Wide hitting area	S	All Flexes	L	$200
	(I)	High toe	S	All Flexes	IC	$360
	Goldentouch #3 (W)	Compact	S	All Flexes	L	$200
	(I)	Flat sole	S	All Flexes	IC	$360
	Goldentouch #1 (W)		S	All Flexes	L	$180
	(I)	Round face	S	All Flexes	IC	$315
Beauwood	Duoflex (W)		LS	All Flexes	P	$ 236
	(I)		LS	All Flexes	IC	$ 369
	Unif. Flex (W)		LS	All Flexes	P	$ 236
	(I)		LS	All Flexes	IC	$ 369
	Bionize-1 (W)	Bionized shafts	B	All Flexes	P	$ 552
	(I)	Bionized shafts	B	All Flexes	IC	$1,062
	Bionize-2 (W)	Bionized shafts	B	All Flexes	P	$ 600
	(I)	Bionized shafts	B	All Flexes	IC	$1,170
	Pro-Model (W)	Bionized shafts	S,LS	All Flexes	P	$ 236

COMPANY	MODEL	FEATURES	SHAFT TYPE	FLEX	CLUB HEAD	PRICE (4 WOODS 9 IRONS)	
Browning	Browning 500 (W)	Clubhead size identical, R&LH	S	All Flexes	P	$234	
	(I)	Non-offset	S	All Flexes	IC	$324	
	Browning 440 (W)	Clubhead size identical, R&LH	S,LS	All Flexes	L	$214	
	(I)	Low profile, offset, R&LH	S,LS	All Flexes	IC	$374	
Cobra	Tour Model (I)	Classic design, R&LH	S,G,TM	All Flexes	IC	$355.50	
	(W)	Classic design, R&LH	S,G,TM	All Flexes	L	$240	
	Cobra Baffler (W)	Double runner soleplate	S,LS,G,	All Flexes	L	$190	
	Cobra (W)	Classic design, R&LH	S,G,TM	All Flexes	L	$196	
	(I)	Perimeter weighted, R&LH	S,G,TM	All Flexes	IC	$355.50	
	L.P. (W)	Backweighted	S,G,LS	All Flexes	L	$196	
	(I)		S,G,TM, LS	All Flexes	IC	$355.50	
Confidence	Visa (W)	One-piece metal face-soleplate	LS	All Flexes	L	$200	
	(I)	Modified profile	LS	All Flexes	IC	$378	
	Solid State (I)	Classic design	S	All Flexes	IC	$378	
	(W)	One-piece metal face-soleplate	S	All Flexes	L	$200	
	Confidence II (I)	Long blade, rocker sole	S	All Flexes	IC	$328.50	
	(W)	Deep faced driver	S	All Flexes	L	$174	
	Custom Persimmon (W)	Hand made	S	All Flexes	P	$240	
Con-Sole	Dynaphase FM (W)	Frequency matched shafts	S	All Flexes	L	$230	
	(I)	Frequency matched shafts	S	All Flexes	IC	$345	
Dunlop	Maxfli Australian Blade (I)	Traditional lines	S	R,S,X	F	$337.50	
	Australian Model (W)	Butterfly sole	S	R,S,X	P	$213	
	Blue Max Alta Shaft (I)	Low profile design, synchronized flex	S,LS (Alta)	M	IC	$342	
	(W)	Low profile fairway woods	S,LS	M	L	$211.70	
	Maxpower (left only) (I)	Classic design	S	R,S,X	IC	$330	
	(W)	Full soleplate, classic design	S	R,S,X	L	$185	
Falcon	Fore/31 (I)	Long blade, flanged sole	S	All Flexes	IC	$395	
	Bench-Made (W)	Compact	S	All Flexes	L	$245	
GAC	Epolyte (W)	Solid polymer head	S,G	All Flexes		$220	
	(I)		S,G	All Flexes	IC&F	$315 (C),	$405 (F)
	Oakmaster (W)	Full epoxy face and soleplate	S,G	All Flexes		$230	
	(I)		S,G	All Flexes	IC&F	$315 (C),	$405 (F)
	Regal (W)	Conventionally poured insert	S,G	All Flexes		$210	
	(I)		S,G	All Flexes	IC&F	$315 (C),	$405 (F)
Golf Design	Power Track (I)	Cavity back, perimeter weighted	S	All Flexes	IC	$378	
	(W)	Perimeter weighted	S	All Flexes	L	$210	
	Auld Classic (I)	Sweet spot marked	S	All Flexes	IC	$378	
	(W)		S	All Flexes	L	$210	
	Oscar Jones (I)		S	All Flexes	IC	$378	
	(W)	Classic design	S	All Flexes	L	$210	
Greenirons	Low Pro (I)	Low profile, strong lofts	ST,LS	All Flexes	IC	$351	
	Honors (I)	Progressive profile	ST,LS	All Flexes	IC	$351	
	(W)		ST,LS	All Flexes	P	$246	
Walter Hagen	Ultraflex (I)	Face slot, classic styling	S,LS	R,S	IC	$398.25	
	(W)	Gamma Fire insert, emerald flecked finish	S,LS	R,S	L	$227	
	Matrix LP (W)	Low c of g, large face area	LS	R,S	L	$220	
	(I)	Optimized profile design	LS	R,S	IC	$387	
	International (W)	Cycolac insert	LS	R	L	$76.50	
	(I)	Low c of g	LS	R	F	$121.50	
	The Haig (W)	Traditional profile	CF,S	R,S	L	$215	
	(I)	Muscleback blade	CF,S	R,S	F	$360	
	Matrix RP (W)	Fore-weighted	LS	R,S	L	$220	
	(I)	Dynamic swing matching	LS	R,S	IC	$387	
Hillerich & Bradsby (Power Bilt)	Citation #322 (W)	Backweighted	S	R,S	P	$240	
	#522 (W)	Backweighted	S	R,S	L	$204	
	#324 (W)		LS (Dynasty)	R,S	P	$260	
	#524 (W)		LS	A,R,S	L	$224	
	#7825 (I)	Classic lines	S	R,S	F	$288	
	#7745 (I)	Low center of gravity	S	R,S	IC	$333	
	#9825 (I)	Classic forging	LS	R,S	F	$324	
	#9945 (I)	Low center of gravity	LS	A,R,S	IC	$369	

COMPANY	MODEL	FEATURES	SHAFT TYPE	FLEX	CLUB HEAD	PRICE	(4 WOODS 9 IRONS)
Ben Hogan	Curved Sole (W)	12° loft in driver, #7 avail.	S,LS (Legend and Apex)	2,3,4	L	$206	
	Tour Woods (W)	11° loft in driver	S,LS	3,4,5	P	$256	
	Medallion (W)	10″ roll & bulge in driver	S,LS	2,3,4	L	$224	
	(I)	Offset, cambered sole	S,LS	2,3,4	F	$378	
	Personal (W)	11½° loft in driver	S,LS	3,4	L	$224	
	Apex II (I)	Short hosel, low profile	S,LS	2,3,4,5	F	$389	
	Director (I)	Heel & toe weighting	S,LS	3,4	F	$356	
Hornung	Ben Sayers Contact (I)	Cut away heel	LS	All Flexes	IC	$393.75	
	(W)	Backweighted	LS		L	$232	
Karsten/Ping	KI (I)		LS,S,G, TM	S	IC	$405	
	KII (W)	Four-way roll sole with ski leading edge	LS,S,G, TM	S	L	$232	
	KII (I)	More rounded sole	LS,S,G, TM	S	IC	$405	
	KIII (W)	More rounded four-way roll sole	LS,S,G, TM	S	L	$232	
	KIII (I)	PING Rail	LS,S,G, TM	S	IC	$405	
	KIV (I)	Rounded edges	LS,S,G, TM	S	IC	$405	
	LH-KII (I)	Left handed only	LS,S,G, TM	S	IC	$405	
Len Kennett	Kennett Classic (I)	Top thin line, compact blade, high flare toe	S	All Flexes	IC	$143.02	(2-9)
Le Master	431 Stainless (I)	Cambered sole, low c of g	S,LS	All Flexes		$598	9I,4W(L)
	(W)			All Flexes		$638	9I,4W(P)
	Cobalt CM 74 (I)	Cast Cobalt	S,LS	All Flexes		$1,605	9I,4W(P)

3 **4**

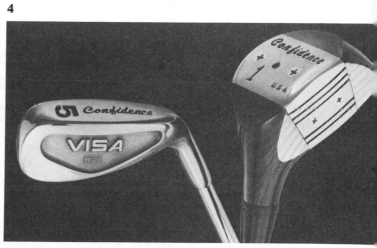

1. **American Precision's low-profile iron retails at $43.**

2. **Persimmon driver head in traditional design from Beauwood.**

3. **Browning's 500 series woods have Dynamic-shafted persimmon heads; iron have low-profile cast heads with straight-set hosel.**

4. **Confidence Visa woods and irons come with lightweight steel shafts in choice of four flexes.**

COMPANY	MODEL	FEATURES	SHAFT TYPE	FLEX	CLUB HEAD	PRICE	(4 WOODS 9 IRONS)
Lynx	Prowler (W)	3-piece sole plate	S,LS	All Flexes	L	$184	
	U.S.A. (W)	Heel & toe weighted	S,LS,TM	All Flexes	P	$224	
	Lynx Master (I)	Offset, broad sole	S,LS,TM	All Flexes	IC	$342	
	Predator (W)	Offset or straight hosel	S,LS,TM	All Flexes	C&L	$228	
	(I)	Low c of g	S,LS,TM	All Flexes	IC	$378	
	U.S.A. (I)	Compact blade	S,LS,TM	All Flexes	IC	$342	
MacGregor	Nicklaus VIP (W)	Classic head shape	S,UCV	S,R	L	$210	
	(I)	Compact blade	S,UCV	S,R	IC	$390	
	Tourney (W)	Compact wood	UCV	S,R	L	$195	
	(I)	Low c of g	UCV	S,R	IC	$345	
	MG Lite (W)	12° loft on driver	UCV	R	L	$180	
	(I)	Low profile	UCV	R	IC	$315	
	DX (W)	Rocker sole	LS	S,R	L	$160	
	(I)	Powerbulge back	LS	S,R	IC	$280	
	300 (W)	Compact uniblock head, rocker sole	UCV	S,R	L	$240	
Matzie	Three Ease (W)	Adjustable lie, low profile	S	All Flexes		$240	
	E-Z Swinger (W)	Extra flexibility	S	All Flexes		$320	
Middleground	#1 (W)	Oil hardened, R & LH	S,G,LS	All Flexes	P	$250	
	(I)	Forged	S,LS	All Flexes	F	$135	
	#2 (W)	R&LH	S,LS	All Flexes	L	$130	
Northwestern	Tour Model (W)	Backweighted	S (Power Kick)	All Flexes	L	$200	
	(I)	Classic design	S	All Flexes	F	$360	
	Thunderbird II (W)	Backweighted	S	All Flexes	L	$160	
	(I)		S	All Flexes	IC	$360	
	Saga (W)	Backweighted	S	All Flexes	L	$160	
	(I)		S	All Flexes	IC	$342	
	Ultimate II (W)	Backweighted	S	All Flexes	L	$160	
	(I)	Classic lines	S	All Flexes	F	$270	
	RB-880 (W)	Bone insert	S	R	L	$104	
	(I)	Low profile	S	R	IC	$198	
	Esquire (W)	Heel & toe weighted	S	R	L	$ 96	
	(I)	Low profile	S	R	F	$180	
	Dorado (W)	Walnut finish	S	R,L	L	$ 96	
	(I)	Semi-low profile	S	R,L	F	$162	
	Regency (W)	Walnut finish	S	R	L	$183	8/3
	(I)	Triple chrome plated	S	R	F		
Pedersen	Persimmon (W)	Traditional pear shape	S,TM,G	All Flexes	P	$196	
	Laminated (W)	Classic design	S,TM,G	All Flexes	L	$164	
	Forged Stainless (I)	Balanced camber	S,TM,G	All Flexes	F	$256	
	XL-7 (I)		S,TM,G	All Flexes	IC	$315	
Tony Penna	Original (I)	Conventional blade	S,G,LS, TM	All Flexes	F	$306	
	(W)		S,G,LS, TM	All Flexes	L	$192	
					P	$240	
Pinseeker	Classic (W)	Heel & toe weighted	LS,TM	All Flexes	P	$256	
	(I)	Traditional blade	S,TM,LS	All Flexes	IC	$342	
	Formula 1 (W)	Heel & toe weighted	TM,S,LS	All Flexes	P	$256	
	(I)	Low profile	TM,S,LS	All Flexes	IC	$378	
	Bombshells (W)	Sole weighted shell	S,G	All Flexes	IC	$200	
	Rebound (I)	Free flex face	TM,S,LS	All Flexes	IC	$396	
	(W)	Backweighted, ebony finish	TM,S, LS,G	All Flexes	L	$216	
Joe Powell Golf	693P (W)	Fiber insert, oil hardened	S,LS, UCV	All Flexes	P	$300	
	PT1 (W)	Fiber insert, aluminum firing pin	S,LS UCV	All Flexes	P	$300	
Pro Group (First Flight)	The Standard (W)	Brass backweight	S	R,S	P	$216	
	(I)	Tour grind	S	R,S	F	$315	
	PhD (W)	Brass backweight	S	R,S	P	$216	
	(I)	Compact blade, low c of g	S	R,S	IC	$330	

COMPANY	MODEL	FEATURES	SHAFT TYPE	FLEX	CLUB HEAD	PRICE	(4 WOODS 9 IRONS)
Rainbow	T-Line Neutralizer (I)	Classic blade	S,UCV, TM	R,S,X	IC	$360	
	Neutralizer (W)	Adjustable swingweight	S,UCV, TM		P	$240	
Ram	Accubar (W)	New weighting system	LS,S	R,S,X	L	$210	
	(I)	Matched sweet spots	LS,S	R,S,X	IC	$360	
	Tradition (W)	Classic shape	LS,S	R,S,X	P	$240	
	(I)	Classic blade	LS,S	R,S,X	IC	$346	
	Aries (W)	Epoxy insert	S	R	L	$158.25	(8I, 3W)
	(I)	Perimeter weighted	S	R	F		
	Accubar Low Profile (W)	Low center of gravity	LS	R,S,X	L	$210	
	(I)	Conventional shape	LS	R,S,X	IC	$360	
	Golden Ram (W)	Classic	S	R,S,X	L	$188	
	Tour Grind (I)	Hand ground	S	R,S,X	F	$270	
	Tom Watson (W)	Custom only	LS,TM UCV,S,G	R,S,X	P	$400	
Rauco Inc.	Modern Classic Raudy (W)	Oil hardened, R&LH	LS,S	All Flexes	P	$225	
	Classic (W)	R&LH	LS,S	All Flexes	P	$165	
	Modern (W)	R&LH, Backweighted	LS,S	All Flexes	L	$135	
Rawlings	RXP (I)	Low profile	S	R,S	IC	$342	
	(W)		S	R,S	L	$152	
	Tour (I)	Classic design	S	R,S	IC	$324	
	(W)		S	R,S	P	$150	
	Omega (W)	Cycolac inserts	S	R,S	L	$128	
	(I)	Low c of g, enlarged sweet spot	S	R,S	F	$184	
	Lee Trevino Pro (W)	Rock-hard maple heads	S	R,S	L	$ 75(3)	
	(I)	Flanged soles	S	R,S	F	$148	
Shamrock	Model 202 (I)	Dual pocket power head	S,LS	All Flexes	ST-IC	$378	
Kenneth Smith	Royal Signet (W)	Hand made	S,G,TM	All Flexes	L	$300	
	(I)	Hand made	S,G,TM	All Flexes	F	$450	
Sounder Sports	Men's Regular (W)	Dynamic & static balance	S	X,S,R	L	$196	
	(I)	Dynamic & static balance	S	X,S,R	IC	$355	
	Pro Loft (W)	Dynamic & static balance	S	X,S,R	L	$196	
	(I)	Dynamic & static balance	S	X,S,R	IC	$355	
Spalding	Executive (W)	1,3½,5,6,7 woods	LS	R	L	$236	
	(I)	4-9 irons,pw	LS	R	IC	$267	
	Top Flite (W)	Classic design	LS (Light Dynamic)	R,S	L	$182	
	(I)	Classic design	LS	R,S	F	$327	

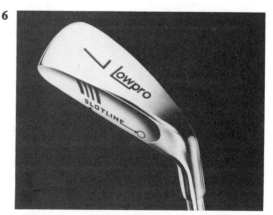

5. Dunlop's Maxpower model for left-handers features laminated wood heads, cast irons, and the Dynamic shaft.

6. Greenirons' Slotline Honors Model features low-profile blade in long irons, conventional shape in 8-iron, 9-iron, and wedge.

COMPANY	MODEL	FEATURES	SHAFT TYPE	FLEX	CLUB HEAD	PRICE (4 WOODS 9 IRONS)	
Spalding	Elite Plus (W)	New set composition	LS	R,S	L	$204	
	Elite Plus (I)	New loft-length relationship	LS	R,S	IC	$380	
	Elite Plus Custom (W)	Backweighted, blonde finish	LS	R,S	P	$254	
Square Two	Square Two (W)	Matched total weight, swingweight	S,G	All Flexes	L,P	$200(L), $240(P)	
	(I)	same as above	S,G	All Flexes	IC	$342	
Stag	Nitro 600 (W)	St and P combo	S,LS	All Flexes	C&P	$268	
	(I)	Progressive face profile	S,LS	All Flexes	IC	$405	
	Classic (I)	New hosel design	S	All Flexes	IC	$405	
	Nova (I)	Shaft over hosel design	S	All Flexes	IC	$405	
Stan Thompson	Ginty (I)	Keel-like sole	S,G	All Flexes	IC	$337.50	
	(W)	Ginty soleplate, 1-6 avail.	S	All Flexes	L	$160	
	Model 22 (W)	Classic head shape	S	All Flexes	P,L	$150	
	RC20X (I)	Conventional	S,G,	All Flexes	IC	$337.50	
Bob Toski	Target (I)	Low profile, slight offset	S,LS,TM, G,UCV	All Flexes	IC	$427.50	
	(W)	Custom designed, backweighted	S,LS,TM, G,UCV	All Flexes	L,P	$280	
	Toski Forging (I)	Conventional blade	S,LS,TM, G,UCV	All Flexes	F	$427.50	
Triumph	Tempo (W)	Backweighted,swingweight adjustment screw	S	All Flexes	P&L	$156(P), $128(L)	
	(I)	Weight distribution system	S	All Flexes	IC	$250	
	Tempo Plus II (W)	Light over-all weight	LS	All Flexes	P	$236	
Tru Stix	#10 Hook Corrector (W)	Self-adjustable swingweight,	S,G	All Flexes	L	All models $189.95	(steel)
	#11 Pro Model	Full rocker sole, special	S,G	All Flexes	L	$299.95	(graphite)
	#12 Fade Corrector	head weighting	S,G	All Flexes	L		
	#13 Slice Corrector		S,G	All Flexes	L		
Unique	Unique (I)	Low c of g	S,LS	All Flexes	IC	$405	
	(W)	Offset	S,LS	All Flexes	IC	$220	
	LP (I)	Semi-low profile	S,LS	All Flexes	IC	$224.55	
	Unique II (W)	Vacuum impregnated heads	S,LS	All Flexes	P	$220	
Victor Golf PGA/Victor	Concept (W)	Deep ebony finish, red Cycolac insert,	S	R,S	L	$200	
	(I)	Flo-weighting (weight shifted in sequence from toe of 2 iron to heel of wedge)	S	R,S	IC	$360	
	Concept LCG (I)	Low profile	S	R,S	IC	$360	
	Tommy Armour (W)	Cycolac insert, rosewood finish	S	R,S	P	$220	
	(W)	Clean back, feel intensifier	S	R,S	F,IC	$200	
	(I)		S	R,S	L	$333	
Wilson	Reflex (W)	Fore-weighted; wide sweetspot	LS	R,S	L	$208.40	
	(I)	Faces flex at impact	LS	R,S	IC	$408.60	
	Staff (W)	Traditional head design	S	R,S	L	$215	
	(I)	Contoured sole	S	R,S	IC	$360	
	X-31 (W)	Clubs can be personalized	S	R,S	L	$185	
	(I)	Sole weighted	S	R,S	F	$319.50	
	1200 Power Sole (W)	Sole weighted	LS	R,S	L	$216	
	(I)	Sole/heel/toe weighted	LS	R,S	IC	$386.55	

7

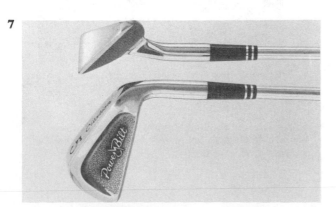

7. H&B's Citation cast-iron head features an extrawide flat sole, offset hosel.

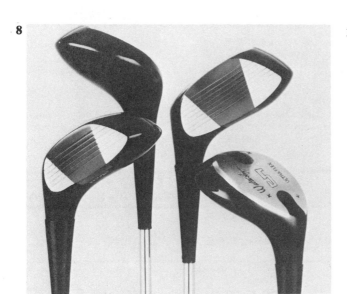

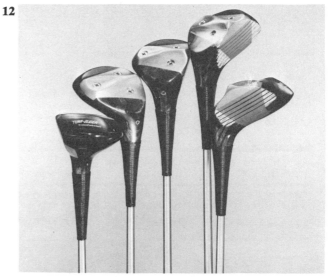

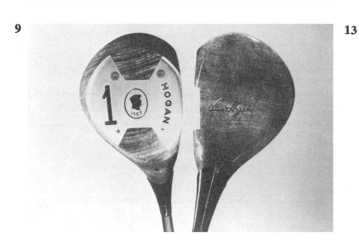

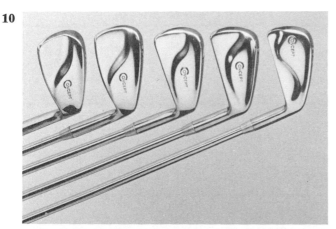

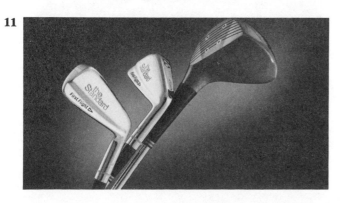

8. Hagen Ultraflex: emerald-finished laminated wood heads; driver has deep face, 11° loft.

9. Ben Hogan Co. has produced this limited-edition driver to commemorate company founder's "triple crown" wins in 1953. Classic-shaped head has 11° loft, 10-inch roll and bulge.

10. PGA/Victor's Concept irons gradually increase in degree of offset hosel and hosel length from 2-iron to wedge.

11. First Flight's Standard woods have brass backweight, dark cherry finish. Irons have forged heads, slightly cambered sole.

12. Northwestern's Turf-Glider woods have unusual knifelike design in soleplate intended to ease playing from difficult lies.

13. The Ben Sayers Contact Model from Hornung's Pro Golf Sales: iron features cutaway-heel design.

WOMEN'S CLUBS

KEY (W) Woods (I) Irons SHAFT TYPES ● (S) Steel (LS) Lightweight steel (ST) Stainless steel (G) Graphite (TM) Titanium (UCV) UCV-304 chrome-vanadium steel (B) Bionize FLEXES ● (L) Ladies (A) Flexible (R) Regular (T), (S) Stiff (X) Extra stiff CLUBHEADS ● (L) Laminated (P) Persimmon (IC) Investment cast (F) Forged (R&LH) Right and Left-Handed ● Prices are suggested retail for steel-shafted clubs unless otherwise indicated. Hogan Shaft Flex Equivalents: 1-L; 2-A; 3-R; 4-S; 5-X.

COMPANY	MODEL	FEATURES	SHAFT TYPE	FLEX	CLUB-HEAD	PRICE	(4 WOODS 9 IRONS)
American Precision	American (W)	Four-way weighting	S,ST,G	L,A,R,	L	$208	
	(I)				IC	$355.50	
	American G-F (I)	Heel-toe weighted, shaft in hosel	S,ST,G, TM	L,A,R	IC	$387	
Cobra	Tour Model (W)	Classic design	S,LS,G, TM	All Flexes	L	$240	
	(I)	R&LH	S,LS,G, TM	All Flexes	IC	$355.50	
	Cobra Baffler (W)	Double runner soleplate	S,LS,G, TM	All Flexes	L	$190	
	L.P. (W)	Backweighted	S,G,TM, LS	All Flexes	L	$196	
	(I)		S,G,TM, LS	All Flexes	IC	$355.50	
Confidence	Ladylite (I)	Low profile	LS	L,A	IC	$212	(8 I)
	(W)	Low center of gravity	LS	L,A	L	$134	
Dunlop	Blue Max (W)	Low profile fairway woods	Alta	Medium	L	$211.70	
	(I)	Low profile, synchronized flex	Alta	Medium	IC	$304	
Walter Hagen	Lady Matrix (W)	14° loft in driver	LS	L,A,R	L	$220	
	(I)	Dynamic swing matching	LS	L,A,R,	IC	$387	
	American Lady (W)	Shallow face	S	L	L	$102	
	(I)	Low c of g	S	L	F	$162	
	Lady Ultraflex (W)	Gamma Fire insert	LS	L	L	$227	
	(I)	Face slot	LS	L	IC	$398.25	
	Onyx LP (W)		LS	L,A	L	$143	
	(I)	Low profile	LS	L,A	IC	$265.50	
Hillerich & Bradsby	Power Bilt (W)		S	R	L	$ 91	
	(I)		S	R	F	$141.75	
	Countess W4722 (W)	Backweighted	S	L	L	$144	
	768T (I)	Shaft over hosel	S	L	F	$238.50	
	5532T (I)	Low c of g	S	L	IC	$288	
	GW4722		G	L	L	$400	
Ben Hogan	Medallion (I)	Offset	S,LS, (Legend)	1	F	$400	
	Director (I)	Heel & toe weighting	Apex	1	F	$239	
	Companion (W)	Midnight blue finish	(Legend)	1	L	$206	
	(W)		Apex	1	L	$194	
	Princess (W)	Cobalt blue Dura-Ply heads	S	1	L	$133	
	(I)		S	1	F	$168	
Karsten/Ping	KI (I)	Original with improvements	LS,S,G, TM	S	IC	$405	
	KII (W)	Patented four-way roll sole with ski leading edge	LS,S,G, TM	S	L	$232	
	(I)	More rounded sole, R & LH	LS,S,G, TM	S	IC	$405	
	KIII (W)	More rounded patented four-way roll sole	LS,S,G, TM	S	L	$232	
Karsten/Ping	KII (I)	PING rail	LS,S,G, TM	S	IC	$405	
	KIV (I)	Rounded edges	LS,S,G, TM	S	IC	$405	
	LH-KII (I)	Left-handed only	LS,S,G TM	S	IC	$405	

14

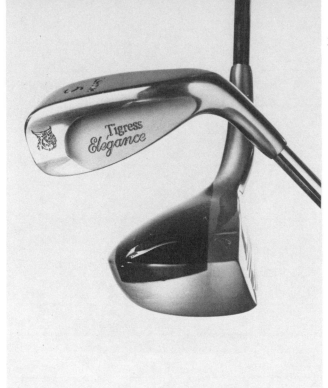

15

17

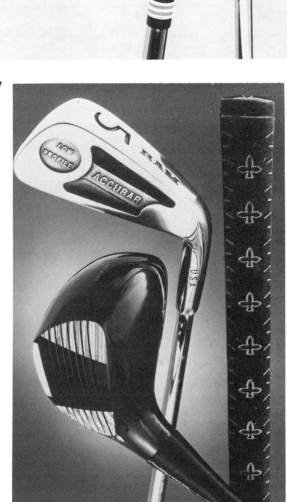

14. Tigress Elegance, the top women's model from Lynx, has cast metal-alloy wood heads and low-profile irons.

15. MacGregor's leading women's model is Spirit-Lite: low-profile clubs with ultralight shaft.

16. Rainbow's T-Line woods retail for $200, set of four.

17. Ram's Lady Accubar low-profile model has calibrated weight bar on irons, heavier brass soleplate on woods.

16

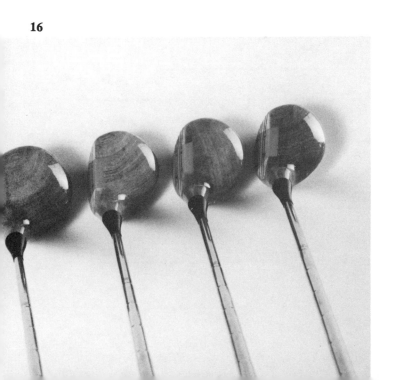

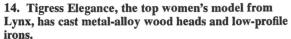

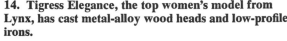

COMPANY	MODEL	FEATURES	SHAFT TYPE	FLEX	CLUB-HEAD	PRICE	(4 WOODS 9 IRONS)
Lynx	Tigress (W)		S	L	L	$124	
	(I)		S	L	IC	$243	
	Tigress Elegance (W)	Offset hosel, blue finish	LS,	L,A,R	C&P	$184	
	(I)	Stainless, slight offset	LS	L,A	IC	$306	
MacGregor	Spirit Lite (W)	Compact head	UCV	L	L	$135	
	(I)	Low profile	UCV	L	IC	$280	
	Finesse (W)	Highly lofted woods	LS	L	L	$108	
	(I)	Low c of g	LS	L	IC	$232	
Northwestern	Saga (W)	Swingweighted, brass sole plates	LS	R	L	$390	(8I, 3W)
	(I)	Tour ground	LS	R	IC		
	Ultimate (W)	Classic design	LS	R	L	$235	(8.I, 3 W)
	(I)	Same as above	LS	R	F		
	Esquire (W)	Walnut finish, red insert	S	R	L	$ 96	
	(I)	Low profile	S	R	IC	$180	
	Dorado (W)	Walnut finish	S	R	L	$ 96	
	(I)	Semi-Low Profile	S	R	F	$162	
Toney Penna	Blue Cloud (W)		LS	L	P	$240	
	Amber Cloud (W)		LS	L	P	$240	
	Original (I)	Custom forged, classic blade	LS	L	F	$298	
Pinseeker	Emerald (W)	Emerald green finish	LS	L	L	$128	
	(I)	Ladies' swingweight, men's head weight	LS	L	IC	$243	
	Rebound (W)	Backweighted, blue finish	LS,TM, S,G	L	L	$216	
	(I)	Free flex face	LS,TM,S	L	IC	$396	
Pro Group	Lady Palmer (W)	Classic design	S	L	L	$ 70	(1,3,5)
	(I)	Classic design	S	L	F	$105	(7 irons)
Ram	Golden Girl (W)	Extra loft	S	L	L	$228.10	(8 I, 3W)
	(I)	Expanded sweetspot	S	L	IC		
	Lady Aries (W)	Extra loft	S	L	L	$158.25	(8 I, 3 W)
	(I)	Wide sweetspot, progressive heel & toe weighting	S	L	F		
	*Lady Accubar (W)	Low c of g	S	L	L	$138	
	(I)	Conventional shapes	S	L	IC	$279	
Rawlings	Honeybee (W)	Low profile	S	L	L	$ 68	(3W)
	(I)	Classic design	S	L	F	$116	
	Lady Omega (W)	Enlarged sweetspot	S	L	L	$128	
	(I)		S	L	IC	$207	
Kenneth Smith	Royal Signet	Custom made	S,LS,G, TM	All flexes	L,P,F	$300 $450	(W) (I)
Sounder Sports	Ladies (W)	Dynamic & static balance	S	All flexes	IC	$324	
	(I)	Same as above	S	All flexes	L	$180	
Spalding	Ladies Executive (W)		LS	L	L	$189	
	(I)	Expanded sweetspot	LS	L	IC	$305	
Square Two	Lady Petite (W)	Driver has 13° loft	S	L		$180	
	(I)	1½" shorter than standard	S	L	IC	$333	
Triumph	Tempo (W)	Backweighted, swingweight adjustment screw	S	L,R,S,X	P L	$156 $128	
	Tempo Plus II (W)		LS	L,R,S	P	$236	
Victor	Butterfly (W)	Composition grip; investment cast soleplate	LS	L	L	$160	
	(I)	Composition grip	LS	L	IC	$276.50	(8 I)
	Ladies Coronation (W)		S	L	L	$100	
	(I)	Lower weight distribution	S	L	F	$168.75	
Wilson	Lady Reflex (W)	Fore-weighted	LS	L	L	$208.40	
	(I)	Face flexes	LS	L	IC	$366.40	(8 I)
	Berg Staff (W)	Mahogany finish	S	L	L	$215	
	(I)	Narrow, contoured sole	S	L	F	$319.50	

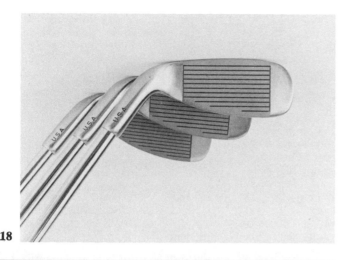

18

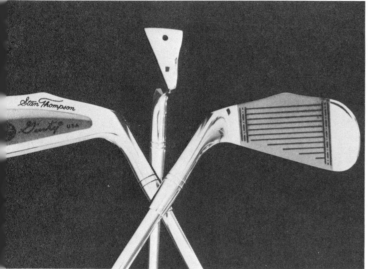

19

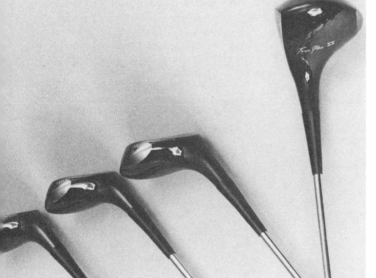

20

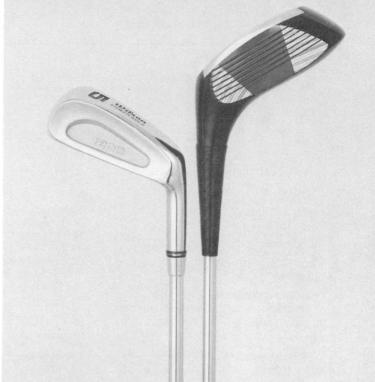

21

18. Stag's low-profile iron is the Nitro 600, available for men and women. Shown here are 1-iron, 6-iron, and pitching wedge.

19. The Ginty iron line from Stan Thompson features keel-shaped sole; Ginty woods available with same sole.

20. Triumph Plus II persimmon wood heads with extralight chrome-vanadium shaft.

21. Wilson's 1200 Power Sole line of irons has low-profile blade, extra-wide sole. Companion woods feature extra-thick soleplate.

22. Tom Watson Woods are available only through Ram's custom program.

22

CLUB TALK

A selected list of equipment and clubfitting terms you should know

bulge: the slightly outward curve, from heel to toe, in the face of a wood club.

camber, cambered sole: the arc or curve in the bottom part of an iron club, whether from heel to toe or front to back.

forging: process by which a type of iron clubhead is formed; a metal bar is heated and placed between two halves of a die. The upper and lower halves of the die squeeze the hot metal into the general shape of an iron head.

investment casting: also referred to as the lost wax process, an operation by which a type of iron clubhead and parts of certain wood clubheads are formed: A waxed pattern is dipped repeatedly into a ceramic mixture. When the ceramic is fired, the wax melts and runs out (hence the lost wax process). Molten metal is poured or invested into the ceramic shell. The shell is then cracked away, leaving the clubhead.

low profile: a term applied usually to irons, which have shallower face heights than the more traditional designs. These clubs are usually sole weighted, with the intent being to lower the center of gravity and facilitate hitting the ball up in the air.

perimeter weighting: process by which weight is removed from the center of the club and placed more in the heel, toe and sole.

roll: the slightly outward curve from crown to sole in the face of a wood club.

tip taper shaft: a type of golf shaft which has a tapered tip and is trimmed to its proper length by cutting from the butt end.

unitized shaft: a type of shaft which has a parallel tip and is trimmed to the proper length by cutting from the tip end. □

GUIDE TO CLUBFITTING

by RALPH MALTBY

GOLF MAGAZINE TECHNICAL ADVISOR

This Master Guide to Clubfitting is not designed to send everyone out to buy a custom set of clubs. Rather, it is intended as a springboard to aid you in making determinations in the fitting variables of lie, flex, material and length of shafts, grip size, swingweight, loft, face angle and clubhead design.

It has long been my contention that far too many people fit their golf games to their equipment. This can lead to compensations, which can, in turn, lead to faulty swing habits.

It is much wiser to fit your equipment to your person, maximizing the effectiveness of your physique and your golf swing. You can do this by going to your pro shop, selecting a set of clubs off the rack and having them altered to your needs. But to do this, you must have some degree of knowledge. This Guide will help you gain that know-how.

Some of the areas that will be discussed will be easily comprehended, with definite guidelines available to

you. Others will require a more subjective interpretation, a gray zone, which can be worked out only through trial and error. My recommendations are just that. They are the result of what I have learned over the years. They are not necessarily axiomatic, nor universally held. They are what I believe to be the best and most practicable methods.

I must caution you, however, that these pages are only a guide; they are not a substitute for the advice and help of a knowledgeable club professional who can measure the specifications of your present clubs and assess your golf swing and potential before fitting you in the most accurate way.

Who needs custom fitting? I would guess that 80 per cent of all golfers would benefit from it, and these people are divided into three categories.
1) Players with unusual physical characteristics, long fingers and/or arms,

for example.
2) Players with a chronic problem, such as hooking, slicing, pushing or pulling.
3) Players whose equipment has changed over the years. This happens more than you realize—a wood, for example, will tend to pick up moisture and with it weight, altering the total weight and the swingweight. Also falling into this category are those golfers who were not fitted correctly at the start. Seventy-five per cent of all golfers play with incorrectly set lofts and lies.

Why is custom fitting important? To produce a highly efficient golf swing, the player, club and ball must mesh like the instruments in a symphony orchestra. Yet each factor, when isolated, is a highly complex item in itself, deserving individual attention. In the following pages, I hope to give you a better focus on how all these parts of your golf club relate to the whole.

continued

LIE ANGLE

The lie angle is that angle formed by the clubhead and the shaft (right). It is an extremely important factor in determining whether or not the face of the club will come into the ball squarely at impact.

Clubs that are too upright will cause you to hit the ball left, either a pulled shot or a hook. Conversely, clubs with a lie angle that is too flat will cause you to hit the ball right, *i.e.,* pushed or sliced shots (below).

You can check your irons to see if they have the proper lie angle simply by engaging the help of a friend. First, sole the club on a hard, smooth surface, and then have your friend slide two pieces of paper under the club, one from the heel toward the center, the other from the toe toward the center. Where the two pieces of paper meet, or equidistant between them, is where the club is touching the ground. Now, if the lie of your clubs is correct, this point will be in the center of the face. If this point is more toward the heel, the lie is too upright; if it is toward the toe, the lie is too flat. Woods can be checked in

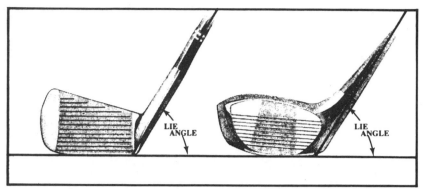

Note, when measuring lie angle on woods, clubhead must be soled slightly toward heel to allow for flattening of lie that results from bowing down during swing.

the same manner. However, a proper lie would be indicated when the papers touch the ground one-half inch toward the heel of the clubhead. This is an allowance for the bowing downward of the shaft during the swing.

You can determine the lie you need by using the following charts and once again engaging the help of a friend. First, take a 5-iron, assume your normal address and measure the height of your "H dimension," which is the distance from your grip cap to the floor (opposite page). Now check this figure against Table 1, which is based on a standard length, or 37-inch 5-iron. As you can see, the standard lie is 60 degrees. So, if your H dimension is 32 inches from the floor, you know

that you are relatively safe with a set of irons bought off the rack. Any deviation in the H dimension should be a warning for you to have your lies rechecked.

Now, if your club is longer than the standard 5-iron, you can calculate the proper lie angle simply by subtracting one degree from the lie angle for each half-inch the club is longer than standard. Likewise, for each one half-inch less than standard add a degree to the lie angle.

Once you have made the determination for your 5-iron, you can fill out the proper lie angles for the rest of your irons by adding one degree as you progress toward the shorter irons and subtracting one degree as you go

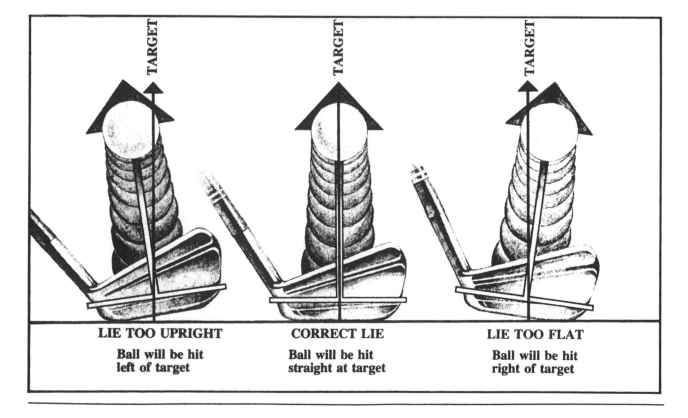

LIE TOO UPRIGHT
Ball will be hit left of target

CORRECT LIE
Ball will be hit straight at target

LIE TOO FLAT
Ball will be hit right of target

toward the longer irons. For example, the set of irons with standard lies, based on this table, would be:

2-iron 57 degrees
3-iron 58 degrees
4-iron 59 degrees
5-iron 60 degrees
6-iron 61 degrees
7-iron 62 degrees
8-iron 63 degrees
9-iron 64 degrees

Standard lies for the fairway woods are: 2-wood, 55½°; 3-wood, 56°; 4-wood, 56½°; 5-wood, 57°; 6-wood, 57½°; 7-wood, 58°.

Calculation of the lie angle is a bit different for the driver as you will see in Table 2. Although you must go through the same procedure of measuring the height of your grip cap from the floor, there is an adjustment, or correction, of two degrees more upright built into the table. This is an allowance for the flattening of lie during the swing. The two-degree differential is due to the bowing downward of the shaft, a result of the centrifugal force exerted during the swing.

Therefore, your driver and fairway woods will be two degrees more upright than the actual measurement. Furthermore, to fit these clubs properly, it is necessary that they be measured when soled ½ inch toward the heel, just as they would be in the natural address position.

continued

Your "H" Dimension tells you proper lie.

TABLE 1

Determining Proper Lie Angle
(standard length 5-iron: 37 inches)

"H" Dimensions (inches)	Degrees Upright (60° standard)	Degrees Flat (60° standard)
30	x	−6°
30¼	x	−5¼°
30½	x	−4½°
30¾	x	−3¾°
31	x	−3°
31¼	x	−2¼°
31½	x	−1½°
31¾	x	−¾°
32	std.	std.
32¼	+¾°	x
32½	+1½°	x
32¾	+2¼°	x
33	+3°	x
33¼	+3¾°	x
33½	+4½°	x
33¾	+5¼°	x
34	+6°	x

Note: for each ½-inch longer than standard, subtract 1¼° from lie angle. For each ½-inch shorter than standard, add 1¼° to lie angle.

TABLE 2

Determining Proper Lie Angle
(standard length driver: 43 inches)

"H" Dimension (inches)	Degrees Upright (55° standard)	Degrees Flat (55° standard)
32	x	-5°
32¼	x	-4½°
32½	x	-4°
32¾	x	-3½°
33	x	-3°
33¼	x	-2¼°
33½	x	-1¾°
33¾	x	-1¼°
34	x	-¾°
34¼	x	-¼°
34½	½°	x
34¾	1°	x
35	1½°	x
35¼	2°	x
35½	2½°	x
35¾	3¼°	x
36	3¾°	x
36¼	4½°	x
36½	5°	x
36¾	5¾°	x
37	6½°	x
37¼	7°	x

Note: For each ½-inch added to standard length, subtract 1° in lie (flatter) and for each ½-inch subtracted from standard length, add 1° in lie (upright).

SHAFT FLEX

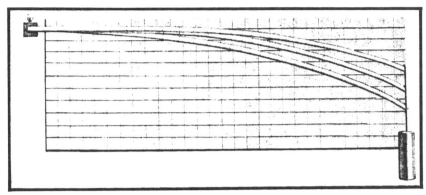

X (EXTRA STIFF)

S (STIFF)

R (REGULAR)

WEIGHT

Shaft flex is measured on a shaft deflection board.

The golf club shaft is perhaps the most complex component to fit properly. Just before impact, it bends and twists in a manner that affects all the other fitting variables.

A shaft that has been properly fitted will enable you consistently to bring the club into a solid impact position. To accomplish this, the shaft must have the flexibility, bend point, curve, torque, weight and length, which complement a particular golfer's swing.

There are very definite guidelines you may follow when selecting a shaft.

First, allow me to say there is no substitute for experimentation with different types of shafts. Only by hitting balls can you determine what feels good and works best for you. However, letting ball flight be your guide, you can use the following as a general rule:

Your shaft is too stiff, if you get:
1) Consistently low shots
2) An unsolid feeling at impact on all but dead center hits
3) A pattern of pushes, slices

Your shaft is too weak if you get:
1) Mostly high shots
2) A whippy feeling
3) Excessive hooking

Shaft flex is affected primarily by the clubhead speed generated in the swing, the location of the center of gravity, the weight distribution in the clubhead and the design of the shaft.

Possibly, just as important as the selection of the proper shaft flex is shaft "curve." The best way I can describe curve is to say that two or three different shafts with the same flex markings actually will perform differently. Three shafts made by

True Temper, for example, are the Dynamic (tr), Pro Fit (tr) and the Jet Step (tr). Let us take one of each type of shaft, all in a stiff flex, and look at the characteristics.

a) Dynamic is weaker than the others in the butt section (grip end) but stronger than the other two in the tip. Consequently, during the swing this shaft does most of its flexing toward the grip end. The Dynamic shaft is used by most of the touring pros and better players who generate a good amount of clubhead speed.

b) Pro Fit is stronger in the butt section than the Dynamic, but has more flex in the tip, allowing the clubhead to kick into the ball at impact. This shaft also will help a player hit the ball a bit higher and give the average golfer a more solid feeling at impact

on off-center hits.

c) Jet Step is even more flexible at the tip end than the Pro Fit and should be investigated by the player who is having difficulty getting the ball airborne.

Again, you must look at your game objectively and make decisions accordingly. Table 3 should aid you in selecting a shaft flex by measuring the distance of your average drive.

If you believe you should be using a shaft flex which lies somewhere between the available shafts, you may wish to specify that your shaft be "tipped." This means trimming the shaft at the tip point. Tipping will make the shaft stiffer. Under normal conditions no more than one-half inch to an inch need be trimmed to obtain the in-between flex.

TABLE 3

RECOMMENDED SHAFT FLEXES

Shaft Flex	Type of Golfer	Carry Distance of Drives
L (Ladies)	Average women golfers	160 yds. or less
A (Flexible)	Senior golfers and stronger women	160 yds. to 185 yds.
R (Medium)	Golfers with average swing speed and strength	175 yds. to 220 yds.
S (Stiff)	Low handicappers, strong players who lack control, most golf pros	210 yds. to 250 yds.
X (Extra Stiff)	Few strong touring pros who generate extremely fast clubhead speeds	240 yds. and over

CLUB LENGTH

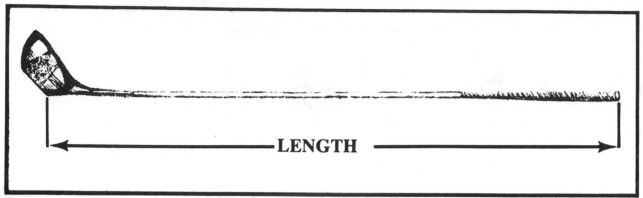

Shaft length is measured from the heel of the sole to the top of the grip cap on both wood and iron clubs.

In all but the most unusual circumstances, length is dictated by comfort.

I suggest that you disregard the talk about longer clubs—longer arc—more distance. Although this basically is true, it is applicable only in the case where a golfer hits the ball just as squarely and with the same amount of clubhead speed with the longer club as with a standard one.

The height of the golfer also matters little as far as club length is concerned. Possibly the single most important element is ability. A tall golfer with an 18 handicap might do better with standard size clubs or even those a bit shorter than normal, spe-cifying a more upright lie to fit him, while a short player with a six handicap might be able to take advantage of the added length of the shaft and adjust to his physique by using a flatter lie. To realize how important this variable is, consider the fact that for each one-half inch off-center the golfer hits the ball, his distance will be decreased by 7 per cent on his woods and 5 per cent on his iron clubs, (below). That is why the average golfer often finds that he gets more distance with shorter clubs.

Keep in mind also that the variables of lie, shaft flex and swingweight as well as total weight are affected when you change the length of your clubs. The more you lengthen the club the more upright the lie becomes, and the more flexible the shaft feels.

As far as swingweight and total weight are concerned, a longer club with the same swingweight as a standard sized club will have less total weight. Conversely, a short club with the same swingweight as one of standard length will have more total weight.

If you decide to make your clubs longer or shorter than standard, experiment with models only one-half inch to an inch in either direction. To check the standard lengths see Table 4.

continued

TABLE 4		
Standard Lengths (Woods and Irons)		
Woods	Men's Length	Ladies' Length
1	43″	42″
2	42½″	41½″
3	42″	41″
4	41½″	40½″
5	41″	40″
6	40½″	39½″
7	40″	39″
Irons		
1	39″	38″
2	38½″	37½″
3	38″	37″
4	37½″	36½″
5	37″	36″
6	36½″	35½″
7	36″	35″
8	35½″	34½″
9	35″	34″
PW	35″	34″
SC	35″	34″

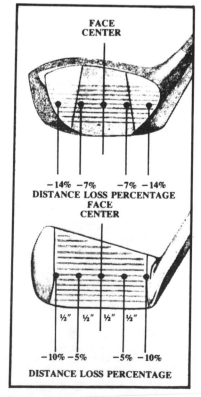

FACE CENTER

−14% −7%   −7% −14%
DISTANCE LOSS PERCENTAGE

FACE CENTER

½″ ½″ ½″ ½″

−10% −5%   −5% −10%
DISTANCE LOSS PERCENTAGE

SHAFT TYPES AND MATERIALS

Although this category is almost entirely a matter of personal preference, I suggest you try out shaft types of different materials and consult your professional before making a decision.

In Table 5 is a list of the shaft types and their properties, with emphasis on step patterns, weight and general characteristics.

TABLE 5

COMMON SHAFT TYPES, MATERIALS AND PATTERNS

Shaft type & Material	Patterns Available	Approx. Shaft Weight Range	General Shaft Characteristics
Traditional tip taper steel	Dynamic (TT) Pro-Fit (TT) Jet Step (TT) Propel I (U) Propel II (U)	4¼ to 4½ oz.	Most popular is Dynamic step pattern. Basically, this is the original steel shaft; it also is the heaviest shaft. The Dynamic is tipstiff, whereas Jet Step is tip weak with Pro-Fit in-between the two.
Tip taper & parallel tip lightweight steel	Dynamic (TT) Dynalite (TT) TT Lite (TT) Pro (U) Tr. Hogan Apex (TT)	3⅞ to 4 oz.	These shafts are about ½ ounce lighter than original steel shaft, approximately the same weight as aluminum.
Parallel tip steel	Dynamic (TT) Jet Step (TT) Comet (TT) Century (TT) Propel I (U) Propel II (U)	4⅛ to 4¼ oz.	Popularized by shaft over hosel assemblies in irons. Weight in-between lightweight and regular steel.
Graphite	Many different mfgs. & types	2¼ to 3¼ oz.	Lightest of popular shafts, the flex and torsional characteristics vary depending on manufacturer.
Titanalloy gold shaft	One pattern	3½ to 4 oz.	Gold color with no stepdowns, these shafts are available for woods and irons. There is some titanium in shaft.
Zirtech titanium 3.25	One pattern	2½ to 3½ oz.	These shafts are comprised of 94½% titanium and in many cases are as light as graphite.
Superlite steel tip taper	One pattern (TT)	3⁷/₁₆ to 3¾ oz.	True Temper's lightest shaft, these are available only for wood clubs and are larger in diameter than other steel shafts.
Chrome vanadium UC V304 tip taper	One pattern	3⅜ to 3⅝ oz.	This is the lightest Union Hardware shaft available for both woods and irons.
.700 butt steel shafts par'll & taper	Hogan Legend (TT) Kinetic (TT)	3⅞ to 4 oz.	The shafts are approximately the same weight as lightweight steel, but have a larger butt diameter. They are available for woods and irons. Specify heavier swingweights when considering this shaft.

The more flexible shafts are represented by the lower numbers in each weight range and the stiffer shafts by the higher numbers in each weight range.

GRIP SIZE

One of the most overlooked elements in fitting a golf club, the proper size grip, is vital if you are to perform your best. Before I get involved in the details of fitting the grip, I will list what an ill-fitted grip can result in.

Grip size too large:
1) Inhibited wrist action, causing the ball to go right
2) Less clubhead feel
3) A tendency to choke down where the grip is more comfortable, thus sacrificing swing speed

Grip size too small:
1) Club turning in hands at impact
2) A tendency to grip the club too hard, thus inhibiting wrist action by creating too much forearm tension
3) A tendency to lose or regrip the club at the top of the backswing.

The best way to determine the proper size grip is to take hold of your club in the playing position. Now release your right hand and check your left to see where your fingertips are positioned (right).

If they are digging into the palm, the grip size is too small; if the fingertips are separated from the heel of the hand by more then one-eighth of an inch then the grips are too large.

For those of you who conclude that your present grip size is too small, and wish to make an adjustment, try this simple test to be sure. Buy some gauze tape and wrap a layer around the grip. Be certain the tape is butting and not overlapping. Now try the grip again. If it is still too small wrap another layer of tape around the grip. Each layer of tape is the equivalent of one-sixty-fourth of an inch added to the diameter.

If, after testing, you believe your present grip size is too large, just choke down on your club until your fingertips are barely touching the heel of your hand. The conversion rate is one-sixty-fourth of an inch reduction for each one-half inch you have

If your left-hand fingertips barely touch your palm, your grip fits properly.

choked down on the handle of the club.

To measure the actual size of the grip you may use either a micrometer, vernier or standard caliper. Measure the diameter of the grip two inches from the top of the butt end of the club.

SWINGWEIGHT

Although the over-all or total weight of a club is definitely a factor in fitting equipment, it is predetermined by the selection of individual components, shaft, head weight, club length, and so on. Swingweight is something else again.

In most cases, swingweight alone is to be specified. The term, which refers to the weight distribution of a golf club about a fixed fulcrum point, is possibly the single most misunderstood element in the selection of golf clubs.

Swingweight usually is expressed in units combining a letter and a numeral, D-1, C-8, etc. Almost everyone has some figure rattling around in his head, but fails to realize the significance of this measurement. For example, each time an adjustment is made in the club, the swingweight must be checked; the same is true after you have had your clubs regripped.

There is no substitute for professional help when attempting to determine the proper swingweight. You may have three woods in your bag all of which you hit well, for example, with three different

shafts and clubhead weights; the result could be three different swingweights.

Although far from infallible, the best way to determine swingweight range is to key on the shaft flex. Table 6 lists recommended swingweights

based on a standard 43-inch driver and 38½-inch 2-iron. For each one-half inch longer the club is than standard, reduce by one swingweight. Conversely, for each one-half inch shorter than standard add one swingweight.

continued

TABLE 6
SWINGWEIGHT RANGE BY SHAFT FLEX

Shaft Flex Designation	Recommended Swingweight Range	Average
L-Ladies	C4-D0	C7
A-Flexible	C7-D3	D0
R-Medium	C9-D5	D2
S-Stiff	D0-D6	D3
X-Extra Stiff	D2-D8	D5

Range is based on standard length clubs (*i.e.*, 43-inch driver and 38½-inch 2-iron). For each ½-inch longer than standard swingweight range should be reduced by one swingweight. For each ½-inch shorter than standard swingweight range should be increased by one swingweight.

LOFT ANGLE

The loft angle is the angle of the club-face in degrees. It is the main factor in determining trajectory.

Ideally, the loft of your clubs should enable you to achieve what is considered normal ball flight for each club. You may, however, wish to order a weak driver, one with more loft than average, and make your fairway woods stronger than the norm (see Table 7). There are any number of combinations in your set, but for the most part you should be concerned with ordering clubs that will allow you maximum efficiency both with the wind and against it, provide adequate backspin on approach shots that land on the green and produce some roll on shots that land short of the putting surface.

As a rule of thumb, increasing the loft (or a weakening of the club) will:
1) Lessen the force applied to the ball at impact
2) Increase backspin
3) Produce higher shots
4) Reduce roll
5) Reduce distance.

Decreasing the loft (or strengthening the club) will:
1) Increase force applied to the ball
2) Reduce backspin
3) Produce lower shots
4) Increase roll
5) Increase distance

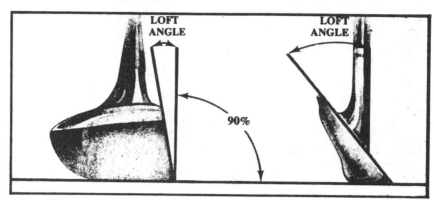

Loft angle as measured for woods and irons.

TABLE 7			
LOFT ANGLES FOR IRONS AND WOODS			
Woods	**Strong Lofts**	**Standard Lofts**	**Weak Lofts**
1	10°	11°	12°
3	15°	16°	17°
4	18°	19°	20°
5	21°	22°	23°
6	24°	25°	26°
7	27°	28°	29°
Irons			
1	16°	18°	20°
2	18°	20°	22°
3	22°	24°	26°
4	26°	28°	30°
5	30°	32°	34°
6	34°	36°	38°
7	38°	40°	42°
8	42°	44°	46°
9	46°	48°	50°
PW	50°	52°	54°
SC	54°	56°	58°

FACE ANGLE OF WOODS

Although it's hard to measure the actual face angle without special equipment, you can visually determine whether your present club is open, square or hooked (right). If it is open and you push or slice consistently, you should consider a square or closed clubface. If it is closed and you have a tendency to pull or hook, ponder a square or open clubface. The face angle of your woods is much more important than just the position that they appear to be in at address. This angle has a direct relationship on the loft of the club at impact as well as an effect on the type of sidespin which will be imparted to the ball.

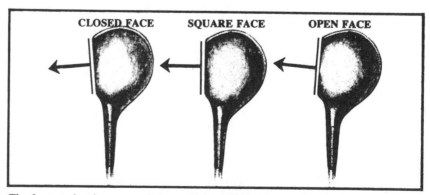

The face angle of your woods has a direct relationship on the loft of the club at the point of impact as well as the sidespin you impart to the ball.

CLUBHEAD DESIGN

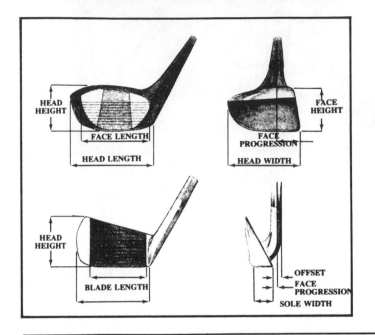

Very few of you, I admit, will have the opportunity to design your own golf clubs. It is important, however, that you understand how features, such as face height, blade length, offset hosel and face progression affect your shotmaking ability. To this end I have included Table 8, below. Depending on what you are looking for in your game, you might decide to try a deeper face and hit the ball lower or a longer bladed iron because you don't feel you hit the ball solidly. Or you might try a shallower head to help you get the ball in the air. Check the table and see which designs fit your performance needs.

continued

Minor adjustments in the features shown at left can have major effects upon the path and trajectory of your golf shots.

TABLE 8

Clubhead Design Variations, Woods and Irons

Clubhead Design Attribute	Applies to: Woods	Irons	Relative Performance Change	Reason	Comments
Deeper head	X	X	Ball will tend to fly lower.	Clubhead's center of gravity is raised.	Loft should be increased slightly.
Shallower head	X	X	Ball will tend to fly higher.	Clubhead's center of gravity is lowered.	Loft may be decreased slightly.
Longer blade length		X	Better chance of square-impact and more solid feel from off-center shots. Less chance of shanking.	Higher moment of inertia (resistance to head twisting on off-center hits) due to better heel-toe weight distribution. Center of gravity usually lower. Increased horizontal hitting area.	Longer blade lengths of iron clubs are usually characterized by an over-the-hosel shaft assembly which aids in weight distribution.
Offset hosel		X	The more offset the easier it is to hit the ball solid, and the lower will be the ball trajectory.	The offset forces the golfer's hands ahead of the ball, enhancing chance of hitting down on it. The offset reduces the face progression and thus results in a lower ball trajectory.	Basically 3 variations of offset irons available. 1. Each iron in the set is offset the same amount. 2. Progressive offset most offset on 9 iron, least on 2 iron. 3. Progressive offset most offset on 2 iron, least on 9 iron.
Face Progression	X		The more face progression the higher trajectory.	Face more in front of center line of the shaft.	Face progression varies among manufacturers.

TROUBLESHOOTING

Now, that you have a basic knowledge of the factors involved in properly fitting a golf club, you can by working backwards effect corrections in your present set of sticks, or if you are going to buy a new set, at least be aware of the priorities.

First, you must have a sound knowledge of your game, and here, I again recommend consulting your club professional.

In Table 9, I have listed possible cures for people who have chronic tendencies. As you will notice, there is more than one way you might try to overcome your problem. However, depending on the intensity of the hook or slice, for example, only one correction may be necessary. This is strictly a matter of trial and error.

Each time you alter your equipment, however, be aware of the effect that change has on the other elements—for example, by changing the size of your grip your club's swingweight automatically has been altered as has its total weight. The same holds true when you switch to a different shaft length or material.

Let's take a case of a golfer who has a hook problem. He now makes his grip size larger, maybe even oversize. When he goes out to the practice range, the grips feel very comfortable, but he is pushing the ball to the right. Now, if he doesn't feel the grips are too large, he might want to look into adding some weight to bring the swingweight back to what it was originally and in turn add to the total weight.

It gets to be like a jigsaw puzzle. And now, you have all the pieces. Go to work. □

TABLE 9

HOW TO CHANGE YOUR SHOTS BY CHANGING YOUR EQUIPMENT

Tendency	With Woods	With Irons
Hook or pull the ball	Open face angle Use stiffer shaft Check for too upright a lie Check for too small a grip Increase swingweight	Use stiffer shaft Check for too upright a lie Check for too small a grip Increase swingweight
Slice or push the ball	Use more flexible shaft Check for too flat a lie Decrease swingweight Check for too large a grip Close face angle Check for weight added to grip end of club	Use more flexible shaft Check for too flat a lie Decrease swingweight Check for too large a grip Check for weight added to grip end of club
Hit ball too high	Decrease loft Lessen face progression Use stiffer shaft Check for excessive vertical face roll Use a deeper faced club Check for excessive hook in face angle Check for backweighted club	Decrease loft Use clubs with more offset Use deeper faced club Use stiffer shaft
Hit ball too low	Increase loft Increase face progression Use more shallow faced club Check for excessive slice in face angle Use backweighted woods	Increase loft Use clubs with minimum offset Use shallower or longer club Use more flexible shaft
Accuracy generally inconsistent in both directions	Check for flexible shaft Check swingsweight Check all lie angles Check for proper grip size Check for weight added to grip end of club	Check all lie angles Check for too flexible shaft Check swingweight Check for proper grip size Center of gravity too high in clubhead, is result of adding excessive weight down shaft
Unsolid feel at impact	Swingweight too light Total weight too light (graphite) Shaft too stiff Center of gravity too high in clubhead, is result of adding excessive weight down shaft.	Swingweight too light Total weight too light (graphite) Shaft too stiff Center of gravity too high in clubhead, is result of adding excessive weight down shaft.

GOLF EQUIPMENT COMPANIES—
ADDRESSES

* Asterisk (*) indicates current catalog will be sent upon request.

ACUSHNET SALES CO. (TITLEIST)
P.O. Box B 965
New Bedford, MA 02741
(617) 997-2811

ALDILA
4883 Ronson Court
San Diego, CA 92111
(714) 279-0074

AMERICAN GOLF OF FLORIDA
1351 S. Federal Highway
Deerfield Beach, FL 33441
(305) 428-3790

AMERICAN PRECISION GOLF CORP.
P.O. Box 601
Worthington, MN 56187
(507) 376-4183

JERRY BARBER GOLF CO.
807 Airway
Glendale, CA 91201
(213) 245-0231 or 245-4849

BEAUWOOD CALIFORNIA, INC.
3122 W. Alpine Avenue
Santa Ana, CA 92704
(714) 751-6740

BELMONT U.S.A.
420 Gulf Boulevard
Belleair, FL 33535

*BROWNING GOLF
Division of Fabrique National
Route One
Morgan, UT 84050
(801) 876-2711

BUTCH BAIRD ENTERPRISES
Box 4503
Hialeah, FL 33014
(305) 757-2971

COBRA GOLF
11045 Sorrento Valley Court
San Diego, CA 92121
(714) 452-1161

*CONFIDENCE GOLF CO.
Division of Life Investors, Inc.
13402 Estrella Avenue
Gardena, CA 90248
(213) 321-4771

CROWN GOLF
1048 E. Burgrove Street
Carson, CA 90746
(213) 537-6690

DELTA GOLF
1735 N. Paulina
Chicago, IL 60622
(312) 278-7422

DUNLOP SPORTS CO.
Division of Dunlop Tire & Rubber Corp.
P.O. Box 1286
Buffalo, NY 14240
(716) 631-5100

GOLF DESIGN & MANUFACTURING, INC.
10869 Portal Drive
Los Alamitos, CA 90720
(714) 995-3612, (213) 430-3586

*GREENIRONS, INC.
15463 Chemical Lane
Huntington Beach, CA 92649
(714) 898-2888

*WALTER HAGEN
Division of Wilson Sporting Goods
2233 West Street
River Grove, IL 60171
(312) 456-6100

HANSBERGER GOLF PRODUCTS
873 Fairway Drive
Bensenville, IL 60106
(312) 595-3241

*HILLERICH & BRADSBY CO.
P.O. Box 35700
Louisville, KY 40232
(502) 585-5226

BEN HOGAN CO.
Division of AMF Inc.
2912 West Pafford Street
Fort Worth, TX 76110
(817) 921-2661

*HORNUNG'S PRO GOLF SALES, INC.
815 Morris Street
Industrial Park
Fond du Lac, WI 54935
(414) 922-2640

LE MASTER PRECISION GOLF EQUIPMENT
1330 East Edinger Avenue
Santa Ana, CA 92705
(714) 542-3996

LOUISVILLE GOLF CLUB CO.
352 Production Court
Louisville, KY 40299
(502) 491-1631

*MACGREGOR GOLF
Division of Brunswick Corp.
One Brunswick Plaza
Skokie, IL 60077
(312) 470-4700

MATZIE GOLF CO.
112 Penn Street
El Segundo, CA 90245
(213) 322-1301

*NORTHWESTERN GOLF COMPANY
4701 N. Ravenswood Avenue
Chicago, IL 60640
(312) 275-0500

TONEY PENNA
Rawlings Golf
15 Industrial Parkway
Hebron, OH 43025
(614) 928-8210

*PING
Karsten Manufacturing Corp.
2201 W. Desert Cove
Phoenix, AZ 85029
(602) 943-7243

PINSEEKER GOLF CORP.
2008 Sunset Drive
Pacific Grove, CA 93950
(408) 373-4148

*PRECISION GOLF EQUIPMENT
A Zurn Company
7302 Adams Street
Paramount, CA 90723
(213) 531-2333

*PRO GROUP, INC. (FIRST FLIGHT)
99 Tremont
Chattanooga, TN 37405
(615) 267-5631

RAINBOW SALES
Yamamoto & Co., Inc.
20130 Hamilton Avenue
Torrance, CA 90502
(213) 321-2808 or 327-0011

RAM GOLF CORP.
Division of Sports & Recreation, Colgate-Palmolive
1501 Pratt Boulevard
Elk Grove Village, IL 60007
(312) 956-7500

*RAUDY GOLF CLUBS
90 Cave Mill Court
Leitchfield, KY 42754
(502) 259-4725

RAWLINGS GOLF
Division of A-T-O Inc.
15 Industrial Parkway
Hebron, OH 43025
(614) 928-8210

*KENNETH SMITH GOLF CLUBS
Box 41
Kansas City, MO 64141
(816) 221-6644

*SOUNDER SPORTS
Division of Pratt-Read
Ivoryton, CT 06442
(203) 767-8234

SPALDING
Division of Questor
Meadow Street
Chicopee, MA 01013
(413) 536-1200

*SQUARE TWO GOLF CORP.
401 E. 9th Street
Orlando, FL 32809

*STAG GOLF PRODUCTS
16224 Garfield Avenue
Paramount, CA 90723

*STAN THOMPSON GOLF CO.
2707 S. Fairfax Avenue
Culver City, CA 90230
(213) 870-7228 or 879-7229

*BOB TOSKI CORP.
160 Essex Street
P.O. Box 576
Newark, OH 43055
(614) 345-9683

TRIUMPH GOLF CO.
Division of Link Development Corp.
3620 105th Street
Orlando, FL 32809
(305) 851-7950

TRU-STIX GOLF CORP.
815 Bearss Avenue
Tampa, FL 33612
(813) 961-8875

UNIQUE GOLF PRODUCTS
68-390 E. Ramon Road
Palm Springs, CA 92262
(714) 328-0878

WILSON SPORTING GOODS CO.
2233 West Street
River Grove, IL 60171
(312) 364-2300

DISCOUNT SOURCES OF CLUBS

BULLSEYE GOLF CENTERS

6602 Menaul Boulevard NE
Albuquerque, NM 87110
(505) 266-3454

852 Middle Road
Duck Creek Plaza
Bettendorf, IA 52722
(319) 359-4853

Merle Hay Driving Range
6107 Merle Hay Road
Des Moines, IA 50131
(515) 276-9557

9006 Maple Street
Omaha, NB 68134
(402) 571-2090

1921 W. Willow Knolls
Peoria, IL 61614
(309) 692-8666

5313 Excelsior Boulevard
Miracle Mile Shopping Center
St. Louis Park, MN 55416
(612) 926-1240

Larpenteur & Snelling Avenues
St. Paul, MN 55113
(612) 647-0233

GOLF AND TENNIS WORLD

1456 South Federal Highway
Deerfield Beach, FL 33441
(305) 428-3780

101 South Military Trail
West Palm Beach, FL 33406
(305) 965-1764

14400 South Military Trail
Delray Beach, FL 33445
(305) 272-2127

1890 South Highway 17
Crescent Beach Section
North Myrtle Beach, SC 29582
(803) 272-6631

6303 North Kings Highway
Myrtle Beach, SC 29577
(803) 449-6322

100 Plantation Center
Highway 278
Hilton Head Island, SC 29928
(803) 785-8005

Town and Country Shopping Center
Aberdeen, NC 28315
(919) 944-7335

MAIL OR PHONE ORDER

340½ Princeton Drive
P.O. Box 1685
Lake Worth, FL 33460
(800) 327-1780
(305) 428-3780 (in Florida)

Catalog available on request. Golf and Tennis World also makes its own custom-club line under the name American Golf of Florida.

WALTER KELLER GOLF SHOPS

2138 Westwood Boulevard
Los Angeles, CA 90025
(213) 479-1547 or 879-9710

Camarillo Springs Golf Club
1 Camarillo Springs Road
Camarillo, CA
(805) 482-6646

LEN KENNETT'S PRO SHOPS

11776 W. Pico Boulevard
Los Angeles, CA
(213) 879-4660

1250 E. Green
Pasadena, CA
(213) 793-3165

101 N. Glassell
Orange, CA
(714) 639-3512

4740 Alvarado Canyon Road
San Diego, CA
(714) 582-2524

PHONE ORDER

(800) 432-7250 (in California)
(800) 854-3687 (elsewhere)

Catalog available on request. Also sells own line of clubs, *Kennett Classic.*

LAS VEGAS GOLF AND TENNIS

4813 Paradise Road
Las Vegas, NV 89109
(702) 736-8030

PHONE ORDER

(800) 634-6745

Brochure and price list available on request.

LOMBARD'S
1861 NE 163 Street
N. Miami Beach, FL 33162
(305) 944-4499

McCAFFERY'S GOLF SHOPS
Passaic County Golf Club
Wayne, NJ

Bethpage State Park
Farmingdale, L.I., NY

Sunken Meadow State Park
Kings Park, L.I., NY

107 Montgomery
San Francisco, CA

NEVADA BOB'S DISCOUNT GOLF & TENNIS
4702 Maryland Parkway
Las Vegas, NV 89109
(800) 634-6202
    Catalog available on request.

PRO SHOP
4550 Oakton Street
Skokie, IL 60076
(312) 675-5286 (Illinois)
(800) 323-4027 (elsewhere)

SAM'S WORLD OF GOLF
7547 Mentor Avenue
Mentor, OH 44060
(216) 946-3392 (Ohio)
(800) 321-7048 (elsewhere)
    Catalog available on request.

SUPREME GOLF
3643 W. Lawrence Avenue
Chicago, IL 60625
(312) 588-3561 (Illinois)
(800) 588-3561 (elsewhere)

SWINGIN' PRO SHOP
Estate Golf Club
Route 1
Lancaster, OH 43130
(800) 282-5013 (Ohio)
(800) 848-5083 (elsewhere)

WEST HILLS PRO SHOP
571 Moon Clinton Road
Coraopolis, PA 15108
(412) 262-4653 (Pennsylvania)
(800) 245-1764 (elsewhere)

EDWIN WATTS GOLF SHOPS
P.O. Drawer 1806
Ft. Walton Beach, FL 32548
(904) 863-1138 (Florida)
(800) 874-0146 (elsewhere)
    Catalog and brochure available on request.

SOURCES OF PRACTICE DEVICES

PRACTICE DEVICES AVAILABLE BY MAIL ORDER

Prices subject to change; shipping extra in some cases.

BERTHOLY SWING PIPE
    Conditions golfing muscles, builds correct positions; $42.50.
        Bertholy Method
        P.O. Box 1867
        Pinehurst, NC 28374

1ST TEE
    Indoor/outdoor individual practice range unit; $46.95, no net required.
        1st Tee Golf Co.
        6015 Gravois
        P.O. Box 22228
        St. Louis, MO 63116

GARY PLAYER'S WRISTRAINER
    To reduce wristiness on short shots; $9.95.
        Gary Player's Wristrainer
        P.O. Box 23231
        31 Donelon Drive
        Harahan, LA 70183

GOLF SWINGER
    Indoor practice club/exerciser; $22.50.
        Swinger/Kerdad Inc.
        P.O. Box 8339
        Salt Lake City, UT 84108

GOLFTEX SWING ANALYZER
    Electronic unit measures clubface alignment, clubhead path and speed, shot shape, estimated carry, etc.; $695.00.
        Golf Technology Inc.
        3406 4th Street
        Lewiston, ID 83501

GOLF MAT—SAM SNEAD AND JOANNE CARNER MODELS
    Stand-on mat shows correct feet-club-ball setup for all clubs; $24.95.
        Stance, Inc.
        1110 Maine
        Quincy, IL 62301

THE GROOVER
Stand-on mat shows clubhead, target lines; $19.95.
Golf Swing Enterprises
P.O. Box 28182
San Diego, CA 92128

LEXR
Swing-plane trainer; $279.95.
Lexr Limited
14044 Ventura Boulevard #209
Sherman Oaks, CA 91423

THE POWER GRIP
Hand-and-finger placement molded into slip-on rubber grip; $6.95.

THE POWER SWINGER
Same as above, plus weighted shaft; $33.90.
Power Grip/Swinger
10239 Monrovia
Lenexa, KS 66215

POWER-PRO
Stand-in device teaches weight shift, braces back leg against sway; $39.95.
Speedmark USA, Inc.
P.O. Box 7496
Van Nuys, CA 91409

POWER-SWING
Shaft unit with sail-like extensions, for building golf muscles.
Power Swing
3333 Camino del Rio South
Suite 210
San Diego, CA 92108

THE SETUP MASTER
Yardstick-type device for building accurate stance consistently; $12.95.
Golf Masters Co.
5182 Avenida Primera
Tucson, AZ 85704

SWING-DING
Corrects head movement during swing; $5.95.
"Swing Ding"
P.O. Box 1061
Muskegon, MI 49443

SWING-GUIDE
A 3′×4′ mat imprinted with lines for proper placement of feet and ball;
Guide Developers, Inc.
1227 Anza Street
San Francisco, CA 94118

SWINGTIMER
Photoelectronic device measures clubhead speed; $89.00.
G.T. Golf Products
Box 370847
Miami, FL 33137

TEACHER PUTTER AND PUTTING CARPET
For training on-sweetspot, on-line contact; $40.00.
Preceptor Golf Ltd.
Suite 727-E
7315 Wisconsin Avenue
Bethesda, MD 20014

TEE-OFF
Indoor/outdoor individual practice range unit; no net required; $17.50.
Tee-Off Co.
Box 15033
Long Beach, CA 90815

PRACTICE DRIVING NETS

Roger J. Auerbach & Son
Box 627
Richboro, PA 18954

Carron Net Co., Inc.
1623 17th Street
Two Rivers, WI 54241

Country Club Golf & Tennis Shops
121 Lakeville Road
New Hyde Park, NY 11040

Custom Golf Clubs (Golfsmith)
10206 N. Interregional Highway
Austin, TX 78753

Eastern Golf Co.
2537 Boston Road
Route One
Bronx, NY 10467

Edwards Sports Nets
Educational Media, Inc.
3191 Westover Drive SE
Washington, DC 20020

Frank's Fisherman's Supply
350 Jefferson Street
San Francisco, CA 94133

Gold Medal Recreational Products
Div. of Blue Mountain, Inc.
Blue Mountain, AL 36201

Great Lakes Golf Ball Co.
4527 Southwest Highway
Oak Lawn, IL 60453

Jayfro Corp.
P.O. Box 400
Waterford, CT 06385

Johnston Ltd., Inc.
Box 12132
Dallas, TX 75225

PRACTICE PUTTING SURFACES

Davis Felt and Carpet Co.
Casimir and Miller Streets
Philadelphia, PA 19137

Eastern Golf Co.
2537 Boston Road
Route One
Bronx, NY 10467

Great Lakes Golf Ball Co.
4527 Southwest Highway
Oak Lawn, IL 60453

Harris Enterprises
Box 243
Wildwood, NJ 08260

Matzie Golf Co.
112 Penn Street
El Segundo, CA 90245

Northern Golf Ball Co.
2350 W. Roscoe Street
Chicago, IL 60618

Par Buster
One E. 26th Place
Tulsa, OK 74114

Par Tee, Inc.
4373 N. Elston Avenue
Chicago, IL 60641

Southern Golf Distributors
P.O. Box 35207
Fayetteville, NC 28300

Sportco, Inc.
3737 Auburn Road
Pontiac, MI 48057

Wittek Golf Range Supply Co.
3650 Avondale Avenue
Chicago, IL 60618

GOLF CART MANUFACTURERS

Harley-Davidson
Motor Co., Inc.
3700 W. Juneau Avenue
Milwaukee, WI 53201

E-Z-Go
P.O. Box 388
Augusta, GA 30903

Davis 500, Inc.
Pelham Road
P.O. Box 1847
Greenville, SC

Yamaha Motor Corp., U.S.A.
Golf Car Division
P.O. Box 6620
Buena Park, CA 90622

Club Car, Inc.
P.O. Box 4658
Augusta, GA 30903

American Continental, Inc.
Box G, Industrial Park
Willmar, MN 56201

Electric Carrier Corp.
8603 Crown Hill Drive
San Antonio, TX 78209

Elmco Inc.
P.O. Box 176
Cooksville, IL 61730

Laher Spring & Electric Car Corp.
2615 Magnolia Street
Oakland, CA 94607

Melex USA, Inc.
1201 Front Street
Raleigh, NC 27609

Nordco Marketeer
Nordco Electric
Vehicle Division
P.O. Box 712
Redlands, CA 92373

Taylor-Dunn
2114 W. Ball Road
Anaheim, CA 92804

GOLF SHOE MANUFACTURERS/DISTRIBUTORS

Dexter Shoe Co.
31 St. James Street
Boston, MA 02116

Etonic
Charles A. Eaton Co.
147 Centre Street
Brockton, MA 02403
(617) 583-9100

Footjoy
144 Field Street
Brockton, MA 02403
(617) 586-2233

Hush Puppies
c/o Morris-Walsh Co.
7815 Airpark Drive
Unit 202
Gaithersburg, MD 20760
(301) 840-0406

Johnston & Murphy
Genesco Park
Nashville, TN 37202

Lazy Bones
7912 Bonhomme Avenue
St. Louis, MO 63105

Pro-Shu
1707 S. Cameron Street
Harrisburg, PA 17105
(717) 223-1688

Ram Golf Corp.
1501 Pratt Boulevard
Elk Grove, IL 60007
(312) 956-7500

Royal Golf
Route 2—Box 70
Farmville, VA 23901
(804) 392-6114

Stylo Matchmaker
Harris International
Weymouth Industrial Park
E. Weymouth, MA 02189
(617) 337-7330

Tretorn Golf
30700 Solon Industrial Parkway
Solon, OH 44139
(216) 248-2199

The Mark V men's model from Etonic is made of sand-colored suede leather uppers and has lightweight crepe sole and sponge inner sole. $39.95

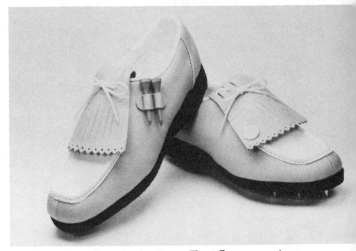

Green-Joys for women, from Foot-Joy, carry tees and ball marker, are guaranteed waterproof. Available in all-white and six color-combinations.

"Jogger" model, from Pro-Shu, is made of synthetic leather with soft-cushion crepe platform sole, quilted lining. $33.50

This men's model made in England by Stylo Matchmakers has a wedge-shaped, flexible, waterproof, composition sole. The uppers are in soft leather with padded collars and insoles. Available in white or tan. $52.00

Travel

One of the challenging tee shots awaiting travelers on Walt Disney World's two championship courses, near Orlando, Fla.

GENERAL GOLF TRAVEL GUIDES—U.S.

PGA GOLFERS ATLAS, 1979, $9.95.
> PGA Golfers Atlas
> P.O. Box 22456
> St. Louis, MO 63126

Not seen. This publication, to be sold through golf shops only, aims to include virtually every course in the country, with details on conditions of play, fees and facilities, and names of golf professionals. Keyed to color maps of 48 states and 65 major metropolitan areas.

PLACES TO PLAY, 50¢.
> *Golf Digest* Reprint Service
> 495 Westport Avenue
> Norwalk, CT 06856

Golf Digest's annual directory lists and briefly describes more than 1,000 courses in the United States, Canada, Mexico, the Caribbean, and Europe, open to public play.

PRIVATE GOLF AND COUNTRY CLUB GUEST POLICY DIRECTORY, 1979, 186 pages, $5.00.
> Compiled by the editors of *Country Club Golfer* magazine.
> Pazdur Publishing Co.
> 2171 Campus Drive
> Irvine, CA 92715

This softbound guide lists about 1500 private country clubs, most in the United States, and is intended primarily for use by the traveling private country club golfer. Contains information on reciprocal guest policies, fees and facilities and details on playing privileges extended to outsiders. Some resort courses and outstanding public courses also included.

GOLF IN HAWAII

Since one never goes to Hawaii for a short *vacation there is always the happy 'dilemma' of figuring out how to cash in the glorious days ahead in such a way that, when it's all over, there's the feeling of having seen enough beaches, golf courses, and other good stuff, to make it all seem worthwhile.*

A two week vacation happened to me recently and since it parlayed into a very satisfying experience I'd like to tell you about it in truncated form as a sort of guide you might use yourself if you like.

With actually 15 days to play with I picked three five-day segments as a good basis, because it gave me three different resorts, three different islands, and three different courses.

My first stop was Oahu, since that's where international flights land. By starting there, I saved the better part of one day in additional traveling time.

Oahu offers a startlingly different opportunity for the vacationer in the Hyatt combination of 'outer island Kuilima' and 'downtown Regency.' One is remote and isolated, the other is smack in the center of Waikiki. Since both are run by Hyatt, they offer a special package situation, in that you can stay at one and use the other, or you can move from one to the other.

Since Kuilima has a George Fazio golf course, that was my headquarters. A superlative course, for openers, it also has a constant wind, and as a result translates into the kind of golfing challenge I like. The first three days I played 18 holes each, and then capping each day with a fine dinner and maybe a touch of revelry thrown in at day's end. Kuilima's gourmet facilities are a natural habitat for hungry golfers (or, romanticists, for that matter), and I especially recommend their seafood fare.

The fourth morning was earmarked: 'beach,' simply because their south beach is one of a kind . . . being a long, soft stretch of white sand that curves along the bay and is a fine place for shucking tension and inhibitions.

Two o'clock found me in the limo on the way to Waikiki and the Hyatt Regency . . . a towering pleasure center only some 100 feet from the water's edge in downtown Honolulu. Outrageously dramatic and modern, one tends to just want to shop and browse, with not a little imbibing of their food and drink as the day wears on. Still, I did walk to the beach for an outrigger ride. Dinner and a show followed, and back to Kuilima by curfew.

Following that round, it was back to the Regency for the afternoon and then a flight to 'the big island' (Hawaii) and check in to Mauna Kea, for a second five day visit.

Mauna Kea is truly isolated. That's fine, however, since there's no reason to leave. The golf is amazingly satisfying, albeit difficult (designed by Robert Trent Jones). Their beach is the most beautiful I've ever seen, and as such will probably keep you from playing as much golf as you've anticipated.

Fly next to Kauai, the Garden Isle, and Princeville at Hanalei . . . for a completely different experience. Princeville is big . . . virtually a ranch. Located on a mesa at ocean's edge, it has no hotel per se. One stays in a luxury condo. The entire complex revolves around an equally luxurious clubhouse, and there are 27 unusually fine golf holes designed by Robert Trent Jones, Jr.

Princeville is a 'different' experience, part of which is due to the great golf course, and part the wondrous beauty of the island itself. The movie, South Pacific, was filmed there, which gives you an idea of the beaches. Buildings don't always have windows because the temperature is so perfect. It's one of the few places I know where one can sort of get re-acquainted with nature while bedding down in modern elegance.

Thus it was that at vacation's end I returned minus tension and inhibitions, with a renewed fix on snobbishness, and somewhat more in tune with my natural rhythms.

—from *Private Golf and Country Club Directory*
Russ Halford

GOLF IN THE GREAT SOUTHEAST, 50¢.
    Travel South USA
    Lenox Towers
    3400 Peachtree Road NE
    Atlanta, GA 30326

A 72-page guide to golf resorts in Southern states, ads included, updated annually.

AMERICA'S GREATEST GOLFING RESORTS by Dick Miller. 1977, 240 pages, $20, Indianapolis: Bobbs-Merrill.

A detailed look at 20 famous resorts, filled with flavorful black/white photos and 16 color-plates. Resorts are categorized as "Seaside," "Mountain," "Inland," and "Desert." Hard-core information on accommodations, rates, etc., tucked away neatly in back.

20 BEST GOLF RESORTS

SEASIDE
The Cloister, Sea Island, Ga.
Casa de Campo, Dominican Republic
Del Monte Lodge, Monterey Peninsula, Calif.
Dorado Beach, Puerto Rico
Mauna Kea Beach Hotel, Hawaii
Princeville at Hanalei, Hawaii
Sea Pines Plantation, Hilton Head Island, S.C.

MOUNTAIN RESORTS
Banff Springs Hotel, Alberta, Canada
Broadmoor G.C., Colorado Springs, Colo.
Concord Hotel, Kiamesha Lake, N.Y.
The Homestead, Hot Springs, Va.
The Otesaga, Cooperstown, N.Y.

INLAND
Bay Hill Club and Lodge, Orlando, Fla.
Doral Hotel and Country Club, Miami, Fla.
Hotel Hershey, Hershey, Pa.
Horseshoe Bay Resort and C.C., Marble Falls, Tex.
La Costa C.C., Rancho La Costa, Calif.
Pinehurst Country Club, Pinehurst, N.C.

DESERT
La Quinta C.C., Palm Springs, Calif.
Wigwam—Goodyear G. & C.C., Litchfield Park, Ariz.
—from *America's Greatest Golfing Resorts*

THE TRAVELER'S GUIDE TO GOLF by the editors of *Golf Digest*. 1976, 192 pages, $4.95.
    Golf Digest Books
    495 Westport Avenue
    Norwalk, CT 06856

Paperback guide reports extensively on about 400 golf resorts worldwide with primary focus on ten major U.S. golfing regions. Listings cover course descriptions, fees and facilities, other recreational offerings, lodging rates, and business-meeting facilities. Color photos and maps, 12 golf lessons from Jack Nicklaus also included.

BEST PUBLIC COURSES IN 45 MAJOR CITIES

Course	Town	Holes/ Par	Yardage	Telephone
Atlanta				
Bobby Jones				
Municipal G. Cse.	Atlanta	18/72	6,178	404-355-9049
Browns Mill G.C.	Atlanta	18/72	6,535	404-627-9310
Stone Mt. G. Cse.	Stone Mt.	18/70	6,831	404-469-9831
Baltimore				
Mt. Pleasant				
Municipal G.C.	Baltimore	18/71	6,730	301-433-1400
Pine Ridge G. Cse.	Lutherville	18/72	6,449	301-252-2011
Birmingham				
Oak Mt. State Park				
G. Cse.	Pelham	18/72	6,423	205-663-6731
Boston				
Colonial-Lynnfield				
C.C.	Wakefield	18/71	6,825	617-245-9300
Easton C.C.	S. Easton	18/72	6,900	617-238-9092
Ponkapoag G.C.	Canton	18/72	6,553	617-828-0645
		18/72	6,300	
Putterham-Meadows				
G. Cse.	Brookline	18/71	6,215	617-556-7794
Buffalo				
Hyde Park Municipal	Niagara Falls	18/70	6,240	716-278-8081
G. Cse.		9/35	3,135	
		9/36	3,275	
Ransom Oaks C.C.	E. Amherst	18/72	6,315	716-688-5454
Chicago				
Buffalo Grove G.C.	Buffalo Grove	18/71	6,500	312-537-5819
Cog Hill G.C.	Lemont	18/71	6,332	312-257-5872
		18/72	6,341	
		18/72	6,431	
		18/72	6,697	
Midwest C.C.	Oak Brook	18/71	6,302	312-654-1320
Silver Lake G.C.	Orland Park	18/70	6,008	312-349-6944
Sportsman C.C.	Northbrook	18/72	6,615	312-272-0272
Cincinnati				
Reeves G. Cse.	Cincinnati	18/72	6,322	513-321-2740
Sharon Woods				
G. Cse.	Sharonville	18/70	6,453	513-769-4325
Cleveland				
Briarwood G. Cse.	Broadview	9/35	2,740	216-237-5271
	Heights	9/36	3,165	
		9/36	3,165	
Seneca Municipal	Broadview	18/71	6,588	216-526-6885
G. Cse.	Heights	18/72	6,691	

Course	Town	Holes/Par	Yardage	Telephone
Columbus				
Blacklick G. Cse.	Columbus	18/72	7,011	614-861-3193
		18/59	3,946	
Minerva Lake G. Cse.	Columbus	18/70	5,905	614-882-9988
Dallas				
Plano Municipal G. Cse.	Plano	18/72	6,400	214-423-5444
Tenison Park Mem. G. Cse.	Dallas	18/70	6,578	214-823-5350
Denver				
Foothills G. Cse.	Lakewood	18/72	6,787	303-989-3901
Detroit				
Palmer Park G. Cse.	Detroit	18/69	5,929	313-869-3069
Rackham G. Cse.	Huntington Woods	18/70	6,445	313-389-6978
El Paso				
Ascarate G. Cse.	El Paso	18/71	6,178	915-772-7381
		9/36	2,934	
Fort Worth				
Lake Arlington G. Cse.	Arlington	18/71	6,490	817-451-6101
Meadowbrook Municipal G. Cse.	Fort Worth	18/71	6,650	817-457-4616
Rockwood G. Cse.	Fort Worth	18/71	6,258	817-624-1771
		9/36	3,689	
Honolulu				
Ala Wai G. Cse.	Waikiki	18/71	6,392	808-737-3066
Houston				
Bear Creek Golf World	Houston	18/70	6,472	713-493-2200
		18/72	7,100	
Memorial Park G. Cse.	Houston	18/72	6,500	713-862-4033
Indianapolis				
Coffin G. C.	Indianapolis	18/70	6,360	317-924-0041
G.C. of Indianapolis	Zionville	18/72	6,016	317-769-6388
Sycamore Springs G. Cse.	Indianapolis	18/70	6,111	317-849-9071
Jacksonville				
Hyde Park G.C.	Jacksonville	18/72	6,698	904-786-5410
Jacksonville Beach G.C.	Jacksonville Beach	18/72	6,170	904-249-8600
Kansas City				
Shamrock Hills G.C.	Lee's Summit	18/71	6,100	816-537-6556
Louisville				
Seneca G. Cse.	Louisville	18/72	6,610	502-458-9298
Los Angeles				
Harding Municipal G. Cse.	Griffith Park	18/71	6,610	213-663-2555
Pancho Park G. Cse.	Los Angeles	18/71	6,600	213-838-7373
Wilson Municipal G. Cse.	Griffith Park	18/72	6,945	213-663-2555
Memphis				
Davey Crockett Park G. Cse.	Razer	18/72	6,125	901-358-3375
McKellar G. Cse.	Memphis	18/72	6,675	901-346-0510
Miami				
Bayshore G.C.	Miami	18/72	6,168	305-673-7705
Biltmore G.C.	Coral Gables	18/71	6,173	305-446-0649
Key Biscayne G.C.	Key Biscayne	18/72	6,212	305-361-2813
Melreese Le Jeune G.C.	Miami	18/72	6,452	305-635-6360
Milwaukee				
Brown Deer Park G.C.	Milwaukee	18/71	7,030	414-352-8880
Minneapolis				
Coon Rapids G.C.	Coon Rapids	18/72	7,100	612-755-4140
Francis Gross G.C.	Minneapolis	18/70	6,361	612-789-2542
Meadowbrook G.C.	Hopkins	18/72	6,474	612-929-2077
Sundance G.C.	Osseo	18/72	6,489	612-425-5757
Nashville				
McCabe Field G. Cse.	Nashville	9/35	2,915	615-297-9138
		9/35	2,865	
		9/36	3,175	
Nashboro Village G. Cse.	Nashville	18/72	6,705	615-367-2311
New Orleans				
City Park G. Cses.	New Orleans	18/73	6,719	504-283-4324
		18/72	6,592	
		18/69	5,891	
		18/68	5,136	
New York				
Clearview Park G. Cse.	Queens	18/68	6,168	212-229-2570
Dyker Beach G. Cse.	Brooklyn	18/70	6,307	212-836-9722
La Tourette Park G. Cse.	Staten Island	18/72	6,589	212-987-9487
Meshone Municipal G. Cse.	Bronx	18/65	6,500	212-655-9842
Pelham G. Cse.	Bronx	18/70	6,405	212-885-1258
Silver Lake G. Cse.	Staten Island	18/69	5,891	212-447-5630
Split Rock G. Cse.	Bronx	18/70	6,462	212-885-1258
Norfolk				
Lake Wright G. Cse.	Norfolk	18/70	6,131	804-461-2246
Ocean View G. Cse.	Norfolk	18/70	6,000	804-587-0632
Sleepy Hole G. Cse.	Suffolk	18/72	6,675	804-485-5874
Oklahoma City				
Kicking Bird G. Cse.	Edmond	18/70	6,130	405-341-5350
Lake Hefner G. Cse.	Oklahoma City	18/70	6,477	405-843-1565
		18/70	6,305	
Lincoln Park G. Cse.	Oklahoma City	18/70	6,508	405-424-1421
		18/70	6,508	
Omaha				
Applewood G. Cse.	Omaha	18/72	6,560	402-339-2020
Benson Park G. Cse.	Omaha	18/72	6,410	402-571-5940
Miracle Hill G. Cse.	Omaha	18/70	6,344	402-498-0220
Philadelphia				
Burn Brae G.C.	Dresher	18/67	6,300	215-659-9917
Center Square G. Cse.	Center Square	18/71	6,465	215-584-4288
Cobbs Creek G. Cse.	Philadelphia	18/70	5,943	215-877-9746
Phoenix				
Encanto Municipal G.C.	Phoenix	18/70	6,245	602-253-3963
Estrella Mt. G.C.	Goodyear	18/70	6,600	602-932-3714
Maryvale G. C.	Phoenix	18/72	6,223	602-846-4022
Papago Park G.C.	Phoenix	18/72	6,690	602-275-8428

Course	Town	Holes/ Par	Yardage	Telephone
Pittsburgh				
Pittsburgh North G.C.	Gibsonia	18/72	6,200	412-443-3800
Portland				
Colwood G.C.	Portland	18/72	6,432	503-254-5515
Glendoveer National G.C.	Portland	18/74	6,368	503-253-7507
		18/72	6,066	
West Delta Park G.C.	Portland	18/72	6,400	503-289-1818
Rochester				
Chili C.C.	Scottsville	18/72	6,310	716-889-9325
Durand-Eastman G. Cse.	Irondequoit	18/69	6,000	716-266-9626
St. Louis				
Paddock C.C.	Florissant	18/72	6,300	314-741-4334
St. Paul				
Keller G.C.	St. Paul	18/72	6,557	612-484-3011
San Antonio				
Olmos Basin Municipal G. Cse.	San Antonio	18/72	6,526	512-826-4041
Pecan Valley C.C.	San Antonio	18/71	6,750	512-333-9018
San Diego				
Carlton Oaks C.C. and Lodge	Santee	18/72	6,426	714-448-8500
Torrey Pines Inn and G.C.	La Jolla	18/72	6,363	714-453-3530
		18/72	6,727	
San Francisco/Oakland				
Alameda Municipal G. Cse.	Alameda	18/71	6,417	415-522-4321
		18/72	6,615	
Harding Park G. Cse.	San Francisco	18/72	6,700	415-564-6058
		9/32	2,500	
Lew. F. Galbraith G. Cse.	Oakland	18/72	6,750	415-568-2012
Seattle				
Port Ludlow G.C.	Port Ludlow	18/72	6,800	206-437-2222
Tampa/St. Petersburg				
Babe Zaharias G.C.	Tampa	18/71	6,124	813-932-8932
Tampa Airport Resort Golf and R.C.	Tampa	18/72	6,211	813-877-6131
Tulsa				
LaFortune Park Municipal Cse.	Tulsa	18/72	6,700	918-627-2822
		18/54	3,000	
Mohawk Park Municipal Cse.	Mohawk Park	18/72	6,400	918-425-6871
		18/68	5,700	
Washington, D.C.				
Algonkian Reg. Park G.C.	Fairfax, Va.	18/72	7,000	703-450-4655
Northwest Park G.C.	Wheaton, Md.	18/72	7,320	301-598-6100
Reston South G. Cse.	Reston, Va.	18/72	6,800	703-620-9333
Washingtonian C.C.	Gaithersburg, Md.	18/72	7,000	301-948-2200
		18/72	7,000	

—from Travelers Guide to Golf.
Reprinted with permission, Golf Digest.
© 1976, Golf Digest, Inc.

GREAT GOLF COURSES YOU CAN PLAY by Robert Scharff and *Golf Magazine*. 1973, 440 pages, $10, N.Y.: Scribner's.

Capsule summaries of thousands of courses open to the public in ten regions of the United States, plus Canada, Mexico, and Central America, the Caribbean Islands, the British Isles and Ireland, Europe, Africa and the Middle East, Asia and the Far East, and Australia and New Zealand. Each section gives a general description of the region followed by an alphabetical listing of the courses available for play along with location, number of holes, par, yardage, and whether the course is classified as resort, public, or semiprivate. Special sections on the most challenging American courses, the most interesting golf holes in the world, and sources of golf travel information. Comprehensive 24-page index. This is the eighth reprint/update.

THE U.S. OPEN COURSES AT A GLANCE

BALTUSROL
Springfield, N.J.

The Baltusrol Golf Club is just that—a club created for the playing of golf. Tennis courts and swimming pools have not been allowed to pollute the pristine atmosphere at this grand and venerable institution in New Jersey's Springfield—an inner suburb of the New York metropolitan region.

There are perhaps 50 clubs in the United States with two or more 18-hole courses, but none has two courses of quality comparable to the Lower and Upper courses of Baltusrol. Members prefer the Upper, which remains much as it was in 1920, but it is the Lower, over the years lengthened and armed with menacing bunkers, that better meets the demands of championship golf today.

Baltusrol's lofty rank in American golf is assured by its role as a host club for the U.S. Open. The 1980 Open on the Lower Course will mark the sixth Open for Baltusrol, which will then go one up on Oakmont in number of Opens hosted.

The original Baltusrol course was the setting for the 1903 and 1915 U.S. Opens. That course was put to the plow after World War I, when the great architect A. W. Tillinghast came in to design the two courses that opened in 1920. The Upper was a worthy site for the 1936 Open. Since then—in 1954 and 1967, and for 1980—the U.S. Golf Association has chosen the Lower for its grand event, while the poor Upper has suffered the indignity of being used as a parking lot.

Tillinghast's works are memorable for their rich variety. The Lower Course is a marvelous example on which no two holes are remotely alike. The par-3 fourth appears on everyone's list of great holes. Its primary elements are a lake, a handsome stone embankment, and a huge, two-tiered green. The contrast between failure and success—a yard short and you get a splash—is stark and riveting. Depending on the tee selected by the USGA, the fourth may call for any club between a 6-iron and a 3-wood.

OAKMONT
Oakmont, Pa.

Oakmont is the apotheosis of a school of golf-course architecture called "penal," which, simply stated, describes a course on which a golfer pays dearly whenever he misses the target, be it a fairway or a green. The payment here is extracted by more than 180 bunkers—an extravagance unmatched in American golf.

The old (1903) course outside Pittsburgh has been the site of five U.S. Opens, four U.S. Amateur Championships, and two PGA Championships. Winners at Oakmont have included Bobby Jones, Ben Hogan, Jack Nicklaus, Sam Snead, and Johnny Miller. It was Miller who delivered a colossal wallop to Oakmont with his closing-round 63 to win the 1973 Open.

Oakmont is distinct in so many ways. On the one hand, there is the glut of sand; on the other, there isn't a drop of water on the course (not counting the drinking fountains). The course is bisected by the Pennsylvania Turnpike, with seven holes on one side and 11 on the other; the practice putting green is simply an extension of the ninth green.

The greens are shaved at 3/32 of an inch for everyday play at Oakmont. Conventional mowers cannot cut that low, so the bedknives have to be specially treated. The USGA uses a gadget called a Stimpmeter to measure the speed of putting greens, and Oakmont's are the fastest ever tested.

The 1962 Open at Oakmont looms ever larger as a milestone. Jack Nicklaus, in his first season as a professional, tied with Arnold Palmer after 72 holes and then won the playoff before an unruly crowd of hometown Palmer fans.

Lew Worsham, Oakmont's pro, is a former Open champion who has been at Oakmont for more than 30 years.

OLYMPIC
San Francisco, Calif.

Many devotees of the U.S. Open count Olympic as the most satisfying and dramatic of all the courses used for the Open. For one thing, it is never hot in San Francisco in June, and for another, Olympic's 18th hole offers the perfect setting for the climax of a great event.

The 18th at Olympic is a tiny thing, a mere 4-wood-and-wedge par-4. The green, however, sits at the bottom of a bowl. An extended and steep slope on the left side of the hole can accommodate thousands, all comfortably seated and looking directly down on the 18th green.

Olympic, as championship courses grow, is very short—only 6,724 yards from the back tees. How misleading yardage can be! In fact, Olympic "plays" as long as any of the Open courses. The fairways are always lush, restricting roll to a matter of a few yards, and the air, heavy with moisture provided by the nearby Pacific Ocean, severely restricts the flight of the ball. The 17th hole, 445 yards long and slightly uphill, makes the best players in the world reach for woods to get home in two if the slightest bit of air is moving toward them.

The 18 holes are distinctly framed by evergreens. The fairways seem like mere swaths in an imperial forest. There are about 30,000 trees on the course—all grown in this century, for the site was once a sandy, barren stretch between Lake Merced and the ocean.

One desirable element lacking at Olympic, however, is fast greens. They never seem to dry up enough to become frightening.

Olympic is unusual in its proximity to the hub of a great city. The third tee offers a stunning view of San Francisco and the Golden Gate Bridge.

MERION
Ardmore, Pa.

The romance of the Merion Golf Club is almost too much.

Merion was designed by Hugh Wilson, a handsome young insurance executive who died before his great work was completed. For decades its superintendent was the legendary Joe Valentine, who discovered behind his 17th tee what we now call Merion bluegrass. And it was at Merion that Bob Jones, in 1930, completed his Grand Slam by winning the U.S. Amateur Championship.

Jones had the impeccable taste to win his 36-hole final match by the lopsided margin of 8 and 7. This meant that he played the last hole of his extraordinary career as an amateur on Merion's sublime 11th, a par-4 with a green enveloped by everyone's dream of what a bubbling brook should be.

At 6,527 yards, Merion is by a good margin the shortest of the important courses in the United States. No less than six of the 14 par-3 and par-4 holes are short holes in the sense that the clubs used to reach the greens by better-than-average golfers will be 7-irons and up.

The truth is that there isn't any room at Merion for extended tees. The course is jammed onto 125 acres, although an area of 200 acres is considered a necessity for the staging of the big events. Merion is so small that the USGA imposes a limit of 14,000 tickets for a round when the Open comes around—as it will in 1981.

Much of Merion's challenge is packed into its three final holes. The 16th is the famous Quarry Hole, a par-4 calling for a big second shot over an expanse of desolation; the 17th is a big, big par-3 into a severely canted green; and the 18th is a majestic par-4. Merion's 18th was the setting for the most famous of golf photographs—that of Ben Hogan, pictured from behind as he finishes a marvelous stroke. *Life* photographer Hy Peskin captured Hogan as he rifled home a 1-iron shot on the 72nd hole of the 1950 Open. That shot enabled Hogan to make his par and finish in a three-way tie for first. He won the playoff.

PEBBLE BEACH
Pebble Beach, Calif.

The Pebble Beach Golf Links, unlike the other U.S. Open courses, is a place of public accommodation, a circumstance it shares with Old Course at St. Andrews, Scotland.

The conditions of playing Pebble Beach have varied over the years, but in recent years, anyone could play *provided* he/she was staying at the adjacent Del Monte Lodge (perhaps $100 a day, American-style) and was also willing to fork over a sizable greens fee. The course, the lodge, and other nearby and plush accouterments were recently acquired by Twentieth Century Fox, flush with surplus cash generated by the movie *Star Wars*.

Pebble Beach is surely one of the world's three most famous courses—the other two being the Old Course at St. Andrews and the Augusta National Golf Club. It is the annual site of the Bing Crosby Pro-Amateur tournament and has entertained the U.S. Amateur and the U.S. Open—both won by Mr. Nicklaus, in 1961 and 1972, respectively.

The course is on the Monterey Peninsula, which slants into the Pacific Ocean about 125 miles south of San Francisco. It was created in 1918 on extraordinary land for golf: The seven holes along the shore of Carmel Bay are photographed about as often as they are played. The wind off the bay can be fierce.

Incidentally, and despite its name, Pebble Beach is not a "links" course. Linksland, as is found on the Scottish seaside courses, is sandy ground formed after the long-ago recession of an ocean. Pebble Beach is on high land, or headland, jutting out into the sea.

INVERNESS
Toledo, Ohio

A funny thing happened to the Inverness Club on its way to staging the 1979 Open. The club had asked architect George Fazio to come by to handle the elementary task of leveling the 17th green, which over the years, had tilted from back to front so as to become unfair, if not ridiculous. Before Fazio had left the premises he made a radical proposal that, perhaps to their own surprise, the Inverness board of directors accepted. Fazio's proposal called for the construction of four entirely new holes, the elimination of four others, and the installation of two new tees. Oh, yes—repair of the 17th green was thrown into the package. And so handsome old Inverness took on a new appearance going into the 1979 Open, the fourth in the club's distinguished history.

Inverness is a quality course. Within the subculture of those who care desperately about golf turfgrass management there rages an argument as to whether the putting greens at Oakmont or at Inverness are the best to be found anywhere.

Inverness is not as highly ranked as it deserves to be because the course lacks a breathtaking hole—or a gimmick. It is, rather, a course of consistency. The makeup of Inverness is different from all other Open courses in that it has only three par-3 holes. There are three par-5s and 12 par-4s. The strength of the course is in the two-shot holes, four of which are 445 yards or longer.

Inverness was the setting for one of the game's social milestones. At the 1920 Open, pros were admitted within a private clubhouse for the first time.

OAKLAND HILLS
Birmingham, Mich.

Prior to the 1951 Open, the members of the Oakland Hills Country Club, in the Detroit suburb of Birmingham, decided they would beef up their nice old Donald Ross course. The club decided to employ the services of architect Robert Trent Jones, who was already well along in his career as the most successful designer of courses in the game's history.

Jones came up with modifications that boggled the mind. The words "harsh" and "severe" were inadequate, so Ben Hogan called it a "monster" and to this day, every time half the field isn't at par or better after 36 holes, a course becomes a "monster," according to the television talkers.

The most significant of Jones' changes had to do with the renovation and addition of fairway bunkers. He installed many in the drive-zone landing areas, restricting the fairway widths on some holes to 25 yards. On the 15th hole, a par-4 dogleg, Jones plopped a bunker right smack in the *middle* of the fairway. The pros blew their minds. Hogan's "monster" coinage came at the prize ceremony. He had just shot a 67 (one of two rounds under 70 in the 1951 Open) to win going away. The course was modified before the Open returned to Oakland Hills, in 1961. Hogan's 67 is regarded as one of a handful of the greatest rounds ever played.

The 16th hole, a 405-yard par-4, is surely the best hole at Oakland Hills and is as alluring and dangerous a hole as you'll find anywhere. It's an acute dog-leg to the right. The key to the hole is a lake that curls from the fairway to the front of the green and then around to the right rear. When the hole is cut to the right, the second shot, perhaps with something on the order of a 5-iron, is menacing. They fish more than 200 balls a month out of that lake.

CHERRY HILLS
Englewood, Colo.

The Cherry Hills course has the distinction of being the highest in altitude of the traditional Open courses, as Englewood is just over the border from mile-high Denver. At that elevation, there is much less resistance to a ball in flight and so the golfer gets a distance bonus at Cherry Hills on the order of 6 percent.

With the snow-capped Rockies as a backdrop, Cherry Hills is also one of the most scenic courses. A lovely blue lake is a critical component of the finishing holes. The green on the par-5 17th is on an island in that lake, and on the 18th, the lake laps against the left side of the fairway. Cherry Hills is also an oddly imbalanced course, in that the front nine includes four short par-4s. That's the nine on which Arnold Palmer shot 30 when he came from seven shots back to win the 1960 Open with a closing 65.

Palmer shot 280 to win the 1960 Open; Andy North won the same event in 1978 with a score of 285. Does this suggest to you that the modern stars are overrated, that they are in fact not as good as we are monotonously told they are during every weekend telecast of a pro tour event? Forget it. The scores shot up in 1978 because the USGA had made the course a more difficult examination of shotmaking for the 1978 Open.

Ray Ainsley became the hero of hackers in the 1938 Open at Cherry Hills, when he put his ball into the creek meandering down the right side of the 16th. He tried to play the ball out of shallow water but found he couldn't. After a couple of serious attempts Ainsley began to swat at the ball. He holed out in 19—the highest number of strokes ever recorded on one hole in a U.S. Open.

WINGED FOOT
Mamaroneck, N.Y.

Winged Foot is one of the two magnificent 36-hole golf complexes designed by A. W. Tillinghast in the 1920s, the other being Baltusrol. Winged Foot is in Mamaroneck, a bedroom community north of New York City.

When Tillinghast got the commission for Winged Foot, he was given simple marching orders: "Give us a mansized course." He certainly did. Both the East and the West courses are notable, but it is the West course that is more renowned, if less charming, because it has been used as the battleground for three Opens.

The West course is characterized by slightly elevated, pear-shaped greens, higher in the back than the front, and by deep bunkers slashed into the sides of the greens. Tillinghast had to elevate the greens because he had to deal with poor drainage conditions.

On a course loaded with big, strong holes, none may be more formidable than the 190-yard, par-3 tenth. From the tee it's hard to conceive that a mere person could hit that green with anything less accurate than a rifle. Ben Hogan once said that playing the tenth was like being asked to hit a 3-iron into a bedroom window.

When the USGA sets up Winged Foot for the Open, it converts two relatively short par-5s, the 9th and the 16th, into brutal par-4s. The West course is not pretty, but it is terribly difficult without being unfair. When Hale Irwin won the 1974 Open at Winged Foot, he finished at seven over par—in terms of par only, the highest score to win an Open since 1963.

SOUTHERN HILLS
Tulsa, Okla.

The Southern Hills course, in Tulsa, is held in greater esteem than any other in the vast states of the Southwest. It has been a happy choice for two U.S. Opens, a PGA Championship, and four other national events including the 1946 Women's Amateur won by Babe Didrikson Zaharias.

Southern Hills was built at a time when golf-course construction had virtually ceased—in the pit of the Great Depression, in 1933. It was backed by optimistic oil men who had the good sense to employ Perry Maxwell as their designer. Maxwell was a Texas banker who decided to get out of the money business and do what he really wanted to do—design golf courses.

There is no getting away from the reality of the mid-June heat in Tulsa. Both of the Southern Hills opens were won by players preconditioned to the climate—native Oklahoman Tommy Bolt in 1958, and Alabaman Hubert Green in 1977.

Southern Hills is relatively flat, with the exception of the first hole, which goes down sharply from the hill near the clubhouse, and the 18th, which goes back up. The 18th is a heroic par-4. Southern Hills had proudly erected a new back tee on the 18th for the 1977 Open, making the hole play to 455 yards. After the first round, when the average score was much closer to 5 than 4, the USGA cried "enough" and went back to the old tee, which is about 25 yards forward.

Southern Hills had the distinction of being the first Open course to be revealed in its entirety on television. In 1977, ABC Sports presented four-hour telecasts of the final two rounds, beginning with the leader on the first tee.

—Frank Hannigan

OTHER SOURCES OF GOLF TRAVEL INFORMATION—U.S.

Much of the material reviewed in this section is in the form of brochures, maps, guides, etc., which are available, usually free, upon request from local and state tourist agencies.

For some states, the only information given here is the name and address of the particular state's tourist bureau. This means that the golf data sent to us was badly outdated, scanty, or nonexistent, but that other potentially useful material of a more general nature, often including detailed state highway maps, was available.

---

50 BEST COUNTRY CLUBS

Town and Country magazine listed these exclusive social/sporting institutions in its August 1978 issue. The golf represented here is as lofty as the membership requirements—according to the editors, the clubs collectively have hosted more than 75 national golf championships.

Allegheny C.C.
  Sewickley, Pa.
Apawamis Club
  Rye, N.Y.
Baltimore C.C.
  Five Farms, Md.
Belmont C.C.
  Belmont, Maine
Birmingham C.C.
  Birmingham, Ala.
Birnam Wood G.C.
  Santa Barbara, Calif.
Brook Hollow G.C.
  Dallas, Tex.
Burlingame C.C.
  Hillsborough, Calif.
Capital City Club
  Atlanta, Ga.
Century C.C.
  Purchase, N.Y.
Charlotte C.C.
  Charlotte, N.C.
Chevy Chase Club
  Chevy Chase, Md.
Cincinnati C.C.
  Cincinnati, Ohio
Columbus C.C.
  Columbus, Ohio
The Country Club
  Brookline, Maine
C.C. of Detroit
  Grosse Pointe Farms, Mich.
C.C. of Indianapolis
  Indianapolis, Ind.

C.C. of Rochester
  Rochester, N.Y.
C.C. of Virginia
  Richmond, Va.
The Creek
  Locust Valley, N.Y.
Denver C.C.
  Denver, Colo.
Everglades Club
  Palm Beach, Fla.
Glen View Club
  Golf, Ill.
Hillcrest C.C.
  Los Angeles, Calif.
Indian Hill Club
  Winnetka, Ill.
La Jolla C.C.
  La Jolla, Calif.
Lakeshore C.C.
  Chicago, Ill.
Los Angeles C.C.
  Los Angeles, Calif.
Maidstone Club
  East Hampton, N.Y.
Memphis C.C.
  Memphis, Tenn.
Midland C.C.
  Midland, Tex.
Milwaukee C.C.
  Milwaukee, Wis.
Morris County C.C.
  Convent Station, N.J.
Myopia Hunt Club
  Hamilton, Mass.

New Orleans C.C.
  New Orleans, La.
Onwentsia Club
  Lake Forest, Ill.
Paradise Valley C.C.
  Scottsdale, Ariz.
Philadelphia C.C.
  Gladwyne, Pa.
Piping Rock Club
  Locust Valley, N.Y.
River Oaks C.C.
  Houston, Tex.
Rockaway Hunting Club
  Cedarhurst, N.Y.
Round Hill Club
  Greenwich, Conn.
St. Louis C.C.
  Ladue, Mo.
Shady Oaks C.C.
  Fort Worth, Tex.
Sleepy Hollow C.C.
  Scarborough-on-Hudson, N.Y.
Somerset C.C.
  St. Paul, Minn.
Somerset Hills C.C.
  Bernardsville, N.J.
Southern Hills C.C.
  Tulsa, Okla.
Waverley C.C.
  Portland, Ore.
Wilmington C.C.
  Wilmington, Del.

ALABAMA

Bureau of Publicity and Information
State of Alabama
Montgomery, AL 36130

ALASKA

State Division of Tourism
Pouch E-907
Juneau, AK 99881

ARIZONA

VALLEY OF THE SUN VISITORS' GUIDE
Phoenix and Valley of the Sun Convention and
    Visitors Bureau
2701 E. Camelback Road, Suite 200-H
Phoenix, AZ 85016
(602) 957-0070

Slick 60-page magazine updated twice a year; covers accommodations and attractions in Phoenix-Scottsdale area; lists approximately 25 resort and public courses with par, yardage, facilities available, and phone numbers; keyed to map.

*TUCSON'S YEAR 'ROUND GOLF AND TENNIS
    FACILITIES*
Tucson Convention and Visitors Bureau
P.O. Box 27210
La Placita Village
Tucson, AZ 85726
(602) 791-4768

Foldout brochure listing nine public and eight private courses, keyed to city map; includes par and yardage, address and phone number, and name of golf professional.

ARKANSAS

*127 GOLF COURSES IN THE NATURAL
    STATE*
Arkansas Department of Parks & Tourism
149 State Capitol
Little Rock, AR 72201

Foldout flyer listing 24 public, 17 semiprivate, and many private courses; includes address, par, yardage.

CALIFORNIA

*NORTHERN CALIFORNIA AND NEVADA
    GOLF COURSES*
Automobile Club of Southern California
P.O. Box 2890, Terminal Annex
Los Angeles, CA 90051

This 44-page booklet, prepared by the Automobile Club of Southern California, lists approximately 320

10 BEST GOLF COURSES—U.S.

Here are the 10 greatest American courses, as named by the editors of *Golf Digest* and a 135-man selection panel of professional and amateur golfing experts. The list is in alphabetical order (within the group, all courses, like Anglican bishops, are ranked equally).

	Yards	Par	Rating
Augusta Nat'l G.C.			
Augusta, Ga.	6,980	72	73.1
Medinah C.C. (#3)			
Medinah, Ill.	7,102	71	75.3
Merion G.C. (East)			
Ardmore, Pa.	6,498	70	70.2
Oakland Hills C.C. (South)			
Birmingham, Mich.	7,088	72	73.7
Oakmont C.C.			
Oakmont, Pa.	6,938	72	73.8
Olympic Club (Lake)			
San Francisco, Calif.	6,669	71	73
Pebble Beach G. Links			
Pebble Beach, Calif.	6,815	72	75
Pinehurst C.C. (#2)			
Pinehurst, N.C.	7,051	72	73
Pine Valley G.C.			
Clementon, N.J.	6,765	70	73
Seminole G.C.			
North Palm Beach, Fla.	6,898	72	72

Reprinted with permission from *Golf Digest*. © 1978 Golf Digest, Inc.

courses located in northern California and 30 courses located in Nevada. Courses are categorized as public, semipublic, and private; information on each covers mailing address and phone number, par and yardage, fees, facilities, and unusually precise travel instructions; maps included.

NOTE: This booklet is *not* available to the general public. It is available free of charge to members of the American Automobile Association (AAA), as well as the Auto Club of Southern California.

SOUTHERN CALIFORNIA GOLF COURSES
A 52-page booklet listing more than 350 courses in the southern half of the state. Same format and restricted availability as above.

*SOUTHERN CALIFORNIA ACTION SPORTS
    MAP*
Action Sports Map
444-A Burchett St.
Glendale, CA 91203

Large foldout map listing and locating 430 golf facilities (including par-3 and executive-length courses) from Monterey Peninsula area south to border. Courses are categorized public, private, or resort; mailing addresses and phone numbers are included; tennis facilities and ski areas also covered. Available for $1.95.

SOUTHERN CALIFORNIA TRAVEL GUIDE

Visitor and Convention Publications
Division of Windsor Publications
21220 Erwin St.
Woodland Hills, CA 91365

Detailed, all-purpose travel and vacation planner; has limited golf information but useful references to visitor attractions, shopping, transportation and tours, and accommodations; 112 pages, $1.95.

SAN DIEGO—GOLFLAND U.S.A.

San Diego Convention and Visitors Bureau
1200 Third Avenue, Suite 824
San Diego, CA 92101
(714) 232-3101

Foldout brochure, keyed to map, listing about 70 courses along with mailing addresses, phone numbers, information on facilities, and brief descriptions of layouts.

PALM SPRINGS LIFE'S GUIDE

Palm Springs Convention & Visitors Bureau
Palm Springs Airport
Palm Springs, CA 92262

A 48-page guide prepared by the editors of *Palm Springs Life* magazine; contains detailed information on local restaurants, entertainment spots, services, air schedules, etc.; also lists Palm Springs' 28 18-hole courses and eight 9-hole courses, private and public, along with par and yardage, address and phone number.

CLUB LIFE IN THE DESERT

The unique role of the private club in the southern California desert life is characterized in this excerpt from the September 1978 issue of *Palm Springs Life*.

Club life is a big and vital part of the desert lifestyle. The club represents more than just a place to have a few drinks with friends, or to play a round of golf or a set of tennis. For most, the club is home. It is activity and sports. It is friends—and the center of one's social calendar.

Clubs have been indigenous to the Desert Empire from the early days of Palm Springs. Visionary men such as Charles Farrell, founder of the Racquet Club, and John Dawson, developer of Thunderbird Country Club, knew that the club life could be the oasis people were in search of when they visited this area.

In the 1920s, when the town was an isolated village, Palm Springs attracted two kinds of people; those who required its arid, sunny climate and healing waters for health reasons, and those who just wanted to get away from the noise and congestion of the city.

At first these visitors flocked to the desert because it offered freedom from pressures, wide open spaces, and a slow tempo. But as time went on, more activity became desirable and the club life began to emerge.

When Farrell and Ralph Bellamy started the Racquet Club in the mid-'30s they did it just to provide a spot for themselves and their friends to play tennis. Later, with the building of the clubhouse, there emerged the first club social life—alive with celebrities and private parties.

Farrell's idea was just the tip of the iceberg. Today there are tennis clubs for every type of player, clubs with permanent and secondary residences, clubs offering overnight accommodations and meeting and conference facilities.

By the late forties, a man named John Dawson felt the area was ripe for an 18-hole championship golf course and country club, with luxury homes built on the perimeter of the course. In 1951, he completed his dream with the desert's first such community: Thunderbird Country Club.

Up until Dawson's unique idea for a community/club concept, small courses had been built around private homes. California oilman Thomas O'Donnell was actually the first to bring golf to the desert area, constructing a 9-hole course in his front yard so that he, his friends and their guests could play their favorite sport as often as desired. Floyd Odlum then added some fairways to his ranch outside of Indio, and the trend spread to hotel premises such as El Mirador and the Biltmore, and to luxury country club settings like Thunderbird.

Dawson's insight about people desiring the club life for both play and good living paid off well, not only for him but also for the desert. After Thunderbird, Dawson just kept on going, developing Eldorado, Seven Lakes, Marrakesh and now the new Desert Country Club at Indian Wells.

Other developers soon to catch on to a good thing would follow suit, building Tamarisk, Indian Wells, Bermuda Dunes, La Quinta, Canyon, Palm Springs Country Club and del Safari.

The concept of club life keeps growing. There are tennis clubs within the main club environs too. Mission Hills, The Springs, Sunrise, Desert Island and Ironwood are a few of the newest country clubs built on this concept. In addition to both tennis and golf, the new Rancho Las Palmas Country Club features a Marriott Hotel on its acreage, offering overnight accommodations, entertainment facilities, and a complete health spa.

Today there is a club in the desert for everyone, no matter what his requirements. There are clubs with an emphasis on the social life, and clubs where sports reign supreme. There are clubs more acceptable to families and those that attract chiefly retired persons. There is one thing, however, that is true of every club in the desert. To its members, each club is still that oasis in the sun offering up all the good things of life. To the majority of people who make the desert a permanent or secondary home, the club life is the only life.

—Toni Alexander

COLORADO

WHERE TO PLAY GOLF IN COLORADO

Rocky Mountain Golf Course Superintendents Association
2222 South Albion, Suite No. 101
Denver, CO 80222

A 16-page foldout brochure describing some 140 courses in the Denver-Boulder area, the "Northeast Plains," the "Southeast Plains," and the "Western Slope"; data provided on par and yardage, fees and facilities.

CONNECTICUT

CONNECTICUT GOLF COURSES

Connecticut Department of Commerce
201 Washington Street
Hartford, CT 06106
(203) 566-3385

Folder listing about 60 courses open to the public; par and yardage, phone numbers; compiled, 1978.

DELAWARE

Delaware State Visitors Service
630 State College Road
Dover, DE 19901

FLORIDA

FLORIDA GOLF GUIDE

Florida Division of Tourism
Collins Building
Tallahassee, FL 32304

An 80-page paperback from the Florida Golf Association with information on over 500 courses arranged by region: Northwest, North, West Gulf Central, etc. Contains some feature material, ads. Updated every year.

GREATER MIAMI GOLF COURSES

Miami-Metro Department of Publicity and Tourism
499 Biscayne Blvd.
Miami, FL 33132
(305) 377-5461

Mimeographed listing of 46 courses within a 35-mile radius of Miami, including 20 semiprivate and 13 public courses; data on par and yardage, fees and facilities; separate brochure keys course locations to map.

GEORGIA

Georgia Department of Industry and Trade
P.O. Box 1776
Atlanta, GA 30301

A request to the State of Georgia got a highway map and brochures on Jekyll Island, St. Simons Island, and Gallaway Gardens, but no detailed or statewide golf information.

HAWAII

GOLF & TENNIS IN HAWAII

Hawaii Visitors Bureau
Waikiki Business Plaza, Suite 801
2270 Kalakaua Avenue
Honolulu, HI 96815

Foldout brochure listing 38 courses open to public play; keyed to map of six islands.

IDAHO

Division of Tourism & Industrial Development
Room 108, Capitol Building
Boise, ID 83720

For information on golf packages at fabled Sun Valley, write:

Sun Valley Resort, Inc.
Sun Valley, ID 83353

ILLINOIS

ILLINOIS GOLF GUIDE

Office of Tourism
Department of Business and Economic Development
222 S. College Street
Springfield, IL 62706
(217) 782-7500

A 45-page booklet listing about 275 municipal or daily-fee courses throughout the state, with data on par and yardage, facilities, phone numbers. No private clubs included.

THE CHIGAGOLAND MAP

"Map"
Chicago Tribune Public Service Office
435 N. Michigan Ave.
Chicago, IL 60611

This 3½″×4″ foldout color map from the *Chicago Tribune* shows Chicago and nearby suburbs on one side, larger area extending to 165 miles on reverse side, and pinpoints golf courses as well as other points of interest. Revised annually. Current mail-order edition available for $2.10.

INDIANA

Tourism Development Division
Indiana Department of Commerce
State House, Room 336
Indianapolis, IN 46204

A 16-page color brochure listing 126 public, private, and semiprivate golf courses, keyed to a small general map of the state. Information on par and yardage, facilities available, plus brief description of playing features of each layout.

IOWA

Iowa Development Commission
250 Jewett Building
Des Moines, IA 50309

KANSAS

Kansas Department of Economic Development
503 Kansas, 6th Floor
Topeka, KS 66603

KENTUCKY

KENTUCKY STATE PARKS GOLF COURSE DIRECTORY
Ed Bignon, Director of Golf
Department of Parks
Capital Plaza Tower
Frankfort, KY 40601

Pamphlet listing 16 courses within or near state parks and affiliated with state-park resorts or privately operated lodging facilities. The five 18-hole courses included are in the Kentucky Dam Village, Lake Barkely, Hawes, General Burnside (an island), and Lincoln Homestead state parks. State highway map and additional brochures describing the individual parks also available.

LOUISIANA

Louisiana Tourist Development Commission
P.O. Box 44291
Baton Rouge, LA 70804

MAINE

FORE ME
Maine Vacations
State of Maine Publicity Bureau
Gateway Circle/Portland, ME 04102

Pamphlet listing 93 courses; sent along with a state highway map.

Courses are more heavily concentrated in the Greater Portland area, but from York to Fort Fairfield picturesque links challenge the golfer. Several courses have been ranked with the most characterful in the nation. Kebo Valley Club at Bar Harbor, Aroostook Valley C.C. at Fort Fairfield, Penobscot Valley C.C. at Orono and York Golf and Tennis Club all are courses of championship length. Some of the most scenic, with spectacular views of lake, mountain or seashore, are Norway C.C., Wilson Lake C.C. at Wilton, Cliff Island C.C. and Presque Isle C.C.

—from *Fore Me*

MARYLAND

Division of Tourist Development
Economic & Community Development Department
State of Maryland
1748 Forest Drive
Annapolis, MD 21401

MASSACHUSETTS

MASSACHUSETTS GOLF COURSES
Massachusetts
Box 1775
Boston, MA 02105

Listing of the state's 294 public, semiprivate, and private courses, keyed to highway map included in information kit. Course distances given in yards and meters; phone numbers also included.

THE BERKSHIRES VACATION GUIDE
Berkshire Vacation Bureau
205 West Street
Pittsfield, MA 01201
(413) 443-9186

This 100-page guide to motels, inns, restaurants, shops, and other attractions in the Berkshires of Massachusetts, New York, and Connecticut lists minimal data on 12 public courses and 10 private courses in the area.

CAPE COD VACATIONER
Cape Cod Chamber of Commerce
Hyannis
Cape Cod, MA 02601
(617) 362-3225

A 64-page directory of activities and attractions, revised annually and including a listing of 23 golf facilities open to the public.

MICHIGAN

WEST MICHIGAN CAREFREE DAYS
West Michigan Tourist Association
Hospitality House
136 Fulton East
Grand Rapids, MI 49503

A 208-page general guide to attractions in the western half of the state; lists twenty 18-hole courses and fifteen 9-holers, with par and yardage.

EAST MICHIGAN GOLF & TENNIS GUIDE
East Michigan Tourist Association
Log Office
Bay City, MI 48706

A brochure listing details on 21 golf resort facilities, keyed to map; also includes names and addresses of over 100 other courses.

GOLF & TENNIS—TRAVERSE CITY AREA
> Traverse City Area Chamber of Commerce
> Traverse City, MI 49684

Flyer with data on sixteen 18-hole courses and four 9-hole courses in Traverse City area, keyed to map.

GOLF COURSES IN SOUTHEAST MICHIGAN
> Southeast Michigan Travel & Tourist Association
> 350 American Center Building
> 27777 Franklin Road
> Southfield, MI 48034
> (313) 357-1663

A 16-page booklet listing 126 golf facilities and 19 driving ranges in nine-county area surrounding and including Detroit.

Request all of the above literature in one fell swoop from:
> Travel Bureau
> Michigan Department of Commerce
> P.O. Box 30226, Law Building
> Lansing, MI 48909

DETROIT AREA GOLF

When a visitor thinks of Detroit and Southeast Michigan the thought usually is of industrial might and automobiles and there's nothing wrong with that—we do have industry and we do make cars.

But the people who design and build the cars like to get into those cars and see the territory and a considerable part of our territory consists of golf courses, well over 100 of them open to the public in Southeast Michigan and we like to play them—this is one of the most active golf areas in the country.

Our courses range from a nine holer and a driving range on Belle Isle, the island park in the middle of the Detroit River, the world's busiest waterway, to fine championship courses.

Donald Ross, one of the game's greatest architects and designer of first magnitude courses such as Oakland Hills, Inverness, Scioto, Pinehurst No. 2, Seminole and so many more, designed Rackham Municipal Golf Course on 10 Mile Rd. in Huntington Woods, next to the Detroit Zoo. Ross was hired by Horace Rackham, one of Henry Ford's early associates, to design the course for the City of Detroit after Rackham became impressed with Ross's design of 36 holes for the private Detroit Golf Club.

Rackham twice has hosted the United States Public Links Championship.

And there's the University of Michigan Golf Course in Ann Arbor, designed by Dr. Alister Mackenzie, a Scottish physician.

Mackenzie also designed the Augusta National Golf Club, home of the world-famed Masters Tournament, and breathtaking Cypress Point on California's Monterey Peninsula.

We have very testy, rolling, tree-lined municipal layouts such as Ann Arbor's 6,690-yard Leslie Park Golf Course, and scenic Kensington Metropark along I-96, northwest of Detroit, where you might see formations of Canada geese honking overhead.

The Huron-Clinton Metropolitan Authority, which operates Kensington, is opening two more 18-hole courses this year, along I-275, south of Metropolitan Airport, at the Willow Metropark, and at Stony Creek near Rochester, north of Detroit.

Salem Hills, just over the Washtenaw-Wayne County line, is renowned as one of the best and toughest public courses in the state and the 7,074-yard course, with its nearby sister course, Godwin Glen, has been used for United States Open and Public Links qualifying.

Holly Greens, Tyrone Hills and Dunham Hills, along the US-23 and I-75 corridors, are well-groomed, demanding courses and an exceptionally fine new course, Rattle Run, has just opened in St. Clair County off the I-94 freeway northeast of Detroit. It was designed and built by former Michigan PGA president Lou Powers who has played some of the world's outstanding courses and utilized that knowledge in building the 6,944-yard course where water comes into play 23 times and there are 57 sand traps and a wide variety of trees.

Detroit has a rich golf heritage—Walter Hagen, Chick Harbert and Walter Burkemo, National PGA champions all, are counted as Detroiters. Four U.S. Opens and four National PGA championships have been played here as well as numerous PGA Tour events and a number of women's professional tournaments.

This is golf country. Tee up with us.
—Jack Berry in Golf Courses in Southeast Michigan

MINNESOTA

Minnesota presently offers no comprehensive listing of its several hundred golf courses, but does have records and information on courses in various regions, i.e., "Arrowhead region," "Pioneerland," "Heartland," "Hiawathaland," "Viking-land," and "Metroland."

There are over 100 courses in the Metroland (St. Paul–Minneapolis) area; a listing of some 40 courses open to the public, containing location and phone number of each is available from:
> Minnesota Department of Economic Development
> 480 Cedar Street
> St. Paul, MN 55101

MISSISSIPPI

MISSISSIPPI GOLF & TENNIS
> Department of Tourism Development
> Mississippi Agricultural and Industrial Board
> P.O. Box 22825
> Jackson, MS 39205

Brochure listing 21 public and 38 private courses,

with locations, facilities, and names of persons to call or write for additional information. Comes with brochures and a handsome 48-page color paperback on various other Mississippi attractions.

For specific information on golf-package plans at various Gulf Coast area resorts, write:

Gulf Coast Visitors Bureau
Drawer CC
Biloxi, MS 39533

MISSOURI

Missouri Tourism
308 E. High Street
Jefferson City, MO 65101

MONTANA

Montana Travel Promotion
Department of Highways
Helena, MT 59601

NEBRASKA

Department of Economic Development
Division of Tourism
Box 94666
Lincoln, NB 68509

NEVADA

RENO HOTEL-MOTEL GUIDE

Greater Reno Chamber of Commerce
Post Office Box 3499
133 N. Sierra Street
Reno, NV 89505
(702) 786-3030

Flyer listing accommodations, 17 hotel casinos; contains simple map indicating location of Reno's three public, one semiprivate, and one private golf course.

LAS VEGAS GOLF AND TENNIS

Las Vegas Convention and Visitors Bureau
3150 Paradise Road
P.O. Box 14006
Las Vegas, NV 89114

Color brochure and list of 12 public, semiprivate, and resort courses, with phone numbers, par and yardage, fees and facilities.

NORTHERN CALIFORNIA AND NEVADA GOLF COURSES

Automobile Club of Southern California
P.O. Box 289, Terminal Annex
Los Angeles, CA 90051

This 44-page booklet, devoted mainly to courses in northern California, also lists 32 Nevada layouts, including 11 in Las Vegas and five in Reno. Prepared by the Automobile Club of Southern California, it covers public, semipublic, and private courses and includes information on mailing addresses and phone numbers, par and yardage, fees and facilities, and precise travel instructions.

NOTE: This booklet is *not* available to the general public. It is available free of charge to members of the American Automobile Association.

NEW HAMPSHIRE

NEW HAMPSHIRE GOLF DIRECTORY

Department of Resources and Economic Development
Division of Economic Development
P.O. Box 856
State House Annex
Concord, NH 03301

Listing of 34 eighteen-hole courses and 43 nine-hole courses, along with locations, par and yardage, fees, phone numbers, and names of golf professionals.

NEW JERSEY

NEW JERSEY GOLF COURSES

New Jersey Division of Travel & Tourism
P.O. Box 400
Trenton, NJ 08625

Booklet prepared in 1973 listing about 200 public, private, and semiprivate courses by county; phone numbers included.

ATLANTIC CITY INFORMATION GUIDE

Visitor's Bureau
Convention Hall, Room LG
Atlantic City, NJ 08401
(609) 348-7044

A 20-page guide to accommodations and attractions; motels and hotels with "golf privileges" are so indicated, but no mention of the one casino now in operation and the various new casinos on the drawing board —even though these facilities comprise the main reason for the city's rebirth.

NEW MEXICO

Tourist Division
Department of Development
Commerce & Industry
Bataan Memorial Building
Santa Fe, NM 87503

NEW YORK

GOLF COURSES IN NEW YORK STATE
Bureau of State Information
Department of Commerce
99 Washington Avenue
Albany, NY 12245

Foldout brochure, prepared in 1977, listing some 300 courses open to the general public, with details on par and yardage, fees and facilities.

GUIDE TO PUBLIC GOLF COURSES IN METROPOLITAN AREA
Sports Department
The New York Times
229 W. 43rd Street
New York, NY 10036

Every spring, usually in March, *The New York Times* runs a full-page listing of about 100 municipal and state golf courses located in New York City, Long Island, Westchester County, southwestern Connecticut, and northern New Jersey. Chart covers par and yardage, addresses and phone numbers, fees and facilities, plus estimated waiting time and playing time.

MET GOLF DIRECTORY
Sports Department
Daily News
220 East 42nd Street
New York, NY 10017

A 38-page booklet compiled by Dana Mozley of the *Daily News;* lists about 400 public and private courses in New York City and surrounding area, including Long Island, Westchester, Connecticut, and New Jersey; names of pros, phone numbers included.

NORTH CAROLINA

NORTH CAROLINA, GOLF STATE U.S.A.
North Carolina Division of Travel and Tourism
Department of Commerce
430 N. Salisbury Street
Raleigh, NC 27611

A slick 16-page color booklet listing the state's 340-odd resort, public, and private courses. There are short pieces on "North Carolina's Great Golfers," "The History of Golf in North Carolina," and "World Golf Hall of Fame." Information on the courses themselves is limited to name, location, par, yardage, and for resort and public courses, phone numbers. Also received: highway map of the state; 32-page guide to hotels, motels, and country inns; and a booklet titled *Tours You Can Take in a Day.*

THE HISTORY OF GOLF IN NORTH CAROLINA

Although North Carolina does have more than 340 golf courses, it is not simply in numbers alone that golf has excelled in the Tar Heel State. Rather, it is a combination of quantity, quality and variety of courses combined with a rich heritage of the game that gives North Carolina unchallenged claim to the title: "Golf State: U.S.A."

Legend has it that the game was first introduced to the Tar Heel scene in 1728 when a resident of Fayetteville was observed swatting at a feather ball in a field near town. Admittedly, this is more than 150 years before the recognized debut of the game in the United States.

Some say that the first North Carolina course was built at the now defunct resort of Hot Springs in Madison County around 1894.

Others say it was about the same time near the site of the present Highland Country Club in Fayetteville. Still another report claims that the state's first golf course was built in Asheville in 1893.

The single most important event in the history of golf in North Carolina was the arrival in 1895 of James W. Tufts who bought 5,000 acres of cut-over sandhills timberland for a dollar an acre.

In 1900 Tufts brought this country's premier golf course architect, Donald Ross, to Pinehurst to be the resort's professional. Ross had served his apprenticeship in Scotland at the famed St. Andrews and had designed some 600 courses across the United States. Ross remained at Pinehurst until his death in 1948.

A few years ago the state's leading professional and amateur golfers were asked to select the best 18 holes of golf in North Carolina. Seventeen of those holes were on courses designed by Ross.

The stimulus of Pinehurst was felt at once from one end of North Carolina to the other. From Asheville and Highlands in the west to Wilmington in the east, golf courses sprouted, players multiplied and golf competition flourished.

The oldest of North Carolina's major competitions is Pinehurst's North and South Amateur, inaugurated in 1901 and today the world's second ranking amateur match play tournament. It rates only behind the British Amateur, now that the USGA Championship has been changed to stroke play.

When the visitor to Pinehurst today winds his way among the stately long leaf pines for a round of golf, he is walking the same ground once covered by nearly all of the game's immortals—Walter Travis, Harry Vardon, Chick Evans, Bobby Jones, Francis Ouimet . . . across the years to Hagen, Sarazan, Nelson, Hogan, Snead, Palmer, Nicklaus et al.

North Carolina's golf heritage, however, is not limited to Pinehurst or even the immediately adjacent area which today boasts of 26 courses all within a 15-mile radius.

Very early the game spread from the sandy beaches in the east to the mountains in the west.

Bobby Jones gave a boost to the early mountain golf

boom. Jones had a summer home at Highlands in southwest North Carolina, often called Land of the Sky. He once shot a 62 on the 6,300-yard Highlands Country Club course which is 4,000 feet above sea level at the clubhouse.

Earlier, Jones and Ouimet had played a great exhibition match at the Asheville Country Club.

The legendary Walter Hagen is credited with a similar early contribution to golf interest in the state's populous Piedmont. He played in the 1932 Carolinas Open at Greensboro's then young Starmount Forest Country Club course, tied for first in a memorable after-dark finish and then lost to Henry Picard in an 18-hole playoff the following day. This, many say, is what launched Picard on a great career of his own.

The very early days are filled with many such stories of the greats and near-greats of the game testing their skills on Tar Heel soil.

One was the playing of the National PGA championship at Pinehurst in 1936, with Denny Shute defeating Jimmy Thompson 3 and 2 in the match play final.

Another was the world-shaking victory by Tony Manero in the 1936 U.S. Open at Baltusrol in New Jersey. Manero was the resident professional at the Sedgefield Country Club in Greensboro and won the Open in a stirring, final-round duel with Lighthorse Harry Cooper in which Manero shot a 67. His victory brought him home as a national hero and golf has never been the same in the Greensboro area.

Still another was the journey of Estelle Lawson Page from the quaint little nine-hole Chapel Hill Country Club course to the high Memphis Country Club for the '37 Women's U.S. Amateur Championship. Mrs. Page won the qualifying medal for the second year in a row and this time went on to destroy Patty Berg 7 and 6 in the title match.

A year later, the Greater Greensboro Open was launched as a PGA tour stop, making it the sixth oldest tournament being played in the United States today. What it has done to spur golf interest in North Carolina is immeasurable.

With the addition of Greensboro as a major tournament stop, by 1940 North Carolina had three such events—the North and South Open at Pinehurst, the GGO and the Land of the Sky Open at Asheville.

Also in 1940 a young professional by the name of Ben Hogan was still trying for his first tour victory. He got it at North Carolina first in Pinehurst, then with another at Greensboro and again in Asheville, winning three in a row.

As the decade of the 1940's came out of wartime, other tour events appeared in North Carolina. Durham was on the schedule briefly; Charlotte for a half-dozen years; then off along with Asheville. Just when it appeared Greensboro and Pinehurst would be going it alone, Wilmington came up with its Azalea Open in 1949. Wilmington survived until 1973.

Pinehurst gave up its North-South Open in 1951 after the 49th annual event but returned to the PGA schedule with the World Open. Charlotte rejoined the circuit with the Kemper Open.

The GGO is still going strong.

In addition there is an outing for the professional lady golfers at the American Defender Golf Classic in Raleigh.

In 1974 the PGA Championship once again returned to North Carolina and was played at Tanglewood near Winston-Salem.

Golf is much more than merely a game in the Tar Heel State. For many, it is a way of life. The significance of the sport is perhaps best summarized by this typical exchange of pleasantries between two Tar Heels:

"Played much golf lately?"

"No, not much. Only in the afternoons."

—from North Carolina, Golf State U.S.A.

SAND AND PINES AND GOLF OF COURSE
Sandhills Area Chamber of Commerce
Box 458
Southern Pines, NC 28387

A 24-page large-format color booklet containing data on the Pinehurst-Southern Pines area's famous golf facilities and the new World Golf Hall of Fame, plus information of general interest to potential visitors. If you send for it, you'll probably also receive separately, as I did, various other promotional pieces from individual resorts in the area.

HIGH WIDE AND CHALLENGING
CAROLINA MOUNTAIN GOLF
Asheville Area Chamber of Commerce
P.O. Box 1011
Asheville, NC 28802

These two brochures contain color photos of and map and guide to 14 courses in the mountains of the western part of the state.

CAROLINA GOLFER
Carolina Golfer
P.O. Box 3
Columbia, SC 29202
(803) 796-9200

Bimonthly magazine reports on golf courses and tournaments in the Carolinas; special Directory issue lists facts and figures on over 450 courses in North and South Carolina. Year's subscription (six issues): $5.00.

NORTH DAKOTA

North Dakota Travel Division
State Highway Department
State Highway Building
Bismarck, ND 58505

OHIO

State of Ohio
Department of Economic and Community Development
P.O. Box 1001
Columbus, OH 43216

A "partial" list of golf courses in the state reports locations, par and yardage, phone numbers and category (public, private, semiprivate) of over 200 eighteen-hole layouts and over 100 nine-holers. You may also receive a colorful magazine, *Ohio is the Greatest,* and a fistful of brochures on various tourist attractions in the state.

OKLAHOMA

Oklahoma Tourist & Recreation Department
500 Will Rogers Building
Oklahoma City, OK 73105

OREGON

OREGON GOLF COURSES
Travel Information Section
Department of Transportation
Transportation Building
Salem, OR 97310

An up-to-date listing of the state's 130-plus courses, in newsletter format.

PENNSYLVANIA

POCONO MOUNTAINS YEAR 'ROUND TRAVEL GUIDE
Pocono Mountain Vacation Bureau
1004 Main Street
Stroudsburg, PA 18560
(717) 421-5791

A 96-page guide to resorts, attractions, vacation homesites, campgrounds, restaurants, etc. Some 32 golf facilities listed with par, yardage, and phone numbers. (Received separately: several brochures from individual resorts, including one with color photos of all 18 holes on the course at Fernwood Resort, Bushkill.)

RHODE ISLAND

GOLFING IN RHODE ISLAND
R.I. Department of Economic Development
One Weybosset Hill
Providence, RI 02903

Booklet with interesting thumbnail sketches of 20 private clubs; and detailed practical information on some 30 semiprivate and public courses.

SOUTH CAROLINA

SOUTH CAROLINA GOLF & TENNIS
South Carolina Division of Tourism
Room 30, Box 71
Columbia, SC 29202

This 18-page brochure presents listings of golf courses as follows: Myrtle Beach-Grand Strand area, 27 courses; Coastal Islands, 15 courses; Swamp Fox area (Florence-Pee Dee region in eastern part of state), 33 courses; Inland courses. The brochure also lists the state's 200 courses by category (resort, public, semiprivate, private, and military). Par, yardage, and phone numbers included.

CAROLINA GOLFER
Carolina Golfer
P.O. Box 3
Columbia, SC 29202
(803) 796-9200

Bimonthly magazine reporting on golf courses and tournaments in Carolinas; special Directory issue lists facts and figures on over 450 courses in North and South Carolina. Year's subscription (six issues): $5.00.

TEE UP!
Greater Myrtle Beach Chamber of Commerce
P.O. Box 2115
Myrtle Beach, SC 29577

A 12-page color brochure describing 30 courses in the 60-mile area of the "Grand Strand."

I also received a 196-page guide to accommodations, and sample copies of two publications:

Coast
"The Vacationer's Guide"
P.O. Drawer 2448
Myrtle Beach, SC 29577

On the Green
"The Golfing Magazine of South Carolina's Grand Strand"
P.O. Box 1463
North Myrtle Beach, SC 29582

Coast is an ad-packed, digest-sized guide to the area's attractions, facilities and services, issued weekly and distributed through motel and hotel rooms. Current issues are available to potential visitors free upon written request. *On the Green* is magazine-sized, focused primarily on golf in the area, and issued six times annually on a subscription basis.

As if the above were not enough, my request to the C. of C. for golf information caused me to receive, over the next two weeks, color brochures from thirty-six motels in the area. I soon wearied of looking at photos of young couples hunting seashells and families playing pinochle in immaculate twin-bed rooms with a view of the sea. I also got a letter from a dentist in Florence offering me his services the next time I was in the area.

HILTON HEAD ISLAND

Hilton Head Island
Chamber of Commerce
P.O. Box 5647-CC
Hilton Head Island, SC 29928

Information kit containing a list of a dozen courses, a restaurant guide, resorts, hotels, rental agents, etc.

SOUTH DAKOTA

Division of Tourism of South Dakota
Pierre, SD 57501

TENNESSEE

GOLFING IN TENNESSEE

Tennessee Tourist Development
505 Fesslers La.
Nashville, TN 37210
(615) 741-2158

A 24-page booklet listing about 150 private, public, and state-park golf courses with mailing addresses, phone numbers, par and yardage, and checklist on facilities available.

TEXAS

Greater Houston Convention & Visitors Council
1522 Main Street
Houston, TX 77002

Mimeographed listing of 14 public and 33 private courses in Houston area; names, addresses, and phone numbers only.

DALLAS GOLF COURSES

Dallas Convention & Visitors Bureau
Dallas Chamber of Commerce
1507 Pacific Avenue
Dallas, TX 75201

One-page flyer with map pinpointing 30 public and private golf courses in immediate Dallas area.

SAN ANTONIO GOLF COURSES

San Antonio Convention & Visitors Bureau
P.O. Box 2277
San Antonio, TX 78298

Listing of 10 private and public courses gives par and yardage, addresses and phone numbers and information on fees.

*Houston City Magazine** ran these amusing insights into golf on the city's five public courses:

GLENBROOK

Measuring 6,081 yards from the men's tees, this is a short course. However, nearly half of its holes run alongside or across a bayou. It took me a year to recognize that I didn't have to sacrifice every third ball to the water gods. On number twelve, a nice-size lake—that can't be seen from the tee—guards the approach to the green. During my first round ever, I chose that hole to hit my best drive of the day. "There's a lake down there," said my partner, as the ball disappeared over the rise.

With 74,351 players in 1977, Glenbrook was second only to Memorial in numbers, but was almost 700 yards shorter. To speed play and save the greens, Glenbrook's pro, Nat Johnson, cut two holes on each green and requests each foursome through to move the flag to the opposite hole.

(8101 Bayou Drive. Can be reached by going out Gulf Freeway to Howard Drive Exit, left on Howard Drive to Radcliff, left on Radcliff to Park and Golf Course. 644-4081.)

GUS WORTHAM

It was here that I experienced my first 130-plus round. No sense being in a hurry, I always say. I like Wortham, but wish it was in better shape. It probably has the worst tee boxes of any public course.

Bought by the city in 1973, the course was built in 1908 as the Houston Country Club, and later became the Executive Country Club. Nowadays, you're more likely to find a derelict selling lost golf balls than you are to find an executive. This course is long, wooded, watered, and well trapped. If some attention were paid to it, this would be a nice place to play.

(7000 Capitol. Can be reached by going out Gulf Freeway to Wayside Exit, left on Wayside to Capitol, right on Capitol to sign that will indicate direction to Golf Course. 921-3227.)

MEMORIAL

Long. It's got Wortham beat by 375 yards. The lakes are set up to accept anybody's slice. During the summer the fairways tend to dry out and harden. It's not uncommon to have a 300-yard drive off a topped ball that ordinarily would have traveled about 100 feet.

Before I'd played Memorial, I'd never been on a course where I had to take my partner's word that there was a green at the end of the fairway. Memorial was the home of the Houston Open from 1947 to 1957 when the cold weather and traffic ruined the winter grass and the Open moved to other pastures. It's currently being played at The Woodlands.

(6001 Memorial Loop Drive. Can be reached by going out Memorial Drive past Shepherd Drive Underpass to Memorial Park, turn right at first traffic signal inside park and continue left to clubhouse. 862-4033.)

* *Houston City Magazine* (November 1978), © 1978 by I.M.H., Inc., 315 W. Alabama, Houston, Texas 77006.

BROCK

Aaagh! Stay away from here unless you hit the ball with a fair degree of accuracy. The home of the City Championship, this course is tough. It's well kept, with greens and fairways in excellent shape. The new clubhouse is open, and it's beautiful. There are lots of trees, water, and distance, along with a rarity in Houston, hills. It walks a lot longer than it plays on the scorecard. Don't expect to run over this course. It demands skill, perseverance, and a dozen extra golf balls.

(8201 John Ralston Road. Go east on Interstate 10 to McCarty Street Exit. Turn left on McCarty—which is also U.S. 90—and follow to John Ralston Road. Sign will indicate direction to Golf Course. 458-1350.)

HERMANN

Constructed in 1923 this was the first course built exclusively for the City of Houston. This is a good beginner's course. There's almost no sand, and skimpy water. The distances are reasonable and the trees that line the fairways aren't too bad if you don't try to hit through them. It's a compact course with the first five holes running cheek by jowl.

Where Wortham has its bums, Hermann has its picnickers. They tend to think the fairways make excellent campsites, and wandering children are a problem. Hermann suffered $10,000 in vandalism last year.

(6110 Golf Course Drive. Course is located in Hermann Park next to the Zoo. 529-9788.)

—*John W. Wilson*

UTAH

UTAH'S PART OF THE EARTH
    Utah Travel Council
    Council Hall/Capitol Hill
    Salt Lake City, UT 84114

Primarily a campground directory, although it does list the state's 60-odd courses (many of them nine-holers).

VERMONT

    Vermont State Chamber of Commerce
    Box 37/Montpelier, VT 05602
    (802) 223-3443 or 229-0154

There are 44 public and semiprivate courses listed on the back of Vermont's official state map and keyed to same.

VIRGINIA

GOLF IN VIRGINIA
    Virginia State Travel Service
    6 North Sixth Street
    Richmond, VA 23219
    (804) 786-4484

A 12-page foldout brochure listing 74 public and semiprivate courses; information includes par and yardage, travel directions and phone numbers, facilities on site, and brief descriptions of layouts. Other tourist information of general interest includes a slick 36-page color booklet and a state highway map.

WASHINGTON

WASHINGTON STATE GOLF
    Department of Commerce & Economic Development
    General Administration Building
    Olympia, WA 98504
Folder listing state's 150 public and private courses.

WEST VIRGINIA

TRAVEL BOOK
    Office of Economic and Community Development
    State of West Virginia
    Charleston, WV 25305
Comprehensive guidebook also listing over 50 courses open to public play in the state.

WISCONSIN

SOUTHERN GATEWAY
    Southern Gateway
    169 W. Garland Street
    Jefferson, WI 53549

Flyer in this packet of general tourist information lists about 75 golf courses open to the public in 10 counties surrounding but not including Milwaukee; names, locations, and phone numbers only.

DOOR COUNTY VACATION GUIDE
    Door County Chamber of Commerce
    Box 219
    Sturgeon Bay, WI 54235
    (414) 743-4456

A 24-page pamphlet devoted to general tourist attractions on this peninsula; also lists seven courses open to public play.

WYOMING

    Wyoming Travel Commission
    Frank Norris, Jr., Travel Center
    Cheyenne, WY 82002

GENERAL GOLF TRAVEL GUIDES— INTERNATIONAL

GENE SARAZEN'S WORLD GOLF DIRECTORY
   1977, 208 pages, $7.50.
   World Sports Publishers, Inc.
   1721 De Sales Street, N.W.
   Washington, D.C. 20036

Originally published in 1973, this expanded and re-vised paperback guide provides thumbnail sketches of 1,600 courses worldwide.

WHERE TO GOLF IN EUROPE, edited by H. Ted
   Ostermann
   European Golf Association
   70 Viale Tiziano 00100
   Rome, Italy

Straightforward guide to golf on the Continent (Austria, Belgium, Czechoslovakia, Denmark, Finland, France, Germany, Great Britain, Greece, Iceland, Italy, Luxembourg, Monaco, Netherlands, Norway, Portugal, Spain, Sweden, Switzerland). Each course is listed with address, telephone, course dimensions, guest privileges, name of professional, golf fees, other facilities, and recommended nearby hotels. Updated every two years.

GOLF IN THE SUN by Michael Gedye. 1977, 160
   pages, Fairgreen Publications, in conjunction with
   British Airways.
   Fairgreen Publications, Ltd.
   Sherborne House, Hadley Highstone,
   Barnet, Herts., England

Appraisals of about 130 resort courses, principally in Europe and the Mediterranean, but also covering Bermuda, the Caribbean, West Indies, South Africa, and Thailand. Firsthand information on particulars not often seen in travel guides. Also includes travel tips, a currency conversion table, photos of each hotel and/or golf course, some course layouts, and scorecards.

THE BRITISH OPEN COURSES AT A GLANCE

The British Open, first played in 1860, is the oldest of the world's golf championships, and remains the major golfing event outside the United States. Only 13 courses have been used for the 107 playings of "The Open" (as the British insist on calling it); nine remain on the modern roster (five in Scotland and four in England). All are true "links" in the sense that they are virtually treeless, windblown, duneland courses either adjacent to or within a short distance of the sea. This type of golf is regarded in Britain as the epitome of the game, which is one reason why the Open has never been played on an inland course. Another, more modern reason is that no British inland course has the support facilities—parking, accommodations, etc.—necessary to stage what has become a massive sports spectacular (some 125,000 people attended the 1978 championship at St. Andrews—probably a world record for golf tournament attendance).

Listed below are the "modern" Open courses.

SCOTLAND

THE OLD COURSE AT ST. ANDREWS
6,960 yards, par 72. The cradle if not the birthplace of golf, and still its traditional "home." The ultimate in nature-made golf; most newcomers either love or loathe the course on first sight, but usually grow fonder of it the more they play it, because of its subtlety and infinite challenge. Open to all comers, but bookings are essential at peak times. Located smack in the center of the beautiful "old gray town" of St. Andrews. Site of 22 Opens.

MUIRFIELD (THE HONOURABLE COMPANY OF EDINBURGH GOLFERS)
Founded in 1744; 6,892 yards, par 71. Modern home of the world's oldest golf club and the game's first rules-makers. Perhaps the best balanced, most mellow and fairest of the Open courses, and always beautifully conditioned. Ultra-exclusive—you definitely need introductions to play. Overlooks the Firth of Forth, 18 miles east of Edinburgh, in the village of Gullane. Site of 11 Opens.

CARNOUSTIE
Club founded in 1842, but golf was played here long before that; 7,065 yards, par 72. This wild, barren-looking course in a stark gray setting is frequently cited as Britain's longest and toughest test. The tigerish finish features the infamous Barry Burn. The town behind the course probably exported more golf pros to the United States than any other Scottish locale. This is a public course but bookings are advisable in peak season. Situated a half-hour drive north of Dundee. Site of five Opens.

ROYAL TROON GOLF CLUB
Founded in 1878; 7,064 yards, par 72. A traditional sea-hugging links with the longest (577 yards) and the shortest (the 126-yard "Postage Stamp") holes of all the Open courses. It's a controversial site for the championship, as its far end adjoins the runways of Glasgow International Airport (Prestwick). Exclusive—an introduction is necessary. In town of Troon. Site of four Opens.

TURNBERRY
Founded in 1903. 6,875 yards, par 70. Majestic oceanside Ailsa Course comes the closest in Great Britain to a Pebble Beach setting. Both courses (the

other is the Arran) are operated on a resort basis by the fine, overlooking Turnberry Hotel, owned by British Rail (proprietors also of Gleneagles). Tom Watson's 1977 winning score here of 268, to beat Jack Nicklaus by one shot after a phenomenal duel, is the Open record. Site of one Open.

ENGLAND

SANDWICH (ROYAL ST. GEORGE'S GOLF CLUB)

Founded in 1887; 6,736 yards, par 72. One of only two courses in southern England to be used for the Open. Off the roster since 1949 because of road-access problems, but returning in 1981, as access difficulties there have been eased. A rugged links burrowing over and through high sandhills overlooking the English Channel. Exclusive—introduction advisable. Lies just south of Sandwich, one of the charming Cinque Ports towns. Site of 10 Opens.

HOYLAKE (ROYAL LIVERPOOL GOLF CLUB)

Founded in 1869; 6,995 yards, par 72. The flattest of the Open courses, built on a former racecourse overlooking Dee Estuary (Wales is what you see on the other side), and featuring unique out-of-bounds "cops" and a notorious finish. The club initiated both the British and English Amateur championships and is one of the country's most historic. It's also one of the most exclusive—introduction advisable. Situated 10 miles west of Liverpool. Site of 10 Opens (last in 1967).

ROYAL LYTHAM AND ST. ANNE'S GOLF CLUB

Founded in 1886; 6,822 yards, par 71. A classic links out of sight of the sea, but with more than 200 bunkers and a par-3 hole to start. Narrow fairways and the widely varying directions of the holes add to the challenge. A private club, so an introduction is advisable. Located five miles south of Blackpool. Site of seven Opens, including the 1979 championship.

ROYAL BIRKDALE GOLF CLUB

Founded in 1889; 7,080 yards, par 72. Comparatively recent addition to the Open roster (1954). The holes thread through high, craggy sandhills dense with barbarous rough, and the finish is long and exacting. The club is perhaps the best equipped for staging the Open. It's private, so get an introduction. Located on southern edge of Southport. Site of five Opens.

Early Open venues no longer used for the championship:

PRESTWICK GOLF CLUB

Founded in 1851; 6,544 yards, par 72. Originator of the Open and site of the first 11 championships. The ultimate in old-time links golf—playing it is perhaps the closest you can come to experiencing the original form of the game. This is a private club, situated between Ayr and Troon, one mile from Prestwick Airport. Site of 24 Opens between 1860 and 1925.

MUSSELBURGH

This course, which was located on the eastern outskirts of Edinburgh, no longer exists, but was the original home of the Honourable Company of Edinburgh Golfers. Site of six Opens between 1874 and 1889.

DEAL (ROYAL CINQUE PORTS GOLF CLUB)

Founded in 1892; 6,659 yards, par 72. An outstanding and nicely sequestered oceanside links adjoining Royal St. George's on the English Channel, with a uniquely tough inward half. A private club situated on the northern outskirts of Deal, about 65 miles from London. Site of two Opens (1909 and 1920).

ROYAL PORTRUSH GOLF CLUB

Founded in 1888; 6,809 yards, par 73. A fine, sprawling, scenically spectacular links on the northern coast of Northern Ireland, and the only course outside the British mainland to host the Open (in 1951). A private club located about 50 miles from Belfast, about 25 from Londonderry.

—Ken Bowden

OTHER SOURCES OF GOLF TRAVEL INFORMATION—INTERNATIONAL

BERMUDA

GOLF IN BERMUDA
Bermuda Department of Tourism
630 Fifth Avenue
New York, NY 10020

Brochure analyzing each of Bermuda's nine courses; provides hole-by-hole par and yardage figures and gives full-color views of the most scenic and challenging holes.

CANADA

GOLF CANADA
Canadian Government Office of Tourism
Travel Information Services
150 Kent Street
Ottawa, Canada K1A OH6

An 84-page directory of the top courses in Canada's 10 provinces and two territories, including many resorts that offer golf packages. Excellent, detailed descriptions on each course layout.

GOLF NOVA SCOTIA

Nova Scotia Department of Tourism
P.O. Box 456
Halifax, Nova Scotia

Brochure listing 38 courses and various tournaments held in province.

GOLFING IN QUEBEC

Direction Generale du Tourisme
150 Est, Boulevard Saint-Cyrille
Quebec, Canada G1R 4Y3

A neat 21-page booklet listing about 240 courses, most of which are open to the public most of the time. Information is listed in chart form, with symbol codes for number of holes, par, length (in meters), who may play, club rentals, cart rentals, practice range and/or net, putting green, restaurant and/or bar, greens, fees, and whether a golf professional is on the premises. Alphabetical index of towns precedes listing.

ONTARIO GOLF COURSES

Ministry of Industry and Tourism
Queen's Park
Toronto, Ontario, Canada M7A 2E5

A 25-page booklet listing more than 500 facilities categorized as private, semiprivate, public, resort, par-3, and driving range. Includes locations, addresses, number of holes, par.

GOLF COURSES IN ALBERTA

Travel Alberta
4th Floor Penthouse
Alberta Hotel Building
808 1 Street S.W.
Calgary, Alberta, Canada T2P 1M9

List of 139 courses (15 classified as "restricted private," all others open for public play). Details include number of holes, grass or sand greens, par, yardage, equipment rentals and sales, food service, dining room, lounge, swimming pool and other recreational facilities.

CARIBBEAN

GOLF AND TENNIS FACILITIES IN THE CARIBBEAN

Caribbean Tourism Association
20 East 46th Street
New York, NY 10017
(212) 682-0435

A 12-page handout listing golf courses throughout the Caribbean, including Barbados (two courses), Jamaica (11 courses, including 4 nine-holers), Puerto Rico (10), U.S. Virgin Islands (one 18-hole course, 3 nines) and Venezuela (4).

BAHAMAS GOLF

Bahamas Tourist Office
30 Rockefeller Plaza
New York, NY 10020

Color brochure providing good thumbnail sketches of 16 courses.

TIPS ON GOLF IN THE BAHAMAS

These island courses are challenging and tricky—and so is the wind. If you want long drives and fairway shots and a chance to score on short chips to the green, here are some tips on strategy from a pro. You have a choice of playing either the English or American ball.

The English ball is smaller, gives more distance and is more easily controlled. On the other hand, the English ball has a tendency to "bury" in soft sand-traps and is harder to hit if it is sitting lower in the grass. The American ball yields less distance and sits up better on turf and won't bury as much in bunkers. With the wind behind you, pick a more lofted club than you would ordinarily. To gain distance off the tee when there's a left-to-right wind, tee the ball high, close your stance, swing from the inside outwards and draw the ball. Against a right-to-left wind, tee ball high, open your stance, swing from the outside inwards and cut the ball. For lower trajectory against the wind, tee ball lower, grip club shorter, play the ball farther back in the stance. Keep hands ahead as you release the clubhead. Do not follow through completely. Definitely play pitch-and-run shots to the green. (Warning: don't lean on your wedge; better leave it untouched in your bag). Use a 7-iron. Keep the ball low, play short of the green, letting the ball run up to the putting surface. On the greens, remember the break of the grass will normally go toward the water. Greens are usually heavy, thick, grainy. Don't be afraid to hit with firmness after lining up in a square stance. Keep the blade square to the line and low. In bunkers with powdery sand, play the regulation bunker shot. Ball off left heel with open stance and open blade. Be sure the left hand is in control and take the sand with a smooth follow-through.

—from *Bahamas Golf*

GOLFING IN JAMAICA

Jamaica Tourist Board
866 Second Avenue
New York, NY 10017

A 16-page special supplement to Air Jamaica's inflight magazine, devoted to golf.

GREAT BRITAIN

GOLFING IN BRITAIN

A 16-page "fact sheet" listing about 100 of the better-known courses in England, Scotland, Wales, and Northern Ireland; indicates the conditions under which each club will welcome visiting golfers.

HOTELS & INNS WITH GOLF

Describes some 750 hostelries; all have either their own golf course or can make arrangements for lodgers to play at a nearby course.

Both publications available free from:

British Tourist Authority
680 Fifth Ave.
New York, NY 10019
(212) 581-4700

AA GUIDE TO GOLF IN BRITAIN

Contains 16 pages of maps showing location of each club and listing over 1,500 courses where visitors are welcome. Illustrated; special descriptions of "50 Top Courses"; $11.75.

SCOTLAND: HOME OF GOLF

Details on some 350 Scottish courses where the visitor may play, with an introduction on the history of golf and a section on golfing hotels; $2.15.

Both publications are available from:

GHS Inc.
Box 1224
Clifton, NJ 07012

SCOTLAND: A VISITOR'S GUIDE TO THE HOME OF GOLF

International Golf
1650 Lincoln Ave.
Montreal, Quebec, Canada H3H 1H1

This 34-page booklet is full of practical and up-to-date information on golf throughout Scotland, including tips on when to go, how to go, what to do before you go, getting around, where to stay, getting a game, where to play. Also contains a revealing and sometimes amusing day-by-day account of an American businessman's golfing fling through Scotland, in 1973; $1.00.

IRELAND

GUIDE TO IRISH GOLF COURSES

Irish Tourist Board
590 Fifth Avenue
New York, NY 10036
(212) 246-7400

Some 171 courses are listed with address, phone number, name of secretary, professional, hole/par/length, when visitors are welcome, nearby lodging accommodations, nearest town. Keyed to map.

MEXICO

Mexican National Tourist Office
405 Park Avenue
New York, NY 10020

General tourist information, but no comprehensive guide to golf facilities.

PORTUGAL

GOLF IN PORTUGAL

Portuguese National Tourist Office
548 Fifth Avenue
New York, NY 10036
(212) 354-4403

This 14-page color booklet captures the romance and challenge of playing golf on 10 courses in Portugal. Includes addresses, phone numbers, greens fees, caddies, dining facilities, playing conditions, course layouts.

ALGARVE: PORTUGAL GOLFER'S PARADISE

Foldout color brochure complements the above with more photos of five of the courses located in the Algarve.

SCANDINAVIA

GOLF IN SCANDINAVIA

Scandinavian National Tourist Office
75 Rockefeller Plaza
New York, NY 10019

Attractive large-format 20-page color booklet produced by Scandinavian Airlines, describing some of the more interesting courses in Sweden, Denmark, Norway and Finland.

Though golf is played in the four countries of Scandinavia, the game is in fact dominated by Sweden which has twice as many courses and three times as many players as Finland, Denmark and Norway added together.

But then Sweden is one of the biggest golfing nations in Europe with more than 110 courses and 45,000 golfers.

Nowhere on the European continent can you find more enthusiastic golfers than in Sweden. With the opening of the first semi-public courses in 1971, it is now expected that the game's popularity will grow at an even faster pace during the next decade.

—*from Golf in Scandinavia*

SPAIN

GOLF IN SPAIN

Spanish National Tourist Office
665 Fifth Avenue
New York, NY 10022
(212) 759-8822

A 24-page color booklet with information on 70 golf courses in Madrid and its environs, the Pyrenees, the Cantabrian Coast and the Firths of Galicia, Costa Brava/Costa Dorada, Costa del Azahar/Costa Blanca, Costa del Sol/Costa de la Luz, the Balearic Islands, and the Canary Islands. The English is stilted, reading like the first draft of a smooth translation, but there are lots of photos.

SOME GOLF TOURS AND PACKAGES—U.S. AND INTERNATIONAL

AFRICAN GOLF/GAME SAFARIS

New England Travel Service
4 Muzzey Street
P.O. Box 439
Lexington, MA 02173
(617) 861-1770

Trips organized by Semjon Lass Associates, travel consultants, for small groups, to Kenya or to Zambia/Malawi, combining golf (Kenya has some 30 courses and Zambia about 10) with tours of the great national game-parks. Land portion of a typical 23-day Zambia/Malawi package costs $1,400.

AMERICAN AIRLINES' GOLF PHOENIX

American Airlines
633 Third Avenue
New York, NY 10017

Color brochure describes golf package plans at Arizona Biltmore, Paradise Inn, San Marcos Resort, and The Wigwam.

ASK MR. FOSTER TRAVEL SERVICE

Ask Mr. Foster
7833 Haskell Avenue
Van Nuys, CA 91406
(213) 988-0181

A wide variety of golf packages developed for American Airlines and TAP (Portugal airlines) are described in detail in the following brochures:

Great Golf & Tennis Resorts. Containing golf tours to Arizona (McCormack Ranch, Scottsdale Conference Resort), California (Rancho Bernardo Inn, Pala Mesa Resort, Carlton Oaks Country Club, Torrey Pines, Canyon Hotel, Marriott's Rancho Las Palmas, Silverado), Mexico (Fiesta Palace, Acapulco Princess, Pierre Marques Hotel), Virgin Islands (St. Croix by the Sea), Jamaica (Half Moon Hotel, Rose Hall Inter-Continental), and the Dominican Republic (Casa de Campo).
The Greens of Portugal and Spain. An assortment of golf holiday packages on the Iberian peninsula and Morocco.

BESTWAYS WONDERFUL WORLD OF GOLF

British Tourist Authority
680 Fifth Avenue
New York, NY 10019

This and other color brochures describing a variety of vacation packages in England, Scotland, and Ireland.

CALTUR

James W. Moss
Caltur
Travel Division of Golf Tour, Inc.
P.O. Box 3080
San Clemente, CA 92672

This firm has been operating group golf tours since 1971, to such places as Spain, Portugal, Scotland, Ireland, Bermuda, Canada, Mexico, Columbia, Venezuela, and New Zealand. The trips emphasize a lot of golf on the best available courses and always include some fun-type tournaments for participants. Golf professionals sometimes accompany groups. A new program to Mexico in 1979 included special golf arrangements in Guadalajara, Mazatlán, Acapulco, Ixtapa, and Mexico City.

FLORIDA SWING

Red Carpet International
6301 International Drive
Orlando, FL 32809
(800) 327-3800 [in Florida call (305) 351-4430]

This is a six-day tour organized by Red Carpet Inns. Participants may play golf daily on any of 12 courses located 2 to 28 miles from the Orlando accommodations. Typical double-occupancy rate of $137 covers room and all golf charges.

GOLFPAC

GOLFPAC
P.O. Box 484
Maitland, FL 32751
(303) 645-0610

A golf package plan involving accommodations at a choice of Days Inn, Quality Inn, Howard Johnson's, or Holiday Inn, and golf at any of 16 Orlando area courses. Variety of package rates, from four to seven days, all of which include room and golf charges.

GOLF INTERCONTINENTAL

Arnold Langer
Golf Intercontinental
424 Madison Ave.
New York, NY 10017
(212) 758-0500
Recent tours:

"GIMME SCOTLAND"

Nine-day tour with accommodations at Gleneagles Hotel for three nights, Turnberry Hotel four nights, and golf at choice of Gleneagles' Kings, Queens courses and/or nearby St. Andrews and Carnoustie, and Turnberry's Ailsa, Arran courses or nearby Troon, Prestwick. British Airways from New York; $1,000.

BRITISH OPEN TOUR

Fifteen-day tour organized around Open week, with plenty of time for spectating as well as playing other courses that have served as venues for the Open. British Airways from New York; $1,575.

"GIMME SPAIN"

Eight-day tour to Costa del Sol, with week-long stay at the grand luxe hotels Melia Don Pepe in Marbella or El Paraiso in Estepona, both of which have their own courses. Iberia Airlines from New York; $675–$875.

GOLF GETAWAYS

Bernie Reumann
Golf Getaways
9465 Wilshire Boulevard, Suite 832
Beverly Hills, CA 90212
(213) 271-3765

Numerous tours to a variety of places: Scotland–England, Spain–Monte Carlo–Tunisia, Pebble Beach, Lake Tahoe, South America, Guadalajara, Canada, and Hawaii.

GUYS AND DOLLS GOLF TOURS

Guys and Dolls
1905 East 17th Street, Suite 308
Santa Ana, CA 92701
(714) 541-9507

Directors Howard and Jeanne Richards escort every tour and oversee the tournament format in which the golf is organized. The Richards have been involved with golfing tours since 1967. Recent offerings:

IRELAND-SCOTLAND-ENGLAND

Seventeen-day tour with six rounds of golf; in Ireland at Lahinch, Ballybunion, and Portmarnock; in Scotland at Turnberry, Gleneagles, St. Andrews. British Airways from L.A.; $2,275.

HAWAII

Fourteen-day tour with five rounds of golf at Princeville, Royal Kaanapali, and Mauna Kea. Continental Airlines from L.A.; $1,495.

CARIBBEAN/PANAMA CANAL

Nineteen-day air cruise tour with four rounds of golf; in Puerto Rico at Dorado Beach and Cerromar, in Mexico at the Acapulco Princess. Delta Airlines from L.A., Pacific Princess from San Juan; $2,570.

HAWAIIAN POLYNESIA TOURS

Hank Spiess, Golf Director
Hawaiian Polynesia Tours
2020 North Broadway
Santa Ana, CA 92706
(714) 558-7633 or (213) 623-3603

4-ISLAND GOLF HAWAII TOUR

Escorted 12-day tour with golf at Kona, Mauna Kea, Waikoloa, Royal Kaanapali, Kauai Surf, Princeville Makai, and Hawaii Kai courses. Western Airlines from L.A.; $950.

CARIBBEAN GOLF/CRUISE PROGRAM

Escorted 12-day trip—seven days at sea, five days at Doral Hotel in Miami. Golf at Upton Country Club, Ocho Rios, Jamaica; Paradise Island, Nassau, Bahamas; and the four-course Doral complex. Western Airlines from L.A., Norwegian Caribbean Line from Miami; $1,000–$1,200.

GOLF & SIGHTSEEING TO MEXICO

Escorted nine-day tour to Guadalajara and Mazatlán, with four rounds of golf on Guadalajara Country Club, San Ysidro Country Club, and El Cid Country Club. Western Airlines from L.A.; $480.

INTERNATIONAL GOLF SAFARIS

Eddie Lewis
International Golf Safaris
4713 Van Nuys Boulevard
Sherman Oaks, CA 91403
(213) 788-5991 or 872-2200

Various tours throughout the world organized and usually escorted by Eddie Lewis. Clientele consists primarily of southern California golfers. Tour participants must hold a Southern California Golf Association handicap or a handicap from a similarly recognized group in order to play in the tournaments, which are the focus of the trips.

INTERNATIONAL GOLF TOURS

International Golf Inc.
1650 Lincoln Avenue
Montreal, Canada H3H 1H1
(514) 933-2771

Specializing in trips to Great Britain, Ireland, France, Portugal, Spain, and Morocco; departing Montreal or New York. Sampling of tours offered below all include airfare, breakfast and dinner daily, golf, and other features. This firm also publishes an interesting practical guide to Scotland called *A Visitor's Guide to the Home of Golf*.

14 days *Morocco & Spain.* Escorted golf tour to Rabat and Marbella, Costa del Sol, several excursions; $1095.

9 days *Costa del Golf,* Spain. Based at two top hotels, Marbella and Sotogrande, car included, several major courses; $775.

8 days *Portugal.* Golf Estoril in Lisbon, three days; then four days at Penina in the Algarve; $729.

8 days *South of France.* Golf and gourmet, deluxe hotel in Cannes, car, and golf at two courses; $795.

8 days *Ireland.* Two hotels and golf at Killarney, Waterville, Ballybunion, and Lahinch; $729.

13 days *Scotland plus Ireland.* Play right across two great golfing countries, from Carnoustie to Killarney, by car or escorted; $1095.

INTERNATIONAL GOLF TRAVEL

Bruce K. Osborne, President
International Golf Travel
13450 Maxella Avenue, Suite 225
Marina del Rey, CA 90291
(213) 821-4511

IGT, with the help of Air New Zealand, has developed a variety of new golf travel programs to the South Pacific, partly in recognition of the existence of a host of eminently playable golf courses in both Australia and New Zealand. Australia ranks fifth in the world in number of golfers, with over 350,000 and third (behind only the United States and Great Britain) in number of courses, with some 1,350. With a population of only 3 million, New Zealand boasts more than 350 courses—in an area about two-thirds the size of California.

Most IGT tours involve at least a day of special competition with local club members, which provides a nice chance to check firsthand the golf techniques prevailing down under.

NEW ZEALAND-AUSTRALIA-FIJI

Sixteen-day tour, golf in New Zealand at Titirangi Golf Club, site of the Air New Zealand Open; Rotorua Golf Club; and Shirley Golf Club. In Australia: Manley Golf Club; New South Wales Golf Club; Yarra Yarra Golf Club, site of the annual Victorian Open; and finally the 36-hole Royal Melbourne, regarded by some as the finest golf facility in Australia. Air New Zealand from L.A. $1875.

Other 16-day tours offered to Australia exclusively, New Zealand exclusively, Australia/Fiji, New Zealand/Fiji. One eight-day trip to Tahiti exclusively.

AROUND-THE-WORLD GOLF PROGRAM

Forty-five day tour planned for 15 countries.

JOHANSEN ROYAL TOURS

Johansen Royal Tours
1406-T Vance Building
Seattle, WA 98101

Week-long golf tours in the Canadian Rockies (Banff Springs Hotel, Jasper Park Lodge), June–August, departures from Calgary. Free 24-page brochure available.

ADD/TOUR/PACKAGES

NATIONAL AIRLINES' ELEGANT ESCAPE

Tour Department
National Airlines
P.O. Box 592055
Miami, FL 33159
(800) 327-4476 (toll-free)

A 12-page color brochure on golf vacations at Boca Raton, Breakers, Doral, Innisbrook, Marco Island, and Ponte Vedra resorts, all in Florida, and the Cloister on Sea Island, GA.

UNITED AIRLINES' THE RESORT WAY IN THE WEST

United Airlines
P.O. Box 27
Glenview, IL 60025

Brochure details golf packages in San Diego (variety of courses and plans offered here), Fallbrook (Pala Mesa Resort), Reno and Sun Valley (Elkhorn Village).

WESTERN GOLF TOURS

Paul Westmiller
Western Golf Tours
1905 E. 17th Street, Suite 308
Santa Ana, CA 92701
(714) 558-0301

This new tour-packager develops custom golf tours working through the PGA professional or manager at any private country club in the United States or Canada. Offers groups individualized trips of any length to such golfing centers as Palm Springs, San Diego, and Monterey/Carmel.

WIDE WORLD OF GOLF

Michael C. Roseto
WIDE WORLD OF GOLF
98 Post Street
San Francisco, CA 94104
(415) 397-0588

About 10 escorted, deluxe golf vacations offered throughout the world every year. This firm has served numerous members of the Northern California Golf Association.

Passport. 20 North Wacker, Chicago, IL 60606; annual subscription $30.

The Travel Advisor. 15 Park Place, Suite 2, Bronxville, NY; annual subscription $20.

GOLF TRAVEL FILMS

ASSOCIATION FILMS, INC.
600 Grand Avenue, Ridgefield, NJ 07657
324 Delaware Avenue, Oakmont, PA 15139
866 Third Avenue, New York, NY 10022, (212) 935-5101
512 Burlington Avenue, La Grange, IL 60525
5797 New Peachtree Road, Atlanta, GA 30340

Come Golf With Me (27 min.). Free/loan. Follows Laura Baugh as she plays the toughest holes on several of Bermuda's golf courses.

BRITISH AIRWAYS
Film Department
245 Park Avenue
New York, NY 10017

Golf in the Sun. Loan.

EASTERN AIRLINES
Film Library
International Airport Branch
Miami, FL 33148
(305) 873-2555

Florida—Golf Capitol, U.S.A. (14½ min.). Sale—$20. Camera roams many of Florida's golf links.

UNITED STATES GOLF ASSOCIATION
Golf House
Far Hills, NJ 07931

Famous Golf Courses: Pinehurst No. 2 (17 min.). Rent—$10. Presents an unusual insight into golfing tactics through analysis of problems created for the players by the architects of the splendid course in North Carolina. Leading players are seen in action in the 1962 USGA Amateur Championship, won by Labron Harris, Jr. Charles Evans, Jr., is shown playing in the championship for the 50th time—an all-time record.

Famous Golf Courses: Scotland (18 min.). Rent—$10. A pictorially breathtaking view of some of Scotland's most famous courses—Muirfield, Carnoustie, Prestwick, Troon, St. Andrews and North Berwick.

St. Andrews, Cradle of Golf (14 min.). Rent—$10. An historic travelogue of the famous Royal Burgh of Scotland and of St. Andrew Old Course, the world's most famous layout.

OTHER TRAVEL SERVICES

THE GOLF CARD

This is an association of 30,000 golfers that provides members complimentary golf at 700 different facilities in the United States and abroad.

A black-and-gold plastic card called "The Golf Card" is issued to members for an annual fee of $49. Participating facilities honor this card by allowing the holder to play two 18-hole complimentary rounds (no greens fees) during the member's 12-month validation period. A member has to play six or seven times to recover his initial investment.

Members also receive a subscription to *The Golf Traveler* magazine, which keeps them up-to-date with a directory of all the places to play. They also benefit from special discounts on Wilson merchandise and Hertz Rent-a-Car services.

For a complete course directory plus membership information, contact:

THE GOLF CARD
1625 Foothill Drive
P.O. Box 8339
Salt Lake City, UT 84108
(800) 453-4260 (toll-free) or (801) 582-8080

TRAVEL NEWSLETTERS

These two excellent newsletters, appearing monthly, furnish up-to-date and general "inside" information of interest to the regular traveler. They rarely report on golf travel specifically.

∘IV∘

Tournaments You Can Watch

PGA TOUR

SPRING (April–May)

TOURNAMENT
Greater Greensboro Open
CONTACT FOR INFORMATION
Forest Oaks C.C.
4600 Forest Oaks Drive
Greensboro, NC 27406
(919) 674-0126

Masters
CONTACT FOR INFORMATION
Augusta National G.C.
P.O. Box 2086
Augusta, GA 30903
(404) 738-7761

Tournament of Champions
CONTACT FOR INFORMATION
La Costa C.C.
Costa del Mar Road
Carlsbad, CA 92008
(714) 438-9111

New Orleans Open
CONTACT FOR INFORMATION
Lakewood C.C.
4801 General De Gaulle Drive
New Orleans, LA 70114
(504) 393-2610

Houston Open
CONTACT FOR INFORMATION
Woodlands C.C.
2301 Millbend Drive
Woodlands, TX 77380
(713) 367-1100

Byron Nelson Classic
CONTACT FOR INFORMATION
Preston Trail G.C.
17201 Preston Trail Drive
Dallas, TX 75240
(214) 239-1371

Colonial National Invitational
CONTACT FOR INFORMATION
Colonial C.C.
3735 Country Club Circle
Fort Worth, TX 76109
(817) 926-4671

Memorial Tournament
CONTACT FOR INFORMATION
Muirfield Village G.C.
Box 565
Dublin, OH 43017
(614) 889-9422

Kemper Open
CONTACT FOR INFORMATION
Quail Hollow C.C.
Box 15224
Charlotte, NC 28210
(704) 364-0914

Atlanta Golf Classic
CONTACT FOR INFORMATION
Atlanta C.C.
Box 28172
Marietta, GA 30060
(404) 971-1200

SUMMER (June–August)

TOURNAMENT
U.S. Open
CONTACT FOR INFORMATION
U.S. Golf Association
Golf House
Far Hills, NJ 07931
(201) 234-2300

Canadian Open
CONTACT FOR INFORMATION
Glen Abbey G.C.
R.R. 2
Oakville, Ontario
Canada L6J 423
(416) 844-1800

Danny Thomas Memphis Classic
CONTACT FOR INFORMATION
Colonial C.C.
2736 Countrywood Parkway
Cordova, TN 38018
(901) 388-5370

Western Open
CONTACT FOR INFORMATION
Butler National G.C.
Oak Brook, IL 60521
(312) 654-4454

Greater Milwaukee Open
CONTACT FOR INFORMATION
    Tuckaway C.C.
    6901 West Drexel Avenue
    Franklin, WI 53132
    (414) 425-4280

British Open
CONTACT FOR INFORMATION
    Royal & Ancient G.C.
    St. Andrews, Fife
    Scotland

Ed McMahon Quad Cities Open
CONTACT FOR INFORMATION
    Oakwood C.C.
    Coral Valley, IL 61240
    (309) 789-3153

Philadelphia Golf Classic
CONTACT FOR INFORMATION
    Whitemarsh Valley C.C.
    Box 297
    Germantown Pike and Thomas Road
    Lafayette Hill, PA 19444
    (215) 247-0900

PGA Championship
CONTACT FOR INFORMATION
    PGA of America
    Box 12458
    Lake Park, FL 33403
    (305) 844-5000

Sammy Davis Jr. Greater Hartford Open
CONTACT FOR INFORMATION
    Wethersfield C.C.
    Wethersfield, CT 06109
    (203) 529-3326

Westchester Classic
CONTACT FOR INFORMATION
    Westchester C.C.
    Rye, NY 10580
    (914) 967-6000

Colgate Hall of Fame Golf Classic
CONTACT FOR INFORMATION
    Pinehurst C.C.
    Box 4000
    Pinehurst, NC 28374
    (919) 295-6181

B.C. Open
CONTACT FOR INFORMATION
    En-Joie G.C.
    Endicott, NY 13760
    (607) 754-2482

FALL (September–November)

TOURNAMENT
American Optical Classic
CONTACT FOR INFORMATION
    Pleasant Valley C.C.
    Armsby Road
    Sutton, MA 01527
    (617) 865-4441

Buick-Goodwrench Open
CONTACT FOR INFORMATION
    Warwick Hills C.C.
    Grand Blanc, MI 48439
    (313) 694-4103

Anheuser-Busch Golf Classic
CONTACT FOR INFORMATION
    Silverado C.C.
    1600 Atlas Peak Road
    Napa, CA 94558
    (707) 255-2970

World Series of Golf
CONTACT FOR INFORMATION
    Firestone C.C.
    452 East Warner Road
    Akron, OH 44319
    (216) 644-8441

San Antonio–Texas Open
CONTACT FOR INFORMATION
    Oak Hills C.C.
    5403 Fredericksburg
    San Antonio, TX 78229
    (512) 341-7234

Southern Open
CONTACT FOR INFORMATION
    Green Island C.C.
    Box 2056
    6500 Standingboy Road
    Columbus, GA 31902
    (404) 324-0411

Pensacola Open
CONTACT FOR INFORMATION
    Perdido Bay C.C.
    #1 Doug Ford Drive
    Pensacola, FL 32507

Walt Disney World National Team Championship
CONTACT FOR INFORMATION
    Magnolia and Palm Courses
    Lake Buena Vista, FL 32830
    (305) 824-2200

WINTER (December–March)

TOURNAMENT
J.C. Penney Mixed Team Classic
CONTACT FOR INFORMATION
Bardmoor C.C.
Largo, FL 33541
(813) 392-1234

Bob Hope Desert Classic
CONTACT FOR INFORMATION
Indian Wells C.C.
46000 Club Drive
Indian Wells, CA 92260
(714) 345-2561

Phoenix Open
CONTACT FOR INFORMATION
Phoenix C.C.
7th Street & Thomas Road
Phoenix, AZ 85014
(602) 263-5208

Andy Williams–San Diego Open
CONTACT FOR INFORMATION
Torrey Pines G.C., North and South Courses
11480 Torrey Pines Road
La Jolla, CA 92037
(714) 453-0380

Bing Crosby National Pro-Am
CONTACT FOR INFORMATION
Pebble Beach Golf Links
17 Mile Drive
Pebble Beach, CA 93953
(408) 624-3811

Hawaiian Open
CONTACT FOR INFORMATION
Waialae C.C.
4997 Kahala Avenue
Honolulu, HI 96816
(808) 734-2151

Joe Garagiola–Tucson Open
CONTACT FOR INFORMATION
Tucson National G.C.
8300 North Club Drive
Tucson, AZ 85704
(602) 297-2271

Glen Campbell–Los Angeles Open
CONTACT FOR INFORMATION
Riviera C.C.
1250 Capri
Pacific Palisades, CA 90272
(213) 454-6591

Bay Hill Citrus Classic
CONTACT FOR INFORMATION
Bay Hill Club
6200 Bay Hill Boulevard
Orlando, FL 32811
(305) 876-2429

Jackie Gleason Inverrary Classic
CONTACT FOR INFORMATION
Inverrary G. & C.C.
Lauderhill, FL 33312
(305) 733-7550

Doral Open
CONTACT FOR INFORMATION
Doral C.C.
4400 Northwest 87th Avenue
Miami, FL 33166
(305) 592-2000

Tournament Players Championship
CONTACT FOR INFORMATION
Sawgrass
3947 Boulevard Center Drive
Jacksonville, FL 32207
(904) 285-2261

Sea Pines Heritage Classic
CONTACT FOR INFORMATION
Harbour Town Golf Links
Hilton Head Island, SC 29948
(803) 671-2446

BOOKS ABOUT THE TOUR
GENERAL

THE WORLD OF PROFESSIONAL GOLF, Mark H. McCormack's *Golf Annual.* 1978, 392 pages, $15.50, N.Y.: Doubleday.

Men's professional golf events of the preceding year are reported in detail, including the U.S. tour and all other pro circuits worldwide. This, plus the fact that the volume has appeared annually since 1967 and presumably will continue to appear, makes the series unique. Some 50 pages list results of all tournaments round by round, including all finishers. Two interesting sets of statistics based on performances on all circuits are "World Stroke Averages" and "World Money List."

SUPERSTARS OF GOLF by Nick Seitz. 1978, 192 pages, $10.95, *Golf Digest;* N.Y. distributor: Simon & Schuster.

Penetrating profiles of the leading touring pros by the editor of *Golf Digest* magazine, along with a swing analysis of each player by Bob Toski. Included: Trevino, Irwin, Watson, Floyd, Palmer, Miller, Geiberger, Nicklaus, Player, and Weiskopf.

GOLF TO REMEMBER by Michael Hobbs, with Peter Alliss. 1978, 168 pages, $10.95, Garden City, N.Y.: Doubleday.

A good companion volume to *Superstars* in that it emphasizes actual tournament play rather than personalities and offcourse life. Exemplary or surprising bursts of shotmaking have been picked for speculative replay, primarily from the annals of the four majors but also, and interestingly, from events such as the Ryder Cup and Picadilly World Match Play championships.

TREVINO AND JACKLIN HEAD TO HEAD

Tony Jacklin played Lee Trevino twice in 1972. Both events would be high up on anybody's list of the great man-to-man encounters of golf history. In July they fought out the Open at Muirfield, watching and matching each other shot for shot as they played round together the final two days. It was perhaps tougher on Jacklin's nerves than Trevino's for this is the Open already a legend for Trevino's holing of everything in sight—particularly if he were off the green, preferably in a bunker.

Jacklin had begun 69, 72 to the American's 71, 70 and had then improved to a 67, during which his fires had been stirred by hitting his second shot at the 558-yard 5th hole to two or three yards and sweeping the putt in. Undeniably that's the ideal way to play a golf hole. Lee Trevino's perfection that day was of a different kind but every bit as effective when it comes to checking what's been written down on the scorecard.

He had gone out in even par—36—but it all happened from the 447-yard 14th onwards. On that hole, Trevino hit a 4 iron to within six or seven yards of the flag and sent the putt in. He repeated the performance on the next. Nothing exceptional about that, you may say. They are all supposed to hit a drive down the fairway, send an iron onto the green and hole some of the medium-length putts. True indeed. For the short hole that followed, Trevino decided on a 6 iron, only to find that the leather grip had unwound. Well most American leather grips these days have a gluey backing and all you have to do is grasp the steel shaft firmly and wind it back on. Nevertheless, it's not quite the job one would choose to pass the time when trying to win an open championship. It seems the task did not distract and soothe Trevino. He pushed his tee shot into a bunker to the right of the flag. He was faced with a shot from a downhill lie and with the back lip of the bunker too close to be dismissed from the mind.

"Oh dear," breathed the gallery. Instead of floating out, Trevino's ball came out low and strong, with enough pace and lack of backspin to carry on through the green and perhaps leave him with the opportunity of trying to do better next time from a bunker the other side of the green. The ball pitched short of the flagstick, skipped sharply on, hit it in the precise middle and duly collapsed into the

hole, all impetus spent. Jacklin's reluctant pencil would have to write down a two, instead of the five he may have begun to have in mind.

Trevino advanced enthusiastically to the next tee, the 542-yard 17th. Afterwards he said, "I really mellowed the drive. I was swinging at the world. Five iron, two putts, another birdie. On 18 I hit the ball as hard as I could and cut a 5 iron through the green. I chipped 30 feet and when it started rolling I knew it was in. Another birdie. I can't remember ever having five birdies in a row."

So at the end of that day Trevino was a shot up on Jacklin, four ahead of Doug Sanders, five on Brian Barnes and six on Jack Nicklaus. All the odds were on a gunfight between the two leaders the next day and so it proved. More or less. Nicklaus confused the issue by going out in 32 and then having a couple more birdies. It all meant that he was six under par with four holes to go. But there were no more birdies and he dropped a shot on the 17th to finish with a stirring 66, one of the great rounds of the Open's history and it could have been at least a couple of shots lower.

Trevino and Jacklin, as they played, knew that one of them must win but there was also the thought that Nicklaus was the bear that might hug them both to death. Indeed, after his birdie at the 10th, he did lead the Championship momentarily.

By the time that Jacklin and Trevino stood on the 17th tee, Nicklaus had faltered. Both knew that to beat him they had to finish in level par and gain one shot on each other. Quite a situation.

This time, Trevino did not "mellow" his drive at all. He pulled his shot into a bunker and had then to watch Jacklin strike long and straight. Jacklin's ball was still ahead of him after the bunker shot and not far behind after Trevino had hit a 3 wood short of the green into long grass. Jacklin failed to reach the green but had only a short pitch left. This pulled up some 15 feet short of the hole but still left him with a fair chance of a birdie. "Well that's that, I've thrown it away," Trevino said to his caddie.

Trevino's pitch from the long grass scuttled through the green. He had now to chip and single putt just to get a six. Trevino reached his ball, examined the lie briefly and seemed unconcerned which club he dragged out of his bag. Equally cursorily he glanced towards the hole and then quickly played the shot. For Trevino, the Championship was over. But a horrified Tony Jacklin saw that it was by no means over. Trevino's ball went into the hole. That was a par five, not the certain six and quite possible seven. And Jacklin had now to hole his 15-feet putt in order to draw level with Trevino. "That," said Trevino to himself, "may be the straw that breaks the camel's back." Perhaps it was. Jacklin's first putt skirted the hole and he had a three-footer return to get in to stay one behind Trevino. By now, the greens were well spiked around the hole for all the final day competitors had passed by. Either a spike mark diverted Tony's short putt or it was never on line for the hole.

Jacklin was a punctured balloon; there was now no hope of winning unless Trevino played the 18th hole more badly than was conceivable. Trevino, full of verve after two gifts from the gods in as many minutes, launched full out into his drive and struck it superbly. Inevitably his following iron shot was to the heart of the green.

—from *Golf to Remember*

TEED OFF by Dave Hill, with Nick Seitz. 1977, 228 pages, $8.95, Englewood Cliffs, N.J.: Prentice-Hall.

A collection of brash, often amusing, always provocative disquisitions on every significant aspect of tour life. Notes on course design, instruction, and equipment show considerable awareness of and sympathy for the average golfer.

THE GREAT, THE GRAND AND THE ALSO RAN: RABBITS AND CHAMPIONS ON THE PRO GOLF TOUR by Dan Gleason. 1976, 238 pages, $7.95, N.Y.: Random House.

Bright writing focused on one year in the life of a journeyman pro.

GOLF'S GOLDEN GRIND: THE HISTORY OF THE TOUR by Al Barkow. 1974, 310 pages, $8.95, N.Y.: Harcourt Brace Jovanovich.

Barkow traces organized pro golf in this country, starting with Harry Vardon's 20,000-mile barnstorming tour of 1900, from a perspective mindful of developments in the broader social and economic life of the country; hence his sometimes controversial views on "elitism" at the Masters, shabby treatment of blacks and foreigners on tour, and the prevalence of materialism in golf generally.

ON TO FLORIDA

The Pro-Am has been run off, and a crowd of over 30,000 have jostled each other and craned necks to see a "host of famous celebrities," including Sammy Davis, Jr., play golf or any form thereof. Davis is run down by a golf-car driver and retires after sixteen holes. Jackie Gleason and Bob Hope play a special match for $25,000, the money donated to a charity. Gleason wears golf knickers with woolen argyle socks, a shirt and tie. Old tradition. Hope dresses as we all do now for golf—slacks and T-shirt. Gleason is not as round of body as in the past, is deeply tanned from much golf here, where he lives. He defeats Hope (82 to 83, no handicaps), does an "away we go" on the last green, and does not appear again until the last two days of the tournament, when he sits at a microphone near the eighteenth green and comments on the play in a soft voice and with no effort to remind everyone that comedy is his business.

The blare of local promotion has simmered. The Fort Lauderdale News and Sun-Sentinel *has scratched the bottom of the "color" build-up with articles on pros who have lost their clubs and are playing with strange instruments, on construction workers who will silence their jackhammers while the pros are putting on greens near the buildings being put up, on gate-crashers at past Inverrarys. The area disk jockeys have done their bit, reminding their listeners, in between spinning sides by Frank and Sammy, that the golf pros are in town. The news is out and a quiet descends. There is a contemplative hush at the start of a professional golf tournament. Neither the players nor the spectators are sure what will happen, but whatever does, that is what it's all about. Each has his own thoughts to think. For the spectators they are not very complicated, dangerous, or worrisome: Who's going to win? Who to watch play? If a fan has played the course, he will compare his best drive on some hole with where the pros hit it.*

The pros have more pertinent considerations, especially since they are now in Florida for the first time this year. Last week, the western portion of the winter tour concluded with the Los Angeles Open. For the pros who have been out west, it is a time for reorientation, adjustments. All have flown east, and the time lag has been easily assimilated. No problem these days. And Ramada Inns have standard beds, bedspreads, rugs on the floors, pictures on the walls—the value of a chain operation.

But during the practice rounds, the pros are reminded that it is always windy in south Florida—a strong wind heavy with subtropical moisture through which golf balls do not zip as they do in California or Arizona. It takes one more club for the distance here—a six instead of a seven iron, or some extra on the seven. Most golfers don't like the wind. It keeps them off balance, is fickle. They can't play their own game and must bend to the will of nature . . . damnit.

—from *Golf's Golden Grind*

PRO: FRANK BEARD ON THE GOLF TOUR by Frank Beard; edited by Dick Schaap. 1969, 32 pages, photos, $6.95, N.Y.: World.

Beard takes his tape recorder with him on tour for a year and collects daily impressions from the viewpoint of a thoughtful but admittedly somewhat mundane journeyman pro. No inspiration or romance, yet the minutiae comes together to give a complete profile of the experience of modern competitive golf.

THE TOUR by Christopher Keane. 1974, 239 pages, $8.95, N.Y.: Stein and Day.

Somewhat superficial treatment of various facets of tour life—press, TV, tournament organizers, player managers, caddies, rabbits, and groupies.

RECENT NOVELS

THE PRO-AM MURDERS by Patrick Cake. 1979, $8.95, Dallas: Proteus Press.

Not seen. Mystery set at the Crosby.

THE 72ND HOLE by Harry Forse. 1976, 190 pages, $7.50, Greenfield, Ind.: Mitchell Fleming.

DEAD SOLID PERFECT by Dan Jenkins. 1974, 234 pages, $7.95, N.Y.: Atheneum.

Texan Kenny Puckett reviews his life and loves in "good-ole-boy" wisecrack style during U.S. Open week at Heavenly Pines Country Club. Slated to be a movie —first significant golf flick since *Follow the Sun.*

THE GOLF BUM by Arthur E. Pickens, Jr. 1970, 223 pages, $5.95, N.Y.: Crown.

Bud Parker overthrows restrictive marriage and lousy putting stroke to forge comeback, get posh club job, launch plans to aid underprivileged youths. Unconvincing.

DRIVE FOR THE GREEN by Anthony Tuttle. 1969, 341 pages, $5.95, N.Y.: Doubleday.

Intertwined lives of three top pros.

PORK, OR THE DAY I LOST THE MASTERS by Thomas Dulack. 1968, 209 pages, $4.95, N.Y.: Dial Press.

Pork Waller's expectations for rookie year on tour include winning all four majors and owning 50 pairs of shoes, but the hulking innocent from Illinois falls in with gamblers.

THE GOLFER by Wayne Greenhaw. 1967, 210 pages, $4.50, Philadelphia: J. B. Lippincott.

Country boy making good in second year on tour encounters problems with women, photographers, and manager during week of Confederate Invitational.

PROMOTERS AND AGENTS

"SIGN 'EM UP, BUCKY"; THE ADVENTURES OF A SPORT AGENT by Bucky Woy with Jack Patterson. 1975, 229 pages, $8.95, N.Y.: Hawthorn Books.

Woy was Lee Trevino's business manager for several years.

UNPLAYABLE LIES by Fred Corcoran with Bud Harvey. 1965, 274, pages, $5.95, N.Y.: Duell, Sloan and Pearce.

Corcoran tells stories about Hogan and Snead and the early years of the ladies' pro tour (which he organized), as well as his experiences with other sports figures.

BOOKS ABOUT THE MASTERS

MASTERS, THE FIRST 41 YEARS
MASTERS, 1978
　　Masters Publications
　　P.O. Box 2086
　　Augusta, GA 30903

Augusta National has gotten into the publishing business: Beginning with the above account of the 1978 Masters, it plans to issue bound illustrated accounts of each year's "Masters Week," at $12.00 apiece. *Masters, The First 41 Years* is a 128-page bound volume covering the event from 1934 through 1977, with photos and brief comments on each tournament by the late Clifford Roberts, longtime Masters tournament chairman; price, $15.00.

THE MASTERS; AUGUSTA REVISITED: AN INTIMATE VIEW by Furman Bisher. 1976, 186 pages, $24.95, Birmingham, Ala.: Oxmoor House.

An elegaic introduction on Bobby Jones and his twin creation, followed by detailed, dramatic accounts of extraordinary Masters performances by Sarazen, Nelson, Snead, Demaret, Hogan, Palmer, and Nicklaus. These latter fulfill the time-warp promise of the title— "Augusta Revisited"—by involving the reader in the present-day perspective of those players who so far have pulled off Augusta's most astonishing rounds of golf. In today's creative writing classes, Bisher might be hooted down as an occasional manufacturer of purple prose and male chauvinist remarks, but I like him anyway.

SPRING AT AUGUSTA NATIONAL

When the day is splashed with sunlight, and there is a touch of syrupy warmth in the air that plays on the horticultural outburst of Augusta National Golf Club grounds, there is no more beautiful place in American sport to be. Spring, it seems, has extracted every strain of color from the plants and shrubs and vines and trees. The green that covers its soil is so green it dazzles.

In this respect, golf has its edge over all the other games at which we spectate. Football rips its grass up in chunks. Horses run on drab, bare earth. Automobiles race on surfaces black with asphalt and stained with oil. Boats leave a wake of sludge on their waters. Baseball is played against a background of girders and concrete and an encirclement of seats for its jury. Basketball and hockey take to the grimness of warehouse life.

Golf wanders out among God's great outdoors, over hill and down into valley, through glen and glade. In no place has the natural beauty of the land been made so much a part of sport as here, where the Masters is played. There are greater golf courses. There are more spectacular golf courses. There are more excruciating tests of golf. There are other beautiful golf courses. But there is no great, spectacular, excruciating test of golf that is so beautiful as Augusta National. The key to it is that both the blossoming of spring and the arrival of the Masters coincide in all their natural and cultivated splendors.

—from The Masters

THE STORY OF AUGUSTA NATIONAL GOLF CLUB by Clifford Roberts. 1976. 256 pages, $25.00, Garden City, N.Y.: Doubleday.

Longtime Masters Tournament chairman Roberts was nothing if not meticulous, and in this exposition of the origins and development of Augusta National, written in the stern and careful prose of a businessman's memorandum, Roberts sets the record straight on a number of subjects of only marginal interest to the average golf nut, such as "Water Color Paintings of the Golf Hole Flowers" and "President Eisenhower's Third Heart Attack." Yet one cannot help admiring the man's thorough devotion to detail—surely this feature in his character was as much responsible for the tournament's ongoing success as was the reputation of founder Bobby Jones. And with a little patience, the true golf fan might well come to appreciate this volume, not only for the light it sheds on the operation of the Masters, but for the glimpses it gives of the role of the elite private club in American business and political life.

WORTHY OF SPECIAL NOTE: Appendix III, an impressive 23-page statistical profile of Jones's life and golfing career, compiled by Bill Inglish.

THE MASTERS: ALL ABOUT ITS HISTORY, ITS RECORDS, ITS PLAYERS, ITS REMARKABLE COURSE AND EVEN MORE REMARKABLE TOURNAMENT by Dawson Taylor. 1973, 159 pages, $8.50, N.Y.: A. S. Barnes.

THE MASTERS: THE WINNING OF A GOLF CLASSIC by Dick Schaap. 1970, 235 pages, $6.95, N.Y.: Random House.

Scatter-shot reportage of the 1969 Masters Week, conveys the experience of a variety of contestants in varying moods and situations, as though viewed by CIA operatives. Casper wins it, anyway.

THE MASTERS: THE STORY OF GOLF'S GREATEST TOURNAMENT by Tom Flaherty. 1961, 150 pages, $7.50, N.Y.: Holt, Rinehart and Winston.

Each year's tournament from 1934 to 1960 is examined in well-chosen detail.

IN THE BEGINNING

Surrounded by a bodyguard of United States Marines a happy young man in knickers moved slowly through the human storm around him toward the clubhouse at Merion. He did his best to acknowledge the accolades that this jubilant mob of 15,000 were offering him. It was September, 1930, and Robert Tyre Jones, Jr., had just won the U.S. Amateur championship, the last leg of the Grand Slam. By winning the British Amateur, the British Open,

the U.S. Open, and now the U.S. Amateur in a single year he had accomplished the "impregnable quadrilateral." No man had done it before, and it seemed unlikely that any man could ever do it again. It was the supreme accomplishment of an already exceptional career.

But at twenty-eight Bob Jones was tired. He had no more golf worlds to conquer. The game which once had brought him so much satisfaction now was a joyless thing for him. Each new victory brought increased demands for still another victory. For fourteen years, just half of his lifetime, Jones had been fighting the battle of tournament golf. He was tired of the psychological strain each victory represented. Tired, too, of living in the public eye like a matinee idol. For years Bob Jones had thought of quitting. If possible he wanted to quit on a high note. If that opportunity did not present itself then he would just slip quietly away. This moment, he knew, was the time he had been waiting for. To the dismay of millions of fans in a dozen lands Bob Jones turned away from tournament golf.

Jones set about rearranging his life with the same concentration he had applied to winning tournaments. He at last was able to devote some time to his law practice and business interests at home in Atlanta, Georgia. He played golf, but on his own terms: weekend foursomes with his old friends at the East Lake Club, where he had learned the game. For the first time he accepted the lucrative commercial offers he had been turning down for years in order to retain his amateur standing. He agreed to design Jones-model clubs for Spalding. He went on the air with a weekly half-hour radio broadcast in partnership with his friend and biographer, O.B. Keeler. He signed a contract with Warner Brothers and made two series of short, instructional movies. They were among the best and most successful movies of their kind ever produced.

At the same time Jones let it be known that he was ready to carry out another plan that had been forming in his mind for years. This plan was to design and build a golf course. After playing on the finest courses in the world for fourteen years Bob had some definite ideas on what a golf course should, and should not, be like. Jones's course would incorporate his ideas, and in a way be his contribution to the game. It would also be a retreat, where Bob and his friends from around the country could enjoy the game they loved in beautiful surroundings and with a degree of blessed privacy.

Promoters and others were quick to propose to Bob a number of sites and schemes for building the new course. They knew that any promotion Jones signed his name to was sure of success. Two basic requirements limited the choice of sites. It must be in the South, where Robert T. Jones was the most popular hero since Robert E. Lee; and it should be in Georgia, Bob's home state, within reasonable distance of Atlanta.

Among those who knew of and understood Jones's desire to build a course was Clifford Roberts of New York. Roberts, tall, bespectacled week-end golfer and successful Wall

Street investment banker, had been introduced to Jones by mutual friends at a tournament a few years earlier. Roberts was an occasional vacationer in Augusta, Georgia, which happened also to be the home of Jones's wife and the site of the Southeastern Open, which Bob had regularly played in and won.

Roberts knew Jones wanted to stay clear of real-estate promotions, and he also knew of a particular piece of property a few miles west of Augusta which was for sale at depression prices. He invited Jones to come over and see it. Jones agreed, and on a December morning in 1930, in company with Cliff Roberts and Alfred Bourne, a member of the Singer Sewing Machine family, who had a winter home in Augusta, Bob had his first look at the land that was to become the Augusta National course.

—from *The Masters*

BOOKS ABOUT THE U.S. OPEN

MASSACRE AT WINGED FOOT: THE U.S. OPEN MINUTE BY MINUTE by Dick Schaap. 1974, 226 pages, $7.95, N.Y.: Random House.

In laconic "you-are-there" style, Schaap and his field-men collect and present a thousand or so snippets of dialogue and anecdote related, sometimes only remotely ("9:35 A.M.: Lee Trevino is fiddling with his gloved hand, flexing it and rubbing it. 'Got a sore hand, Lee?' a spectator calls. 'No,' says Supermex, 'a sore glove.' "), to the shotmaking ups and downs of Hale Irwin's Open week. A good orientation to the flotsam and jetsam of events during a typical major tournament.

THE OPEN COURSE

Against an awesome array of mercenaries—actually, only one hundred and thirty-eight are mercenaries; the other twelve are amateurs—Winged Foot looks almost defenseless. The West Course stretches 6,961 yards, which is lengthy, but not gigantic. Twenty-nine bunkers guard the fairways, and forty-four protect the greens, an ample, but not prodigious number. Not a single water hole mars the layout, not a lake to clear, not a pond to fear, only a harmless little stream that meanders briefly into play.

Poor Winged Foot.

The Alamo looked sturdier.

Except . . . that this is no ordinary tournament that is about to be played at Winged Foot. This is the United States Open, the seventy-fourth renewal, and the U.S. Open has a way of turning even mild courses into man-eaters.

This is no accidental transformation. The United States Golf Association, the group that sponsors and conducts the Open, at a different site each year, deliberately toughens up its Open courses. The greenskeeper at the host club is instructed many weeks before the event to forget about trimming the rough along the fairways. He is encouraged instead to concentrate on razor-cutting the greens, creating

a surface slightly sparser than an Earl Morrall crew cut and slightly fuller than a Yul Brynner scalp. As a result, any shot that wanders off an Open fairway is doubly or triply penalized, and any putt that is stroked too firmly may roll forever.

Besides jungle rough and icy greens, the USGA loves narrow fairways and lengthy holes. If an Open fairway is deemed too wide—if two Volkswagens can squeeze through side by side—the USGA will have it narrowed. If a par-three or a par-four appears too accessible, the USGA will suggest the construction of a new and more distant tee or a new trap at a critical spot. The USGA has a less troublesome way of dealing with short par-fives. Don't lengthen the hole; just reduce the par. Hardly an Open goes by without a 430- to 470-yard par-four to stretch the muscles of the pros.

The reasoning of the USGA is simple: The U.S. Open is the most coveted title in golf and, logically, should be the most difficult to win. It should be a stern and true test of skill, of intellect (golf intellect, that is), of courage and of stamina (until a decade ago, the USGA placed a special premium on stamina by playing the Open in three days, with two rounds on the final day; the format was changed to one round a day for four days to satisfy the demands, and the rewards, of television).

The West Course of Winged Foot lends itself perfectly to the needs of the USGA. It is the kind of course that can be shaped easily into a fortress.

—from *Massacre at Winged Foot*

THE U.S. OPEN: 1895–1965 by Tom Flaherty. 1966, 242 pages, N.Y.: E. P. Dutton.

First-rate recapitulation of the high points in the Open's first hundred years, focusing particularly on the feats of Ouimet in 1913 ("The Magnificent Upset"), Hagen, Jones, Hogan, and the "new giants"—Palmer, Player, Nicklaus.

PALMER'S OPEN

What happened in the afternoon that lovely June Saturday at Cherry Hills was the making of the Arnold Palmer legend. Here is what Palmer did:

On the first hole, a 346-yard par 4, he drove the green and two-putted for a birdie 3. On the second hole, 410 yards, Arnie was just short of the green in 2. He chipped in from 30 feet for a birdie 3. Now Palmer was aroused and charging. "I knew I was on my way," he said later. At the third hole, 348 yards, Arnie put his wedge stiff to the pin and canned his birdie putt of less than a yard. On the fourth, 426 yards, he stuck his wedge 18 feet from the cup and got the putt for still another birdie. He parred the long fifth after driving into the rough, but at the sixth, 174 yards, par 3, he hit the center of the green with a seven-iron and curved a 25-foot sidehill putt into the hole for a deuce. At the seventh, a 411-yard dogleg, Palmer played a lovely wedge to within six feet and ran in the putt. That made it six birdies in seven holes. The great streak ended at the eighth green where Arnie missed the short putt he needed for par. But at the next hole he got his par and his score for the first nine was an astonishing 30, five strokes below par. It was a total matched only once before in the Open, by Jimmy McHale in 1947.

Now Palmer's name was back on the scoreboard with the leaders and as the field turned into the home stretch the advantage of impetus was all his. Souchak was cracking. He missed a putt from 18 inches at the 10th hole and another of similar length on the finishing hole. He faded to 75 and 283. So much for Mike. But there were a dozen others jamming for the lead. Palmer, certain that the word of his tremendous rally had reached his rivals, coolly switched to a conservative brand of golf and waited for the pressure to have its effect. One by one the others wilted. Jack Fleck proved his 1955 victory was no fluke by going out in 32. But on the home nine he bogeyed two of the last three holes and fell back to a tie with Souchak and four others at 283. For a few minutes young Jack Nicklaus had the lead to himself, five under par for the tournament. But at the 13th (or 67th) hole Jack took three putts from 10 feet and at the next hole he three-putted again. Cancel Jack. For Ben Hogan, playing with Nicklaus, the tournament was two exhausting holes too long. After 70 holes Ben was tied with Palmer at four under. He had hit 34 consecutive greens this day in par or better. But on the next to last hole, a 548-yard par 5, Ben chose to gamble for a birdie on the third shot, a difficult 50-yard pitch over a creek to an island green where the pin was at the front. His soft shot fell just a shade too short. It landed at the edge of the water on the far bank. Hogan took off his right shoe and sock, stood with one foot in the water and splashed the ball to within 18 feet of the pin. He two-putted for a bogey 6. On the 18th hole Hogan hooked his drive into the lake and later missed a short putt that gave him an inglorious 7 and a score of 284. Once again Ben's bid for a fifth championship ended in frustration.

Palmer was playing behind Nicklaus and Hogan and he realized that he needed only to hold onto the gains he had made. Arnold reached the green of the 563-yard 11th hole in two shots and holed out in two putts for his seventh birdie of the round. After that he was content to knock off par after steady par right to the finish. At the 18th, where Hogan had met disaster, Palmer drove with a No. 1 iron and was safe. His four-iron approach was 80 feet to the left of the flag. From there he chipped to within a yard and dropped the putt for his par 4. Arnie's second nine was 35, his round was 65 and his 280 total, four under par, earned him the championship by two strokes.

Palmer's spectacular charge, the unforgettable manner in which he took command of a tournament which he surely had lost, elevated him to the steepletop of world golf. He claimed the throne that Hogan had occupied for so long. But the new emperor had only to glance over his shouder to see where his next challenge was coming from. Jack Nicklaus, a full 10 years younger than Palmer, had finished second to Arnie by just two strokes. His 282 was the lowest score any amateur had ever made in the Open— including the amateur who won it four times, Bobby Jones.

—from The U.S. Open: 1895–1965

BOOKS ABOUT THE BRITISH OPEN

A CENTURY OF OPENS by Geoffrey Cousins and Tom Scott. 1971, 232 pages. London: Frederic Muller, Ltd.

Two veteran British golf writers/editors trace the growth of the hundred Opens held between 1851 and 1971 "from the simple, unpretentious promotions of the 1860s to the flamboyant richness of the 1970s."

"THE OPEN"

Many great sporting events are "open" in the sense that anyone in the world can compete in them. Some have the word in their titles. But when sportsmen generally speak of "The Open" they mean only one competition, which began in a simple and humble way more than a hundred years ago and ever since has been acknowledged as the greatest and most important event in the world of golf.

In 1860 a handful of professional golfers—men who made clubs and balls, carried clubs for amateurs, played with their patrons for fees and often helped in the care of golf courses—went to Prestwick to play for a Belt. There were only eight players, the competition was over thirty-six holes, or three rounds of the Prestwick twelve-hole links, and there was no prize money. But these men had no conception of the importance and glamour with which this competition was to be invested in later years, or of the immense sums which would be won by golfers of the 1960s. They were keen, appreciated the goodwill of the Prestwick Golf Club members who had subscribed £30 to provide the Belt, and did their best to please the patrons. It was impossible for them to visualise how their new competition, carried through rather haphazardly in one day, was to grow into a large-scale international promotion involving more than five hundred players, thousands of spectators, many thousands of pounds in prize money, an encampment of marquees, TV towers, grandstands, car parks glittering with glass and chromium and all the other paraphernalia of a great sporting occasion.

Those sturdy professionals of mid-Victorian days, with their bearded faces, baggy trousers, seafaring caps, rude-looking clubs and solid gutta-percha golf balls, were pioneers paving the way for the lords of the links—Arnold Palmer, Gary Player, Jack Nicklaus, Tony Jacklin and others who were to win the Open three or four generations later and enjoy six-figure incomes from the game. If Willie Park and Old Tom Morris were to make ghostly visitations to the scene of a modern Open Championship they would be too amazed to do anything but stare. But they would be perfectly justified in saying to the present-day contenders for the title: "Good luck, boys, but don't forget we started it." —from *A Century of Opens*

ANDERSON AND FERGUSON

The outstanding players of the next few years were Jamie Anderson of St. Andrews and Bob Ferguson of Musselburgh, who each held the Championship for three years in succession, the St. Andrews man from 1877 to 1879, the Musselburgh hero from 1880 to 1882. One of the most exciting finishes the event has ever known saw Anderson gain his second Championship in 1878 at Prestwick. Four holes from home he learned that J. O. F. Morris had finished in 161, which meant that Anderson had to do these last four holes in seventeen to tie. "I can dae't," he remarked, "wi' a five, a fower, a three, and a five." At the first of the four holes, a weak drive fell short of a bunker, but he had a fine brassie for his second, and followed this up by holing a full iron shot for a 3. He got his 4 all right at the next, but at the "Short" hole, a fortunate iron shot, a shade too strong, pitched on a small mound at the far edge of the green, hesitated a moment, and then trickled back and into the hole, for the first "ace" in the Open Championship. With a steady 5 for the home hole Anderson finished in 157—four strokes better than his schedule. Yet he needed every stroke of his luck in the end, for Bob Kirk, coming behind him, had been "burning up the course" and on the last green had a longish putt for a 4 to tie. He made a tremendous effort to get it down, but was a trifle too strong, the ball hitting the back of the hole and jumping out again. Unfortunately Kirk in his disappointment did not take enough care with the short one and somehow managed to miss that also, so that he actually finished two strokes behind the leader.

Ferguson came nearer than any other champion has ever done to equalling "Young Tom's" record of four championships in a row, being beaten on the fourth occasion only after a tie. His career was a typical example of the way in which the professionals of that generation rose to fame. Born within sight of Musselburgh links, he was only eight years old when he earned his first wages as a caddie there. And he was still no more than a boy—only eighteen—when he took his courage and a bag of borrowed clubs in his hand and went out to conquer the world in an open professional tournament at Leith. Leith was then a seven-hole course and four rounds were played. Ferguson's score was 131, and deservedly carried off what in those days was regarded as the generous first prize of £10. It is on record that after this victory an enthusiastic patron offered to present him with a set of clubs, and when the set was duly bought in the shop of Douglas McEwan—an ancestor of the well-known Lancashire professionals, now in their sixth generation—the eight clubs were chosen with such care that they lasted him all through his championship career.

—from *A History of Golf* by Robert Browning

BOOKS ABOUT THE CROSBY

THE CROSBY: GREATEST SHOW ON EARTH by Dwayne Netland. 1975, 160 pages, $9.95, Garden City, N.Y.: Doubleday.

Everything you ever wanted to know about the Crosby—the fabulous three-course venue on Monterey Peninsula, the perennial bad weather, and the pros, celebs, and business types who take part. Lots of photos; year-by-year tournament summaries and leading scorers, 1937–1975.

COMEDY AT THE CLAMBAKE

One of the primary reasons for the Crosby's enormous appeal, in the view of television people, is the prospect of watching a personality like Jack Lemmon taking three swipes at a ball buried in a bunker. The celebrities have long recognized the publicity value of television exposure in the Crosby, but that has to be measured against the chance of making an absolute fool of one's self in front of millions.

Nobody has experienced both to a more substantial degree or taken the ordeal more graciously than Jack Lemmon. Lemmon is fifty years old and has spent the greater part of his adult life performing in front of audiences and cameras. But the prospect of hitting golf shots in a televised tournament terrifies him.

"I would rather play Hamlet with no rehearsal in an opera house than play golf on television," Lemmon admits. "On the stage or a movie set, I'm in control on familiar ground. On the golf course, I'm playing someone else's game."

Lemmon's first exposure to the cameras at Pebble Beach came on the 14th hole of the third round in 1959. Chopping and dubbing frightfully, he finally came within TV range. "And now here's Jack Lemmon, about to hit that all-important eighth shot," remarked Jim McKay from the tower behind the green.

After chunking a wedge, Lemmon skulled his chip shot from just off the green. The ball rolled uphill toward the hole and died, then began rolling back, gathering momentum until it trickled off the green and between Jack's legs. ABC replayed the sequence over and over.

"Jack's getting more footage here today," observed Bing, "than he has in his last three films."

Byron Nelson the ABC analyst, broke down Lemmon's swing in slow motion—and detected eleven major flaws.

Lemmon continued to botch up his round that day, as the cameras kept returning to him. "When we got to 17, the long par-3, we had a little wind behind us," he says. "I cranked up and hit a driver. It went forty yards over the green. 'That's the only good shot you've hit all day, Jack,' Jim Garner said. 'Unfortunately it's in the ocean.'"

Standing in the water and rocks, Lemmon swung a wedge and flailed the ball 130 yards farther out into the ocean.

On the 18th hole he knocked two tee shots out of bounds, reached the green in 9 and carefully surveyed his 35-foot putt. Asked which way it broke, Lemmon's caddie replied, "Who cares?"

Andy Williams endured a similar embarrassment in 1966, his first year in the Crosby. "On the 18th hole at Pebble Beach," Andy says, "I hit a low hard shot that bored into the side of a trap, against a wall of sand two feet high. I didn't know how to get out of that kind of a lie. I tried to blade the shot, and left it in the sand. The next week I got several hundred letters from TV viewers, explaining how to hit that shot.

"When I finally did get it onto the green, I was lying seven. I looked up at the television tower and there were Bing and several of my friends from NBC. I was so nervous I couldn't focus on the ball. I missed the ball completely with the putter and hit the toe of my shoe instead."

Singer Robert Goulet experienced the horrors of a duffer on TV the following year. Driving off the 16th tee, he toed a shot which nearly decapitated announcer Chris Schenkel in the tower at the 15th green. "I've seen bad shots," Schenkel laughed, "but never one that endangered my life."

On the 18th hole, Goulet scraped and hacked his way up the fairway with the cameras homing in on him. He heeled one shot off his left foot and took four to get out of a seawall trap. Attempting to laugh his anguish away, Goulet skipped over the gallery rope near the green, tripped and fell.

—from *The Crosby: Greatest Show on Earth*

THE BOGEY MAN by George Plimpton. 1968, 306 pages, $5.95, N.Y.: Harper & Row; an Avon paperback, $1.25.

Inspired deadpan reporting of author's uninspired play during Crosby, Hope, and now defunct Lucky International pro-am events, fleshed out with setpieces on instructional material, temper tantrums, yips, tour caddies, driving ranges, and a particularly nice exegesis of odd golfing happenings as collected in *The Golfer's Handbook,* which I suspect is the resting place Golfer Plimpton secretly wishes for.

FILMS ABOUT THE TOUR

THE MASTERS

Commercially-sponsored color highlight films of the Masters tournament have been produced every year since 1960 under the direction of Augusta National. They run 30–60 minutes. For terms and availability, contact Augusta National G.C., P.O. Box 2086, Augusta, GA 30903.

THE MEMORIAL TOURNAMENT

A film has been made of the tournament every year since its inception, in 1976. For availability and terms, contact Muirfield Village G.C., Box 565, Dublin, OH 43017.

THE U.S. OPEN

Films about each year's Open championship since 1962 run 30–50 minutes and may be rented for $15.00 to $25.00 per film. For details contact:

Film Library
USGA
Far Hills, NJ 07931

THE CANADIAN OPEN

This event has been documented in film form every year since 1954. For terms and availability of specific films, contact Royal Canadian Association, R.R. 2, Oakville, Ontario, Canada L6J 423.

THE PGA CHAMPIONSHIP

Color documentary films of past tournaments, running 30–40 minutes. For terms and availability, contact PGA headquarters, Box 12458, Lake Park, FL 33403.

NEWSPAPER AND MAGAZINE COVERAGE OF THE TOUR

MAGAZINES

Golf World, a weekly throughout most of the year, reports in detail on every PGA and LPGA event—complete scores, money winnings, etc.

Sports Illustrated runs a dozen or so full-length features on the major golf events throughout the year, usually written by Dan Jenkins, Barry McDermott, or Sarah Pileggi. Also does occasional star profiles and major championship previews.

The New Yorker usually carries each year two very long articles—frequently over 10,000 words—by Herbert Warren Wind, one after the Masters and the other after the U.S./British opens. These articles "cover" the major events but also touch on numerous other facets of golf.

Golf and *Golf Digest,* being monthlies, generally *preview* the major events with special articles or sections and confine their reportage to back-of-the-book capsule summaries of past tournaments and year-to-date money-winning tables.

NEWSPAPERS

The only newspaperman on the PGA Tour full-time in recent years has been Bob Green, who reports on every event for the Associated Press. United Press International also covers nearly every tour event but uses various writers on a regional basis. The most extensive year-round coverage of pro golf by daily papers is provided by *The New York Times* (John Radosta) and the New York *Daily News* (Dana Mozley).

Many other major dailies limit their staff coverage to the major tournaments and to six to eight events taking place in their general area, although almost all provide wire-service coverage of the tour in varying degrees. Foremost among papers with golf specialists are:

> Boston *Globe*
> Quincy (MA) *Patriot-Ledger*
> *The New York Times*
> New York *Daily News*
> Pittsburgh *Post Gazette*
> Cleveland *Plain Dealer*
> Columbus (OH) *Dispatch*
> Columbus (OH) *Citizen Journal*
> *Washington Post*
> Washington *Star*
> Charlotte (NC) *News*
> Atlanta *Journal*
> Orlando *Sentinel*
> Dallas *Morning News*
> Dallas *Times Herald*
> Fort Worth *Star Telegram*
> San Diego *Union*
> *Los Angeles Times*
> San Francisco *Examiner*
> San Francisco *Chronicle*
> San Jose *Mercury-News*
> *Kansas City *Star*
> *Detroit *News*
> *Augusta (GA) *Chronicle*
> *Philadelphia *Inquirer*
> *Philadelphia *Bulletin*
> *Philadelphia *News*
> *Newsday*
> *Houston *Post*

* Amount of coverage seems to vary from year to year.

THE TOUR'S GREATEST SHOTS

This article by PGA Tour Information Director Tom Place is reprinted with permission from the 1978 *World Golf Hall of Fame Annual*.

Ben Hogan absorbed the question, thought about it for a moment, and commented:

"In almost every tournament, there was a key shot."

As true as that may be, everyone who has played the game usually can reach back and pull out the shot they will never forget, a Hall of Fame shot, if you please.

There was Gene Sarazen's three wood for the double eagle at the 15th in the 1935 Masters Tournament; Jerry Pate's five iron on the final hole of the 1976 United States Open; Tom Watson's seven iron on the 72nd hole of the

1977 British Open; the eight footer that gave Al Geiberger the historic 59 in the 1977 Danny Thomas-Memphis Classic; Jack Nicklaus' one iron into the final hole of the 1967 United States Open; Hogan's incredible nine iron on the fifth hole of the 1953 British Open on the last day.

Arnold Palmer has had more than his share of brilliant shots, too, and he said, "I remember those shots that helped me to win, but the one I'll never forget was the one that cost me the 1961 Masters."

It was the seven iron that drifted into the right bunker, and, before he finished the final hole, he had a double bogey six and the tournament belonged to Gary Player.

Let us re-create that moment. Player was in the clubhouse with an eight-under par 280, but Palmer, still with a few to play, seemed to be in control.

By the time he reached the 18th tee, he had a one-stroke lead and then he laced an absolutely perfect drive, dead in the center of the fairway.

As he walked toward his ball, his legions were cheering, shouting "Congratulations" to their hero, their king, the champion to be. He was about to win his third Masters. All he needed was a par to win. Even a bogey (perish the thought) would give him a tie.

There are those who believe all the tumult and the shouting may have caused him to lose a little of his concentration. Whatever, he came off the seven iron and saw it drop into the right greenside bunker and the ball came to rest in a slight depression.

"That was the shot I'll never forget," Palmer said with ever so slight a wince. The memory still burned.

On the bunker shot, he said he "half skulled it," and the ball bounced across the green, into the gallery and down the bank. It took him three more to get home and the double-bogey six gave Player the Masters.

It is something of a surprise that Hogan could single out one shot that he considered better than the others. It was at Carnoustie in the 1953 British Open.

"It was in the last round," he started, "on the par four fifth hole, a lay-up hole. I went with a two or three iron off the tee and then a seven iron into the double-level green. The pin was in the upper back, on the right side, over a hump. The ball hit to the left of the hole and then backed all the way off the green.

"It came to rest on a bias and I couldn't tell if it was in the bunker or not, even after examining it closely. I didn't know whether to pick the ball off or blast it out.

"It required a shot I seldom practiced, but I decided to pick it off," he continued, as if it had happened yesterday. "I had to strike it clean, hitting the ball into the bank and then have it jump up on top.

"I used a nine iron and the ball hit absolutely perfect into the bank, scooted up on the top level and grabbed. As it did, it died right in the hole.

"At that time, I was either tied or one shot ahead of Antonio Cerda, who was playing two or three groups behind me. But, when I made that, I thought, 'It looks as if I have luck with me.' I birdied the next hole and went on to win the championship."

Byron Nelson always was known for his exceptional talent with the long irons, and he knows one of the reasons why.

"It is difficult to boil it down to one great shot," he said, "but I remember in the 1939 U.S. Open at the Philadelphia Country Club, Craig Wood, Denny Shute and I were tied after 72 holes. We had an 18-hole playoff and Craig and I still were tied.

"On the fourth hole of the second 18-hole playoff—it was a 460-yard hole—I hit a good drive down the left side. There was a plateau out there that would give me a better shot at the green and I put my tee shot exactly where I wanted it to be. I had a one iron left to the green. I hit it and the shot never varied from the flag. It landed about 15 feet from the hole and rolled right on in for an eagle two. That put me three shots ahead and that was the way it finished. But, from that day forward, I was known as a good long iron player."

Nicklaus believes his greatest shot was a one iron, too. Many people recall the one he hit on the par three 17th at Pebble Beach in the 1972 U.S. Open. The wind was howling off Carmel Bay and he nailed it right at the hole. "It came up about four inches away," Jack says, smiling at the thought of it, "but that was a shot that just happened. Actually, I made a bad swing."

Another magnificent one iron that Nicklaus pulled off under extreme pressure was at Augusta National's par 5 15th hole during the 1975 Masters tournament. Nicklaus had to hit an absolutely perfect shot to carry a lake guarding the green some 220 yards away. This he did, the ball coming to rest 20 feet directly behind the hole. He two-putted from there for a birdie four and went on to capture his fifth Masters in a dramatic stretch duel with Johnny Miller and Tom Weiskopf.

His first choice as his greatest shot, however, came on the 72nd hole of the 1967 Open at Baltusrol. You may recall he surprised everyone by hitting a one iron off the tee on the par five hole, "to play it safe, and make certain I got my five. If I broke Ben Hogan's Open record of 276, fine, but my first objective was to win the tournament.

"The one iron shot, unfortunately, rolled into some sort of hole and I had to play an eight iron to get it out. I didn't hit it very good, but I wanted to lay up short of the water and I hit it fat.

"I left myself with 232 yards uphill against the wind. I didn't want to hit a wood and take a chance of spraying it, so I decided on the one iron again. I'll never forget how hard I swung at it and the ball went zinging off the club, carried over the bunker and stopped about 20 feet from the hole.

"I made the putt for a birdie and that gave me the record at 275."

Hale Irwin must have hit 264 brilliant shots when he won the 1977 Colgate-Hall of Fame Classic on famed Pinehurst No. 2 as he destroyed tournament and course records, but he believes his best came in the 1974 U.S. Open at Winged Foot on the final hole the last afternoon.

"Actually, it was a succession of three shots," he explained. "I made a 12-foot putt for a par at the 17th that was a very difficult putt and that helped my mood on the 18th tee. It gave me a two-stroke lead, but I knew I had to drive the ball in the center of the fairway because the left side kicked into the heavy rough.

"I hit the drive exactly where I wanted it and that set up the more spectacular shot, the one people still remember. It was a two iron. At the moment of contact, I knew for all intents and purposes, the tournament was over. I just knew it was. It was solid contact and the flight of the ball was exactly where I wanted it. I had allowed for a little left to right drift in the winds and the ball landed on top of the crest and rolled about 18 feet past the hole."

Three players—Al Geiberger, Dave Stockton and Gary Player listed putts for their most memorable.

Al's was an eight footer on his final hole at the Colonial Country Club in the 1977 Danny Thomas-Memphis Classic that gave him the first "59" in PGA Tour history.

"I wasn't worried about my stroke," he said, "I just told myself not to leave it short. It was uphill and on hybrid Bermuda greens, so there would be that tendency. I aimed just outside the left edge, hit it firm and it went in the center of the hole. When I think about it now, I sometimes wonder how I made it."

Stockton's was on the final green of the 1976 PGA Championship at Congressional Country Club. He had played a two iron short of the green rather than challenge the water that protected three sides of the putting surface.

He placed his approach just about where he wanted, about 15 yards short of the green, only to discover he had a difficult chip, off a downslope before the upslope of the green.

He used a sand wedge, "and I hit it a fraction heavy. I wanted to leave it short of the hole, but not 13 feet or so short."

He needed to make the putt to win his second PGA championship. If he two-putted, he would drop back into a tie with Don January and Ray Floyd.

"The green was slick and I knew it wouldn't break much," he said. "It was inside the hole to the right. I hit it perfectly. When it was halfway there, I knew it was going in. It was a putter's putt."

Gary said, "I have to go with the putt on the 18th green at the Masters this year. That won the tournament for me. In 1970, I had a six-foot putt on the exact same line to tie Billy Casper and Gene Littler, but it didn't break as much as I thought it would.

"This year, I had it about 18 feet, and I recalled that six footer vividly. That all flashed through my mind as I got ready to putt and I didn't allow quite as much break and I holed it to win."

He has had some other great shots, too, such as the nine

iron he hit over the willow tree on the 16th hole at Oakland Hills en route to the 1972 PGA Championship; and the three wood at the 14th hole at Carnoustie in the 1968 British Open that stopped 15 inches from the cup. He made it for an eagle and went on to victory.

Tom Watson's greatest came in the British Open, too. "It was on the 72nd hole at Turnberry in 1977," he said. "I was one up on Jack Nicklaus and playing with Jack. I had to hit first, and had 178 yards slightly downwind to a hard green. I hit a seven iron about 2½ feet from the hole. That was the best I have ever hit."

Billy Casper, the newest member of the World Golf Hall of Fame, returns to the Augusta National and the 1970 Masters for his choice.

"It was on the second hole of the playoff with Gene Littler," he recalls. "I hit a terrible hook down in the hazard in the trees. There was a piece of wood, about the size of a baseball bat about four-or-five inches behind my ball and I couldn't move it. I could make six, seven, eight or even nine from there.

I only had one shot, a nine iron. I had to get the club down in front of the wood and under the ball to hit it over the trees and back onto the fairway. It was the only shot I had.

"It had to be a precise, perfect swing," he said. It was absolutely perfect, as he hit the ball about 120 yards and went on to make a par five on the hole and eventually win the playoff.

Littler hit the perfect shot into the 14th in the 1975 Westchester Classic. "I was about three behind Julius Boros at the time," Gene said ever so slowly, and he proceeded to ACE it. "I don't know if it was the greatest I've ever hit," he said, "but it was the most timely." He went on to birdie the 18th to tie Boros and then won the playoff.

Jerry Pate struck one of the great shots in U.S. Open history when he ripped a five iron through the rough on the right side of the fairway on the 72nd hole at the Atlanta Athletic Club in the 1976 Championship.

"The ball was sitting up a little and I had about 190 yards to the flag," Jerry remembers. "I had to go over water to a well-trapped green. The pin was about 10 yards from the left edge and there was a little left to right wind.

"I had been fading the ball all day, so I set the ball right at the hole. I knew it was going to fly out of the rough and besides, I was pumped up. I hit the ball high and it came out straight. It didn't fade at all. It never left the pin all the way and landed about 15 feet short and rolled up there about three feet from the cup.

"The shot must have shocked a lot of people, because it did shock me," he added, a huge grin breaking across his handsome face. "I hit the perfect shot at the most pressure-packed point of the entire championship."

He made the putt, of course, to win it all.

Hubert Green is another who has struck many outstanding shots that paved the way to victory. However, he remembers the eight iron he hit on the 18th hole at Augusta this year in the Masters. He needed a birdie to tie Player.

"I had about 137 yards to the flag," Hubert said. "It was a great shot that stopped about three feet from the hole. It may not be looked on as that great a shot since I missed the putt, but, in my mind, it was a pressure shot that had to be hit and it came off perfectly. Under the situation, it was my greatest."

Doug Sanders likes to recall the bunker shot he played on the 71st hole of the 1970 British Open at St. Andrews. "I was in position to win, and should have won," he said. "On that hole, I put the ball in the left-side bunker on the downslope. It is such a short bunker you have to get the ball straight up and have it drop straight down.

"My sand wedge had no bounce on it, but I stopped the ball two-and-a-half feet from the hole. I could drop 500 balls there and not do that. If I had gone on to win, it probably would have gone down as one of the greatest bunker shots that has ever been played, anywhere. But, as you know, I missed a putt at the last hole to drop into a tie with Jack Nicklaus and he won the playoff."

But, Doug, like all the others, you'll never forget "The Greatest Shot I've Ever Played."

—Tom Place

LEADING PLAYERS ON THE PGA TOUR

MILLER BARBER

BORN: Mar. 31, 1931, Shreveport, La.

HEIGHT: 5'11"   WEIGHT: 210

RESIDENCE: Sherman, Tex.

FAMILY: Wife, Karen Harrison; Casey (8/24/62); Douglas (8/17/64); Brad (12/16/65); Larry (10/28/71); Richard (6/13/74)

COLLEGE: U. of Arkansas (1954, Business)

SPECIAL INTERESTS: Football

TURNED PROFESSIONAL: 1959   JOINED TOUR: 1959

CAREER EARNINGS THROUGH 1978: $1,351,053   PLAYOFF RECORD: 3–4

TOUR VICTORIES: (TOTAL: 11): **1964** Cajun. **1967** Oklahoma City. **1968** Byron Nelson. **1969** Kaiser. **1970** New Orleans. **1971** Phoenix. **1972** Tucson. **1973** World Open. **1974** Ohio Kings Island. **1977** Anheuser-Busch Classic. **1978** Phoenix Open.

MONEY & POSITION:

1959—$ 2,008—79	1969—$ 90,107—14
1960—$ 2,533—82	1970—$ 99,963—17
1961—$ 3,398—85	1971—$117,359— 6
1962—$ 3,330—95	1972—$ 73,664—31
1963—$ 20,764—38	1973—$184,014— 6
1964—$ 20,234—36	1974—$ 95,207—22
1965—$ 28,183—35	1975—$ 81,993—21
1966—$ 44,168—21	1976—$106,675—23
1967—$ 60,304—17	1977—$148,320— 8
1968—$105,845— 9	1978—$101,189—24

Barber remains one of the busiest players on the tour. In 1976 he played in 34 events and made money in 26, the same number he cashed checks from in 1975 while playing in 33. He hasn't missed the top-60 money list since 1962, his fourth year on tour.

Barber first ventured out on the tour in 1959, but he did not make it a full-time occupation until members of the Apawamis Club in Rye, N.Y., where he was serving as pro, urged him to give it his best effort. Starting in 1963 he never was close to falling out of the top 60.

In 1973 he lost playoffs to Jack Nicklaus at New Orleans and to Bert Greene in the L&M Open, but the year was to wind up as his most lucrative. In the first World Open at Pinehurst, N.C., which carried the first half-million-dollar total purse, Barber won the record $100,000 first prize at the end of 144 holes.

ANDY BEAN

BORN: March 13, 1953, Lafayette, Ga.
HEIGHT: 6'4"   WEIGHT: 210
RESIDENCE: Lakeland, Florida
FAMILY: Wife, Debbie
COLLEGE: Univ. of Florida (1975, Marketing-Business)
SPECIAL INTERESTS: Hunting and fishing
TURNED PROFESSIONAL: 1975   Q. SCHOOL: Fall 1975
CAREER EARNINGS THROUGH 1978: $405,315.   PLAYOFF RECORD: 2–0
TOUR VICTORIES (TOTAL: 4): **1977** Doral-Eastern Open. **1978** Kemper Open, Danny Thomas Memphis Classic, Western Open.
MONEY & POSITION:

1976—$ 10,761—139	1978—$267,241—3
1977—$127,312— 12	

In his first tour victory, at Doral, Andy led all four days on the Blue Monster course, shooting 67-67-71-72—277. The win became a birthday present; he turned 24 on the final day, March 13.

During his rookie year of 1976, Bean's play was disappointing, especially to himself. "It was mainly temperament," he says. "I knew I had the game to play out here, but when I'd make a mistake I'd get hot at myself, and that would make everything worse. I wasn't able to manage my game."

Andy certainly had the background to become a professional golfer. As a youngster, he lived on Jekyll Island, Ga., where his father was associated with a golf course. When he was 15, the family moved to Lakeland, Fla., where his father bought a course.

GEORGE BURNS, III

BORN: July 29, 1949, Brooklyn, N.Y.
HEIGHT: 6'2"   WEIGHT: 210
RESIDENCE: Quail Ridge, Delray Beach, Fla.
FAMILY: Wife, Irene; Kelly Ann (4/2/76)
COLLEGE: Univ. of Maryland (1972, Phys. Ed. & Recreation)
SPECIAL INTERESTS: Traveling, reading
TURNED PROFESSIONAL: 1975   Q. SCHOOL: Fall 1975
CAREER EARNINGS THROUGH 1978: $259,256
TOUR VICTORIES: None
MONEY & POSITION:

1975—$ 6,344—154	1977—$102,026—25
1976—$85,732— 30	1978—$ 71,498—38

Burns was too busy playing all sports in high school on Long Island to concentrate on golf. He lettered in football and basketball and entered the University of Maryland with the primary purpose of playing football, in addition to earning a degree.

He was a defensive end for the Terps, but recalls, "I realized I wasn't going to go anywhere in football." He concentrated on golf from his freshman year forward.

However, it was a full year after his graduation before he blossomed as a force in amateur golf. While working for two years in the New York City area in sales and promotion, he had a chance to play often, and in 1973 he won the Canadian Amateur. The following year Burns won the Porter Cup, North-South Amateur and the New York State Amateur.

REX CALDWELL

BORN: May 5, 1950, Everett, Wash.
HEIGHT: 6'2"   WEIGHT: 177
RESIDENCE: Tallahassee, Fla.
FAMILY: Wife, Marjorie; Michael (1/9/77)
COLLEGE: San Fernando Valley State
SPECIAL INTERESTS: Basketball, jogging
TURNED PROFESSIONAL: 1972   Q. SCHOOL: 1974
CAREER EARNINGS THROUGH 1978: $108,151
TOUR VICTORIES: None
MONEY & POSITION:

1975—$ 3,094—178	1977—$11,693—137
1976—$24,912— 87	1978—$68,451— 42

Caldwell didn't start to play the game until he was 14, but it only took a few trips to the country club with his father to convince him that this was his sport.

He made his Lompoc (Calif.) High School varsity golf team as a sophomore. He went to junior college for two years and then on to San Fernando Valley State College on a golf scholarship. That's when he started to work on his game seriously.

He had dreams of being on the tour, but knew his game wasn't good enough. He worked one summer at the Arnold Palmer Golf Academy in Stratton, Vt., and played the mini-tours for two years. It wasn't until after his second year that he decided to give the tour a try. He entered the 1974 Fall School and made it. In fact, he was leading going into the final round at the Canyon Club in Palm Springs and finished tied for seventh.

BEN CRENSHAW

BORN: Jan. 11, 1952, Austin, Tex.

HEIGHT: 5'9" WEIGHT: 170

RESIDENCE: Austin, Tex.

FAMILY: Wife, Polly

COLLEGE: U. of Texas

SPECIAL INTERESTS: Fishing, bird watching, and collecting golf artifacts

TURNED PROFESSIONAL: 1973 Q. SCHOOL: 1973

CAREER EARNINGS THROUGH 1978: $696,633 PLAYOFF RECORD: 0–1

TOUR VICTORIES (TOTAL: 6): **1973** San Antonio–Texas Open. **1976** Bing Crosby National Pro-Am, Hawaiian Open, Ohio Kings Island Open. **1977** Colonial Invitational. **1979** Phoenix Open.

MONEY & POSITION:

1973—$76,749—34	1976—$257,759— 2
1974—$71,065—31	1977—$123,841—16
1975—$63,528—32	1978—$108,305—21

Crenshaw came to the tour in the fall of 1973 after compiling an amateur record seldom authored by anyone. It didn't include the U.S. Amateur title, but he did win the NCAA championship three years running, sharing it with U. of Texas teammate Tom Kite in 1972.

In his first appearance after earning his approved Tournament Player's card for the PGA Tour, he won the San Antonio–Texas Open. He followed with a second place in the 1973 World Open, then a 144-hole, $500,000 event, and wound up the short year with more than $76,000 earned in only nine tournaments. He also averaged 69.9 strokes for 42 competitive rounds.

He was winless the next two years while undergoing a thorough examination of his long swing, but he placed in the top 10 in three 1974 events, and in 1975 he finished only a shot back in the U.S. Open at Medinah after his two iron from the 71st tee splashed in the lake and resulted in a double-bogey five.

DAVE EICHELBERGER

BORN: Sept. 3, 1943, Waco, Tex.

HEIGHT: 6'1" WEIGHT: 180

RESIDENCE: Fort Worth, Tex.

FAMILY: Wife, Linda; Laura (5/6/68); Martin 9/28/69); Clinton (3/14/73)

COLLEGE: Oklahoma State U. (1965, Business Administration)

TURNED PROFESSIONAL: 1966 Q. SCHOOL: 1967

CAREER EARNINGS THROUGH 1978: $440,653 PLAYOFF RECORD: 0–1

TOUR VICTORIES (TOTAL: 2): **1971** Greater Milwaukee. **1977** Greater Milwaukee.

MONEY & POSITION:

1967—$ 3,076—143	1973—$60,515— 49
1968—$ 15,473— 95	1974—$33,640— 79
1969—$ 9,423—132	1975—$12,780—117
1970—$ 23,455— 88	1976—$25,780— 86
1971—$108,312— 9	1977—$59,702— 51
1972—$ 37,543— 67	1978—$63,405— 49

Dave Eichelberger is proud to be a Texan, but he will always have a special place in his heart for Milwaukee.

He has won two events since joining the PGA Tour in 1967 and both were the Greater Milwaukee Open, in 1971 and in 1977. In the years around those victories, he admits he has had to do some struggling.

Dave started in the game at age 13 in the junior program at his family's club in Waco, Texas. It wasn't until he went on to Oklahoma State University that he decided that he wanted to make a career in the game.

LEE ELDER

BORN: July 14, 1934, Dallas, Tex.

HEIGHT: 5'8" WEIGHT: 175

RESIDENCE: Washington, D.C.

FAMILY: Wife, Rose

SPECIAL INTERESTS: Football and tennis

TURNED PROFESSIONAL: 1959 Q. SCHOOL: 1967

CAREER EARNINGS THROUGH 1978: $733,537 PLAYOFF RECORD: 2–2

TOUR VICTORIES (TOTAL: 4): **1974** Monsanto. **1976** Houston Open. **1978** Greater Milwaukee Open, Westchester Classic.

MONEY & POSITION:

1968—$31,691—54	1974—$ 71,986—30
1969—$53,679—38	1975—$ 26,809—81
1970—$20,734—93	1976—$113,263—21
1971—$49,933—49	1977—$ 75,945—41
1972—$70,401—32	1978—$152,198—13
1973—$84,730—30	

Lee Elder enjoyed his finest season on the PGA Tour in 1978. In truth, however, Lee's season boiled down to an absolutely torrid stretch in July and August, during which he won two events and earned more than $116,000.

Elder qualified for the PGA Tour in the fall of 1967 and in his first full year he caused a stir by tying for first in the American Golf Classic and taking Jack Nicklaus to the fifth extra hole before losing.

RAY FLOYD

BORN: Sept. 4, 1942, Fort Bragg, N.C.
HEIGHT: 6'1" WEIGHT: 200
RESIDENCE: Miami, Fla.
FAMILY: Wife, Maria; Raymond, Jr. (9/20/74); Robert Loran (1/23/76)
COLLEGE: U. of North Carolina
TURNED PROFESSIONAL: 1961 JOINED TOUR: 1963
CAREER EARNINGS THROUGH 1978: $1,116,763 PLAYOFF RECORD: 2–4
TOUR VICTORIES (TOTAL: 11): **1963** St. Petersburg Open. **1965** St. Paul Open. **1969** Jacksonville Open, American Golf Classic, PGA Championship. **1975** Kemper Open. **1976** Masters, World Open. **1977** Byron Nelson Classic, Pleasant Valley Classic. **1979** Greensboro Open

MONEY & POSITION:

1963—$ 10,529—58		1971—$ 70,607—32
1964—$ 21,407—30		1972—$ 35,624—70
1965—$ 36,692—25		1973—$ 39,646—77
1966—$ 29,712—32		1974—$119,385—18
1967—$ 25,254—47		1975—$103,627—13
1968—$ 63,002—24		1976—$178,318— 7
1969—$109,957— 8		1977—$163,261— 7
1970—$ 47,632—24		1978—$ 77,595—30

Floyd grew up in Ft. Bragg, N.C., the son of an Army man who is now co-owner of the Cypress Lakes Club in Fayetteville. Although he was exposed to golf at an early age, Ray almost chose to pursue baseball, until he won the National Jaycees Junior Golf Title in 1960. He turned pro the following year, joined the tour in 1963, won the St. Petersburg Open as a rookie and only twice has failed to finish among the top 60 money-winners since.

In 1972 and 1973 Raymond was in a slump, but he rebounded smartly with more than $100,000 in earnings in 1974 and then started to win again. Perhaps his most notable victory was in the 1976 Masters. Raymond won it by eight strokes, tying Jack Nicklaus' tournament record of 17-under 271.

ROD FUNSETH

BORN: Apr. 3, 1933, Spokane, Wash.
HEIGHT: 5'10" WEIGHT: 170
RESIDENCE: Napa, Calif.
FAMILY: Wife, Sandi; Lisa Ann (11/16/66); Mark Robert (11/11/67)
COLLEGE: U. of Idaho
SPECIAL INTERESTS: Fishing, horses
TURNED PROFESSIONAL: 1956 JOINED TOUR: 1961
CAREER EARNINGS THROUGH 1978: $595,627 PLAYOFF RECORD: 0–1
TOUR VICTORIES (TOTAL: 3): **1965** Phoenix. **1973** Glen Campbell Los Angeles Open. **1978** SDJ–Greater Hartford Open.

MONEY & POSITION:

1961—$ 1,495—114		1970—$44,972—53
1962—$ 2,806—101		1971—$63,567—34
1963—$ 5,378— 80		1972—$48,238—52
1964—$10,620— 65		1973—$89,145—29
1965—$30,647— 30		1974—$27,507—89
1966—$19,011— 55		1975—$48,453—49
1967—$23,604— 51		1976—$32,800—73
1968—$27,011— 66		1977—$25,400—92
1969—$33,111— 59		1978—$83,731—28

Funseth worked as an assistant pro for five years before joining the tour in 1961, and it was another four years before he garnered his first victory—the 1965 Phoenix Open—and made it to the top 60. From that year through 1973, a season he started by winning the Glen Campbell Los Angeles Open, he dropped out of the top 60 just once.

When he finished second in the 1978 Masters, it was further proof to many that this soft-spoken Californian always plays the tough courses well—but not well enough to win. He was a fellow, they said, who could keep it around par on any course; thus, his history of good finishes at venues where higher scores are the order.

But Rod fooled them all by winning the Sammy Davis, Jr.–Greater Hartford on a Wethersfield C.C. layout where even-par in 1978 meant a tie for 73rd and no check. Funseth not only paced the field by four strokes to claim the $42,000 winner's reward, but he did so with the lowest score of the year on the PGA Tour.

AL GEIBERGER

BORN: Sept. 1, 1937, Red Bluff, Calif.
HEIGHT: 6'2" WEIGHT: 170
RESIDENCE: Santa Barbara, Calif.
FAMILY: Wife, Lynn Butler; Lee Ann (9/14/63); John (5/20/68); Robby (10/11/63); Bryan (9/28/76)
COLLEGE: U. of So. Calif. (1959, Business)
SPECIAL INTERESTS: Photography, tennis
TURNED PROFESSIONAL: 1959 JOINED TOUR: 1960
CAREER EARNINGS THROUGH 1978: $1,098,449 PLAYOFF RECORD: 1–1
TOUR VICTORIES (TOTAL: 11): **1962** Caracas Open, Ontario Open. **1963** Almaden Open. **1965** American Golf Classic. **1966** PGA Championship. **1974** Sahara. **1975** Tournament of Champions, Tournament Players Championship. **1976** Greater Greensboro Open, Western Open. **1977** Danny Thomas Memphis Classic.

MONEY & POSITION:

1960—$10,511—37	1970—$ 21,233— 91
1961—$18,656—30	1971—$ 20,848— 99
1962—$26,045—20	1972—$ 29,710— 80
1963—$34,126— 8	1973—$ 63,467— 45
1964—$36,323—13	1974—$ 91,628— 23
1965—$59,699— 8	1975—$175,693— 6
1966—$63,220—10	1976—$194,821— 5
1967—$63,315—14	1977—$ 88,645— 30
1968—$64,931—22	1978—$ 20,477—107
1969—$26,868—65	

In January 1978, Al Geiberger underwent surgery for the removal of a growth in the lower-intestine area. Fortunately, the growth was benign, yet Al was unable to rejoin the PGA tour until the Greater Greensboro Open in April.

Though Geiberger's showing at Greensboro was certainly respectable—he shot even-par 288 to finish tied for 28th—it became evident as the year wore on that Al was not in top form. He never placed in the top ten and, though he was in the money in nearly every tournament he entered, his earnings dipped substantially in this curtailed campaign.

An off-year could not overshadow, however, Geiberger's record-smashing achievement of 1977, when he shot the lowest score in the history of the PGA tour. That incredible 59, carded in the second round of the Danny Thomas Memphis Classic (June 10), included 11 birdies, one eagle and six pars.

His victory in the 1966 PGA Championship at Firestone, where he won by a comfortable four-stroke margin, is not easily forgotten, either. But after gaining that title, Al endured a succession of personal and physical problems, the latter sending him home to California for long periods.

GIBBY GILBERT

BORN: Jan. 14, 1941, Chattanooga, Tenn.
HEIGHT: 5′9″ WEIGHT: 185
RESIDENCE: Chattanooga, Tenn.
FAMILY: Wife, Judy; Jeff (11/14/63); Gibby (10/21/66); Mark (5/31/70)
SPECIAL INTERESTS: Fishing, hunting
TURNED PROFESSIONAL: 1964 Q. SCHOOL: 1967
CAREER EARNINGS THROUGH 1978: $543,773 PLAYOFF RECORD: 1–0
TOUR VICTORIES (TOTAL: 3): **1970** Houston. **1976** Danny Thomas–Memphis Classic. **1977** Disney World National Team Play (with Grier Jones).
MONEY & POSITION:

1968—$ 1,752—203	1974—$69,992—33
1969—$ 2,814—197	1975—$56,279—38
1970—$65,618— 27	1976—$97,476—25
1971—$62,501— 35	1977—$27,892—88
1972—$34,144— 73	1978—$72,758—35
1973—$60,636— 48	

Despite the lack of a given name, Gibby began to make a name for himself in golf early in his native Chattanooga, after taking up the game at age 13. In 1962 he quit the University of Chattanooga, married and two years later became an assistant pro in Hollywood, Fla.

Gilbert finished second to Bobby Cole in the 1967 Qualifying School but struggled for 2½ years before winning the Houston Champions tournament.

In 1971 he recorded six straight birdies in the Westchester Classic and finished the year again over the $60,000 level. But he slipped badly in 1972, and by the following spring he was considering giving up the tour, when his play improved suddenly.

A highlight of 1973 was a course-record 62 at Pinehurst No. 2 during the World Open. It shattered the record on the famed course by three strokes, although Tom Watson matched it a week later during the 144-hole event.

BOB GILDER

BORN: Dec. 31, 1950, Corvallis, Ore.
HEIGHT: 5′9½″ WEIGHT: 165
RESIDENCE: Corvallis, Ore.
FAMILY: Wife, Peggy; Bryan, (3/24/75); Cammy Lynn (6/10/77)
COLLEGE: Arizona State (1973, Business Administration)
SPECIAL INTERESTS: All sports
TURNED PROFESSIONAL: 1973 Q. SCHOOL: Fall 1975
CAREER EARNINGS THROUGH 1978: $211,527
TOUR VICTORIES (TOTAL: 1): **1976** Phoenix Open.
MONEY & POSITION:

1975—$ 905—224	1977—$36,844—72
1976—$101,262— 24	1978—$72,515—36

It took Bob Gilder three years to qualify for the PGA tour, but once he made it, he let everyone know he was here to stay. He won the second tournament of his rookie year, the 1976 Phoenix Open, and went on to become only the fourth first-year player to break the $100,000 mark.

Bob starred for the Arizona State golf team and was a teammate of tour regulars Tom Purtzer, Howard Twitty, and Morris Hatalsky. After he was graduated in 1973, he tried for his tour card three times without success. Meanwhile, in 1974 he went "down under" and won the New Zealand Open in a playoff over Bob Charles and Jack Newton.

DAVID GRAHAM

BORN: May 23, 1946, Windsor, Australia
HEIGHT: 5′10″ WEIGHT: 162
RESIDENCE: The Hamlet, Delray Beach, Fla.
FAMILY: Wife, Maureen Burdett; Andrew (11/8/74); Michael (10/8/77)

SPECIAL INTERESTS: Hunting, golf club design
TURNED PROFESSIONAL: 1962   Q. SCHOOL: 1971
CAREER EARNINGS THROUGH 1978: $525,093   PLAYOFF
RECORD: 1–1

TOUR VICTORIES (TOTAL: 3): **1972** Cleveland. **1976** Westchester, American Golf Classic.

MONEY & POSITION:

1971—$10,062—135		1975—$ 51,642—44	
1972—$57,827— 38		1976—$176,174— 8	
1973—$43,062— 71		1977—$ 72,086—44	
1974—$61,625— 41		1978—$ 66,909—43	

OTHER ACHIEVEMENTS: Winner 1970 World Cup team championship (with Bruce Devlin) for Australia. Foreign victories include 1970 French Open, 1970 Thailand Open, 1971 Caracas Open, 1971 Japan Open, 1975 Wills Masters, 1976 Chunichi Crowns Invitational (Japan), 1976 Picadilly World Match Play, 1977 Australian Open and 1977 South African PGA.

Graham was only 16 when he turned pro, but his tournament career did not begin until the late 1960s in his native Australia and on the Far East circuit. A tournament-record 62 helped him tie for first in the 1969 Singapore Open but he lost the playoff. He came to America the following year and failed to earn his playing card at the 1970 Qualifying School, but the very next week he and Bruce Devlin won the World Cup for Australia.

In 1971, in addition to winning the Caracas Open and the Japan Air Lines Open, Graham succeeded in the Tour School. In his rookie year of 1972, a full decade after turning pro, he won the Cleveland Open by beating Devlin on the second playoff hole.

LOU GRAHAM

BORN: Jan. 7, 1938, Nashville, Tenn.
HEIGHT: 6'   WEIGHT: 175
RESIDENCE: Nashville, Tenn.
FAMILY: Wife, Patsy; Louann (4/1/61); Phyllis (10/4/62)
COLLEGE: Memphis State U.
TURNED PROFESSIONAL: 1962   JOINED TOUR: 1964
CAREER EARNINGS THROUGH 1978: $959,145   PLAYOFF
RECORD: 2–1

TOUR VICTORIES (TOTAL: 3): **1967** Minnesota Classic. **1972** Liggett & Myers. **1975** U.S. Open.

MONEY & POSITION:

1964—$ 2,322—130		1972—$ 96,077—19	
1965—$11,093— 73		1973—$ 94,854—19	
1966—$11,312— 79		1974—$ 74,898—29	
1967—$42,556— 27		1975—$ 96,425—15	
1968—$36,108— 47		1976—$107,008—22	
1969—$27,208— 68		1977—$128,676—11	
1970—$53,665— 37		1978—$105,617—23	
1971—$82,575— 23			

Graham turned pro after discharge from the Army in 1962 and worked at two clubs near Baltimore before striking out on the tour in 1964. He won his first tour event, the Minnesota Classic, three years later and only once since then, when he needed surgery to repair tendonitis in his left hand in 1969, has he failed to finish among the top 60 money-winners.

HUBERT GREEN

BORN: Dec. 28, 1946, Birmingham, Ala.
HEIGHT: 6'1"   WEIGHT: 180
RESIDENCE: Shoal Creek, Ala.
FAMILY: Wife, Karen; Patrick (10/17/78)
COLLEGE: Florida State U. (1968)
SPECIAL INTERESTS: Bridge, fishing
TURNED PROFESSIONAL: 1970   Q. SCHOOL: 1970
CAREER EARNINGS THROUGH 1978: $1,143,102   PLAYOFF RECORD: 2–2

TOUR VICTORIES (TOTAL: 16): **1971** Houston. **1973** Tallahassee Open, B.C. Open. **1974** Bob Hope, Gr. Jacksonville, Philadelphia, Disney. **1975** Southern Open. **1976** Doral-Eastern, Jacksonville Open, Sea Pines Heritage Classic. **1977** U.S. Open. **1978** Hawaiian Open, Sea Pines Heritage Classic. **1979** Hawaiian Open, New Orleans Open.

MONEY & POSITION:

1970—$ 1,690—218		1975—$113,569—12	
1971—$ 73,439— 29		1976—$228,031— 4	
1972—$ 44,113— 58		1977—$140,255— 9	
1973—$114,397— 11		1978—$247,406— 5	
1974—$211,709— 3			

Green was never out of first place in the 77th U.S. Open Championship at Southern Hills in Tulsa, and millions recall that he beat Lou Graham by a stroke after playing the final four holes knowing there had been a telephoned threat to his life.

JAY HAAS

BORN: Dec. 2, 1953, St. Louis, Mo.
HEIGHT: 5'10½" WEIGHT: 160
RESIDENCE: Belleville, Ill.
FAMILY: Wife, Janice
COLLEGE: Wake Forest
SPECIAL INTERESTS: All sports
TURNED PROFESSIONAL: 1976 Q. SCHOOL: Fall 1976
CAREER EARNINGS THROUGH 1978: $109,502
TOUR VICTORIES (TOTAL: 1): **1978** Andy Williams–San Diego Open.
MONEY & POSITION:
1977—$32,326—77   1978—$77,176—31

It was a foregone conclusion that Jay Haas would become a professional golfer. His uncle, Bob Goalby, started him in the game at an early age and helped him through every stage of his career.

Jay was seven when he played in his first tournament —and won his first trophy. It was the National Pee Wee championship in Orlando, Fla. "We played five holes each day and I scored 26-26—52 to finish third," he said.

Under the tutelage of Goalby, Jay went on to win the Illinois state high school championship in 1972 and then headed for Wake Forest. His junior year was the big one. "I had one stretch when I played some of the best golf of my life," he said. It started with him winning three of his Walker Cup matches, then advancing to the fifth round of the British Amateur; the third week he was low amateur in the U.S. Open at Medinah; and finally, he won the NCAA championship at Ohio State University.

PHIL HANCOCK

BORN: October 30, 1953, Greenville, Ala.
HEIGHT: 5'10" WEIGHT: 160
RESIDENCE: Pensacola, Fla.
FAMILY: Wife, Kitty
COLLEGE: U. of Florida (1976, Journalism)
SPECIAL INTERESTS: Fishing, all sports
TURNED PROFESSIONAL: 1976 Q. SCHOOL: Spring 1977
CAREER EARNINGS THROUGH 1978: $91,526
TOUR VICTORIES: None
MONEY & POSITION:
1977—$24,450—95   1978—$66,460—44

Phil Hancock enjoyed his days of glory while playing varsity football and basketball at Greenville High in Alabama, but there never was any doubt in his mind which sport was number one. It was golf, all the way.

"I enjoyed the other sports," Phil says, "but I knew golf would be my sport in college and that one day I would turn professional."

He started to play golf as a nine-year-old through the encouragement of his father and an older brother and has been successful all along the way. He won both the Alabama State Junior and Amateur crowns; went on to the University of Florida and twice won the Southeastern Conference title. While at Florida, he was a teammate of Andy Bean and Gary Koch.

MARK HAYES

BORN: July 12, 1949, Stillwater, Okla.
HEIGHT: 5'11" WEIGHT: 170
RESIDENCE: Edmond, Okla.; plays out of Oak Tree G.C.
FAMILY: Wife, Jana
COLLEGE: Oklahoma State U.
SPECIAL INTERESTS: Fishing
TURNED PROFESSIONAL: 1973 Q. SCHOOL: 1973
CAREER EARNINGS THROUGH 1978: $510,754
TOUR VICTORIES (TOTAL: 3): **1976** Byron Nelson Golf Classic, Pensacola Open. **1977** Tournament Players Championship.
MONEY & POSITION:
1973—$ 8,637—160   1976—$151,699—11
1974—$40,620— 68   1977—$115,749—19
1975—$49,297— 47   1978—$146,456—15

Hayes arrived on the PGA tour in the fall of 1973 and he arrived as a genuine star in his third full year on the circuit, 1976, when he led the Byron Nelson Classic from the opening bell, playing the first 43 holes without a bogey. He also won the Pensacola Open that year.

Mark's most recent victory was also his most significant. In a gutsy finish, Hayes won the 1977 Tournament Players Championship and the 10-year exemption and $60,000 first prize that go with the title. His highest round of the tournament was a two-over 74 on the second day, but in the gale winds of that Friday at Sawgrass a 74 was remarkable. Mark was a stroke behind co-leaders Tom Watson and Mike McCullough starting the last round, and shot 72 to win by a pair.

Mark started playing golf at age six under the eye of his father, a high school physical education teacher and golf coach. Not many years passed before he picked out his career. "One of the reasons I was so dedicated," Hayes said not long ago, "was that I was small for my age and couldn't do anything else. I practiced every day. I never thought of doing anything else for a living but play golf."

JERRY HEARD

BORN: May 1, 1947, Visalia, Calif.
HEIGHT: 6' WEIGHT: 190
RESIDENCE: Visalia, Calif.
COLLEGE: Fresno State
SPECIAL INTERESTS: Trout fishing and duck hunting
TURNED PROFESSIONAL: 1968 Q. SCHOOL: Fall 1968
CAREER EARNINGS THROUGH 1978: $732,024 PLAYOFF RECORD: 0–1

TOUR VICTORIES (TOTAL: 5): **1971** American Golf Classic. **1972** Florida Citrus, Colonial. **1974** Florida Citrus. **1978** Atlanta Classic.

MONEY & POSITION:

1969—$ 10,236—129	1974—$145,788— 8
1970—$ 44,919— 54	1975—$ 81,687— 22
1971—$112,389— 7	1976—$ 28,236— 79
1972—$137,198— 5	1977—$ 5,955—173
1973—$ 94,223— 20	1978—$ 79,511— 29

Heard began playing golf at age 11, and he was scoring around par a year later, the result of constant practice on a municipal course operated by his father in California. He dropped out of Fresno State College in 1968 in order to try the Tour Qualifying School. He passed, and he earned barely $10,000 in his rookie year of 1969.

Heard started out 1970 by earning $133 in his first five events, but his game improved suddenly and he recorded five top 10 finishes and crashed the top 60 money list.

He won four tournaments in the next four years and topped $100,000 each year he won, including the two-victory year of 1972.

DAVE HILL

BORN: May 20, 1937, Jackson, Mich.

HEIGHT: 5′11″ WEIGHT: 145

RESIDENCE: Denver, Colo.

FAMILY: Wife, Sandie

SPECIAL INTERESTS: Hunting, records, bridge

TURNED PROFESSIONAL: 1958 JOINED TOUR: 1959

CAREER EARNINGS THROUGH 1978: $1,059,679 PLAYOFF RECORD: 4–2

TOUR VICTORIES (TOTAL: 13): **1961** Home of the Sun Open, Denver. **1963** Hot Springs. **1967** Memphis. **1969** Memphis, Buick, Philadelphia. **1970** Memphis. **1972** Monsanto. **1973** Danny Thomas–Memphis. **1974** Houston. **1975** Sahara Invitational. **1976** Greater Milwaukee Open.

MONEY & POSITION:

1959—$ 1,655—84	1969—$156,423— 2
1960—$ 7,424—46	1970—$118,415— 10
1961—$21,560—22	1971—$ 61,410— 36
1962—$22,731—25	1972—$ 98,464— 18
1963—$18,906—25	1973—$ 95,574— 17
1964—$13,333—56	1974—$133,674— 11
1965—$14,674—58	1975—$ 80,533— 24
1966—$26,857—35	1976—$116,606— 19
1967—$49,774—23	1977—$ 17,058—116
1968—$34,036—48	1978—$ 3,781—177

One year after Dave joined the PGA tour in 1959, he climbed into the top 60 money list and was to remain there for 17 straight years. Ten years after coming on the tour he won three tournaments, finished second to Frank Beard in the money rankings and won the Var-

don Trophy for 1969 with a stroke average of 70.344 for 90 rounds.

He won $100,000 again in 1970, then began to reduce his playing schedule. He limited his appearances still further in 1972 but he played more efficiently, winning the Monsanto Open and placing in the top 10 in seven other events.

In 1973, Hill won at Memphis for the fourth time and recorded nine top-10 finishes, missed the cut only once and qualified for his second Ryder Cup team. Dave underwent surgery in late 1973 for removal of cartilage in a knee which had troubled him for some time, and that decision probably contributed to his second most profitable year in 1974, when he won at Houston.

LON HINKLE

BORN: July 17, 1949, Flint, Mich.

HEIGHT: 6′2″ WEIGHT: 215

RESIDENCE: Dallas, Tex.

FAMILY: Wife, Edith; Monique (8/10/78)

COLLEGE: San Diego State (1972)

SPECIAL INTERESTS: Reading

TURNED PROFESSIONAL: 1972 Q. SCHOOL: 1972

CAREER EARNINGS THROUGH 1978: $229,939 PLAYOFF RECORD: 1–1

TOUR VICTORIES (TOTAL: 2): **1978** New Orleans Open. **1979** Bing Crosby Pro Am.

MONEY & POSITION:

1972—$7,350—145	1976—$ 11,058—138
1973—$7,539—164	1977—$ 51,494— 60
1974—$6,509—162	1978—$138,388— 16
1975—$8,420—136	

Hinkle's improvement over the last few seasons has come in quantum leaps and bounds. During his first five years on the PGA tour, Lon lolled in the lower depths of the money list. In 1977, when he won more than $51,000 and squeaked into the top 60, things started to roll.

Lon started in the game at age 13, shortly after his family moved from Granville, Ohio, to the San Diego area. "I was a good baseball player," he says, "but I started to have trouble with my eyes, so I switched to golf. I'd play all day, whenever I could. I loved it."

He was the oldest of seven children, and his entire family played in those days; in junior tournaments around Southern California, it wasn't unusual to find half a dozen Hinkles in the field.

HALE IRWIN

BORN: June 3, 1945, Joplin, Mo.

HEIGHT: 6′ WEIGHT: 170

RESIDENCE: Frontenac, Mo.

FAMILY: Wife, Sally Stahlhuth; Becky (12/15/71); Steven Hale (8/6/74)

COLLEGE: U. of Colorado (1968, Marketing)
SPECIAL INTERESTS: Fishing, hunting, photography
TURNED PROFESSIONAL: 1968   Q. SCHOOL: 1968
CAREER EARNINGS THROUGH 1978: $1,425,896
TOUR VICTORIES (TOTAL: 11): **1971** Heritage. **1973** Heritage. **1974** U.S. Open. **1975** Western Open, Atlanta Golf Classic. **1976** Glen Campbell–Los Angeles, Florida Citrus. **1977** Atlanta Golf Classic, Hall of Fame, San Antonio-Texas. **1979** U.S. Open.

MONEY & POSITION:

1968—$ 9,093—117		1974—$152,529—7
1969—$ 18,571— 88		1975—$205,380—4
1970—$ 46,870— 49		1976—$252,718—3
1971—$ 99,473— 13		1977—$221,456—4
1972—$111,539— 13		1978—$191,666—7
1973—$130,388— 7		

Irwin left the University of Colorado in 1968 with a degree in marketing, an NCAA golf title and the honor of having been selected twice as an All-Big Eight Conference defensive back. He joined the PGA Tour that fall and climbed steadily on the money list each year through 1976.

Although he twice won the Heritage Classic on the demanding Harbour Town Links on Hilton Head Island, S.C., Hale was among the less familiar U.S. Open champions when he captured that major championship in 1974 at Winged Foot.

In 1975 he won his first Atlanta Classic and also the Western Open at Butler National. In 1976 he won two weeks apart, at Los Angeles and Orlando. His second place in the 1976 World Series lifted him over $1 million in career earnings.

Perhaps 1977 was Hale's most satisfying of 10 years on the tour. He won three tournaments—a personal high—and his most notable performance came in the Colgate Hall of Fame Classic. In that event, Irwin devastated Pinehurst's revered No. 2 course in a record smashing 264—20 under par—to win by five strokes.

He also passed the $200,000 mark for the third consecutive time, a feat equaled in the same years by just one other player, Jack Nicklaus.

BARRY JAECKEL

BORN: Feb. 14, 1949, Los Angeles, Calif.
HEIGHT: 5'10½"   WEIGHT: 160
RESIDENCE: Los Angeles, Calif.
COLLEGE: Santa Monica College
SPECIAL INTERESTS: Surfing, antiques, UCLA basketball
TURNED PROFESSIONAL: 1971   Q. SCHOOL: Spring 1975
CAREER EARNINGS THROUGH 1978: $137,696   PLAYOFF RECORD: 1–0
TOUR VICTORIES (TOTAL: 1): **1978** Tallahassee Open.
MONEY & POSITION:

1975—$ 8,883—133	1977—$19,504—108
1976—$36,888— 70	1978—$72,421— 37

One of the truisms of golf holds that it is impossible to play well in a PGA tour event when it is competed in the player's hometown. Barry Jaeckel proved to be an exception to that rule in the 1978 Glen Campbell Los Angeles Open.

Playing before family, friends and fellow club members at Riviera Country Club, Barry scored 285 and tied for fourth place. It was his highest finish in a PGA Tour event—he pocketed a check for $7,800—since he earned his playing privileges in the 1975 Spring Qualifying School. The week's experience boosted his confidence.

He played well the following week in the Jackie Gleason Inverrary Classic and again in the Sea Pines Heritage and Greater Greensboro Open. He capped the year by winning the 1978 Tallahassee Open.

He is the son of Richard Jaeckel, a character actor who has had roles in dozens of movies and many television series.

DON JANUARY

BORN: Nov. 20, 1929, Plainview, Tex.
HEIGHT: 6'   WEIGHT: 165
RESIDENCE: Dallas, Tex.
FAMILY: Wife, Patricia; Timothy (11/15/54); Cherie Lynn (7/8/58); Richard (9/25/61)
COLLEGE: North Texas State U. (1953)
TURNED PROFESSIONAL: 1955   JOINED TOUR: 1956
CAREER EARNINGS THROUGH 1978: $945,231   PLAYOFF RECORD: 3–5
TOUR VICTORIES (TOTAL: 12): **1956** Dallas Open, Apple Valley Clambake Championship. **1959** Valencia Open. **1960** Tucson Open. **1961** St. Paul Open. **1963** Tucson Open. **1966** Philadelphia Golf Classic. **1967** PGA Championship. **1968** Tournament of Champions. **1970** Jacksonville Open. **1975** San Antonio–Texas Open. **1976** Tournament of Champions.

MONEY & POSITION:

1956—$17,731—16	1967—$ 61,103— 15
1957—$ 4,540—47	1968—$ 61,732— 25
1958—$13,337—25	1969—$ 65,631— 27
1959—$12,956—29	1970—$ 49,116— 46
1960—$23,319—16	1971—$ 66,388— 33
1961—$24,108—16	1972—$ 25,833— 89
1962—$21,384—28	1973—$ 3,971—200
1963—$33,754— 9	1975—$ 69,034— 30
1964—$22,339—27	1976—$163,622— 9
1965—$28,540—33	1977—$ 73,715— 43
1966—$55,280—11	1978—$ 52,703— 62

In 1972, Don left the tour to devote his time to golf course construction in the Dallas area. When financing became difficult during the recession, he rejoined the tour in 1975, soon after his 45th birthday. His remarkable comeback season was highlighted in his home state, when he defeated Larry Hinson in a playoff to win the San Antonio–Texas Open.

GRIER JONES

BORN: May 6, 1946, Wichita, Kan.
HEIGHT: 5'10" WEIGHT: 165
RESIDENCE: Wichita, Kan.
FAMILY: Wife, Jane; Carey and Corey (2/26/68); Grier (5/17/71); Casey (9/9/72); Brian (9/13/75)
COLLEGE: Oklahoma State U. (1968)
TURNED PROFESSIONAL: 1968 Q. SCHOOL: Fall 1968
CAREER EARNINGS THROUGH 1978: $631,065 PLAYOFF RECORD: 2–0
TOUR VICTORIES (TOTAL: 3): **1972** Hawaiian Open, Robinson Fall Golf Classic. **1977** Disney Team Championship (with Gibby Gilbert).

MONEY & POSITION:

1968—$ 1,313—223	1974—$54,861— 50
1969—$ 37,194— 50	1975—$15,719—112
1970—$ 55,913— 36	1976—$69,087— 40
1971—$ 30,929— 72	1977—$80,021— 35
1972—$140,177— 4	1978—$76,930— 32
1973—$ 83,871— 31	

Jones arrived on the tour in 1968 with impressive credentials. While at Oklahoma State, he won the 1966 NCAA championship, the Big Eight Conference title, the Oklahoma Intercollegiate and the Oklahoma Invitational. He led the Fall 1968 Qualifying School and in 1969 was named Rookie of the Year with more than $37,000 in earnings.

Two of Grier's tour wins came in 1972 after playoffs: he defeated Bob Murphy in the Hawaiian Open and Dave Marad in the Robinson Classic. After topping $140,000 that year, he began suffering physical problems with his back and right hand. In one stretch in the summer of 1974 he was forced to withdraw from six of seven tournaments. In 1975, he missed 10 weeks after catching pneumonia the week following the PGA Championship.

TOM KITE

BORN: Dec. 9, 1949, Austin, Tex.
HEIGHT: 5'8½" WEIGHT: 153
RESIDENCE: Austin, Tex.
FAMILY: Wife, Christy
COLLEGE: U. of Texas
SPECIAL INTERESTS: Fishing, golf club repair
TURNED PROFESSIONAL: 1972 Q. SCHOOL: 1972
CAREER EARNINGS THROUGH 1978: $624,680 PLAYOFF RECORD: 1–0
TOUR VICTORIES (TOTAL: 2): **1976** IVB–Bicentennial Golf Classic. **1978** B.C. Open

MONEY & POSITION:

1972—$ 2,582—233	1976—$116,180—21
1973—$54,270— 56	1977—$125,204—14
1974—$82,055— 26	1978—$161,370—11
1975—$87,045— 18	

Kite's life in golf began at age six, when his father put a club in his hand for the first time and urged him to take a swipe. At 11 he won his first tournament, an age-group event at the Country Club of Austin, Tex. He began to take the game seriously three years later.

Before his 21st birthday in 1970, Tom was medalist in the Western Amateur, runner-up to Lanny Wadkins in the U.S. Amateur, second in the Southern Amateur and was named to the four-man U.S. team in the World Amateur Team Championship.

The following year he was chosen on the U.S. Walker Cup team and, in 1972, he shared the NCAA title with his U. of Texas schoolmate, Ben Crenshaw, before turning pro and joining the Tour. In 1973, Tom won the Hope of Tomorrow second-tour event and was named Rookie of the Year after missing the cut in only three of 35 events.

BILL KRATZERT

BORN: June 29, 1952, Quantico, Va.
HEIGHT: 6' WEIGHT: 190
RESIDENCE: Fort Wayne, Ind.

FAMILY: Wife, Cheryl Ann; Rebecca Brea (9/6/78)
COLLEGE: U. of Georgia (1974, General Business)
SPECIAL INTERESTS: Following all sports
TURNED PROFESSIONAL: 1974   Q. SCHOOL: Spring 1976
CAREER EARNINGS THROUGH 1978: $339,695   PLAYOFF
RECORD: 1–1

TOUR VICTORIES (TOTAL: 2): **1976** Walt Disney World National Team Play (with Woody Blackburn). **1977** Greater Hartford Open.

MONEY & POSITION:
1976—$ 21,253—102   1978—$183,683—8
1977—$134,758— 10

Kratzert was practically born into the game, the son of the head pro at Fort Wayne, Ind., C.C. for the last 19 years. "I didn't start to play until I was about 13," Bill says. "My dad never pushed me into it. It was just always there. It wasn't until I `was 14 or 15 years old that I decided that golf was my game."

He won the Indiana State Amateur at age 16 and the Indiana Open a year later. Allen Miller, who befriended Bill when he became ill during the Sunnehanna Amateur, influenced him to going to the University of Georgia, where he was chosen All-Southeastern Conference all four years and All-American his last two.

After he failed in his first try in the Tour Qualifying School, Kratzert quit the game in frustration, went home to Fort Wayne and worked six months as a forklift operator. But in the spring of 1975 he accepted an assistant pro's job at a club and returned to the game to stay.

BRUCE LIETZKE

BORN: July 18, 1951, Kansas City, Kan.
HEIGHT: 6'2"   WEIGHT: 195
RESIDENCE: Beaumont, Tex.
COLLEGE: U. of Houston
SPECIAL INTERESTS: Fishing, racing cars
TURNED PROFESSIONAL: 1974   Q. SCHOOL: Spring 1975
CAREER EARNINGS THROUGH 1978: $416,070   PLAYOFF
RECORD: 1–2

TOUR VICTORIES (TOTAL: 4): **1977** Tucson Open, Hawaiian Open. **1978** Canadian Open. **1979** Tucson Open.

MONEY & POSITION:
1975—$30,780—74   1977—$202,156— 5
1976—$69,229—39   1978—$113,905—18

Lietzke started playing the game at age five when brother Duane, then an assistant pro in Wichita, Kan., gave him a cut-down set of clubs. While at Forest Park High School in Beaumont, Tex., he won the Texas State scholastic title as a sophomore and helped the team to one championship and three seconds in his four years. At the University of Houston he captured the 1971 Texas State Amateur.

Late in the spring of 1973, Bruce closed the closet door on his golf clubs and declared he was finished with the game. "I had played so much through high school and in college I was tired of it. I suppose in the back of my mind I knew I would come back, but at that point I was tired mentally of the competition and needed the time to think about some other things."

His retirement lasted six months and he turned pro in 1974. He missed by a stroke in his first try in the Tour School but made it in the spring of 1975.

GENE LITTLER

BORN: July 21, 1930, San Diego, Calif.
HEIGHT: 5'9½"   WEIGHT: 160
RESIDENCE: La Jolla, Calif.
FAMILY: Wife, Shirley Warren; Curt (3/11/54); Suzanne (10/16/57)
COLLEGE: San Diego State
SPECIAL INTERESTS: Antique cars
TURNED PROFESSIONAL: 1954   JOINED TOUR: 1954
CAREER EARNINGS THROUGH 1978: $1,439,348   PLAYOFF
RECORD: 3–8

TOUR VICTORIES (TOTAL: 29): **1954** San Diego. **1955** Los Angeles, Phoenix, Tournament of Champions, Labatt. **1956** Tournament of Champions, Texas, Palm Beach Round Robin. **1957** Tournament of Champions. **1959** Phoenix, Tucson, Arlington Hotel Open, Insurance City, Miller Open. **1960** Oklahoma City, Eastern. **1961** U.S. Open. **1962** Lucky International, Thunderbird. **1965** Canadian Open. **1969** Phoenix, Greensboro. **1971** Monsanto, Colonial. **1973** St. Louis. **1975** Bing Črosby Pro-Am, Danny Thomas Memphis Classic, Westchester Classic. **1977** Houston Open.

MONEY & POSITION:
1954—$ 8,327—28   1967—$ 38,086— 32
1955—$28,974— 5   1968—$ 61,631— 26
1956—$23,833— 6   1969—$112,737— 6
1957—$13,427—18   1970—$ 79,001— 22
1958—$12,897—27   1971—$ 98,687— 14
1959—$38,296— 2   1972—$ 11,119—135
1960—$26,837— 8   1973—$ 95,308— 18
1961—$29,245— 9   1974—$102,822— 20
1962—$66,200— 2   1975—$182,883— 5
1963—$32,566—12   1976—$ 60,471— 43
1964—$33,173—15   1977—$119,759— 17
1965—$58,898— 9   1978—$ 55,576— 59
1966—$68,345— 7

Littler's battle with cancer is a story that bears repeating. He underwent surgery for cancer of the lymph glands in the spring of 1972, and the then winner of 24 tour events in 18 years appeared at the end of his career. However, he rejoined the tour that October and in July of 1973, about 16 months after his surgery, he won the St. Louis Children's Hospital Classic.

He did not win again in 1974 but he did top $100,-000 in official purses for the second time in his long career, and 1975 was truly remarkable. He won three times in 1975, including the Westchester Classic in a playoff with Julius Boros, two weeks after his 45th birthday.

MIKE McCULLOUGH

BORN: March 21, 1945, Coshocton, Ohio
HEIGHT: 5′9″   WEIGHT: 160
RESIDENCE: Scottsdale, Ariz.
FAMILY: Wife, Cheryl; Jason (4/24/74)
COLLEGE: Bowling Green University (1968)
SPECIAL INTERESTS: Outdoor activities
TURNED PROFESSIONAL: 1970   Q. SCHOOL: 1972
CAREER EARNINGS THROUGH 1978: $226,865
TOUR VICTORIES: None
MONEY & POSITION:

1972—$ 227—437	1976—$29,491—76
1973—$17,076—114	1977—$79,413—36
1974—$31,961— 83	1978—$56,066—57
1975—$17,706—109	

Mike is one of the game's more tenacious players. As a boy, he played all sports. It wasn't until after he was graduated from Bowling Green State University in 1968 that he decided to devote more time to golf.

His first year out of college, he taught physical education in the Monroe (Mich.) school system; then he headed for Florida to play the mini-tours. Before doing so, he won the 1970 Ohio Amateur championship.

Twice, he tried to obtain his PGA Tour card and missed, in the fall of 1970 and again in 1971. Finally, he made it in 1972.

JERRY McGEE

BORN: July 21, 1943, New Lexington, Ohio
HEIGHT: 5′9½″   WEIGHT: 160
RESIDENCE: East Palestine, Ohio
FAMILY: Wife, Jill; Roxanne (5/30/64), Jerry Michael (11/12/74)
COLLEGE: Ohio State U.
SPECIAL INTERESTS: All sports and fishing
TURNED PROFESSIONAL: 1966   Q. SCHOOL: 1966
CAREER EARNINGS THROUGH 1978: $661,506   PLAYOFF RECORD: 0–1
TOUR VICTORIES (TOTAL 3): **1975** Pensacola Open. **1977** IVB—Philadelphia Classic. **1979** Kemper Open.

1967—$ 4,212—125	1973—$ 46,927—67
1968—$ 6,969—114	1974—$ 54,506—51
1969—$13,833—102	1975—$ 93,569—16
1970—$22,965— 90	1976—$130,986—16
1971—$54,359— 46	1977—$124,584—15
1972—$47,751— 55	1978—$ 71,228—39

McGee, for years better known for his quick wit than being one of Ohio State's gang of standout golf products, suffered pulled ligaments in his thumb in the summer of 1971, an injury which seriously disrupted his steady progress since joining the PGA tour in 1967.

He sat out the last several months of 1971, and the injury apparently continued to bother him for about two more years. "The longer I was home," he said, "the more I wondered if I'd ever play again." However, he pulled out of his long slump in 1974 by earning checks in 25 of 35 tournaments and regaining a spot in the top-60 list. And the following year he won his first PGA tour event.

MAC McLENDON

BORN: Aug. 10, 1945, Atlanta, Ga.
HEIGHT: 6′2½″   WEIGHT: 180
RESIDENCE: Birmingham, Ala.; plays out of Pine Harbor Resort, Pell City, Ala.
FAMILY: Wife, Joan; Lance (10/24/71); Amy (12/14/73)
COLLEGE: Louisiana State U. (1967, Accounting)
SPECIAL INTERESTS: Fishing, bridge
TURNED PROFESSIONAL: 1968   Q. SCHOOL: Spring 1968
CAREER EARNINGS THROUGH 1978: $526,718   PLAYOFF RECORD: 1–0
TOUR VICTORIES (TOTAL: 4): **1974** Walt Disney World National Team Championship (with Hubert Green). **1976** Southern Open. **1978** Florida Citrus Open, Pensacola Open.
MONEY & POSITION:

1968—$40,469— 40	1974—$ 34,870—76
1969—$34,074— 57	1975—$ 76,971—26
1970—$19,810— 96	1976—$ 72,390—35
1971—$23,376— 92	1977—$ 86,135—32
1972—$40,250— 62	1978—$107,299—22
1973—$24,379—101	

McLendon won the first PGA tour event he competed in, the 1968 Magnolia Classic, a second-tour tournament which did not contribute to his official earnings. However, he did place in the top 60 at the end of his first two years on tour.

Then he found himself in a five-year slump which caused him to consider a more rewarding career, such as, perhaps, using his accounting degree from Louisiana State to more advantage. However, at the end of 1974, Mac hooked up with Hubert Green to win the Walt Disney World National Team Championship and an exemption for the following 12 months.

Given that opportunity, Mac more than doubled his official earnings in 1975 and twice almost won, when he tied for second at Jacksonville and placed second alone in the Pleasant Valley Classic.

JOHN MAHAFFEY

BORN: May 9, 1948, Kerrville, Tex.

HEIGHT: 5'9" WEIGHT: 150

RESIDENCE: Houston, Tex.; plays out of Riverhill C.C., Kerrville

FAMILY: Wife, Susie

COLLEGE: U. of Houston (1970, Psychology)

SPECIAL INTERESTS: Fishing

TURNED PROFESSIONAL: 1971 Q. SCHOOL: 1971

CAREER EARNINGS THROUGH 1978: $664,364 PLAYOFF RECORD: 1–1

TOUR VICTORIES (TOTAL: 4): **1973** Sahara Invitational. **1978** PGA Championship, American Optical Classic. **1979** Bob Hope Desert Classic.

MONEY & POSITION:

1971—$	1,010—230		1975—$141,471—	8
1972—$	57,779— 39		1976—$ 77,843—	33
1973—$112,536—	12		1977—$	9,847—150
1974—$122,189—	16		1978—$153,520—	12

John Mahaffey must be convinced of the verity of the old adage, "When it rains, it pours." After nearly five years' absence from the winner's circle and a dismal campaign in 1977, Mahaffey returned to the spotlight in August 1978 with stunning, back-to-back victories in the PGA Championship and the American Optical Classic.

All this came just a year after John had hit the depths. After a sparkling collegiate career at the University of Houston, Mahaffey immediately made his presence felt on the tour. In his first full year, 1972, he was among the top 60, and for the next three seasons he topped $100,000 in earnings.

The physical problems began, ironically, during the 1976 PGA Championship at Congressional, when he suffered what was later diagnosed as a hyperextended tendon in the left elbow. His earnings that year dipped from a career-high $141,471 in 1975 to "just" $77,843.

Recovery was slow. He was virtually unable to compete during the first part of 1977, and just days before his expected return to action, Mahaffey fell off a ladder in his garage and broke the little finger on his right hand. He finally rejoined the tour in July, but finished the year with less than $10,000, having made a check in just five of 15 events.

JOHNNY MILLER

BORN: Apr. 29, 1947, San Francisco, Calif.

HEIGHT: 6'2" WEIGHT: 185

RESIDENCE: Napa, Calif.

FAMILY: Wife, Linda Strouse; John S. (6/2/70); Kelly (12/26/72); Casi (7/30/74); Scott (5/12/76); Brent (2/3/78)

COLLEGE: Brigham Young U. (1969, Phys. Ed.)

SPECIAL INTERESTS: Fishing, church work, duck hunting

TURNED PROFESSIONAL: 1969 Q. SCHOOL: Spring 1969

CAREER EARNINGS THROUGH 1978: $1,161,505 PLAYOFF RECORD: 1–1

TOUR VICTORIES (TOTAL: 17): **1971** Southern. **1972** Heritage Classic. **1973** U.S. Open. **1974** Bing Crosby Pro-Am, Phoenix, Dean Martin-Tucson, Heritage Classic, Tournament of Champions, Westchester Classic, World Open and Kaiser International. **1975** Phoenix, Dean Martin-Tucson, Bob Hope Desert Classic, Kaiser International. **1976** NBC Tucson Open, Bob Hope Desert Classic.

MONEY & POSITION:

1969—$	8,364—135	1974—$353,021—	1
1970—$	52,391— 40	1975—$226,118—	2
1971—$	91,081— 18	1976—$135,887—	14
1972—$	99,348— 17	1977—$ 61,025—	48
1973—$127,833—	9	1978—$ 17,440—111	

OTHER ACHIEVEMENTS: 1974 PGA Player of the Year. 1973 individual and team (with Jack Nicklaus) World Cup champion. Winner 1974 Dunlop Phoenix Open (Japan). 1975 World Cup and Ryder Cup teams. 1976 British Open champion.

Miller's arrival as a star has always been tied to his '73 Oakmont triumph. But he enjoyed his finest season the following year, winning eight tournaments and $353,021, a record sum until 1978, when Tom Watson earned $362,429. Johnny opened that amazing campaign with 23 consecutive rounds of par or better, winning the first three events of the year, the Bing Crosby Pro-Am, the Phoenix Open, and the Tucson Open.

In 1978, Miller's performance fell off drastically. He failed to crack the top 60 for the first time since his rookie year of 1969—and in that campaign he played only the second half of the season. In 15 events—the fewest he's ever played—Johnny had but one top-ten finish, a tie for sixth in the U.S. Open. In that event, Miller showed—for two rounds—a flash of the brilliance he'd displayed from 1971 to 1976, when he won 17 tournaments and more than a million dollars.

ORVILLE MOODY

BORN: December 9, 1933, Chicasha, Okla.

HEIGHT: 5'10" WEIGHT: 200

RESIDENCE: Plano, Tex.

FAMILY: Wife, Beverly Meyers; Michelle (11/24/69); Sabreena (2/7/70); Kelley Rhea (9/14/73); Jason (4/17/75)

COLLEGE: U. of Oklahoma

SPECIAL INTERESTS: Hunting and fishing

TURNED PROFESSIONAL: 1967 Q. SCHOOL: 1967

CAREER EARNINGS THROUGH 1978: $319,372 PLAYOFF RECORD: 0–2

TOUR VICTORIES (TOTAL: 1): **1969** U.S. Open.

MONEY & POSITION:

1968—$12,950—103	1974—$13,283—130
1969—$79,176— 21	1975—$ 2,813—185
1970—$50,086— 44	1976—$ 2,866—195
1971—$25,256— 83	1977—$15,521—121
1972—$13,672—126	1978—$44,204— 73
1973—$74,286— 36	

There have been numerous highlights to Orville Moody's long career in golf, including his victory in the 1969 U.S. Open Championship, joining with Lee Trevino to give Uncle Sam the 1969 World Cup team title, as well as triumphs in the 1958 All-Army Championship and the 1962 All-Service Championship.

Times have not been easy for him the last few years. He left the PGA tour for most of 1975 and 1976 to devote his energies to his golf course business in the Denver area, but rejoined the tour as a full-timer in 1977 and plans to stay with it for awhile.

Orville's father was greens superintendent in Chickasha, Okla. "I grew up on the golf course and have played the game since I was about three," he said. "I never played on anything but sand greens until I was 13 or 14."

Orville, who is part Cherokee Indian, joined the army in 1953 and stayed for 14½ years. He saw duty in both the European and Pacific zones and was a staff sergeant (E-6), when he was discharged.

GIL MORGAN

BORN: Sept. 25, 1946, Wewoka, Okla.

HEIGHT: 5′10″   WEIGHT: 165

RESIDENCE: Wewoka, Okla.; plays out of Oak Tree Country Club, Edmond, Okla.

FAMILY: Wife, Jeanine

COLLEGE: East Central State College (1968, B.S.), Southern College of Optometry (Doctor of Optometry, 1972)

SPECIAL INTERESTS: Hunting and fishing

TURNED PROFESSIONAL: 1972   Q. SCHOOL: 1973

CAREER EARNINGS THROUGH 1978: $502,195   PLAYOFF RECORD: 1–0

TOUR VICTORIES (TOTAL: 4): **1977** B.C. Open. **1978** Glen Campbell Los Angeles Open, World Series of Golf. **1979** Memphis Classic.

1973—$ 3,800—204	1976—$ 61,372—42
1974—$23,880— 94	1977—$104,817—24
1975—$42,772— 60	1978—$267,459— 2

The way he's been going lately, Dr. Gil Morgan will have to put off plans of a full-time optometry practice for quite a while.

In 1978, Gil established himself as one of the true stars of the PGA tour. His steady climb up the money list since joining the tour has been impressive, and in '78 he nearly made it to the pinnacle. Overall, he notched 11 top ten finishes in 1978, more than double his output of a year earlier.

Gil began playing golf at about age 15 and decided he would pursue it as a career along with optometry when he was a junior at East Central State College in Oklahoma. He won the Oklahoma collegiate championship before graduation in 1968 but he did not turn pro until after earning his doctorate four years later.

He was second in the Western Amateur and Porter Cup before entering the fall 1972 Tour Qualifying School. He failed to win his player's card, but a year later, after subsisting on the mini-tour circuit, Morgan passed.

BOB MURPHY

BORN: Feb. 14, 1943, Brooklyn, N.Y.

HEIGHT: 5′10″   WEIGHT: 210

RESIDENCE: Delray Beach, Fla.

FAMILY: Wife, Gail; Kimberly (1/11/69)

COLLEGE: U. of Florida (1966, Phys. Ed.)

SPECIAL INTERESTS: Fishing

TURNED PROFESSIONAL: 1967   Q. SCHOOL: 1967

CAREER EARNINGS THROUGH 1978: $882,491   PLAYOFF RECORD: 1–4

TOUR VICTORIES (TOTAL: 4): **1968** Philadelphia, Thunderbird. **1970** Hartford. **1975** Jackie Gleason Inverrary Classic.

MONEY & POSITION:

1968—$105,595—10	1974—$ 59,048—44
1969—$ 56,526—32	1975—$127,471—11
1970—$120,639— 9	1976—$ 47,627—60
1971—$ 75,301—27	1977—$ 52,874—58
1972—$ 83,259—26	1978—$ 73,598—34
1973—$ 93,442—22	

Murphy's introduction to competitive golf was little short of miraculous. He entered the University of Florida in the early 1960s as a baseball prospect but he turned to golf when an injury kept him off the diamond his freshman year. Suddenly he won the 1965 U.S. Amateur championship, then the following spring the NCAA title as a senior.

He almost exploded as a pro, too, after gaining his player's card in 1968. As a rookie, he won the Philadelphia and Thunderbird tournaments on consecutive weeks and more than $100,000 for the year, easily the most money banked by a rookie to that time.

In his first six years on the tour, Murphy wound up no lower than 32nd on the money list. He dropped to 44th position at the end of 1974, the result of a thumb injury which sidelined him for four months and limited him to 19 events.

Murphy's performance in 1976 and 1977 was not characteristic of his professional career. A painful hand, finally diagnosed as a uric acid condition, damaged his game for most of the summer of 1976, and that year he maintained his top-60 streak by a margin of just $250.

LARRY NELSON

BORN: Sept. 10, 1947, Ft. Payne, Ala.
HEIGHT: 5'9"   WEIGHT: 155
RESIDENCE: Kennesaw, Ga.
FAMILY: Wife, Gayle; Drew (10/7/76); Josh (9/28/78)
COLLEGE: Kennesaw Junior College (1970)
SPECIAL INTERESTS: Fishing
TURNED PROFESSIONAL: 1971   Q. SCHOOL: 1973
CAREER EARNINGS: $294,770
TOUR VICTORIES (TOTAL: 1): **1979** Inverrary Classic.
MONEY & POSITION:

1974—$24,022—93	1977—$99,876—26
1975—$39,810—66	1978—$65,686—45
1976—$66,482—41	

There are not many stories on the PGA tour more unusual than Nelson's. Only four years after he started to play golf, and after playing only one 72-hole tournament, he had his Approved Tournament Player's card. "I really wasn't ready," he said later, but he got ready in a hurry, as witness his steady climb up the money rankings since then.

Larry lettered in baseball and basketball in high school and attended Southern Tech for a year before he was drafted and spent two years in the military. After his discharge in 1968, he tried school again and also worked as an illustrator at the Lockheed plant near his home.

He went to a driving range one day in 1969, liked hitting balls so much that he went to work in pro Bert Seagraves' shop at the Pine Tree club in Kennesaw, Ga., turned pro six months after that. He tried the mini-tours briefly and, in 1973, finished bogey-bogey in the Florida State Open to lose by a shot. That was his lone 72-hole event before earning his tour card that fall.

JACK NICKLAUS

BORN: Jan. 21, 1940, Columbus, Ohio
HEIGHT: 5'11"   WEIGHT: 180
RESIDENCE: North Palm Beach, Fla. and Muirfield Village, Ohio
FAMILY: Wife, Barbara Bash; Jack II (9/23/61); Steven (4/11/63); Nancy Jean (5/5/65); Gary (1/15/69); Michael (7/24/73)
COLLEGE: Ohio State U.
SPECIAL INTERESTS: Fishing, hunting, tennis and skiing
TURNED PROFESSIONAL: 1961   JOINED TOUR: 1962
CAREER EARNINGS THROUGH 1978: $3,349,393   PLAYOFF RECORD: 12–8
TOUR VICTORIES (TOTAL: 66): **1962** U.S. Open, Seattle World's Fair, Portland. **1963** Palm Springs, Masters, Tournament of Champions, PGA Championship, Sahara. **1964** Portland, Tournament of Champions, Phoenix, Whitemarsh. **1965** Portland, Masters, Memphis, Thunderbird Classic, Philadelphia. **1966** Masters, Sahara, National Team (with Arnold Palmer). **1967** U.S. Open, Sahara, Bing Crosby, Western, Westchester. **1968** Western, American Golf Classic. **1969** Sahara, Kaiser, San Diego. **1970** Byron Nelson, Four-Ball (with Arnold Palmer). **1971** PGA Championship, Tournament of Champions, Byron Nelson, National Team (with Arnold Palmer), Disney World. **1972** Bing Crosby, Doral-Eastern, Masters, U.S. Open, Westchester, Match Play, Disney. **1973** Bing Crosby, New Orleans, Tournament of Champions, Atlanta, PGA Championship, Ohio Kings Island, Walt Disney. **1974** Hawaii, Tournament Players Championship. **1975** Doral-Eastern Open, Heritage Classic, Masters, PGA Championship, World Open. **1976** Tournament Players Championship, World Series of Golf. **1977** Gleason Inverrary, Tournament of Champions, Memorial. **1978** Gleason Inverrary, Tournament Players Championship, IVB-Philadelphia Classic.

MONEY & POSITION:

1962—$ 61,869—3	1971—$244,490—1
1963—$100,040—2	1972—$320,542—1
1964—$113,285—1	1973—$308,362—1
1965—$140,752—1	1974—$238,178—2
1966—$111,419—2	1975—$298,149—1
1967—$188,998—1	1976—$266,438—1
1968—$155,286—2	1977—$284,509—2
1969—$140,167—3	1978—$256,672—4
1970—$142,149—4	

OTHER ACHIEVEMENTS: PGA Player of the Year five times (1967, 1972, 1973, 1975 and 1976). U.S. Amateur champion in 1959 and 1961. NCAA champion in 1961. Winner of British Open in 1966, 1970 and 1978. Six-time winner Australian Open (1964, 1968, 1971, 1975, 1976 and 1978). Member of six winning World Cup teams (1963, 1964, 1966, 1967, 1971 and 1973). Winner of World Series of Gold (old format) four times (1962, 1963, 1967 and 1970). Member of five Ryder Cup teams (1969 through 1977). Has total of 17 international titles.

ANDY NORTH

BORN: Mar. 9, 1950, Thorp, Wisc.
HEIGHT: 6'4" WEIGHT: 210
RESIDENCE: Madison, Wisc.
FAMILY: Wife, Susan; Nichole (11/30/74); Andrea (8/22/78)
COLLEGE: U. of Florida (1972)
SPECIAL INTERESTS: All sports
TURNED PROFESSIONAL: 1972 Q. SCHOOL: 1972
CAREER EARNINGS THROUGH 1978: $486,781
TOUR VICTORIES (TOTAL: 2): **1977** American Express–Westchester Classic. **1978** U.S. Open.

MONEY & POSITION:

1973—$48,672—64	1976—$ 71,267—37
1974—$58,409—46	1977—$116,794—18
1975—$44,729—53	1978—$150,398—14

Andy North abruptly thrust himself into the spotlight in 1978 by winning the U.S. Open at Cherry Hills. Although a constant member of the top 60 money-winners since 1974, his second year on the PGA tour, North's only previous victory came in the 1977 Westchester Classic.

An unusual ailment helped lead North to golf when he was in the seventh grade in Madison, Wis. A bone in his knee had stopped growing and was disintegrating. While on crutches for 18 months he was told to give up his pursuit of basketball and football but that he could play golf—if he rode in a car.

Since Andy's father was a low-handicap golfer, the game was no stranger to the family and he progressed quickly. He also returned to basketball and was chosen all-state as a high school senior, but by then golf was his dominant sport.

North won the Wisconsin high school championship in 1966 and 1967, the State Amateur in 1969 and placed second in the Wisconsin Open in 1968 and 1969. After entering the University of Florida he was chosen All-American for three years and won the 1971 Western Amateur.

ARNOLD PALMER

BORN: Sept. 10, 1929, Latrobe, Pa.
HEIGHT: 5'10½" WEIGHT: 190
RESIDENCE: Latrobe, Pa.
FAMILY: Wife, Winifred Walzer; Margaret (2/26/56); Amy (8/4/58)
COLLEGE: Wake Forest
SPECIAL INTERESTS: Flying, tennis, business, club-making
TURNED PROFESSIONAL: 1954 JOINED TOUR: 1955
CAREER EARNINGS THROUGH 1978: $1,789,155 PLAYOFF RECORD: 14–10

TOUR VICTORIES (TOTAL: 61): **1955** Canadian. **1956** Insurance City, Eastern. **1957** Houston, Azalea, Rubber City. San Diego. **1958** St. Petersburg, Masters, Pepsi Golf. **1959** Thunderbird (Calif.) Invitational, Oklahoma City, West Palm Beach. **1960** Insurance City, Masters, Palm Springs Classic, Baton Rouge, Pensacola, U.S. Open, Mobile Sertoma. **1961** San Diego, Texas, Baton Rouge, Phoenix, Western. **1962** Masters, Palm Springs Classic, Texas, Phoenix, Tournament of Champions, Colonial National, American Golf Classic. **1963** Thunderbird, Pensacola, Phoenix, Western, Los Angeles, Cleveland, Philadelphia. **1964** Oklahoma City, Masters. **1965** Tournament of Champions. **1966** Los Angeles, Tournament of Champions, Houston Champions International, PGA Team (with Jack Nicklaus). **1967** Los Angeles, Tucson, American Golf Classic, Thunderbird Classic. **1968** Hope Desert Classic, Kemper. **1969** Heritage, Danny Thomas—Diplomat. **1970** Four-Ball (with Jack Nicklaus). **1971** Hope Desert Classic, Citrus, Westchester, National Team (with Jack Nicklaus). **1973** Hope Classic.

MONEY & POSITION:

1955—$ 7,958—32	1967—$184,065— 2
1956—$ 16,145—19	1968—$114,602— 7
1957—$ 27,803— 5	1969—$105,128— 9
1958—$ 42,606— 1	1970—$128,853— 5
1959—$ 32,462— 5	1971—$209,603— 3
1960—$ 75,263— 1	1972—$ 84,181— 25
1961—$ 61,091— 2	1973—$ 89,457— 27
1962—$ 81,448— 1	1974—$ 36,293— 72
1963—$128,230— 1	1975—$ 59,017— 36
1964—$113,203— 2	1976—$ 17,017—115
1965—$ 57,770—10	1977—$ 21,950—101
1966—$110,467— 3	1978—$ 27,073— 94

OTHER ACHIEVEMENTS: 1954 U.S. Amateur champion. Winner of 18 foreign titles, including 1961 and 1962 British Open, 1966 Australian Open, 1975 Spanish Open, and 1975 British PGA. 1961, 1965, 1967, 1971, and 1973 Ryder Cup team. 1960, 1962, 1963, 1964, 1965, 1966, and 1967 World Cup team.

JERRY PATE

BORN: Sept. 16, 1953, Macon, Ga.

HEIGHT: 6′   WEIGHT: 165

RESIDENCE: Pensacola, Fla.

FAMILY: Wife, Soozi; Jennifer (10/5/78)

COLLEGE: U. of Alabama

SPECIAL INTERESTS: Water skiing, hunting, fishing

TURNED PROFESSIONAL: 1975   Q. SCHOOL: Fall 1975

CAREER EARNINGS THROUGH 1978: $427,504   PLAYOFF RECORD: 1–1

TOUR VICTORIES (TOTAL: 5): **1976** U.S. Open, Canadian Open. **1977** Phoenix Open, Southern Open. **1978** Southern Open.

MONEY & POSITION:

1975—$ 3,250—176	1977—$ 98,152—27
1976—$153,102— 10	1978—$172,999—10

Pate literally burst into world-wide attention as a PGA tour rookie in 1976. His last swing in the U.S. Open, a five-iron from the rough at Atlanta Athletic Club, left him a two-foot birdie putt for a two-shot victory, and his closing 63 in the Canadian Open was good for a four-stroke victory over Jack Nicklaus. His total of $153,102 in official earnings was the most ever won by a rookie.

Conrad Rehling, who developed Bob Murphy while coaching at the University of Florida in the early 1960s, found another champion-to-be about a decade later while coaching at a small college near Pensacola. Pate was still in high school when he came under Rehling's wing. When Rehling moved to the University of Alabama, Pate followed. In 1974, like Murphy nine years earlier, Pate won the U.S. and Florida amateur titles.

Jerry also helped the U.S. win the 1974 World Amateur Team championship and the 1975 Walker Cup matches. As an amateur he finished sixth in the Pensacola Open and tied for 18th in the U.S. Open, both in 1975.

GARY PLAYER

BORN: Nov. 1, 1935, Johannesburg, South Africa

HEIGHT: 5′7″   WEIGHT: 150

RESIDENCE: Johannesburg, South Africa

FAMILY: Wife, Vivienne Verwey; Jennifer ('59); Mark (3/61); Wayne (4/62); Michelle (12/63); Theresa ('65); Amanda ('73)

SPECIAL INTERESTS: Raising horses on his farm, physical fitness

TURNED PROFESSIONAL: 1953   JOINED TOUR: 1957

CAREER EARNINGS THROUGH 1978: $1,506,643   PLAYOFF RECORD: 3–11

TOUR VICTORIES (TOTAL: 21): **1958** Kentucky Derby Open. **1961** Lucky International Sunshine, Masters. **1962** PGA Championship, San Diego. **1963** Pensacola. **1964** 500 Festival. **1965** U.S. Open. **1969** Tournament of Champions. **1970** Greater Greensboro. **1971** Jacksonville, National Airlines. **1972** New Orleans, PGA Championship. **1973** Southern. **1974** Masters, Danny Thomas-Memphis. **1978** Masters, Tournament of Champions, Houston Open.

MONEY & POSITION:

1957—$ 3,286—	1968—$ 51,950—33
1958—$18,591—	1969—$123,897— 5
1959—$ 5,694—58	1970—$101,212—15
1960—$13,879—28	1971—$120,916— 5
1961—$64,540— 1	1972—$120,719— 7
1962—$45,838— 6	1973—$ 48,878—63
1963—$55,455— 5	1974—$108,372—19
1964—$61,449— 7	1975—$ 73,943—27
1965—$69,964— 5	1976—$ 53,668—53
1966—$26,391—38	1977—$112,485—21
1967—$55,820—18	1978—$177,336— 9

OTHER ACHIEVEMENTS: Winner of 114 tournaments around the world, including the 1959, 1968 and 1974 British Opens. Winner of South African Open 11 times since 1956. Seven-time winner Australian Open and five-time winner World Picadilly Match Play. Individual titlist in 1965 and 1977 World Cup. Winner of World Series of

Golf (old format) in 1965, 1968 and 1972. Other victories include: 1957 Australian PGA, 1972 and 1974 Brazilian Open, and 1976 South African Dunlop Masters.

VICTOR REGALADO

BORN: April 15, 1948, Tijuana, Mexico
HEIGHT: 5'10½" WEIGHT: 185
RESIDENCE: San Diego, Calif.
FAMILY: Wife, Carol
SPECIAL INTERESTS: Fishing
TURNED PROFESSIONAL: 1971 Q. SCHOOL: 1972
CAREER EARNINGS THROUGH 1978: $290,414
TOUR VICTORIES (TOTAL: 2): **1974** Pleasant Valley Classic. **1978** Ed McMahon Quad Cities Open.

MONEY & POSITION:

1973—$ 9,512—154	1976—$53,686—52
1974—$61,848— 39	1978—$62,621—50
1975—$25,833— 85	

Victor grew up in Tijuana, Mexico, two blocks from the Tijuana C.C. and started in golf at age 11. The first tournament he entered was the Pan-American Juniors at his course and he won it at age 14.

The most impressive of his early titles throughout Central America were the Mexican Amateur in 1970, the Mexican PGA in 1972 and the Mexican Masters in 1972 and 1973. He represented Mexico in the World Amateur Team Championships of 1968 and 1970, the latter year winning the individual title in Spain. He also represented his country in the 1972 and 1973 World Cup tournaments.

JACK RENNER

BORN: July 6, 1956, Palm Springs, Calif.
HEIGHT: 6' WEIGHT: 160
RESIDENCE: San Diego, Calif.
COLLEGE: College of the Desert
SPECIAL INTERESTS: Reading, all sports
TURNED PROFESSIONAL: 1976 Q. SCHOOL: Spring 1977
CAREER EARNINGS THROUGH 1978: $86,833.
TOUR VICTORIES: None
MONEY & POSITION:

1977—$12,837—128	1978—$73,996—33

Jack Renner has been told that he was "about two years old" when he started to chip around the back yard with a golf club, and he knows he was about six when he started to play golf competitively. He won two important junior titles, the 1972 World Junior and the 1973 United States Junior. During his school days, he chose not to play varsity golf, because he felt he could improve faster by working on his own.

The Renners are an avid golfing family. Sister Jane has been part of the LPGA tour for four years, and younger brother Jim turned professional last year.

BILL ROGERS

BORN: Sept. 10, 1951, Waco, Tex.
HEIGHT: 6' WEIGHT: 145
RESIDENCE: Texarkana, Tex.
FAMILY: Wife, Beth
COLLEGE: U. of Houston
SPECIAL INTERESTS: Hunting and fishing
TURNED PROFESSIONAL: 1974 Q. SCHOOL: 1974
CAREER EARNINGS THROUGH 1978: $257,516 PLAYOFF RECORD: 0–1
TOUR VICTORIES (TOTAL: 1): **1978** Bob Hope Desert Classic.

MONEY & POSITION:

1975—$29,302—78	1977—$ 88,707—29
1976—$24,376—88	1978—$114,206—17

When Bill Rogers was attending the University of Houston, he was nicknamed the "Panther" by his roommate, Bruce Lietzke. "I was the jumpy type," he said. "I never wanted to miss anything.

"I was still that way during my first two years on the PGA tour," he continued, "and they were something of a disappointment to me. I had to learn to adjust."

Bill turned things around in 1977, finishing in the top 10 nine times and earning more than $88,000. Though he had only five finishes among the top 10 in 1978, he increased his income by more than $25,000 and garnered his first PGA tour victory.

Bill started to play the game at age nine in Montgomery, Ala., and was playing competitively by the time he was 13 and the family was living in Texarkana, Tex. Although his father and brother started him, it was Jerry Robinson, professional at the North Ridge Country Club in Texarkana, who taught him the fine points of the game.

Bill's father was a lieutenant colonel in the air force, and, from age three to six, he lived in Germany; from ages six through eight, he lived in Morocco, North Africa. "Dad is retired from the air force now, and he still is a good player. He played in a lot of the major air force tournaments when he was in the service."

JOHN SCHROEDER

BORN: Nov. 12, 1945, Great Barrington, Mass.
HEIGHT: 5'10½" WEIGHT: 170
RESIDENCE: La Jolla, Calif.
FAMILY: Wife, Kathleen; Patricia (2/18/74); Molly (4/17/76)
COLLEGE: U. of Michigan (1968, Business Administration)
TURNED PROFESSIONAL: 1969 Q. SCHOOL: 1969
CAREER EARNINGS THROUGH 1978: $361,058
TOUR VICTORIES (TOTAL: 1): **1973** U.S. Professional Match Play.

MONEY & POSITION:

1969—$10,584—122	1974—$23,685— 95
1970—$32,059— 72	1975—$25,520— 86
1971—$25,181— 84	1976—$16,205—119
1972—$27,797— 83	1977—$69,333— 45
1973—$67,257— 42	1978—$70,707— 40

John is the son of Ted Schroeder, one of the greats in tennis history. Ted won the 1949 Wimbledon championship and was a standout performer on 10 U.S. Davis Cup teams.

Tendonitis in the left hand hindered John's progress periodically from 1974 through 1976, but he believes that is a thing of the past.

Since joining the tour in 1969, he has one victory, in the 1973 U.S. Professional Match Play championship. Along the way, in order, he defeated Grier Jones, Bud Allin, Lee Trevino (one up) and, in the 18-hole final, DeWitt Weaver, two up. He enjoyed his most profitable season in ten years on the PGA Tour in 1978.

JIM SIMONS

BORN: May 15, 1950, Pittsburgh, Pa.
HEIGHT: 5'10½"   WEIGHT: 170
RESIDENCE: Tequesta, Fla.
FAMILY: Wife, Sherry; Bradley (1/15/77)
COLLEGE: Wake Forest (1972)
SPECIAL INTERESTS: Hunting, fishing and water sports
TURNED PROFESSIONAL: 1972   Q. SCHOOL: Fall 1972
CAREER EARNINGS THROUGH 1978: $319,107
TOUR VICTORIES (TOTAL: 2): **1977** First NBC New Orleans Open. **1978** Memorial.

MONEY & POSITION:

1972—$ 2,030—248	1976—$44,727—62
1973—$26,493— 93	1977—$81,397—34
1974—$30,710— 87	1978—$90,218—26
1975—$47,724— 50	

Jim's father started him in golf at Butler, Pa., Country Club at the age of nine. He lived on a farm and says now, "I'd ride over to the club on my bike in the morning and either play or hit balls most of the day and ride back in the evening."

He started competition at the age of 13 and his progress was rapid. He first enrolled at the University of Houston but, after a year, transferred to Wake Forest. He was on the 1971 Walker Cup team and remained overseas for the 1971 British Amateur, reaching the final round where he lost to Steve Melnyk.

In the 1971 U.S. Open, at Merion, he gained national attention by leading the tournament after the third round. He finished in a tie for fifth and was low amateur. He also was low amateur in the 1972 Open at Pebble Beach. He turned pro that fall.

LEE TREVINO

BORN: Dec. 1, 1939, Dallas, Tex.
HEIGHT: 5'7"   WEIGHT: 180
RESIDENCE: Dallas, Tex.
FAMILY: Wife, Claudia Fenley; Richard (11/21/62); Lesley Ann (6/30/65); Carl (12/31/68); Tony Lee (4/13/69); Troy (9/10/73)
SPECIAL INTERESTS: Fishing
TURNED PROFESSIONAL: 1960   JOINED TOUR: 1967
CAREER EARNINGS THROUGH 1978: $1,849,446   PLAY-OFF RECORD: 5–4
TOUR VICTORIES (TOTAL: 21): **1968** U.S. Open, Hawaiian. **1969** Tucson. **1970** Tucson, National Airlines. **1971** Tallahassee, Danny Thomas-Memphis, U.S. Open, Canadian Open, Sahara. **1972** Danny Thomas-Memphis, Hartford, St. Louis. **1973** Gleason, Doral-Eastern. **1974** New Orleans, PGA Championship. **1975** Florida Citrus Open. **1976** Colonial Invitational. **1977** Canadian Open. **1978** Colonial Invitational.

MONEY & POSITION:

1966—$ 600—	1973—$210,017— 4
1967—$ 26,472—45	1974—$203,422— 4
1968—$132,127— 6	1975—$134,206— 9
1969—$112,418— 7	1976—$136,963—13
1970—$157,037— 1	1977—$ 85,108—33
1971—$231,202— 2	1978—$228,723— 6
1972—$214,805— 2	

In 1978, Lee Trevino left no doubts that he was totally recovered from the back surgery he underwent in November of 1976. Though he won just one tournament, Lee piled up a remarkable total of five runnerup finishes and came within a few thousand dollars of his best year ever, 1971.

Trevino, with more than $1.8 million in career earnings, also moved past Billy Casper and Arnold Palmer into second place on the all-time list.

Trevino tied for 54th in the 1966 U.S. Open at Olympic Club in San Francisco, and he didn't try the tour again until a year later at Baltusrol. He placed sixth in that U.S. Open, and was on the tour to stay. He was chosen Rookie of the Year for 1967. Twelve months after Baltusrol, the quick-quipping Merry Mex from Dallas was entertaining everyone at a margarita party in the clubhouse at Oak Hill C.C., Rochester, where he had just won the 1968 U.S. Open.

Lee won the U.S. Open again in 1971, defeating Jack Nicklaus in a playoff at Merion, and in a span of five weeks that summer he added the Canadian and British Open titles to his fast-growing collection. He was named player of the year practically by acclamation.

J. C. SNEAD

BORN: Oct. 14, 1941, Hot Springs, Va.
HEGHT: 6'2"   WEIGHT: 200
RESIDENCE: Hot Springs, Va.
FAMILY: Wife, Sue Bryant; Jason (10/10/78)
COLLEGE: East Tennessee State U.`
SPECIAL INTERESTS: Fishing and hunting
TURNED PROFESSIONAL: 1964   JOINED TOUR: 1968
CAREER EARNINGS THROUGH 1978: $888,332   PLAYOFF RECORD: 1–1

TOUR VICTORIES (TOTAL: 6): **1971** Tucson, Doral-Eastern. **1972** Philadelphia. **1975** Andy Williams San Diego Open. **1976** Andy Williams San Diego Open, Kaiser International.

MONEY & POSITION:

1968—$	690—280	1974—$164,486—	6
1969—$	10,640—121	1975—$ 91,822—17	
1970—$	11,547—122	1976—$192,645—	6
1971—$	92,929— 17	1977—$ 68,975—46	
1972—$	87,435— 22	1978—$ 63,561—47	
1973—$103,601— 14			

Jesse Carlyle Snead, although still constantly mentioned as the nephew of legendary Sam Snead, can stand on his own performance record. After growing up in Hot Springs, Va., he sought a career in baseball and served in the Washington Senators' farm system before turning to golf as a pro in 1964.

He worked for head pro Charlie Beverage at the Century C.C. Westchester County, N.Y., while twice failing to pass the PGA Tour Qualifying School, and it was four years before he earned his card. Following three so-so years on the tour, J.C. burst into golf's consciousness by winning twice in a three-week period, at Tucson and Doral, immediately before and after the PGA Championship in Florida.

SAM SNEAD

BORN: May 27, 1912, Hot Springs, Va.
HEIGHT: 5'11"   WEIGHT: 185
RESIDENCE: Hot Springs, Va.
FAMILY: Wife, Audrey; Sam, Jr. (6/30/44); Terrance (5/27/52)
SPECIAL INTERESTS: Hunting, fishing
TURNED PROFESSIONAL: 1934   JOINED TOUR: 1937
CAREER EARNINGS THROUGH 1978: $615,455   PLAYOFF RECORD: 8–6

TOUR VICTORIES (TOTAL: 84): **1936** Virginia Closed Professional. **1937** St. Paul Open, Nassau Open, Miami Open, Oakland Open. **1938** Greensboro Open, Inverness Four-Ball, Goodall Round Robin, Chicago Open, Canadian Open, Westchester 108 Hole Open, White Sulpher Springs Open. **1939** Miami Open, St. Petersburg Open, Miami-Biltmore Four-Ball, Ontario Open. **1940** Inverness Four-Ball, Canadian Open, Anthracite Open. **1941** Canadian Open, St. Petersburg Open, North and South Open, Rochester Times Union Open, Henry Hurst Inv. **1942** St. Petersburg Open, PGA Championship, Corduba Open. **1944** Richmond Open, Portland Open. **1945** Los Angeles Open, Gulfport Open, Pensacola Open, Jacksonville Open, Dallas Open, Tulsa Open. **1946** Miami Open, Greensboro Open, Jacksonville Open, Virginia Open, World Championship. **1948** Texas Open. **1949** Greensboro Open, PGA Championship, Masters, Washington Star Open, Dapper Dan Open, Western Open. **1950** Texas Open, Miami Open, Greensboro Open, Inverness Four-Ball, North and South Open, Los Angeles Open, Western Open, Miami Beach Open, Colonial National Inv., Reading Open. **1951** Miami Open, PGA Championship. **1952** Inverness Four-Ball, Masters, Greenbrier Inv., All American, Eastern Open, Julius Boros Open. **1953** Texas Open, Greenbrier Inv., Baton Rouge Open. **1954** Masters, Palm Beach Round Robin. **1955** Miami Open, Greensboro Open, Palm Beach Round Robin, Insurance City Open. **1956** Greensboro Open. **1957** Dallas Open. **1958** Greenbrier Inv. **1959** Sam Snead Festival. **1960** Greensboro Open, De Soto Open. **1961** Sam Snead Festival, Tournament of Champions. **1964** Haig and Haig Scotch Mixed Foursome Inv. **1965** Greensboro Open.

MONEY & POSITION:

1937—$10,243—	3	1954—$ 7,889—	29
1938—$19,534—	1	1955—$23,464—	7
1939—$ 9,712—	2	1956—$ 8,253—	36
1940—$ 9,206—	3	1957—$28,260—	4
1941—$12,848—	2	1958—$15,905—	18
1942—$ 8,078—	3	1959—$ 8,221—	45
1943		1960—$19,405—	19
1944—$ 5,755—	7	1961—$23,906—	17
1945—$24,436—	4	1962—$ 9,169—	59
1946—$18,341—	6	1963—$28,431—	16
1947—$ 9,703—12		1964—$ 8,383—	74
1948—$ 6,980—18		1965—$36,889—	24
1949—$31,593—	1	1966—$12,109—	72
1950—$35,758—	1	1967—$ 7,141—104	
1951—$15,072—	6	1968—$43,106—	39
1952—$19,908—	4	1969—$15,439—100	
1953—$14,115—15		1970—$25,103—	85

1971—$22,258— 94
1972—$35,462— 71
1973—$38,685— 78
1974—$55,562— 49

1975—$ 8,285—138
1976—$ 2,694—198
1977—$ 488—256
1978—$ 385—265

OTHER ACHIEVEMENTS: Credited with 135 victories by independent record keepers. 1949 Player of the Year. 1938, 1949, 1950, 1955 Vardon Trophy winner. 1937, 1939, 1941, 1947, 1949, 1951, 1953, and 1955 Ryder Cup team. Member winning World Cup team in 1956, 1960 and 1961 (won individual title in 1961). Winner 1964, 1965, 1967, 1970, 1972, and 1973 PGA Seniors. Winner 1964, 1965, 1970, 1972, and 1973 World Seniors.

ED SNEED

BORN: Aug. 6, 1944, Roanoke, Va.
HEIGHT: 6′2″ WEIGHT: 190
RESIDENCE: Pompano Beach, Fla.
FAMILY: Wife, Nancy Kay; Mary Elisa (8/16/74); Erica Kathryn (4/21/77)
COLLEGE: Ohio State (1967, Marketing)
SPECIAL INTERESTS: Chess, bridge, billards, backgammon
TURNED PROFESSIONAL: 1967 Q. SCHOOL: Fall 1968
CAREER EARNINGS THROUGH 1978: $399,939 PLAYOFF RECORD: 2–0
TOUR VICTORIES (TOTAL: 3): 1973 Kaiser International Open. 1974 Milwaukee. 1977 Tallahassee Open.

MONEY & POSITION:
1969—$ 4,254—170
1970—$ 3,186—189
1971—$10,716—133
1972—$16,945—118
1973—$67,990— 40

1974—$66,376—34
1975—$46,634—51
1976—$71,675—36
1977—$50,638—61
1978—$86,510—27

While serving a so-called four-year apprenticeship on the PGA tour, during which Sneed never came close to cracking the top-100 money list, Sneed was told more than once by his fellow Ohio State alumnus, Tom Weiskopf, that there was no reason he shouldn't be among the top 60. Long Tom proved right, it turned out.

Sneed won the New South Wales Open in Australia late in 1973, grabbed a plane for San Francisco and —gaining a day via the international dateline—arrived in Napa, Calif., in time for Monday qualifying for the Kaiser International. The following Sunday he beat John Schlee in a playoff for his first tour triumph. The following July, in 1974, Ed led all four rounds at Milwaukee.

Sneed started golf at age 13 in his native Roanoke, Va. He earned his privileges to play the tour in 1969 but it was another two years before he decided to play full time.

CRAIG STADLER

BORN: June 2, 1953, San Diego, Calif.
HEIGHT: 5′10″ WEIGHT: 210
RESIDENCE: La Jolla, Calif.
COLLEGE: U. of Southern Cal.
SPECIAL INTERESTS: Fishing, snow skiing, stock market
TURNED PROFESSIONAL: 1975 Q. SCHOOL: Spring 1976
CAREER EARNINGS THROUGH 1978: $109,138.
TOUR VICTORIES: None
MONEY & POSITION:
1976—$ 2,702—196
1977—$42,949— 66

1978—$63,486—48

Craig first played the game at age five with the assistance of his father, and really became interested in the game at age "eight or nine." Along the way, he won such titles as the World Junior championship, the San Diego City Amateur, the Southern California Interscholastic, and the 1973 U.S. Amateur at the Inverness Club in Toledo.

DAVE STOCKTON

BORN: Nov. 2, 1941, San Bernardino, Calif.
HEIGHT: 5′11½″ WEIGHT: 180
RESIDENCE: Westlake Village, Calif.
FAMILY: Wife, Catherine Fay; David Bradley (7/31/68); Ronald Edwin (9/16/70)
COLLEGE: U. of Southern Cal. (1964, General Management)
SPECIAL INTERESTS: Hunting and fishing
TURNED PROFESSIONAL: 1964 JOINED TOUR: 1964
CAREER EARNINGS THROUGH 1978: $1,032,801 PLAYOFF RECORD: 0–1
TOUR VICTORIES (TOTAL: 11): 1967 Colonial, Haig Scotch Foursome (with Laurie Hammer). 1968 Cleveland, Milwaukee. 1970 PGA Championship. 1971 Massachusetts. 1973 Milwaukee. 1974 Glen Campbell–Los Angeles, Quad Cities, Sammy Davis-Hartford. 1976 PGA Championship.

MONEY & POSITION:
1964—$ 1,203—167
1965—$ 5,410— 99
1966—$ 10,115— 82
1967—$ 54,333— 19
1968—$100,402— 14
1969—$ 70,707— 26
1970—$108,564— 12
1971—$ 85,738— 19

1972—$ 66,342—34
1973—$ 96,207—16
1974—$155,105— 6
1975—$ 72,885—28
1976—$ 94,973—27
1977—$ 58,328—53
1978—$ 65,016—46

Stockton graduated from the University of Southern California in 1964, turned professional immediately and struggled for three years on the PGA tour before winning the prestigious Colonial National Invitation in 1967. He hasn't been out of the top 60 since.

He won his first PGA Championship in 1970, when

he fought off extreme heat and a stretch challenge from Arnold Palmer at Southern Hills in Tulsa. Three victories in 1974 resulted in his most productive year. Dave's first win that year was at Los Angeles, where his 235-yard 3-wood shot on the 72nd hole set up a 12-foot birdie putt which beat Sam Snead and John Mahaffey.

He didn't win after 1974, however, until the 1976 PGA at Congressional. "I probably was heading for my poorest year," Stockton said, "and I can't tell you why. I was in the best physical condition of my life. I guess it was mental."

Stockton shot 70-72-69 at Congressional, and was four strokes back entering the last round. But he forged in front entering the last nine and then, on the water-guarded 72nd green, rolled in a 13-foot putt to beat Ray Floyd and Don January by a shot each.

HOWARD TWITTY

BORN: Jan. 21, 1949, Phoenix, Ariz.
HEIGHT: 6'5" WEIGHT: 220
RESIDENCE: Phoenix, Ariz.
FAMILY: Wife, Linda; Kevin Scott (10/2/76)
COLLEGE: Arizona State U. (1972, Business Administration)
SPECIAL INTERESTS: All sports
TURNED PROFESSIONAL: 1973 Q. SCHOOL: Spring 1975
CAREER EARNINGS THROUGH 1978: $215,303
TOUR VICTORIES: None
MONEY & POSITION:

1975—$ 8,211—139		1977—$60,091—49	
1976—$54,268— 51		1978—$92,409—25	

Twitty believes now that his ample physical proportions probably slowed his progress in golf at the start. He started to play at age 10 but it wasn't until he was a senior in high school in Phoenix that his game started to develop.

"I was about 6-3 when I was a sophomore," he recalls, "and I was terrible. I guess I just needed time to catch up with my body. I didn't have the coordination that I needed."

As a sophomore and junior at Arizona State, Twitty really showed progress, however. He won the important Sunnehanna and Porter Cup amateur events and, when a senior, he finished right behind the Texas co-champions, Ben Crenshaw and Tom Kite, in the NCAA championship.

Twitty turned pro in 1973 and twice failed in the PGA Tour Qualifying School before meeting success in June 1975. That was the same year he also won the Thailand Open during a second trip to the Far East circuit.

BOBBY WADKINS

BORN: July 26, 1951, Richmond, Va.
HEIGHT: 6'1" WEIGHT: 180
RESIDENCE: Richmond, Va.
FAMILY: Wife, Terry
COLLEGE: East Tennessee State (1973, Health and Phys. Education)
SPECIAL INTERESTS: Water skiing, duck and goose hunting
TURNED PROFESSIONAL: 1973 Q. SCHOOL: 1974
CAREER EARNINGS THROUGH 1978: $138, 134
TOUR VICTORIES: None
MONEY & POSITION:

1975—$23,330—90		1977—$20,867—103	
1976—$23,510—93		1978—$70,426— 41	

Bobby is approximately 20 months younger than his brother, Lanny, and while Lanny was more spectacular on the national amateur level and during his first couple of years on the tour, they both were standouts in junior golf around their home territory of Richmond, Va.

They kept the city junior title in the family for six straight years, with Lanny winning four.

Today Bobby and Lanny usually practice together, and when one needs help, he almost always goes to his brother.

After high school—where he also was a standout basketball player—Bobby headed for the University of Houston and his two closest friends there—and now—were Bill Rogers and Bruce Lietzke.

After one year, though, he transferred to East Tennessee State and earned All-America status in 1972 and 1973.

He earned his tour card in the fall of 1974, and was "satisfied" with his first-year earnings of $23,330. He stayed at approximately the same level the next two years and that was disappointing.

LANNY WADKINS

BORN: Dec. 5, 1949, Richmond, Va.
HEIGHT: 5'9" WEIGHT: 160
RESIDENCE: Advance, N.C.; plays out of Bermuda Run, N.C.
FAMILY: Wife, Penelope; Dawn (10/14/73)
COLLEGE: Wake Forest
SPECIAL INTERESTS: Fishing, other sports
TURNED PROFESSIONAL: 1971 Q. SCHOOL: 1971
CAREER EARNINGS: $737,154 PLAYOFF RECORD: 2–1
TOUR VICTORIES (TOTAL: 7): **1972** Sahara Invitational. **1973** Byron Nelson, USI Classic. **1977** PGA Championship, World Series of Golf. **1979** Los Angeles Open, Tournament Players Championship.
MONEY & POSITION:

1971—$ 15,291—111		1973—$200,455— 5	
1972—$116,616— 10		1974—$ 51,124— 54	

1975—$ 23,582—88	1977—$244,882— 3
1976—$ 42,849—64	1978—$ 53,811—61

Lanny enjoyed a brilliant amateur career, highlighted by a victory in the 1970 U.S. Amateur. It wasn't any surprise when he became an immediate success on the PGA tour. After earning his players' card in the fall of 1971, he went on to win the 1972 Sahara Invitational.

His superb play continued through 1973, winning $200,455, with victories in the Byron Nelson Classic in Dallas and the USI Classic in Sutton, Mass. His game started to sag in 1974. As the year progressed, he found it difficult to maintain his energy. In the fall his ailment was diagnosed as a diseased gall bladder and in early December, he underwent an operation for its removal.

Going against doctor's orders, he returned to the PGA tour in less than three months. Still weak, he developed bad habits and he admits it wasn't until mid-1976 that he was able to get his game back in its original groove.

TOM WATSON

BORN: Sept. 4, 1949, Kansas City, Mo.
HEIGHT: 5′9″   WEIGHT: 160
RESIDENCE: Kansas City, Mo.
FAMILY: Wife, Linda
COLLEGE: Stanford U. (1971)
SPECIAL INTERESTS: Hunting, fishing, guitar
TURNED PROFESSIONAL: 1971   Q. SCHOOL: 1971
CAREER EARNINGS THROUGH 1978: $1,201,391   PLAYOFF RECORD: 1–1

TOUR VICTORIES (TOTAL: 15): **1974** Western Open. **1975** Byron Nelson Golf Classic. **1977** Bing Crosby Pro-Am, San Diego Open, Masters, Western Open. **1978** Garagiola-Tucson Open, Bing Crosby Pro-Am, Byron Nelson Classic, Colgate Hall of Fame Classic, Anheuser-Busch Classic. **1979** Heritage Classic, Tournament of Champions, Byron Nelson Classic, Memorial.

MONEY & POSITION:

1972—$ 31,081—79	1976—$138,202—12
1973—$ 74,973—35	1977—$310,653— 1
1974—$135,474—10	1978—$362,429— 1
1975—$153,795— 7	

OTHER ACHIEVEMENTS: 1975 and 1977 British Open champion. Winner 1975 World Series of Golf. 1977 Ryder Cup team.

Watson was only six years old when his father, a scratch golfer, exposed him to the game. He became a four-time winner of the Missouri Amateur and played three years at Stanford University before graduating in 1971 with a degree in psychology.

Tom first gained national attention in 1974. He led the U.S. Open at Winged Foot after three rounds, but a final 79 dropped him to a share of fifth. Shortly thereafter, however, he scored his first PGA tour victory, coming from six shots back with a closing 69 to win the Western Open.

After winning four PGA tour events and the British Open in 1977, Tom cemented his reputation as one of the world's premiere golfers in 1978. Watson won five times, breaking a pair of PGA tour records—both previously held by Johnny Miller—along the way. His official earnings of $362,429 topped Miller's old mark of $353,021, set in 1974.

Watson also earned his first million dollars faster than anyone ever had on the tour. His career winnings passed seven figures with his victory in the Byron Nelson Classic, approximately six years and seven months after his first check on the tour. That broke Miller's old standard of six years, nine months.

TOM WEISKOPF

BORN: Nov. 9, 1942, Massillon, Ohio
HEIGHT: 6′3″   WEIGHT: 185
RESIDENCE: Phoenix, Ariz.
FAMILY: Wife, Jeanne Ruth; Heidi (3/20/71); Eric (1/10/73)
COLLEGE: Ohio State U.
SPECIAL INTERESTS: Hunting and all sports
TURNED PROFESSIONAL: 1964   JOINED TOUR: 1965
CAREER EARNINGS THROUGH 1978: $1,664,157   PLAYOFF RECORD: 2–2

TOUR VICTORIES (TOTAL: 13): **1968** Williams–San Diego, Buick. **1971** Kemper, IVB-Philadelphia. **1972** Jackie Gleason. **1973** Colonial, Kemper, IVB-Philadelphia, Canadian Open. **1975** Greater Greensboro Open, Canadian Open. **1977** Kemper Open. **1978** Doral-Eastern Open.

MONEY & POSITION:

1964—$ 1,008—	1968—$152,946— 3
1965—$ 11,264—72	1969—$ 81,594—18
1966—$ 37,166—27	1970—$ 95,287—19
1967—$ 40,069—30	1971—$106,538—12

1972—$129,422— 6	1976—$131,331—15
1973—$245,463— 3	1977—$197,639— 6
1974—$127,529—13	1978—$110,331—19
1975—$219,140— 3	

OTHER ACHIEVEMENTS: 1963 Western Amateur champion. 1972 World Picadilly Match Play champion. 1973 British Open, World Series of Golf and South African PGA champion. 1973 and 1975 Ryder Cup team. 1972 World Cup team.

Long regarded as one of the most talented players on the tour, Weiskopf proved in one dazzling spell in 1973 that he is capable of reaching unusual heights. During eight weeks that spring and summer he won five tournaments, including the British and Canadian opens. Carrying over to two other tournaments, he shot in the 60s in exactly half of his 40 rounds.

Later in 1973, Weiskopf also won the World Series of Golf and the South African PGA Championship. Although failing to win in 1974, Weiskopf passed the $1 million barrier in career earnings and finished in the top 10 in nine of 21 events. In 1975 he was a winner again and easily topped $200,000 for the second time.

FUZZY ZOELLER

BORN: Nov. 11, 1951, New Albany, Ind.
HEIGHT: 5'10" WEIGHT: 190
RESIDENCE: New Albany, Ind.
FAMILY: Wife, Dianne
COLLEGE: Edison Junior College in Ft. Myers, Fla., and U. of Houston
SPECIAL INTERESTS: All sports
TURNED PROFESSIONAL: 1973 Q. SCHOOL: 1974
CAREER EARNINGS THROUGH 1978: $245,347
TOUR VICTORIES (TOTAL: 2): **1979** Williams–San Diego Open. Masters.
MONEY & POSITION:

1975—$ 7,318—146	1977—$ 76,417—40
1976—$52,557— 56	1978—$109,055—20

Fuzzy Zoeller's statistics have improved geometrically since he joined the PGA tour after the 1974 Qualifying School. From 1975 through 1978 his money-winnings have jumped by $45,239, $23,860 and $32,638, respectively. During that span, he has lowered his position on the money list by 90, 16 and 20 places.

Zoeller grew up alongside a fairway at the Valley View C.C. in New Albany, Ind., and it seemed natural when he started swinging a golf club at age three. He entered his first tournament two years later. He enjoyed all sports while growing up, but when he was eight his father said to him, "Son, all we're doing is running back and forth between the golf course and the baseball diamond. You had better choose one."

Fuzzy chose golf, but during his days in high school he played varsity basketball, mainly, he said to "keep in shape for golf, and in Indiana in the winter you can't play golf."

He was second in the state scholastic golf tournament in 1970 and went to Edison Junior College in Florida, where he won the State Junior College title before entering the University of Houston.

LPGA TOUR

The LPGA tour, unlike the more firmly established PGA tour, makes numerous schedule changes and attracts a high number of new sponsors every year, with the result that the women's pro circuit is more difficult to pin down to a predictable annual pattern. Nevertheless, there is a core of stable tournament sites and dates. In the schedule below, dates indicated in parentheses indicate the year an event was first held—though not necessarily under its present name. These are the more established events. Golf courses listed are the "permanent" sites for those tournaments.

SPRING (April–May)

TOURNAMENT
Colgate–Dinah Shore Winners Circle (1972)
CONTACT FOR INFORMATION
　　Mission Hills C.C.
　　Palm Springs, CA
　　(714) 328-6502

Florida Ladies Citrus

Otey Crisman Classic (1972)
CONTACT FOR INFORMATION
　　Green Valley C.C.
　　Birmingham, AL
　　(205) 822-0647

Women's International (1976)
CONTACT FOR INFORMATION
　　Moss Creek Plantation
　　Hilton Head, SC
　　(803) 785-4488

Lady Michelob Classic (1970)
CONTACT FOR INFORMATION
　　Brookfield West G. & C.C.
　　Roswell, GA
　　(404) 993-1990

Coca-Cola Classic (1976)

Corning Classic

Golden Lights Championship (1976)
CONTACT FOR INFORMATION
  Wykagyl C.C.
  New Rochelle, NY
  (914) 636-8700

SUMMER (June–August)

TOURNAMENT
Ladies PGA Championship (1955)
CONTACT FOR INFORMATION
  LPGA
  919 Third Avenue
  New York, NY 10022
  (212) 751-8181

Sarah Coventry Classic (1973)
CONTACT FOR INFORMATION
  Locust Hill C.C.
  Rochester, NY
  (716) 586-3930

Lady Keystone Open (1975)
CONTACT FOR INFORMATION
  Hershey C. C.
  Hershey, PA
  (717) 533-2360

Lady Stroh's Open (1978)
CONTACT FOR INFORMATION
  Dearborn C.C.
  Dearborn, MI
  (313) 561-0800

Mayflower Classic (1976)
CONTACT FOR INFORMATION
  Harbour Trees G.C.
  Noblesville, IN
  (217) 896-3611

U.S. Women's Open (1946)
CONTACT FOR INFORMATION
  U.S. Golf Association
  Golf House
  Far Hills, NJ 07931
  (201) 234-2300

Greater Baltimore Golf Classic (1963)
CONTACT FOR INFORMATION
  Pine Ridge G.C.
  Timonium, MD
  (301) 252-0211

Peter Jackson Classic (1973)

Colgate European Open (1974)
CONTACT FOR INFORMATION
  Sunningdale G.C.
  Berkshire, England

WUI Classic (1978)

Barth Classic (1974)
CONTACT FOR INFORMATION
  Plymouth C.C.
  Plymouth, IN
  (219) 936-4543

Patty Berg Classic (1973)
CONTACT FOR INFORMATION
  Keller G.C.
  St. Paul, MN
  (612) 484-9154

Rail Charity Golf Classic (1976)
CONTACT FOR INFORMATION
  Rail G.C.
  Springfield, IL
  (217) 525-0365

FALL (September–December)

TOURNAMENT
Columbia Savings Classic (1972)
CONTACT FOR INFORMATION
  Green Gables C.C.
  Denver, CO
  (303) 985-4433

Ping Team Classic (1977)
Sept. 14–16
CONTACT FOR INFORMATION
  Portland G.C.
  Portland, OR
  (503) 292-2651

ERA Kansas City Classic
Sept. 20–23
CONTACT FOR INFORMATION
  Brookridge C.C.
  Kansas City, MO
  (913) 648-1600

United Virginia Bank Golf Classic
Sept. 27–30
CONTACT FOR INFORMATION
  Cedar Point C.C.
  Portsmouth, VA
  (804) 238-2275

Dallas (1956)
Oct. 4–7
CONTACT FOR INFORMATION
　　Bent Tree C.C.
　　Dallas, TX
　　(214) 233-7908

Houston
CONTACT FOR INFORMATION
　　Newport Yacht & C.C.
　　Crosby, TX
　　(713) 328-3511

Colgate Far East Open (1974)

Japan Classic

J. C. Penney Mixed Team Classic (1977)
CONTACT FOR INFORMATION
　　Bardmoor C.C.
　　Largo, FL 33541
　　(813) 392-1234

WINTER (February–March)

TOURNAMENT
Colgate Triple Crown

LPGA Match Play Championship (1975)
CONTACT FOR INFORMATION
　　Mission Hills, C.C.
　　Palm Springs, CA
　　(714) 328-6502

Elizabeth Arden Classic

Orange Blossom Classic (1954)
CONTACT FOR INFORMATION
　　Pasadena G.C.
　　St. Petersburg, FL
　　(813) 345-9329

Bent Tree Classic (1976)
CONTACT FOR INFORMATION
　　Bent Tree G.C.
　　Sarasota, FL
　　(813) 371-5854

Sunstar Classic (1978)
CONTACT FOR INFORMATION
　　Rancho Park C.C.
　　Los Angeles, CA
　　(213) 838-7373

Honda Civic Golf Classic (1977)
CONTACT FOR INFORMATION
　　Rancho Bernardo Inn
　　San Diego, CA
　　(714) 487-1611

Sahara National Pro-Am

Women's Kemper Open

BOOKS ABOUT THE LPGA TOUR

"WHATTA-GAL"—THE BABE DIDRIKSON STORY by William Oscar Johnson and Nancy P. Williamson. 1977, 224 pages, $8.95, Boston: Little, Brown.

The authors rightfully deplore the sentimentalism of a major TV special on the life of history's greatest woman athlete, which was morbid in its fascination with the Babe's death by cancer. Curiously, this hardnose bio, relying a great deal on apparently unedited oral history, is just as disappointing. One gets to know the Babe warts and nothing else. Nevertheless the sophisticated treatment is of great interest for the light it sheds on the first years of the LPGA, and as a kind of document of an early superstar. Half is about golf.

EARLY DAYS

The charter membership of the Ladies Professional Golf Association numbered six. They were Babe Didrikson Zaharias, Patty Berg, Helen Dettweiler, Betty Jameson, Betty Hicks and Bea Gottlieb. This was a select but relatively deprived little group. None was in any way prospering from the sport, except for Babe and Patty Berg. Patty had turned professional in 1940 when she was twenty-two and, like Babe, had a contract with L. B. Icely's Wilson Company. In January 1948, Babe, Patty, George and Fred Corcoran got together at the Venetian Hotel in Miami and in a couple of afternoons laid out the new L.P.G.A. Patty volunteered to be president that first year. L. B. Icely put up the prize money—$15,000.

And that was all there was in 1949—$15,000 over nine tournaments. Babe Zaharias ended up as the leading money-winner with a mere $4,300. Despite its puny beginning, it was obvious that the L.P.G.A. was an excellent idea whose time had come: it grew with astounding rapidity, attracting dozens of new members and thousands of new dollars in the first year. In 1950 Babe was the leading winner with

$13,450 and in 1951 she won $15,087—more than they had for the whole tour two years before. In the first five years, the total L.P.G.A. prize money multiplied fifteenfold—to $225,000.

As the money poured in and more women began competing, rivalries were born. Babe's most intense rival was Louise Suggs, a chunky brunette from Atlanta. Louise was stoic, very serious, a colorless person who was almost completely humorless. She was, however, a superb golfer and her record was almost as good as Babe's. Because of her withdrawn personality, Louise never got the adoring press coverage that Babe did. Suggs won the British Women's Amateur in 1948, the year after Babe, and the feat received about half the coverage Babe's victory had, and there was certainly no tugboat full of reporters to greet Louise when she returned. Even when she defeated Babe, the headlines as often as not said BABE LOSES rather than LOUISE WINS. These things grated on her, naturally. She also disapproved of Babe's loud, flamboyant behavior; she believed that golf should be a dignified game and that Babe's quips and tricks on the course were disgraceful.

Once Louise was silently frowning over a crucial putt on the eighteenth green of a tournament. The gallery was hushed, Louise lined it up, poised to hit it and at the instant she took her putter back to strike the ball Babe and Betty Dodd suddenly cut loose on the clubhouse porch with a hillbilly song, Babe tootling her harmonica and Betty twanging her guitar. Louise jerked, hit the ball, missed the putt. She was enraged and stalked off the course. Babe and Betty swore it was an accident, that they hadn't known she was on the green. Louise refused to talk to either of them for days, convinced they had done it purposely to ruin her shot.

—from *"Whatta-Gal"*

THE GUTS TO WIN by Jane Blalock, with Dwayne Netland. 1977, 158 pages, $7.95, *Golf Digest;* N.Y. distributor: Simon and Schuster.

Focus here is on Blalock's struggle (successful) to free herself of the cheating charges that were brought against her by several other LPGA members in 1972. But along the way she provides numerous glimpses of other more interesting aspects of life on today's growing women's tour.

CONTROVERSY

The next tournament was the Titleholders, held at the Pine Needles resort that Warren and Peggy Kirk Bell own in Southern Pines, N.C. On the drive to Southern Pines, Sandra and I stopped at Greensboro to see Ernie Vossler, Sandra's instructor. Ernie and his partner, a lawyer named John Russell, were building a golf course called the Cardinal.

Ernie had played the PGA tour before he got into the golf architecture business, and I trusted him. I told him the whole story about what happened at Louisville. "I'm

not perfect," I said. "I may have marked my ball wrong at times. You know how difficult it is to put it back in the same spot every time. But I've never done anything intentionally wrong, and I can honestly tell you I've never tried to cheat."

I showed him how I prefer to mark the coin well behind the ball, so that if I'm nervous or tense under tournament pressure I would be sure not to touch it. Then I'd carefully return the ball to its previous position. It's something I had always done on the tour.

Ernie advised me to take that approach with the board at Pine Needles if they called me into another meeting. "Tell them you're sorry if you've done anything wrong," he said, "and promise them it will never happen again."

It wasn't the best advice I've ever received.

At Pine Needles I met with Cynthia Sullivan, Judy Rankin, Sharon Miller and Gene McCauliff. Penny Zachivas and Linda Craft were not there because they weren't eligible to play in that tournament.

Before we had to really discuss the situation, they told me I had been put on probation and fined $500. I still didn't think the situation was all that serious. They asked me if there was anything I wanted to say. Remembering what Ernie had told me, I apologized for anything I had unintentionally done wrong and then added, "If all these things you say are true, I guess I've dug my own grave and I'll just have to live with it."

While the meeting was taking place in the dining room, several of the women, including Marlene Hagge and Louise Suggs, were sitting in the bar awaiting the news. Someone went right from the meeting to the bar and told them exactly what I had said. Shortly after, Jan Ferraris and Sally Little rushed up to me. "Janie," Jan said, "there's a lot of talk going on. They said you've admitted your guilt. They're talking now about suspending you."

After hearing this, I became desperate. I went up to Judy Rankin and asked her what was going on. She didn't say much. Neither did Cynthia. Marlene Hagge walked by and she gave me the most chilling, devastating look I've ever seen. I'll never forget that look.

Betsy Rawls was there at the tournament. We all respected her. I went to her room and pleaded my case. I discovered I had been accused of moving the ball as much as two inches ahead of the marker. That was stupid, because I always had big galleries and there was no way I could get away with doing that during my two years on the tour. Betsy seemed to understand.

Then I heard some more rumors from Jan Ferraris. That night I went to see Sharon Miller, who was staying in a trailer park near the course, and I threw a tantrum. "Sharon," I screamed, "tell me what is going on! I thought you were my friend!"

I finally got Sharon to admit that I might be suspended. She said that I had cheated the LPGA and that by doing so I was taking money out of her pocket.

My next stop was Kathy Whitworth. I was trying to get

some answers from people I respected. "Kathy," I said, "you know I don't ever recall doing what they say. If I have ever mis-marked, it wasn't intentional and it certainly was minimal."

Kathy looked at me and replied, "Well, there's no such thing as being a little bit pregnant."

—from *The Guts to Win*

LEADING PLAYERS ON LPGA TOUR

AMY ALCOTT

BORN: Feb. 22, 1956, Kansas City, Mo.
RESIDENCE: Santa Monica, Calif.
TURNED PROFESSIONAL: 1975
CAREER EARNINGS THROUGH 1978: $221,596
LOWEST CAREER ROUND: 67
TOUR VICTORIES: 6

Professional Career: Right from the start Amy has been one of the consistently impressive players on tour. She was Rookie-of-the-Year in 1975 and she won the third tournament she played as a pro. She has won at least one tournament each year she has been on tour and in 1978 had her best season financially, with more than $75,000 in earnings for ninth place on the money list.

Style of Play: An accomplished scrambler, Amy is capable of extraordinary birdie streaks. She is one of the tour's hardest workers and is dedicated to being the best.

Personal: Writes the "Alcott Report," a column for *Golf World Magazine* . . . Hopes for a career in broadcasting when she leaves the tour . . . Is a member of Riviera C.C. . . . Likes to jog, play tennis, cook, and collect wine.

DEBBIE AUSTIN

BORN: Feb. 1, 1948, Oneida, N.Y.
RESIDENCE: Boynton Beach, Fla.
TURNED PROFESSIONAL: 1968
CAREER EARNINGS THROUGH 1978: $285,863
LOWEST CAREER ROUND: 66
TOUR VICTORIES: 6

Professional Career: Consistency had always been Debbie's strength as she finished among the top 25 money winners each year since 1971, but not until 1977 was she able to crack the winner's circle. Her first victory came in the Birmingham Classic and she continued on to win four more titles that year, including three in a four-week span. 1978 was not quite as lucrative but she did win almost $45,000 and one tournament, the American Cancer Society Classic.

Style of Play: A long hitter with a smooth, fluid swing, Debbie's consistency enables her to hit a lot of greens in regulation. When she is putting well she is always in contention.

Personal: 5'4", 150 lbs. Credits Al Reynolds with refining her game and Sherry Wilder with teaching her how to win . . . Torn tendons in her left shoulder hampered her in 1978 . . . At the end of 1978 she attended Travel Agents school . . . Was *Golf Digest's* Most Improved Player and *Golf Magazine's* Player-of-the-Year in 1977.

LAURA BAUGH

BORN: May 31, 1955, Gainesville, Fla.
RESIDENCE: Delray Beach, Fla.
TURNED PROFESSIONAL: 1973
CAREER EARNINGS THROUGH 1978: $181,621
LOWEST CAREER ROUND: 65

Professional Career: Because of the LPGA's minimum age requirement of 18, Laura was unable to play the tour in her first six months as a pro, but in her first LPGA event—the Lady Tara in Atlanta—she made her presence known immediately by leading for two rounds before finishing tied for second. She was named Rookie-of-the-Year in '73, and continued to improve in '74, when she finished in the top ten 13 times and was 12th on the money list. She had her best season financially in 1977, when she won $46,373, finishing in the top four in three consecutive tournaments and equaling the LPGA record for most birdies in a round with nine at the Borden Classic. That elusive first victory still did not come her way in 1978 but her consistency remained as she had five top ten showings and finished 25th on the money list.

Personal: 5'4½", 110 lbs. . . . Credits her father, mother and brother with teaching her golf and guiding her career . . . Father Hale played golf at the Univer-

sity of Florida and brother Beau is a golf professional
. . . A former Los Angeles Woman-of-the-Year . . .
Attended Long Beach City College and California State
University . . . Enjoys modeling, dance, acting and
music.

SILVIA BERTOLACCINI

BORN: Jan. 30, 1950, Rafaela, Argentina
RESIDENCE: Dallas, Tex.
TURNED PROFESSIONAL: 1975
CAREER EARNINGS THROUGH 1978: $150,209
LOWEST CAREER ROUND: 65
TOUR VICTORIES: 2

Professional Career: After winning her first tournament as a professional in the 1977 Colgate Far East
Open, Silvia captured her first U.S. pro victory during
1978 when she outbattled Kathy Whitworth for the
Civitan Open title. She finished the season with almost
$54,000 in official earnings for 14th place on the money
list. In 1977 she tied the LPGA 36-hole record of 131
by shooting 66-65 in the Lady Keystone Open.

Style of Play: A good wind player who hits the ball
long and with a draw, Silvia plays particularly well on
long, difficult courses requiring placement.

Personal: 5'8", 126 lbs. . . . Both her parents were
avid golfers and got her started playing at the age of 10
. . . Graduated in 1968 from the National College of
Argentina . . . Her favorite athlete is native country-
man Roberto de Vicenzo . . . Enjoys playing tennis
and listening to music.

JANE BLALOCK

BORN: Sept. 19, 1945, Portsmouth, N.H.
RESIDENCE: Highland Beach, Fla.
TURNED PROFESSIONAL: 1969
CAREER EARNINGS THROUGH 1978: $593,709
LOWEST CAREER ROUND: 67
TOUR VICTORIES: 23

Professional Career: From her first season on the
LPGA Tour when she was chosen Rookie-of-the-Year,
Jane has grown steadily into one of the toughest competitors and most accomplished players on tour. She
won her first professional title in 1970 at the Lady
Carling, won twice the following year and has captured
21 more assorted titles in the years since. Only twice in
the last eight seasons has she failed to finish among
the top five money winners, and she completed her best
year ever in 1978 by winning four events and more
than $117,000, going over $100,000 for the second
straight year. Jane has been named to *Golf Magazine*'s
All-American team for her play with Middle Irons in
1977 and '78.

Style of Play: An aggressive player who performs
well in the wind, Jane seems to thrive on pressure. She
is an excellent putter who reads greens well and seldom
three-putts.

Personal: 5'6", 120 lbs. . . . Started playing golf at
age 13 and credits Bob Toski and Tom Nieporte for
helping develop her game . . . Pigtails have been her
trademark . . . Graduated in 1967 from Rollins College with a B.A. in History . . . Is a former school-
teacher.

PAT BRADLEY

BORN: March 24, 1951, Arlington, Mass.
RESIDENCE: Westford, Mass.
TURNED PROFESSIONAL: 1974
CAREER EARNINGS THROUGH 1978: $320,188
LOWEST CAREER ROUND: 64
TOUR VICTORIES: 5

Professional Career: When Pat took medalist honors
at the January 1974 Qualifying School, it was a portent
of things to come. She won the Colgate Far East Open
in 1975 for her first professional victory, and won one
tournament each in 1976 and 1977 before emerging
as one of the LPGA's most dominant players in 1978,
when she won four tournaments and well over $100,-
000. She was named Most Improved Player in 1976
and was named to *Golf Magazine*'s All-America Team
for long irons in both 1977 and 1978. Also won '78
J. C. Penney Classic (unofficial mixed team event) with
Lon Hinkle.

Style of Play: Above average in strength, Pat is one of the longer players off the tee. Her low, drawing shot is effective in the wind. Improvement in course management was a key to her success in the last three years.

Personal: Taught by John Wirbal, pro at Nashua, N.H. C.C. . . . Lists her father, Richard J. Bradley, Jr., as a major influence . . . He owns a sports shop in Westford, Mass. . . . Enjoys skiing during the winter months . . . A great sports fan, she is loyal to all the pro teams in Boston . . . Has played golf with former President Ford at Vail, Colo., in the last three years . . . Graduated from Florida International University in 1974 with a B.S. in Physical Education.

JERILYN BRITZ

BORN: Jan. 1, 1943, Minneapolis, Minn.
RESIDENCE: Luverne, Minn.
TURNED PROFESSIONAL: 1973
CAREER EARNINGS THROUGH 1978: $82,696
LOWEST CAREER ROUND: 67

Professional Career: Having improved steadily each year since joining the tour in 1974 Jerilyn had by far her best season in 1978 as she won almost $40,000 and finished in 23rd position on the money list. She had seven top ten finishes in '78, including six in a ten-week span.

Personal: Academically oriented, she earned a B.S. from Mankato State College in Minnesota and an M.S. in physical education from the University of New Mexico. She then taught for five years at St. Anthony's High School in Minneapolis, two years at the University of New Mexico and one at New Mexico State . . . Credits JoAnne Winter and Joe Nichols with refining her game . . . Has a pilot's license and tries to fly as often as possible.

JOANNE CARNER

BORN: Apr. 4, 1939, Kirkland, Wash.
RESIDENCE: Lake Worth, Fla.
TURNED PROFESSIONAL: 1970

CAREER EARNINGS THROUGH 1978: $551,761
LOWEST CAREER ROUND: 64
TOUR VICTORIES: 22

Professional Career: Joanne won a tournament in her first year on tour when she captured the 1970 Wendell West Open in Ocean Shores, Wash. She earned $15,000 that season and was named Rookie-of-the-Year. In 1971 she stopped Donna Caponi Young's bid to win three consecutive U.S. Opens by taking that coveted title at the Kahkwa C.C. in Erie, Pa. JoAnne was winless the next two years but blossomed with six tournament victories in 1974 and was named Player of the Year. She has been one of the tour's most consistently dominant players ever since. She won three times in 1978, including the unofficial Colgate Triple Crown where she utilized the match-play skills learned as an amateur, and became the first player ever to win more than $100,000 in three successive years.

Style of Play: Because of her great strength, JoAnne prefers the longer courses. She is aggressive, at times to the point of recklessness, and likes to go for broke.

Personal: 5'7" . . . Travels the Tour in a plush trailer with her husband, Don . . . Started playing at age 10 and has been tutored by Gordon Jenkins, John Hoetmer and, most recently, Gardner Dickinson . . . Credits Billy Martin with developing proper mental attitude . . . One of the longest hitters ever in women's golf.

GLORIA EHRET

BORN: Aug. 23, 1941, Allentown, Pa.
RESIDENCE: Richardson, Tex.
TURNED PROFESSIONAL: 1965
CAREER EARNINGS: $212,545
LOWEST CAREER ROUND: 66
TOUR VICTORIES: 2

Professional Career: It did not take Gloria long to make a name for herself on tour as she finished fifth in the LPGA Championship in 1965, her rookie year. She won that prestigious title the following year and was subsequently named Most Improved Player on tour. A few lean years followed but she broke through with victory again in 1973, capturing the Birmingham Classic, and has been a consistent finisher ever since. She had her most lucrative season in 1978, winning more than $42,000 and finishing 22nd on the money list.

Personal: 5'8", 135 lbs. . . . Turns to Gail Davis of Dallas when any phase of her game needs work . . . Enjoys reading, writing and collecting coins . . . Attended St. Petersburg Junior College.

BETSY KING

BORN: Aug. 13, 1955, Reading, Pa.
RESIDENCE: Limekiln, Pa.

TURNED PROFESSIONAL: 1977
CAREER EARNINGS THROUGH 1978: $48,101
LOWEST CAREER ROUND: 67

Professional Career: In her first professional tournament, the Long Island Charity Classic, Betsy carded a 67 in the second round to take the 36-hole lead. This convincing debut was clearly no fluke as she came out in 1978 and had a great year, winning nearly $45,000 and finishing 20th on the money list. She had eight top-ten showings, including a tie for second in the Borden Classic.

Style of Play: Betsy is an aggressive player who swings hard and hits the ball long for her size. She manages her game well, is a fine strategist, and possesses a lot of composure and control for her age.

Personal: 5'6", 120 lbs. . . . Graduated from Furman University in 1977 with a B.A. in Physical Education . . . At Furman she was named both Athlete of the Year and Woman Scholar-Athlete of the Year . . . Also played basketball and field hockey in college . . . John Gerring has been her teacher the last five years.

SALLY LITTLE

BORN: Oct. 12, 1951, Cape Town, South Africa
RESIDENCE: Dallas, Tex.
TURNED PROFESSIONAL: 1971
CAREER EARNINGS THROUGH 1978: $236,820
LOWEST CAREER ROUND: 65
TOUR VICTORIES: 3

Professional Career: Sally joined the tour in 1971 after finishing fifth in an LPGA event as an amateur. She was subsequently named Rookie-of-the-Year, although she played in only seven tournaments. The next four years were part of the learning process for Sally and she improved gradually. In 1976 she broke through with a dramatic victory in the Women's International, where she holed a bunker shot on the final hole to edge Jan Stephenson by one. The past two years she has finished among the top ten money winners and has

added another title, the '78 Kathryn Crosby/Honda Civic Classic.

Style of Play: A potential superstar who has had to deal with a series of nagging injuries, Sally is capable of some incredible rounds, evidenced by her 65 in the 1978 U.S. Open.

Personal: 5'8" . . . Her father, Percy, was her only teacher before she turned pro . . . Eldrige Miles and Peter Kostis have worked with her game more recently . . . Attended secretarial college . . . Enjoys tennis and music.

NANCY LOPEZ

BORN: Jan. 6, 1957, Torrance, Calif.
RESIDENCE: Harrisburg, Pa./Roswell, N.M.
TURNED PROFESSIONAL: 1977
CAREER EARNINGS THROUGH 1978: $212,952
LOWEST CAREER ROUND: 65
TOUR VICTORIES: 11

Professional Career: Nancy finished second in the 1977 U.S. Open, her first tournament as a professional, before qualifying for the tour. After successfully making it through the qualifying school the following week she finished second in two more events, the Colgate European Open and the Long Island Charity Classic. It was all merely a prelude to 1978, though, when Nancy captured the fancy of golf fans throughout the world by winning nine tournaments and setting numerous records, never losing her grace and her glowing smile.

— Won $161,235 in her rookie year (August '77 through July '78), the most by any rookie ever, with five consecutive tournaments in which she was entered.
— Through 1978 has not finished lower than tied for 25th in any event in her professional career.

Style of Play: Nancy's swing is characterized by superb rhythm, and her ability to carry the ball a long way gives her an advantage on soft or hilly courses. It is her excellent putting, though, that makes her a threat in every tournament she enters.

Personal: 5'7" . . . Attended Tulsa University two years on a Colgate Scholarship . . . Was named Most Valuable Player and Female Athlete of the Year at Tulsa two years . . . Took up golf at age eight under influence of her father, Domingo.

DEBBIE MASSEY

BORN: Nov. 5, 1950, Grosse Pointe, Mich.
RESIDENCE: Bethlehem, Pa.
TURNED PROFESSIONAL: 1977
CAREER EARNINGS THROUGH 1978: $117,175
LOWEST CAREER ROUND: 67
TOUR VICTORIES: 1

Professional Career: With her impressive amateur record it was not surprising that Debbie came out in her first year on tour and immediately established herself as a quality professional. She won nearly $47,000, won the Mizuno Japan Classic and was named Rookie-of-the-Year, her rookie earnings setting a new standard at the time. She continued to improve in 1978, finishing with over $70,000 in winnings for 11th place on the money list.

Style of Play: Noted for her strength, composure under fire and intelligent play, which makes her a frequent contender.

Personal: 5'8", 140 lbs. . . . Graduated in 1972 from the University of Denver with a B.A. in Elementary Education . . . Former professional ski instructor . . . Lists Dorothy Porter, Morry Holland, and Joe Dey as major influences on her career . . . Enjoys tennis, squash, and bike riding.

PAT MEYERS

BORN: May 8, 1954, Beverly, Mass.
RESIDENCE: Ormond Beach, Fla.
TURNED PROFESSIONAL: 1976
CAREER EARNINGS THROUGH 1978: $77,212
LOWEST CAREER ROUND: 67

Professional Career: Regarded by her peers as one of the most underrated players on tour, Pat has yet to break into the win column but in the past two years has finished second no less than five times. She is consistently in the top ten and it is only a matter of time before she takes her first title as a professional.

Style of Play: Good fundamentals and a solid swing insure consistency, occasional low scores, and a bright future.

Personal: 5'4" . . . Formerly Pat Roy, married Bob Meyers in 1974 . . . Attended Daytona Beach Community College . . . Lists Mike O'Sullivan as her only teacher . . . Enjoys bridge and backgammon.

SANDRA PALMER

BORN: March 10, 1941, Ft. Worth, Tex.
RESIDENCE: Boca Raton, Fla.
TURNED PROFESSIONAL: 1964
CAREER EARNINGS THROUGH 1978: $545,128
LOWEST CAREER ROUND: 66
TOUR VICTORIES: 18

Professional Career: The 1978 season was a bit of a disappointment for Sandra as she failed to win a tournament for the first year since 1970, but her record in prior years certainly establishes her as one of the LPGA's true stars. She did not win a tournament for her first seven years on tour, and did not win fewer than two per year for the next seven. Her best season came in 1975, when she was the leading money winner and was named LPGA Player of the Year. Despite not winning in '78 she had nine finishes in the top ten.

Style of Play: One of the tour's hardest workers, Sandra gets remarkable distance for her size. A good pressure player, she is one of the best putters and sand players on tour.

Personal: 5'1½", 117 lbs. . . . Full name Sandra Jean. . . Graduated from North Texas State in 1964 with a degree in physical education . . . Started playing golf at age 13 in Bangor, Maine, where she worked as a caddy . . . Teachers have included Harry Pressler, Harvey Penick, Johnny Revolta and Ernie Vossler . . . Was an all-district basketball player in high school . . . Was named North Texas State's Alumna of the Year in 1977.

SANDRA POST

BORN: June 4, 1948, Oakville, Ontario, Canada
RESIDENCE: Boynton Beach, Fla.
TURNED PROFESSIONAL: 1968
CAREER EARNINGS THROUGH 1978: $346,840
LOWEST CAREER ROUND: 65
TOUR VICTORIES: 3

Professional Career: Sandra got off to an auspicious start in her career by winning the LPGA Championship in her rookie year at the tender age of 19, defeating veteran Kathy Whitworth in an 18-hole play-off. She was subsequently named Rookie-of-the-Year. She was not to win another official tournament for ten years, but she broke through as a double winner in 1978, capturing the prestigious Colgate–Dinah Shore Winner's Circle, in which she shot her low career round of 65, and the new Lady Stroh's Open. She finished seventh on the money list with over $92,000.

Style of Play: Her strength lies in fairway woods, mid-irons and putting. Sandra is a consistent top-ten finisher, and performs particularly well on courses that require positioning.

Personal: 5'4", 120 lbs. . . . Inspired by watching LPGA tournaments in Florida, she took up the game at age five . . . Instructed throughout her career by her father, Cliff, and Elmer Prieskorn . . . Enjoys gardening, needlepoint, and traveling.

KATHY POSTLEWAIT

BORN: Nov. 11, 1949, Norfolk, Va.
RESIDENCE: Sylacauga, Ala.
TURNED PROFESSIONAL: 1972
CAREER EARNINGS THROUGH 1978: $100,223
LOWEST CAREER ROUND: 67

Professional Career: Steady progression each year has been Kathy's trademark and in 1978 she moved into the tour's elite, finishing 17th on the money list with over $45,000 in earnings. She had nine finishes in the top ten, her best showing a solo fourth at Houston, where she also had her best tournament in 1977.

Style of Play: Kathy has a sound and simple swing, which results in accuracy and consistency. She gains confidence with each good performance and should be a good player for a long time.

Personal: 5'8", 135 lbs. . . . Her father, Ken, a golf pro, has been her most important teacher and motivator . . . Has recently worked with Davis Love . . . Graduated from East Carolina University in 1971 . . . A car accident caused a slump after a good start in 1976 . . . Likes to work on cars and tinker with her motorhome.

PENNY PULZ

BORN: Feb. 2, 1953, Melbourne, Australia

RESIDENCE: Palm Springs, Calif.
TURNED PROFESSIONAL: 1973
CAREER EARNINGS THROUGH 1978: $115,943
LOWEST CAREER ROUND: 65

Professional Career: Penny showed marked improvement in each of her first four seasons on the U.S. tour, but made a most remarkable leap to prominence in 1978 as she won more than $71,000 and finished tenth on the money list. She finished in the top ten in one out of every three tournaments she entered, her best showing a second-place in the Colgate–Dinah Shore Winners Circle, where she lost in a play-off to Sandra Post.

Style of Play: With a mechanically sound swing and a good mental approach, Penny should soon break into the win column.

Personal: 5'3", 125 lbs. . . . Loves rock music, waterskiing and playing squash.

JUDY T. RANKIN

BORN: Feb. 18, 1945, St. Louis, Mo.
RESIDENCE: Midland, Tex.
TURNED PROFESSIONAL: 1962
CAREER EARNINGS THROUGH 1978: $652,618
LOWEST CAREER ROUND: 63
TOUR VICTORIES: 25

Professional Career: A consistent player and frequent champion throughout her career, Judy really emerged as one of the LPGA's all-time greatest players in 1976, when she became the first woman ever to earn over $100,000 in a single season. She accomplished the feat again in '77 and in both years was the LPGA Player of the Year and winner of the Vare Trophy for low scoring-average. She was also the Golf Writers Association of America Player of the Year in 1977. A chronic back problem plagued her during the 1978 season.

Style of Play: Patience and perseverance characterize Judy's game. A strong fairway-wood and medium-iron player, her success in '76 was the result of vastly improved putting. She is a great wind player.

Personal: 5'3½", 110 lbs. . . . Maiden name Torluemke, married Yippy Rankin in June 1967 . . . They have a son, Tuey, 10 . . . Started playing golf at age six under guidance of her father, Paul, and received instruction also from Eddie Held, Bob Greene and, most recently, Bob Toski . . . Joined the tour at age 17.

ALEXANDRA REINHARDT

BORN: May 19, 1953, Albuquerque, N.M.
RESIDENCE: Albuquerque, N.M.
TURNED PROFESSIONAL: 1974
CAREER EARNINGS THROUGH 1978: $51,316
LOWEST CAREER ROUND: 64

Professional Career: Perseverance has paid off for Alex, who lost her playing card at the end of 1975. She came back to regain her playing privileges and had a banner year in 1978, finishing 24th on the money list with almost $38,000. She shot a spectacular 64 at the Houston Exchange Clubs Classic which led to a second-place finish, her best of the year.

Personal: 5'8" . . . Likes all sports, music and art . . . Teachers who have helped polish her game are E. Oldfield, Joanne Winter and Jim Hardy.

HOLLIS STACY

BORN: March 16, 1954, Savannah, Ga.
RESIDENCE: Savannah, Ga.
TURNED PROFESSIONAL: 1974
CAREER EARNINGS THROUGH 1978: $239,279
LOWEST CAREER ROUND: 65
TOUR VICTORIES: 5

Professional Career: After maturing steadily through her first three years on tour, Hollis assumed a role as one of the LPGA's finest players in 1977, when she won three official events and finished fifth on the money list. In the process she broke Kathy Whitworth's 11-year-old record for low 72-hole total by carding 271 at Springfield. She was just as solid in 1978, entering the history books again by becoming only the fourth woman ever to win two consecutive U.S. Open titles. In both '77 and '78 she displayed her consistency by recording 12 finishes in the top ten.

Style of Play: An adept player with long irons, Hollis will frequently use a 1-iron off the tee. She is a flamboyant, aggressive player, which makes her a big favorite with the galleries.

Personal: 5'5" . . . Attended Rollins College in Florida but left school to turn pro.

JAN STEPHENSON

BORN: Dec. 22, 1951, Sydney, Australia
RESIDENCE: Palm Springs, Calif.
TURNED PROFESSIONAL: 1973
CAREER EARNINGS THROUGH 1978: $233,017
LOWEST CAREER ROUND: 65
TOUR VICTORIES: 3

Professional Career: Before coming to America, Jan won four events on the Australian LPGA circuit, including the Australian Championship. In the U.S. she was named Rookie-of-the-Year in 1974, moved into the top 25 money winners in '75 and broke through in '76 with two tournament victories. Although she didn't win in 1977 she continued to be a consistent top-ten finisher and in '78 she won the Women's International and had her best year for earnings to date.

Style of Play: Jan has a mechanically sound swing and good tempo, which allows her to control the ball well. She has a fine putting stroke as well. Her low rounds tend to come in bunches.

Personal: 5'5", 115 lbs. . . . Graduated from Hales Secretarial College in Sydney . . . Is interested in journalism, and wrote columns for the *Daily Mirror* in Sydney and *Australian Golf* magazine . . . A great sports enthusiast, she likes to ski and surf.

DONNA CAPONI YOUNG

BORN: Jan. 29, 1945, Detroit, Mich.
RESIDENCE: Los Angeles, Calif.
TURNED PROFESSIONAL: 1965
CAREER EARNINGS THROUGH 1978: $477,315
LOWEST CAREER ROUND: 67
TOUR VICTORIES: 13

Professional Career: Donna's first victory was the 1969 U.S. Open, and the following year she became only the second woman ever to win that title in consecutive years. She was named Most Improved Player by *Golf Digest* in '69 and the *L.A. Times* Woman Golfer of the Year in '70. Her best was yet to come, however, and in 1976 she was one of three players to break the $100,000 barrier for the first time. She also won four events that year including three in a row. After a mild slump in 1977 she came back in '78 to win twice and finish with $96,000 in earnings, fifth on the money list.

Style of Play: A slow takeaway makes her an accurate driver, and her real strength is in the fairway woods and long irons. Donna tends to gain confidence and momentum from good performances, which often leads to consecutive wins.

Personal: 5'5" . . . In high school earned varsity letters in seven sports . . . Married Ken Young in 1971, and he is tournament manager for several LPGA events . . . Sister Janet Caponi LePera also competes on the LPGA Tour . . . Loves music and dancing.

JO ANN WASHAM

BORN: May 24, 1950, Auburn, Wash.
RESIDENCE: Dallas, Tex.
TURNED PROFESSIONAL: 1973
CAREER EARNINGS THROUGH 1978: $137,869
LOWEST CAREER ROUND: 66
TOUR VICTORIES: 2

Professional Career: Progressing rapidly after joining the tour in 1973, Jo Ann emerged as a player of quality in 1975, when she won two events and finished 12th on the money list. She has been a consistent top-ten performer since and in 1978 had her best year ever financially, winning more than $45,000.

Style of Play: Despite an effortless-looking swing, Jo Ann is one of the tour's longest hitters. She is an aggressive player who likes to take chances and she has the ability to play spectacular rounds.

Personal: 5'3", 120 lbs. . . . Graduated from Washington State University with a B.S. in Recreation . . . Attended college three years on an Evans caddie scholarship . . . A very long hitter despite her size.

KATHY WHITWORTH

BORN: Sept. 27, 1939, Monahans, Tex.
RESIDENCE: Richardson, Tex.
TURNED PROFESSIONAL: 1959
CAREER EARNINGS THROUGH 1978: $822,214
LOWEST CAREER ROUND: 65
TOUR VICTORIES: 80
LPGA HALL OF FAME MEMBER

Professional Career: Surely one of the greatest players in the history of the LPGA, Kathy is the leading all-time money winner with $822,214 in career earnings. She has 80 official tour victories, second only to Mickey Wright, who has 82. She has won three LPGA Championships, has been leading money winner eight times, and has been Player of the Year and has won the Vare Trophy for low scoring average seven times each. The only gap in her record is that she has never won the U.S. Open; second place in 1972 is her best Open performance. Kathy has won nine tournaments in a year once, eight in a year three times, and has won at least one tournament in each of the last 17 seasons. In 1978 she won the National Jewish Hospital Open in

Denver and teamed with Donna Young to win the Ping Classic Team Championship.

Style of Play: Kathy is one of the greatest putters in the history of women's golf. She can maneuver the ball and can play all kinds of shots, and is particularly adept at saving strokes around the greens. She adapts well to all conditions and is at her best under pressure.

Personal: 5'9", 140 lbs. . . . Started golf at age 15, has been tutored by Harvey Penick and Hardy Loudermilk . . . Attended Odessa Junior College . . . A former president of the LPGA Executive Board.

CHARITIES SUPPORTED BY PGA AND LPGA EVENTS

Not all the money generated by the professional golf tours winds up in the bank accounts of Nicklaus, Watson, Lopez, et al. In fact in 1978, the PGA and LPGA combined helped raise $8 million for the various charities listed below. No other pro sport is so solidly linked to fund-raising. In fact, all other professional sports *combined* usually fail to raise $1 million a year for charities. This summary of charities benefiting from 1978 tour events appeared in the November-December 1978 issue of *Golf Journal* and is reprinted here with permission. © 1978 *Golf Journal.*

PGA TOUR

Joe Garagiola–Tucson Open, Tucson, Ariz.
    Proceeds go through the Conquistadors, a civic group, to a variety of youth endeavors in the Tucson area
Phoenix Open, Phoenix, Ariz.
    Through the Thunderbird Foundation and the Thunderbird Youth Foundation to Arizona Special Olympics for the handicapped and many other local and state programs
Bing Crosby National Pro-Am, Pebble Beach, Calif.
    Crosby Youth Fund; Community Hospital of Monterey
Bob Hope Desert Classic, Palm Springs, Calif.
    Eisenhower Medical Center, Palm Springs
Glen Campbell–Los Angeles Open, Pacific Palisades, Calif.
    Through Jaycees to 130 charities in greater Los Angeles, including foster families, scholarships, annual fishing trip for blind youths, etc.
Jackie Gleason–Inverrary Classic, Lauderhill, Fla.
    Boy Scouts of America; Boys' Clubs of South Florida; others
Florida Citrus Open, Orlando, Fla.
    Scholarships to Florida colleges (five students are currently in school)
Doral-Eastern Open, Miami, Fla.
    American Cancer Society; Boys' Clubs of South Florida

Tournament Players Championship, Jacksonville, Fla.
  Through Jaycees to a variety of Jacksonville charities

Sea Pines Heritage Classic, Hilton Head Island, S.C.
  Hilton Head Island Hospital; Camp Hope, for the mentally retarded; Camp Leo, for blind children; other local charities

Greater Greensboro Open, Greensboro, Tenn.
  Through Jaycees to 250 projects each year, including home repair for the aged, housing insulation for needy families, etc.

Magnolia Classic, Hattiesburg, Miss.
  Boy Scouts of America; Jaycees; University of Southern Mississippi ROTC; others

MONY Tournament of Champions, Carlsbad, Calif.
  North County YMCA

Tallahassee Open, Tallahassee, Fla.
  United Way

Houston Open, Conroe, Tex.
  Boys' Harbor, a home for orphans; other local charities

Byron Nelson Golf Classic, Dallas, Tex.
  Through Dallas Salesmanship Club to youth camps for boys and girls with emotional problems

Oklahoma City Open, Oklahoma City, Okla.
  Heart Fund; Newborn Care Unit of Mercy Health Center

Memorial Tournament, Dublin, Ohio
  Children's Hospital of Columbus; Boy Scouts of America; *Columbus Dispatch* Charities of Franklin County; others

Atlanta Classic, Atlanta, Ga.
  Paul Anderson Home for Boys; Atlanta Junior Golf Association; Tallulah Falls School for underprivileged children; others

Kemper Open, Charlotte, N.C.
  In odd-numbered years, Boys' Clubs of America; in even-numbered years, a variety of local charities

Danny Thomas–Memphis Classic, Memphis, Tenn.
  St. Jude Children's Research Hospital

Western Open, Oak Brook, Ill.
  Evans Scholars Foundation

Greater Milwaukee Open, Franklin, Wis.
  Greater Milwaukee Charities, Inc.

IVB Philadelphia Classic, Lafayette Hill, Pa.
  National Multiple Sclerosis Society; St. Christopher's Hospital for Children

Sammy Davis, Jr.,–Greater Hartford Open, Wethersfield, Conn.
  Hartford Jaycees

American Optical Classic, Sutton, Mass.
  Local Boy Scouts; Leukemia Society; St. Vincent's Hospital; American Cancer Society; Worcester Lions Club; others

American Express–Westchester Classic, Harrison, N.Y.
  Six hospitals in Westchester County

Colgate Hall of Fame Classic, Pinehurst, N.C.
  World Golf Hall of Fame

B.C. Open, Endicott, N.Y.
  Through Broome County Charities Foundation, Inc., to orphanages, hospitals, Special Olympics, Boys' Clubs, Girls' Clubs, many others

Southern Open, Columbus, Ga.
  Boy's Club of Columbus; Bob Jones Scholarships for the exchange program between Emory University in Atlanta and St. Andrews University, St. Andrews, Scotland

San Antonio Open, San Antonio, Tex.
  Children's Hospital Endowment Fund of the Santa Rosa Hospital

Walt Disney World National Team Championship, Lake Buena Vista, Fla.
  Orange County Memorial Hospital

Anheuser-Busch Golf Classic, Napa, Calif.
  Napa Boys' Club; Community Projects, Inc.

World Series of Golf, Akron, Ohio
  Akron *Beacon-Journal* Charities Fund; Children's Hospital of Akron; Akron Jaycees; Akron Regional Development Board

J.C. Penney Mixed Team Classic, Largo, Fla.
  University Community Hospital and St. Joseph's Hospital in Tampa; Morton Plant Hospital in Clearwater; Bayfront Medical Center and St. Anthony's Hospital in St. Petersburg

LPGA TOUR

Colgate Triple Crown, Palm Springs, Calif.
  Boys' Club of Palm Springs

American Cancer Society Classic, Miami, Fla.
  Dade County Unit of American Cancer Society

Orange Blossom Classic, St. Petersburg, Fla.
  All Children's Hospital, St. Petersburg

Bent Tree Classic, Sarasota, Fla.
  Girls' Club of Sarasota

Sunstar Classic, Los Angeles, Calif.
  Boys' Club of Hollywood

Kathryn Crosby–Honda Civic Classic, San Diego, Calif.
  Children's Hospital and Health Center of San Diego

Colgate–Dinah Shore Winners Circle, Palm Springs, Calif.
  Desert Hospital; United Way of the Desert

Birmingham Classic, Birmingham, Ala.
  Alabama Sheriffs' Boys and Girls Ranch

American Defender Classic, Raleigh, N.C.
  Tammy Lynn Center for Mentally Retarded Children; Boys' Club of Wake County

Lady Tara Classic, Roswell, Ga.
  Georgia Special Olympics Foundation

Women's International, Hilton Head Island, S.C.
  Boy Scouts of America; four area schools

Greater Baltimore Golf Classic, Lutherville, Md.
  Children's Hospital Rehabilitation Center

LPGA Coca Cola Classic, Jamesburg, N.J.
    N.J. Hospital Association; N.J. Association for Retarded Citizens; Hemophilia Association; Jaycees; Elks
Golden Lights Championship, New Rochelle, N.Y.
    Westchester County Firefighters Burn Center
Peter Jackson Classic, Toronto, Canada
    Jean Belliveau Fund for Needy Kids
Bankers Trust Classic, Rochester, N.Y.
    The TWIG Organization of Rochester General Hospital
Lady Keystone Open, Hershey, Pa.
    Harrisburg Hospital
Mayflower Classic, Noblesville, Ind.
    Riley Children's Hospital
Wheeling Classic, Wheeling, W. Va.
    King's Daughters Building Fund; other community development projects
Borden Classic, Dublin, Ohio
    Aid to Retarded Children; Cystic Fibrosis
Hoosier Classic, Plymouth, Ind.
    Local charities
WUI Classic, Manhasset, N.Y.
    Major Long Island charities
Lady Stroh's Open, Dearborn, Mich.
    Leader Dogs for the Blind
Patty Berg Classic, St. Paul, Minn.
    St. Paul Jaycees; Special Olympics; School Police
Rail Charity Classic, Springfield, Ill.
    Friends of Memorial Medical Center; St. John's Hospital
National Jewish Hospital Open, Denver, Colo.
    National Jewish Hospital and Research Center
The Sarah Coventry, Alamo, Calif.
    Children's Home Society of California
Ping Classic, Portland, Ore.
    Waverly Children's Home; Evans Scholars Foundation
Golden Lights Championship, Los Angeles, Calif.
    City of Hope National Medical Center
Dallas Civitan, Dallas, Tex.
    Angels, Inc.; Callier Center for Communication Disorders; Children's Development Center; Children, Inc.; others
Houston Exchange Clubs Classic, Houston, Tex.
    Through the Exchange Clubs and Women's Golf Charities to a variety of local charities

OTHER MAJOR SPECTATOR EVENTS

SPRING

EVENT
The Legends of Golf
Onion Creek Club
Austin, TX

CONTACT FOR INFORMATION
    Bob Rule, Tournament Director
    Onion Creek Club
    2510 Onion Creek Parkway
    Austin, TX 78747
    (512) 282-3148

The Legends is no nostalgia trip, mainly because old golf pros keep on trying to win. In the inaugural of this event, in fact, a lot of highly competitive golf was displayed. Sam Snead produced a few key birdies in the home stretch to lift him and his partner Gardner Dickinson into first place and $100,000 in prize money, which beats Social Security. If you missed these and other stars of yesteryear in their heyday, here is a time and place* to fill that gap. Tournament week also includes a celebrity pro-am.

Walker Cup Matches
CONTACT FOR INFORMATION
    U.S. Golf Association
    Far Hills, NJ 07931
    (201) 234-2300
        or
    Royal and Ancient Golf Club
    St. Andrews, Fife, Scotland

A team event arranged once every two years (1979, 1981, 1983, etc.), pitting leading U.S. amateurs against Great Britain's brightest hopes, and burdened with just the right amount of the spirit of patriotic combat. I happened to be in attendance when opposing flags were raised over the Old Course at St. Andrews, in 1971 (the event alternates between various high-caliber British and U.S. sites). The unusually strong American side, including the likes of Lanny Wadkins, Tom Kite, Allen Miller, Steve Melnyk, and Jim Simons, lost 11 matches to 13, in a great upset. It was our first defeat since 1938. The night after the final matches, I came across two jovial figures in the dimming cobbled streets of the university town: John Jacobs, the British team coach, and Pat Ward-Thomas, the distinguished golf correspondent for *The Guardian*. They were wobbling along arm-in-arm and singing something from Robert Burns, I suppose it was. "You'll have to forgive us this one evening," said Jacobs in passing, impeccably mannered even while half in his cups. "It is not often anymore that we can celebrate at your expense!" Shortly after I myself found a pub, challenged a local lad to darts, promptly lost, and so completed the American debacle.

The series was launched in 1921 with the donation of the cup by George H. Walker, a former USGA president.

---

* Two other similar suitable occasions: the annual PGA Seniors and the new U.S. Senior Open (described on pages 165 and 166).

Curtis Cup Matches
CONTACT FOR INFORMATION
U.S. Golf Association
Golf House
Far Hills, NJ 07931
(201) 234-2300
or
Royal and Ancient Golf Club
St. Andrews
Fife, Scotland

Similar to Walker Cup in format, except that women compete, and biennial in even years (1980, 1982, 1984, etc.). Harriot and Margaret Curtis of Boston gave the cup that started the series in 1932. The sisters were both former U.S. Women's Amateur champions.

SUMMER

EVENT
National Long Driving Championship
CONTACT FOR INFORMATION
Roger Casl/*Golf Digest*
297 Westport Avenue
Norwalk, CT 06856
(203) 847-5811

Golf's Incredible Hulks gather early in the week of the PGA Championship for this unusual event. Conducted by *Golf Digest* and the PGA, the contest is actually open to every golfer in the country, amateur or pro; about a dozen contestants (most of them non-household names) survive sectional and regional qualifiers and earn spots in the final at the year's PGA Championship site. Along with 5,000 or so other distance-obsessed golf fans, I had the chance to see the 1978 Long Drive at Oakmont. I enjoyed every minute of the hour-long competition, even though I was hanging from a tree branch most of the time in order to see the action. At last—a format where it is all right to try to hit the ball as far as you possibly can with no instructor telling you "Accuracy is more important than power!" or "Play for position!" Of course, some of the contestants knock all their shots OB, but no right-minded spectator at these things fails to partake of a certain amount of vicarious visceral pleasure upon seeing a USGA-approved golf ball go well in excess of 300 yards, which the shots of most finalists do, no matter where it ends up. The various sectional qualifiers for this event are also fun to watch, and less crowded to boot.

FALL

EVENT
Ryder Cup Matches
CONTACT FOR INFORMATION
PGA/Box 12458
Lake Park, FL 33403
(305) 844-5000

The Ryder Cup Matches developed from a match played between representatives of the American and British Professional Golfers' Association in England in 1926. That unofficial match, incidentally, was won by the British 13½ to 1½.

Following this highly successful exhibition, Samuel A. Ryder, a wealthy British seed merchant, offered to donate a solid gold trophy bearing his name to be competed for in a series of matches between professionals of two nations.

From the start of the series through the 1959 Ryder Cup matches, the competition was comprised of four foursomes matches one day and eight singles matches the other day, each at 36 holes.

In 1961, the format was changed to provide for four 18-hole foursomes the morning of the first day and four more that afternoon, then for eight 18-hole singles the morning of the second day and eight more that afternoon. As in the past, one point was at stake in each match, so the total number of points was doubled.

In 1963, for the first time, a day of four-ball matches augmented the program to add new interest to the overall competition. This brought the total number of points to 32.

In 1977, the format was altered once again. This time there were five foursomes on the opening day, five four-ball matches on the second day, and ten singles matches on the final day. This reduced the total number of points to 20.

For 1979, eligibility for the Great Britain-Ireland side was expanded to include all British PGA/European TPD members who are residents of European nations.

The above is a U.S. PGA description. What might be added is that the latest change is a long-overdue effort to reduce American dominance of the event, which in the U.K. is a premier sports and media happening, but which over here gets scant attention from either fans or press.

U.S. Senior Open
CONTACT FOR INFORMATION
U.S. Golf Association
Far Hills, NJ 07931
(201) 234-2300

This new USGA event is open to all amateur and professional golfers 55 years of age and older with a maximum handicap of eight strokes. Qualifying rounds at various sites determine the starting field of 150 for the stroke-play event. Former U.S. Open, U.S. Amateur, British Open and Masters winners are exempt.

WINTER

EVENT
J.C. Penney Mixed Team Classic
CONTACT FOR INFORMATION
Bardmoor C.C.
Largo, FL
(213) 393-3423

Traditionally held in the first week in December, this mixed-team event involves 52 pairings made up from leading players on the PGA and LPGA tours. Even with its substantial $300,000 purse, the tournament has a genial, fun-type atmosphere. The men and women pros rarely compete with each other or in a team format and they appear to enjoy it, especially as it comes at the end of the year-long grind of the regular tours. Format: On the par-4 and par-5 holes, each partner drives, the men from the back tees and the women from their own tees. Then partners hit each other's drive for the second shot. For the third shot, they decide which ball is in a better position and then play that ball with alternate strokes until they hole out. On par-3 holes, both players hit tee shots, then pick the ball with which they will finish the hole.

National Football League Players Ass'n Golf Classic
January
CONTACT FOR INFORMATION
Frank Woschitz
NFL National Headquarters
1300 Connecticut Ave. N.W.
Washington D.C. 20036
(202) 833-3335
The Superbowl is over and quarterbacks, cornerbacks, wide receivers, and Too Tall Jones's can get down to serious business.

American Airlines Golf Classic
February
CONTACT FOR INFORMATION
David H. Lobb
Director, Public Relations & Marketing
American Airlines
633 Third Avenue
New York, NY 10017
Pro football *and* baseball stars take part in this one.

PGA Seniors
February
CONTACT FOR INFORMATION
PGA/Box 12458
Lake Park, FL 33403
(305) 844-3000
Many of the top pros of the past are in the field, for this event, first played in 1937, and held in conjunction with other winter activities of the PGA.

Tony Lema Memorial Tournament
Marco Island C.C.
Marco Island, Fla.
March
CONTACT FOR INFORMATION
Jim Stackpoole, Tournament Director
500 Nassau Boulevard
Marco Island, FL 33937
(813) 394-3151

This is one of the most successful pro-ams in operation and attracts galleries of nearly 20,000 every year. The field consists of about 50 touring pros, 50 celebrities from sports and show business, and 100 amateur golfers whose entry fees constitute donations to the Tony Lema Memorial Fund. It's held on the first or second Monday of March, depending on the year's PGA tour schedule. Lema, who died in a plane crash in 1966, was Marco Island's first pro.

World Cup
CONTACT FOR INFORMATION
International Golf Association
101 West 50th Street, Room 4018
New York, NY 10020
(212) 581-2200
Colorful annual event pits in competition two-man teams from dozens of nations.

GOLF'S ENTERTAINERS

The following golfers perform regularly in uniquely entertaining ways at clinics, exhibitions, outings, etc.

PAUL BUMANN—"GOLF COMEDY WITH A PURPOSE"

Bumann, a Georgia native and former Georgia PGA president, calls himself the clown prince of golf, performs 100 different trick shots with the 47 clubs in his oversized bag, and has entertained in Europe and Far East as well as throughout the United States. Associated with Callaway Gardens, he won Horton Smith Award in 1972 for contributions to education and promotion of golf in Georgia. For more information:
Paul Bumann
6375 Montainview Drive
Columbus, GA 31904
(404) 327-3488

BUDDY DEMLING—"THE KING OF CLUBS"

Professional since 1954, spent 12 years putting act together, now appears frequently with his 52 clubs and 90-pound bag at club outings, club functions, tournaments and fund-raising events. Charges $400–$600 per show, depending on location.
Buddy Demling
3512 Kirby Lane
Jeffersontown, KY 40299
(502) 491-1891

PAUL HAHN, JR.—"GOLF'S MOST VERSATILE STAR"

His one-hour combination trick-shot show and educational clinic has been seen in 46 states and 43 countries. A $1,000 fee covers TV film, open-end radio interview, posters, press releases, photos, tickets, souvenir programs, one-hour audience warm-up before show, and the formal clinic followed by social hour with sponsors and/or club members. Contact:

Paul Hahn, Jr.
Palmetto Dunes Golf Courses
P.O. Box 5849
Hilton Head Island, SC 29928

MIKE SMITH—"TRICK SHOT SPECTACULAR"

Smith is golf director for Princess Hotels International and on the Lynx staff. Among his 30 routines are driving the ball 240 yards while in a chair, hitting a shot 300 yards from tees ranging in height from six inches to three feet, driving the ball with a rubber-shafted club, and driving a ball that is teed in a person's mouth. Contact:

Mike Smith
c/o Lynx Golf Co.
7302 Adams Street
Paramount, CA 90723
(213) 531-2333

DENNIS WALTERS—"GOLF'S MOST UNIQUE SWING"

Walters won the 1977 Ben Hogan Award for his courageous return to golf after a freak golf cart accident rendered him a paraplegic in 1974. He uses a special swivel chair mounted to a golf car to give clinics and exhibitions which demonstrate fundamentals of golf and various trick shots. He also gives demonstrations at rehabilitation centers designed to introduce golf as a wheelchair sport and to inspire participants to start using golf both as recreation and therapy. Contact:

Dennis Walters
250 Jacaranda Drive
Plantation, FL 33324
(305) 472-1511
or
63 E. Overlook Way
Englishtown, NJ 07726
(201) 536-5071

EVAN "BIG CAT" WILLIAMS—TWO-TIME NATIONAL LONG DRIVE CHAMP

Shows given by the 6'6" Williams center on his wry sense of humor and his prodigious length off the tee with any club. In a typical exhibition, he starts by hitting balls 150 yards with his wedge, then moves through his set until he takes out his graphite-shafted "contest driver" and hits the final three or four shots 330 yards or more. Contact:

Evan Williams
413 Hillside Avenue
Leonia, NJ 07605
(201) 944-9043
or
c/o Hans Kramer
International Management
767 Fifth Avenue, Suite 601
New York, NY 10022
(212) 832-4763

V

Tournaments You Can Play In

TEAM EVENTS FOR THE SERIOUS AMATEUR GOLFER
PROMINENT MEN'S AMATEUR TOURNAMENTS
PROMINENT WOMEN'S AMATEUR TOURNAMENTS
SPECIAL PARTICIPATION TOURNAMENTS
OTHER PARTICIPANT PROGRAMS FOR THE AMATEUR GOLFER
INFORMATION ON RUNNING YOUR OWN TOURNAMENTS
SOME GAMES GOLFERS PLAY, BY PATTY FISHER

TEAM EVENTS FOR THE SERIOUS AMATEUR GOLFER

SUMMER

TOURNAMENT
Gold Cup International
Desert Inn C.C.
Las Vegas, Nev.
 June

CONTACT FOR INFORMATION
 Harry Williams
 Special Events Director
 Desert Inn and C.C.
 3145 Las Vegas Boulevard South
 Las Vegas, NV 89109

World Golf Hall of Fame Pro-Am
Pinehurst C.C.
Pinehurst, N.C.
 August

CONTACT FOR INFORMATION
 Randy Collett
 Tournament Director
 World Golf Hall of Fame
 P.O. Box 908
 Pinehurst, NC 28374

FALL

TOURNAMENT
Amateur of Americas Tournament
Dorado Beach Hotel
Puerto Rico
 September

CONTACT FOR INFORMATION
 Tournament Director
 Dorado Beach Golf & Tennis Club
 Dorado Beach, PR 00646

Casa de Campo Invitational
Cajuiles I and Cajuiles II
Golf Courses, La Romana Resort
Dominican Republic
 November

CONTACT FOR INFORMATION
 Dr. Norman G. Becker, Jr.
 150 Spring Lane
 Winter Park, FL 32789

South Ocean International Pro-Am
South Ocean Beach Hotel and G.C.
Nassau, Bahamas
 November

CONTACT FOR INFORMATION
 Ted Maude
 South Ocean Beach Hotel & G.C.
 P.O. Box N8191
 Nassau, Bahamas

Castle Harbour Invitational Pro-Am
Castle Harbour G.C.
Bermuda
 December

CONTACT FOR INFORMATION
 John Mason, Director of Golf
 Castle Harbour G.C.
 Tucker's Town 2–01, Bermuda

St. Croix Pro-Am Invitational
Fountain Valley G.C.
St. Croix, U.S. Virgin Islands
 December

CONTACT FOR INFORMATION
 Carl Seiffer
 Box 1407, Kingshill, St. Croix
 U.S. Virgin Islands 00850

Bermuda Goodwill
Mid-Ocean Club,
Castle Harbour G.C.,
Port Royal G.C., and Belmont Golf & C.C.
Bermuda
 December

CONTACT FOR INFORMATION
 Mrs. Muriel Parker, Secretary
 Bermuda Golf Association
 P.O. Box 433
 Hamilton 5, Bermuda

WINTER

TOURNAMENT
Jamaica Jamboree
Rose Hall Inter-Continental G.C., Half Moon G.C.,
Montego Bay; and Tryall G.C., Sandy Bay, Jamaica
 January

CONTACT FOR INFORMATION
 Richard Munson
 Jamaica Tourist Board
 866 Second Avenue
 New York, NY 10017

Cajuiles International Pro-Am
Santo Domingo Country Club, Cajuiles G.C., and
Ocean Pines G.C.
Dominican Republic
 January

CONTACT FOR INFORMATION
Dan Pesant
c/o Hugh Stevens and Associates
One Gulf + Western Plaza
New York, NY 10023

Mid-Florida Golf Festival
Harder Hall Golf and Tennis Resort
Sebring, Fla.
January

CONTACT FOR INFORMATION
Ben Roman
Tournament Director
Harder Hall Golf & Tennis Resort
Sebring, FL 33870

Castle Harbour Bermuda Classic
Castle Harbour Golf Club
Bermuda
February

CONTACT FOR INFORMATION
John Mason
Director of Golf
Castle Harbour G.C.
Tucker's Town 2–01, Bermuda

World Invitational Pro-Am
Pebble Beach and Spyglass Hill Courses
Monterey Peninsula, Calif.

CONTACT FOR INFORMATION
Dick Farley
Tournament Director
Box 200
Shawnee-on-Delaware, PA 18356

PROMINENT MEN'S AMATEUR TOURNAMENTS (U.S. only)

SPRING

TOURNAMENT
American Amateur Classic

CONTACT FOR INFORMATION
American Amateur Classic
P.O. Box 4337
Pensacola, FL 32507
(904) 456-7661

North and South Amateur
Pinehurst, N.C.

CONTACT FOR INFORMATION
North and South Amateur
c/o Mr. Ken Schroeder
Pinehurst C.C.
Pinehurst, NC 28374
(919) 295-6181

Southwestern Amateur
Arizona C.C.
Phoenix, Ariz.

CONTACT FOR INFORMATION
Southwestern Amateur
c/o Dave Askins
3955 E. Exposition Avenue, Suite 416
Denver, CO 80209
(303) 744-3149

SUMMER

TOURNAMENT
Northeast Amateur
Wannamoisett C.C.
Rumford, R. I.

CONTACT FOR INFORMATION
Northeast Amateur
c/o Edward Perry
Rhode Island Golf Association
710 Hospital Trust Boulevard
Providence, RI 02903
(401) 272-1350

Sunnehanna
Sunnehanna C.C.
Johnstown, Pa.

CONTACT FOR INFORMATION
Sunnehanna Amateur
c/o William Price
Sunnehanna C.C.
Johnstown, PA 15905
(814) 255-4121

PNGA Amateur

CONTACT FOR INFORMATION
Pacific Northwest Golf Association
c/o Eugene C.C.
Eugene, OR

Trans-Mississippi Amateur

CONTACT FOR INFORMATION
Trans-Mississippi Amateur
c/o Mr. Loren Lamberth
5353 Nall Avenue
Shawnee Mission, KS 66202
(913) 432-3939

USGA Public Links

CONTACT FOR INFORMATION
USGA
Far Hills, NJ 07931
(201) 234-2300

Southern Amateur
C.C. of North Carolina
Pinehurst, N.C.

CONTACT FOR INFORMATION
Southern Golf Association
Box 9151
Birmingham, AL 35213
(205) 328-9405

Broadmoor Invitational
The Broadmoor
Colorado Springs, Colo.

CONTACT FOR INFORMATION
Broadmoor Invitational
c/o Dow Finsterwald
The Broadmoor
Colorado Springs, CO 80901

Southeastern Amateur

CONTACT FOR INFORMATION
Southeastern Amateur
c/o Madden Hatcher
Box 2707
Columbus, GA 31902
(404) 324-0201

Western Amateur

CONTACT FOR INFORMATION
Western Golf Association
Golf, IL 60029
(312) 724-4600

Pacific Coast Amateur

CONTACT FOR INFORMATION
Southern California G.A.
3740 Cahuenga Boulevard
North Hollywood, CA 91604
(213) 980-3630

Porter Cup

CONTACT FOR INFORMATION
Dr. William McMahon
515 Third Street
Niagara Falls, NY 14301
(716) 284-8250 (office)

Eastern Amateur

CONTACT FOR INFORMATION
Mr. Richard F. Woods
Box 3343
Portsmouth, VA 23701
(804) 488-6605 (club)

Worsham Memorial

CONTACT FOR INFORMATION
Frank Emmet
3807 Williams Lane
Chevy Chase, MD 20015
(301) 652-0200

U.S. Amateur

CONTACT FOR INFORMATION
USGA
Far Hills, NJ 07931
(201) 234-2300

FALL

TOURNAMENT
National Amateur Invitational

CONTACT FOR INFORMATION
Western Amateur Golf Association
33681 Capstan
Laguna Niguel, CA 92677
(714) 661-3006

Middle Atlantic Amateur

CONTACT FOR INFORMATION
Middle Atlantic Amateur
c/o Ralph M. Bogart
4829 Fairmont Avenue
Bethesda, MD 20014
(301) 654-2277

WINTER

TOURNAMENT
Florida International Four Ball

CONTACT FOR INFORMATION
Florida International Four Ball
c/o Mickey Van Gerbig
Box 2227
Palm Beach, FL 33480

Dixie Amateur

CONTACT FOR INFORMATION
Dixie Amateur
c/o Frank Perpich
1770 N.E. 171st Street
N. Miami Beach, FL 33162
(305) 947-6874

PROMINENT WOMEN'S AMATEUR TOURNAMENTS (U.S. only)

SPRING

TOURNAMENT
Southern Amateur

CONTACT FOR INFORMATION
Mrs. Wilbur C. Barnhart
Women's Southern Golf Association
2050 Country Side Circle North
Orlando, FL 32804

North and South
Pinehurst (N.C.) C.C.

CONTACT FOR INFORMATION
North and South Tournament Bureau
P.O. Box 4000
Pinehurst, NC 28374
(919) 295-6181

SUMMER

TOURNAMENT
Eastern Amateur

CONTACT FOR INFORMATION
Women's Eastern Golf Association
27 Longmeadow Road
Milton, MA 02186

USGA Women's Public Links

CONTACT FOR INFORMATION
USGA
Far Hills, NJ 07931
(201) 234-2300

Broadmoor Amateur
Broadmoor G.C.
Colorado Springs, Colo.

CONTACT FOR INFORMATION
Broadmoor G.C.
Colorado Springs, CO 80901
(303) 634-7711

Western Amateur

CONTACT FOR INFORMATION
Mrs. Addison A. Wakeford, Jr.
5449 N. Diversey Boulevard
Milwaukee, WI 53217

Trans National

CONTACT FOR INFORMATION
Mrs. Bruce Gilliland
Box 122
Kimball, NB 69145

USGA Women's Amateur

CONTACT FOR INFORMATION
USGA
Far Hills, NJ 07931
(201) 234-2300

WINTER

TOURNAMENT
Harder Hall
Harder Hall G.C.
Sebring, Fla.

CONTACT FOR INFORMATION
Ben Roman, Tournament Director
Harder Hall G.C.
Sebring, FL 33870
(813) 385-0151

South Atlantic

CONTACT FOR INFORMATION
Mrs. Marjorie Bernstein
Oceanside C.C.
P.O. Box 367
Ormond Beach, FL 32074
(904) 677-7200

Doherty Challenge Cup

CONTACT FOR INFORMATION
Eileen Goodman
Coral Ridge C.C.
P.O. Box 24099
Fort Lauderdale, FL 33307
(305) 564-1271

International Four Ball

CONTACT FOR INFORMATION
Jim Keat
Orangebrook C.C.
Hollywood, FL

SPECIAL PARTICIPATION
TOURNAMENTS

TOURNAMENT
National Amateur Left-Handed Championship

CONTACT FOR INFORMATION
Frank Elder, Executive Secretary
National Association of Left-Handed Golfers
P.O. Box 489
Camden, SC 29020

National Clergymen's Tournament

CONTACT FOR INFORMATION
George Peters
499 Biscayne Boulevard
Miami, FL

Annual Ecumenical Open

CONTACT FOR INFORMATION
C. Scott Marozan
Ext. No. Kingsboro Avenue
Box 106
Gloversville, NY 12078

Blind Golfer's Championship

CONTACT FOR INFORMATION
> Pat W. Browne, Jr.
> President, U.S. Blind Golfers' Association
> 225 Baronne Street, 28th Floor
> New Orleans, LA 70112

Braille Institute Blind Golfers' Classic

CONTACT FOR INFORMATION
> Ben Hoberman
> c/o KABC Radio
> 3321 S. LaCienega Boulevard
> Los Angeles, CA 90016
> (213) 663-3311

U.S. Deaf Golfers' Championship

CONTACT FOR INFORMATION
> Bernard P. Brown
> U.S. Deaf Golfers' Association
> 16 Miller Road
> Glastonbury, CT 06033

Little People's Celebrity Golf Tournament
(*This event raises money for the study of dwarfism.*)

CONTACT FOR INFORMATION
> Little People Invitational
> 916 E. Nearfield Street
> Azusa, CA 91702

National Senior Amputee Golf Championship

CONTACT FOR INFORMATION
> c/o Mrs. Eleanor Ramage
> 420 Hopkins Street
> Lakeland, FL 33801

OTHER PARTICIPANT PROGRAMS FOR THE AMATEUR GOLFER

EVENT
Women Golfers Week

CONTACT FOR INFORMATION
> Golf Digest
> Box 5000
> Norwalk, CT 06856

National Hole-in-One Weekend

CONTACT FOR INFORMATION
> Arthur Brill
> Big Brothers/Big Sisters of America
> 215-03 17th Avenue
> Bayside, NY 11360

National Golf Day

CONTACT FOR INFORMATION
> PGA of America
> Box 12458
> Lake Park, FL 33403

Golf Digest Clearing House

CONTACT FOR INFORMATION
> *Golf Digest*
> 495 Westport Avenue
> Norwalk, CT 06856

GOLF DIGEST PROGRAMS

Golf Digest runs the programs listed below to foster recognition of the achievements made in golf by ordinary folks. A regular column in the magazine ("Records and Rarities," by John P. May) also is devoted to the outstanding or more unusual feats reported.

MOST IMPROVED GOLFER

To increase the desire to play more and better golf, to inspire players with a season-end goal, and to encourage them to use the instruction facilities at their clubs, *Golf Digest* makes available the Most Improved Golfer awards.

WORLD GOLF HALL OF FAME

Each ace and acer will be recorded on special computer in the archives of the World Golf Hall of Fame in Pinehurst, N.C. This also makes you eligible for the special "Acers of Fame" drawing (in addition to the *Golf Digest* annual Sweepstakes). The winner receives trip prizes valued at $350.

CLUB CHAMPION

Golf Digest recognizes club champions by publishing their names in the February "Annual" issue.

DOUBLE EAGLE

Double eagles—three-under-par on a hole—are rewarded with a personalized certificate, suitable for framing, and a tie clasp for men or a double-eagle pin for women, upon receipt of the official Double Eagle form.

RULES	*Par-4 holes*	*Par-5 holes*
For men:	At least 251 yards	At least 471 yards
For women:	At least 211 yards	At least 401 yards

AGE SHOOTER

In recognition of a golfer's rarest feat, shooting his or her age or better in 18 holes, *Golf Digest* awards a personalized certificate suitable for framing and a tie clasp.

RULES: Courses for age shooters must be at least 6,000 yards for men and 5,250 yards for women. Copy of scorecard must be included and Age Shooter form signed by golf professional or manager. Form available from golf professional or *Golf Digest*.

HOLE-IN-ONE

When an ace is made and the completed, verified form returned to the Clearing House, the acer receives a bag tag from *Golf Digest*. He also becomes eligible for individual awards from participating manufacturers whose equipment he used when scoring his ace and is automatically entered in the annual Sweepstakes. The drawing is conducted in January and the winners are published in the March issue of *Golf Digest*.

GOLF DIGEST HOLE-IN-ONE RECORDS

The following hole-in-one records have been established from reported aces made on regulation golf courses, defined as 18-holers with no more than six par 3s and nine-holers with no more than three par 3s.

ALL-TIME RECORDS

Longest by a man—447 yards, by Robert Mitera, Omaha, on the 10th hole at the Miracle Hills Golf Club, Omaha, on Oct. 7, 1965.

Longest by a woman—393 yards, by Marie Robie, Wollaston, Mass., on the first hole at the Furnace Brook Golf Club, Wollaston, on Sept. 4, 1949.

Longest on dogleg—480 yards, by Larry Bruce, Hope, Ark., on the fifth hole at the Hope Country Club on Nov. 15, 1962.

Oldest man—George Henry Miller, 93, Anaheim, Calif., on the 116-yard 11th hole at the Anaheim Municipal Golf Course on Dec. 4, 1970; also William H. Diddel, 93, Naples, Fla., on the 142-yard eighth hole at the Royal Poinciana Golf Club, Naples, on Jan. 1, 1978.

Oldest woman—Maude Hutton, 86, Sun City Center, Fla., on the 102-yard 14th hole at the Kings Inn Golf and Country Club, Sun City Center, on Aug. 7, 1978.

Youngest boy—Tommy Moore, 6 (plus 1 month and 1 week), Hagerstown, Md., on the 145-yard fourth hole at Woodbrier Golf Course, Martinsburg, W.Va., on March 8, 1969.

Youngest girl—Rebecca Ann Chase, 8, Dallas, Ore., on the 125-yard fifth hole at the Oak Knoll Golf Course, Independence, Ore., on Aug. 15, 1977.

* On straightaway hole.

HOLE-IN-ONE ODDS
(On 18-hole course with four par 3s.)

In one round

Average golfer	10,738 to 1
PGA Tour pro	927 to 1
LPGA Tour pro	1,162 to 1

On one hole

Average golfer	42,952 to 1
PGA Tour pro	3,708 to 1
LPGA Tour pro	4,648 to 1

INFORMATION ON RUNNING YOUR OWN TOURNAMENTS

The following two publications are available from:
National Golf Foundation
200 Castlewood Drive
N. Palm Beach, FL 33408

PLANNING AND CONDUCTING COMPETITIVE GOLF EVENTS

This booklet offers comprehensive guidelines for planning and conducting all types of tournaments for all ages, both novelty events and serious tests of championship skill. Designed for club-tournament chairman, recreation director, school golf instructor, and coach. Sections include major tournament procedure, club-level tournament planning, types of tournaments, team and league play, junior and senior programs, business-meeting and convention tournaments—over 90 special events in all. Cost: $4.00.

HOW TO SECURE AND MAINTAIN A GOLF LEAGUE

Details on organizing a league program. Cost: $1.25.

The following three publications are available from:
USGA
Golf House
Far Hills, NJ 07931

TOURNAMENTS FOR YOUR CLUB

Four-page pamphlet describes formats for early-season events, individual events, team events, and season events. Cost: 25¢.

GOLF COMMITTEE MANUAL AND USGA GOLF HANDICAP SYSTEM

A 57-page booklet. Cost: $1.00.

HANDICAPPING THE UNHANDICAPPED

The Callaway System of automatic handicapping for occasional players in a single tournament. Cost: 25¢.

HANDICAPPING SERVICE

For public course golfers who do not otherwise have the chance to establish an official handicap, this service costs $10 annually. Subscribers file scores and receive updated handicap cards monthly.
National Publinks Handicaps, Inc.
Box 9147
Providence, RI 02940

TOURNAMENT ORGANIZING SERVICE

The Avis rental car agency, in conjunction with Tournament Services, Inc., will locate a site for your outing, register the players, administer the program, set the tees, cut the pin placements, keep the scores, procure prizes and trophies, etc. For more information, write:

Avis Tournament Service
9710 South La Cienega Blvd.
Inglewood, CA 90301

SOME GAMES GOLFERS PLAY

Here are some popular formats used by golfers to organize a friendly round of golf, usually on a modest-wager basis.

ALIBI GOLF

Golfer may replay the same number of shots as his handicap, but not more than one on any single hole.

BEST-BALL TWOSOME

Two persons play as a team, taking handicaps as they fall on the card. Lowest score on the hole with handicap counts toward team's best-ball score for round. Only the lowest score on the hole is counted. Team having the lowest ball score wins.

BINGLE-BANGLE-BUNGLE

You can win three points on each hole. What each point is worth depends on the players. One point goes to the person whose ball comes to rest on the surface of the green first. The second point to the person whose ball is nearest the cup after all players are on the green. The third point goes to the player who gets his ball in the hole first.

BLIND HOLES

The winning score is based on only nine holes—selected at random after all the players have teed off, so they have no knowledge of the holes that will count. Half of the handicap is used to compile net totals.

BOBS AND BIRDS

Bobs are points given to the person landing closest to the point on par-3 holes, and birds are points given for birdies on any hole. The points can be worth whatever you feel your pocketbook can handle.

BLIND PARTNERS

Players may play with anyone of their choice but partners are drawn at random after everyone has teed off so that players don't know their partners until they finish. Full handicap is used and the team with the lowest best-ball score wins.

FLAG TOURNAMENT

Each player is given a small flag with his name attached. Using his full handicap, he plays until he has used the number of strokes equaling par plus his handicap. Wherever this occurs on the course, he plants his flag. The winner is the player who plants his flag the farthest around the course.

GET-ACQUAINTED TOURNAMENT

Play is 18-hole medal with full handicaps. Each player is teamed with a partner with whom he has not previously been paired.

GREENIES

A point is given for the player who lands his tee shot closest to the pin on par-3 holes.

HIGH AND LOW

Playing with a partner against another partnership, with two points at stake: one for the best ball and individually, the other for the best ball of partners.

KICKERS

The committee draws a number that it announces after the tournament. Players select a handicap without knowing what number will be drawn. The player whose net score equals or is closest to the number drawn, is the winner.

LOW NET FOURSOME

In a large field of contestants, the total score of one foursome of players, less handicaps, determines the winner.

MIXED SCOTCH

Partners consist of a man and a woman, with the man driving on the odd-numbered and the woman on the even-numbered holes (or the other way around). Partners play every other shot from tee to green, allowing half of combined handicaps.

MONKEY FOURSOME

Each player of the foursome carries a single club, those selected generally being a wood, 2-iron, 5-iron and sand wedge. Each player in rotation plays the one ball of his foursome from wherever it lies with his chosen club. Thus, a player may be forced to drive with a wedge, putt with a 5-iron, etc. The low foursome in the field wins.

NASSAU

Three points are involved: one point for the front nine, the second point for the back nine, and the third point for the 18. The low score with full handicap on the front nine wins, and the same on the back nine. The player who wins the most holes on either nine wins the nassau, the 18-hole point.

ODD-EVEN TOURNAMENT

Played in foursomes with two players to a team, one of whom plays all the even-numbered holes and the other all the odd-numbered holes. One half of combined handicaps for each team is deducted from total score and low net is the winner.

POINTS

Players receive three points for each birdie, two points for each par, and one point for bogies. Played at full handicap, the winner is the golfer with the most points.

REMORSEFUL GOLF

Each golfer has the privilege of making his opponent replay any four shots during the 18 holes. These may be shots that he considers lucky or feels cannot be duplicated.

ROUND-ROBIN

Played in foursomes. Partners change every six holes, so each player engages in three six-hole matches with each of the others in the foursome as a partner.

SCRATCH AND SCRAMBLE

Four-ball stroke play. On each hole, the partners' scores are added and divided by two to obtain the team score. The full handicap for each player is used.

SELECTED SCORE

Each golfer plays 36 holes. He selects his best score on each hole from the two scorecards and applies his handicap. The golfer with the lowest net score for 18 holes is the winner.

SHOTGUN TOURNAMENT

Each team, twosomes or foursomes, tees off from one of the 18 tees. Low-gross and low-net winners.

SKINS

Skins is a match-play tournament. The "skin" is a point given to the player with the low score. If three players in the foursome tie and the fourth player has a higher score than the others, no skin is won, nor is the high scorer penalized.

SPECKS

Played individually or as a team. Specks are awarded for the following on each hole: longest drive on the fairway, first on the green, closest on approach to the pin, one-putt greens, and lowest total for the hole. Winner is the person or team with most specks.

SPLASH TOURNAMENT

Players must contribute one new golf ball for every one they hit into a water hazard. A player not turning in his card is fined three balls just on suspicion. The three lowest net scores divide up the balls on a 60–30–10 basis.

STRING TOURNAMENT

Each player is given a piece of string in lieu of a handicap. The string is measured to allow one foot for each handicap stroke. The player is allowed to advance the ball by hand to a more favorable spot, measuring the distance with the string and cutting off the length used. When the string is used up, the player is on his own. The string may be used to advance the ball on the fairway or putting surface, out of a hazard or away from an obstruction, etc.

THROW-AWAY TOURNAMENT

Played at full handicap under medal play, each golfer may throw out his three worst holes of the 18.

WIN, PLACE, SHOW

Golfers play with full handicap. The low score wins three points, the second lowest wins two points, and the third lowest wins one point. The player with the most points at the end of 18 is the winner.

—Patty Fisher

VI

Senior Golf

THE FAST-GROWING WORLD OF SENIOR GOLF

> Mirror, mirror on the locker room wall,
> Which senior group is fairest of all?

Which one, indeed! We certainly hope all of them are "fair" to both their members and outside foes. And we're sure they are.

Picking out the "best" would be fraught with editorial peril, and perhaps inconclusive. Besides, there is a great deal of overlapping membership, and who would play for whom?

The largest? Well that's easier: It's the Southern Seniors Golf Association—hands down. This organization once boasted a roster numbering well above 2,000. Of late they've pared that down around the 1,800 mark —still enough to stake a claim to being number one, however.

There's no question as to the "grandaddy" of the seniors organizations, though. The United States Seniors Golf Association, which traditionally holds its championship during the first week in June, was founded in 1905.

In addition to its seniority, the U.S. Seniors also has a reputation for moving its players around the two courses it uses with more dispatch than any other. It is a model for "playing without delay."

Seniors golf groups come in all sizes and all ages, and have interesting boundaries. Take the Southern Seniors, for example, founded in 1930. A recent tabulation showed members living in 37 states as well as Canada, Mexico, and the District of Columbia. Hardly a truly Rebel group anymore.

For contrast to the U.S. and Southern seniors, there's the new and different Tri-State Seniors Golf, Inc., a meld of golfers—mostly from Tennessee, North Carolina, and Florida—boasting few low handicappers and joined together for monthly outings. The group quickly reached 500 members and branched out to other states.

The Nevada State Seniors Golf Club was founded in 1975 by amateur Art Hansen and professional Leon Pounders with the Black Mountain Golf Club in Henderson, Nev., as its home. The Nevada men also play on a once-a-month schedule in the Las Vegas area and have formed a Reno-area branch club.

The Great Lakes Senior Golf Association got started in 1969, and it has grown to include more than 450 members from those states and Canadian provinces bordering the Great Lakes.

The American Seniors Golf Association traces its history back to 1935, when a group of men who spent winter months at the Kenilworth Lodge in Sebring, Fla., put on an event called the Winter Seniors Golf Tournament. In fact, it was sort of a winter version of the summertime U.S. Seniors competition. The tournament was moved to the Ponce de Leon Golf Club in St. Augustine, Fla., in 1953, after the Kenilworth was sold. Actually, the American Seniors was formally organized in October 1952, during the playing of the North and South Seniors at Pinehurst, N.C. Fred L. Riggin, Sr., was the first American Seniors president.

Longevity citations are due a number of seniors groups, certainly the New England Senior Golfers Association, which began competition in 1922 following a locker-room conversation in June 1921 at the Woodland Golf Club in Auburndale, Mass. It produced a handsome 50th anniversary book in 1972 and is still going, stronger than ever.

The original Tri-State Seniors, involving golfers from Texas, Oklahoma, and New Mexico, employs a unique format in which 32 men qualify for the championship flight. They have two rounds of matches, then the remaining eight quarterfinalists have an 18-hole stroke round to determine the winner and runnerup.

An even older group is the Michigan Seniors Golf Association, headed toward its sixth decade. Like many northern seniors organizations, Michigan members have a spring tourney and a fall championship (although some, such as the New York Seniors, reverse this, with a championship first, then a fall tournament).

The Senior Golf Association of Northern California played its 50th annual championship in 1979. It was organized in 1929 and skipped the 1943 meet because of World War II.

The California Seniors Golf Association, launched in 1944 as its northern neighbor resumed, met for the 36th time in 1979.

The Western Senior Amateur Association, now in its 19th year, has a membership of 600 and attracts about 360 men and 150 women to its annual tournament, held yearly in one of 11 Western states.

The Indiana State Senior Golf Association was born, according to its history, on June 12, 1929, at French Lick, Ind. Original members were 18 men 50 years or older who had failed to qualify in the Indiana State Amateur tournament. Because they were at French Lick for a vacation and didn't care to go home so early, they banded together for a tournament of their own. That fall they gathered for another tourney at Martinsville, and by 1931 the group was meeting three times during the year. With interest a proven fact, the Association was incorporated in 1939.

Like Indiana's, a great many of the seniors groups, located in almost every state, started out with a minimum age of 50 years. When the roster filled and a waiting list developed, officers "bought some time" by raising the lower limit to 55. Today, virtually every seniors' association employs a minimum age of 55 years—and they all have waiting lists, some larger than the membership roster. Most require membership in a country club and applications to be submitted by current members.

The age-old links issue of match play versus stroke play is generally taken care of by holding tournaments with both formats. The American Seniors, for instance, stages its regular championship in the early spring at match play, but 14 years ago started a stroke-play tournament that now draws an equally large and competitive field.

Perhaps the newest wrinkle to senior golf is the birth of organizations with an older entry-age including the Three Score and Ten Club, which holds an annual championship at Pinehurst C.C. in the North Carolina Sandhills. The great Chick Evans has maintained that senior golf should start at 65 years and to prove his point makes that the minimum age for his Golden 65 Seniors each fall in Chicago, although he has added a Silver Division for some of his younger friends. Also, the new National Super Seniors Texas Invitational, with a minimum age of 65, had its inaugural in Galveston two years ago and became an instant success.

Senior golf's major mix of professional and amateur players is the U.S. National Senior Open Golf Association, headquartered in Los Angeles, which stages an annual fall championship. This classic has been contested at Reno, Las Vegas, and most recently, at Scottsdale, Ariz. The 22nd Open, held in 1978, brought out the usual field of 500 men—125 pros aged 50 or older, and 375 amateurs with the same age-minimum. Past U.S. Senior Open kings have included Dutch Harrison, Tommy Bolt, Chandler Harper, and Willie Barber.

—Chuck Albury, Editor, *Senior Golfer*
Reprinted with permission from *Senior Golfer*

BOOKS FOR SENIOR GOLFERS

GOLF BEGINS AT FORTY by Sam Snead, with Dick
    Aultman; illustrated by Jim McQueen. 1978, 175
    pages, $9.95, N.Y.: Dial Press.

Lots of clear-cut advice that studiously avoids overhauling the older player's swing (on the theory that it wouldn't run better after any overhaul, anyway), stresses various "advantages" of age, and entertains with stories of how Snead and other golfers learned to cope successfully with problems of seniority. If the remarkable Snead had chosen to call this handsomely produced volume "Golf Begins at Seventy," we'd still have to take it quite seriously, of course.

TURNING EXCESS POUNDS INTO EXTRA YARDS

I could go on and on about the troubles of the overweight golfer, but it's time to start coming up with some

solutions. Obviously the first and best answer is simply to lose weight. Short of that, however, there are some other things that will help. If you tend to slice most of your long shots—you may occasionally pull one to the left on a straight line—or if you pull your short irons to the left, I advise you try what I suggest. The same would be true if you sometimes pop your drives high into the air or scoot them along the ground to the left, or if you often feel like you've "looked up." All of these results are symptomatic of the fat man's chop.

First you should understand that your goal is to sweep your shots forward. That goal demands that your clubhead move into the ball on a path that is from your side of the target line, not from out beyond it. The inside path will help give your clubhead a shallower approach into the ball. It will send the force of the blow forward instead of downward.

You must address the ball in a way that will let you swing the clubhead into it on this path. You may need to align your shoulders—but not your feet—more to the right than you have been. You may need to play the ball a bit farther back in your stance, a bit inside your left heel.

See where your shots start out. If they still start out to the left—regardless of where they curve to after that— you're still not getting that clubhead moving from inside to along the line. Visualize that path before you swing and keep trying to swing back to the ball along it.

Another thing to do before you swing is to start with more weight on your right foot. One big problem of the overweight golfer is moving out of his own way on his downswing. His left side never turns clear in time for his arms to swing freely forward. It helps to start with more weight on the right side at address. Then it's much easier to shift and turn to the left during the downswing. If your weight doesn't get to the right in the backswing, it can't move to the left when you shift directions.

Beyond that, here are some additional tips that will help most older, overweight golfers who tend to slice their long shots from left to right and pull the short ones to the left.

—Hold the club lightly at address and keep it light throughout the swing.

—Hold the club more in the fingers of your left hand.

—Toe out the left foot to the left, more toward the target.

—Narrow the width of the stance.

—Be sure to make a forward press.

—Make a longer, slower backswing.

—Try to point the clubshaft toward the target at the top of the backswing, rather than off to the left. Again, hold it lightly.

Obviously you can't think about all these things at the same time. Pick one or two and work on them in your practice sessions. Just keep working to create as much freedom of arms and body motion as you can, and to swing the clubhead into the ball from inside—your side— of the target line.

Finally, I suggest you follow this simple drill. At every meal, before dessert is served, place both hands firmly against the edge of the table and push yourself backward and upward, with a full extension of both arms.

—from *Golf Begins at Forty*

SENIOR GOLF by Robert O'Byrne. 1977, 174 pages, $8.95, N.Y.: Winchester Press.

This is a once-over-lightly treatment on all aspects of senior golf, including some instruction. Fairly detailed coverage of golf courses particularly suitable for the vacationing senior, based on knowledge gained by the author in playing some 1,500 layouts worldwide in the course of his work as travel writer for *Sports Afield*. Among the U.S. courses listed, he notes those that in his view make excellent retirement spots.

MAINTAINING A SHARP SHORT GAME

Probably the best bit of advice for senior players has to do with their philosophy in chipping: whether to use one club and vary the way you hit or use several clubs with the same type of hit. Jack Nicklaus, Bobby Locke, and others have had great success using just one club, and you can too. It's much easier to practice with just one club than with several, and if you rely on one club you can "get to know" it as you would a putter. Which club you choose is up to you, but I would recommend something in the 7-iron to pitching wedge range. Clubs with less loft than the 7-iron are not versatile enough, and the sand wedge with its thick, heavy flange is both difficult and dangerous to use for the finesse shots.

When you do practice with your club, try to make it hit all sorts of shots—high ones, low ones, stoppers, and runners. You can vary the trajectory of the shot by moving the ball up or back in your stance. Be sure to grip down on the club, for optimum feel.

One good way to practice on a putting green is to try to chip balls directly into one of the holes, on the fly. There's no better practice for your hand-eye coordination.

Most of us know the basics of the chip shot, so I won't go into them here, but each of us at one time or another just loses his touch completely around the green. If this should happen in the middle of a round, try this trick. Make believe your chipping club is a putter, and stroke your chips exactly as you would a putter. Many people do this all the time, and with great success.

—from *Senior Golf*

GOLF BEGINS AT FORTY by Earl Stewart, Jr. and Dr. Harry ("Bud") Gunn. 1977, 163 pages, paperback, Matteson, Ill.: Greatlakes Living Press.

Stewart is a well-known teaching pro and golf coach; Gunn a clinical psychologist and scratch golfer. Unlike Paul Runyan, this team thinks a smaller pivot and shorter swing-arc are inevitable as muscles grow old, but believes the resultant more-compact swing improves consistency anyway, even if it cuts down on yardage. Considerable emphasis is placed on address position, keeping the head over the ball, adopting a swing style that is "natural" for the individual (some players *should* take the club back fast).

SET-UP

Older persons frequently have some difficulty with their concentration. This may perhaps be a part of the aging process, but I believe that it is primarily related to numerous business interests. There is also a great tendency in our society to dwell upon ill health, however, and this too becomes a distraction.

The first thing this means for an older golfer is that he should not take an excessively long period of time in setting up over the ball. He should plan his shot, select his club, and then get right to his set-up. He should work to get to the point where he quickly and easily sets up—in exactly the same way for every shot. He may have to devote more concentration in the beginning to establish the right pattern for him. He may, for example, practice his set-up procedure a few minutes in his home in the evenings. He will definitely need to work harder on the mental aspect of his set-up. If he allows negative thoughts to creep into his mind he will very likely tense up and in some manner change his set-up pattern or procedure. This is why we believe he should not take an undue period of time to set up over the ball. Too much time allows for too much thinking, whereas a good set-up should be natural and automatic. As the set-up becomes more automatic it will also become more consistent and self-repeating.

I am reminded of one of my older students who was constantly concerned about distance. He seemed to believe that he had lost many yards as he had aged. I did not see evidence of that on the practice tee. One day, however, I joined him on the course just at the time when he was fretting about a long approach shot to the green. I could figuratively see the wheels going around in his head as he worried about his club selection. Tension set in, and by the time he finally hit the shot he was too tense to make a smooth movement through the ball. It was obvious to me that he had lost yardage, not because of age but because of worry. His set-up was slow because of his enormous indecision, and the very slowness of the process gave him far too much time to worry.

I am not advocating quickness at the expense of thoroughness. I have already stated that I believe the set-up to be the most vital part of the swing—and perhaps even the entire game. It is even more crucial for the older person because he must attain maximum result from minimum effort. The younger person can sometimes make up for error by utilizing brute force. If he hits the ground behind the ball, for example, he may have sufficient strength to force the club through the ball—and compensate for the fat shot. The older man probably won't have that kind of strength. Perhaps, too, the older man must use everything he has in order to drive the ball 250 yards. The younger man may be able to get that with a weak hit.

There is another point to be stressed too. Perhaps with age an individual finds that he can no longer bend over the ball with as much agility as he could when he was younger. This dictates a postural change for the older player. He needs to recognize this so that he can find his normal, comfortable position. It may be very different from what it was when he was younger. That's fine according to my principle of building the game around the individual, not the individual around the game.

All of this adds up to a special need for mental discipline by the older player. He should find the set-up that works well and feels comfortable. Then he should find some way of duplicating it each time he sets up to the ball. And he should adopt a pace in setting up that is unhurried enough to allow for care but quick enough to facilitate mental and physical relaxation.

—from *Golf Begins at Forty*

BETTER GOLF AFTER FIFTY by Gene Sarazen, with Roger Ganem. 1967, 120 pages, N.Y.: Harper & Row.

The Squire discusses in a businesslike manner common senior ailments and how to deal with them, and describes various shots (such as the fairway wood) that the older golfer must fall back on.

LOFTED PUTTER

When your putter starts to feel strange, or your putting goes sour, it may be a good idea to change putters for a while. You may return to your original first love, or you may find the right putter for you. The change may also help you get back in the right groove with the old. Just walk into your pro shop and buy another. It isn't unusual to have a half dozen putters. If there is any rule of thumb to go by in selecting the putter that is right for you, it starts with your knowing something about the greens you play. Greens today are generally slower than they were in my tournament days. They were really fast then. But nowadays they pour a shower bath over the putting surface, that really slows them up. There are a few exceptions, of course, like Pebble Beach and Oakmont, where the greens are lightning fast. If your greens are slow, you might do well to use a mallet-head putter. On fast greens the pros switch to blade putters, the same kind Jones and Hagen used to use.

With a putter that fits you, you should be able to close your left eye and be able to see the whole face of it. If you can, you know you have ample loft. If you have to move forward to look at the face it means that your putter does not have enough lift.

When my putting was great, I used a blade putter with a slight loft. This enabled the ball to leave the ground within four inches of where I struck it, so that the ball was well on the way to the direction I was aiming. So many putters these days are made with very little loft so that you're actually driving the ball into the ground instead of getting it started. If there is any little thing that could interfere with the ball within four inches of where you hit it, like somebody's footprint or a ball's pit mark that you can't see, it could knock the ball off line very easily.

—from *Better Golf After Fifty*

PAUL RUNYAN'S BOOK FOR SENIOR GOLFERS by Paul Runyan. 1962, 149 pages, N.Y.: Dodd, Mead.

From one of the game's most successful "little men," absorbing instruction that actually would be of interest and relevance to ordinary golfers of any age. He emphasizes hand action and pivoting in the full swing, scrambling skills, wrist-free putting stroke. Older players should keep a honey pot in their bag (for emergency energy source) and carry no iron longer than a 4. He writes clearly and precisely about complex matters such as grip construction and swing plane, but relieves the inevitable tedium with anecdotes from his tour experience in the 1930s and 1940s, and later as a PGA Seniors champ.

GARDEN RAKE DRILL

So in my middle fifties I have found that a constant program of simple exercises has not only helped me hold my ground, but has actually enabled me to hit the ball harder than I ever did before. These exercises are not strenuous. They do not tax the heart. After doing them I do not even breathe more heavily. They are designed to affect and strengthen only those muscles in the hands and arms which are so important for accelerating the clubhead in the hitting area.

The best way to reach these particular muscles is to swing just as you do in golf, with something considerably heavier than your golf clubs. I have found an ordinary garden rake to be ideal for this purpose. Swing it out of sight somewhere, or in the dark, so your neighbors won't think you've suddenly lost your mind. The rake should be very heavy and very stiff. The stiffness makes your hands and arms do all the work of starting and stopping the rake as you move it through the normal arc of a golf swing, and its great length, with the weight so far removed, helps tire the muscles very quickly.

The average iron rake is probably fifteen or twenty times the swing weight of the average golf club. By using it for no more than two or three minutes a night just before going to bed you can prevent your hands from losing their strength and snap during long periods when you are not playing and you can also add considerably to the flexibility and quickness of the hands.

Other related exercises undoubtedly condition you over all, but do not have as much specific golfing benefit, at least for me. The rake is much better for this purpose than the weighted golf clubs often advertised. Such clubs, or the specially weighted head covers placed on conventional clubs, certainly have a useful function; they are primarily warmer-uppers, or the golf version of the two or three bats a baseball player uses just before he steps into the batting box. But they are not heavy enough to give your arms and hands the stretching and strengthening produced by a rake. Rakes are also stiffer to swing; with them, the hands and arms must do all the work, because there is no "give" to the shaft as there is with a weighted club.

This hand strengthening program can, of course, be overdone. Perhaps a lighter object, a garden hoe, or broom, should be used initially. And then when a rake is taken up it should be swung very slowly at first. If it is kept from hitting the ground at the bottom of the arc you can be sure your hands are bearing the brunt of the work. You want to tire them out as rapidly as you can. As you find your hands becoming stronger, you should swing the rake faster.

—from *Paul Runyan's Book for Senior Golfers*

GOLF BEGINS AT 45 by Tom Scott and Geoffrey Cousins. 1960, 208 pages, $4.95, N.Y.: A. S. Barnes.

This book was written by two long-time British golfer/journalists with a British audience in mind, but if you can see through the gorse and heather of their references, there's a lot of common-sense notes on holding one's own after 45.

OTHER SENIOR-GOLF REFERENCES

SENIOR GOLFER
   P.O. Box 4716
   Clearwater, FL 35518
   (813) 442-2509
   Charles B. Albury, editor and publisher
   STARTED PUBLICATION: 1964.
   FREQUENCY: 6 times annually (bimonthly).
   AVG. CIRCULATION: 10,000.
   AVG. NO. OF PAGES PER ISSUE: 16.
   SUBSCRIPTION: $2.50 for one year, $4.50 for two years.
   CONTENTS: *Senior Golfer* previews and reports on all types of senior events, maintains an up-to-date schedule of events, and runs seniors-oriented instruction by noted teacher Irv Schloss.

SENIOR CITIZENS AND GOLF
   National Golf Foundation
   200 Castlewood Drive
   North Palm Beach, FL 33408

This 24-page booklet is designed to help towns and cities set up their own senior golf programs and includes several detailed case histories. Cost: $1.25.

SPECIAL SENIORS SECTION
   Golf Digest Reprint Service
   495 Westport Avenue
   Norwalk, CT 06856

Reprint of *Golf Digest* senior editor John P. May's 1978 roundup on senior activities; called "More Competition and Fun for the Booming 55-and-Over Group." Includes short personality features on leading senior golfers, instruction geared to seniors, and a directory of senior associations and events. Cost: 60¢.

SIMPLE EXERCISES FOR SENIORS
   Golf Digest Reprint Service

Reprint of 1978 article by Paul Runyan on shaping up or shipping out. Cost: 50¢.

RETIREMENT IN THE SUNBELT

This passage is reprinted with permission from an article by Peter A. Dickinson in the October–November 1978 issue of *Modern Maturity*. © 1978 by *Modern Maturity*.

Whatever you're looking for—lower cost of living, improved health, new friends and activities—you'll find it more easily in the Sunbelt than in any other part of the United States. It's an area that welcomes older people with hopes as well as young people with dreams.

The Sunbelt lies in the South and West, including Hawaii. Snow is rare, winter is short, and the weather is mild and sunny, averaging a comfortable 55 degrees throughout the year.

I traveled 7,000 miles through the region researching a newly published book. 'Sunbelt Retirement' (E. P. Dutton, New York). Here is what I found, plus some reasons why you should consider Sunbelt living in your retirement plans.

LOWER COST OF LIVING

Because living is easier, Sunbelt costs are lower. Using a Bureau of Labor Statistics index in which 100 represents the average cost of living for retired couples, cities and towns in the West and South, except for Los Angeles and Honolulu, score consistently in the 80s and 90s.

A retired couple is defined as a husband 65 or older and his wife. They are assumed to be self-supporting, in reasonably good health and able to take care of themselves. Budgets include food, housing, transportation, clothing, personal care and medical care, but not personal income taxes. Annual budgets at 1978 prices: Lower, $5,000; Intermediate, $7,500; Higher, $12,000.

All Sunbelt states offer some tax relief to the elderly, usually according to income.

However, first of all you must establish legal residency in the state, and then you must apply for the exemption.

SUNBELT IS HEALTHIER

Your body functions best when the temperature is about 66 degrees with a relative humidity of about 55 percent, and a temperature-humidity index (a combination of factors) of under 72.

Ideally, there should be gentle breezes and beaming sunshine.

You'll find most of this "perfect" weather in the Sunbelt states.

A good climate makes fewer demands upon your body and pocketbook. And the milder weather makes you feel and behave better psychologically because changes in weather affect your pulse rate, urine, body temperature, and metabolic processes.

Northern cities—with their weather extremes, noise, congestion and pollution—strain nerves and the body. Colds and other respiratory diseases abound in winter when people stay indoors in artificially heated air.

More than 50 percent of deaths in the U.S. occur during the winter.

Another common ailment, diabetes, appears more controllable in hot climes. Stress diseases—ulcers, certain heart problems, hardening of the arteries—are also less frequent in warm zones. Doctors frequently recommend these regions for relief from the following ailments:

HEALTH PROBLEM	WHERE TO FIND RELIEF
Hay Fever	*Arizona, Southern Calif., Florida beach resorts, North Carolina mountain resorts, El Paso, Tex.*
Heart trouble, hardening of the arteries, hypertension	*Florida, Gulf Coast of Alabama, Mississippi, Louisiana, Texas*
Rheumatism, arthritis	*Southern parts of Arizona and New Mexico*
Sinus and respiratory problems	*Southern Calif., central Arizona, and at moderate elevations*
Kidney and liver ailments	*Ozone Belt of Louisiana*

If you're contemplating a change of climate for health reasons, consult your doctor first. He knows your medical history and emotional patterns, and would help you evaluate whether a move would be helpful. Also, remember that even within states of the Sunbelt, you're likely to find many climatic variations. Moving to Arizona for your health works only if you find the right spot in that state.

Also, be sure to investigate the availability of doctors and hospitals. Ideally, there should be at least five hospital beds per 1,000 residents, and at least one doctor per 750 residents. You won't always find these ideal conditions in the Sunbelt, especially in rural areas. Here are the best retirement places I found for hospital facilities and availability of doctors:

NORTH CAROLINA—Charlotte, Asheville, Chapel Hill; SOUTH CAROLINA—Charleston; FLORIDA—Miami, Sarasota, St. Petersburg; ALABAMA—Fairhope; LOUISIANA—New Orleans, Baton Rouge; ARKANSAS—Hot Springs, Fayetteville; TEXAS—Brownsville, Kerrville; NEW MEXICO—Albuquerque; ARIZONA—Tucson, Phoenix; CALIFORNIA—San Diego (area), Los Angeles (area), Palm Springs.

If the average national rate for a semiprivate room is about $100 a day, here are what Sunbelt states would charge:

North Carolina—$68.67	*Louisiana—$69.59*
South Carolina—$63.95	*Arkansas—$66.71*
Georgia—$76.59	*Texas—$74.84*
Florida—$89.11	*New Mexico—$86.80*
Alabama—$71.18	*Arizona—$88.68*
Mississippi—$54.06	*Southern Calif.—$127.90*
	Hawaii—$110.71

LOWER-COST HOUSING

Generally, two- and three-bedroom retirement houses in the Sunbelt sell for 20 to 50 percent less than in the North and East. One- and two-bedroom apartments rent for $100 to $200 a month in the Sunbelt compared to $150 to $300 elsewhere.

Also, you don't need as much shelter because you spend more time outdoors. Sunbelt houses don't require full basements for central heating systems (space, floor, wall heaters, etc., suffice), nor do they require as much insulation, or enclosed garages.

The Sunbelt offers more developments and retirement villages than other parts of the country including groups of single-family houses, townhouses, apartments or mobile homes surrounding a garden, swimming pool, or recreation area. Many developments include a golf course, bowling green and tennis courts.

STIMULATING LIVING

Social life in the Sunbelt is more person-to-person and less centered on social or economic status than elsewhere. Entertaining is less formal. Major activities are outdoors. You can enjoy golf, tennis, lawn bowling, shuffleboard and boating.

There are many opportunities to continue learning. Colleges such as the Universities of Texas, North Carolina and South Carolina offer free or low-cost classes for older persons. Most community colleges will provide a course and instructor if 10 or more older persons sign up.

Sunbelt residents value personal contact. While some "Southern hospitality" might be superficial, it's a way of life that can charm even the most confirmed Northerner. Some people, of course, would miss the folks back home. But they're only seconds away by telephone or a few hours away by jet plane. And you'll always find plenty of former Northerners and Midwesterners in the Sunbelt.

SERVICES FOR OLDER PERSONS

Each Sunbelt state has state, area and local agencies on aging that work directly with local and community groups in housing, health, transportation, nutrition, recreation, and legal services. While many programs are aimed at helping the poor elderly, other services such as transportation (minibuses) and nutrition (inexpensive hot meals) appeal to higher income persons because the services are convenient and often stimulate social contact.

Many communities with large retirement populations have private organizations that supply special services and programs for older persons. Such communities include cities like New Bern, Southern Pines, Hendersonville, Tryon, N.C.; Myrtle Beach and Charleston, S.C.; St. Petersburg, Miami, Sarasota, Fla.; Fairhope, Ala.; El Paso, Tex.; Rosewell, N.M.; Prescott, Ariz.; Los Angeles.

SOME DISADVANTAGES

I found pitfalls in this paradise, and I'd like to balance the advantages with some disadvantages:

· Perpetual summer. Though I prefer moderate temperatures, I also like distinct seasons to add variety. But only in northwestern North Carolina and Arkansas and in the high plateaus of New Mexico and Arizona is there a four-season climate.

· Lack of transportation. With few exceptions (perhaps Miami, Albuquerque, N.M., Los Angeles, Honolulu), public transportation in the Sunbelt is poor or lacking. A car is a must.

· Too many insects. Because average temperatures are higher in the Sunbelt states, annoying insects are more prevalent. Such pests include cockroaches, mosquitoes and fire ants. Snakes are more common, too.

· Less culture. There are fewer opportunities to enjoy classical music, museums, libraries, and art galleries in the Sunbelt states than in more cosmopolitan cities elsewhere. However, there are good opportunities for continuing education in community and local colleges in the Sunbelt.

WHERE TO GET MORE INFORMATION

You and only you know what housing you need, want and can afford. To help find housing I suggest:

· Pinpoint the area you'd like to settle in. Also, write the Administration on Aging, Department HEW, Washington, D.C. 20201 or the U.S. Department of Housing and Urban Development (HUD) Information Center, 7th & D Sts. S.W., Washington, D.C. 20410 for housing suggestions. If health is a factor, check with your doctor.

· After you've pinpointed the area, write to the specific state units on aging (located in state capitals). Ask about location and availability of housing; cost of living and taxes; climate and environment; special facilities for older persons, including tax exemptions. Be specific.

· Then write to the chambers of commerce of the various cities and towns you're interested in. No street address necessary, but the zip code is desirable. Again, specify what you're looking for. A friendly (or no) answer will give you an idea if the welcome mat is out.

· Subscribe to weekly or Sunday papers to learn about the area's business and social life and cost of food, clothing, and real estate.

· Vacation there—off season as well as on. Get the pulse of the town. Is it brisk in the morning but dull in the evening? Are weekdays somber and weekends lively?

· Get to know the people—the postman, grocer, real estate agent, librarian, chamber of commerce people, the people you meet in clubs, town meetings and houses of worship. Are they friendly or do they avoid strangers? How long would it take you to go from "stranger to neighbor"? (Two years is about average.)

· Rent before buying, or swap houses. Rent your home "back home." If you decide you don't like your new community, you can always go back.

Four major home-exchange clubs will list your home in their directories for about $15. They leave it to you to make any arrangements. Write to:

Vacation Exchange Club
350 Broadway
New York, N.Y. 10013

Loan-A-Home
18 Darwood Place
Mt. Vernon, N.Y. 10553

Holiday Home Exchange Bureau
Post Office Box 555
Grants, N.M. 87020

Adventures in Living
Post Office Box 278
Winnetka, Ill. 60093

For catalogs of retirement housing in the Sunbelt write:

Strout Realty
Plaza Towers
Springfield, Mo. 65804

United Farm Agency
612 West 47th St.
Kansas City, Mo. 64112

SENIOR (OVER 55) GOLF EVENTS

Results in tournaments marked with an asterisk (*) are weighed by *Golf Digest* in compiling annual senior rankings. Among these, the most competitive fields are usually found at the USGA Senior, the North & South, the U.S. Seniors, and the American Senior (both stroke and match).

SPRING

EVENT
*American Sr. Golf Ass'n
Match Play Championship
Belleview Biltmore Hotel
Belleair, Fla.
CONTACT FOR INFORMATION
ASGA
P.O. Box 241
Palm Beach, FL 33480

Breakers Senior
Breakers Hotel C.C.
Palm Beach, Fla.
CONTACT FOR INFORMATION
Tournament Director
Breakers Hotel
Palm Beach, FL 33480

SUMMER

EVENT
*World Sr. Golf Association International
Team and Individual Golf Championship
Broadmoor Hotel
Colorado Springs, Colo.
CONTACT FOR INFORMATION
WSGA
Broadmoor G.C.
Colorado Springs, CO 80906

*U.S. Seniors Golf Association Championship
Apawamis Club
Rye, N.Y.
CONTACT FOR INFORMATION
USSGA
60 E. 42nd Street
New York, NY 10017

*International Senior Amateur Golf Society
Gleneagles, Scotland
CONTACT FOR INFORMATION
ISAGS
1775 Broadway, Suite 2505
New York, NY 10019

*Curtis Person Invitational
Colonial C.C.
Memphis, Tenn.

*Eastern Seniors Golf Association Championship
CONTACT FOR INFORMATION
ESGA
c/o Rupert H. Johnson
7 Red Oak Road
Bronxville, NY 10708

*Great Lakes Senior Golf Association
(Site varies)
CONTACT FOR INFORMATION
GLSGA
c/o Hank Meiers
Heights-Rockefeller Building
2483 Lee Boulevard
Cleveland Heights, OH 44118

*Canadian Senior Championship
(Site varies)
CONTACT FOR INFORMATION
Royal Canadian G.A.
RR #2
Oakville, Ontario
Canada, LGJ 423

FALL

EVENT
*Southern Seniors Golf Association Championship
CONTACT FOR INFORMATION
SSGA
c/o Robert Fowler
P.O. Box 1629
Winter Park, FL 32790

National Super Senior Texas Invitational
Galveston (TX) C.C.
CONTACT FOR INFORMATION
Bud McKinney
8104 Meadow Road, Apt. 205
Dallas, TX 75231

Caribbean Seniors Golf Championship
Casa de Campo
La Romana
Dominican Republic
CONTACT FOR INFORMATION
Irv Schloss
P.O. Box 6504
Clearwater, FL 35518

*USGA Senior/USGA Women's Senior
CONTACT FOR INFORMATION
U.S. Golf Association
Far Hills, NJ 07931

*Western Senior
CONTACT FOR INFORMATION
Western Golf Association
c/o Charles Donaldson
903 Chanticleer Lane
Hinsdale, IL 60521

*North and South Seniors/North & South Senior
  Women's
Pinehurst (N.C.) C.C.
CONTACT FOR INFORMATION
  Tournament Director
  Pinehurst, C.C.
  Pinehurst, NC

U.S. National Senior Open
Scottsdale, Ariz.
CONTACT FOR INFORMATION
  Tournament Chairman
  USNSGA
  2140 Westwood Boulevard, Suite 19
  Los Angeles, CA 90025

Western (WSAA)
CONTACT FOR INFORMATION
  John B. Olson
  Western Senior Amateur Association
  25115 Kirby, Sp. 335
  Hemet, CA 92343

Senior Women's Invitational
Palmetto Dunes C.C.
Hilton Head Island, S.C.
CONTACT FOR INFORMATION
  Tournament Director
  Palmetto Dunes C.C.
  Hilton Head Island, SC

WINTER

EVENT
*American Senior Golf Association Stroke Play
  Championship
Breakers Hotel C.C.
Palm Beach, Fla.
CONTACT FOR INFORMATION
  ASGA
  P.O. Box 241
  Palm Beach, FL 33480

* Belleair Seniors Invitational
Belleview Biltmore Hotel G.C.
Belleair, Fla.
CONTACT FOR INFORMATION
  Tournament Director
  Belleview Biltmore Hotel
  Belleair, FL 33516

*International Senior Champions Tournament
Belleview Biltmore Hotel G.C.
Belleair, Fla.

CONTACT FOR INFORMATION
  Tournament Director
  Belleview Biltmore Hotel
  Belleair, FL 33516

Lakewood Seniors Invitational
Lakewood C.C.
Point Clear, Ala.
CONTACT FOR INFORMATION
  c/o Jim Pope, General Manager
  Grand Hotel
  Point Clear, AL 36564

Golf Wing-Ding
Valley C.C.
Scottsdale, Ariz.
CONTACT FOR INFORMATION
  E. D. Bailey
  c/o Jokake Inn
  6000 E. Camelback Road
  Phoenix, AZ 85018

Invitational Golf Rodeo
Valley C.C.
Scottsdale, Ariz.
CONTACT FOR INFORMATION
  E. D. Bailey
  c/o Jokake Inn
  6000 E. Camelback Road
  Phoenix, AZ 85018

*Suncoast Seniors Invitational
Sunset G.C.
St. Petersburg, Fla.
CONTACT FOR INFORMATION
  Billy Watts
  c/o Sunset G.C.
  St. Petersburg, FL

American Association of Retired Persons (AARP)
  Championship
CONTACT FOR INFORMATION
  American Golf Association
  Box 1103
  Morgantown, NC 28655

STATE, REGIONAL, AND SPECIAL-INTEREST SENIOR GROUPS

Alabama Seniors Golf Association
P.O. Box 1167
Florence, AL 35630

Arizona Seniors Golf Association
P.O. Box 34
Scottsdale, AZ 85252

Arkansas Senior Golf Association
1800 East Roosevelt
Little Rock, AK 72206

Arkansas Senior Women's Golf Association
Pine Bluff, AK 71601

Bay State Seniors Golf Association
Box AF
Duxbury, MA 02332

California Seniors Golf Association
P.O. Box 96
Danville, CA 94526

Central States Senior Golf Association
2782 S. Wentworth Avenue
Milwaukee, WI 53207

Colorado Senior Golf Association
9340 E. Center Avenue
Denver, CO 80231

Eastern States Seniors Golf Association
5020 Citadel Avenue
Columbia, SC 29206

Florida Senior Golf Association
Box 616
Holly Hill, FL 32017

Free State Seniors Golf Association of Maryland
11008 Inwood Avenue
Silver Spring, MD 20902

Georgia Senior Golfers Association
P.O. Box 90151
East Point, GA 30364

Georgia Senior Women's Golf Association
P.O. Box 342
Blackspear, GA 31516

Gulf Coast Seniors Golf Association
P.O. Box 83
Valparaiso, FL 32580

Illinois Seniors Golf Association
105 W. Adams Street, Room 600
Chicago, IL 60603

Indiana State Seniors Golf Association
5641 East 72nd Street
Indianapolis, IN 46250

Iowa Senior Golf Association
130 Thompson Drive SE
Cedar Rapids, IA 52403

Kansas Senior Inv. Golf Association
3403 Burlingame Road
Topeka, KS 66611

Long Island Senior Golf Association
60 E. 42nd Street
New York, NY 10017

Louisiana Senior Golf Association
813 Carolina Avenue
Bogalusa, LA 70427

Maine Seniors Golf Association
c/o Mr. Edmund C. Ritchie
38 Richardson Street
Portland, ME 04103

Michigan Seniors Golf Association
2084 Bordeaux Drive
W. Bloomfield, MI 48033

Mississippi Seniors Golf Association
P.O. Box 12412
Jackson, MS 39211

Missouri Senior Golf Association
108 Burnan
Columbia, MO 65201

Missouri Senior Women's Golf Association
1915 W. Boulevard South
Columbia, MO 65201

New Jersey State Seniors' Golf Association
382 Springfield Avenue
Summit, NJ 07901

Nebraska Senior Golf Association
2453 St. Marys
Omaha, NB 68105

Nevada State Seniors Golf Club
P.O. Box 19444
Paradise Valley Station
Las Vegas, NV 89119

New England Senior Golfers Association
252 Fairview Avenue
Brockton, MA 02401

New Hampshire Senior Golf Association
109 Riddle Street
Manchester, NH 03103

New York Seniors Golf Association
243 Overbrook Road
Rochester, NY 14618

North Carolina Seniors Golf Association
Dan Poole, Secretary
Durham, NC 27707

North Texas Senior Golf Association
9578 Spring Branch
Dallas, TX 75238

Ohio Seniors Golf Association
1098 Springmill Road
Mansfield, OH 44906

Ohio Valley Seniors Golf Association
P.O. Box 327
Steubenville, OH 43952

Oklahoma State Senior Golf Association
P.O. Box 70
Guthrie, OK 73044

Oregon Senior Women's Golf Association
2246 N.E. 31st Street
Portland, OR 97212

Oregon Senior Golfers Association
Box 3414
Portland, OR 97208

Philadelphia Seniors Golf Association
7380 Ridge Avenue
Philadelphia, PA 19128

Retired Military Golfers Association
P.O. Box 2444
Laguna Hills, CA 92653

Rhode Island State Senior Golf Association
715 Hospital Trust Building
Providence, RI 02903

Senior Social Golf Association
P.O. Box 51
Oswego, NY 13827

Senior Golf Association of Wisconsin
5856 N. Port Washington Road
Milwaukee, WI 53217

Senior Golf Association of Southern California
(West Section)
610 Kentwood Drive
Oxnard, CA 93030

Senior Golfers Association of Eastern New York
15 Snowden Avenue
Elsmere, NY 12054

Senior Golfers of South Carolina
Box 4705
Columbia, SC 29240

Seniors Golf Association of Southern California
3740 Cahuenga Boulevard
N. Hollywood, CA 91604

Society of "55" Gentlemen Golfers
17985 Sky Park Circle, Suite H
Irvine, CA 92714

South Mississippi Senior Golf Association
410 Forest Avenue
Biloxi, MS 39531

Southern California Senior Golf Association
1041 Huasna Road
Box 870
Arroyo Grande, CA 93420

Southern Illinois Senior Golf Association
P.O. Box 222
Murphysboro, IL 62966

Southwest Florida Seniors Golf Association
662 Allegheny Drive
Sun City Center, FL 33570

St. Louis Senior Golf Association
8715 Sturdy Drive
St. Louis, MO 63126

Tarheel State Senior Golf Association
P.O. Box 7263
Greensboro, NC 27407

Triangle Seniors Golf Association
1504 Ruffin Street
Durham, NC 27701

Tri-State Senior Golf Association
1016 Austin
Amarillo, TX 79102

Tri-State Seniors Golf
P.O. Box 3834 C.R.S.
Johnson City, TN 37601

U.S. Senior Women's Golf Association
Wellesley Hills, MA 02181

Utah Senior Golf Association
1935 S. Main Street
P.O. Box 30030
Salt Lake City, UT 84125

Vermont Senior Golf Association
15 Wilson Street
Burlington, VT 05401

The Virginia Senior Golf Association
P.O. Box 27
Charleston, WV 25321

Volunteer State Seniors Golf Association
1634 Fairway Drive
Johnson City, TN 37601

Washington State Senior Women's Golf Association
Box 1309
Bellevue, WA 98009

Washington State Seniors Golf Association
P.O. Box 2035
Bellingham, WA 98225

Westchester Senior Golf Association
60 E. 42nd Street
New York, NY 10017

Women's New Jersey Senior Golf Association
342 Richmond
South Orange, NJ 07079

Zanesville Seniors Golf Association
2771 West Drive
Zanesville, OH 43701

VII

Junior Golf

ADVICE FOR PARENTS
ESTABLISHED TOURNAMENTS FOR JUNIORS
SOURCES OF INFORMATION ON JUNIOR GOLF PROGRAMS
INCENTIVE PROGRAMS FOR JUNIORS
JUNIOR GOLF SCHOOLS AND CAMPS
BOOKS FOR BEGINNERS

ADVICE FOR PARENTS

The most important thing to remember about junior golf, or any other junior level sport for that matter, is it must be fun and enjoyable to have merit.

At the younger ages, parents should try to encourage young people to play. Not push. Just encourage the kids to go out on the golf course and enjoy the game and what it has to offer. At a certain time you will find out just how interested the kid has become, and then it comes the time for guidance.

The guidance stage is one all parents have to handle properly. The guidance should again be loaded with encouragement but completely without pressure. Being pushy is the quickest way to turn away the would-be superstar who is learning the character-building aspects of the game of golf.

Entering competition is something that is good for some, bad for others. If the competition is properly organized and the perspectives maintained, competition can come at most any age. Once that competition begins, the parents should remain in the background. Let the officials handle the program and the situations that develop therein. Be supportive but let that support take the proper route.

Finding a good competitive program is not that easy. Try your club, your golf professional or others in your area who have had their children go through the program. Find out what the motivations are. If the program is overly oriented toward winning or is a pressurized situation, it might be wise to wait until later to enroll the player. Make sure he or she will benefit from the participation.

Competition is a way of life and kids will learn sooner or later how to survive. In golf. In business. In life. Once you have made sure your golfer can handle the competitive nature of organized junior golf, let 'em go and wish 'em well.

—Mike Bentley, President,
American Junior Golf Association

ESTABLISHED TOURNAMENTS FOR JUNIORS

In addition to the events listed below, most of which attract strong national fields, numerous other junior tournaments are held every year for essentially statewide or citywide fields. For information on these local events, contact your state golf association (addresses and numbers begin on page 258).

Events designated with two asterisks (**) are classified as "major tournaments" by *Golf Magazine* in the selection process it uses to name Junior All-America teams every year. Performances in events designated with one asterisk (*) are also considered in the voting.

SUMMER

TOURNAMENT
Women's Western Golf Association Junior (girls)
Rockford (IL) C.C.
CONTACT FOR INFORMATION
    Mrs. Mark Cox
    Women's Western Golf Association
    108 Lakeshore Drive
    North Palm Beach, FL 33408

*National High School All-American Tournament
    (boys)*
CONTACT FOR INFORMATION
    Carey McDonald, Executive Director
    National High School Athletic Coaches
        Association
    P.O. Box 357
    Ocala, FL 32670

Little Peoples Golf Championships (girls and boys)
CONTACT FOR INFORMATION
    Little Peoples Golf Championships
    P.O. Box 80
    Quincy, IL 62301

Southern Junior (girls and boys)
CONTACT FOR INFORMATION
    Southern Golf
    P.O. Box 1368
    Southern Pines, NC 28387
    Attn.: Rodney Williams

Texas and Oklahoma Junior (boys)
CONTACT FOR INFORMATION
    Weeks Park Men's Golf Association
    P.O. Box 343
    Wichita Falls, TX 76307

Bluebonnet Junior (boys)
CONTACT FOR INFORMATION
    Chuck Klein
    P.O. Box 6528
    San Antonio, TX 78209

International Junior Masters
CONTACT FOR INFORMATION
    East Aurora C.C.
    Buffalo, NY

Doug Sanders International Junior
Woodlands C.C.
Houston, TX
CONTACT FOR INFORMATION
    Golf Services Ltd.
    2301 Millbend Drive
    Woodlands, TX 77380

Bobby Bowers Memorial
CONTACT FOR INFORMATION
Springfield G. and C.C.
8601 Old Keene Mill Road
Springfield, VA 22152

Western Junior (*boys*)
CONTACT FOR INFORMATION
Western Golf Association
Golf, IL 60029

North-South Junior (*girls and boys*)
CONTACT FOR INFORMATION
Southern Golf
P.O. Box 1368
Southern Pines, NC 28387
Attn.: Rodney Williams

NIMAGA Junior Match Play Championship
CONTACT FOR INFORMATION
North Illinois Men's Golf Association
P.O. Box 162
Golf, IL 60029

**Junior World Golf Championship* (*girls and boys*)
San Diego, CA
CONTACT FOR INFORMATION
Mrs. A. S. Smith
4375 Temecula Street
San Diego, CA 92107

International Pee Wee (*girls and boys*)
CONTACT FOR INFORMATION
Pee Wee Golf Championships, Inc.
P.O. Box 2047
Orlando, FL 32802

**USGA Junior* (*boys*)
CONTACT FOR INFORMATION
United States Golf Association
Golf House
Far Hills, NJ 07931

**National PGA Junior Golf Championship* (*girls and boys*)
CONTACT FOR INFORMATION
Mr. Gary Ellis
PGA National Junior Golf Championship
Box 12458
Lake Park, FL 33403

New England Junior
CONTACT FOR INFORMATION
Ponkapoag G.C.
2167 Washington Street
Canton, MA

International Junior Tournament of Champions
CONTACT FOR INFORMATION
Southern Junior Golf
Box 1368
Southern Pines, NC 28387

Tournament of Champions (*girls and boys*)
CONTACT FOR INFORMATION
American Junior Golf Association
P.O. Box 33565
Decatur, GA 30033

Insurance Youth Classic Golf Championship (*girls and boys*)
CONTACT FOR INFORMATION
Insurance Youth Classic
Independent Insurance Agents of America, Inc.
85 John Street
New York, NY 10038

USGA Junior (*girls*)
CONTACT FOR INFORMATION
United States Golf Association
Golf House
Far Hills, NJ 07931

All-American Junior (*boys*)
CONTACT FOR INFORMATION
Southern Golf
P.O. Box 1368
Southern Pines, NC 28387
Attn.: Rodney Williams

Southern Junior Championship (*boys*)
CONTACT FOR INFORMATION
Pensacola Sports Association
P.O. Box 4337
32 North Navy Boulevard
Pensacola, FL 32507

All-American Junior (*girls*)
CONTACT FOR INFORMATION
All-American Golf
P.O. Box 1368
Southern Pines, NC 28387

Worsham Memorial (*boys*)
CONTACT FOR INFORMATION
Junior Golfers of Washington
3807 Williams Lane
Chevy Chase, MD 20015
Attn.: Frank Emmet

WINTER (Christmas–New Year's Week)

TOURNAMENT

Orange Bowl International Junior (boys)
CONTACT FOR INFORMATION
> City of Coral Gables
> Community Development Dept.
> 405 Biltmore Way
> Coral Gables, FL 33134

National Junior Team Classic
CONTACT FOR INFORMATION
> North Illinois Men's Golf Association
> P.O. Box 162
> Golf, IL 60029

All-American Tournament (girls and boys)
CONTACT FOR INFORMATION
> American Junior Golf Association
> P.O. Box 33565
> Decatur, GA 30033

World Series of Junior Golf
CONTACT FOR INFORMATION
> Indigo G. & C.C.
> Daytona Beach, FL

SOURCES OF INFORMATION ON JUNIOR GOLF PROGRAMS

AMERICAN JUNIOR GOLF ASSOCIATION

The American Junior Golf Association was founded in 1977 to promote junior golf on all levels in the nation. Its primary goal is the dissemination of information about junior golf, to inform the players of what is available in their area and on a national scale. The association is also interested in fostering interest on the local level and in trying to improve the quality of golf programs available to juniors in various areas.

In its first year, over 3,000 young people from 49 states joined the AJGA, which sponsors tournaments and publishes the *Junior Golf Newsletter* eight times each year and the *Junior Golf America* tab newspaper four times each year.

For information, write:
> American Junior Golf Association
> P.O. Box 33565
> Decatur, GA 30033

PGA NATIONAL JUNIOR GOLF FUND

New program of the PGA raises money for junior golf schools, clinics and tournaments, makes available booklets and films showing how to run such events locally. For name of current PGA junior golf chairman in your area, contact below, or nearest PGA Section office (see page 264).
> PGA National Junior Golf Fund
> PGA of America
> Box 12458
> Lake Park, FL 33403

PUBLICATIONS AVAILABLE

To receive the following publications, write:
> National Golf Foundation
> 200 Castlewood Drive
> North Palm Beach, FL 33408

PLANNING AND CONDUCTING JUNIOR GOLF PROGRAMS, with a foreword by Jack Nicklaus.

This booklet tells how to build a program to satisfy the needs of all juniors. Includes the concept of junior golf; basic planning procedures; guidelines for private clubs, municipal recreation departments, and schools; organization of junior tournaments and junior golf associations. Also has a question-and-answer section and a list of resources for further help. Cost: $3.00.

DIRECTORY OF JUNIOR GOLF ASSOCIATIONS AND RESOURCE PERSONS

Sixteen-page listing of over 250 key contacts in every state and Canada. Free.

HOW LINCOLN, NEB., PROVIDES GOLF FOR ITS JUNIOR CITIZENS

Case history of a 1,116-yard, nine-hole course built strictly for youngsters, which now records some 30,000 paid rounds per season. Cost: 25¢.

THE GARNER MIDDLE SCHOOL GOLF PROGRAM

Case history of a successful golf program developed in a San Antonio, Texas, middle school. Cost: 25¢.

HOW TO BECOME A GOLFER

Short flyer on personal conduct, care of the course, safety, and speed of play, plus some comments directed to members of school team or class that is granted playing privileges. Cost: 25¢.

JUNIOR GOLF REFERENCES

Three pages of information on books, pamphlets, periodicals, and films of interest to junior golfers and organizers of junior golf programs. Free.

To receive the following publication, write:
> U.S. Golf Association
> Golf House
> Far Hills, NJ 07931

A JUNIOR GOLF PROGRAM FOR YOUR CLUB AND DISTRICT

A 16-page brochure aimed at a private-club audience, outlining format and goals of a program for youngsters. Also offers guidelines on caddie programs, rules of amateur status, and gambling. Cost: 25¢.

The following reprints are available from:
> *Golf Digest* Reprint Service
> 495 Westport Avenue
> Norwalk, CT 06856

HOW YOU SHOULD TEACH YOUR CHILD TO PLAY GOLF by Bob Toski. 50¢.

SPECIAL INSTRUCTIONS FOR JUNIORS by Gary Wiren. 50¢.

INCENTIVE PROGRAMS FOR JUNIORS

OFFICIAL PGA WIN-MARK JUNIOR INCENTIVE SYSTEM

Instructional motivational-reward system for golf, in which juniors move through levels of achievement in putting, chipping, pitching, fairway driving, and sand shots. Includes instructional material and record book, walnut achievement-plaque, and progress awards for each skill. Available to PGA professionals through:

PGA Bookstore
P.O. Box 12458
Lake Park, FL 33403

Others contact:
Win-Mark, Inc.
309 Greenwich Avenue
Greenwich, CT 06830

BOY SCOUTS GOLF MERIT BADGE PROGRAM

This program was introduced in 1976 (merit badges were first passed out in 1911) and includes a 72-page paperback on rules, history and (largely) instruction edited by Joseph C. Dey. For more information, contact:

Scouting Division
Boy Scouts of America
North Brunswick, NJ 08902
(201) 249-6000

JUNIOR GOLF SCHOOLS AND CAMPS

See page 49 for a directory of golf schools and camps for youngsters reprinted from *Golf Digest* magazine. Upon request, most schools will mail to interested golfers brochures and other descriptive literature, as well as up-to-date sites, dates, and costs.

TYPICAL JUNIOR GOLF CAMP PROGRAM

(The following is taken from a letter from Crimson Tide Golf Academy to an interested parent.)

Crimson Tide Golf Academy *director Conrad H. Rehling is the University of Alabama coach, a recipient of the Horton Smith Award from the PGA and heralded as "the teacher of champions" by* Golf Digest. *Coach Rehling is primarily responsible for developing the educational services at the U of A Golf Center. The modern clubhouse is equipped with video-taping equipment, a sequence camera and super-8 filming facilities. The course itself is an attractive 18-hole facility complete with driving range and practice greens. Coach Rehling's mainstay for success is simply hard work and definite purpose. Believing there are no overnight miracles in golf, Coach Rehling cautions students to have patience with their games. Golf requires steady, regulated practice, and in time all the things the student works on will show up and make him or her a better player.*

The main goals of the camp are to teach:
- *Basic Concepts of the Golf Swing*
- *Basic Golf Rules*
- *Basic Golf Etiquette*
- *Basic Practice Habits*
- *Basic Course Management*
- *The Five Basic Shots of Golf: Putting, Chipping, Pitch Shot, Short Iron, Wood*
- *To Give Each Camper a Tournament Experience*

The Academy schedule runs in weekly units through the month of June.

Housing and meals are provided by the University of Alabama as part of the registration fee. An unlimited food service is available to each camper.

Your child has 24-hour-a-day supervision. The staff includes dorm counselors and an on-site director who resides in the dorm.

Transportation is provided for all campers from Tuscaloosa and Birmingham bus, train, and air terminals as well as from the dorms to the camp facilities during the encampment.

An insurance plan is contracted by the University for all campers and is included in the cost of the camp.

Your child's limited free time is filled with miniature golf, roller skating, bowling, cookouts, and other appropriate activities.

The camp fee is $175, with a $75 registration fee applied to the total cost. Cancellations prior to May 1 will receive a $50 refund with $25 retained for an application processing fee. Campers who return for additional weeks of instruction pay only $150.

A TYPICAL DAY IN JUNIOR GOLF CAMP

(The following is reprinted with permission from the September 1978 *PGA magazine.*)

A typical day at the PGA National Academy of Golf started with a 6:30 early-bird jog or swim, followed by breakfast, and then on to the practice range for the morning session.

Once at the range, the students reported to preassigned stations, such as chipping and pitching or sand play, or full swing. The students were divided into groups based on skill level, so that the instructors could tailor their presentations accordingly. After a midmorning refreshment break, the students rotated to a different station with another instructor. Before departing the range for lunch break, all students spent 45 minutes practicing the basic skills under the watchful eyes of the instructors.

During each session, the participants were treated to a clinic by a touring professional and a past PGA Champion. For many, this was the highlight of the week. Andy North led off the guest slots during the first session, less than 72 hours after ramming home a 4-foot putt for the 1978 U.S. Open title in Denver. He was followed by Chick Harbert, Ed Sneed, and Dow Finsterwald, with Jim Simons wrapping up the special appearances in the third and final session of the Academy.

Why the guest appearanecs? Gary Wiren put it best, when he told the students, "We can't think of any better models for you to pattern your games and your lives after, than these men. They are representative of the people who have dedicated their lives to the game and are giving to its future, by being here with you to share what they have learned."

And the opportunity to learn was there, right into the afternoon and evening sessions. After lunch and a rest period, all the students reported to a classroom for a lecture. These sessions consisted of films and slides on a variety of subjects.

At the end of the lecture period, the students reported to their respective stations and instructors for further assignments. Built into the afternoon sessions was time for open play on the course before heading back for dinner and the evening program.

Perhaps the one part of the week-long program which brought out the team spirit and competition among the youngsters more than any other, was the evening intramural. For the first four days of the Academy, all the students would meet out on the athletic fields of St. Andrews to plot team strategy with their staff counselors for that day's events.

All students were assigned to one of six teams upon arrival, and each day there were events in which they earned points for their teams. Teams contended for the top prize at the conclusion of the Academy.

The day's program concluded with the classroom session, which includes quizzes (one of the ways to earn team points), a lecture on the principles of the golf swing, a film, and finally, an open forum on the day's instruction at the course and a discussion of plans for the next day's

schedule. Then it was off to the dorm lounges for a little TV, a rehash of the day's events and finally, "lights out."
—John Zurek

BOOKS FOR BEGINNERS

Some recent and inexpensive books covering the basics of the game for youngsters and other newcomers to golf are listed below.

GOLF GUIDE, edited by Joseph Gambatese. 1978, 96 pages, $1.25; Snibbe Publications, 7119 Exfair Road, Bethesda, MD 20014.

Pocket-sized book with simple playing and practice tips, rules, customs and lore, tour records and schedules.

GOLF PRIMER by Dick Aultman. 1977, 48 pages, 50¢; *Golf Digest* Reprint Service, 495 Westport Avenue, Norwalk, CT 06856.

This booklet, containing excerpts from the excellent magazine series of the same name, presents four "procedures" for mastering the full swing: developing tempo and rhythm, creating leg and body motion, a steady head position, and putting your swing in the slot.

GOLF LESSONS, illustrated by Dom Lupo. 1976, 48 pages, $2.50; National Golf Foundation, 200 Castlewood Drive, North Palm Beach, FL 33408.

An attractive large-format paperback with 12 easily understood and professionally illustrated lessons (see excerpt on pages 14–21.

GOLF FUNDAMENTALS by Richard D. Gordin and Roderick W. Myers. 1973, 73 pages, Columbus, Ohio: Charles E. Merrill.

Gordin and Myers coach golf at Ohio Wesleyan and Duke, respectively.

GOLF FOR BEGINNERS by Mac Hunter. 1973, 94 pages, $1.95, N.Y.: Grosset and Dunlap.

Hunter is a well-known teaching pro and clubmaker.

SO YOU WANT TO BE A GOLFER? by Jerry Vroom. 1973, 48 pages, $3.50.

Paperback by the San Jose State golf coach.

GOLF by Gary Wiren. 1971, 118 pages, Englewood Cliffs, N.J.: Prentice-Hall.

Presents basic instruction but also discusses history of the game, theory of the swing, current scientific appraisals, and practice principles.

SPORTS ILLUSTRATED BOOK OF GOLF by Charles Price. 1970, 73 pages, $3.50, N.Y.: Lippincott.

Concise, comprehensive yet uncluttered, well illustrated.

GOLF by Bruce Fossum and Mary Dagraedt. 1969, Boston: Allyn & Bacon.

Two noted coaches created this book for the publisher's Basic Concepts of Physical Activity series.

·VIII·

College Golf

COLLEGE GOLF: THE SELECTION PROCESS AND SCHOLARSHIP OPPORTUNITIES

Collegiate golf, regardless of the level, is a far cry from what most boys and girls experience in high school. Match play has become extinct and dual matches are few and far between. The level of play is naturally much stronger, since collegiate teams are comprised of the best high-school players from throughout the country.

College golf is tournament golf. It is the breeding place for the future tour stars and the battlefield for hundreds of others who enjoy the competition that this game has to offer. Each tournament finds between 12 and 24 teams battling it out over 36 or 54 holes of stroke-play competition. Normally, five or six players comprise each of these competing teams. At the conclusion of the spring season, district selection committees determine the teams to be represented in the national championships on the basis of these tournament records.

Golf is no longer restricted to a short spring season, but has grown to encompass the fall as well. For many schools, golf is now a year-round activity, and the emphasis on excellence is very great.

Strong junior-golf programs throughout the country have improved the caliber of college golf tremendously, and the number of qualified young golfers has increased proportionately. Therefore, it is necessary for each high-school student to play enough tournament golf to be able to evaluate his or her game, potential for improvement, and desire to excel. The final task will be to select the college and the golf program that will satisfy these needs.

The best way to get information about universities is to write directly to the admissions office for a bulletin, an application, and related materials. A personal note to the golf coach requesting information about the golf program will start the ball rolling. He will send schedules, brochures, and a questionnaire to be completed. Be sure to follow up with those schools that interest you. Recommendations from the high-school coach, a golf professional, or outstanding amateur alumni should be forwarded both to the admissions office and to the college coach. A résumé containing both academic and tournament records should also be included. This mailing should be done by the fall of senior year at the latest. Many universities have early deadlines for the filing of applications and coaches also like to make early decisions regarding scholarships or priority requests to the admissions office.

The selection process can become very involved. Therefore, it becomes very important to narrow down choices by becoming familiar with some important characteristics of each university:

(1) Size of school
(2) Location
(3) Quality of education
(4) Cost (tuition, travel, etc.)
(5) Scholarships and financial aid
(6) Type of golf program
(7) NCAA, NAIA, or AIAW affiliation

To become better informed about each school's golf program, the applicant will need answers to the following questions:

(1) Are scholarships available? How many? What qualifications are necessary?
(2) What are the available golf facilities? Does the school have its own course? If not, where does the team play? What is the proximity to campus? Is a car necessary?
(3) How extensive is their fall and spring schedule?
(4) What was their team's competition record the last few years?
(5) How many players are on the team? Where are they from and what year are they in school?
(6) How does the coach select his team?
(7) What type of equipment is provided?
(8) Is the coach a PGA professional? Does he attempt to help his players with their golf swings?

Once the student-athlete has surveyed the various schools, it is important to visit the campus. During the visit, appointments should be scheduled with the admissions office, golf coach, etc. Most of your detailed questions can be answered at this time. Also find time to question team members and/or students. I must re-emphasize that applications should be filed with those schools that fit your qualifications. Check deadline dates and file as early as possible.

Scholarship limitations, recruiting rules, etc., will differ among the various organizations that control college athletics. The rules for the AIAW (Association for Intercollegiate Athletics for Women) differ greatly from those of the NCAA (National Collegiate Athletic Association).

The NCAA limits major colleges (Divisions I and II) to *only* five scholarships, or the dollar equivalent, in effect at any one time. Scholarships at small colleges (Division III) are based on financial need only. Therefore, it is very important to realize that golf scholarships are limited and the competition is very keen.

The AIAW has limited the number of scholarships to eight, and with the boost for women's sports from Title

IX, more and more universities are beginning to offer aid to girls.

Scholarships are great and many students would not be able to go to college without them, but their true value must be kept in proper perspective and egos kept under control. Each college or university should be evaluated very closely and selections made for the right reasons. The school that best fits the needs of the student should be chosen, not just the one that has offered the most money.

Each parent and student must realize that there will be very few scholarships available. These scholarships will be awarded to the national champions, state champions, scratch handicappers, and those who have established successful junior records. Therefore, all those involved should be very realistic and not be disappointed if that scholarship doesn't materialize.

The college years will be extremely important to each student athlete, because they will be very instrumental in determining the student's future. Therefore, the college selection process should be given ample time and serious concern. It will be a most important decision involving these young people.

—Rod Myers, Golf Director, Duke University; Chairman, NCAA Golf Committee

SOURCES OF INFORMATION ON COLLEGE GOLF PROGRAMS, COACHES, AND FINANCIAL AID

NATIONAL DIRECTORY OF COLLEGE ATHLETICS, 1978–79
   Men's Edition, 432 pages, $10.00.
   Women's Edition, 208 pages, $6.00.
   Ray Franks Publishing Ranch
   P.O. Box 7068
   Amarillo, TX 79109

Comprehensive listings of four-year, junior, and Canadian colleges and universities, including names of coaches in every sport offered by each institution. *Women's Edition* indicates schools that offer golf scholarships.

1979 AIAW HIGH SCHOOL BROCHURE
   Association for Intercollegiate Athletics for
   Women
   1201 16th Street, NW
   Washington, DC 20036

This eight-page brochure provides clear, up-to-date information for young women student-athletes, coaches, parents, and school personnel on rules of eligibility for financial aid, auditions, letters of intent, and transfer-student procedures. Spells out *do*s and *don't*s under AIWA rules for both students and schools. Available free from AIWA or local Coca-Cola bottler.

AIWA DIRECTORY, 1978–79. 170 pages, $5.00.
   AAHPER Publication Sales
   1201 Sixteenth Street NW
   Washington, DC 20036

Lists some 825 two- and four-year member colleges and universities and summarizes sports offered for women by each institution, including those that provide financial aid based on athletic ability. Of the 174 schools listed here that offer golf to undergraduates, some 67 also provide financial aid to talented golfers who qualify.

COLLEGIATE SPORTS ORGANIZATIONS
NATIONAL COLLEGIATE ATHLETIC ASSOCIATION (NCAA)

   U.S. Highway 50 & Nall Avenue
   Box 1906
   Shawnee Mission, KS 66222
   (913) 384-3220
   Walter Byers, executive director

ASSOCIATION FOR INTERCOLLEGIATE ATHLETICS FOR WOMEN (AIAW)

   1201 16th Street NW
   Washington, DC 20036
   (202) 833-5485
   Bonnie Slatton, acting executive director

NATIONAL ASSOCIATION OF INTERCOLLEGIATE ATHLETICS (NAIA)

   1221 Baltimore Street
   Kansas City, MO 64105
   (816) 842-5050
   Dr. Harry G. Fritz, executive director
For smaller-enrollment schools.

NATIONAL LITTLE COLLEGE ATHLETIC ASSOCIATION (NLCAA)

   P.O. Box 367
   Marion, OH 43302
   (614) 389-4818
   Del Noble, commissioner

For schools with enrollment under 500.

NATIONAL JUNIOR COLLEGE ATHLETIC ASSOCIATION (NJCAA)

   12 East 2nd Street
   Hutchinson, KS 67501
   (316) 663-5445
   George E. Killian, executive director

TOP COLLEGE GOLF TEAMS AND THEIR COACHES

MEN'S TEAMS

Listed below are the schools that qualified for the men's 1978 NCAA Division I and Division II tournaments, along with the names of their golf coaches. Only first-rate players are selected for the Division I championships but it should be noted that in order to have a representative national field, the selection process is accomplished on an allotment basis by region. For example, the Southeast region, which stretches from Maryland down to Florida and across to Louisiana, can send no more than 42 players to the championship. Some strong teams from this golf-intensive region frequently do not get a chance to compete, even though they may well be superior to some teams named out of other regions. For all that, this listing provides a sampling of where the collegiate golf action is.

DIVISION I

Arizona State University
Tempe, AZ 85281
George Boutell
Bowling Green State University
Bowling Green, OH 43403
John Piper
Brigham Young University
Provo, UT 84602
Karl Tucker
University of California, Los Angeles (UCLA)
405 Hilgard Avenue
Los Angeles, CA 90024
Ed Merrins
University of Florida
Box 14485
Gainesville, FL 32604
Buster Bishop
University of Georgia
P.O. Box 1472
Athens, GA 30603
Dick Copas
Georgia Southern College
Statesboro, GA 30458
Buddy Alexander
University of Houston
4800 Calhoun Boulevard
Houston, TX 77004
Dave Williams
University of Nebraska
Lincoln, NE 68588
Larry Romjue
University of New Mexico
Athletic Department
Albuquerque, NM 87131
Dwaine Knight
University of North Carolina, Chapel Hill
P.O. Box 2675
Chapel Hill, NC 27514
Devon Brouse

Ohio State University
410 West Woodruff
Columbus, OH 43210
James Brown
Oklahoma State University
Stillwater, OK 74074
Mike Holder
Oral Roberts University
7777 South Lewis Avenue
Tulsa, OK 74171
Bill Brogden
University of Oregon
McArthur Court
Eugene, OR 97403
Jim Ferguson
San Diego State University
San Diego, CA 92182
Frank Scott
San Jose State University
145 South Seventh Street
San Jose, CA 95192
Jerry Vroom
University of South Carolina
Columbia, SC 29208
Bobby Foster
University of Southern California
University Park
Los Angeles, CA 90007
Stan Wood
Stanford University
Stanford, CA 94305
Bruce Summerhays
Temple University
McGonigle Hall
Philadelphia, PA 19122
John MacDonald
Texas A & M University
College Station, TX 77843
Bob Ellis
University of Texas, Austin
AHG 106
Austin, TX 78712
George Hannon
Wake Forest University
P.O. Box 7265
Winston-Salem, NC 27109
Jesse Haddock
Weber State College
3750 Harrison Boulevard
Ogden, UT 84408
Mac Madsen
Wichita State University
Campus Box 18
Wichita, KS 67208
Al Littleton
Yale University
402-A Yale Station
New Haven, CT 06520
David Paterson

DIVISION II

University of Arkansas, Little Rock
33rd and University
Little Rock, AR 72204
Dudley Beard

University of California, Davis
Davis, CA 95616
Joe Carson

California State University, Sacramento
6000 J Street
Sacramento, CA 95819
Harvey Roloff

California State University, Northridge
18111 Nordhoff Street
Northridge, CA 91330
Bill Cullum

Columbus College
Algonquin Drive
Columbus, GA 31907
Dr. Mike Taylor

Edinboro State College
Edinboro, PA 16444
Jim McDonald

Florida Southern College
Lakeland, FL 33802
Charley Matlock

Indiana University of Pennsylvania
Indiana, PA 15701
Dr. Edward Sloninger

Nicholls State University
P.O. Box 2032
Thibodaux, LA 70301
Bob Gros

University of Northern Iowa
23rd & College
Cedar Falls, IA 50613
Dr. Ken Green

Roanoke College
College Avenue
Salem, VA 24153
Elwood Fox

Rollins College
Winter Park, FL 32789
Joseph Justice

Southeastern Louisiana University
North Hazel Street
Hammond, LA 70402
Ken Kenelly

University of Southern Colorado
2200 North Bonforte Boulevard
Pueblo, CO 81001
Marshall Springer

Southern Connecticut State College
501 Crescent Street
New Haven, CT 06515
Tony Martone

Southern Illinois University (at Edwardsville)
Edwardsville, IL 62026
Harry Gallatin

Southwest Missouri State University
901 South National
Springfield, MO 65802
Jay Kinser

Troy State University
University Avenue
Troy, AL 36081
Mike Griffin

Western Illinois University
Macomb, IL 61455
Harry Mussatto

Wright State University
Dayton, OH 45435
Chuck Licher

WOMEN'S TEAMS

The schools listed below participated in last year's AIWA championship, the premier event for collegiate women golfers.

University of Alabama
P.O. Box K
University, AL 35486
Bob Montgomery

University of Arizona
SUPO Box 211106
Tucson, AZ 85720
JoAnne Lusk

Arizona State University
Tempe, AZ 85281
Judy Whitehouse

University of Florida
Box 14485
Gainesville, FL 32604
Mimi Ryan

Florida International University
Tamiami Trail
Miami, FL 33199
Mary Dagraedt

Florida State University
Tallahassee, FL 32306
Verlyn Giles

Furman University
Poinsett Highway
Greenville, SC 29613

University of Georgia
P.O. Box 1472
Athens, GA 30603
Liz Murphey

University of Kentucky
Memorial Coliseum
Lexington, KY 40506
Alan Steinberg

Lamar University
Box 10038
Beaumont, TX 77710
Pat Park

University of Miami
Box 248167
Coral Gables, FL 33124
Lesley Holbert

Michigan State University
East Lansing, MI 48824
Mary Fossum

University of Minnesota
516-15th Avenue SE
Minneapolis, MN 55455
Carol Isaacs Davy

University of New Mexico
Athletic Department
Albuquerque, NM 87131
Henry Sandles

University of North Carolina, Chapel Hill
P.O. Box 2126
Carmichael Auditorium
Chapel Hill, NC 27514
Dot Gunnells

Ohio State University
410 West Woodruff
Columbus, OH 43210
William Ables

University of Oklahoma
180 West Brooks
Room 201
Norman, OK 73019
Joan Blumenthal

Oklahoma State University
Stillwater, OK 74074
Ann Pitts

Pennsylvania State University
University Park, PA 16802
Annette Thompson

San Jose State University
145 South Seventh Street
San Jose, CA 95192
Mark Gale

University of South Florida
4202 East Fowler Avenue
Tampa, FL 33620
Rick Christie

Southern Methodist University
Dallas, TX 75275
Earl Stewart

Texas A & M University
College Station, TX 77843
Mary C. Halley

University of Tulsa
600 South College
Tulsa, OK 74101
Dale McNamara

University of Washington
Graves Building
Seattle, WA 98105
Edean Ilhanfeldt

RECENT TOP COLLEGE GOLFERS AND CONFERENCE CHAMPIONS

ALL-AMERICAN COLLEGE GOLFERS

The 1978 picks by NCAA golf coaches:

FIRST TEAM

David Edwards	Oklahoma State
Lindy Miller	Oklahoma State
Chip Beck	Georgia
John Cook	Ohio State
John Stark	Houston
Gary Hallberg	Wake Forest
Bobby Clampett	Brigham Young
Mike Gove	Weber State
Curt Worley	San Diego State

SECOND TEAM

Britt Harrison	Oklahoma State
Lenny Clements	San Diego State
Griff Moody	Georgia
Brent Murray	Oregon
Scott Hoch	Wake Forest
Scott Watkins	Arizona State
Don Levin	San Jose State
Dan Croonquist	Arizona State
Mike Peck	Stanford
Mitch Mooney	New Mexico
Scott Steger	Ball State
Joe Rassett	Oral Roberts
Ron Commans	Southern Cal
Mike Brannan	Brigham Young

THIRD TEAM

Mark Balen	Ohio State
Terry Snodgrass	Houston
Peter Teravainen	Yale
Don Lee	Wichita State
Jon Chaffee	Texas
David Ogrin	Texas A&M
Gary Trivisonno	Alabama
Robert Donald	Georgia
Jack Hubbert	Temple
Larry Collins	Southern Cal
Chuck White	UCLA
Doug Clarke	Stanford
John McGough	North Carolina

SOME RECENT MAJOR-CONFERENCE GOLF CHAMPIONS (1977–1978, MEN)

Atlantic Coast: Wake Forest
Big Eight: Oklahoma State
Big Ten: Ohio State
East Coast: Temple
Far Western: Cal State, Davis
Great Lakes: Ferris State
Ivy League: Dartmouth
Mid-American: Bowling Green
Pacific Ten: USC
Rocky Mountain: Southern Colorado
Southeastern: Georgia
Southwest: Houston
Western: Arizona State

COLLEGIATE GOLF CHAMPIONSHIP TEAMS SINCE 1970—MEN

NCAA DIVISION I

1970: Houston	1975: Wake Forest
1971: Texas	1976: Oklahoma State
1972: Texas	1977: Houston
1973: Florida	1978: Oklahoma State
1974: Wake Forest	

NCAA DIVISION II

1970: Rollins
1971: LSU, New Orleans
1972: LSU, New Orleans
1973: Cal State, Northridge
1974: Cal State, Northridge
1975: U. of California, Irvine
1976: Troy State
1977: Troy State
1978: Columbus

NAIA

1970: Champbell (N.C.)
1971: St. Bernard
1972: U.S. International U. (San Diego)
1973: Wofford (S.C.)
1974: U.S. International
1975: Texas Wesleyan
1976: Gardner-Webb (N.C.)
1977: Gardner-Webb
1978: Sam Houston (TX)

NJCAA

1970: Miami Dade C.C. (North)
1971: Brevard J.C.
1972: Miami Dade
1973: Miami Dade
1974: Broward C.C. (Central)
1975: Miami Dade
1976: Brevard
1977: Brevard
1978: Brevard

NATIONAL LITTLE COLLEGE ATHLETIC AS-SOCIATION

1972: U. of South Carolina, Aiken
1973: Steed (Tenn.) College
1974: U. of South Carolina, Spartanburg
1975: U. of South Carolina, Aiken
1976: U. of South Carolina, Aiken
1977: Ambassador (Tex.) College
1978: Southern Union (Ala.) College

COLLEGIATE GOLF CHAMPIONSHIP TEAMS —WOMEN

AIAW

1973: University of North Carolina, Greensboro
1974: Rollins
1975: Arizona State University
1976: Furman University
1977: University of Miami
1978: University of Miami

NJCAA

1976: Temple J. C.
1977: Broward C. C. (Central)
1978: Miami Dade C. C. (North)

CADDIE-SCHOLARSHIP PROGRAMS

SPONSORS

Listed below are 29 major golf associations that sponsor caddie-scholarship programs.

Note that 17 of the associations are a part of the Evans Scholars Foundation, sponsored and administered by the Western Golf Association. Qualifications and terms are identical: full tuition and housing; renewable for four years; average value, $6,000.

Evans scholars are enrolled in 27 universities. However, 95 percent attend 14 universities where the foundation owns chapter houses. The scholars reside in these houses, which operate like a fraternity. Evans chapters are among the foremost groups on each such campus.

The 12 other associations listed have no common ties, either with the Evans Scholars Foundation or with each other. Each operates independently, and each awards cash grants ranging from $100 to $1,500 a year, or a tuition grant.

In all 29 programs, a boy or girl may qualify with a two-year record as an outstanding caddie. He competes with other applicants on the basis of academic record and financial need, and the latter requirement is documented in detail. These are *not* golf scholarships.

The WGA serves as the clearinghouse for information pertaining to caddie scholarships. Material on the Evans program is furnished upon request; the names and addresses of the operating officials of the other programs are supplied upon request to the WGA.

The caddie-scholarship program is the foremost charity carried out in the name of sports today. A record total of 2,042 ex-caddies currently hold grants that totaled $2,056,751 in the 1977–78 school year. This is possible only because officials of golf associations provide leadership and 400,000 club members provide financial support. All 29 programs receive an annual National Golf Fund grant from National Golf Day proceeds.

For further information, contact:

Marshall Dann
Western Golf Association
Golf, IL 60029
(312) 539-4600

Organization	Year Founded	Current Scholars	1977–1978 Expenses
Western Golf Assn.*	1930	256	$ 542,034
Cleveland District Golf Assn.	1940	142	43,125
Western Pennsylvania Golf Assn.	1941	71	58,000
Rhode Island Golf Assn.	1947	38	33,400
Wisconsin State Golf Assn.*	1947	64	76,413
Golf Assn. of Michigan*	1948	112	162,443
Pacific Northwest Golf Assn.*	1948	53	65,149
Illinois Women's Golf Assn.*	1949	6	15,142
Massachusetts Golf Assn.	1949	295	152,650
Minnesota Golf Assn.*	1950	57	79,241
New Jersey State Golf Assn.	1951	65	39,000
Connecticut State Golf Assn.	1954	31	24,000
Kansas City Golf Assn.*	1954	46	54,883
Maine State Golf Assn.	1954	27	8,100
New Hampshire Golf Assn.	1955	21	5,400
Westchester County Golf Assn.	1956	83	49,800
Golf Assn. of Philadelphia	1958	259	92,100
Northeastern Wisconsin Golf Assn.*	1960	38	50,228
Long Island Golf Assn.	1962	58	29,000
Ohio Golf Assn.*	1962	150	238,624
Colorado Golf Assn.*	1963	34	44,313
Indiana Golf Assn.*	1963	58	100,373
Vermont State Golf Assn.	1964	22	8,800
Northern California Golf Assn.*	1966	2	4,990
St. Louis District Golf Assn.*	1967	34	38,676
Kentucky State Golf Assn.*	1969	4	6,296
Arizona Golf Assn.*	1972	6	6,862
South Dakota Golf Assn.*	1975	4	9,963
Buffalo District Golf Assn.*	1975	6	17,746
TOTALS		2,042	$2,056,751

* Affiliated with Evans Scholars Foundation

FACTS ABOUT EVANS SCHOLARSHIPS
WHO IS ELIGIBLE TO APPLY FOR AN EVANS SCHOLARSHIP?

In order to be nominated for an Evans scholarship, a candidate must:

(1) Have completed his junior year in high school and rank in the upper 25 percent of his class.

(2) Have a superior caddie record for a minimum of two years and be recommended by club officials.

(3) Require financial assistance in order to attend college.

(4) Have outstanding personal character.

Scholarships are awarded on a competitive basis, taking all these factors into consideration.

WHAT ARE THE POLICIES OF THE EVANS SCHOLARS PROGRAM?

(1) Residence on the college campus is required.

(2) An Evans scholarship is an outright grant, renewable for four years provided that the program's standards are maintained.

(3) An Evans scholarship covers tuition and housing at the 14 universities where the Evans Scholars Foundation maintains an "Evans Scholar Chapter House"—Colorado, Illinois, Indiana, Kansas, Marquette, Miami (Ohio), Michigan, Michigan State, Minnesota, Missouri, Northwestern, Ohio State, Purdue, and Wisconsin.

(4) In other states, tuition and rooming costs are covered at the candidate's state university.

(5) An Evans scholarship is limited to the candidate's state university in those states where an Evans Scholar Chapter House is maintained. However, because of the large number of applicants each year from Illinois, candidates from that state are requested to indicate a first and second choice of universities from those listed under (3) above.

HOW DOES A CANDIDATE APPLY FOR AN EVANS SCHOLARSHIP?

(1) Obtain a standard "Scholarship Application Form." This is available from the club or sponsoring association, or it can be obtained by writing to the WGA at Golf, IL 60029.

(2) Submit a letter of recommendation from each of the four following club officials: president, caddie committee chairman, golf professional, and caddie superintendent.

(3) Arrange for your high school to submit a transcript of grades for your first three years.

(4) Request from the WGA a "Parents' Confidential Financial Statement," which must be completed by your parents and submitted as directed.

(5) Arrange to take the morning Scholastic Aptitude Test (SAT) of the College Entrance Examination Board in April of your junior year in high school, or in the following June, or at the latest, in November of your senior year. Request that the scores be sent to Evans Scholars Foundation, Golf, IL 60029.

WHEN IS A SCHOLARSHIP AWARDED?

(1) Applications should be submitted to the WGA as soon as possible after July 1, following completion of the junior year in high school.

(2) Candidates who reach the finals in scholarship competition *may* be asked to appear before a scholarship committee at selection meetings held in late fall or early winter. Each finalist will be considered on the basis of his overall record and financial need.

(3) Each candidate is advised promptly thereafter of the decision of the scholarship committee.

GIRL GOLFERS SCHOLARSHIPS

Since 1971 the Women's Western Golf Foundation has awarded $1,500 scholarships to young women selected on the basis of worthiness, character, financial need, and golf involvement. The WWGF is an outgrowth of the Women's Western Golf Association, which has 400 member clubs representing 30,000 active woman golfers. The number of scholarships awarded each year varies according to the amount of money generated by the various WWGF fund-raising activities. During the 1978–1979 school year, 15 young women were recipients of the award. WWGA scholarships are open to:

(1) Girls of excellent character.

(2) Girls who meet entrance requirements at an accredited state or private school.

(3) Girls who are recommended by one or more high-school officials.

(4) Girls who have participated in local, state, or national golf events.

(5) Girls who submit an application by April 1 of their senior year in high school. Incomplete or late applications will not be considered.

Candidates will be selected on the basis of worthiness and financial need. Scholarships will not be awarded solely on golfing excellence. Award of scholarships will be made by the Scholarship Committee of the Women's Western Golf Foundation. Applications may be obtained from:

Mrs. John L. Palmer
780 E. Ravine Lane
Milwaukee, WI 53217

°IX°

Careers in Golf

OUTLOOK FOR GOLF IN THE 1980s

Since its resurgence following World War II, golf has developed a pattern of steady growth, largely free of the boom-or-bust characteristics of some come-lately past-times which proliferated in the same period.

To be sure, there have been banner years in both the development of golf facilities and golfers and, conversely, there have been lean years. Particularly in the early and middle 70's did the impact of various economic crises produce a distinct slowing effect upon golf's growth.

Golf has shaken them off, however, on the strength of its enduring popularity with mature sportsmen, its continuing attraction for young players, increased activity among municipalities in providing needed public facilities and the restored happy marriage of golf course and real estate development. For these and other reasons, golf at the close of the decade is well, happy and living in every nook and cranny of the nation.

There is further evidence that the game will charge into the 80's with renewed vigor in every aspect of growth and development. For example, National Golf Foundation records show more than 350 golf course projects currently under construction. These include new golf courses and additions to existing facilities with activity on record in all but two states.

Admittedly, the under-construction figure is somewhat inflated because of the freakish weather conditions in 1978 which placed many projects in holding situations. The result has been a downturn in openings for the year and an expected rash of ribbon-cutting beginning in spring, 1979.

But do not write of 1979 as artificially overactive in this area. Along with the 356 projects under construction, the Foundation also counts more than 700 "prospectives" in its file. These are likely golf course development projects which have been uncovered by the Foundation's field staff and through scores of requests for information and assistance which pour into the organization's Florida headquarters weekly.

Foundation research personnel have come to regard the prospect list as the most accurate gauge in predicting the growth of golf.

The Foundation's ambitious campaign to deliver 500,000 new golfers to the game and increase play across the country by 5% in 1978 was rained out—literally. Monsoon conditions in the Sun Belt and lingering spring storms in the Northwest and Midwest took their tolls on play during the first five months of the year. NGF surveys showed participation in the game was down 8.3% for the first quarter and 3.4% for the second quarter compared to the same periods in 1977. These quarterly decreases led to a 7.0% decline at mid-year.

During the third quarter of 1978, however, participation increased a robust 4.7% and was still growing. These substantial gains brought play up to levels nearer recent year totals. In fact, by the end of September the decrease was only 1.8%. Further increases should be realized during the fourth quarter, due to excellent fall weather, resulting in end of year figures equal to or greater than 1977's total of 332,000,000 rounds played.

Assuming something close to normal weather conditions and economic patterns in 1979, the Foundation is predicting attainment of another 500,000 new-golfer goal and a substantial upturn in play.

The promised bonanza in new course openings—as many as two dozen each could open in Florida and California, for example—includes some of the most enticing creations ever carved from a landscape. The impact they will have on the game will be evident in the early 80's once golfers have discovered them and filled their fairways with humanity.

Added impetus is expected in new golfer development from the cooperative efforts of the Foundation's educational arm, allied associations and existing golf course operations. A leveling off of the past several years, measured in terms of golf equipment sales, rounds of golf, sometimes diminishing golf opportunity in schools and public recreation systems under budgetary duress, has brought with it a reawakened recognition of the importance of promotion.

Moved to the top of many priority lists in 1978, these promotional and recruitment efforts can be expected to show substantial results in 1979.

—Don A. Rossi, executive director,
National Golf Foundation

U.S. GOLF FACTS & FIGURES*

STATISTICS AS OF JAN. 1, 1979

Number of golf courses in the United States:

Regulation 10,974

Executive 692

Par-3 1,018

TOTAL COURSES 12,684

Estimated number of golfers in the United States:

Number playing 15 or more rounds
a year each 12,655,000

Number of casual players 3,200,000

TOTAL GOLFERS IN U.S. 15,855,000

Estimated number of rounds of golf
played in 1978 336,600,000

Estimated number of acres devoted
to golf facilities 1,273,000

Estimated capital invested in
golf facilities $4,800,000,000

Estimated annual maintenance costs $778,000,000

Estimated number of motorized golf cars
in use in 1978:

Electric 404,500

Gasoline 173,300

TOTAL GOLF CARS IN USE 577,800

* Source: National Golf Foundation

ESTIMATED NUMBER OF GOLFERS IN THE UNITED STATES PLAYING 15 OR MORE ROUNDS A YEAR

GROWTH SINCE 1947

Year	Number of Golfers	Year	Number of Golfers
1947	2,516,506	1963	6,250,000
1948	2,742,234	1964	7,000,000
1949	3,112,000	1965	7,750,000
1950	3,215,160	1966	8,525,000
1951	3,237,000	1967	9,100,000
1952	3,265,000	1968	9,300,000
1953	3,335,632	1969	9,500,000
1954	3,400,000	1970	9,700,000
1955	3,500,000	1971	10,000,000
1956	3,680,000	1972	10,400,000
1957	3,812,000	1973	11,000,000
1958	3,970,000	1974	11,660,000
1959	4,125,000	1975	12,036,000
1960	4,400,000	1976	12,328,000
1961	5,000,000	1977	12,451,000
1962	5,500,000	1978	12,655,000

FOR 1978 ADD AN ADDITIONAL 3,200,000 CASUAL PLAYERS.

RELATIVE GROWTH OF TYPES OF GOLF FACILITIES

YEAR	TOTAL	Private	Daily Fee	Municipal	YEAR	TOTAL	Private	Daily Fee	Municipal
1931	5,691	4,448	700	543	1960	6,385	3,236	2,254	895
1934	5,727	4,155	1,006	566	1961	6,623	3,348	2,363	912
1937	5,196	3,489	1,070	637	1962	7,070	3,503	2,636	931
1939	5,303	3,405	1,199	699	1963	7,477	3,615	2,868	994
1941	5,209	3,288	1,210	711	1964	7,893	3,764	3,114	1,015
1946	4,817	3,018	1,076	723	1965	8,323	3,887	3,368	1,068
1947	4,870	3,073	1,061	736	1966	8,672	4,016	3,483	1,173
1948	4,901	3,090	1,076	735	1967	9,336	4,166	3,960	1,210
1949	4,926	3,068	1,108	750	1968	9,615	4,269	4,110	1,236
1950	4,931	3,049	1,141	741	1969	9,926	4,459	4,192	1,275
1951	4,970	2,996	1,214	760	1970	10,188	4,619	4,248	1,321
1952	5,026	3,029	1,246	751	1971	10,494	4,720	4,404	1,370
1953	5,056	2,970	1,321	765	1972	10,665	4,787	4,484	1,394
1954	5,076	2,878	1,392	806	1973	10,896	4,720	4,710	1,466
1955	5,218	2,807	1,534	877	1974	11,134	4,715	4,878	1,541
1956	5,358	2,801	1,692	865	1975	11,370	4,770	5,014	1,586
1957	5,553	2,887	1,832	834	1976	11,562	4,791	5,121	1,650
1958	5,745	2,986	1,904	855	1977	11,745	4,847	5,203	1,695
1959	5,991	3,097	2,023	871	1978	11,885	4,872	5,271	1,742

NOTE: Figures include Regulation, Executive, and Par-3 facilities.

ESTIMATED ROUNDS OF GOLF (1978)

TYPE OF COURSE:	Rounds Played	Men (Ages 18–64)	Women (Age 18–64)	Juniors (under 18)	Seniors (65 & over)
Private	111,000,000	62,200,000 (56.0%)	24,200,000 (21.8%)	7,100,000 (6.4%)	17,500,000 (15.8%)
Daily Fee	147,200,000	87,600,000 (59.5%)	25,200,000 (17.1%)	10,400,000 (7.1%)	24,000,000 (16.3%)
Municipal	78,400,000	47,200,000 (60.2%)	11,600,000 (14.8%)	6,000,000 (7.7%)	13,600,000 (17.3%)
U.S. TOTAL	336,600,000	197,000,000 (58.5%)	61,000,000 (18.1%)	23,500,000 (7.0%)	55,100,000 (16.4%)

COMPARATIVE STUDY: PRIVATE, DAILY FEE, MUNICIPAL

	1975	1976	1977	1978
At Private Clubs:				
Men	1,122,000	1,133,000	1,144,000	1,160,000
Women	534,000	571,000	577,000	591,000
Juniors	284,000	287,000	290,000	286,000
TOTAL	1,940,000	1,991,000	2,011,000	2,037,000
At Daily Fee Courses:				
Men	3,403,000	3,437,000	3,471,000	3,560,000
Women	1,195,000	1,279,000	1,292,000	1,339,000
Juniors	810,000	818,000	826,000	814,000
TOTAL	5,408,000	5,534,000	5,589,000	5,713,000
At Municipal Courses:				
Men	2,985,000	3,015,000	3,045,000	3,093,000
Women	1,130,000	1,209,000	1,221,000	1,237,000
Juniors	573,000	579,000	585,000	575,000
TOTAL	4,688,000	4,803,000	4,851,000	4,905,000
At All Courses:				
Men	7,510,000	7,585,000	7,660,000	7,813,000
Women	2,859,000	3,059,000	3,090,000	3,167,000
Juniors	1,667,000	1,684,000	1,701,000	1,675,000
TOTAL IN U.S.	12,036,000	12,328,000	12,451,000	12,655,000

TOURING PRO (PGA)

Young men seeking to join the PGA tour must successfully pass the Qualifying School for Approved Tournament Players. It has been called the most unique school in all professional sports, and in truth, there is nothing else to compare with it.

According to the PGA Tour's Regulations and By-laws:

Candidates for a Qualifying School must apply on application forms furnished by PGA Tour and must pay the application fee prescribed by PGA Tour. PGA Tour shall conduct qualifying rounds at the School and will offer classroom instruction on subjects pertaining to professional golf. The number of applicants who qualify for tournament playing privileges shall be determined by the Commissioner on the basis of playing and other performance.

Application forms for the school, usually held in the spring and fall of each year, can be obtained from PGA tour headquarters. In recent years, the entry fee has been $300. That sum is subject to change.

The heart of the qualifying school is competition, just as it is on the PGA tour itself. The format normally starts with a 72-hole Regional Qualifying Round, which serves to reduce the list of applicants to approximately 120 players, who then compete in a 72-hole tournament at the school proper. All dates, sites, and requirements are announced about six months in advance.

The number of membership cards issued at each school is determined by the commissioner, Deane R. Beman, and is announced before the start of play. In recent years, the number of cards issued has varied between 22 and 32. Approximately 500 applications are received for each school.

Prize money is usually awarded to the low scorers at the school proper. The size of the purse and its breakdown is determined at the end of play. Successful qualifiers must be prepared to pay PGA tour dues as well as apprentice dues in the PGA of America. These fees have totalled approximately $200 in recent years.

Successful qualifiers must attend the PGA Tour Business School, which follows immediately after the competition and includes three days of classroom instruction. Subjects discussed by experts in the various fields include the rules of golf, contracts and legal matters, relations with golf-equipment and apparel manufacturers, a tournament-sponsor's view of the PGA tour, human relations, public relations, personal views of the tour as recalled by touring professionals, and regulations.

A successful candidate receives a membership card that permits him to qualify for cosponsored events on the PGA tour for the following year. At the end of that period, each player's tournament record is reviewed. Under the current performance guidelines, a first-year player must win $8,000 to retain his membership for the next year. If a player has been injured or has been ill for an extended period of time during the year and has failed to meet the dollar minimum, the commissioner takes these facts into consideration at the annual review; extensions of membership are granted under such circumstances.

All players are reviewed annually, and in subsequent years, under the current regulations, a player must earn $12,000 to retain his membership.

For further information, contact:

PGA Tour
100 Nina Court
Ponte Vedra Beach, FL 32082
(904) 285-3700

—Joe Schwendeman,
PGA Tour Information Director

TOURING PRO (LPGA)

Young women seeking to join the LPGA tour must successfully compete in the LPGA Qualifying School conducted by the LPGA Tournament Players Corporation.

The school is held twice a year, in winter and summer. The 1978 Summer Qualifying School had an enrollment of 67; eight applicants qualified for the tour. Competition is conducted at stroke play, over 72 holes. The field is reduced after 36 holes of play to the 50 players having the lowest scores, including those tied for 50th place.

The number of golfers invited to join the LPGA and granted LPGA tournament-playing privileges is determined by the LPGA commissioner, with the advice of the LPGA tournament director, on the basis of playing and other performance. The number of qualifiers is set during tournament week. Prize money is awarded to the five low-scorers.

Following the school, there is a meeting for all those who qualify according to the standards set. The meeting includes an informal introduction to the LPGA, along with a written exam on the Rules of Golf.

Annual dues for those accepting invitations to join the LPGA/TPC is $150. Foreign qualifiers must pay dues of $300. Dues must be paid before entering an LPGA tournament.

The basic application requirements for the Qualifying School are as follows:

(1) Applicants must be at least 18 years of age, or have special permission from the commissioner to petition for membership.

(2) Applicants must have an approved and authenticated USGA handicap of 3 or better.

(3) Application must be accompanied by two letters from recognized golf professionals testifying to applicant's tournament ability at the time of application for the school.

(4) Applicants must be able to show proper financial responsibility for maintenance on tour, as determined by commissioner and player council.

All documents requested above must accompany the application form upon submission. The Qualifying School entrance fee is $200.

For application form and/or further information, contact:

Ladies Professional Golf Asssociation
919 Third Avenue
New York, NY 10022
(212) 751-8181

TEACHING PRO (PGA)

Chances are, the major appeal of golf as a profession stems from the fact that you like to play the game and that you play it reasonably well. At one time or another, you may have even given some consideration to tournament golf, but have since decided that you are not quite that talented or that a life of living out of a suitcase is not for you or your family. Now, having eliminated playing for a living, you are exploring other means of making golf your profession, and your quest makes you curious about becoming an assistant golf professional.

If it's not playing that has hooked you, maybe it's just that you love to be around a golf course. In either instance, there is no doubt that earning a living at doing what you enjoy most has a lot of attraction as well as many advantages, especially if you find your present job unexciting or routine. Or maybe you are just out of school and in the job marketplace, golf looks glamorous. In any case, before you delude yourself, you should be fully aware of what being a golf professional involves.

Though it is true that the popularity of the game is today at an all-time peak in the United States, with more than 12 million active golfers playing 15 rounds or more annually on more than 11,000 golf courses, behind these encouraging statistics remains the fact that golf has been as severely affected by the economy in recent years as other business. Not only has the growth of golf slowed, but many of its existing facilities are facing grave problems that demand immediate solutions.

This situation has had its effect on the golf professional, who has watched competitive pressure erode his income, while, ironically, being asked to perform better. Fortunately, most of the 8,200 PGA professionals have proved themselves equal to the challenge, although it has required ability—and a good deal of ingenuity— to change their method of operation. It has made head professionals demand top performance from their staffs, and to be especially selective when hiring new people.

And prospective assistants abound. Never in the history of golf have there been more people interested in golf as a profession. At the present time, there is a record surplus of young men and women competing for an opportunity to get into golf, so be prepared for no easy task if you choose golf as your business. There are more people than jobs and there are more average jobs than there are posh jobs.

The financial prospects for a golf professional are usually limited by his employer—unless, of course, the professional is the employer and owns his own course. Should you be interested in serving at a private club, you'll discover that most of the members make more money than you do. Should you be quite successful and begin making more than many of them, they may reduce your opportunities. Public operations are controlled by a governmental employee (city manager, county park director, state conservation department, federal administration, etc.) or citizens appointed to boards or committees. Your income or projected income will be closely monitored in these circumstances, with nonstated but real limits on your financial rewards. In corporate or military jobs, remuneration is prescribed by the rank accorded the position of golf professional; there is no way you will earn as much as the company president or commanding officer. At the daily-fee facility, you work for an owner who will pay you according to your value to him, but never more than what he makes.

Golf professionals don't get rich. Roughly speaking, one third of all golf professionals net over $25,000; another third nets between $17,000 and $25,000; and the final third, less than $17,000. The point is that if only the highest rungs of the economic ladder are acceptable in your eyes, you should look elsewhere.

Most PGA club professionals have at least one assistant. Many have as many as five or six, each with highly specialized responsibilities. An assistant might be employed as a teaching professional, a shop manager, a golf-car manager, or even a driving-range boss, etc. Of course, there is turnover in these jobs, but it is not so great as in most other businesses. Consequently, if you are seriously interested in applying for such an opening, you should approach it just as you would any other job.

First, it must be a matter of record that you are interested, and so you should seek an opportunity for a personal interview. A further prerequisite is a written resume that includes not only all your vital and personal statistics, educational background, etc., but also a detailed record of your golf background and experience.

Since it is very likely that there will be many others interested in the same job, it is important to determine exactly what the head professional will be looking for. The following are five highly probable areas that his appraisal of you will include.

First, he will want to know why you want to be an assistant professional or what is truly motivating your interest in the job. Although your playing ability is important, the head professional will be suspect of anyone who is more interested in his own game than the members'. Service is what the golf business is about, and that means being more interested in others than yourself.

Second, he will want to know your educational background. Both your formal schooling and your business training are more important than you realize. Most head professionals can always use someone who has a solid background in merchandising, marketing, or accounting, and preferably all of them, to assist them in running a more efficient and profitable operation.

Next, he will consider your overall appearance, and even more important, your personality. Why? Because being a golf professional means dealing directly with people. If you have never had experience meeting the public, you should know that it is a constant challenge requiring special personality traits. A personality that reflects getting great satisfaction from serving others, a personality that wants others to enjoy the time they devote to golf more than anything else, is the personality that a professional must have to be successful, or even to survive. If you know that doing for others is not one of your strengths, you would be wise to forget golf as a profession, although you may find it difficult to escape this obligation completely in any profession.

If you are married, the head professional will also try to determine whether your wife or husband is willing and able to adapt to the rigors imposed by such a demanding profession. In fact, it is critical that your spouse fully understands, before you take a job in golf, that you may be working six days a week, 60 to 70 hours a week, will have "lost weekends," will be away on holidays while other families are playing, have a starting pay which may not be much above the minimum wage, plus all the other things that are peculiar to the golf profession. It takes an unusual mate to accept these conditions, especially if you have been working a nine-to-five job. Full understanding of how demanding the golf profession can be is essential, or you will face a far more serious problem down the road. Before hiring a new staff member, some head professionals require that the applicant's wife or husband be present for a joint discussion about the business. You would be wise to request this if the employer does not.

The fifth highly probable area the head professional will try to evaluate is your seriousness about making golf a lifetime profession, and specifically, whether you are committed enough to do all that is necessary to stay in the game. Keep in mind that in addition to the demands the job will place on you, you will be expected to take advantage of every opportunity to improve yourself, including attending educational and PGA business functions.

It takes a minimum of three years and possibly as many as six to become eligible for PGA membership, and there are also stringent educational requirements, including two exacting Business Schools. In addition you must pass a playing-ability test, an oral examination, and serve a given length of time in your apprenticeship. It would be wise to request a copy of the *PGA Apprentice Handbook* and read it thoroughly before making any decisions about becoming a professional. This and other pertinent information may be obtained by contacting:

> PGA of America
> Box 12458
> Lake Park, FL 33403
> (305) 844-5000

SAN DIEGO GOLF ACADEMY

This school (not affiliated with the PGA) offers courses in managing and operating various facets of a golf complex, including teaching, course maintenance, club operations, personnel management, and retailing. For catalog and application, mail $2.00 to:

> San Diego Golf Academy
> P.O. Box 1937
> Rancho Santa Fe, CA 92067

TEACHING PRO (LPGA)

Application for membership in the Teaching Division of the LPGA is open to female golf teachers at golf and country clubs, approved driving ranges, and approved golf organizations, and to other persons exceptionally qualified and actively involved with golf instruction, leadership, and service. Application forms may be obtained from LPGA headquarters.

Once her application is reviewed and approved, the applicant must pass a written and practical examination. Teaching Division exams are administered by LPGA area representatives; the applicant is assigned to the representative nearest to her place of residence. The written portion of this examination is comprehensive, covering golf rules, teaching golf, golf-shop operations, merchandising, golf-course operations and maintenance, golf-car operations and maintenance, and new and old terminology.

Classifications for membership in the Teaching Division are as follows:

APPRENTICE: An LPGA Teaching Division member who is serving a 12-month apprenticeship period. Within this 12 months, an apprentice must earn 8 points in order to upgrade her classification.

CLASS B: An LPGA member who has served a 12-month apprenticeship and is eligible for testing. A member will serve in the "B" classification for a two-year period. During this period, she must earn 24 points.

FERRIS STATE COLLEGE PROFESSIONAL GOLF MANAGEMENT PROGRAM

The Professional Golfers' Association of America and Ferris State College have jointly developed a college-degree program in which a person can prepare for the many aspects of a career in golf. It is the first program of its kind in the United States. It requires 4½ years to complete the program. Successful completion of the program leads to a Bachelor of Science Degree in Business (Marketing) awarded by Ferris. The 4½ year program combines alternating periods of six months on campus and six months in golf on-the-job internships. During the 4½ years a student will spend a total of 34 months in college and approximately 20 months in golf on-the-job internships.

A graduate of this program wishing to become a member of the PGA will be awarded 24 credits toward membership for a Ferris State degree. The graduate will then have to obtain a full-time eligible position in the golf profession, register in the PGA Apprentice Program to complete requirements, and attend a special one-week training course for which six additional credits will be given upon successful completion.

For detailed information regarding this program contact:

Ferris State College
305 Business
Big Rapids, Michigan 49307

CLASS A: An LPGA member of three or more years who has been tested and classified as Class A within the required time allotment. Within each three-year time span, each Class A member is required to earn 32 points.

MASTER PROFESSIONAL: An LPGA member of 10 or more years who has earned the specified accumulation of points.

LIFE MEMBER: An LPGA Class A member no longer employed who had 20 years' service in the association.

HONORARY MEMBER: A member of the Teaching Division who in the opinion of the Teaching Committee, has made an outstanding contribution to the Teaching Division.

The LPGA Teaching Division is divided regionally into five sections. Each section has a sectional president, vice-president, secretary, and treasurer. The sections and sectional presidents are as follows:

Northeast	Carrie Russell 46 Ann Avenue Dover, DE 19901
Southeast	Marge Burns Box 317 North Myrtle Beach, SC 29582
Midwest	Goldie Bateson 1701 Coachlight Drive New Berlin, WI 53151
Central	Betty Dodd 310 Columet Place San Antonio, TX 78209
Western	Shirley Englehorn 39740 Kirkwood Court Rancho Mirage, CA 92270

Further information may be obtained by contacting sectional officials or:

Ladies Professional Golf Association
919 Third Avenue
New York, NY 10022
(212) 751-8181

REQUIRED READING LIST FOR LPGA TEACHING DIVISION APPLICANTS

GOLF: A NATURAL COURSE FOR WOMEN by Sandra Haynie.
HOW TO PLAY GOLF THE WRIGHT WAY by Mickey Wright.
GOLF MY WAY by Jack Nicklaus.
SHAPE YOUR SWING THE MODERN WAY by Bryon Nelson.
GOLF by Gary Wiren.
BOBBY JONES ON GOLF by Robert Tyre Jones.
THE SEARCH FOR THE PERFECT SWING by Alistair Cochran and John Stobbs.
PREPARING COURSE FOR TOURNAMENT PLAY (USGA).
THE PROFESSIONAL GOLF SHOP (National Golf Foundation).
PGA HOME STUDY COURSE I AND II (PGA).
GOLF MAGAZINE YEARBOOK.

GOLF COURSE ARCHITECT

Here's what the would-be golf course architect should be aware of in order to prepare for the profession and to become technically qualified to join the American Society of Golf Course Architects, which defines membership as follows:

A member . . . is one who by virtue of his knowledge of the game, training, experience, vision and inherent ability, is in all ways qualified to design and prepare specifications for a course of functional and aesthetic perfection. He is further qualified to execute and oversee the implementation on the ground of his plans and specifications to create an enjoyable layout that challenges golfers of all abilities and exemplifies the highest standards and traditions of golf. He will counsel in all phases of the work to protect the best interests of his client.

Today's golf course architect, then, must be proficient in many fields, including the following:

(1) GOLF: A thorough understanding of the game and shot values.

(2) CIVIL ENGINEERING: An ability to read and work with contour maps in order to develop efficient route plans and prepare cut and fill plans and drainage plans.

(3) HYDRAULIC ENGINEERING: How to design manual and automatic golf-course irrigation systems and pumping stations.

(4) LANDSCAPE ARCHITECTURE: For the development of aesthetically designed plans that work with the existing natural conditions; for an understanding of plant materials for preservation of trees during clearing and for the preparation of planting plans.

(5) AGRONOMY: Soil fertility and drainage and the selection of the proper grass types for the different climatic areas of the country and the world.

(6) SOIL CHEMISTRY: Fertilizers, fungicides, and weed killers for turf-establishment specifications and post-construction maintenance assistance.

(7) SURVEYING: An ability to operate an engineer's transit for staking and checking grades in the field.

(8) HEAVY CONSTRUCTION: A thorough understanding of heavy and light equipment and its operation for clearing and grubbing, earthmoving, drainage, irrigation installation, and seedbed preparation.

(9) COST ESTIMATING: Detailed figures for itemizing costs so that realistic budgets and adequate financing can be obtained.

The study of landscape architecture is generally regarded as the best educational background for a career in golf course architecture. However, the existing curriculum should be supplemented with courses in agronomy and basic civil engineering. Golf course architecture is a very specialized profession and for this reason on-the-job experience with a golf course architect and/or a golf course contractor is almost imperative. Becoming and being a good golf-course architect involves a continuing learning process, and the best possible foundation can be obtained by working with an established architect.

—Rees Jones, President,
American Society of Golf
Course Architects

RECOMMENDED READING

The following works are taken from a bibliography on golf course design compiled by Gary L. Sorensen.

GENERAL LANDSCAPE DESIGN

INTRODUCTION TO THE STUDY OF LANDSCAPE DESIGN, Hubbard and Kimbel, 1917.
LANDSCAPE FOR LIVING, Garrett Eckbo, 1950.
AN APPROACH TO DESIGN, Norman Newton, 1951.
GARDENS ARE FOR PEOPLE. Thomas Church, 1951.
LANDSCAPE ARCHITECTURE, John O. Simons.
THE GARDEN, Julia Barrall.
DESIGN ON THE LAND, Norman Newton.
DESIGN WITH NATURE, Ian McHarg.
URBAN LANDSCAPE DESIGN, Garrett Eckbo.

GOLF COURSE DESIGN

ARCHITECTURAL SIDE OF GOLF, Wethered and Simpson, 1929.
DESIGN FOR GOLF, Wethered and Simpson, 1929.
GOLF AND COUNTRY CLUBS, Wendebach, 1929.
GOLF ARCHITECTURE, Mackenzie, 1920.
GOLF ARCHITECTURE IN AMERICA, Thomas, 1927.
HAZARDS, Bauer, 1913.
LINKS, Hunter, 1926.
SOME ESSAYS ON GOLF COURSE ARCHITECTURE, Colt and Allison, 1920.

OTHER SOURCES OF READING MATERIAL

National Golf Foundation, American Society of Golf Course Architects, U.S. Golf Association, Golf Course Superintendents Association of America.

ACCREDITED PROGRAMS IN LANDSCAPE ARCHITECTURE

A comprehensive, up-to-date listing of universities offering a variety of landscape-architecture programs is available through the ASGCA, 221 N. LaSalle Street, Chicago, IL 60601.

GOLF COURSE SUPERINTENDENT

In this age of specialization, there is typically one individual directly responsible for the playing conditions of our modern golf courses. Although the title varies in different sections of the country, he is generally known as the Golf Course Superintendent. Joining with the clubhouse manager and the golf professional to provide the finest in recreation, the golf course superintendent is charged with managing the entire area where golf is played.

To be more specific, the superintendent must be familiar with many facets of golf courses, and how they relate to the game itself. To produce and maintain the specialized turfgrass required, he must have a knowledge of the available types and varieties of turfgrass, as well as possessing the technical information required to produce the desired results. He must know and understand the complexities and interrelationships of soils, fertilizers, irrigation, drainage, insects, insecticides, turf diseases, fungicides, weeds, herbicides, tools, and equipment ranging from hand tools to complex, hydraulically-operated fairway moving units.

He must be able to secure, train, and supervise labor and work intelligently with his employees and employers. He must be able to maintain accurate records covering everything from weather reports to short- and long-term budgets. He must know how and where to obtain information relating to all aspects of his job, and he must read technical publications almost constantly, for no man can keep pace with the rapid developments in this field without outside contacts and assistance.

The superintendent's personal characteristics must include integrity, understanding, and humility. As the trusted custodian of much of the course's property and future, the superintendent's integrity will dictate that he must do what is good for the course, not what may seem best for his personal interests. He must have an understanding of the golfer's feelings, which enables him to accept blame for missed putts, lost balls, and "unplayable" lies.

Working with the forces of nature tends to instill a great sense of humility in most men, and consequently requires that they be flexible in their planning and actions. Superintendents know full well that their best planning can easily be altered or reversed by a natural phenomenon such as drought, flood, insects, or disease. Therefore, he will continue with his original plan as long as possible, keeping in mind that the need to react immediately is ever present.

Add to these qualifications the knowledge required to deal with the problems related to roadways, trees, flowers, buildings, tennis courts, skeet ranges or other maintenance phases of a golf course, and it becomes more apparent that the superintendent carries a tremendous responsibility in presenting pleasurable recreation facilities.

A commonly held misconception is that the superintendent is always directly responsible to the clubhouse manager or the golf professional for the management of the golf course playing area. In fact, these three parties are usually individually responsible for their distinct areas of management, which when combined will result in the total operation of the clubhouse facilities, pro shop, and golf course.

On most courses, there will be committees to establish policy as it pertains to each segment of the total facility operation. Thus, the superintendent would respond to the general policy, guidance and suggestions of the "green committee." In addition, the superintendent's areas of responsibility would include:

(1) Golf course management (the entire playing surface of the course, to include all tees, fairways, roughs, greens, and surrounding areas).

(2) Area management (entrance roads, parking lots, practice putting green and driving range).

(3) Landscaping (planning, planting, and removal).

(4) Structures (buildings, fences, bridges, and shelters).

(5) Equipment (purchase, storage, inventory, and maintenance).

(6) Personnel (working staff, procurement, training and supervising).

(7) Materials (purchase, storage, inventory, and application).

(8) Budget (preparation, explanation, and execution).

(9) Recordkeeping (expenses, weather, material application, and inventories).

(10) Knowledge of golf (participation, rules, and regulations).

(11) Reporting and advising (periodic contact with "green committee" and golfers).

For more information, contact:

Golf Course Superintendents Association
of America
1617 St. Andrews Drive
Lawrence, KS 66044

RECOMMENDED READING

TURF-MANAGEMENT PROGRAMS

A listing of some 90 U.S. universities offering a variety of turf-management programs. Available free through the GCSAA.

TURFGRASS BIBLIOGRAPHY by James B. Beard, Harriet Beard, and David P. Martin. 1978, $35.

Michigan State University Press
Room 25
Manly Miles Building
1405 So. Harrison Road
East Lansing, MI

The USGA's *Golf Journal* described this book as follows: ". . . the first comprehensive listing of turfgrass literature produced in an organized reference format in a single publication. It contains more than 16,000 references listed alphabetically by author and cross-referenced in a subject index of more than 40,-000 entries. Included are scientific, semitechnical, and popular writings covering turfgrass science, culture, and management from 1672 to 1972."

USGA GREEN SECTION RECORD

A 16-page magazine published six times a year. Annual subscription: $2.00. Available from the USGA, Golf House, Far Hills, NJ 07931

DICTIONARY OF TURFGRASS TERMS

Pamphlet defining the vocabulary of a good greenskeeper, from *acid soil* to *winterkill*. Cost: 50¢. Available from the USGA.

GOLF CLUB MANAGER

The following questions are ones asked most frequently concerning the opportunities, educational requirements and potential in the club industry today. The answers have been prepared to help you decide whether or not you have the interest, desire, and drive to become a part of one of the most challenging and expanding professions open to a young person today.

What are the general duties and traits of an effective club manager?

A club manager should be an efficient organizer. A club should be well organized from top to bottom in order to function properly and satisfactorily to meet the needs of the members. His expertise should qualify him to go into every department of the club and function knowledgeably and effectively. He should know whether those whom he places in positions in various departments are themselves functioning properly, efficiently, and honestly.

A club does indeed have a business side. It has revenue out of which it operates and pays its bills. It must maintain an unquestioned credit rating in the community. It is the duty of the manager to choose the personnel of the club's business organization, and to attend to the collection of its revenue, dues, and fees. Within the bounds of fiscal stability, he must manage to meet all obligations of the club.

The manager must be a buyer. He should be able to go out into the marketplace and buy food supplies and equipment at proper prices that are competitive. He must know how much to buy, how much not to buy, how much to pay, and how much not to waste.

The manager must staff his kitchen with experts. It would even be desirable for the manager to put on the chef's hat if the need should ever arise. He must see that the equipment in the kitchen is updated, in the best condition, and is operating efficiently and economically. He should be so meticulous that he sees to it that every area of the clubhouse, grounds, and all properties of the club are well maintained and scrupulously clean.

The manager must have his dining-room staff expertly trained and see that they are attractive in appearance and exhibit a warm, friendly, and concerned personality. The manager is responsible for the development and the implementation of a menu that is always well balanced, seasonal, varied, and interesting. The menu prices should be adequate but highly competitive to those in the public marketplace.

TYPICAL WORKSHOPS & SEMINARS SPONSORED BY PGA FOR GOLF PROFESSIONALS

How to Build, Buy or Lease a Golf Facility

- What Makes a Professional Take the Step
- Preliminary Study of the Golf Potential of an Area
- Considerations in Selecting a Site—Land Cost and Layouts, Water Availability, Zoning, and Power Supplies
- Identifying the Operating Costs—Maintenance, Debt Retirement, Insurance, Utilities, Personnel, and Cost of Construction
- Financing—Sources of Funds, Meeting the lenders, and Tax Considerations
- Legal Considerations—Contract Length, Conditions, Clauses, Renewal Options
- Considerations in Building the Golf Course—Selecting an Architect and Builder, Scheduling Work, and Planning the Overall Layout
- Equipping the Course and Shop—Food and Beverage, Displays, Maintenance Requirements
- First Year Operations—Staffing and Training, Condition of Play, Advertising and Promotion of Play, Membership Programs
- The Bottom Line—Go/No-Go Decision—Cost versus Revenue

The Golf Car Fleet—Acquisition, Management

- Professional's Role in Golf Car Operation
- Selecting a Fleet
- Gas versus Electric
- Leasing versus Owning—Advantages, Disadvantages, Lease Agreements, Purchase Contracts
- Insurance, Safety, Legal Liability
- Hiring and Training Your Staff on Golf Cars
- Golf Car Housing, Winter Storage
- Merchandising the Fleet
- Policies on Damages and Breakdowns
- Rental Rates, Tournament Fleets
- Privately Owned Cars

PGA-USGA Rules Workshops and Tournament Management

- How to Use the Rule Book and Decisions Book
- Definitions—1 to 36
- Rules 1 to 41
- Strategies for Increasing Your Responsibilities and Revenue from Golf Cars
- Maintenance—16 hours of practical, hands-on, professionally offered training on preventive maintenance (steering, brakes, body work, motors, and batteries)

General Club and Course Management Seminar

- Personnel Management—Hiring Your Staff, Labor Costs and Controls, Wage and Hour Law—OSHA, and Developing Work Schedules
- Physical Plant—Care and maintenance of facilities, purchasing equipment, internal vs. external contracts, and planning for new facilities
- Recordkeeping, Legal and Financial Matters
- Membership and Programs—Membership drives, Outside Business, Attracting your members' business, Reporting to members and staff, and Special assessments and dues
- Bar Operation—Bar and beverage services, Purchasing and storage, Inventory control, Legal responsibilities, and Cost control methods
- Restaurant Operation—Food purchasing and storage, inventory management, Cost control methods, Methods of grading food, and Cost to price relationship
- Turfgrasses, Soils and Construction
- Golf Car Problems
- Establishment of Turfgrasses and Fertility Programs

A manager needs an unusual and flexible personality. He should be able to meet everyone who comes to the club and to astutely recognize their needs and effectively accommodate them. He ought to attract people, be magnetic in personality. He must command respect from his staff and exercise discipline at all times. He must use tact and politeness with members and their guests. He can only do these things if he is working in compatible partnership with the club and its officers, directors, and members.

What is the average salary of a club manager and an assistant manager?

MANAGER—$20,000–$62,000. Many clubs offer bonuses, fringe benefits, housing, vacation allowances, etc., bringing the TOTAL job value to $25,000–$80,000! Salaries, of course, depend on the size, type, and location of a club as well as the manager's experience and education.

ASSISTANT MANAGER—$12,000–$25,000 annually depending on experience, education, size, and type of club and location. Again, add to this the benefits usually offered, and the total enlarges significantly.

What is the potential in the club field for someone with a high school diploma? With a college degree?

A high school education is a prerequisite for almost any position today. A person who has the right temperament and aptitude can make successful progress in the club industry. It would be to your advantage to continue your education through on-the-job training, industry related subjects in adult education courses, and other techniques for educational development.

For the person with a college degree, doors may open a little more quickly. A college graduate would have a good preparation for the club-management field if he had a strong background in business administration as well as courses in hospitality management. He would

- Cultural Maintenance (Principles and Practices
- The Maintenance Center
- Personnel Management
- Local Rules
- Marking the Course and Course Preparation
- Duties of Rules Officials and Committees
- Tournament Management & Operation
- Tournaments—Scheduling and Handicapping
- Promotion of Play—Juniors, Teams, Leagues, Seniors, Outside Events
- Golf Course Conditioning, Preparation for Play and Rating
- Processing the Tournament—Entry Forms, Pairings, Scorecards, Scoreboards
- Prizes and Awards; Publicity
- Proper Play—Etiquette, Safety, Slow Play

Teaching and Playing Workshops

- "What I Believe About the Principles of the Golf Swing"
- Lesson Scheduling, Promotion, and Pricing; Selling Golf Equipment in Today's Market
- "How I Conduct a Private Lesson"
- Presentation of "My Best Teaching Ideas" by participants
- "How I Apply My Principles and Preferences in Teaching the Golf Swing"
- Pitching and Chipping, Putting, and Sand Play
- Teaching Juniors and Groups
- Individual Improvement and Ball Hitting
- Error Correction for Pupils in All Handicap Ranges

The Job of a Professional at a Private Facility, Resort, or Daily Fee/Municipal Facility

- Writing a Policy, Procedures, and Operations Manual
- Staffing the Shops and Initiating a Training Program
- Shop Operation—Starting Times, Lesson Promotion, Slow Play, Bag Storage, Driving Range, Golf Cars, Junior Programs, and Tournaments
- Golf Shop Display, Layout, and Traffic Patterns
- Golf Shop Services—Class Discussion and Idea Sharing on Customer Relations and Service Policy, Special Rates, Loss Leaders, Seasonal Merchandise, Custom Orders, Trade-Ins, Gift Certificates, Advertising, Promotions, and Mailings
- Budgeting, Cash Flows, Record-keeping Systems, Profit and Loss Statements

- Manufacturers' Views of the Professional—Working with Your Representative, Credit Lines, and Shipping and Return Policy
- Product Knowledge—Features and Benefits—Women's Apparel, Men's Apparel, Accessories, Equipment
- Pricing, Inventory Management and Reorder Practices
- What An Employer Looks for in a Professional
- Resume Writing
- Evaluating the Specifics of a Job Opportunity
- The Interview Process
- Negotiating and Contracting

Club Repair and Custom Fitting

- Getting Organized—ticketing, charges, warranty, and policies on breakage
- Refinishing
- Inserts
- Refacing
- Reshafting Woods
- Reshafting Irons
- Gripping
- Lengthening and Shortening Shafts
- Bent Shaft
- Weighting
- Loose Heads
- Rattles
- Whipping

be better prepared to meet the challenges that will confront him. Advancement would most likely be more rapid and the opportunities for higher earnings would be greater.

However, an individual must still expect to earn his promotions by continuing to expand his knowledge by on-the-job experience and through courses designed specifically within the industry for the club manager.

A recent survey by Club Managers Association of America (the professional association for managers of private clubs) indicates that over 52 percent of their members have at least one college degree. The average CMAA member has had over 14 years of full-time schooling.

How many jobs or positions are there in a typical club?

A recent book published by CMAA indicates that there are over 200 possible job descriptions for people employed at a private club. In a small club employing only a few people, the manager must be a "jack of all trades." On the other hand, a large country club operation with 500–2,000 members may require some 120 paid personnel. The manager's responsibilities are always great no matter what size the club, for he is the executive in charge.

What is the employment potential?

The total employment in the private club industry today is almost 826,000 with an annual payroll of $3,200,000,000. The total annual club revenue in recent years has exceeded 9.2 billion dollars. This represents in excess of 1 percent of the national Personal Consumption Expenditures per year. There is every indication that growth will continue and the demand for qualified managers today already far exceeds the supply.

How does a job as a club manager for a private club differ in scope from that as a hotel or restaurant man-

ager? Is there a chance to switch from one area of the hospitality field into club management?

Managers of clubs, restaurants, hotels, and motels must all have a knowledge of administration, public relations, and operational procedures. The manager of a private club, however, must have a more personal and closer working relationship with a specific group of people—the members. He has a chance to form a stronger bond with his "customer" than managers in other hospitality-related fields, because his club members are not transient. A club manager has a greater chance to personally express his imagination and talents. If you decide to enter any area of the hospitality industry, you will gain experience which will be helpful to you should you later decide a career in club management would better fit your needs and goals.

How should a young person prepare for a career in club management?

A person planning to make a career as a club manager should have a thorough understanding of the work with which he or she will be involved. Certain requirements are necessary but in general, any club will look for the person with a strong moral sense, a good appearance, personal integrity, loyalty, and a sense of humor. High personal standards are looked upon as a must. Academically, a student should receive his or her training in an accredited school with a curriculum of courses aimed toward the hospitality industry. A typical 4-year curriculum at a University will cover:

Basic business courses such as:
    Accounting, Business Law, Economics, Marketing, Finance, Statistics, Corporate Development, Real Estate.
General education courses such as:
    English, Oral and Written Communications, Psychology, Sociology, Government, and various cultural courses.
Professional courses such as:
    Food and Beverage Preparation and Control, Management and Personnel Procedures, Sanitation, Purchasing, Specialized and Classical Foods and Beverage, Facilities Planning, and Interior Design.

The high-school student, who for financial reasons may not be able to attend college, should consider continuing his education at night school taking courses in business administration. Many students may qualify for financial assistance and be eligible for scholarships.

Scholarships were mentioned. How do you apply?

Check with your counsellor at your school. There are many types of grants and aid available today and the competition is keen. Academically, a student should maintain a good scholastic average, be active in school and community life, and show a definite financial need. Club Managers Association of America annually provides substantial funds to different educational institutions for distribution.

How can you gain practical experience while attending school?

Through part-time employment during the school year, and during summer vacations. Many clubs offer intern programs for students featuring on-the-job training. Any type of experience is useful, whether you work as a doorman, caddy, laborer, on the golf course, as an assistant to the tennis, swimming or golf pro, waiter, busboy, or work in the club manager's office. Any and all of these areas will provide you with useful experience.

Do some schools and universities specialize in courses designed to prepare one for a career in club management?

Yes, indeed! Some of the more well known are:

    City College of San Francisco
    San Francisco, California
    Cornell University
    Ithaca, New York
    University of Denver
    School of Hotel & Restaurant Management
    Denver, Colorado
    Florida International University
    Miami, Florida
    Florida State University
    Tallahassee, Florida
    Michigan State University
    East Lansing, Michigan
    Northern Virginia Community College
    Annandale, Virginia
    Oklahoma State University
    Stillwater, Oklahoma
    Pennsylvania State University
    University Park, Pennsylvania
    University of Houston
    School of Hotel, Restaurant and Club Management
    Houston, Texas
    University of Massachusetts
    Amherst, Massachusetts
    University of New Hampshire
    Durham, New Hampshire
    Washington State University
    Pullman, Washington

The complete list of vocational high schools, adult trade schools, and two-year and four-year colleges is too long to list here. A complete directory may be obtained by writing:

Council on Hotel Restaurant and Institutional Education
1522 K Street N.W.
Washington, DC 20005

Further information on a club management career may be obtained by writing:

Club Managers Association of America
7615 Winterberry Place
P.O. Box 34482
Washington, DC 20034

X

Good Reading

GOOD READING IN BOOKS

U.S. GOLF PERIODICALS

BEST GOLF STORIES, 1944–1978, BY EDWARD EHRE

CHARLES BARTLETT MEMORIAL AWARDS

GOOD READING IN BOOKS

As novelist John Updike has noted, "Golf converts oddly well into words." In this section, we draw your attention to some of the books that have helped the conversion along over the years. There are gaps in the listing which follows, and there are probably some egregious errors of commission as well. Nevertheless, I hope the samplings are sufficiently broad and entertaining to send readers off to the original sources.

I've divided the books into short- and long-form reading. The short-form books are mostly collections and require a relatively short attention span, a sense of humor, and no particular credentials as a weightlifter. The long-form books are the monumental cocktail-table variety—heavy in theme, range, size, and weight, but not necessarily in style.

Some of the books cited elsewhere, on tournaments or players or technique, also make very good reading. I do not mean to slight them by leaving them out here.

SHORT-FORM BOOKS

THE BEST OF HENRY LONGHURST by Henry Longhurst. 1978, 206 pages, $9.95, *Golf Digest;* N.Y. distributor: Simon & Schuster.

Longhurst, who died before this collection came out, wrote for the London *Sunday Times* for many years but was more familiar to Americans for his gracefully terse, or tersely graceful, commentary on various U.S. golf telecasts. The following excerpt, from the foreword to the book, written by Alastair Cooke, explains nicely why Longhurst can hardly be fully appreciated through TV alone:

. . . Longhurst wrote about the game as an entirely familiar exercise in human vanity. It is why, of all sportswriters, he had for so many years the highest proportion of non-sporting readers. Izaak Walton on fishing, Dickens on lawyers, Mark Twain on steam-boating, Cardus on cricket: they have appealed for generations to people who know nothing about baiting a hook, filing a suit, taking a sounding or flighting a googly. Longhurst is of their breed. He is recognizable in the first few sentences as a sly, wry, rheumy-eyed observer of human beings who happened to choose golf to illustrate their fusses and follies. He might just as well have chosen oil-drilling, toboggan racing, military service, being a member of Parliament or the motives that propelled an old lady over Niagara in a barrel. That, in fact, he wrote about all these things only went to prove his particular virtue: a curiosity that centered not on a game but zoomed in on whatever was bold, charming, idiotic or eccentric about human behavior. After due meditation, he decided early on that as a weekly exercise of this curiosity, golf would do as well as anything.

FIRST PRINCIPLES

I often think that one's attitude to the game of golf is subconsciously conditioned for a lifetime by the circumstances in which one is first introduced to it. Those of us who see it first in its elementary, primitive form, knocking a ball along with one club, or perhaps even two or three, cheerfully encountering all manner of unorthodox hazards on the way until eventually we get it into the hole, seem to me to have captured a basic outlook on the game which can never later be revealed to those who travelled first class from the start.

My own beginnings were primitive in the extreme. I was introduced to the game before breakfast one morning on the common at Yelverton, Devon, by two other small boys whose parents were taking their holiday in the same hotel. They had devised a triangular course of three holes—no tees, flags, fairways or any other such nonsense, of course —and with luck we could get in two rounds before breakfast.

None of us, therefore, was baptised in the faith that, if we drove onto the fairway, we were entitled to a "fairway lie," and that, if we did not get it, we had been robbed. Ours was a simple creed. You played the ball where you found it. The only true disaster in golf was when you could not find it.

—from *The Best of Henry Longhurst*

THE PLEASURES OF THE GAME by Colman McCarthy. 1977, 150 pages, $7.95, N.Y.: Dial Press.

By turns charming and persnickety, the author shares his reflections on the many different corners of golf he has snooped into over the years, including caddying for Tommy Bolt, playing in PGA tour events himself, predicting winners of major championships for *The Washington Post* (with a modicum of success), and slyly introducing his own children to the game he embraced as a boy and still has not let go. At times he is a bit dogmatic and perhaps even dubious in some of his more direct advice to other golfers—he is death on waggling, for example. But his attacks on golf carts and overlong backswings are sensible enough and his tips on club selection and chipping stand out as most valuable. I wish he were not opposed to the tradition of the 19th hole; instead, he brings a can of fruit juice from home with him for his solitary postround refreshment. On days when he anticipates long waits between holes, he also packs a banana or two, and a copy of Darwin, Bob Jones, or P. G. Wodehouse. Well, if we can't have McCarthy at the bar, we can at least have him in the book.

COMMISERATION

Some years ago, when I was qualifying for the U.S. Amateur, I received a well-deserved dressing down from one of those in my threesome. He was in the midst of a wretched round, his moods shifting from fury to despair and self-mockery. While his game was falling apart, he threw clubs, swore at his caddy and strung out a litany of blasphemy. Meanwhile, I was playing well. On the north course of the Montclair club in New Jersey, I was one under after six holes. Sunnily, I kept up a steady flow of commiseration: what a bad bounce, the wind took it, it would have made the green but for that limb. Finally, he could take no more of me. "Just keep quiet, will you," he cried out. I started to mumble an explanation, that I really was rooting for him, but I trailed off in mid-sentence. Commiseration was not what he needed, at least not the verbal kind.

The fates were merciless to my friend that day. Not even his blast at me brought his game around. But I had learned something, that on the golf course misery doesn't necessarily love company; it loves only relief, and if relief isn't forthcoming, then what misery loves next is silence. I kept mine for the remainder of the round, breaking it only at the end when my dejected friend handed me the score-card. "You kept score well," I offered. He had no comment, except to stomp off morosely. But that hardly ruined my mood. I had qualified for the Amateur—played that year (1959) in Colorado Springs.

The problem of commiseration requires that we be alert to the sensibilities of disgrace. That may mean that we keep silent for a few holes. Deciding when to say nothing involves making a judgment on whether or not your partner's psyche can bear a comment—not immediately after a bad shot, but perhaps before the next one. If your partner has topped three consecutive shots, you might say as you walk the 10 yards to the next shot, "Keep the weight on the right side a little longer." If by magic, providence, or the law of averages, the next shot is well hit, your partner's spirit will not only be lifted from the slough of despond, but you will gain credit for astute observation.

—from *The Pleasures of the Game*

DAVIE by Donald McDougall. 1977, 254 pages, $8.95, N.Y.: St. Martin's Press.

Wee Carnoustie-born David Crombie emigrates to America to test himself in pro golf, but his soul belongs to the highlands. The story of this shy, likable young man is set in the 1920s and 1930s. Unlike those pro-tour novels listed elsewhere, this book sets out more to define a character than to document or exploit the "material" of the pro tour life, and it succeeds.

THE CROMBIE STYLE

The Golf Mechanic was an annual journal designed to help the less proficient players. In pictures and prose, it dissected the styles and swing, the methods and movements of the top players, pointing out the tricks and mannerisms, the anxious-to-improve might adopt with profit.

In the 1928 edition, Lee Bendon wrote:

Dave Crombie, the 'Whistling Snowflake,' the Gallery's idol, is undoubtedly the master shotmaker on the present American scene. He is the exception to the rule that a good big 'un always beats a good little 'un—And, while it is interesting to note just how he has overcome his lack of inches, the study is profitless—no one could copy him. No one can hope to attack the ball in the Crombie style. The method is his alone.

The advantage of a tall man, is, naturally, the extra leverage he can bring to bear by reason of the larger diameter circle his club head describes. As will be brought out by the slow motion film.

Crombie has offset this by flattening both top and bottom ellipses, and thus stretching it sideways. On the back swing, with club vertical, hands at shoulder height, there is a decided rock sideways of the trunk from the hip upwards, and this, with the completion of the back swing in this plane, gives a terrific wind up preparatory to hitting.

The downswing starts in the usual Crombie manner, until the hitting area is reached, then the trunk snaps back to the vertical, giving extra, added force to an already mighty wallop. But the terrific force he has generated must be curbed slowly, else he would be swept off his feet. At the moment of impact, the trunk sways back, away from the line of flight, and, at the same time, the hands go straight out and up, still with both elbows straight. Then, as the hands reach the apex of their swing, the body snaps back to its upright plane, the elbows bend, and he comes round to that lovely hands high pose so beloved of photographers but with the little extras he alone can give, like that tiny snapping twitch of the right shoulder, and his habit of turning his head along with his shoulders in the follow through, and following the ball's flight with the corners of his eyes.

To players and non-players alike, to watch Crombie drive is a thrilling experience. Laymen, knowing nothing of the game, see him, and talk about the poetry of motion, the ballet-like grace of Dolin and Martinez.

—from *Davie*

MOSTLY GOLF: A BERNARD DARWIN ANTHOLOGY, edited by Peter Ryde. 1976, 198 pages, London: A. & C. Black; U.S. distributor: Transatlantic Arts.

In addition to writing on golf for the *Times* from 1907 to 1953, Darwin also produced scholarly works on Dickens and books for youngsters. Collections of his golf columns have appeared frequently in Great Britain but are hard to find in this country. The present volume is worth the trouble of importing as a sampler of Darwin's marvelous essays over the years, as well as for the thoughtful 20-page foreword on the man himself prepared by Ryde, his successor at the *Times*.

JEKYLLS AND HYDES

Every golfer has a dual nature, in every one of us a Jekyll and a Hyde are constantly contending. The Jekyll of the story was a fine, well-grown man, while Hyde was light and dwarfish. Of most golfers I am afraid that the converse is much more nearly true: Jekyll is small, sickly, puny; Hyde a lusty monster. Yet even the worst of us have our moments, not in which we are wholly virtuous, but in which the good for all too short a while conquers the evil. It is then that we display the temperate smoothness, the suavity and rhythm of a Jekyll, that all unseemly haste and passion are temporarily absent from our swing, that we stand up to the ball as though we feared to look no man in the face. And then there comes over us swiftly the dreadful change, and it is our own doing. Sometimes we have, like that unhappy doctor, 'smarted in the fires of abstinence' too long, so that there catches us by the throat a sudden lust to hit the ball hard, as hard as ever we can. At others we 'lick the chops of memory,' contrasting with our present and insipid methods the gorgeous carefree driving of some unforgettable summer evening, when it did not seem to matter how we stood or how quickly we swung or even whether we looked at the ball.

Again it may happen that we do not fall through any active wickedness, but suffer only, as did Dr Jekyll at the outset of his career, from 'a certain impatient gaiety of disposition.' We want some new and comparatively innocent experience; we grow tired, however modestly successful it may be, of our own style and think it would be amusing to imitate somebody else's or to try only for a stroke or two on insidious advice that we have read in a book. It matters not precisely how our fall is accomplished; we ourselves have precipitated it, and our devil, long caged, comes out roaring.

All too easily can we recognize the marks of change. The Hyde in us is unmistakable. Observe his tense muscles, his evil crouch, his furious address to the ball, his reckless loss of balance, his ape-like contortions. For a moment or two we find a hideous enjoyment in his antics, we leap at the ball with a misbegotten confidence, but too soon the spirit of hell awakes in us and we lash and slash till, on a sudden, tragedy and destruction overtake us. Then realising our danger, even as Hyde did after battering Sir Dancers Carew to death, we fly back to Jekyll as our city of refuge, only to find that we are cut off from it, that we have not got the key.

—from *Mostly Golf*

HOW TO PLAY DOUBLE BOGEY GOLF by Hollis Alpert, Ira Mothner, and Harold Schonberg; illustrated by David Harbaugh. 1975, 177 pages, $7.95, N.Y.: Quadrangle.

The authors gang up on golf like erudite Marx Brothers, developing their instructional ideas from various sources such as the Scots teacher MacTeague ("The swing never ends"); Herbert de Simplement

Woozler ("To slice, sir, is no sin"); the I Ching; a Bach fugue; Chaucer's "The Golfer's Tale"; and a Japanese classic on Zen, "The Golfing Travels of the Sage Wopei." Other useful items for duffers include a proposal for a new handicap system awarding strokes on the least-difficult holes instead of the hardest (because high-handicappers shoot 8s and 9s on tough holes and so get no benefit from the odd extra stroke), and an enumeration of the 23 different minerals contained in a typical sand bunker.

THE GOLF OMNIBUS by P. G. Wodehouse. 1973, London: Barrie & Jenkins.

WODEHOUSE ON GOLF, by P. G. Wodehouse. 1940, N.Y.: Doubleday.

Both are complete collections of the master's wacky golf stories.

HERBERT WARREN WIND'S GOLF BOOK by Herbert Warren Wind. 1971, 317 pages, $7.50, N.Y.: Simon & Schuster.

A collection of pieces on a wide range of topics, appearing originally mainly in *The New Yorker* and *Sports Illustrated* and done with Wind's usual acumen, thoroughness and sly humor.

19TH HOLE

When the charms of golf are listed, a priority consideration must be given to the game's uniqueness in not being played on a field or court of specified dimensions with set regulation appointments. Each golf course possesses its own distinct and recognizable character. On a first-rate course, every hole—or almost every hole—has its own especial character. When a golfer speaks of the third at Augusta, the fifteenth at North Berwick, the sixteenth at Oakland Hills, the eighth at Pebble Beach, the fifth at Mildenhall, or the thirteenth at Myrtle Beach, in his mind's eye is an image every bit as individual and defined as the face of a friend. The traveling golfer is always bumping into new faces or renewing old acquaintances, and both experiences can be tremendously enjoyable.

The more a golfer travels, the clearer it becomes that, though each golf course has a separate personality, there is an inescapable sameness to practically all nineteenth holes. Antigolf men have the nineteenth hole in mind when they call golf "the hoof-and-mouth disease," their point being that after a golfer hoofs his eighteen holes, he comes in and tells you about his round at length and boringly. This charge is not entirely true. At the nineteenth hole, men talk at length and boringly on a wide variety of subjects.

—from *Herbert Warren Wind's Golf Book*

THE DOGGED VICTIMS OF INEXORABLE FATE by Dan Jenkins. 1970, 298 pages, Boston: Little, Brown.

Among the funniest pieces in this collection: "The Glory Game," an account of the author's early experiences playing golf on a public course in Fort Worth with people named Cecil the Parachute, Magoon, Foot the Free, Weldon the Oath, John the Band-Aid, and Moron Tom; "The Game of Golfe," during which the author assays the championship courses of Scotland ("Heather, Whin, Bracken & Broom, Inc.") for the first time; and "Lockwrist and Cage Cases," an account of various pro theories on the short game that begins, "The devoted golfer is an anguished soul who has learned a lot about putting just as an avalanche victim has learned a lot about snow."

THE GOLF IMMORTALS by Tom Scott and Geoffrey Cousins. 1968, 272 pages, $6.95, N.Y.: Hart.

Excellent, well-informed short profiles of Vardon, Hagen, Sarazen, Lady Heathcoat-Amory (Joyce Wethered), Jones, Armour, Cotton, Nelson, Babe Zaharias, Locke, Snead, Hogan, Palmer, Casper, Player, and Nicklaus.

JOYCE WETHERED

She played for Surrey in the first post-war women's county championship, but attracted little public attention. But before that year was out, Joyce Wethered had become famous by beating Cecil Leitch in the final of the English championship. She won that title five more times in succession and the British championship four times, before making her final withdrawal into the pleasant pastures of friendly golf.

Her record was due as much to her calm unflappability of temperament as to the consistent excellence of her golf. And we must look again at the similarity between Miss Wethered and Bobby Jones to note that there was a strong resemblance in swings, allowing of course for the difference in physique. They both played with great economy of movement, in the lateral sense; both used a narrow stance without loss of balance; and both had the ability and the instinct to pivot freely and fully. Indeed, Miss Wethered achieved tremendous and consistent accuracy by avoiding any suggestion of lateral sway. Her timing was so good that she was as long, if not longer, than the hardest hitters among her contemporaries.

Another of her secrets, and again one she shared with Jones, was her ability to concentrate on her own game to the exclusion of all else, including the activities of her opponent. There were several occasions when she was trailing at one stage in a match but won in the end by a wearing-down process in which the abrasive agent was the ability to maintain a constant succession of par or better figures. The first notable occasion of this kind was in the English Ladies' Championship at Sheringham in 1920 when she was six down to Cecil Leitch after 20 holes and seemed to be going the way of all the champion's victims of that week. But Miss Wethered continued to reel off good figures. Then Miss Leitch made some errors, and Miss Wethered won her first national title at the 35th hole.

This ability to pursue a set path irrespective of what the opponent is doing has a complementary quality—that gift of being able to shut one's mind, eyes, and ears to all extraneous thoughts and sounds. It has gone on record that on more than one occasion Miss Wethered was so wrapped up in her own game as to be unaware on holing the winning putt, that the match was over. And of course there is the famous and oft-told story of that Sheringham final when, with a train rushing past on the nearby railway, she holed the winning putt on the 17th green. "What train?" she is said to have asked, in reply to inquires as to why she did not wait until the noise had subsided.

—from The Golf Immortals

SPORTS ILLUSTRATED'S BEST 18 GOLF HOLES IN AMERICA by Dan Jenkins. 1966, 160 pages, $15.00. N.Y.: Delacorte Press.

Entertaining reportage on individual holes that have brought great golfers and the author to their knees.

PINE VALLEY

Any man who has ever waggled a wedge with serious intent knows about Pine Valley. He knows from books, articles, photographs, films and plain old locker-room conversation that this is the golf course with the largest sand traps and funniest footprints in the world. He also knows that Pine Valley—just the sound of it can make you shank —has more trees, bushes, Scotch broom, poverty grass, hawthorn and mountain laurel lying around those traps, and in them, than any course ever devised. And finally, he knows that if he ever is fortunate enough to be invited to play there he probably will not be able to break 100, because Pine Valley is the science-fiction monster of golf courses.

All of this is true, to some extent, depending on which way your shots bounce off the pine trees. Located in the New Jersey shore area east of Philadelphia near a little town called Clementon, Pine Valley is the most difficult course anywhere for the man who makes a lot of mistakes. Almost every fairway landing area and every putting surface is an island of lawn surrounded by unraked sand through which footprints lead in and then out again, mute and memorable testimony to the trials and determination of those who have gone before. In this sense, Pine Valley is the epitome of target golf, for each drive must reach the sanctity of a fairway island, and each approach must reach the green. Fail, and you tear up your score card and retire to the gin-rummy table for the afternoon.

—from Sports Illustrated's Best 18 Golf Holes in
America

THE AMERICAN GOLFER, edited by Charles Price. 1964, 244 pages, $9.95, N.Y.: Random House.

The American Golfer magazine, started by Walter Travis and edited for many years by Grantland Rice, attracted numerous articulate contributors including Bobby Jones, O. B. Keeler, Bernard Darwin, Paul Gallico, and Ring Lardner. Selections by these and others from issues appearing during the years 1920–1935 (when the magazine finally succumbed to the Depression economy) remain eminently readable today. My personal favorite: Rube Goldberg's hilarious "Left-Handed Golf Courses: Our Greatest Need." A lot of the instructional material here, devoid of the benefits of high-priced artwork and high-speed sequence cameras, is nevertheless easier to figure out than some of our modern fare.

DOCTOR GOLF by William Price Fox; drawings by Charles Rodrigues. 1963, 176 pages, Philadelphia: J. B. Lippincott.

Dr. Golf, an archconservative transplanted Scot, answers letters from the golflorn; peddles devices to keep the left arm straight, head down, etc.; and conspires to replace the USGA with his own governing body, "Eagle-Ho."

IS THERE A GOLF TYPE?

Yes, there is a golf type. Just as tall, dark men make good surgeons and pianists, and short, fat small-headed men become leaders of industries, there is a definite golf type. You will find him standing alone at parties. He is taller, his outward appearance can be called sadder, his hands hang quietly, and often he is gazing at a window or an object in the distance. There is a seriousness around the eyes and an honest brooding strength about the set of his jaw. I call this look the look of eagles. His mind is not on the petty, the commonplace, the Dow-Jones averages; he does not converse easily with women. If he drinks, it is the straight whiskeys—the bourbons, the Scotches, the Irish; never mixed drinks—the cocktail, the Manhattan or the Martini. He holds his head a little higher than the average. His cephalic index is 86.

There will be an absence of flesh, a high threshold of nervousness, and little inclination to entertain in the low manner of jokes, tricks with glasses, spoons, etc. He does not dance and seldom cares for any type of so-called modern music. He is, in short, a leader and since there is now so little to lead he remains on the periphery of the crowd. Economics and family require that he conform to a degree, but he keeps this to a minimum. And in his inner self, where he excludes all save golf and his golfing friends, he is gazing at the lovely green, the flowing fairway and the arching ball.

—from *Doctor Golf*

ON TOUR WITH HARRY SPRAGUE by Herbert Warren Wind. 1958, 94 pages, N.Y.: Simon & Schuster.

Harry's semiliterate letters home to sponsors catch the raw young driving-range pro in varying moods and situations as he makes his assault on the winter circuit, principally with a No. 1 wood and a variety of sweaters. His short game is so bad that we forgive him his natural impudence—as when he offers to help Hogan with his swing, or tells Bobby Jones that the 13th at Augusta National needs redesigning.

LIFE AT HAPPY KNOLL by John P. Marquand. 1955, 167 pages, Boston: Little, Brown.

This witty commentary on country-club internal politics, pecadilloes, cliques, and above all, deficits, holds up amazingly well after all these years—perhaps because novelist Marquand couldn't help giving a touch of character even to his most ridiculous golfing figures, all of whom are with us today.

MONUMENTAL-VARIETY

GOLF: THE PASSION AND THE CHALLENGE by Mark Mulvoy and Art Spander; special photography by Ellen Griesedieck. 1978, 256 pages, $25.00, Englewood Cliffs, N.J.: Prentice-Hall.

Mainly a documentation of the U.S. male pro experience, this book has a great many fabulous color pictures; setpiece writing; a couple of chapters that may date quickly (one on architecture focusing almost entirely on Pete Dye, and another on the workings of the Kaiser Open); and above all, an imaginary match-play championship among 16 all-time greats, which the authors administer to a ringing conclusion using four different courses: Pebble Beach, St. Andrews, Oakmont, and Merion. (But wild cards at least should have been extended to Tommy Armour, Henry Cotton, Jimmy Demaret, Lloyd Mangrum, and Tom Watson.)

GOLF SUPERBOWL

FIRST ROUND—PEBBLE BEACH
MONTEREY, CALIFORNIA

Ben Hogan	Gene Sarazen	Byron Nelson
Billy Casper	Julius Boros	Gary Player
Lee Trevino	Walter Hagen	Sam Snead
Peter Thomson	Harry Vardon	Jack Nicklaus
Arnold Palmer	Bobby Jones	Cary Middlecoff
Bobby Locke		

—from *Golf: The Passion and the Challenge*

WORLD ATLAS OF GOLF by Pat Ward-Thomas, Herbert Warren Wind, Charles Price, and Peter Thomson. 1977, 208 pages, $25.00, N.Y.: Random House.

Lavish, large-format book by impressive team of authors on 170 outstanding courses around the world, with stunning graphics that "explain" the aesthetics and tactics of golf holes extremely well. Originally published in Britain, it begins with a probe of 25 European courses, complete with full-color photographs, course layouts, and scorecards. Each course's unique history, architecture, and memorable playing moments are told. Other sections cover 27 courses in North America, eight in Asia, five in Australia, three in Africa and two in South America. A "Gazeteeer" gives brief rundowns on another 100 outstanding courses.

A HISTORY OF GOLF by Henry Cotton. 1975, 240 pages, $16.95, Philadelphia: Lippincott.

Lamentably unknown in the United States (understandably—he rarely came here to compete), Henry Cotton is one of golf's few men for all seasons—player (three-time British Open winner), teacher, course architect, and writer. This latest, somewhat rambling account of golf through the years may not be the best of the 10 books on golf he has authored, and indeed parts of it appear to have been picked up from his earlier works, but it still repays the reading, especially if you've been deprived of the man's knowledge and pointed opinionating until now. He thinks some of the best instructional material in the sport may be found in *The Art of Golf*, by Sir Walter Simpson—published back in 1887. Gambling is on the increase because so much monotony has been designed into modern courses. He is death on "square-to-square," and not too keen on the sand wedge, either. Interesting photos.

STEEL SHAFTS ARRIVE

In 1928, at the age of twenty-one, I went to the States to see why they were beating our home players so regularly and found that steel shafts were already legal and one type of bigger ball was in use, and I actually played my first tournaments in America with hickory shafts. About this time, Horton Smith, aged twenty, a tall skinny young man from Joplin, Missouri, was cleaning up on the Winter Circuit. He had not known anything but golf with steel shafts and had knocked all the fancy shot-making frills off by just simply scoring low, using the same swing and same shot for practically all his strokes—a gently hooking ball which was to be the dread of the experienced golfers he was later to succeed. He used a slow, deliberate three-quarter swing, which he repeated mechanically for every shot. He somehow never took three putts and he holed a lot of good ones under the greatest pressure; he became renowned as a super putter.

This was rather like the way Bobby Locke played in the 1950s, though Locke's swing was longer and faster. Seeing Horton Smith play was quite a revelation, for I saw straightaway that the day of learning to play all the shots was almost over—the steel shafts had made golf an easier game. Only one swing was necessary, and I had to find out as soon as possible the swing which would suit me. The soft, watered greens, a necessity in a country where the fixed fine weather periods of spring, summer and autumn meant many successive sunny days and no rain, showed that one shot, if you could repeat it, was good enough to win any event, if you could putt. This fact did not really register in Britain until the steel shaft was legalized. At last everyone could have the exact set used by his favourite champion, a set which would not vary with the weather, as was always the case with hickory shafts when iron heads got loose if kept in too dry a place overnight.

Gradually the top golfers began to realize that golf was a more simple game with this new standard link between the hands and the clubhead. It was not necessary to know or to practice all the shots as in the hickory-shaft days in order to know your clubs individually, though some of the older players never quite adapted themselves to steel. Abe Mitchell, whose play I have always admired and who was a great golfer and wonderful striker himself of the ball, never got to like steel. He could not make himself play just one stroke; he liked among other things to fade many shots up to the flag and found the steel shaft could let him down when he attempted to play a controlled fade, or any special stroke for that matter. I guess he missed the torsion of the hickory shaft. His contemporary, George Duncan, was also too much of an artist to enjoy steel. They would both have rejoiced at the coming of the carbon-fibre shafts.

—from *A History of Golf*

THE INTERNATIONAL ENCYCLOPEDIA OF GOLF, edited by Donald Steel and Peter Ryde; advisory editor, Herbert Warren Wind. 1975, 480 pages, $25.00, N.Y.: Viking Press.

This is one of those books you want to test on the bathroom scale before looking inside—according to the jacket, it contains 400,000 words, 900 b/w illustrations and 32 pages in color. There are entries on players from Aaron, Tommy, to Zaharias, Babe, exceptionally apt descriptions of over 400 courses worldwide, and clear explanations of terminology in the areas of technique, equipment, and rules. Usually, few readers have the time or inclination to find out how encyclopedic an encyclopedia really is. My own random sampling in the present volume leaves me dismayed to find golfing artist Clare Briggs included, but not, say, A. B. Frost, and Sir Walter Simpson missing when much is made (deservedly so) of the writings of Darwin and Hutchinson. Also, I like *Monty Python* and *Upstairs, Downstairs* as much as the next American, but there are a shade too many British references and terms in this tome, which comes to us via a London publisher. Does one David W. Frame deserve five lines because he won the Worplesdon Foursomes (with the Vicomtesse de Saint Sauveur as partner) and then went on to take the Hampshire Hog?

THE PGA: THE OFFICIAL HISTORY OF THE PROFESSIONAL GOLFERS' ASSOCIATION OF AMERICA by Herb Graffis. 1975, 559 pages, $16.95, N.Y.: T. Y. Crowell.

The internal politics and growth (from 1,100 members in 1930 to 7,392 in 1974) of the PGA organization may be of doubtful interest to average golf fans, but there is also much first-rate research here on the early history of the game, on modern club-design and ball-development, and on events in the commercial side of golf (Graffis and his brother Joe started *Golfdom*, the sport's first business magazine, in 1927), plus thoughtful pieces on Hagen and Sarazen.

HIGH-PROOF BRAWL

The minutes of the Edinburgh Burgess Golfing Society record pleasant hoistings of champagne at the expense of a member soon to be married. The Musselburgh Golf Club limited the wagering on "club day" to sixpence (about 15 cents) a hole. It also restricted charges on members' liquor bills to "port wine and sherry, rum, brandy, gin and small beer." This was in 1788, when Scotch whisky was presumably served in lieu of water, and golfers could be a rough, roistering lot.

A story of the period tells of a stalwart laird who became involved in a high-proof brawl with other Highland noblemen in an Edinburgh hotel to which a golfers' fiesta had transferred after a lusty day on the links. Unfortunately a waiter aroused the vigorous displeasure of his lordly clients, and the laird was the leader in flinging him out of the nearest window. The party went on merrily, and soon the golfers needed refills and clamored for a waiter. Finally the landlord opened the door carefully and told the merrymakers, "You'll just have to be patient. You killed the other waiter we sent up here." The laird shrugged at the news. "Too bad," he said. "Put him on the bill and send us a fresh waiter!" —from *The PGA*

THE STORY OF AMERICAN GOLF by Herbert Warren Wind. 1975, 591 pages, $20.00, N.Y.: Knopf.

Updated and greatly expanded since its first appearance in 1956, this is the definitive account of the events, personalities, and larger (and sometimes smaller) themes, issues, and meanings of the game of golf in this country. As a glance at the table of contents (following) reveals, the great players are well attended to, but so too are many of golf's lesser lights. The chronicle is rounded out at intervals with well-considered views of changes and trends in the game at large. A masterpiece of sound research and clear writing— so good I sometimes wonder if merely a game deserves it.

CONTENTS

PART SIX

THE AGE OF HOGAN
1948–1955

The Champion Who Came Back—A Greater Champion

PART SEVEN

PALMER, NICKLAUS, PLAYER, AND A NEW ERA
1955–1975

*Arnold Palmer, the Man Who Made Charisma
a Household Word
The Golden Hours of the Golden Bear
Gary Player and the Other New Champions
The Scene Changes
High Drama in the Seventies, at Home and Abroad*

GREAT GOLF COURSES OF THE WORLD by William H. Davis. 1974, 288 pages, $19.95, *Golf Digest;* N.Y. distributor: Harper & Row.

Nearly half of this unique book is devoted to full-color views of great and famous courses from around the world. Individual tournament and resort courses are authoritatively explored and explained by various contributors. Provocative listings include "America's 100 Greatest Tests of Golf" (from the biennial rankings of *Golf Digest* magazine), "Canada's Top 25," and "Europe's Top 40."

THE GLORIOUS WORLD OF GOLF by Peter Dobereiner; special photography by Norman Snyder. 1973, 250 pages, $20.00, N.Y.: McGraw-Hill, a Ridge Press Book.

This is an exquisitely produced volume containing stunning color views of golf in all its manifestations, and if that were not enough, the text, organized around loosely conceived themes such as "How Golf Invented the Scots," and "Secrets of the Great Courses," is by Peter Dobereiner, still another in a long succession of superb British interpreters of the game—all of whom have been able to report quite seriously and dramatically on golf as it is played by the best, without losing the knack of covering the scene where ordinary golfers lurk—with hilarious effect.

GOLF: ITS HISTORY, PEOPLE AND EVENTS by Will Grimsley. 1966, 331 pages, Englewood Cliffs, N.J.: Prentice-Hall.

A well-organized series of informative short features on the important individuals and tournaments in golf history and the reasons for their color and permanence. Associated Press columnist Grimsley probably has logged as many hours on the pro tour as Sam Snead, and always writes with a fresh ribbon in his machine. Also included: "Ten Great Courses" (a selection made by the ubiquitous Robert Trent Jones) and "Ten Shots That Rocked the World."

GOLF ORIGINS

Golf is a game with a shady past. Its actual birth is shrouded in mystery. No one is quite certain when or where it drew its first tortured breath. Historians only know that the first anguished squalls of the infant came rolling over the moors of Scotland in the fifteenth century. Golf cannot point to a legal father, such as baseball in the case of Abner Doubleday and basketball in the case of Dr. James A. Naismith. In fact, there is a question that golf was ever born at all. As some scientists contend in regard to man himself, the game may have just evolved.

Even the source of the name, which originally came out as "golfe" or "goff," has thrown researchers into a tizzy. Some attach to it a kinship with the German word "kolbe," meaning club. Others associate it with the Gothic word "kulban," a stick with a thick knob at the end. The majority opinion, however, is that "golf" is a Celtic form. In some old manuscripts, there are references to "golfdrum."

If you take the word of some historians, who are disinclined to give latter-day generations credit for anything of an inventive or creative nature, golf was first played by Adam in the Garden of Eden. The first man may have fashioned a club from an extra rib, which he drew from his apparently surplus supply, and amused himself by belting apples from one tree to another. This, of course, made Eve the first golf widow. Half in despair and half in boredom, she gorged herself on the forbidden fruit and every school child knows what happened after that.

—from *Golf: Its History, People and Events*

THE WORLD OF GOLF by Charles Price. 1962, 307 pages, N.Y.: Random House.

The great men and women players, amateur and professional, from the days of Old Tom Morris to the appearance of Nicklaus, with particularly good portraits of Vardon, Travis, Ouimet, Hagen, Jones, and Hogan. Pleasurable popular history from one of America's top golf writers, with a bonus of a large selection of b/w photos.

A HISTORY OF GOLF by Robert Browning. 1955, 236 pages, N.Y.: E. P. Dutton.

"A history of golf and not of golfers"—so promises the esteemed long-time (1910–1955) editor of the British magazine *Golfing* in his preface to this fascinating and thoroughly researched chronicle of the game, including notable moments in the British Open. Don't be put off by the occasional foray into totally arcane debate, such as the question of whether or not the Royal Wimbledon Club is in fact junior to Clapham Common Golf Club in history's roll of London's distinguished layouts. (Pshaw, let them both in.) See sample excerpt on page 124.

BOOK CLUBS FOR GOLFERS

GOLFER'S BOOK CLUB

P.O. Box 14606
Cincinnati, OH 45214

Golf Digest operates this, the only book club for golfers, and runs ads on its offerings in nearly every issue. The book club issues up to six bulletins a year announcing main and alternate selections as well as choices from a backlist of more than 30 titles. A new member gets to buy one book from a wide selection for $1.95, agrees to buy four more books during the next 12 months (1978–1979 terms). All books are offered at from 10 to 25 percent off list price.

U.S. GOLF PERIODICALS

Consumer magazines only, *Golf and Golf Digest,* the two giant monthlies, devote the bulk of their editorial space to ingeniously conceived instruction articles, service articles, and personality features on the winningest pros. *Golf Journal* and *Country Club Golfer* are much smaller and geared primarily to a private-club membership audience. As America's only golf weekly, *Golf World* is heavily relied upon for detailed tournament coverage and current trade-news.

COUNTRY CLUB GOLFER

2171 Campus Drive
Irvine, CA 92715
(714) 752-6474

FREQUENCY: monthly.
YEAR ESTABLISHED: 1972.
NO. READERS (avg. circulation per issue in 1978): 70,000.
NO. OF PAGES PER ISSUE (in 1978): 50.
YEAR'S SUBSCRIPTION: $10.00.
REMIT TO:
Country Club Golfer
Suite E
9420 Activity Road
San Diego, CA 92116

Contents include instruction "intended for the average country club golfer, whom we know is around 50 years of age, has been playing golf some 25 years, and carries a computerized 18 handicap," and articles on issues of interest to members of private clubs.

Editor/Publisher: Edward F. Pazdur
Associate Editor: Russ Halford
Golf Instructor: Kathy Whitworth
Golf Rules Editor: Norman G. Meyers
Seniors' Advisor: Chick Evans

GOLF

380 Madison Avenue
New York, NY 10017
(212) 687-3000

FREQUENCY: monthly.
YEAR ESTABLISHED: 1959.
NO. READERS (avg. paid circulation per issue in 1978): 705,000.
NO. PAGES PER ISSUE (1978): 140.
YEAR'S SUBSCRIPTION: $9.94.
REMIT TO:
Golf Magazine
P. O. Box 2786
Boulder, CO 80302

Contents include periodic instruction by Arnold Palmer, monthly columns by Charles Price and Oscar Fraley. Special theme issues include:

January: Men's, Women's, and Junior All-American teams
February: Yearbook
March: Buying Guide
April: Masters Preview
May: Junior Golf
June: U.S. Open Preview
October: College Golfers of the Year

Editor: George Peper
Senior Editors: Vincent J. Pastena, Travel/Fashion; Desmond Tolhurst, Instruction; Lew Fishman, Features/Equipment
Production Copy Editor: Pauline Crammer
Associate Editor: P. J. Boatwright III
Consulting Editor: Herb Graffis
Director of Instruction: Arnold Palmer
Professional Advisors: Severiano Ballesteros; Ben Crenshaw; Bill Kratzert; Carol Mann; Johnny Miller; Jan Stephenson; Ken Venturi; Hubert Green
Instruction Editors: Dick Farley; John Jacobs; Harry Obitz; Harvey Penick; Ernie Vossler
Technical Consultant: Ralph D. Maltby

GOLF DIGEST

495 Westport Avenue
Norwalk, CT 06856
(203) 847-5811

FREQUENCY: monthly.
YEAR ESTABLISHED: 1950.
NO. READERS (avg. paid circulation per issue in 1978): 928,000.
NO. PAGES PER ISSUE (1978): 165.
YEAR'S SUBSCRIPTION: $9.50.
REMIT TO:
Golf Digest
P.O. Box 10180
Des Moines, IA 50340

Contents include regular monthly instruction by Jack Nicklaus and columns by Peter Dobereiner, Joseph C. Dey, and Frank Beard. Special-theme issues include:

January: Most Improved Golfers
February: Annual Recordbook
March: Equipment Preview
April: Masters Preview
June: U.S. Open Preview
December: Rookies of the Year

Editor: Nick Seitz
Managing Editor: Jay Simon
Senior Editor: John P. May
Associate Editors: Larry Dennis; Ross Goodner; Dwayne Netland; Jerry Tarde; Don Wade
Assistant Editor: Nick Romano
Professional Teaching Panel: Jim Flick; Peter Kostis; Davis Love; Paul Runyan; Bob Toski
Professional Advisory Staff: Cary Middlecoff; Byron Nelson
Playing Editors: Andy Bean; Frank Beard; Al Geiberger; Hale Irwin; Nancy Lopez; Jack Nicklaus; Jerry Pate; Gary Player; Sam Snead; Tom Watson
Technical Editor: John Baymiller

GOLF JOURNAL

Golf House
Far Hills, NJ 07931
(201) 235-2300

FREQUENCY: 8 times a year.
YEAR ESTABLISHED: 1947.
NO. READERS (avg. paid circulation per issue in 1978): 80,000.
NO. PAGES PER ISSUE (1978): 28.
YEAR'S SUBSCRIPTION: $6.00.
REMIT TO: above address.

As the official publication of the USGA, the magazine is strong on coverage of USGA events, rules of golf, amateur status, golf history, etc. Accepts no advertising.

Editor and Publisher: Robert Sommers
Managing Editor: Charles Brome

GOLF SCORE

606 Wilshire Boulevard
Santa Monica, CA 90401
(213) 451-1423

FREQUENCY: monthly.
NO. READERS (avg. paid circulation per issue in 1978): 80,000.

Editor: Steve Werner
Managing Editor: Larry Collier

GOLF WORLD

Box 2000
Southern Pines, NC
(919) 692-6856

FREQUENCY: weekly, Jan.–Sept.; biweekly, Oct.–Dec.; total issues per year, 45.
YEAR ESTABLISHED: 1947.
NO. READERS (avg. paid circulation per issue in 1978) 48,000.
NO. PAGES PER ISSUE: 32.
YEAR'S SUBSCRIPTION: $19.50.
REMIT TO: above address.

Contents include detailed reports on current professional and major-amateur events, some instruction, and industry news. Special issues include previews and round-by-round coverage of major tournaments, a PGA Merchandise Show number, and annual year-end review.

Chief Editor: Dick Taylor
Managing Editor: Ron Coffman
Contributing Editors: Amy Alcott; Clive Clark; David Graham; Harvie Ward

BEST GOLF STORIES, 1944–1978

The excellent E. P. Dutton anthology, *Best Sports Stories,* edited by Irving T. Marsh and Edward Ehre, has appeared every year except one since 1944, and in nearly every volume, several stories about golf have an honored place. These stories and their authors are listed below—thanks to the fine cooperation of co-editor Ehre and his publisher.

1944

"Fairway Fairy Tale" by Charles Stark, Jr., *Spokesman Review* (Oregon).
  Bob Hamilton wins $3,500 in his first tournament, beating Byron Nelson 1 up in 36 holes.
"The Humbling Game" by Jack Wade, Charlotte *Observer.*

1945

"A Jinx is Broken" by Harry Robert, Philadelphia *Bulletin.*
"Caddy's Eye View of a Champion" by Leo Fischer, Chicago *Herald-American.*

1947*

"Thunder on the Links" by Oscar Fraley, United Press.
  Purple Heart hero Lloyd Mangrum wins National Open.
"They Also Serve Who Knit and Wait" by Howard Preston, Cleveland *News*
  An interview with Mrs. Mangrum.

* No book published in 1946.

1948

"Golf's Bad Boy" by Tom Siler, *Collier's*.

Frank Stranahan, an abrasive competitor, gives the galleries something to mutter about.

"The King Is Riegel" by Art Rosenbaum, San Francisco *Chronicle*.

Robert Henry Riegel becomes the 47th national amateur golf champ by beating Johnny Dawson, 2 and 1.

1949

"Little Ben" by Lincoln Werden, *The New York Times*.

Hogan wins PGA with record-breaking 276.

1950

"Cigar Store Indian" by Harold Classen, Associated Press.

Charles Coe defeats Rufus King to become amateur champ and bring the title to the Southwest for the first time.

"The Life of Cary Middlecoff" by Bill Fay, *Collier's*.

From the beginning, Cary had class and was in the money.

1951

"Again Little Ben" by Lincoln A. Werden, *The New York Times*.

Ben Hogan, miraculous survivor of an auto smashup, beats Lloyd Mangrum and George Fazio in an 18-hole playoff in the 1950 Open.

"The Bauer Girls" by Roger Pippin, Baltimore *News-Post*.

Man leaves White Russia, settles in America, and sires two pretty daughters, Marlene and Alice, who become extraordinary golf talents.

"The Comeback of a Champion" by Grantland Rice, *Sport*.

Another story of golf's most famous comeback and the winning of the Los Angeles Open in 1950.

"Sam's Song" by Bill Carson, Minneapolis *Sunday Tribune*.

Rich young spark-plug-fortune heir Frank Stranahan is undone by the son of a janitor, Sam Urzetta, in the golden anniversary USGA championship.

1952

"Still the Champion" by Lincoln A. Werden, *The New York Times*.

Hogan retains the Open title, overcoming nearest challengers Bobby Locke and Jimmy Demaret.

"Valley of Despair" by Franklin Lewis, Cleveland *Press*.

A description of Pine Valley, a course 15 miles from Philadelphia and depicted here as the dead end of every golfer's ambition.

1953

"Miracle Putter" by Bill Rives, Dallas *News*.

Julius Boros demonstrates his prowess with the putter in capturing the U.S. Open. Porky Oliver finishes second. Hogan, gunning for his fourth Open, is way back.

"I Can Still Win the Open" by Sam Snead and Tom Siler, *Saturday Evening Post*.

Snead confesses to weaknesses: gambling, overconfidence, beer-drinking, and rages. Underneath these venalities emerges an honest human being.

"Lawmaker of the Links" by Art Rosenbaum, San Francisco *Chronicle*.

A 47-year-old Congressional campaigner, Jack Westland of Everett, Wash., becomes the oldest winner of the National Amateur trophy—and it's done between speeches in the boondocks.

"Lady Golfer" by Maxwell Stiles, Los Angeles *Mirror*.

The radiant story of Women's Open champ Jackie Pung.

1954

"Worsham's Shot" by John Carmichael, Chicago *Daily News*.

Lew Worsham's spectacular wedge shot wins for him at Tam O'Shanter.

"It's Hogan Again!" by Lincoln Werden, *The New York Times*.

Ben wins the U.S. Open for fourth time.

"This Is Ben Hogan" by Art Rosenbaum, San Francisco *Chronicle*.

"Ike and His Friends" by Will Grimsley, Associated Press.

The late president's golfing style and cronies.

1955

"Dizzy Dean of the Links" by David Eisenberg, New York *Journal-American*.

Snead had just beaten Hogan in 1954 Masters, but it was Billy Joe Patton who made the copy with his amusing comments in the locker room.

"Winning the Open Changed My Life" by Ed Furgol and Will Grimsley, *Saturday Evening Post*.

Ed Furgol, handicapped by his crooked arm, tells a few truths about himself and the game.

1956

"Jack the Giant Killer" by Herbert Warren Wind, *Sports Illustrated*.

Newcomer Jack Fleck pops up at the 55th U.S. Open and prevents Hogan from becoming first five-time winner.

"The Biggest Victory" by Whitney Martin, Associated Press.

Essay on four players waylaid by misfortune—Jones, Hogan, Zaharias, and Furgol.

"Brooklyn's Mad Golf Course" by Jane Perry, *Sports Illustrated*.

Dyker Beach and its variegated collection of human beings.

1957

"Fidgeter of the Fairways" by Don Selby, San Francisco *Examiner*.

Cary Middlecoff wins the Open in spite of tension and tics.

"Do Ye Ken Venturi" by Furman Bisher, Atlanta *Constitution*.

Venturi's presence as an amateur at Augusta gives the author a chance to depict a colorful character.

"All Golfers Are Mad" by Melvin Durslag, *Saturday Evening Post*.

"The Trouble with Golf" by Howard Preston, Cleveland *News*.

The author insists that it is impossible for a golfer to improve if he insists on playing the game.

1958

"Saved from Wall Street" by Harry Hayward, San Francisco *Examiner*.

Dick Mayer leaves the stockbroker profession to make a few dollars on tour.

"Golf Wife" by Bill Rives, Dallas *Morning News*.

Another story in which a man doesn't go it alone.

"Golf with No Holds Barred" by James A. Skardon, *Saturday Evening Post*.

No other recreational activity matches golf for blowing off steam, claims the author.

"Master of the Masters" by Gene Gregston, Fort Worth *Star-Telegram*.

Doug Ford wins 21st Masters and proves that class and style isn't always necessary, but that rough golfing courage is.

"Wonder Workman of the Publinx," by John Travers, Harrisburg (Pa.) *Patriot-News*.

An 18-year-old stringbean from Indianapolis becomes king of America's public-course players.

1959

"The Open Was His" by Dan Jenkins, Fort Worth *Press*.

Tommy Bolt easily wins the 1958 U.S. Open.

"I'll Take a Mulligan" by Roger O Gara, *Berkshire Eagle*.

Controversial article on that shot on the house.

"The Guy She Loved" by Dave Gordon, Chicago *Tribune*.

Connie Venturi describes following her husband as he plays and wins the 1957 Chicago Open.

"What Golf Means to Me" by Branen Dyer, Los Angeles *Times*.

Almost as sentimental as Elizabeth Barrett Browning's "How do I love thee . . ."

1960

"An Exhibition of Scrambling," by Jim Trinkle, Fort Worth *Star-Telegram*.

Billy Casper sweats out his pursuers at the 1959 Open.

"Open Rebellion on the Links," by Blackie Sherrod, Dallas *Times-Herald*

More on the Casper win.

"Hacker's Dream" by Art Rosenbaum, San Francisco *Chronicle*.

The writer, a 15-handicap, is teamed with George Bayer, then the longest hitter in golf.

1961

"For Love and Money" by Jim Atwater, *Time*.

Palmer's pro debut.

"Lightning Strikes Twice" by Maxwell Stiles, Los Angeles *Mirror*.

A lesser-known pro tells how he fell apart during the L.A. Open.

"Golf Magic" by Jim Cuneo, Erie *Times*.

A panoramic view of the PGA Championship.

1962

"Master to Duffer," by Joe Schwendeman, Philadelphia *Evening Bulletin*.

Palmer blows the Masters on the 72nd hole.

"On the Road with the Girls" by Barbara Heilman, *Sports Illustrated*.

Sandra Haynie is 17 and Carol Mann 20 at the time of this look at life on the LPGA tour.

"Charles Sifford, Professional Golfer" by Ray Haywood, Oakland *Tribune*.

Charlie lights up a cigar and tees off at exclusive Cypress Point—the first black to do so.

1963

"Sweet Birds of Palmer" by Jeff Cadou, Indianapolis *Star*.

Arnie's sizzling spurt on the last nine holes of the Masters.

"Arnie's Army" by Bud Shrake, Dallas *Morning News*.

The subway mentality of Arnie's Army.

"That Big Strong Dude" by Alfred Wright, *Sports Illustrated*.

The beginning of the Nicklaus-Palmer golf showdowns.

1964

"The World Is His Fairway" by Will Grimsley, Associated Press.

Another look at a fairway Croesus.

"It's a Long Walk from Thompson St. to Elmsford" by Laurence Robinson, *Golf Digest*.

Vitale Turnesa's humble hegira to his dad's farm and some nostalgia concerning his other six brothers in the lore of golfing achievements.

"Golf Intermediary" by Wirt Gammon, Chattanooga *Times*.

A caddy studies Barbara Romack's game and gives her enough pointers to win first prize at her first PGA.

1965

"He Refused to Quit" by Lincoln Werden, *The New York Times*.

Ken Venturi wins Open in punishing heat.

"The Secret Life of Juan Rodriguez" by Gary Cartwright, *Golf Digest*.

A penetrating look at an unusual man.

1966

"He Pays off a Debt" by Lincoln Werden, *The New York Times*.

Gary Player gives his Open winnings to junior golf.

"Prelude to the Thunderbird" by Dick Schaap, New York *Herald-Tribune*.

A Ford dealer enters a golf tournament at Westchester accompanied by 17-handicap and somehow manages to win.

"Green Stands for Mint" by Morton Moss, Los Angeles *Times*.

Last line: "Columbus Fats is the Jolly Green Giant of golf today."

"Follow the Sun" by Jim Browder, Fort Worth *Press*.

"Some golfers die a slow death . . . some strike it rich." A bittersweet story of a once ambitious golfer.

"The Varied Reception" by Blackie Sherrod, Dallas *Times-Herald*.

The many ways in which Gary Player's charity was received by the cynics.

1967

"From Arnie's Army to Casper's Crowd" by Jack Murphy, San Diego *Union*.

Casper is U.S. Open champ for the second time in seven years.

"Koch Choked" by John Garrett, Sarasota *Herald-Tribune*.

Losing pro gives himself a merciless mental thrashing.

"Masterful Again" by Kaye Kessler, Columbus *Citizen-Journal*.

Nicklaus becomes the first repeat champion in 30-year history of the Masters.

1968

"Nicklaus Nullifies Arnie's Army" by Harlan Wade, Dallas *Morning News*.

He "murdered" challengers in an avalanche of birdies to win second Open with a record-shattering five-under-par 65.

"Why the Fans Don't Love Nicklaus" by Nick Seitz, *Sport*.

The main reason is that he began to beat Palmer.

1969

"The Fickle Pencil of Fate" by Kaye Kessler, Columbus *Citizen-Journal*.

A playing partner of De Vicenzo's inscribes a 4 for Roberto on the 17th hole instead of a 3.

"The Beautiful Guy" by Francis Stann, Washington *Star*.

The Open had become dullsville until Trevino emerged.

"Is This the Man to Succeed Palmer?" by Nick Seitz, *Golf Digest*.

The author puts his money on Tom Weiskopf, for various reasons.

"The Longest Gams in the Tournament" by Al Cartwright, Wilmington *News*.

Carol Mann, 6'3" professional golfer.

"A Pairing for History" by Jim Trinkle, Fort Worth *Star*.

More on the 1968 Masters scorecard fiasco.

1970

"Frank Beard Is Dull" by Nick Seitz, *Golf Digest*.

Beard is actually depicted with many splendid facets to his character.

"Not with Power, but with Poise" by Art Spander, San Francisco *Chronicle*.

Archer's remarkable poise in winning the 1969 Masters.

"A Profitable Bag" by Mark Radbovsky, Newspaper Enterprise Association.

The tribulations of pro tour caddies.

"A Sergeant Outshoots the General" by Jesse Outlar, Atlanta *Constitution*.

Moody, longshot NCO, hits the jackpot in 1969 Open.

"Purgatory with 18 Holes" by Furman Bisher, *The Atlanta Journal*.

Described is a golf course where you don't retrieve your misses unless you are on good terms with alligators.

1971

"The Intoxicating Moment" by Shirley Povich, Washington *Post*.

Club pro makes the cut in a big tournament.

"Florida Fats" by Stan Hochman, Philadelphia *Daily News*.

Bob Murphy doesn't mind being overweight or in the winner's circle.

"Ben Hogan Today" by Nick Seitz, *Golf Digest*.

Nothing is omitted in this depiction of one of the greats.

"Foreplay" by William Murray, *Playboy*.

At a tournament in Palm Springs, the author notes the guys and dolls who mingle among the celebrities.

1972

"The White Faces of Merion" by Art Spander, San Francisco *Chronicle*.

These white faces are large, deep bunkers that frustrated Jack Nicklaus in his quest for the 1971 Open.

"The Locker Room" by Larry Sheehan, *Golf Digest*.

Small talk, jibes, and jokes of the contenders as they get ready to play the 1970 Open at Hazeltine.

"Mr. Nobody's Somebody Now" by Phil Taylor, Seattle *Post-Intelligencer*.

Charles Coody wins the Masters.

1973

"Nicklaus Didn't Win, He Merely Survived" by Art Spander, San Francisco *Chronicle*.

Swirling gusts, rain, and cold buffet the Open field.

"How Trevino Makes Life Simpler" by Ray Dedinger, Philadelphia *Bulletin*.

Supermex eases the strain by jabbering and joking with galleries.

"Television's Underground Classic" by Larry Sheehan, *Golf Digest*.

A tournament put on by CBS and shown four months later is analyzed.

"The Race Was for Second" by Ben Garlikov, Dayton *Daily News*.

The fight for second place in the Masters was more exciting than the win.

"How I Cured My Hated Shank" by Nick Seitz, *Golf Digest*.

Lots of advice is received by the author. He tries every tip. One day the shank disappears—but he doesn't know why.

1974

"Tommy Aaron Is Finally #1" by Phil Taylor, Seattle *Post-Intelligencer*.

Much maligned as a "bridesmaid," Aaron wins.

"Weiskopf Conquers Himself" by Bob Addie, Washington *Post*.

The golfer long known as his own devil's advocate has finally straightened himself out with the help of his wife and family.

"A $500,000 Tournament . . . and Who Cares?" by Hubert Mizell, *Golf Digest*.

Many reasons are given by the top pros for begging off from the World Open at Pinehurst.

"Where's Ken Venturi?" by Phil Jackman, Baltimore *Evening Sun*.

"Golf Paralysis . . . From Analysis" by Ted Green, Los Angeles *Times*.

A golfer can't get out of the 80s, so he consults four pros, each of whom locates a different problem and an absolute cure.

1975

"A Magnificent 9-Iron Shot Wins Masters" by Art Spander, San Francisco *Chronicle*.

"The Greatest Golfer in the World" by Nick Seitz, *Golf Digest*.

Gary Player is put under a microscope.

1976

"The Only-ness" by Nick Seitz, *Golf Digest*.

Hale Irwin coined this catchy title in answer to the question, "What makes golf unique?"

"The Quiet Golfer from Nashville," by Bob Addie, Washington *Post*.

Lou Graham proves that the Open is within reach of the common man.

"Women's Golf . . . The Rewards are Elusive" by Joan Ribman, *Wall Street Journal*.

The hard life on the road and the meager purses have made Jan Ferraris a bit cynical.

1977

"The Anticlimatic Masters" by Edwin Pope, *Miami Herald*.

Ray Floyd's lead kept building all the way through the '76 event.

"The Witwams Go to the Masters" by Jolee Edmondson, *Golf Magazine*.

A California couple satisfy a lifelong desire to visit Augusta National in the spring.

"Arnie's Still The Man," by Art Spander, San Francisco *Chronicle*.

An appreciation of the aging Arnold Palmer.

1978

"Watson Is the Master" by Phil Taylor, Seattle *Post Intelligencer*

The kid who was supposed to choke makes the entire golf world gag on a mouthful of birdies at the 1977 Masters.

"Nicklaus!" by Nick Seitz, *Golf Digest*.

Nicklaus epitomizes mental discipline more than any other athlete in any other sport.

"Women's Golf Tour: Stained by Tears and Drudgery" *The New York Times.*

Says Carol Mann: "Soon life becomes nothing more than a mattress, a box spring, a bathroom, and four walls. Is that all there is? You cry a lot."
—compiled by Edward Ehre

CHARLES BARTLETT MEMORIAL AWARDS

Prizes for outstanding golf reporting/writing are given annually by the Golf Writers Association of America. Winners since the program was initiated by MacGregor Golf Corp. in 1957 are listed below.

YEAR　　　　　　*WINNER*

1957　NEWS: Gene Gregston, Ft. Worth *Star-Telegram*
　　　FEATURE: Dan Jenkins, Ft. Worth *Press*
1958　NEWS: Dana Mozley, New York *Daily News*
　　　FEATURE: Tom Davison, Houston *Post*
1959　NEWS: Wally Wallis, Oklahoma City *Daily Oklahoman*
　　　FEATURE: Gary Cartwright, Dallas *Times-Herald*
1960　NEWS: Dana Mozley, New York *Daily News*
　　　FEATURE: Ray Haywood, Oakland *Tribune*
1961　NEWS: Charles Bartlett, Chicago *Tribune*
　　　FEATURE: Ray Haywood, Oakland *Tribune*
1962　NEWS: Irwin Smallwood, Greensboro (N.C.) *News*
　　　FEATURE: Dan Jenkins, Dallas *Times-Herald*
1963　NEWS: Irwin Smallwood, Greensboro (N.C.) *News*
　　　FEATURE: Jack Murphy, San Diego *Union*
1964　NEWS: Irwin Smallwood, Greensboro (N.C.) *News*
　　　FEATURE: Frank Hannigan, USGA *Journal*
1965　NEWS: Bruce Phillips, Raleigh *Times*
　　　FEATURE: Jerry Izenberg, Newark *Star-Ledger*
1966　NEWS: Sam Blair, Dallas *Morning News*
　　　FEATURE: Phil Taylor, Seattle *Post-Intelligencer*
　　　MAGAZINE: Gwilym S. Brown, *Sports Illustrated*
1967　NEWS: Art Spander, San Francisco *Chronicle*
　　　FEATURE: Joe Schwendeman, Philadelphia *Evening Bulletin*
　　　MAGAZINE: Herbert Warren Wind, *Golf Digest*

YEAR　　　　　　*WINNER*

1968　NEWS: Jim Trinkle, Ft. Worth *Star*
　　　FEATURE: Jack Patterson, Akron *Beacon-Journal*
　　　MAGAZINE: Cal Brown, *Golf Digest*
1969　NEWS, A.M.: Jim Trinkle, Ft. Worth *Star-Telegram*
　　　NEWS, P.M.: Gene Roswell, *New York Post*
　　　FEATURE: Doug Mintline, Flint *Journal*
　　　MAGAZINE: Dan Jenkins, *Sports Illustrated*
1970　NEWS, A.M.: Art Spander, San Francisco *Chronicle*
　　　NEWS, P.M.: Blackie Sherrod, Dallas *Times-Herald*
　　　FEATURE: Sam Blair, Dallas *Morning News*
　　　MAGAZINE: Dan Jenkins, *Sports Illustrated*
1971　NEWS, A.M.: Phil Taylor, Seattle *Post-Intelligencer*
　　　NEWS, P.M.: Fred Russell, Nashville *Banner*
　　　FEATURE: Maury White, Des Moines *Register and Tribune*
　　　MAGAZINE: Dan Jenkins, *Sports Illustrated*
1972　NEWS, A.M.: D. L. Stewart, Dayton *Journal-Herald*
　　　NEWS, P.M.: Fred Russell, Nashville *Banner*
　　　FEATURE: Bill Beck, St. Louis *Post-Dispatch*
　　　MAGAZINE: Lee Mueller, *Golf*
1973　NEWS, A.M.: D. L. Stewart, Dayton *Journal-Herald*
　　　NEWS, P.M.: Blackie Sherrod, Dallas *Times-Herald*
　　　FEATURE: Dave Nightingale, Chicago *Daily News*
　　　MAGAZINE: Jim Trinkle, *Golf*
1974　NEWS, A.M.: Marvin Moss, Montreal *Gazette*
　　　NEWS, P.M.: Bill Beck, St. Louis *Post-Dispatch*
　　　FEATURE: Blackie Sherrod, Dallas *Times-Herald*
　　　MAGAZINE: Ross Goodner, *Golf*
1975　NEWS: Marino Paracenzo, Pittsburgh *Post-Gazette*
　　　FEATURE, A.M.: Ronald Green, Charlotte *News*
　　　FEATURE, P.M.: Gary Nuhn, Dayton *Daily News*
　　　MAGAZINE: Jolee Edmondson, *Golf*
1976　NEWS: Gary Nuhn, Dayton *Daily News*
　　　FEATURE: Larry Bush, Palm Beach *Times;* Bob Green, Associated Press
　　　MAGAZINE: Dick Taylor, *Golf World*
1977　NEWS: Bruce Phillips, Raleigh *Times*
　　　FEATURE: Ronald Green, Charlotte *News;* Tim Horgan, Boston *Herald-American*
　　　MAGAZINE: Charles Price, *Golf*

XI

Golfiana

THE GOLF COLLECTORS' SOCIETY, BY JOE MURDOCH
REFERENCES FOR COLLECTING BOOKS
COLLECTING ART
REFERENCES FOR COLLECTING EQUIPMENT
HISTORIC GOLF COLLECTIONS

THE GOLF COLLECTORS' SOCIETY

GOLF COLLECTORS' SOCIETY

638 Wagner Road
Lafayette Hill, PA 19444

The Golf Collectors' Society was formed in 1970 and now has 470 members. The purpose of the society is simply to encourage collectors of *golfiana* (primarily clubs, books, prints, balls, and scorecards, plus numerous miscellaneous items) to meet each other. Annual dues is $10.00, which goes to the printing and mailing costs of an annual *Membership Directory* and periodic *Society Bulletins*. The bulletins are not published on any set schedule, because I write them at my own pleasure. They attempt to circulate to the members news and information that I think would be of interest to collectors. We hold an annual meeting (usually in October) and in the early part of the year hold a Trade Fair. The latter is strictly a swap, sell, and buy session, while the annual meeting is more programmed, although trading activity also goes on. Membership requirements are not very strict—more or less, an expression from the applicant that he is a collector. We prefer that the applicant be sponsored by a current member, but if he or she does not know a member, a statement from the applicant will be accepted as evidence of his collecting interests.

—Joe Murdoch, co-founder (with Bob Kuntz) of the Golf Collectors' Society

REFERENCES FOR COLLECTING BOOKS

The best references for building or organizing your own collection of golf books are the following works.

THE LIBRARY OF GOLF by Joseph S. F. Murdoch. 1968, 314 pages, $12.50, Detroit: Gale Research Company.

Bibliography of almost 1,000 books published on or about golf from 1943 to 1966, along with useful chronological, alphabetical, and subject-matter listings. Delightful introduction devoted to "the madness known as collecting" cites numerous interesting antique and modern writers on the game. Murdoch is the same fellow who started Golf Collectors'.

THE LIBRARY OF GOLF by Joseph S. F. Murdoch. 1978, 56 pages (paperback), $10.00. Write to:
Joseph S. F. Murdoch
638 Wagner Road
Lafayette Hill, PA 19444

This privately printed, limited edition corrects and adds to the 1943–1966 coverage of titles in the previous volume and reports on about 100 new titles appearing in 1967–1977. Also a recommended-reading list of about 50 books "for collectors."

GOLF: A GUIDE TO INFORMATION SOURCES, edited by Janet Seagle and Joseph S. F. Murdoch. 1979, $22.00, Detroit: Gale Research Company.

Not seen. Combines a selected group of important books in the Murdoch bibliographies, plus compilation of wide range of information sources in golf world.

BOOK COLLECTING: A MODERN GUIDE, edited by Jean Peters. 1977, 288 pages, $15.95, Ann Arbor, Mich.: R. R. Bowker.

This volume covers the whole spectrum of book collecting; suggests directories and periodicals to use for information on book dealers; lists auction houses, recommended suppliers, bibliographical societies, etc.

THE LIBRARY OF CONGRESS, Washington, DC 20540.

There are approximately 1,075 cards in the library's main catalog listed under the subject heading "Golf" and its subdivisions. Three ways to find out more about these books:

· Go there in person (the reading room is well-organized, well-lighted, etc.)
· Order photocopies of the cards (at 8¢ each) or 16-mm microfilm (at 4¢ each) from the library's Photoduplication Service department.
· Consult the Library of Congress *Subject Catalog* (published quarterly beginning in 1950), available in many large libraries. This publication describes works represented on the Library's printed catalog cards.

TWO READING LISTS

Touring pro Ben Crenshaw has been an avid collector of old and secondhand golf books. In discussing his hobby in an article in *Golf* magazine, he suggested the titles listed below as a starting point for the would-be serious collector:

Golf Courses of the British Isles, by Bernard Darwin
Mostly Golf, essays by Bernard Darwin, edited by Peter Ryde
The World of Golf, by Charles Price
James Braid on Golf, by James Braid
Fifty Years of American Golf, by H. B. Martin
Golf Is My Game, by Robert Tyre (Bobby) Jones, Jr.
A Game of Golf, by Francis Ouimet

Golfing, by W. R. Chambers
The Story of American Golf, by Herbert Warren Wind
Golf, by Horace Hutchinson

Robert Cromie's recommended starter list (from *Bartlett's World Golf Encyclopedia*):

Bobby Locke on Golf
The Bogey Man, by George Plimpton
Chick Evans Golf Book
Down the Fairway, by Robert T. Jones, Jr.
The Duffer's Handbook of Golf, by Grantland Rice and Clare Briggs
The Education of a Golfer, by Sam Snead, with Al Stump
Fifty Years of American Golf, by H. B. Martin
Golf, by Horace Hutchinson
Golfer's Gold, by Tony Lema, with Gwilym S. Brown
Golf for Women, by Louise Suggs et al.
The Golf Immortals, by Tom Scott and Geoffrey Cousins
Golf Magazine's Pro Pointers and Stroke Savers, edited by Charles Price
Golfing Memories and Methods, by Joyce Wethered
How to Play Your Best Golf All the Time, by Tommy Armour
It's the Damned Ball, by Ike Handy
My Partner, Ben Hogan, by Jimmy Demaret
A New Way to Better Golf, by Alex J. Morrison
The Nine Bad Shots of Golf and What to Do About Them, by Jim Dante and Leo Diegel
Par for the Course: A Golfer's Anthology, edited by Robert Cromie
The Story of American Golf, by Herbert Warren Wind
Swinging into Golf, by Ernest Jones and Innis Brown
Tee Shots and Others, by Bernard Darwin
Thirty Years of Championship Golf, by Gene Sarazen, with Herbert Warren Wind
This Life I've Led, by Babe Didrikson Zaharias
The Walter Hagen Story, by Walter Hagen, as told to Margaret Seaton Heck
The World of Golf, by Charles Price

SECONDHAND BOOKSTORES IN THE U.S.

You may come upon an old or rare golf book in any good used-book store. The names and locations of some 275 such stores can be found in *American Book Trade Directory* (R. R. Bowker) available in the reference section of most good-sized libraries.

DEALERS SPECIALIZING IN OLD GOLF BOOKS

Contact these firms for specific titles—some will put your name on mailing list and send you all future notices of old golf books available.

UNITED STATES

Hollywood Book City
6627 Hollywood Boulevard
Hollywood, CA 90028

Charles J. Tatro
60 Goff Road
Wethersfield, CT 02109

Reel Yardage
1600 S. Main #574
Las Vegas, NV 89401

Nicklas & Parker
24 Lake Street
Cooperstown, NY 13326

Old Golf Shop
325 W. Fifth Street
Cincinnati, OH 45202

Philip G. LeVan
2443 Liberty Street
Allentown, PA 18104

GREAT BRITAIN

W. G. Foyle, Ltd.
119–125 Charing Cross Road
London, England

Hatchcard's
Piccadilly
London, England

Philip A. Truett
"Woodbine House"
12 Spencer Street
South Croydon, England

David White
Hampden House
84 Kingsway
London WC2, England

John Grant Booksellers
Dundas Street
Edinburgh, Scotland

Quarto Bookshop
St. Andrews
Fife, Scotland

The following excerpt is from a typical price list from Reel Yardage:

The Duffer's Handbook of Golf, Grantland Rice and Clare Briggs, Macmillan Co., N.Y. 1926, 8 × 10″, ill. by Briggs, very good. $40

Scotland's Gift, Golf, Charles Blair Macdonald, Scribner's Sons, N.Y., 1928, 1st ed. ill. with fotos, color frontispiece of author, & pull-out map of the National Golf Links, Shinnecock Hills, L.I. 8 × 10″, 340 p., almost fine (cover rubbed slightly over 1 sq. inch), extremely scarce. $110

Picture Analysis of Golf Strokes, James M. Barnes, J.B. Lippincott, Phil., 1919, 9 × 11″, ill. (fotos by L.F. Deming), 252 p. Mostly fotos, this book features Mr. Barnes' fine swing and excellent teaching, very good. $75

Golf Fundamentals, Seymour Dunn, Saratogian Printing, N.Y. 1922, 8 × 12″, ill. with lots of fotos, this is an instruction book featuring the author. Scarce book features pull-out specification chart by author who was golf director at Laurel C.C., Saranac Inn, and Lake Placid Club. 281 pages, fine, 1st ed. $100

Fifty Years of American Golf, H.B. Martin, Dodd, Mead, N.Y. 1936, 7 × 9″, lots of fotos of golf champions esp. 19th century. 423 p. Binding broken, repaired, otherwise fine, 1st ed. $35

A Guide to Good Golf, James M. Barnes, Dodd, Mead & Co., N.Y. 1926, 6 × 8″, ill. with line drawings, 137 p., very good. $25

Nine Holes of Golf, Royal Cortissoz, Scribner's Sons, N.Y. 1922, 6 × 8″, 1st ed. 97 p. Author 1st published these 9 essays in New York Tribune, fair-poor. $10

So This is Golf, Harry Leon Wilson, Cosmopolitan, N.Y. 1923, 5 × 7″, 46 p. ill. by M.L. Blumenthal (line drawings), very good. $20

Down the Fairway, Robert T. Jones, Jr. & O.B. Keeler, Minton Balch & Co., N.Y. 1927, 1st ed. 239 p. ill. with fotos, 6 × 9″, good. $20

Golf Without Tears, P.G. Wodehouse, Geo. Doran Co.,

N.Y. 1924, 6 × 8″, 330 p. An early novel on golf, very good. $30

Golf Without Tears, exactly as above except cond. is good ex. binding fixed. $15

COLLECTING ART

GALLERIES AND FIRMS OFFERING GOLF PRINTS AND PAINTINGS

Arthur Ackermann & Son, Inc.
50 East 57th Street
New York, NY 10022
Old prints and reproductions.

Argosy Books and Prints
116 East 59th Street
New York, NY 10022
Old prints and reproductions.

Cottage Door
190 NE 5th Street
Delray Beach, FL 33444

Crossroads of Sport, Inc.
5 East 47th Street
New York, NY 10017
Old and new prints and reproductions; representative for Weaver, Mawicke.

Oestreicher's Prints, Inc.
43 West 46th Street
New York, NY 10036
Old and new prints and reproductions.

Old Golf Shop, Inc.
325 W. 5th Street
Cincinnati, OH 45202
Claims world's largest collection of golf art, antiques, and collectibles, as well as a wide selection of golf books, old and new.

Old Print Center of Phyllis Lucas
981 Second Avenue
New York, NY 10022
Old and new prints and reproductions.

The Old Print House
139 East 53rd Street
New York, NY 10019
Old prints.

Old Print Shop, Inc.
150 Lexington Avenue
New York, NY 10016
Old prints, drawings, and watercolors.

Palm Valley Arts
P.O. Box 174
Jacksonville Beach, FL 32050
Prints and reproductions.

Pebble Beach Gallery
Box 325/Pebble Beach, CA 93953
"Gus the Golfer" series; Phillips watercolors.

"PEGASUS" (Robert F. Lee)
Pitts Bay Road
Pembroke, Bermuda
P.O. Box 1551
Hamilton, 5 Bermuda
Specializes in Vanity Fair Prints and has some golfers.

The Sporting Life
Chickasaw Oaks Plaza
3092 Poplar Street
Memphis, TN

The Sporting Life
3029 M Street NW
Washington, DC 20007

Sportsman's Eyrie
Spread Eagle Village
Wayne, PA 19087
Reproductions; "Golf in America."

World-Famous Golf Holes
Box 2506
Palos Verdes Pen., CA 90274
Oil-color wall pictures of famous and scenic golf holes.

The following excerpt is from a list of offerings of rare art, books and clubs by the Old Golf Shop:

A. Limited-edition lithograph of 300 numbered copies of the original oil painting by Clement Fowler done in 1913, featuring Harry Vardon, James Braid and J. H. Taylor, known as "The Triumvirate."
B. Original Vanity Fair lithographs of John Ball, James Braid, Sam Fergusson, Harold Hilton, Horace Hutchinson, Robert Maxwell dated 1890–1907, $30–$75.
C. Hand-painted leaded-glass windows on walnut base, five different ones available, each a limited edition of 50. Size 8½ × 10″, $85 each.
D. Various leather-bound books ranging from *Fifty Years of American Golf* by Martin at $45 to *Encyclopedia of Golf* edited by Steel and Ryde, $58.50.
E. Antique golf clubs priced at $20 and up depending on club maker, condition, age, and availability.
F. Antique Royal Doulton china with golf designs, $50 and up.
G. Original golf art, watercolor or oil, $350.

OTHER SOURCES OF ORIGINAL ART

MUSEUM OF CARTOON ART
Comly Avenue
Port Chester, NY 10573
Jack Tippit, director
(914) 939-0234

This group will make available on a first-come first-served basis the original art for such popular newspaper strips as "Beetle Bailey," "Hi & Lois," and "Hagar the Horrible" (some of which have been drawn with a golf theme). Prices are $75 for a daily strip and $125 for a Sunday; full-size copies are also available for $15. Preferred approach is to request desired date and alternates.

SOCIETY OF ILLUSTRATORS
128 East 63rd Street
New York, NY 10021
(212) 838-2560
Arpi Ermoyan, executive director

This group represents many of the top artists and commercial illustrators in the country and is willing to recommend artists for specific golf commissions.

SOURCES OF GOLF ART REPRODUCTIONS

U.S. GOLF ASSOCIATION
Golf House
Far Hills, NJ 07931

Offers variety of color reproductions of artwork on display in Golf House from $5.00 to $30.00 unframed. Send for brochure.

GOLF DIGEST SPECIAL SERVICES
495 Westport Avenue
Norwalk, CT 06856

Color Prints of Famous Courses. Reproductions of architect's drawings of layouts of Augusta National, Carnoustie, Cypress Point, Glen Abbey, Gleneagles, Oakmont, Pebble Beach, Spyglass Hill, and Winged Foot. Cost: $2.50 per print.

Infamous Golf Holes. Color lithographs of fantastical holes from the golfing nightmares of artist Loyal H. Chapman, with names like "Larsen Ice Shelf, Antarctica C.C." and "No. 10, Alps International Golf & Climbing Club."

Ben Hogan in Bronze. Twelve-inch-high bronze sculpture of Hogan just before impact on a 2-iron shot, by David Earle Goodrich. Cost: $650.

Golf Digest also carries diaries, calendars, and other gift items.

THE GALLERY ARTISTS
3935 Blackstone Avenue
Riverdale, NY 10471

Golf. Reproduction of Leroy Nieman montage of Snead, Hogan, Player, Trevino, Palmer, Nicklaus. Cost: $50 unframed; $90 framed.

THOUGHT FACTORY
P.O. Box 1515
Sherman Oaks, CA 91413

Gary Patterson Golf Prints. Humorous figures.

SCULPTORS FOUNDRY
13280 Murphy Rd.
Stafford, TX 77477

Bronze abstract sculpure of golf swing by Ted McKinney; 9″ high on walnut base. Cost: $175.

GOLF GRAPHICS LTD.
Coval Court
Sunningdale, Berkshire, England

Limited-edition reproductions of oil or watercolor landscapes of golf holes at St. Andrews, Troon, Turnberry, Kings and Queens, Gleneagles, Sunningdale, Moor Park, and Wentworth. Cost: £27.50 unsigned; £32.50 signed.

ST. ANDREWS GOLF COMPANY OF AMERICA
13131 Champions Drive
Houston, TX 77069

Hickory-shafted reproductions of putters, jiggers, and chippers, from $65.

WESTPORT COLLECTIBLES
P.O. Box 28384
West Branch
Creve Coeur, MO 63141

Five-inch-high porcelain figurines based on whimsical golf characters of cartoonist Gary Patterson. Cost: $10.

CHIEF & TIGER CO.
Box 1969
Covina, CA 91722

Twenty-two carat gold-leafed golf ball balanced on tee and set into black walnut base, designed by Emerson D. Conklin. Cost: $35.

TRUE DISTANCE
5818 Beverly Hill Lane
Houston, TX 77057

Replicas made in St. Andrews of various putters and play clubs.

BORDER ENTERPRISES
2112 11th Avenue South
Birmingham, AL 35205

Reproductions of turn-of-century clubs, made in St. Andrews.

SOURCES OF GOLF PHOTOGRAPHS, POSTERS AND BUMPER STICKERS

GOLF PORTFOLIO
140 Seventh Avenue, Apt. 5-F
New York, NY 10011

Selection of five 11×14″ top-quality color prints, suitable for framing, of evocative golfing scenes captured by camera of Leonard Kamsler, "the foremost photographer in golf today" according to *Golf* magazine. Cost: $500.

LIMITED EDITION PHOTOGRAPHS
1711 N. Grismer, No. 52
Burbank, CA 91504

Hand-printed color photographs, by accomplished golf editor/photographer Will Hertzberg, of dramatic holes at Pebble Beach, Cypress Point, and Mauna Kea, in choice of three sizes. 9¾×14″, $24.95; 14×20″, $49.94; 16×24″, $69.95.

SPORTS ILLUSTRATED
c/o Marketcom, Lockbox 2257
Hampton Bank
4301 Hampton Avenue
St. Louis, MO 63109

"Signature Poster Series." Color blowups (2×3′) of Hale Irwin, Laura Baugh, Jan Stephenson, Nancy Lopez. Cost: $3.00.

IBUS CORP.
P.O. Box 1026
Flagler Beach, FL 32036

Humorous bumper stickers with golf motif. Cost: 3 for $3.95.

REFERENCES FOR COLLECTING EQUIPMENT

The following list contains some pertinent references for collectors of clubs and balls.

GOLF IN THE MAKING by Ian T. Henderson and David I. Stirk. 1979, 328 pages, 250 ill., $40.00, West Yorkshire, England: The Manningham Press.

Orders accepted through:
Old Golf Shop, Inc.
325 W. Fifth Street
Cincinnati, OH 45202

Not seen. History of the evolution of golf up to the outbreak of World War I. Chapters include "The Golf Ball," "The Clubmakers," "The Wooden Clubs," "The Cleekmakers," "Styles and Methods of Play," and "The Patents." Golfiana section offers advice on identification of old clubs and balls and tips on preserving books, ceramics, paintings, prints, etc.

ENCYCLOPEDIA OF COLLECTIBLES, VOL. 7. 1979, 160 pages, $6.95, Alexandria, Va.: Time-Life Books.

This volume in the series, subtitled *Folk Art to Horse-Drawn Carriages,* includes a short, illustrated section on rare golf art and clubs, with text by Joseph S. F. Murdoch.

THE AMAZING GOLF BALL. 1978, 16 pages, AMF Ben Hogan Co.

This 16-page booklet entertainingly reports on the golf ball's history, types, performance characteristics, and method of manufacture. Also, tips on how to select a ball for play and a glossary of ball terms. Copies available free through any Ben Hogan professional.

THE CURIOUS HISTORY OF THE GOLF BALL: MANKIND'S MOST FASCINATING SPHERE by John Stuart Martin. 1968, 192 pages, $6.95, N.Y.: Horizon Press.

The flight of the golf ball over 600 years, from featherie through rubber-wound to solid. The only complete chronicle of the golf ball, told in a lively style, with useful drawings and photos.

SOURCES OF CLASSIC* CLUBS

Golf Classics
Box 1202
Studio City, CA 91604
(213) 348-4086

Kennedy's Classics
Box 112
Stevensville, MI 49127

Vintage Golf
Box 90
Glencoe, IL 60022
(312) 835-0025

Coveted Clubs
P.O. Box 12364
Jackson, MS 39211

Golf Exchange
Rt. 6, Box 731-C
Charlotte, NC 28208

Peninsula Golf
14357 Old Courthouse Way
Newport News, VA 23602

Ye Olde Golf Shoppe
1238 N. 28th Place
Phoenix, AZ 85008

Orlando Classic Golf
4680 North Lane
Orlando, FL 32808

Wood Works
Box 50180
Nashville, TN 37205

The following excerpt is from a typical price list from Vintage Golf:

TOMMY ARMOUR, 1-3-4-5, #925, SUPER EYE O MATIC, Original "D" shaft, D-4 leather grips, Sit square, Refinished to BETTER THAN NEW by POWELL. $500.00

JIMMY DEMARET, #3532 Master, 1-2-3, Black Square, D-2 Excellent. $150.00

JIMMY DEMARET #352CW, Super grain, original grip & shaft, refinished. $100.00

BEN HOGAN, #1652, 1-2-3-4, Speedwoods, all original, Excellent. $100.00

* Playable, high-quality clubs from the 1940s and 1950s.

TONEY PENNA, TP1W, 1-3-4, Velocitized, D-3 Green Victory, Refinished Fawn. $400.00

TONEY PENNA, P40W, 1-3-4, Super EyeOmatic, all original, never refinished. $300.00

ALL OF THE ABOVE CLUBS ARE "OIL HARDENED"

TOURNEY PT3W, 1-3-4, *NEW* dynamic Stiff shaft, red fiber inserts, & Green Victory Sit square, outstanding grain, Armour Red. $300.00

TOURNEY PT1W, 1-3-4 PROPEL #1 Shaft, Green Victory, D-2, Refin. walnut square. $300.00

TOURNEY, EyeOmatic 60, 1-3-4-5 Stiff, D-2, Refin. Fawn, Brown Victory Super. $450.00

A GUIDE TO MCGREGOR GOLF CLUBS, 1950–1968 by Jim Kaplan. 1978, 4 pages, $3.00. Write Vintage Golf, address on page 249.

Index to wood and iron sets made by McGregor—including Tommy Armour, Toney Penna, Byron Nelson, and Tourney models—that gives accurate identification of year of manufacture, name, model number, shaft and flex, grip, and insert.

GOLF CLASSICS PRICE AND IDENTIFICATION GUIDE by Mike Doherty. 1978, 200 pages, $19.95. Write Golf Classics, address on page 249.

A "blue book" approach to metal-shafted classic clubs. Numerous photos, listings, and prices on clubs dating from 1935 to the present; information on buying, selling, and restoring; and identification of clubs the touring pros are *really* using. The book is actually a three-ring vinyl binder containing 8½ × 11″ printed material. The publisher intends to send supplement pages to update individual chapters in the future. See following excerpt.

"CLASSIC" CLUBS—NOT THE SAME AS "ANTIQUE" CLUBS

This excerpt, reprinted with permission, from Mike Doherty's *Golf Classics Price and Identification Guide*, will clear up any confusion a would-be collector may have about "old" golf clubs.

Because of some confusion over what the fervor for older golf clubs is all about, a clarification of terms is in order before delving into the Price and Identification Guide's *subject matter. To that end Webster's New World Dictionary was employed for the following definitions.*

> *Antique—Of ancient times. A piece of furniture, etc. made in a former period, generally more than 100 years ago.*
> *Classic—Of the highest class, being a model of its kind.*
> *Special-interest—Exceptional. Highly regarded or valued. A feeling of concern or curiosity about something.*

The term "antique," as used in this book, describes pre-1935 clubs, usually hickory-shaft models. This is quite different from a "classic," which may be from years past, but is among the best ever in appearance and performance. Example: McGregor Tommy Armour 693 woods.

"Special-interest" clubs are, as Webster's says, exceptional in quality and design, and certainly do inspire concern and curiosity, yet may not be classics in the sense of Webster's definition. Example: Power-Bilt woods with brass bar inserts.

Because both classic and special-interest clubs appeal to the same enthusiasts, and because it is a fine line separating them, the terms are used rather interchangeably in the Price and Identification Guide.

The most important thing to understand when buying or selling clubs—even if only disposing of the bagful in a late uncle's estate—is that clubs have no special value simply because they are old.

Hundreds of brands and thousands of models have been sold to golfers around the world and of these only a minute percentage has attained more than ordinary value. Yet of the numerous inquiries received by Golf Classics a majority ask for details and values of oldies that aren't really playable and are nothing unusual to collectors. Example: Spalding Robt. T. Jones irons with yellow-coated shafts and long leather grips of some 40 years ago. There seem to be so many of these still in existence that everyone who even recognizes a golf club has some in an attic or basement. Until the owner becomes a little knowledgeable about this field he figures that with a famous signature, a major manufacturer, and forty years of age they must be valuable. In fact, they have almost no value except sentimental. Light blades, outdated shafts, and slender, slippery grips make them undesirable for play. And, since they are so common, collectors do not seek them for rarity or anticipated appreciation.

This brings us to another basic but often overlooked fact governing the buying and selling of clubs: The value of a club is only what someone else is willing to pay for it. Not what someone talks about, but the amount of cash they will actually pay. Just as fishermen exaggerate "the one that got away," golfers fill the pro shops of the world with a lot of empty boasts. The proud owner of a set of forty-year-old brown-shaft Wilson woods in mint original condition says they were played by Denny Shute and he wouldn't sell them for $500. He needn't worry. Because the head shape is not popular no one is likely to step up and pay more than $50 for the set.

There is a solid, continuing demand for certain clubs and they maintain a high value. However, clubs which may seem very similar often have little value. Example: The Bristol Geo. Low Wizard 600 putter which often sells for $500. The other Geo. Low models, with the same quality of manufacture, same shaft and grip, usually trade in the $35 range.

Another example of how carefully one must be in figuring values: The Wilson Helen Hicks sand iron of the late

1930s sells for $150 and up but none of the other clubs in the set would bring more than a few dollars. Reason? The sand wedge, like the Wilson R-90 and R-20 models, is considered the best of shapes, and it plays superbly. The rest of the Hicks irons are not out of the ordinary.

Classics' values are determined to quite an extent by their playability, i.e. better in some respects than new clubs. There are other factors, of course, but if the clubs can't be played successfully their worth for display or mere possession is usually not large.

Only an occasional putter or wedge among hickory-shaft clubs has the great playing characteristics sought in classics. By and large, the antique collectors, as opposed to the classic, seek hickory-shaft clubs but are used to buying most of them at garage sales for a dollar each. Some of the old Forgan-made clubs and splice-head woods of the 1800s may change hands at $50 to $250 but they are rare indeed.

Therefore, as a rule, wooden-shaft clubs are not worth acquisition by classic collectors or anyone looking for marketable items.

Anyone with an interest in the real antiques should contact the Golf Collectors' Society. Its membership is the hard core of antique club and memorabilia collecting.

—Mike Doherty

HISTORIC GOLF COLLECTIONS

Museums, libraries and/or "halls of fame" with interesting collections open to the public are listed below.

GOLF HOUSE LIBRARY AND MUSEUM
U.S. Golf Association
Far Hills, NJ 07931
(201) 234-2300

Janet Seagle, librarian and museum curator

The headquarters for amateur golf's governing body also houses a superb collection of golf books, art, and artifacts. (A 16-page booklet, *A Brief Introduction to Golf House,* which describes the museum and library in detail, is available from the USGA for 50¢.)

The library contains some 8,000 volumes organized in the following categories: architecture, club histories, fiction, history, humor, instruction, poetry, records, reference, rules, and turf management. Numerous rare and offbeat volumes. There is also a large collection of golf periodicals, some dating back to the 1890s.

The museum collection has a broad range of antique and/or storied golf equipment; numerous paintings, sketches, and photographs; and such charming exhibits as a turn-of-the-century clubmaker's bench complete with tea cabinet.

Located on New Jersey Route 512 about a mile east of U.S. Route 202, near the intersection of I-78 and I-287.

GOLF HOUSE TOUR

A circular tour will take you through the rooms of the museum and library that contain the various exhibits.

The origins of the USGA, photographs and charter papers of the first member clubs and photographs of its presidents are displayed in a room that features the international trophies won by the teams representing the United States. The World Amateur Golf Council is explained and illustrated. Also to be seen in this room is the history of the Rules of Golf and photographs of those individuals who have worked in their behalf through the years.

Scattered through the rooms are paintings of a number of golf courses, and the visitor may very well recognize his own course. Contributors have been very generous in providing golf course scenes.

There is a room containing an interesting exhibit of golfing memorabilia from Presidents of the United States who have played golf, one item of which is a painting of the 16th hole at Augusta National Golf Club by President Dwight D. Eisenhower.

Also in this room is a display of early golfing attire, bright red jackets with brass buttons of their respective clubs.

And speaking of change, probably one of the most interesting exhibits is the next one on the "tour," the display of golf clubs and balls as they have evolved through the eras of the feathery ball, the gutta percha ball and the rubber ball of today. As the ball changed, so did the clubs. A complete clubmaker's bench with all his tools as well as the equipment used to make the early golf balls is on display. There is also testing equipment from that era when equipment was made to order for each player. For the imaginative golfer, and who isn't, there is the "trick shot" equipment of Joe Kirkwood and Paul Hahn; the unusual designs of clubmakers that have been submitted for approval by the USGA Implements and Ball Committee; and the clubs and balls used by USGA Champions, such as Arnold Palmer, Jack Nicklaus, Ben Hogan, Gene Sarazen, Byron Nelson, Babe Didrikson Zaharias and Patty Berg as well as the earliest champions. Other items that relate to the champions of all years are their medals and pictures, which are located on a balcony gallery.

The approach to the Library is made along a light and spacious hall on the wall of which are paintings of golfing greats of the past such as Chick Evans, Walter Hagen and Glenna Collett Vare.

There is a small room off the gallery hall where the mementos of Francis Ouimet are on view, including the red coat he wore as Captain of the Royal and Ancient, the first American to be so honored.

The last room on this circular tour of the first floor of Golf House is decorated with wood paneling believed to be hundreds of years old and is named for Robert T. Jones, Jr. In this room are his magnificent collection of championship medals, his portrait by Thomas E. Stephens, Calamity Jane II (his famous putter) and many photos and other items relating to his career.

—Janet Seagle

CANADIAN GOLF HALL OF FAME, MUSEUM, AND LIBRARY
> Golf House
> Royal Canadian Golf Association
> Glen Abbey G.C.
> RR #2, Oakville, Ontario, Canada L6J 4Z3
> (416) 844-0516

> Lorne Rubenstein, curator

Glen Abbey is the headquarters of the Royal Canadian Golf Association and permanent site of the Canadian Open.

DIRECTIONS: From Toronto, take the Gardiner Expressway or Lakeshore Boulevard westbound to the Queen Elizabeth Way West. Exit upon reaching Oakville at the Dorval Drive exit, then go north to the North Service Road and continue west (left) a few hundred yards to the first exit on the right, the Glen Abbey Golf Club. Coming up the long drive, bear to the right at a fork in the road, and you will be at the Hall of Fame, Museum, and Library. From Buffalo, the nearest major U.S. city, take the Queen Elizabeth Way toward Toronto and proceed as above. Oakville is located 25 miles southwest of Toronto.

CANADIAN GOLF HOUSE TOUR

In the museum the visitor will find golf balls that span the game's history, from the featherie, made with leather sewn over a hatful of feathers, to the gutta-percha, an almost indestructible ball which became popular in 1848, through the modern rubber-core ball, developed in 1904 by a Cleveland golfer named Coburn Haskell.

Also on view is a selection of antique golf bags, including one that looks like a pouch mounted on a tripod, fashionable in the 1880's; the meticulously crafted silver trophy won by Canada's George S. Lyon in winning the golf championship of the 1904 Olympics at St. Louis; in a cabinet are unusual clubs including a toothed niblick for those troublesome shots from water hazards, a club made from whalebone, and a homespun wood created from a tree trunk by Albert Murray, early Canadian golf course professional and designer, when he was nine years old.

The first clubs, with their elongated shafts that called for a very flat swing, were quite deep in the blade to help extract the ball from ruts and tracks on the course. Hence the name rut-iron, an example of which can be seen at Golf House. The earliest club on display dates from 1750, possesses no markings, and was made by an ironworker in the course of his day's work. Not until the 1800's were identifying marks put on clubs, when men like Hugh Philp took up the craft of club-making. On view is a baffy spoon by Jackson of Perth; a play club or driver of Robert Forgan's; and an assortment of smooth-faced irons from the featherie and guttie eras.

Clubs that Canadians have used in important victories are on display. C. Ross (Sandy) Somerville contributed the irons he used in winning the 1932 United States Amateur while Gary Cowan gave the 9 iron with which he holed out a 135 yard shot to win the 1971 United States Amateur on the final hole. Nick Weslock, four times the Canadian Amateur champion, donated his bite wedge, and Marlene Stewart Streit gave the four wood she used in winning the 1973 British Women's Amateur. Pat Fletcher, 1976 inductee to the Hall of Fame and the last Canadian to win the Canadian Open, gave the putter that was so successful for him.

Upstairs in Golf House is the library, where what is believed to be the only complete edition of Canadian Golfer magazine, first published in 1915, is shelved. As a place for research or quiet study, the library is a mecca to the visitor who appreciates that golf has inspired a well-written literature, with more than 2,500 books having been published.

Golf House is open to the visitor free of charge, Monday through Friday year-round, 9:00–4:30, and during the entire week of the Canadian Open.

—Lorne Rubenstein

AMERICAN GOLF HALL OF FAME
> Foxburg Country Club
> Box 1, Route 58
> Foxburg, PA 16036

> Kenneth A. Christy, executive secretary

Foxburg claims to have the oldest golf course in the United States and an extensive collection of vintage golf memorabilia for viewing by the general public. The collection includes feather balls; gutta-percha balls and molds; feather-ball clubs; Joe Kirkwood's complete collection of trick clubs; six generations of McEwan clubs dating from 1770, as well as other European clubs; clubs of venerable champions such as Old Tom Morris, James Braid, J. H. Taylor; and more.

Approximately 55 miles northeast of Pittsburgh, four miles off I-80 at Exit 6. Open between April and November only.

WORLD GOLF HALL OF FAME
> P.O. Box 1908
> Pinehurst, NC 28374
> (919) 295-6651

> Donald C. Collett, president

This combination shrine/museum (golf books are not a significant part of the exhibit) was built by the Diamondhead Corporation, the owners of Pinehurst, and became a nonprofit foundation in 1976.

WORLD GOLF HALL OF FAME TOUR

Approaching the Hall of Fame, the visitor is impressed by the sparkling fountain, flags snapping in the breeze, white-columned porticoes and towering pines.

It overlooks Pinehurst Country Club's famous No. 2

course and covers thirty thousand feet of exhibit and display space.

Even before you enter the hall you glimpse, through glass doors, the 10-foot statue of Bobby Jones that dominates the big room.

In the main exhibit building is the world's finest collection of golfing artifacts and memorabilia, including the collection of Laurie Auchterlonie, honorary professional at the Royal and Ancient Golf Club in St. Andrews, Scotland. There is also a Golf History Wall, a 90-foot display depicting the evolution of the game over the past 500 years. This wall gives solid credence, in a fascinating visual manner, to the fact that golf was being played in Scotland before Columbus discovered America.

Other displays show the development of the game. Items of golf equipment include the feathery golf balls which were in common use from 1750 to 1850. These balls were made from tanned animal hides stuffed with a hatful of feathers.

Another attraction is the theater where golf films are shown. These films feature instruction on how to play the game as well as highlights of major tournaments played around the world.

Behind the exhibit hall is the actual shrine with plaques of the golfers who are inducted into the Hall of Fame each year. The shrine is completely surrounded by water. Shooting geysers frame the serene tall-columned structure which stands like a sentinel guarding the No. 2 course, the favorite of its designer, Donald Ross.

—Sandhills Area Chamber of Commerce

GOLF'S GREATEST: THE LEGENDARY WORLD GOLF HALL OF FAMERS by Ross Goodner. 1978, 240 pages, $11.95, *Golf Digest;* N.Y. distributor: Simon & Schuster.

Short but entertaining profiles that sum up the careers of 35 of golf's legends; nostalgia value is further enhanced by dozens of vintage b/w photos.

Members of the World Golf Hall of Fame and year elected:

MODERN ERA CATEGORY

Arnold Palmer—1974	Walter Hagen—1974
Jack Nicklaus—1974	Patty Berg—1974
Gary Player—1974	Babe Zaharias—1974
Bobby Jones—1974	Mickey Wright—1976
Sam Snead—1974	Tommy Armour—1976
Ben Hogan—1974	Bobby Locke—1977
Byron Nelson—1974	Billy Casper—1978
Gene Sarazen—1974	

DISTINGUISHED SERVICE CATEGORY

Fred Corcoran—1975	Herb Graffis—1977
Joseph C. Dey—1975	Bing Crosby—1978
Donald Ross—1977	Clifford Roberts—1978

PREMODERN ERA CATEGORY

Harry Vardon—1974	J. H. Taylor—1975
Francis Ouimet—1974	Tom Morris, Sr.—1976
Willie Anderson—1975	James Braid—1976
Tom Morris, Jr.—1975	Jerome Travers—1976
Glenna Collett—1975	John Ball, Jr.—1977
Joyce Wethered—1975	Harold Hilton—1978
Chick Evans—1975	Dorothy Campbell Hurd—1978

GOLF MUSEUM

James River Country Club
1500 Country Club Road
Newport News, VA 23606
(804) 595-3327

Burr Melvin, curator

A room in the clubhouse exhibits several hundred clubs, some dating back to the early 1600s; balls from every stage in the evolution of the game; approximately 1,000 books; and a number of paintings.

The collection was gathered in 1932 through funds provided by Archer Huntington, son of the founder of the Chesapeake & Ohio Railroad. Huntington had the old equipment brought from various sources in Scotland and England and paid for the construction of the special room to display it in.

GOLF MUSEUM

3920 New Bern Avenue (off Highway 64)
Raleigh, NC 27610
(919) 832-5131

Burr Patchell, owner and operator

On display here are some 10,000 golf clubs, including 3,000 putters, as well as balls, bags, and trophies. Earliest artifacts date from the 19th century. One of the most prized items: a set of three woods built in 1921 and made of ivory.

PGA HALL OF FAME, LIBRARY, AND MUSEUM

c/o PGA of America
Box 12458
Lake Park, FL 33403
(305) 848-3481

Dr. Gary Wiren

This 55,000-piece collection is scheduled to go public by 1982, when the facility to house it will have been built, as part of the PGA's new headquarters in Palm Beach Gardens, Fla.

THE PGA'S COLLECTION

The object of the PGA Hall of Fame is to depict the evolution of the game where visitors may take a quick overview of the game and then focus on individual items of interest.

It will house golf art works throughout a 10,000-square-foot complex and provide an extensive library and research facility for people interested in delving into the history of the game.

The PGA received its first major private collection about 20 years ago when Judge Earle F. Tilley of Chicago donated his library to the Association. Some of Tilley's books date to the 1400s and 1500s. Some contain records of Scottish Parliament when golf was outlawed in the 1400s because the King thought people should be practicing archery for defense instead of playing golf.

The cornerstone of the Hall of Fame collection came from Col. R. Otto Probst of South Bend, Indiana. The 88-year-old Probst began collecting golf artifacts about 1922 when most people hadn't even thought of the idea. His collection never has been displayed in public and contains a wide range of items: 16,000 bound volumes of rare golf magazines and books, art, vases, plates created by prominent early 20th century illustrators, clubs, Walter Hagen's bronzed shoes, trophies, a golf pinball machine, jewelry and countless other pieces of golf history. It's estimated the collection is now worth $500,000.

Last year the PGA received several dozen antique golf clubs from the McEwan family, a Scottish clan that hand-crafted golf clubs continuously from the 1700s until 1971. They are the oldest clubs in the PGA collection and show the evolution of golf clubmaking by a single family.

Chick Harbert, the 1954 PGA Champion, recently made a donation of golfing artifacts that date back more than 100 years. The items were gathered over the years by Harbert and his late father and include old splice-shafted baffies, one-piece drivers, hickory-shafted jiggers, a prototype steel shaft, tee molds, ready-tees, golf balls of early 20th century vintage and the first set of clubs Harbert's clubmaker father made about 1920.   —PGA magazine

RALPH W. MILLER GOLF LIBRARY

Industry Hills Civic & Recreational Facility
111 S. Azusa Avenue
P.O. Box 32877
City of Industry, CA 91744
(213) 333-2211

Jean Bryant, director

Ralph Miller, a prominent figure in southern California amateur golf for many years, built one of the world's finest private golf libraries before he died in 1974. His collection consists of over 2,000 books and 5,000 journals, plus volumes of clippings, hundreds of art objects, and thousands of photos, postcards, and miscellaneous articles. Open to the public for reference and research.

THE MILLER COLLECTION

At the library you will see some of the rarest books in the world; books like "The Goff" (1743), a 22-page volume which was the first known book to be entirely devoted to golf and "The Lawes and Actes of Parliament, Maid be King James The First, And His Successors King of Scotland," the first book to mention golf. Scottish subjects of King James read in 1597 that "Fute-ball and golfe be abused in time cummin," and, "It is statute and ordained that in a place of the Realme there be used futeball, golfe, or uther sik unprofitable sportes." There is also an 1866 volume of Chamber's Useful Hand-Books "Gymnasics, Golf, Curling." The original price of the book was a sixpence. An 1893 romantic fiction titled "Won at the Last Hole" is among the rare collection.

—Fore magazine

XII

Major Golf Groups

UNITED STATES GOLF ASSOCIATION

WESTERN GOLF ASSOCIATION

STATE GOLF ASSOCIATIONS

NATIONAL GOLF FOUNDATION

NATIONAL CLUB ASSOCIATION

PGA TOUR

LPGA TOUR

TOURING-PRO MANAGEMENT GROUPS

PROFESSIONAL GOLFERS ASSOCIATION OF AMERICA

GOLF COURSE SUPERINTENDENTS ASSOCIATION OF AMERICA

CLUB MANAGERS ASSOCIATION OF AMERICA

AMERICAN SOCIETY OF GOLF COURSE ARCHITECTS

GOLF COURSE BUILDERS OF AMERICA

PROFESSIONAL GOLF CLUB REPAIRMEN'S ASSOCIATION

GOLF COACHES ASSOCIATION OF AMERICA

GOLF WRITERS ASSOCIATION OF AMERICA

MAJOR TELEVISION NETWORKS

TRADE ASSOCIATIONS

PROMINENT INTERNATIONAL GOLF ORGANIZATIONS

UNITED STATES GOLF ASSOCIATION

Golf House
Far Hills, NJ 07931
(201) 234-2300

KEY OFFICIALS:

P. J. Boatwright, Jr., executive director
John D. Laupheimer, deputy executive director
Alexander M. Radko, national director, USGA Green Section

OTHER KEY STAFF MEMBERS:

Stephen M. Foehl, regional affairs
George V. Grady, amateur status
Tom Meeks, rules and competitions
C. Edmund Miller, tournament entries
Peter A. Schaible, communications
Janet Seagle, museum and library
Charles W. Smith, membership and services
Robert T. Sommers, editor and publisher, *Golf Journal*
Frank Thomas, balls and implements

The USGA is an organization run by golfers for the benefit of golfers. It was formed on December 22, 1894, a year that saw two clubs proclaiming different U.S. amateur champions. Realizing the need for a central governing body to establish uniform rules for championships and to nurture the virtues of sportsmanship in golf, five clubs joined together to form the USGA.

Thus, from the beginning, the USGA has been an association of member clubs. Today, membership stands at approximately 4,800 clubs and courses.

As a nonprofit association dedicated to servicing the game of golf and individual golfers, the USGA acts in cooperation with local and regional golf associations in areas of mutual interest. It also serves as the representative of American golf in relations with the governing bodies in other countries.

The USGA is managed by an executive committee of 15 members, elected annually by the regular member-clubs. There are 24 standing subcommittees, composed of nearly 600 men and women throughout the country. All USGA committeemen donate their services and pay their own expenses.

The USGA's single most important goal is preserving the integrity and values of the game. Perhaps foremost among its activities is its rules-making responsibility. Through the years, the *Rules of Golf,* as approved by the USGA and the Royal and Ancient Golf Club of St. Andrews, Scotland, have been refined into a code that carefully guards the traditions of the sport. These rules are used in every golf-playing country of the world.

The USGA also developed and now maintains the national system of handicapping, which allows every golfer to compete on an equitable basis with other golfers.

Preservation of the element of skill in golf is also a goal of the USGA. This calls for constant testing of new balls, clubs, and other equipment, so that the traditional character of the game remains paramount. Without this maintenance of standards, "freak" balls and implements could make a mockery of individual skills and change the nature of the game.

Of course, amateurism is at the core of the USGA, which actively pursues its obligation to support the rules of amateur status, which define who is and who isn't an amateur.

Competition is the incentive for playing the game. In that interest, the USGA conducts 11 national championships annually:

CHAMPIONSHIP	HANDICAP LIMITS
Open	2
Amateur Public Links	None
Women's Amateur Public Links	None
Women's Open	4
Junior Amateur	9
Girls' Junior	16
Women's Amateur	5
Amateur	3
Senior Amateur	11
Senior Women's Amateur	16
Senior Open (starts in 1980)	8

MEMBERSHIP REQUIREMENTS: The Amateur, Senior Amateur, Women's Amateur, and Senior Women's Amateur are open to members of USGA regular member-clubs. The other championships have no membership requirement.

The USGA also sponsors four international amateur events:

· WITH GREAT BRITAIN: the Walker Cup for men and the Curtis Cup for women.
· WITH THE WORLD AMATEUR GOLF COUNCIL: the Eisenhower Trophy for the Men's World Amateur Team Championship and the Espirito Santo Trophy for the Women's World Amateur Team Championship.

Another function of the USGA has to do with turf and turf management. It provides on-the-course visits by experienced agronomists to USGA member-clubs subscribing to the Turfgrass service. These visits cover the entire range of golf-course maintenance, including soil testing, turf culture, seed, fertilizer, watering and control of pests, diseases, and weeds. Assistance by correspondence and telephone is available at no charge. The USGA Green Section Research and Education Fund, Inc., awards grants to universities and other recognized experimental centers to insure better turfgrasses, better maintenance and management practices, better playing conditions, and better golf courses for the future.

USGA ASSOCIATE PROGRAM FOR INDIVIDUAL GOLFERS

The Associate concept grew out of a study that recommended greater efforts by the USGA to inform the golfing public about who it is and what it does. The Associate program seeks to establish the USGA's work for golf clearly and to bridge the gap between USGA leadership and the golfing public by inviting individual golfers to become part of the new Associate category.

For a fee of $15.00 ($9.75 of which is tax-deductible), which goes to support the work of the USGA, the individual receives copies of the *Rules of Golf*, a subscription to the USGA's *Golf Journal*, a bagtag, decal and pocket patch marking the golfer as an Associate who supports the work of the USGA. Men, women and children can join the program.

Send fee or request for more information to:

> USGA Associates
> Golf House, Box 708
> Far Hills, NJ 07931

WESTERN GOLF ASSOCIATION
> Golf, IL 60029
> (312) 439-4600 and 724-4600

KEY OFFICIALS:

Marshall Dann, executive director
Roland F. McGuigan, educational director

This group, founded in 1899, now has a membership of some 500 private clubs, most of which are located in the Midwest. It conducts the Western Open, Amateur, and Junior championships every year, and sponsors and administers Evans Scholars Foundation (see Caddie Scholarships, p. 208).

STATE* GOLF ASSOCIATIONS
ALABAMA GOLF ASSOCIATION
> P.O. Box 1010
> Auburn, AL 36830
> Buddy Davidson, executive director

ALASKA STATE GOLF ASSOCIATION
> 1691 Crescent Drive
> Anchorage, Alaska 99504

ARIZONA GOLF ASSOCIATION
> P.O. Box 13236
> Phoenix, AZ 85002
> (602) 264-7607
> John W. Riggle, executive director

ARKANSAS STATE GOLF ASSOCIATION
> P.O. Box 943
> Little Rock, AK 72203
> (501) 378-1284
> Charles E. Wade, executive director

* Some active sectional and city groups are also included.

NORTHERN CALIFORNIA GOLF ASSOCIATION
> P.O. Box NCGA
> Pebble Beach, CA 93953
> (408) 625-GOLF
> Robert E. Hanna, executive director

Conducts numerous events and provides other services for 265 member-clubs representing 67,000 golfers. Currently building its own championship course on land purchased in Del Monte Forest.

SOUTHERN CALIFORNIA GOLF ASSOCIATION
> Golf House West
> 3740 Cahuenga Boulevard
> North Hollywood, CA 91604
> (213) 980-3630 or 877-0901
> Newell O. Pinch, executive director
> Thomas A. Morgan, assistant director

Has about 240 member-clubs representing 80,000 golfers in southern California. Conducts numerous tournaments and other activities in behalf of membership and golf generally. Publishes *Fore,* slick quarterly magazine (available to members only).

COLORADO GOLF ASSOCIATION
> Cherry Creek Drive
> 3955 E. Exposition Avenue
> Suite 416
> Denver, CO 80209
> (303) 744-3149

CONNECTICUT STATE GOLF ASSOCIATION
> 95 Howe Street
> New Haven, CT 06511
> (203) 562-4171
> W. H. Neale, executive director

DELAWARE STATE GOLF ASSOCIATION
> P.O. Box 325
> Wilmington, DE 19899
> (302) 652-8263
> Anthony L. Dominelli, secretary

DISTRICT OF COLUMBIA GOLF ASSOCIATION
> 3142 Patrick Henry Drive
> Falls Church, VA 22044

FLORIDA STATE GOLF ASSOCIATION
> 1734 Main Street
> P.O. Drawer 1298
> Sarasota, FL 33578
> (813) 958-6673
> W. P. Carey, executive director

GEORGIA STATE GOLF ASSOCIATION
> P.O. Box 6322
> Macon, GA 31208
> (912) 474-1146
> Floyd Doss, executive director

HAWAIIAN GOLF ASSOCIATION
P.O. Box 103
Honolulu, HI 96821

IDAHO GOLF ASSOCIATION
458 Highland
American Falls, ID 83211
(208) 226-2922
Ken Vanderhoff, executive director

NORTHERN ILLINOIS GOLF ASSOCIATION
P.O. Box 211
Golf, IL 60029

SOUTHERN ILLINOIS GOLF ASSOCIATION
1907 Logan Street
Murphysboro, IL 62966

CHICAGO DISTRICT GOLF ASSOCIATION
2100 Clearwater Drive
Suite 300
Oak Brook, IL 60521
(312) 920-0130
Denny Davenport, executive director
Carol McCue, associate executive director

INDIANA GOLF ASSOCIATION
316 S. Range Line Road, Suite D
Carmel, IN 46032
(317) 844-7271
Ray McDonald, executive director

IOWA GOLF ASSOCIATION
P.O. Box 837
Des Moines, IA 50304

KANSAS AMATEUR GOLF ASSOCIATION
1658 Withdean
Topeka, KS 66611
(913) 234-4293
E. J. Skradski, executive secretary

KANSAS CITY GOLF ASSOCIATION
5353 Nail Avenue
Shawnee Mission, KS 66202
(913) 432-3939
Loren Lamberth, executive director

KENTUCKY STATE GOLF ASSOCIATION
366 Starks Building
Louisville, KY 40202
(502) 583-1661
Martin J. Iuler, executive director

LOUISIANA STATE GOLF ASSOCIATION
1428 Johnston Street
Lafayette, LA 70503
(318) 235-4340
Frank Leach, executive director

MAINE STATE GOLF ASSOCIATION
156 Highland Avenue
Scarborough, ME 05074
Blaine Davis, tournament director

MARYLAND STATE GOLF ASSOCIATION
3 East Lexington Street
Baltimore, MD 21202
John A. Emich, executive director

MASSACHUSETTS GOLF ASSOCIATION
190 Park Road
Weston, MA 02193
(617) 891-4300
Richard D. Haskell, executive director

GOLF ASSOCIATION OF MICHIGAN
29563 Northwestern Highway, Suite 10
Southfield, MI 48034
(313) 353-0330
James D. Standish III, executive director

MINNESOTA GOLF ASSOCIATION
6550 York Avenue S, Suite 301
Edina, MN 55435
(612) 927-4644
Warren J. Rebholz, executive director

MISSISSIPPI GOLF ASSOCIATION
c/o *The Clarion-Ledger*
P.O. Box 40/Jackson, MS 39205
Carl Walters, executive director

MISSOURI STATE GOLF ASSOCIATION
Box 1425 S.S.S.
Springfield, MO 65805

ST. LOUIS DISTRICT GOLF ASSOCIATION
465 Mason Road South
Creve Coeur, MO 63141
(314) 434-2233
Jim Benson, secretary

MONTANA STATE GOLF ASSOCIATION
660 Dewey Boulevard
Butte, MT 59701
(406) 792-0463
Fraser MacDonald

NEBRASKA AMATEUR GOLF ASSOCIATION
211 West 3rd, Box 1492
Grand Island, NB 68801
(308) 382-2330
Del W. Ryder, executive secretary

NEVADA STATE GOLF ASSOCIATION
P.O. Box 2231
Reno, NV 89505
Del Machabee, president

NEW HAMPSHIRE GOLF ASSOCIATION
45 Kearney Street
Manchester, NH 03104

NEW JERSEY STATE GOLF ASSOCIATION
539 Valley Road
Upper Montclair, NJ 07043
(201) 744-1010
Carol Rhodes, executive director

SUN COUNTRY (NEW MEXICO) GOLF
ASSOCIATION
　　1605 Carlisle Boulevard NE
　　Albuquerque, NM 87106
　　(505) 262-1497
　　Jeff Rivard, executive director

NEW YORK STATE GOLF ASSOCIATION
　　Drawer J, Lansingburg Station
　　Troy, NY 12182

METROPOLITAN GOLF ASSOCIATION
　　60 E. 42nd Street
　　New York, NY 10017
　　(212) 867-0740
　　James E. McLoughlin, executive director

CAROLINA GOLF ASSOCIATION
　　Box 844
　　Clemmons, NC 27012
　　(919) 766-5992
　　Hale B. Van Hoy, Jr., executive director

NORTH DAKOTA STATE GOLF ASSOCIATION
　　P.O. Box 2231
　　Fargo, ND 58102
　　Lou Miller, secretary-treasurer

OHIO GOLF ASSOCIATION
　　50 West Broad Street, Suite 2920
　　Columbus, OH 43215
　　(614) 221-7661
　　Nicholas Popa, executive director

GREATER CINCINNATI GOLFERS LEAGUE
　　P.O. Box 6218
　　Cincinnati, OH 45206
　　(513) 321-8193
　　Ben F. Turner, executive director

CLEVELAND DISTRICT GOLF ASSOCIATION
　　2483 Lee Boulevard
　　Cleveland Heights, OH 44118
　　(216) 932-3900
　　Henry J. Meiers, executive director

TOLEDO DISTRICT GOLF ASSOCIATION
　　P.O. Box 6313
　　Toledo, OH 43614
　　(419) 381-1391
　　Mrs. Jan Taylor, executive director

OKLAHOMA STATE GOLF ASSOCIATION
　　1501 Classen Avenue, Room 106
　　Oklahoma City, OK 73106
　　(405) 755-3070
　　Joe V. Evans, executive secretary

OREGON GOLF ASSOCIATION
　　614 Executive Building
　　Portland, OR 97204
　　(503) 222-1139
　　Dale Johnson, executive director

PENNSYLVANIA GOLF ASSOCIATION
　　Box 2
　　King of Prussia, PA 19406
　　(215) 265-9520
　　James D. Sykes, executive director

WESTERN PENNSYLVANIA GOLF
ASSOCIATION
　　1378 Freeport Road, Suite 1D
　　Pittsburgh, PA 15238
　　(412) 963-9806
　　A. J. Luppino, executive director

PUERTO RICO GOLF ASSOCIATION
　　GPO Box G 3862
　　San Juan, PR 00936

RHODE ISLAND GOLF ASSOCIATION
　　710 Hospital Trust Building
　　Providence, RI 02903
　　Edward Perry, secretary

SOUTH CAROLINA GOLF ASSOCIATION
　　314 Cheyenne Road
　　North Augusta, SC 29841
　　(803) 593-9910
　　Happ Lathrop, executive director

SOUTHERN GOLF ASSOCIATION
　　P.O. Box 9151
　　Birmingham, AL 35213
　　(205) 328-9405
　　Grantland Rice II, executive secretary

Some 400 member-clubs from 14 southern states;
conducts Southern Amateur, Senior, Junior and Southern States Four-Ball championships.

SOUTH DAKOTA GOLF ASSOCIATION
　　P.O. Drawer T
　　Sioux Falls, SD 57101
　　(605) 336-2720
　　Don H. Platt, executive secretary

TENNESSEE GOLF ASSOCIATION
　　P.O. Box 50574
　　Nashville, TN 37205
　　(615) 353-0903
　　Dick Horton, executive director

TEXAS GOLF ASSOCIATION
　　3914 Live Oak
　　Dallas, TX 75204
　　(214) 823-6004
　　Wally Murray, executive director

HOUSTON GOLF ASSOCIATION
　　710 N. Post Oak Road, Suite 100
　　Houston, TX 77024
　　(713) 688-7100

UTAH GOLF ASSOCIATION
1518 South 11th East
Salt Lake City, UT 84105
(801) 466-1132
Richard H. Alexander, executive director

VERMONT GOLF ASSOCIATION
61 Elm Street
Springfield, VT 05156

VIRGINIA STATE GOLF ASSOCIATION
Box 5527
Charlottesville, VA 22902
(804) 977-2348
Wallace W. McDowell, executive director

WASHINGTON STATE GOLF ASSOCIATION
308 Columbia Street
Seattle, WA 98104

WEST VIRGINIA GOLF ASSOCIATION
P.O. Box 431
Charleston, WV 25322
Albert Schwabee II, president

WISCONSIN STATE GOLF ASSOCIATION
7630 W. Capitol Drive
Milwaukee, WI 53222
(414) 463-0455
Eugene Haas, executive director

WYOMING STATE GOLF ASSOCIATION
726 North Gould Street
Sheridan, WY 82801
(307) 672-9553
Bernard Speilman, president

NATIONAL GOLF FOUNDATION
200 Castlewood Drive
North Palm Beach, FL 33408
(305) 844-2500

KEY OFFICIALS:
Don A. Rossi, executive director
Harry Eckhoff, information services
Priscilla Pilgrim, educational services coordinator
Ed Wells, research

REGIONAL DIRECTORS:

Lorraine Abbott	Joe Much
1017 North Euclid Avenue	938 Alberta Avenue East
Oak Park, IL 60302	Monmouth, OR 97361
(312) 386-4960	(503) 838-0136
Mark DePalma	Steve V. Mrak
1675 Eleanor Avenue	5814 Cary Grant Drive
St. Paul, MN 55116	San Antonio, TX 78240
(612) 699-1032	(512) 681-1703
David B. Hueber	Larry Smith
6707 Clover Court	2413 Timbercrest Circle West
Carlsbad, CA 92008	Clearwater, FL 33515
(714) 438-5369	(813) 733-5714
John LaPoint	Syl Wagasky
75 Waterville Street	527 Williamsburg Lane
North Grafton, MA 01536	Odenton, MD 21113
(617) 839-3367	(301) 674-6098

CLUB MANAGEMENT:
Gerald V. Marlatt
435 Deerfield Road
Deerfield, IL 60015
(312) 945-5182

The purpose of the NGF is to maintain a national clearinghouse for golf information and to initiate and operate programs that will enhance the growth of golf, specifically by:

· Increasing golf play
· Assisting in the development of golf facilities of all types wherever they are needed
· Offering consultant service and information pertaining to the instructional aspects of the game
· Conducting necessary research

The NGF was founded in 1936 as a nonprofit organization by the major manufacturers of golf equipment to stimulate golf activity, and is today supported by these same sponsors and others interested in the sound and continued growth of golf. The NGF coordinates its efforts with all the major national golf groups. It has expended $8 million for golf promotion and development, and its annual budget has grown from $10,000 in 1936 to over $800,000 today.

Trained regional directors of the NGF are available to golf-course planning groups. Their duties include:

· Meeting with individuals, private groups, or community organizations to assist in the preliminary planning of new golf facilities.
· Providing overall guidance in determining need, feasibility, and potential use of planned facilities.
· Presenting facts and figures on construction costs, methods of financing, and operation.
· Keeping abreast of the golf market in their respective areas.

The NGF Instruction Service for schools, colleges, golf facilities, and any other sponsoring group offers various programs involving outstanding PGA or LPGA professionals or noted physical educators. Programs include teaching teachers, discussing coaching methods, instructing golfers, lecture/demonstrations, workshop/seminars, and player clinics.

The NGF has published numerous planning and operational aids available to interested persons at low cost. Titles include the following:

Planning and Building the Golf Course
Planning Information for Private and Daily Fee Golf Clubs
Organizing and Operating Municipal Golf Courses
Golf Operations Handbook
Par-3 and Executive Golf Course Manual
Miniature Putting Course Manual
Golf Driving Range Manual

The Professional Golf Shop
Golf Coach's Guide
Golf Instructor's Guide
Golf Lessons
Planning and Conducting Competitive Golf Events
Planning and Conducting Junior Golf Programs
Easy Way to Learn Golf Rules

Also available are over 140 new or updated NGF Information Sheets on specific subjects pertaining to various phases of golf-facility planning, financing, maintenance, operation, statistics, activities, and research.

NATIONAL CLUB ASSOCIATION

1129 Twentieth Street NW
Washington, DC 20036
(202) 466-8424

KEY OFFICIALS:
Gerald F. Hurley, executive director
Steven N. Ahlberg, director of public affairs

Founded in 1961, the National Club Association represents the tax, legal, legislative, and policy interests of private-club officers, directors, and owners. Sixty percent of NCA members are golf clubs; the remainder are city, yacht, athletic and other types of social/recreational clubs.

The NCA has three goals: promoting private-club interests, informing private-club leaders, and solving common private-club problems. As the lobbying arm of the club industry, NCA represents club interests before Congress and the various federal agencies to minimize governmental intrusion into club operations. NCA members also have access to the latest in-depth information specifically tailored to private clubs, via monthly newsletters and bimonthly reference-series articles. Through the NCA's Golf, City, and Yacht Club divisions, members can work together to solve common problems such as escalating property taxes. The NCA also has a group-officers and directors liability-insurance program for member clubs.

The NCA is directed by a 17-man board composed of club owners, attorneys, association executives, executive managers, and corporate officers.

PGA TOUR

100 Nina Court
Ponte Vedra Beach, FL 32082
(904) 285-3700

KEY OFFICIALS:
Deane R. Beman, commissioner
Clyde Mangrum, deputy commissioner for tour operations
Jack Tuthill, tournament director
Labron Harris, Jr., director of tournament administration
Richard Wammock, tournament manager
Judith Dixon, executive assistant

COMMUNICATIONS STAFF:
Joe Schwendeman, director
Tom Place, public information director
John Goldstein, media official
Mrs. Lou Bressler, public information secretary

The PGA tour, with the cooperation of interested local organizations throughout the country, governs and administers tournaments nearly every week for 10 months of the year. Policy for the tour is set by a 10-man tournament policy board. Four players, known as player directors, are included on this board. Three independent businessmen sitting on the board—all avid amateur golfers—are known as indepedent directors. Three elected officers of the PGA of America also serve on the board.

The tour evolved slowly and sometimes painfully over the last 60 years, starting from an unorganized number of tournaments that were operated independently by resort owners, businessmen with an eye to free advertising, chambers of commerce with visions of headlines to lure people to their cities, and interested golfers who had the funds to put up for the fun of seeing how professional golfers handled—or were handled—by their courses.

The present structure for the tour was laid down in 1969. At that time, the annual purse was just over $5 million. A decade later, the total hit $13 million.

LADIES PROFESSIONAL GOLF ASSOCIATION

919 Third Avenue
New York, NY 10022
(212) 751-8181

KEY OFFICIALS:
Ray Volpe, commissioner
Chip Campbell, director of public relations
Jeff Adams, public relations coordinator
Ruffin Beckwith, publicity coordinator
Betsy Rawls, tournament director

MARKETING SERVICES (PEOPLE & PROPERTIES, INC.):
Tony Andrea, president
Edd Griles, VP, director of creative/broadcasting services
Ron Cotrone, VP, marketing

The LPGA is a nonprofit association, now in its 28th year, whose purpose is to promote and publicize the professional side of women in golf. Its membership presently consists of 155 touring pros and 200 club pros. Of the 155 touring professionals, 65 percent have been on tour less than three years, and 50 percent are under the age of 25, which is indicative of the growth and youthfulness of the tour.

In 1979, the LPGA played for a record $4.2 million in prize monies. This represents nearly a 400 percent increase since 1975.

TOURING-PRO MANAGEMENT GROUPS

MEN

MANAGERS AND THEIR CLIENTS

William C. Boone, Jr.
3300 First National Tower Building
Louisville, KY 40202
(502) 589-4200
> Frank Beard
> Homero Blancas
> Charles Coody
> Al Geiberger
> Bobby Nichols
> Dave Stockton

W. E. (Gene) Bushman
P.O. Box 3918
Brownsville, TX 78520
(512) 350-4000 ext. 2237
> John Schlee

James F. DeLeone, Esq.
17 South High Street
Columbus, OH 43215
(614) 221-2341
> Ed Sneed
> Tom Weiskopf

Lee Elder Enterprises, Inc.
1725 K Street NW, Suite 1201
Washington, DC 20006
(202) 857-0745
> Lee Elder

Eddie Elias Enterprises
1720 Merriman Road
Akron, OH 44313
(216) 836-9321; NYC, (212) 245-1710
> Marty Fleckman
> Hubert Green
> Bill Kratzert
> John Mahaffey
> Chi Chi Rodriguez

Golden Bear, Inc.
1208 US Highway One
North Palm Beach, FL 33408
(305) 626-3900
> Jack Nicklaus

David Gramm, Esq.
Wisconsin Bank Building #410
One South Pickney Street
Madison, WI 53701
(608) 257-9521
> Andy North

Ed Hardin
413 21st Street, N
Birmingham, AL 35216
(205) 328-2674
> Mac McLendon

International Management Group
One Erieview Plaza, Suite 1300
Cleveland, OH 44114
(216) 522-1200

Tommy Aaron	Dave Marr
Buddy Allin	Graham Marsh
George Burns	Jim Nelford
Bob Byman	Peter Oosterhuis
Bob Charles	Arnold Palmer
Ray Floyd	Gary Player
Buddy Gardner	Bill Rogers
Phil Hancock	Bob Rosburg
Jerry Heard	Bill Sander
Hale Irwin	Curtis Strange
Peter Jacobsen	Lanny Wadkins
John Lister	

International Golf Travel, Inc.
13450 Maxella Avenue
Marina del Rey, CA 90291
(213) 821-4511
> Craig Stadler

O'Neil-Simkowki Marketing Group
711 South Boulevard
Oak Park, IL 60302
(312) 383-2070
> Andy Bean

Arnold Palmer Enterprises
P.O. Box 52
Youngstown, PA 15696
(412) 537-7751
> Arnold Palmer

Karsten-Ping Management
10416 N. 46th Drive
Glendale, AZ 85302
(602) 247-0861

Danny Edwards	Joe Inman, Jr.
Bill Garrett	Tom Jenkins
Bob Gilder	Doug Tewell

Pros, Inc.
One James River Plaza
P.O. Box 673
Richmond, VA 23206
(804) 643-7600

Tom Kite	Allen Miller
Gary Koch	Jerry Pate
Roger Maltbie	Eddie Pearce
Lee Mikles	Bobby Wadkins

Charles Rubin, Esq.
1726 Commerce Tower
Kansas City, MO 64105
(816) 421-4770
> Tom Watson

Eugene Selvage
Box 2420
Reno, NV 89505
(702) 826-4300
     George Archer

TAP
Technical Athletic Programs
777 N. First Street, Suite 270
San Jose, CA 95112
(408) 297-2213

| Larry Nelson | Bob E. Smith |
| Jack Renner | Bob Wynn |

Lee Trevino, Inc.
1341 West Mockingbird Lane, Suite 718E
Dallas, TX 75247
(214) 634-2432
     Lee Trevino

Uni-Managers International
10880 Wilshire Blvd., Suite 1800
Los Angeles, CA 90024
(213) 475-9555

Severiano Ballesteros	Orville Moody
Billy Casper	Mark Pfeil
Lou Graham	Mike Reid
Bert Greene	John Schroeder
Morris Hatalsky	Jim Simons
Dave Hill	Sam Snead
Barry Jaeckel	

WOMEN

MANAGERS AND THEIR CLIENTS
International Management Group
One Erieview Plaza
Cleveland, OH 44114
(216) 522-1200

Laura Baugh	Nancy Lopez
Janet Coles	Michelle Walker
Marlene Floyd	Donna C. Young
Lauren Howe	

Pros, Inc.
536 Granite Avenue
Richmond, VA 23226
(804) 282-7607
     Debbie Massey

Anthony Rivizzigno
647 S. Warren Street
Syracuse, NY 13202
(315) 422-1321
     Silvia Bertolaccini
     Jane Blalock
     Sally Little
     Cathy Mant
     Mary Bea Porter
     JoAnn Washam

PROFESSIONAL GOLFERS ASSOCIATION OF AMERICA

804 Federal Highway
Box 12458
Lake Park, FL 33403
(305) 844-5000

KEY OFFICIALS:
Mark H. Cox, executive director
Kevin Foley, assistant executive director

OTHER KEY STAFF MEMBERS:
Barbara Bell, apprentice program
Thomas Boyle, comptroller, PGA Merchandise Show director
Earl Collings, communications director
Dick Hale, editor, *Professional Golfer* magazine
Lloyd Lambert, executive secretary
Linda Leister, membership department
Joe O'Brien, education director
Jim Warters, news director
Gary Wiren, club and professional relations

The PGA was organized in 1916 to elevate standards of the profession and to promote golf. Most of its 8,200 members are club professionals who run the business of golf at local clubs and courses. The PGA has more than 4,000 apprentices in membership-training programs and spends more than $500,000 annually on educational programs. From a headquarters staffed by over 50 employees, it runs national and local tournaments and junior golf schools, and sponsors the PGA championship and the World Series of Golf with its partner, the PGA tour. Publishes *PGA* magazine (monthly), *Book of Golf* (annual), and a large assortment of booklets and other literature.

The PGA is organized on a regional basis into 36 sections, each with its own officers and officials, as listed below.

PGA SECTION EXECUTIVE DIRECTORS AND SECRETARIES

ALOHA
     Jim Reilly, executive director
     Box 10657
     Honolulu, HI 96816

CAROLINAS
     John Derr, executive director
     P.O. Box 209
     North Myrtle Beach, SC 29582

CENTRAL NEW YORK
     John LaValle, executive director
     111 Chapel Drive
     Syracuse, NY 13219

COLORADO
Myran Craig, executive director
40 Inverness Drive, East Suite 50
Englewood, CO 80110

CONNECTICUT
Robert Shea
P.O. Box 660
Niantic, CT 06357

DIXIE
Chick Ritter, executive secretary
Prattville C.C.
Highway 82
Prattville, AL 36067

FLORIDA
Roger Ganem, executive director
4381 Sandlering Circle E.
Quail Ridge 725
Boynton Beach, FL 33436

GATEWAY
Bonnie J. Davis, executive secretary
P.O. Box 5699
St. Louis, MO 63121

GEORGIA
Bob Bonifay, executive director
P.O. Box 5601/Macon, GA 31208

GULF STATES
Oliver Counce, executive secretary
c/o Southern Specialty Sales
P.O. Box 19965
New Orleans, LA 70179

ILLINOIS
Ken Boyce, executive director
2021 Spring Road, Suite 417
Oak Brook, IL 60521

INDIANA
Ray McDonald, executive director
316 South Range Line Road, Suite D
Carmen, IN 46032

IOWA
Joan Wilhite, executive secretary
1015 West State
Mason City, IA 50401

KENTUCKY
Ernest Denham, executive secretary
366 Starks Building
Louisville, KY 40402

METROPOLITAN
Charles Robson, executive director
Box C-25, Wykagyl Station
New Rochelle, NY 10804

MICHIGAN
Douglas M. Findlay, executive director
Golf House, 29563 Northwestern Highway
Southfield, MI 48075

MIDDLE ATLANTIC
David M. Leonard, executive director
8218 Wisconsin Avenue, Suite 405
Bethesda, MD 20014

MID-WEST
Carol McGinnis, executive secretary
1000 West 88th Street
Kansas City, MO 64114

NEBRASKA
John Schumacher, executive director
2453 St. Marys Avenue
Omaha, NB 68105

NEW ENGLAND
George Wemyss, executive director
P.O. Box 81
Wakefield, MA 01880

NEW JERSEY
Robert Comstock, executive director
1 Bank Street
Rockaway, NJ 07866

NORTHERN CALIFORNIA
Lyle Wehrman, executive director
P.O. Box N
Sunol, CA 94586

NORTHERN OHIO
Detra Macheskee
24816 Aurora Road
Bedford Heights, OH 44146

NORTHERN TEXAS
James McAfee, executive director
2815 Valley View Lane, Suite 214
Dallas, TX 75234

PACIFIC NORTHWEST
Dale Johnson, executive secretary
614 Executive Building
Portland, OR 97204

PHILADELPHIA
John W. Klein, executive director
354 W. Lancaster Avenue
Haverford, PA 19041

ROCKY MOUNTAIN
William L. Korns, executive director
P.O. Box 1363
Provo, UT 84601

SOUTH CENTRAL
Eleanor Drew, executive secretary
3015 E. Skelly Drive
300 Center Suite 280
Tulsa, OK 74105

SOUTHERN CALIFORNIA
Ronald E. O'Connor
3740 Cahuenga Boulevard, Suite 104
North Hollywood, CA 91604

SOUTHERN OHIO
Bill Miller, executive director
317 Colonial Lane
Dayton, OH 45429

SOUTHERN TEXAS
Wilbur Wright
P.O. Box 23176
San Antonio, TX 78223

SOUTHWEST
Vi Wahl, executive secretary
204 W. Buist Avenue
Phoenix, AZ 85041

SUN COUNTRY
Jeffery L. Rivard, executive director
1605 Carlisle Boulevard NE
Albuquerque, NM 87106

TENNESSEE
Dick Horton, executive director
Box 50574
Nashville, TN 37205

TRI-STATE
Dennis Darak, executive director
221 Sherwood Dr.
Monaca, PA 15061

WISCONSIN
Robert Brandenburg, executive director
3489 North 76th Street
Milwaukee, WI 53222

GOLF COURSE SUPERINTENDENTS ASSOCIATION OF AMERICA

1617 St. Andrews Drive
Lawrence, KS 60644
(913) 841-2240

KEY OFFICIALS:
Conrad L. Scheetz, executive director
Palmer Maples, Jr., education
James R. Brooks, marketing and sales
John M. Schilling, communications

The Golf Course Superintendents Association of America, formed in 1926, is a professional organization that helps superintendents attain educational and professional growth. The GCSAA hosts an annual international turfgrass conference and frequent educational seminars. It sponsors research projects; produces numerous publications, including *Golf Course Management* (formerly *The Golf Superintendent*); and administers a lending library. Its employment-referral service helps those members seeking a club assignment or a challenging new position. In 1971, GCSAA established its certification program to identify progressive superintendents and to formulate standards of excellence in the golf-turf management profession.

CLUB MANAGERS ASSOCIATION OF AMERICA

7615 Winterberry Place
Washington, DC 20034
(301) 229-3600

Horace G. Duncan, executive director

This group represents 3,000 managers of private membership clubs (about 50 per cent within the golf industry), encourages the education and advancement of members, and assists club officers and members to secure efficient and successful operation through their managers. Publishes *Club Management* (monthly).

AMERICAN SOCIETY OF GOLF COURSE ARCHITECTS

221 North La Salle Street
Chicago, IL 60601
(312) 372-7090

Paul Fullmer, executive secretary

The society is an association of course-architects dedicated to high standards in that profession and in the game of golf. It works toward this goal through both internal and external programs. Internally, the society conducts a series of ongoing informational programs, primarily in the area of professional development. These programs culminate at the annual meeting in seminar programs where critical questions are discussed by experts from within the society, as well as outside speakers.

Externally, the society publishes brochures that assist communities and developers in planning new golf courses. It also publishes material that aids those planning to remodel their present courses. Sample titles: *Selecting Your Golf Course Architect, Planning the Real Estate Development Golf Course,* and *Planning the Municipal Golf Course.*

The society also provides speakers for those golf-oriented groups that would like to know more about design, and presents the Donald Ross Award annually to those who have furthered the understanding of golf course architecture.

GOLF COURSE BUILDERS OF AMERICA

725 15th Street NW
Washington, DC 20005
(202) 638-0555

Harry J. Lambeth, executive director

1978 MEMBERSHIP

H. E. Bishop Co., Inc.
1025 N. West End Boulevard
Quakertown, PA 18951

Robert Vincent Co., Inc.
Benton, PA 17814
(717) 925-6411

Underwood Golf Course Construction
P.O. Box 571
Bowie, TX 76230
(817) 872-2241 or 872-1809

David Canavan, President
Moore Golf, Inc.
P.O. Drawer 916
Culpeper, VA 22701
(703) 825-9211

Edward A. Hunnicutt, Inc.
1811 E. Holyoke, Unit 6
P.O. Box 7283
Spokane, WA 99211
(509) 487-5459

Cellsystem
986 Baycrest Drive
North Vancouver, B.C., Canada V7G 1N8
(604) 929-7215

Siemens' Contracting, Inc.
2559 S. East Avenue
Fresno, CA 93706
(209) 233-8461

Robert L. Elder & Sons, Inc.
Rt. 2, Box 438, Durberry Road
Smithsburg, MD 21783
(301) 739-0032

White Turf Engineering, Inc.
3 Summer Drive
Winchendon, MA 01475

Barnard Construction Co., Inc.
289 Sunset Road
Pompton Plains, NJ 07444
(201) 835-0888

Nielsen Construction Co.
56 Forester Avenue
Warwick, NY 10990
(914) 986-2232

Hendrix and Dail, Inc.
Box 631
Greenville, NC 27834
(919) 758-4263

R & G Construction Co.
P.O. Box 5524, 1700 N. Graham Street
Charlotte, NC 28206

OTHER CONTRACTORS

Keith V. Dewar
Keith Dewar Construction
73-525 Dalea Lane
Palm Desert, CA 92260

George Fazio
308 Tequesta Drive
Tequesta, FL 33458

Golden Bear, Inc., and Golforce, Inc. (Jack Nicklaus)
1208 U.S. Highway #1
North Palm Beach, FL 33408

Joseph Lee
P.O. Drawer 1270
Boynton Beach, FL 33435

Stanley Wadsworth
The Wadsworth Company
Van Dyke Road
Plainfield, IL 60544

Robert D. Beard, President
Robert D. Beard, Inc.
1241 Pinehurst Drive
Fort Wayne, IN 46805

Irwin R. Venske & Jack Murray
U.S. Golf Course Const. Co.
7330 Indianapolis Boulevard
Hammond, IN 46324

L. R. Fleming, Jr.
Fleming Irrigation, Inc.
6511 Line Avenue
Shreveport, LA 71106

Russell Roberts
Russell Roberts Co., Inc.
Turkey Foot Road
Gaithersburg, MD 10760

Loren Youngblood
Youngblood's Excavating & Well Drilling Co.
P.O. Box 47
Reeds Spring, MO 65737

William M. Kubly
Landscapes Unlimited, Inc.
6125 Andrews Court
Lincoln, NE 68512

William Parker
Midwest Golf
4904 Swisher Road
Cable. OH 43009

James T. Robinson
Tait, Inc.
500 Webster Street
Dayton, OH 45401

X. G. Hassenplug
Hassenplug Associates
1300 Freeport Road
Pittsburgh, PA 15238

Wallace Gunderson
Gunderson's, Inc.
2820 West Main
Rapid City, SD 57701

PROFESSIONAL GOLF CLUB REPAIRMEN'S ASSOCIATION

P.O. Box 6504
Clearwater, FL 33518

Irv Schloss, executive director

This group was organized in 1978 for men and women who either work full-time at golf-club repair or custom clubmaking, or do repairs in their jobs as professionals. Its purpose is to exchange ideas, techniques, methods, etc., among members, as well as keep abreast of new materials and equipment used in repair. Founder Irv Schloss is a veteran golf professional and golf businessman of Dunedin, Fla. The *Pro Golf Club Repairman,* the group's official publication, appears quarterly, edited by Chuck Albury.

GOLF COACHES ASSOCIATION OF AMERICA

c/o Dick Gordin, secretary/treasurer
Ohio Wesleyan University
Department of Athletics
Delaware, OH 43015
(614) 369-4431, Ext. 500

Composed of about 140 top college-golf coaches.

GOLF WRITERS ASSOCIATION OF AMERICA

1720 Section Road, Suite 210
Cincinnati, OH 45237
(513) 631-4400

Bob Rickey, secretary

The GWAA has about 400 members, meets twice a year, publishes newsletters and a membership directory, and annually presents the Ben Hogan Award (for the golfer who has overcome physical handicaps to play), the William Richardson Award (for service to golf), and the Charlie Bartlett Award (for humanitarian service outside golf).

GWAA MEMBERS

Listed below are GWAA members working for daily newspapers, as shown in current membership directory.

CALIFORNIA
Shav Glick
Los Angeles Times
Times Mirror Square
Los Angeles, CA 90053

Bill Shirley
Los Angeles Times
Times Mirror Square
Los Angeles, CA 90053

John Nettles
San Diego *Union*
350 Camino de la Reina
San Diego, CA 92108

Richard Smith
San Diego *Union*
4502 Berwick Drive
San Diego, CA 92117

Nelson Cullenward
San Francisco *Examiner*
P.O. Box 3100, Rincon
   Annex
San Francisco, CA 94119

Art Spander
San Francisco *Chronicle*
901 Mission Street
San Francisco, CA 94119

Ira Miller
San Francisco *Chronicle*
901 Mission Street
San Francisco, CA 94119

Fred Merrick
San Jose *Mercury*
750 Ridder Park Drive
San Jose, CA 95131

Steve Mona
Tri-Valley *Herald*
325 S. I Street
Livermore, CA 94550

Hal Davee
Poway *News*
P.O. Box 685
Poway, CA 92064

COLORADO
Ralph Moore
Denver *Post*
P.O. Box 1709
Denver, CO 80201

CONNECTICUT
Bruce Berlet
The Hartford Courant
285 Broad Street
Hartford, CT 06115

William Guthrie
Register & Journal-Courier
367 Orange Street
New Haven, CT 06503

Dave Solomon
New Haven *Register*
367 Orange Street
New Haven, CT 06503

John O'Brien
New London *Day*
17 High Street
Hartford, CT 06103

DELAWARE
Tom Tomashek
News-Journal
831 Orange Street
Wilmington, DE 19899

FLORIDA
Mike Jamison
Boca Raton *News*
34 S.E. Second Street
Boca Raton, FL 33432

Vince Smith
Fort Myers *News-Press*
P.O. Box 10
Fort Myers, FL 33902

Rex Edmondson
Jacksonville *Journal*
1 Riverside Avenue
Jacksonville, FL 32202

Greg Larson
Florida *Times-Union*
Box 1949
Jacksonville, FL 32201

Fred Seely
Florida *Times-Union*
Box 1949
Jacksonville, FL 32201

Stuart Schneider
Lakeland *Ledger*
Box 408
Lakeland, FL 33802

Edwin Pope
Miami *Herald*
1 Herald Plaza
Miami, FL 33101

James Achenbach
Sarasota *Herald-Tribune*
Drawer 1719
Sarasota, FL 33578

Hubert Mizell
St. Petersburg *Times*
P.O. Box 1121
St. Petersburg, FL 33731

Dr. Don Veller
Tallahassee *Democrat*
Tallahassee, FL 32304

Tom McEwen
Tampa *Tribune*
P.O. Box 191
Tampa, FL 33602

Richard Mudry
Tampa *Times*
P.O. Box 191
Tampa, FL 33601

Larry Bush
Palm Beach *Times*
2751 S. Dixie Highway
West Palm Beach, FL 44302

GEORGIA
Furman Bisher
Atlanta *Journal*
P.O. Box 4689
Atlanta, GA 30302

Al Ludwick
Augusta *Chronicle*
P.O. Box 936
Augusta, GA 30903

Harley Bowers
Macon *Telegraph*
Broadway at Riverside
Macon, GA 31208

Mike Waldron
Marietta *Daily Journal*
P.O. Box 449
Marietta, GA 30060

ILLINOIS
John Husar
Chicago Tribune
435 N. Michigan Boulevard
Chicago, IL 60611

Forrest R. Kyle
Decatur *Herald-Review*
Box 311
Decatur, IL 62525

L. Allan Klope
Alton *Telegraph*
631 Broadway
East Alton, IL 62024

INDIANA
Bill Fluty
Evansville *Courier*
201 N.W. Second Street
Evansville, IN 47705

Jim Costin
Ft. Wayne *News-Sentinel*
600 West Main Street
Fort Wayne, IN 46802

Wayne Fuson
Indianapolis *News*
307 W. Pennsylvania St.
Indianapolis, IN 46204

Eugene Pulliam
Indianapolis *News*
307 Pennsylvania Street
Indianapolis, IN 46206

IOWA
Maury White
Des Moines *Register & Tribune*
P.O. Box 957
Des Moines, IA 50304

Gus Schrader
Cedar Rapids *Gazette*
Cedar Rapids, IA 52406

KANSAS
Bob Hentzen
Topeka *Capital-Journal*
Sixth & Jefferson
Topeka, KS 66607

KENTUCKY
Julian Pitzer
Daily News
Chester Avenue
Middlesboro, KY 40965

MARYLAND
Bob Maisel
Baltimore *Sun*
Calvert & Center Streets
Baltimore, MD 21043

John W. Stewart
Baltimore *Morning Sun*
2904 Knoll Acres Drive
Baltimore, MD 21234

MASSACHUSETTS
William Brotherton
Beverly *Evening Times*
Dunham Road
Beverly, MA 01915

John Ahern
Boston *Globe*
135 Morrissey Boulevard
Boston, MA 02107

Ray Fitzgerald
Boston *Globe*
135 Morrissey Boulevard
Boston, MA 02107

Ray Fitzgerald
Boston *Globe*
135 Morrissey Boulevard
Boston, MA 02107

John E. McCarthy
Boston *Herald-American*
300 Harrison Avenue
Boston, MA 02106

Ernest A. Roberts
Boston *Globe*
135 Morrissey Boulevard
Boston, MA 02107

Frank Stoddard, Jr.
Brockton *Enterprise*
60 Main Street
Brockton, MA 02401

Nancy O'Connell
Transit-Telegram
120 Whiting Farm Road
Holyoke, MA 01040

George McGuane
The Lowell Sun
15 Kearney Square
Lowell, MA 01852

Roger Barry
The Patriot-Ledger
13 Temple Street
Quincy, MA 02169

Gary S. Larrabee
The Salem Evening News
155 Washington Street
Salem, MA 01970

Gerry Finn
Springfield *Union*
P.O. Box 2350
Springfield, MA 01101

Stan Hunt
Springfield *Union*
1860 Main Street
Springfield, MA 01101

Stephen Kelly
Springfield *Daily News*
1860 Main Street
Springfield, MA 01101

James Regan
Springfield *News*
P.O. Box 2499
Springfield, MA 01101

James F. Cunningham
Worcester *Telegram*
20 Franklin Street
Worcester, MA 01601

MICHIGAN
Jack Saylor
Free Press Sports Dept.
321 West Lafayette
Detroit, MI 48231

Jack Berry
Detroit *News*
615 Lafayette Boulevard
Detroit, MI 48231

Bruce L. Johns
The Flint Journal
200 E. First Street
Flint, MI 48501

Bill Cornwell
Grand Rapids *Press*
Press Plaza, Vandenberg
  Center
Grand Rapids, MI 49502

Fred Stabley
The State Journal
120 East Lenawee
Lansing, MI 48910

MINNESOTA
Carl Peterson
St. Paul *Pioneer Press*
63 E. Fourth Street
St. Paul, MN 55101

MISSISSIPPI
Jerry Potter
The Clarion-Ledger
Box 40
Jackson, MS 39205

Danny McKenzie
The Daily Journal
P.O. Box 909
Tupelo, MS 38801

MISSOURI
Bill Beck
St. Louis *Post-Dispatch*
1133 Franklin Avenue
St. Louis, MO 63101

NEVADA
Bob Coffin
Las Vegas *Review-Journal*
1820 E. Desert Inn Road
Las Vegas, NV 89109

NEW JERSEY
John S. Brodhead
The Courier-News
Box 6600
Bridgewater, NJ 08807

Al DeSantis
Times Herald-Record
40 Mulberry Street
Middletown, NJ 07748

Jack Lutton
The Home News
P.O. Box 551
New Brunswick, NJ 08903

NEW YORK
Ben Danforth
Knickerbocker *News-Union
  Star*
645 Shaker Road
Albany, NY 12211

Joseph D. Ravella
Capital Newspapers
645 Shaker Road
Albany, NY 12201

Al Mottau
The Saratogian
Route #1
Ballston Spa, NY 12020

Dan Lauck
Newsday
550 Stewart Avenue
Garden City, NY 11530

Ed Golemboski
Times *Herald-Record*
40 Mulberry Street
Middletown, NY 10940

Dave Anderson
New York Times
229 W. 43rd Street
New York, NY 10036

Dana Mozley
New York *Daily News*
220 East 42nd Street
New York, NY 10017

Norman Miller
Daily News
220 East 42nd Street
New York, NY 10017

John S. Radosta
New York Times
229 West 43rd Street
New York, NY 10036

Tony Destino
Democrat and Chronicle
55 Exchange Street
Rochester, NY 14614

Lou Torre
Schenectady *Gazette*
332 State Street
Schenectady, NY 12305

Guido Cribari
Westchester Rockland
  Newspapers
One Gannett Drive
White Plains, NY 10604

NORTH CAROLINA
Ronald Green
Charlotte *News*
P.O. Box 360
Charlotte, NC 28201

Whitey Kelley
Charlotte *Observer*
P.O. Box 2138
Charlotte, NC 28233

Richard Sink
Charlotte *Observer*
P.O. Box 2138
Charlotte, NC 28233

Howard Ward
Fayetteville *Observer*
P.O. Box 849
Fayetteville, NC 28302

Smith Barrier
The Daily News
P.O. Box 20848
Greensboro, NC 27420

Jim Pettit
High Point *Enterprise*
210 Church Street
High Point, NC 27261

Cletus Brock
Mt. Olive *Tribune*
P.O. Box 27
Mount Olive, NC 28365

Bruce Phillips
Raleigh *Times*
P.O. Box 191
Raleigh, NC 27602

OHIO
Jack Patterson
Akron *Beacon-Journal*
44 East Exchange Street
Akron, OH 44328

John Seaburn
Akron *Beacon Journal*
44 East Exchange Street
Akron, OH 44328

Terry Galvin
Akron *Beacon Journal*
44 E. Exchange Street
Akron, OH 44328

Dick Forbes
Cincinnati *Enquirer*
617 Vine Street
Cincinnati, OH 45202

Terry Armour
Cincinnati *Enquirer*
617 Vine Street
Cincinnati, OH 45202

Pat Harmon
Cincinnati *Post*
800 Broadway
Cincinnati, OH 45202

Mark Purdy
Cincinnati *Enquirer*
617 Vine Street
Cincinnati, OH 45201

Tim Rogers
Cleveland *Press*
901 Lakeside Avenue
Cleveland, OH 44114

George Sweda
Cleveland *Plain Dealer*
1801 Superior Avenue
Cleveland, OH 44114

Paul Hornung
Columbus *Dispatch*
34 S. Third Street
Columbus, OH 43216

Kaye Kessler
Columbus *Citizen-Journal*
34 S. Third Street
Columbus, OH 43216

Tom Pastorius
Columbus *Citizen-Journal*
34 S. Third Street
Columbus, OH 43216

John Albers
Dayton *Journal-Herald*
Dayton, OH 45401

Gary Nuhn
Dayton *Daily News*
4th & Ludlow Streets
Dayton, OH 45401

Jim Taylor
Toledo *Blade*
541 Superior Street
Toledo, OH 43604

Tom Loomis
Toledo *Blade*
541 Superior Street
Toledo, OH 43640

Joel H. Walker
Troy *Daily News*
224-226 South Market Street
Troy, OH 45373

OKLAHOMA
Bob Hurt
The Daily Oklahoman
500 North Broadway
Oklahoma City, OK 73125

Tom Lobaugh
Tulsa *Daily World*
P.O. Box 1770
Tulsa, OK 74102

OREGON
Vern Putney
Portland *Press-Herald*
P.O. Box 1460
Portland, OR 97207

PENNSYLVANIA
Gordon Smith
Call-Chronicle Newspapers
8th & Ludlow Streets
Allentown, PA 18105

John Kunda
Call-Chronicle
P.O. Box 1260
Allentown, PA 18105

Jack Polancy
Erie *Morning News*
205 W. 12th Street
Erie, PA 16501

Paul Weimer
Harrisburg *Patriot-News*
P.O. Box 2265
Harrisburg, PA 17105

Felix (Red) McCarthy
Norristown *Times-Herald*
410 Markley Street
Norristown, PA 19404

Joseph Greenday
Philadelphia *News*
400 N. Broad Street
Philadelphia, PA 19101

Marino A. Parascenzo
Pittsburgh *Post-Gazette*
50 Boulevard of Allies
Pittsburgh, PA 15222

Jimmy Calpin
The Scrantonian & Scranton
   Times
338 N. Washington Avenue
Scranton, PA 18501

Al Williams
The Scrantonian & Scranton
   Tribune
338 N. Washington Avenue
Scranton, PA 18501

Joseph Miegoc
Pocono *Record*
511 Lenox Avenue
Stroudsburg, PA 18360

RHODE ISLAND
Ambrose R. Smith
Pawtuxet Valley *Times*
1353 Main Street
West Warwick, RI 02893

Bill Cawley
Westerly *Sun*
59 Main Street
Westerly, RI 02891

SOUTH CAROLINA
Bob Gillespie
Charleston *News & Courier*
P.O. Box 758
Charleston, SC 29402

Harold Martin
The State
P.O. Box 1333
Columbia, SC 29202

Dan Foster
Greenville *News*
P.O. Box 1688
Greenville, SC 29602

Wilfrid G. Binette
The Sun News
Box 406
Myrtle Beach, SC 29577

Luther Gaillard
Spartanburg *Herald-Journal*
P.O. Drawer 1657
Spartanburg, SC 29301

Leslie Timms
Spartanburg *Herald-Journal*
P.O. Drawer 1657
Spartanburg, SC 29301

TENNESSEE
Eddie Davidson
Chattanooga *Times*
117 E. 10th Street
Chattanooga, TN 37401

Sam Woolwine
Chattanooga *News-Free
   Press*
400 East 11th Street
Chattanooga, TN 37401

Al Dunning
Commercial Appeal
495 Union Avenue
Memphis, TN 38101

Mike Fleming
Commercial Appeal
495 Union Avenue
Memphis, TN 38101

Bobby Hall
Commercial Appeal
495 Union Avenue
Memphis, TN 38101

Wayne Thompson
Commercial Appeal
495 Union Avenue
Memphis, TN 38101

Steve Kelley
Memphis *Press-Scimitar*
495 Union Avenue
Memphis, TN 38103

John Bibb
Nashville *Tennessean*
1100 Broad
Nashville, TN 37202

Edgar Allen
Nashville *Banner*
1100 Broad
Nashville, TN 37202

Fred Russell
Nashville *Banner*
1100 Broad
Nashville, TN 37202

TEXAS
Sam Blair
Dallas *Morning News*
Communications Center
Dallas, TX 75222

Blackie Sherrod
Dallas *Times-Herald*
P.O. Box 5445
Dallas, TX 75222

Jack Agness
Houston *Post*
4747 Southwest Freeway
Houston, TX 77001

Jack Gallagher/Houston *Post*
4747 Southwest Freeway
Houston, TX 77001

UTAH
Lee Benson/*Deseret News*
P.O. Box 1527
Salt Lake City, UT 84110

VIRGINIA
Mark Hyman
Norfolk *Ledger-Star*
150 W. Brambleton Avenue
Norfolk, VA 23501

Harold D. Pearson
Richmond *Times-Dispatch*
333 E. Grace Street
Richmond, VA 23219

Douglas Doughty
Roanoke *Times World News*
P.O. Box 2491
Roanoke, VA 24014

WASHINGTON
Phil Taylor
Seattle *Post-Intelligencer*
Sixth & Wall
Seattle, WA 98111

Jack Sareault
Tacoma *News-Tribune*
Box 11000
Tacoma, WA 98411

WASHINGTON, D.C.
Richard Slay
Washington *Star-News*
225 Virginia Avenue, SE
Washington, DC 20061

Merrell Whittlesey
Washington *Star-News*
225 Virginia Avenue SE
Washington, DC 20061

Dave Kindred
Washington Post
1150 15th Street, NW
Washington, DC 20071

WEST VIRGINIA
Bob Baker
Charleston *Gazette*
P.O. Box 2993
Charleston, WV 25330

WISCONSIN
Glenn Miller
Wisconsin *State Journal*
Box 8058
Madison, WI 53708

CANADA
Garry McKay
The Spectator
Hamilton, Ontario, Canada

Bev Tyrrell
Winnipeg *Free Press*
300 Carlton Street
Winnipeg, Manitoba, Canada

MAJOR TELEVISION NETWORKS

ABC

American Broadcasting Co.
1330 Avenue of the Americas
New York, NY 10019
(212) 581-7777

SPORTS HEAD: Roone Arledge

Golf Telecasts

PRODUCER: Chuck Howard

ANNOUNCERS: Jim McKay, Chris Schenkel, Dave Marr, Peter Alliss, Bob Rosburg, Rhonda Glenn

CBS

Columbia Broadcasting System
51 W. 52nd Street
New York, NY 10019
(212) 975-4321

SPORTS HEAD: Frank M. Smith, Jr.

Golf Telecasts

PRODUCER: Frank Chirkinian

DIRECTOR: Bob Bailey

ANNOUNCERS: Jack Whitaker, Vin Scully, Ben Wright, Jim Thacker, Pat Summerall, Ken Venturi

NBC

National Broadcasting Co.
30 Rockefeller Plaza
New York, NY 10020
(212) 664-4444

SPORTS HEAD: Chester Simmons

Golf Telecasts

ANNOUNCERS: John Brodie, Arnold Palmer, Carol Mann, Jim Simpson, Cary Middlecoff

TRADE ASSOCIATIONS

NATIONAL ASSOCIATION OF GOLF CLUB MANUFACTURERS

200 Castlewood Drive
North Palm Beach, FL 33408
(305) 842-4100
Arthur W. Goettler, executive secretary

GOLF BALL MANUFACTURER'S ASSOCIATION

(Same as above.)

SPORTING GOODS MANUFACTURERS ASSOCIATION

(Same as above.)

NATIONAL SPORTING GOODS ASSOCIATION

717 North Michigan Avenue
Chicago, IL 60611
(312) 944-0205
G. Marvin Shutt, executive director

Represents sports shops, sporting-goods stores, etc.

NATIONAL INDUSTRIAL RECREATION ASSOCIATION

20 North Wacker Drive
Chicago, IL 60606

NATIONAL RECREATION & PARK ASSOCIATION

1601 North Kent Road
Arlington, VA 22209

PROMINENT INTERNATIONAL GOLF ORGANIZATIONS

INTERNATIONAL GOLF ASSOCIATION

101 West 50th Street
Room 4018
New York, NY 10020
(212) 581-2200
John Ross, director

Conducts annual World Cup.

INTERNATIONAL ASSOCIATION OF GOLF ADMINISTRATORS

c/o Chris Gribbin, Executive Director
Quebec Golf Association
3300 Cavendish Boulevard, Room 250
Montreal, Quebec, Canada H4B 2M8
(514) 481-0471

Group of about 45 individuals who direct major golf organizations in the United States and Canada.

ROYAL AND ANCIENT GOLF CLUB OF ST. ANDREWS

St. Andrews
Fife, Scotland
KY169JD

Conducts British Open and other championships; maintains (with USGA) *Rules of Golf.*

ROYAL CANADIAN GOLF ASSOCIATION
RR 2, Oakville
Ontario, L6J 4Z3, Canada
(416) 844-0516

The RCGA conducts the Canadian Open, Amateur, Senior, and Junior championships and works with provincial golf associations in furthering the development of golf across Canada. It also provides information in such areas as golf administration, golf-course management, greenskeeping, junior development, rules, handicapping and course rating, amateur status, golf history, and long-range planning for Canadian golf projects. Approximately 1,000 member clubs.

CANADIAN LADIES GOLF ASSOCIATION
333 River Road
Ottawa, Ontario, Canada
KIJ 7T5
(613) 746-5564

CANADIAN PGA
59 Berkeley Street
Toronto, Ontario, Canada
M5A 2W5

MEXICAN GOLF ASSOCIATION
Asociacion Mexicana de Golf A.C.
Apartado Postal 59
Mexico I., D.F.

MEXICAN PGA
Plaza Patria, Zona 1
Guadalajara, JAL
Mexico

ASIA GOLF CIRCUIT
P.O. Box 271
Manila, Philippines

The Asian pro tour includes about 10 events scheduled from February to April.

JAPAN PROFESSIONAL GOLF ASSOCIATION
4-4, Toranomom-1 Chome
Minato-Ku
Tokyo 105, Japan

The Japanese tour runs from April to November and includes some 40 events.

PGA OF AUSTRALIA
PGA House
102 Alexander Street
Crows Nest, 2065, N.S.W.
Australia

The Australian pro tour has about 20 events and runs February–November every year.

EUROPEAN PGA
The Kennington Oval
London SELL 5ST
England

The Great Britain/Continental pro tour consists of 25–30 events scheduled from April to October.

PGA OF SOUTH AFRICA
c/o Wanderers Golf Club
C/r. Corlett Drive & Rudd Road
Illovo, Johannesburg, 2001
South Africa

A half-dozen tournaments in October and November constitute the South African tour.

·XIII·

Argument Settlers

THE RULES OF GOLF

This excellent summation of basic golf rules appears in the National Golf Foundation's publication, *Golf Lessons*. For more information on rules, see list of publications which follows.

Golf is one of the unique sports where rules are self-governed. Knowing the rules is to your advantage — rules are friends. Playing by the rules makes conditions equal for everyone but not everyone equal. Because rules change, it is wise to keep a current copy of them.

In the beginning, you need not concern yourself with all rule technicalities but you should be aware of the regulations which apply to situations that will most often confront you during play.

First of all, there are two types of competition. In stroke play, *the winner completes his round in the fewest number of strokes. In* match play, *he wins more holes than does his opponent; each hole is figured separately as having been won, halved (tied) or lost.*

Some rules will vary with the type of competition involved.

Whether competing in match or stroke play, an underlying principle to remember is this: Do not touch your ball, except by striking it with the club, until you have holed out on the green. *True, there are situations for which the rules permit you to lift your ball, with or without penalty, but most of the time you are expected to play the ball as it lies, counting a stroke each time you intentionally swing at the ball, even if you miss it completely.*

On the tee, the player who is entitled to hit first has the honor, which is determined by draw on the first tee, and thereafter by the lowest score on the previous hole (or on the last hole not tied).

You may tee your ball anywhere in a rectangular space bounded in front by a line formed by the outside limits of the tee markers and two club-lengths in depth directly behind.

If you tee up anywhere outside this rectangle, your opponent in match play may recall your shot and oblige you to replay properly, without penalty. In stroke play, you must shoot again and count your strokes from the incorrect position. If you accidentally move the ball off the wooden or plastic tee before making your stroke, you may replace it without penalty.

After teeing off, play is continued toward the green with the player farthest from the flag hitting first. This hitting order continues until the balls are in the hole.

If your ball moves after you have addressed it at any time other than for the tee shot, naturally or accidentally, add one penalty stroke to your score for the hole.

You may not remove or press down any irregularities of the ground (except when on the teeing ground) which could in any way affect your lie, swing or line of play; nor can you improve the position of your ball by moving, bending or breaking anything fixed or growing. You must play around or over trees, bushes, large boulders and other immovable natural objects. However, you may remove loose natural impediments such as stones, twigs, or fallen leaves (except in a hazard), and man-made obstructions, such as paper, bottles, boxes and greenkeeping equipment.

Should your ball be lost outside a water hazard, or be out of bounds, you must drop another ball as close as possible to the spot from which it was hit, counting that stroke and adding a penalty stroke to your score.

If you think the ball you have just hit may be in either of these states, you may play a provisional ball providing: (1) you do so before going forward to look for your first ball, and (2) you inform your opponent or your marker of your intention before hitting again. If you discover your first ball not lost or out of bounds, it remains the ball in play and the provisional ball must be abandoned. If, however, your first ball is lost or out of bounds, the provisional ball is in play and you count both strokes played (first plus provisional) and add a penalty stroke to your score.

Officially to drop a ball, stand erect, face the hole, and drop it over your shoulder, allowing it to come to rest naturally, within two club lengths of the spot where it is to land.

Officially to drop a ball, stand erect, face the hole, and drop it over your shoulder, allowing it to come to rest naturally, within two club lengths of the spot where it is to land.

You may deem your ball unplayable anywhere except in a water hazard. You have three alternatives: (1) hit a second ball from the point at which you hit the first, count both shots and add a penalty stroke; (2) drop the ball within two club-lengths of the point where the ball lies, but no nearer the hole, and count one penalty stroke; or (3) drop a ball behind the unplayable lie in line with the hole (as far back as desirable), and count one penalty stroke.

(Note: if options #2 or #3 are used in a bunker, the ball must remain in the bunker.)

Hazards *include permanent water areas (ponds, brooks, ditches, whether filled or dry), their banks and the exposed soil or sand in a bunker (sand trap). Grass areas within a bunker are not considered parts of a hazard.*

When your ball lies in a hazard, you may not touch the ground, sand or water with the club until making the forward swing. Except for movable, artificial obstructions which interfere, and may be removed, play the hazard as you find it in order to avoid the penalty of loss of hole in match play and two strokes in stroke play.

If your ball enters a water hazard, *you may play it as it is; or, under a stroke penalty, either (1) drop a ball behind the hazard in line with the hole and the point at which the ball last crossed the margin of the hazard, or (2) drop a ball at the point from which your original ball was hit.*

When your ball enters a lateral water hazard (i.e. one which runs approximately parallel to the line of play), the choices are the same as a regular water hazard with one addition: you may drop a ball within two club-lengths of the point where the ball last crossed the hazard margin (or a point on the opposite margin of the hazard which is equidistant from the hole) but not closer to the hole.

You may lift your ball from a man-made *obstruction which interferes with your swing or stance, such as a water pipe, protective screen or sprinkling outlet (even when in a hazard) but not from an out-of-bounds stake or fence. Drop the ball over your shoulder within two club-lengths of the nearest point which provides relief from the obstruction. The ball must come to rest not nearer the hole than the spot where it originally lay.*

If through the green your ball lies in casual water, ground under repair *or in a hole made by a burrowing animal, or if such area interferes with your stance or swing, you may lift it without penalty and drop it within two club-lengths of the nearest point of relief which avoids the situation and which is not nearer the hole.*

But if in a bunker your ball lies in casual water, ground under repair, or in a hole made by a burrowing animal, you have a choice of playing it as it lies or lifting it without penalty and dropping it in the hazard as near as possible to the spot where the ball lay but not nearer the hole, so as to get the most relief possible from the bad condition. Or . . .

. . . under penalty of one stroke you may lift it and drop it outside the hazard, but not nearer the hole, keeping the spot where the ball lay between yourself and the hole. All this applies also if your ball is in a water hazard except that there is no casual water in a water hazard.

When your ball is on the putting green, if it lies in casual water, ground under repair, or in a hole made by a burrowing animal, or if such conditions intervene with the ball and the hole, you may lift the ball and place it without penalty in the nearest position to where it lay which affords maximum relief from these conditions, but not nearer the hole.

If your ball strikes the flagstick *when played from anywhere on the putting green, your penalty is loss of hole in match play and two strokes in stroke play.*

Fig. 103

Fig. 102

On the putting green, you may not touch the line of your putt *except to (1) repair ball marks, (2) remove loose impediments and/or (3) clean your ball. Nor can you test the surface of the putting green by rolling a ball or scraping the surface. In match play the penalty is loss of hole; in stroke play, two strokes.*

Before lifting a ball on the putting green, *you should mark its position by placing a small coin or other object directly behind it. Should your marker interfere with another player's line of putt, use your putterhead as a measuring instrument to move the marker to one side. However, be sure to replace your ball on its original position.*

In match play there is no penalty for your ball hitting your opponent's ball on the green. He may play the ball from its new position or immediately replace it. In stroke play, however, when both balls lie on the green, if your ball then strikes a fellow competitor's ball, you must take a two-stroke penalty and the displaced ball must be returned to its original position.

Should your ball land on the wrong putting green, *you must lift and drop it off the green without penalty within two club-lengths of the nearest point providing relief but no nearer the hole you are playing.*

As your interest, skill, and frequency of play increase, you will learn more about special situations not mentioned here.

INFORMATION ON THE RULES

THE RULES OF GOLF, as approved by the U.S. Golf Association. Booklet, 50¢. Hardcover edition (6×9″), $3.00.

DECISIONS ON THE RULES OF GOLF BY THE USGA (1956–1977). Interpretations of the rules of golf, including the complete rules and index; hard cover, two volumes, $25.00. Annual fee for new and revised *Decisions,* $12.50.

GOLF RULES IN PICTURES. Published by Grosset and Dunlap, compiled by Joseph C. Dey, Jr., former USGA executive director; 96 pages 8½ × 10¾″; $2.95.

GOLF RULES IN PICTURES ON 35 MM FILM. Set of 46 slides, $25.00.

GOLF RULES IN BRIEF. Four-page weather-resistant pamphlet featuring some basic rules in easy-to-understand language; $5.00 per 100.

HOW TO BEHAVE AS A GOLFER. Twelve-page picture folder on golf course etiquette; $5.00 per 100.

DUTIES OF OFFICIALS UNDER THE RULES OF GOLF. Contains a checklist of the duties of the referee and other committee members on the course; no charge.

THE GOLF CART AND THE RULES. Pamphlet; 25¢.

WHAT TO DO ABOUT OBSTRUCTIONS. Contains useful information on proper procedures under the rules of golf pertaining to obstructions; 25¢.

AT SEA IN A WATER HAZARD. A 12-page picture folder on rules pertaining to water hazards; 25¢.

All of above available from:

U.S. Golf Association
Golf House
Far Hills, NJ 07931

EASY WAY TO LEARN GOLF RULES. Pocket-size USGA-approved booklet updated annually, with more than 50 explanatory drawings by Dom Lupo.

GOLF RULES WALL CHART. Complete reproduction of "Easy Way to Learn Golf Rules" on a 23×35″ wall chart printed in two colors on heavy paper; $1.75.

Both of above available from:
National Golf Foundation
200 Castlewood Drive
North Palm Beach, FL 33408

MAJOR TOURNAMENT RECORDS

MAJOR MEN'S CHAMPIONSHIP WINNERS

MASTERS (APRIL, AUGUSTA, GA., NATIONAL G.C.)

YEAR	WINNER	SCORE
1934	Horton Smith	284
1935	Gene Sarazen	282–144
1936	Horton Smith	285
1937	Byron Nelson	283
1938	Henry Picard	285
1939	Ralph Guldahl	279
1940	Jimmy Demaret	280
1941	Craig Wood	280
1942	Byron Nelson	280–69
1943–45	no championships held	
1946	Herman Keiser	282
1947	Jimmy Demaret	281
1948	Claude Harmon	279
1949	Sam Snead	282
1950	Jimmy Demaret	283
1951	Ben Hogan	280
1952	Sam Snead	286
1953	Ben Hogan	274
1954	Sam Snead	289–70
1955	Cary Middlecoff	279
1956	Jack Burke	289
1957	Doug Ford	283
1958	Arnold Palmer	284
1959	Art Wall	284
1960	Arnold Palmer	282
1961	Gary Player	280
1962	Arnold Palmer	280–68
1963	Jack Nicklaus	286
1964	Arnold Palmer	276
1965	Jack Nicklaus	271
1966	Jack Nicklaus	288–70
1967	Gay Brewer	280
1968	Bob Goalby	277
1969	George Archer	281
1970	Billy Casper	279–69

YEAR	WINNER	SCORE
1971	Charles Coody	279
1972	Jack Nicklaus	286
1973	Tommy Aaron	283
1974	Gary Player	278
1975	Jack Nicklaus	276
1976	Ray Floyd	271
1977	Tom Watson	276
1978	Gary Player	277
1979	Fuzzy Zoeller*	280

* Won sudden death playoff

U.S. OPEN (JUNE)

YEAR	SITE	WINNER	SCORE
1895	Newport (R.I.) G.C.	Horace Rawlins	173
1896	Shinnecock Hills G.C., Southampton, N.Y.	James Foulis	152
1897	Chicago G.C.	Joe Lloyd	162
1898	Myopia Hunt C., Hamilton, Mass.	Fred Herd	328
1899	Baltimore C.C.	Willie Smith	315
1900	Chicago G.C.	Harry Vardon	313
1901	Myopia Hunt C.	Willie Anderson	331-85
1902	Garden City (N.Y.) C.C.	L. Auchterlonie	307
1903	Baltusrol G.C., Springfield, N.J.	Willie Anderson	307-82
1904	Glen View (Ill.) C.	Willie Anderson	303
1905	Myopia Hunt C.	Willie Anderson	314
1906	Onwentsia C., Lake Forest, Ill.	Alex Smith	295
1907	Phila. (Pa.) Cricket C.	Alex Ross	302
1908	Myopia Hunt C.	Fred McLeod	322-77
1909	Englewood (N.J.) G.C.	George Sargent	290
1910	Phila. (Pa.) Cricket C.	Alex Smith	298-71
1911	Chicago G.C.	J. McDermott	307-80
1912	C.C. of Buffalo, N.Y.	J. McDermott	294
1913	The C.C., Brookline, Mass.	*F. Ouimet	304-72
1914	Midlothian (Ill.) C.C.	Walter Hagen	290
1915	Baltusrol G.C., Springfield, N.J.	*J. D. Travers	297
1916	Minikahda C., Minneapolis, Minn.	*C. Evans, Jr.	286
1917–18—No championship			
1919	Brae Burn C.C., W. Newton, Mass.	Walter Hagen	301-77
1920	Inverness C., Toledo, O.	Edward Ray	295
1921	Columbia C.C., Chevy Chase, Md.	James M. Barnes	289
1922	Skokie (Ill.) C.C.	Gene Sarazen	288
1923	Inwood (N.Y.) C.C.	*R. T. Jones, Jr.	296-76
1924	Oakland Hills C.C., Birmingham, Mich.	Cyril Walker	297
1925	Worcester (Mass.) C.C.	W. MacFarlane	291-75-72
1926	Scioto C.C., Columbus, O.	*R. T. Jones, Jr.	293
1927	Oakmont (Pa.) C.C.	Tommy Armour	301-76
1928	Olympia Fields C.C., Matteson, Ill.	Johnny Farrell	294-143
1929	Winged Foot G.C. Mamaroneck, N.Y.	*R. T. Jones, Jr.	294-141
1930	Interlachen C.C., Minneapolis, Minn.	*R. T. Jones, Jr.	287
1931	Inverness C. Toledo, O.	Billy Burke	292-149-148
1932	Fresh Meadow C.C. Flushing, N.Y.	Gene Sarazen	286
1933	North Shore G.C., Glenview, Ill.	*John Goodman	287
1934	Merion Cricket C. Ardmore, Pa.	Olin Dutra	293
1935	Oakmont (Pa.) C.C.	Sam Parks, Jr.	299
1936	Baltusrol G. C., Springfield, N.J.	Tony Manero	282
1937	Oakland Hills C.C., Birmingham, Mich.	Ralph Guldahl	281
1938	Cherry Hills C. Denver, Colo.	Ralph Guldahl	284
1939	Phila. C.C., W. Conshohocken, Pa.	Byron Nelson	284-68-70
1940	Canterbury G.C., Warrensville, O.	Lawson Little	287-70
1940	Colonial C.C., Ft. Worth, Tex.	Craig Wood	284
1942–45—No championship held			
1946	Canterbury C.G., Warrensville, O.	Lloyd Mangrum	284-72-72
1947	St. Louis C.C., Clayton, Mo.	Lew Worsham	282-69
1948	Riviera C.C., Los Angeles, Calif.	Ben Hogan	276
1949	Medinah C.C., Chicago, Ill.	Cary Middlecoff	286
1950	Merion Cricket C., Ardmore, Pa.	Ben Hogan	287-69
1951	Oakland Hills C.C., Birmingham, Mich.	Ben Hogan	287
1952	Northwood C., Dallas, Tex.	Julius Boros	281
1953	Oakmont C.C., Oakmont, Pa.	Ben Hogan	283
1954	Baltusrol G.C., Springfield, N.J.	Ed Furgol	284
1955	Olympic C.C., S. Fran., Calif.	Jack Fleck	287-69
1956	Oak Hill C.C., Rochester, N.Y.	Cary Middlecoff	281
1957	Inverness C., Toledo, O.	Dick Mayer	282-72
1958	Southern Hills, Tulsa, Okla.	Tommy Bolt	283
1959	Winged Foot, Mamaroneck, N.Y.	Bill Casper	282
1960	Cherry Hills C.C., Denver, Colo.	Arnold Palmer	280
1961	Oakland Hills C.C., Birmingham, Mich.	Gene Littler	281
1962	Oakmont (Pa.) C.C.	Jack Nicklaus	283-71
1963	The C.C., Brookline, Mass.	Julius Boros	293-70
1964	Congressional C.C., Wash. D.C.	Ken Venturi	278
1965	Bellerive C.C., Creve Coeur, Mo.	Gary Player	282-71
1966	Olympic C.C., S. Fran., Cal.	Billy Casper	278-69
1967	Baltusrol G.C., Springfield, N.J.	Jack Nicklaus	275
1968	Oak Hill C.C., Rochester, N.Y.	Lee Trevino	275

YEAR	SITE	WINNER	SCORE
1969	Champions G.C., Houston, Tex.	Orville Moody	281
1970	Hazeltine Ntl. Chaska, Minn.	Tony Jacklin	281
1971	Merion G.C., Ardmore, Pa.	Lee Trevino	280-68
1972	Pebble Beach, Calif.	Jack Nicklaus	290
1973	Oakmont (Pa.) C.C.	John Miller	279
1974	Winged Foot G.C., Mamaroneck, N.Y.	Hale Irwin	287
1975	Medinah C.C., Chicago, Ill.	Lou Graham	287-71
1976	Atlanta Athletic Club, Atlanta, Ga.	Jerry Pate	277
1977	Southern Hills, Tulsa, Okla.	Hubert Greene	278
1978	Cherry Hills C.C., Denver, Colo.	Andy North	285
1979	Inverness C. Toledo, O.	Hale Irwin	284

* Denotes Amateur

BRITISH OPEN (JULY)

YEAR	SITE	WINNER	SCORE
1860	Prestwick	Willie Park	174
1861	Prestwick	Tom Morris	163
1862	Prestwick	Tom Morris	163
1863	Prestwick	Willie Park	168
1864	Prestwick	Tom Morris	160
1865	Prestwick	A. Strath	162
1866	Prestwick	Willie Park	169
1867	Prestwick	Tom Morris	170
1868	Prestwick	Tom Morris, Jr.	154
1869	Prestwick	Tom Morris, Jr.	157
1870	Prestwick	Tom Morris, Jr.	149
1872	Prestwick	Tom Morris, Jr.	166
1873	St. Andrews	Tom Kidd	179
1874	Musselburgh	Mungo Park	159
1875	Prestwick	Willie Park	166
1876	St. Andrews	Bob Martin	176
1877	Musselburgh	Jamie Anderson	160
1878	Prestwick	Jamie Anderson	157
1879	St. Andrews	Jamie Anderson	169
1880	Musselburgh	Bob Ferguson	162
1881	Prestwick	Bob Ferguson	170
1882	St. Andrews	Bob Ferguson	171
1883	Musselburgh	W. Fernie	159
1884	Prestwick	Jack Simpson	160
1885	St. Andrews	Bob Martin	171
1886	Musselburgh	D. Brown	157
1887	Prestwick	W. Park, Jr.	161
1888	St. Andrews	Jack Burns	171
1889	Musselburgh	W. Park, Jr.	155
1890	Prestwick	John Ball	164
1891	St. Andrews	Hugh Kirkaldy	166
1892	Muirfield	Harold Hilton	305
1893	Prestwick	W. Auchterlonie	322
1894	Sandwich	J. H. Taylor	326
1895	St. Andrews	J. H. Taylor	322
1896	Muirfield	Harry Vardon	316
1897	Hoylake	Harold Hilton	314
1898	Prestwick	Harry Vardon	307
1899	Sandwich	Harry Vardon	310
1900	St. Andrews	J. H. Taylor	309

YEAR	SITE	WINNER	SCORE
1901	Muirfield	James Braid	309
1902	Hoylake	Alex Herd	307
1903	Prestwick	Harry Vardon	300
1904	Sandwich	Jack White	296
1905	St. Andrews	James Braid	318
1906	Muirfield	James Braid	300
1907	Hoylake	Arnaud Massey	312
1908	Prestwick	James Braid	291
1909	Deal	J. H. Taylor	295
1910	St. Andrews	James Braid	299
1911	Sandwich	Harry Vardon	303
1912	Muirfield	Ted Ray	295
1913	Hoylake	J. H. Taylor	304
1914	Prestwick	Harry Vardon	306
1915–1919—No championships held			
1920	Deal	George Duncan	303
1921	St. Andrews	Walter Hagen	300
1922	Sandwich	A. G. Havers	295
1923	Troon	Jock Hutchison	296
1924	Hoylake	Walter Hagen	301
1925	Prestwick	Jim Barnes	300
1926	Royal Lytham & St. Annes	R. T. Jones	291
1927	St. Andrews	R. T. Jones	285
1928	Sandwich	Walter Hagen	292
1929	Muirfield	Walter Hagen	292
1930	Hoylake	R. T. Jones	291
1931	Carnoustie	Tommy Armour	296
1932	Prince's, Sandwich	Gene Sarazen	283
1933	St. Andrews	Denny Shute	292
1934	Sandwich	Henry Cotton	283
1935	Muirfield	A. Perry	283
1936	Hoylake	A. H. Padgam	287
1937	Carnoustie	Henry Cotton	290
1938	Sandwich	R. A. Whitcombe	295
1939	St. Andrews	R. Burton	290
1940–45—No championships held			
1946	St. Andrews	Sam Snead	290
1947	Hoylake	Fred Daly	293
1948	Muirfield	Henry Cotton	284
1949	Sandwich	Bobby Locke	283
1950	Troon	Bobby Locke	279
1951	Portrush	Max Faulkner	285
1952	Royal Lytham & St. Annes	Bobby Locke	287
1953	Carnoustie	Ben Hogan	282
1954	Royal Birkdale	Peter Thomson	283
1955	St. Andrews	Peter Thomson	281
1956	Royal Liverpool	Peter Thomson	286
1957	St. Andrews	Bobby Locke	279
1958	Royal Lytham & St. Annes	Peter Thomson	278-139
1959	Muirfield	Gary Player	284
1960	St. Andrews	Kel Nagle	278
1961	Royal Birkdale	Arnold Palmer	284
1962	Troon	Arnold Palmer	276
1963	Royal Lytham & St. Annes	Bob Charles	277-140
1964	St. Andrews	Tony Lema	279
1965	Royal Birkdale	Peter Thomson	285
1966	Muirfield C.	Jack Nicklaus	282
1967	R. Liverpool C.	Roberto de Vicenzo	278
1968	Carnoustie	Gary Player	289
1969	Royal Lytham & St. Annes	Tony Jacklin	280

YEAR	SITE	WINNER	SCORE
1970	St. Andrews	Jack Nicklaus	283-72
1971	Royal Birkdale	Lee Trevino	278
1972	Muirfield	Lee Trevino	278
1973	Troon	Tom Weiskopf	276
1974	Royal Lytham & St. Annes	Gary Player	282
1975	Carnoustie	Tom Watson	279-71
1976	Royal Birkdale	Johnny Miller	279
1977	Turnberry	Tom Watson	268
1978	St. Andrews	Jack Nicklaus	281
1979	Royal Lytham & St. Annes	Severiano Ballesteros	283

PGA CHAMPIONSHIP (AUGUST)

YEAR	SITE	WINNER	SCORE
1916	Siwanoy C.C., Bronxville, N.Y.	James Barnes	1 up
1917–18—No tournament			
1919	Engineers C.C., Roslyn, L.I., N.Y.	James Barnes	5&4
1920	Flossmoor (Ill.) C.C.	Jock Hutchison	1 up
1921	Inwood C.C., Far Rockaway, N.Y.	Walter Hagen	3&2
1922	Oakmont (Pa.) C.C.	Gene Sarazen	4&3
1923	Pelham (N.Y.) C.C.	Gene Sarazen	1 up (38)
1924	French Lick (Ind.) C.C.	Walter Hagen	2 up
1925	Olympia Fields (Ill.) C.C.	Walter Hagen	6&5
1926	Salisbury G.C., Westbury, N.Y.	Walter Hagen	5&3
1927	Cedar Crest C.C., Dallas, Tex.	Walter Hagen	1 up
1928	Five Farms C.C., Baltimore, Md.	Leo Diegel	6&5
1929	Hillcrest C.C., Los Angeles, Calif.	Leo Diegel	6&4
1930	Fresh Meadows C.C., Flushing, N.Y.	Tommy Armour	1 up
1931	Wannamoisett C.C., Rumford, R.I.	Tom Creavy	2&1
1932	Keller G.C., St. Paul, Minn.	Olin Dutra	4&3
1933	Blue Mound C.C., Milwaukee, Wis.	Gene Sarazen	5&4
1934	Park C.C., W'msville, N.Y.	Paul Runyan	1 up (38)
1935	Twin Hills C.C., Okla. City, Okla.	Johnny Revolta	5&4
1936	Pinehurst (N.C.) C.C.	Denny Shute	3&2
1937	Pittsburgh C.C., Aspinwall, Pa.	Denny Shute	1 up (37)
1938	Shawnee (Pa.) C.C.	Paul Runyan	8&7
1939	Pomonok C.C., Flushing, N.Y.	Henry Picard	1 up (37)
1940	Hershey (Pa.) C.C.	Byron Nelson	1 up
1941	Cherry Hills C.C., Denver, Colo.	Vic Ghezzi	1 up (38)
1942	Seaview C.C., Atlantic City, N.J.	Sam Snead	2&1
1943—No tournament			
1944	Manito G. & C.C., Spokane, Wash.	Bob Hamilton	1 up
1945	Moraine C.C., Dayton, O.	Byron Nelson	4&3
1946	Portland (Ore.) C.C.	Ben Hogan	6&4
1947	Plum Hollow C.C. Detroit	Jim Ferrier	2&1
1948	Norwood Hills C.C. St. Louis	Ben Hogan	7&6
1949	Hermitage C.C., Richmond, Va.	Sam Snead	3&2
1950	Scioto C.C., Columbus, O.	Chandler Harper	4&3
1951	Oakmont (Pa.) C.C.	Sam Snead	7&6
1952	Big Spring C.C., Louisville, Ky.	Jim Turnesa	1 up
1953	Birmingham (Mich.) C.C.	Walter Burkemo	2&1
1954	Keller G.C., St. Paul, Minn.	Chick Harbert	4&3
1955	Meadowbrook, Detroit, Mich.	Doug Ford	4&3
1956	Blue Hill C.C., Canton, Mass.	Jack Burke	3&2
1957	Miami Valley, Dayton, O.	Lionel Hebert	2&1
1958	Llanerch C.C., Haverford, Pa.	Dow Finsterwald	276
1959	Minneapolis G.C., St. Louis Park, Minn.	Bob Rosburg	277
1960	Firestone C.C., Akron, O.	Jay Hebert	281
1961	Olympia Fields Chicago, Ill.	Jerry Barber	277-67
1962	Aronimink G.C., Newtown Sq., Pa.	Gary Player	278
1963	Dallas (Tex.) A.C., C.C.	Jack Nicklaus	279
1964	Columbus C.C., Columbus, O.	Bobby Nichols	271
1965	Laurel Valley G.C., Ligonier, Penna.	Dave Marr	280
1966	Firestone C.C., Akron, O.	Al Geiberger	280
1967	Columbine C.C., Denver, Colo.	Don January	281-69
1968	Pecan Valley C.C., San Antonio, Tex.	Julius Boros	281
1969	N.C.R. G.C., Dayton, O.	Ray Floyd	276
1970	So. Hills C.C., Tulsa, Okla.	Dave Stockton	279
1971	PGA Ntl. G.C., Palm Beach, Fla.	Jack Nicklaus	281
1972	Oakland Hills C.C., Birmingham, Mich.	Gary Player	281
1973	Canterbury C.C., Cleveland, O.	Jack Nicklaus	277
1974	Tanglewood C.C., Clemmons, N.C.	Lee Trevino	276
1975	Firestone C.C., Akron, O.	Jack Nicklaus	276
1976	Congressional C.C.	Dave Stockton	281
1977	Pebble Beach G.L., Monterey Pen., Calif.	Lanny Wadkins	282
1978	Oakmont C.C., Oakmont, Pa.	John Mahaffey	276
1979	Oakland Hills C.C., Birmingham, Mich.	David Graham*	272

* Won sudden-death playoff.

LEADING MONEY-WINNERS—MEN

1934	Paul Runyan	. . . .	$ 6,767
1935	Johnny Revolta	. . . .	9,543

1936	Horton Smith	7,682
1937	Harry Cooper	14,138
1938	Sam Snead	19,534
1939	Henry Picard	10,303
1940	Ben Hogan	10,655
1941	Ben Hogan	18,358
1942	Ben Hogan	13,143
1943	(None compiled)	
1944	Byron Nelson	*37,967
1945	Byron Nelson	*63,335
1946	Ben Hogan	42,556
1947	Jimmy Demaret	27,937
1948	Ben Hogan	32,112
1949	Sam Snead	31,594
1950	Sam Snead	35,759
1951	Lloyd Mangrum	26,089
1952	Julius Boros	37,033
1953	Lew Worsham	34,002
1954	Bob Toski	65,820
1955	Julius Boros	63,122
1956	Ted Kroll	72,836
1957	Dick Mayer	65,835
1958	Arnold Palmer	42,607
1959	Art Wall	53,168
1960	Arnold Palmer	75,263
1961	Gary Player	64,540
1962	Arnold Palmer	81,448
1963	Arnold Palmer	128,230
1964	Jack Nicklaus	113,284
1965	Jack Nicklaus	140,752
1966	Billy Casper	121,945
1967	Jack Nicklaus	188,998
1968	Billy Casper	205,169
1969	Frank Beard	175,223
1970	Lee Trevino	157,037
1971	Jack Nicklaus	244,490
1972	Jack Nicklaus	320,542
1973	Jack Nicklaus	308,362
1974	Johnny Miller	353,021
1975	Jack Nicklaus	298,149
1976	Jack Nicklaus	266,438
1977	Tom Watson	310,653
1978	Tom Watson	362,429

* Computed in War Bonds.

VARDON TROPHY WINNERS

The PGA Vardon Trophy, named in honor of Harry Vardon, was placed in competition among American professionals in 1937 as a successor to the Henry E. Radix Trophy, which, prior to that time, had been awarded annually to the professional having the finest tournament record in play in this country.

Today, the Vardon Trophy, a bronze-colored plaque measuring 39″ × 27″ is awarded each year to the member of the PGA of America maintaining the finest playing average in those events cosponsored or so designated by the PGA in each such period. A minimum of 80 rounds in tournaments considered official by PGA is required to win.

YEAR	WINNER	AVERAGE
1937	Harry Cooper	*
1938	Sam Snead	*
1939	Byron Nelson	*
1940	Ben Hogan	*
1941	Ben Hogan	*
1942–		
1946	No award—World War II	
1947	Jimmy Demaret	69.90
1948	Ben Hogan	69.30
1949	Sam Snead	69.37
1950	Sam Snead	69.23
1951	Lloyd Mangrum	70.05
1952	Jack Burke	70.54
1953	Lloyd Mangrum	70.22
1954	E. J. (Dutch) Harrison	70.41
1955	Sam Snead	69.86
1956	Cary Middlecoff	70.35
1957	Dow Finsterwald	70.30
1958	Bob Rosburg	70.11
1959	Art Wall	70.35
1960	Billy Casper	69.95
1961	Arnold Palmer	69.85
1962	Arnold Palmer	70.27
1963	Billy Casper	70.58
1964	Arnold Palmer	70.01
1965	Billy Casper	70.85
1966	Billy Casper	70.27
1967	Arnold Palmer	70.18
1968	Billy Casper	69.82
1968	Dave Hill	70.34
1970	Lee Trevino	70.64
1971	Lee Trevino	70.27
1972	Lee Trevino	70.89
1973	Bruce Crampton	70.57
1974	Lee Trevino	70.53
1975	Bruce Crampton	70.51
1976	Don January	70.56
1977	Tom Watson	70.32
1978	Tom Watson	70.16

* Point system used 1937–'41.

MAJOR WOMEN'S CHAMPIONSHIP WINNERS

U.S. WOMEN'S OPEN (JULY)

YEAR	SITE	WINNER	SCORE
1946	Spokane C.C., Spokane, Wash.	Patty Berg d. Betty Jameson	5&4
1947	Starmount Forest C.C., Greensboro, N.C.	Betty Jameson	295

YEAR	SITE	WINNER	SCORE
1948	Atlantic City C.C., Northfield, N.J.	Babe Zaharias	300
1949	Prince Georges G. & C.C., Landover, Md.	Louise Suggs	291
1950	Rolling Hills C.C., Witchita, Kan.	Babe Zaharias	291
1951	Druid Hills G.C., Atlanta, Ga.	Betsy Rawls	293
1952	Bala G.C., Philadelphia, Pa.	Louise Suggs	284
1953	C.C. of Rochester, Rochester, N.Y.	Betsy Rawls	302–71
1954	Salem C.C., Peabody, Mass.	Babe Zaharias	291
1955	Wichita C.C., Wichita, Kansas	Fay Crocker	299
1956	Northland C.C., Duluth, Minn.	Kathy Cornelius	302-75
1957	Winged Foot G.C., Mamaroneck, N.Y.	Betsy Rawls	299
1958	Forest Lake C.C., Bloomfield Hills, Mich.	Mickey Wright	290
1959	Churchill Valley C.C., Pittsburgh, Pa.	Mickey Wright	287
1960	Worcester C.C., Worcester, Mass.	Betsy Rawls	292
1961	Baltusrol G.C., Springfield, N.J.	Mickey Wright	293
1962	Dunes G. and Beach C., Myrtle Beach, S.C.	Murle Lindstrom	301
1963	Kenwood C.C., Cincinnati, Ohio	Mary Mills	289
1964	San Diego C.C., Chula Vista, Calif.	Mickey Wright	290-70
1965	Atlantic City C.C. Northfield, N.J.	Carol Mann	290
1966	Hazeltine Nat'l G.C., Minneapolis, Minn.	Sandra Spuzich	297
1967	Va. Hot Springs G. & Tennis Club, Hot Springs, Va.	Catherine Lacoste	294
1968	Moselem Springs G.C., Fleetwood, Pa.	Susie Maxwell Berning	289
1969	Scenic Hills C.C., Pensacola, Fla.	Donna Caponi	294
1970	Muskogee C.C., Oklahoma	Donna Caponi	287
1971	Kahkwa Club, Erie, Penn.	JoAnne Gunderson Carner	288
1972	Winged Foot G.C., Mamaroneck, N.Y.	Susie Maxwell Berning	299
1973	C.C. of Rochester, Rochester, N.Y.	Susie Maxwell Berning	290
1974	LaGrange C.C., LaGrange, Ill.	Sandra Haynie	295
1975	Atlantic City C.C. Northfield, N.J.	Sandra Palmer	295
1976	Rolling Green G.C., Springfield, Pa.	JoAnne Gunderson Carner	292-76
1977	Hazeltine Nat'l G.C., Minneapolis, Minn.	Hollis Stacy	292
1978	C.C. of Indianapolis, Indianapolis, Ind.	Hollis Stacy	289
1979	Brooklawn C.C., Fairfield, Conn.	Jerilyn Britz	284

LPGA CHAMPIONSHIP (JUNE)

YEAR	SITE	WINNER	SCORE
1955	Orchard Ridge C.C., Ft. Wayne	Beverly Hanson d. L. Suggs	4&3
1956	Forest Lake C.C., Detroit, Mich.	*Marlene Hagge Patty Berg	291 291
1957	Churchill Valley C.C., Pittsburgh	Louise Suggs	285
1958	Churchill Valley C.C., Pittsburgh	Mickey Wright	288
1959	Sheraton Hotel C.C., French Lick, Ind.	Betsy Rawls	288
1960	Sheraton Hotel C.C., French Lick, Ind.	Mickey Wright	292
1961	Stardust C.C., Las Vegas, Nev.	Mickey Wright	287
1962	Stardust C.C., Las Vegas, Nev.	Judy Kimball	282
1963	Stardust C.C., Las Vegas, Nev.	Mickey Wright	294
1964	Stardust C.C., Las Vegas, Nev.	Mary Mills	278
1965	Stardust C.C., Las Vegas, Nev.	Sandra Haynie	279
1966	Stardust C.C., Las Vegas, Nev.	Gloria Ehret	282
1967	Pleasant Valley C.C., Sutton, Mass.	Kathy Whitworth	284
1968	Pleasant Valley C.C., Sutton, Mass.	Sandra Post Kathy Whitworth	294-68 294-75
1969	Concord G.C., Kiamesha Lake, N.Y.	Betsy Rawls Shirley Englehorn	293 285-74
1970	Pleasant Valley C.C., Sutton, Mass.	Kathy Whitworth	285-78
1971	Pleasant Valley C.C., Sutton, Mass.	Kathy Whitworth	288
1972	Pleasant Valley C.C., Sutton, Mass.	Kathy Ahern	293
1973	Pleasant Valley C.C., Sutton, Mass.	Mary Mills	288
1974	Pleasant Valley C.C., Sutton, Mass.	Sandra Haynie	288
1975	Pine Ridge G.C. Towson, Md.	Kathy Whitworth	288
1976	Pine Ridge G.C., Towson, Md.	Betty Burfeindt	287
1977	Baytree Myrtle Beach, S.C.	Chako Higuchi	279
1978	Jack Nicklaus G.C., Kings Island, Ohio	Nancy Lopez	275
1979	Jack Nicklaus G.C., Kings Island, Ohio	Donna C. Young	279

* Won sudden-death playoff

LEADING MONEY-WINNERS—WOMEN

YEAR	PLAYER	AMOUNT
1948	Babe Zaharias	$ 3,400*
1949	Babe Zaharias	4,650*
1950	Babe Zaharias	14,800*
1951	Babe Zaharias	15,087*
1952	Betsy Rawls	14,505

1953	Louise Suggs	19,816
1954	Patty Berg	16,011
1955	Patty Berg	16,492
1956	Marlene Hagge	20,235
1957	Patty Berg	16,272
1958	Beverly Hanson	12,639
1959	Betsy Rawls	26,774
1960	Louise Suggs	16,892
1961	Mickey Wright	22,236
1962	Mickey Wright	21,641
1963	Mickey Wright	31,269
1964	Mickey Wright	29,800
1965	Kathy Whitworth	28,658
1966	Kathy Whitworth	33,517
1967	Kathy Whitworth	32,937
1968	Kathy Whitworth	48,379
1969	Carol Mann	49,152
1970	Kathy Whitworth	30,235
1971	Kathy Whitworth	41,181
1972	Kathy Whitworth	65,063
1973	Kathy Whitworth	82,854
1974	JoAnne Carner	87,094
1975	Sandra Palmer	76,374
1976	Judy T. Rankin	150,734
1977	Judy T. Rankin	122,890
1978	Nancy Lopez	189,813

* Approximate Figure

VARE TROPHY WINNERS

The Vare Trophy was presented to the Ladies Professional Golf Association by Betty Jameson in 1952, in honor of the great American player, Glenna Collett Vare.

Miss Jameson requested that this trophy be awarded to the player with the lowest scoring average at the end of each year.

Vare Trophy Scoring Averages are computed on the basis of a player's total yearly score in official LPGA tournaments divided by the number of official rounds she played during the year. A further requirement is that a player must compete in 70 official rounds of tournament competition during the LPGA tour year.

YEAR	PLAYER	AVERAGE
1953	Patty Berg	75.00
1954	Babe Zaharias	75.48
1955	Patty Berg	74.47
1956	Patty Berg	74.57
1957	Louise Suggs	74.64
1958	Beverly Hanson	74.92
1959	Betsy Rawls	74.03
1960	Mickey Wright	73.25
1961	Mickey Wright	73.25
1962	Mickey Wright	73.67
1963	Mickey Wright	72.81
1964	Mickey Wright	72.46

1965	Kathy Whitworth	72.61
1966	Kathy Whitworth	72.60
1967	Kathy Whitworth	72.74
1968	Carol Mann	72.04
1969	Kathy Whitworth	72.38
1970	Kathy Whitworth	72.26
1971	Kathy Whitworth	72.88
1972	Kathy Whitworth	72.38
1973	Judy T. Rankin	73.08
1974	JoAnne Carner	72.87
1975	JoAnne Carner	72.40
1976	Judy T. Rankin	72.25
1977	Judy T. Rankin	72.16
1978	Nancy Lopez	71.76

GALLERY OF CHAMPIONS

ALPHABETICAL LISTING OF MAJOR MEN'S CHAMPIONSHIP WINNERS

Tommy Aaron—1973 Masters.

Jamie Anderson—1877, 1878, and 1879 British Opens.

Willie Anderson—1901, 1903, 1904 and 1905 U.S. Opens.

George Archer—1969 Masters.

Tommy Armour—1927 U.S. Open, 1930 PGA Championship, 1931 British Open.

Laurence (Laurie) Auchterlonie—1902 U.S. Open.

William Auchterlonie—1893 British Open.

John Ball—1890 British Open.

Severiano Ballesteros—1979 British Open.

Jerry Barber—1961 PGA Championship.

James Barnes—1916 and 1919 PGA Championships, 1921 U.S. Open, 1925 British Open.

Tommy Bolt—1958 U.S. Open.

Julius Boros—1952 and 1963 U.S. Opens, 1968 PGA Championship.

James Braid—1901, 1905, 1906, 1908, and 1910 British Opens.

Gay Brewer—1967 Masters.

David Brown—1886 British Open.

Billy Burke—1931 U.S. Open.

Jack Burke—1956 Masters and PGA Championship.

Walter Burkemo—1953 PGA Championship.

Jack Burns—1888 British Open.

Richard Burton—1939 British Open.

Billy Casper—1959 and 1966 U.S. Opens, 1970 Masters.

Bob Charles—1963 British Open.

Charles Coody—1971 Masters.

Henry Cotton—1934, 1937, and 1948 British Opens.

Tom Creavy—1931 PGA Championship.

Fred Daly—1947 British Open.

Jimmy Demaret—1940, 1947, and 1950 Masters.

Roberto de Vicenzo—1967 British Open.

Leo Diegel—1928 and 1929 PGA Championships.

George Duncan—1920 British Open.

Olin Dutra—1932 PGA Championship, 1934 U.S. Open.

Charles (Chick) Evans, Jr.—1916 U.S. Open.

Johnny Farrell—1928 U.S. Open.

Max Faulkner—1951 British Open.

Robert Ferguson—1880, 1881, and 1882 British Open.

Willie Fernie—1883 British Open.

Jim Ferrier—1947 PGA Championship.

Dow Finsterwald—1958 PGA Championship.

Jack Fleck—1955 U.S. Open.

Ray Floyd—1969 PGA Championship, 1976 Masters.

Doug Ford—1955 PGA Championship, 1957 Masters.

James Foulis—1896 U.S. Open.

Ed Furgol—1954 U.S. Open.

Al Geiberger—1966 PGA Championship.

Vic Ghezzi—1941 PGA Championship.

Bob Goalby—1968 Masters.

Johnny Goodman—1933 U.S. Open.

David Graham—1979 PGA Championship.

Lou Graham—1975 U.S. Open.

Hubert Green—1977 U.S. Open.

Ralph Guldahl—1937 U.S. Open, 1938 U.S. Open, 1939 Masters.

Walter Hagen—1914 and 1919 U.S. Opens; 1921, 1924, 1925, 1926, and 1927 PGA Championships; 1922, 1924, 1928, and 1929 British Opens.

Bob Hamilton—1944 PGA Championship.

Melvin (Chick) Harbert—1954 PGA Championship.

Claude Harmon—1948 Masters.

Chandler Harper—1950 PGA Championship.

Arthur Havers—1923 British Open.

Jay Hebert—1960 PGA Championship.

Lionel Hebert—1957 PGA Championship.

Alexander Herd—1902 British Open.

Fred Herd—1898 U.S. Open.

Harold H. Hilton—1892 and 1897 British Opens.

Ben Hogan—1946 and 1948 PGA Championships; 1948, 1950, 1951, and 1953 U.S. Opens; 1951 and 1953 Masters; 1953 British Open.

Jock Hutchison—1920 PGA Championship, 1921 British Open.

Hale Irwin—1974 and 1979 U.S. Opens.

Tony Jacklin—1969 British Open, 1970 U.S. Open.

Don January—1967 PGA Championship.

Robert T. (Bobby) Jones, Jr.—1923, 1926, 1929, and 1930 U.S. Opens; 1926, 1927, and 1930 British Opens.

Herman Keiser—1946 Masters.

Tom Kidd—1873 British Open.

Hugh Kirkaldy—1891 British Open.

Tony Lema—1964 British Open.

Lawson Little—1940 U.S. Open.

Gene Littler—1961 U.S. Open.

Joe Lloyd—1897 U.S. Open.

Arthur d'Arcy (Bobby) Locke—1949, 1950, 1952, and 1957 British Opens.

John McDermott—1911 and 1912 U.S. Opens.

William MacFarlane—1925 U.S. Open.

Fred McLeod—1908 U.S. Open.

John Mahaffey—1978 PGA Championship.

Tony Manero—1936 U.S. Open.

Lloyd Mangrum—1946 U.S. Open.

Dave Marr—1965 PGA Championship.

Robert Martin—1876 and 1885 British Opens.

Arnaud Massy—1907 British Open.

Dick Mayer—1957 U.S. Open.

Cary Middlecoff—1949 and 1956 U.S. Opens; 1955 Masters.

Johnny Miller—1973 U.S. Open, 1976 British Open.

Orville Moody—1969 U.S. Open.

Tom Morris, Jr.—1868, 1869, 1870, and 1872 British Opens.

Tom Morris, Sr.—1861, 1862, 1864, and 1867 British Open.

Kel Nagle—1960 British Open.

Byron Nelson—1937 and 1942 Masters; 1939 U.S. Open; 1940 and 1945 PGA Championships.

Bobby Nichols—1964 PGA Championship.

Jack Nicklaus—1962, 1967, and 1972 U.S. Opens; 1963, 1965, 1966, 1972, and 1975 Masters; 1963, 1971, and 1973 PGA Championships; 1966, 1970, and 1978 British Opens.

Andy North—1978 U.S. Open.

Francis Ouimet—1913 U.S. Open.

Alfred Padgham—1936 British Open.

Arnold Palmer—1958, 1960, 1962, and 1964 Masters; 1960 U.S. Open; 1961 and 1962 British Opens.

Jerry Pate—1976 U.S. Open.

Mungo Park—1874 British Open.

Willie Park, Jr.—1887 and 1889 British Open.

Willie Park, Sr.—1860, 1863, 1866 and 1875 British Opens.

Sam Parks, Jr.—1935 U.S. Open.

Alfred Perry—1935 British Open.

Henry Picard—1938 Masters, 1939 PGA Championship.

Gary Player—1959, 1968, and 1974 British Open; 1961, 1974, and 1978 Masters; 1962 and 1972 PGA Championships; 1965 U.S. Open.

Horace Rawlins—1895 U.S. Open.

Edward (Ted) Ray—1912 British Open, 1920 U.S. Open.

Johnny Revolta—1935 PGA Championship.

Bob Rosburg—1959 PGA Championship.

Alex Ross—1907 U.S. Open.

Paul Runyan—1934 and 1938 PGA Championships.

Gene Sarazen—1922 and 1932 U.S. Opens; 1932 British Open; 1933 PGA Championship; 1935 Masters.

George Sargent—1909 U.S. Open.

Herman Densmore (Denny) Shute—1933 British Open; 1936 and 1937 PGA Championships.

Jack Simpson—1884 British Open.

Alex Smith—1906 and 1910 U.S. Opens.

Horton Smith—1934 and 1936 Masters.

Willie Smith—1899 U.S. Open.

Sam Snead—1942, 1949, and 1951 PGA Championships; 1946 British Open; 1949, 1952, and 1954 Masters.

Andrew Strath—1865 British Open.

Dave Stockton—1970 and 1976 PGA Championship.

John H. Taylor—1894, 1895, 1900, 1909, and 1913 British Opens.

Peter Thomson—1954, 1955, 1956, 1958, and 1965 British Opens.

Jerome Dunstan (Jerry) Travers—1915 U.S. Open.

Lee Trevino—1968 and 1971 U.S. Opens; 1971 and 1972 British Opens; 1974 PGA Championship.

Jim Turnesa—1952 PGA Championship.

Harry Vardon—1896, 1898, 1899, 1903, 1911, and 1914 British Opens; 1900 U.S. Open.

Ken Venturi—1964 U.S. Open.

Roberto de Vicenzo—1967 British Open.

Lanny Wadkins—1977 PGA Championship.

Cyril Walker—1924 U.S. Open.

Art Wall—1959 Masters.

Tom Watson—1975 and 1977 British Opens; 1977 Masters.

Tom Weiskopf—1973 British Open.

Reginald A. Whitcombe—1938 British Open.

Jack White—1904 British Open.

Craig Wood—1941 Masters and U.S. Open.

Lew Worsham—1947 U.S. Open.

Fuzzy Zoeller—1979 Masters.

BEST AMATEUR RECORD—BOB JONES

(Statistics compiled by Bill Inglish. Excerpted from *THE STORY OF THE AUGUSTA NATIONAL GOLF CLUB* by Clifford Roberts. Copyright © 1976 by Clifford Roberts. Reprinted by permission of Doubleday & Company, Inc.)

Beginning in 1916 at the age of fourteen, and ending in 1930 at the age of twenty-eight, Robert Tyre Jones, Jr., played in thirty-one major championships for which amateurs are eligible. His first victory came in the U.S. Open in 1923 at the age of twenty-one. During eight consecutive years, 1923–30, he held one or more major titles every year. In those eight years he entered a total of twenty-eight tournaments, an average of only 3.6 per annum. Twenty-one of these tournaments were major events, an average of 2.5 per annum. He won thirteen of the twenty-one major tournaments.

Jones won the U.S. Amateur five times in thirteen starts, the U.S. Open four times in eleven starts, the British Open three times in four starts, and the British Amateur once in three starts.

Jones averaged 73.61 strokes for fifty-six rounds in the two National Opens, not counting play-offs, and won fifty-nine matches in match-play while losing only ten—almost six out of every seven.

In 1930, Jones captured all four major championships, the British Amateur, British Open, U.S. Open, and U.S. Amateur, in that order. This was golf's Grand Slam. He then retired from competition at the age of twenty-eight.

However, a finer achievement than the Grand Slam, in the opinion of O. B. Keeler, was Jones's performance in the two National Open Championships.

In the last nine years of his career, from 1922–30, Jones played in twelve National Open Championships, nine in this country and three in Britain. He finished first or second eleven times in those twelve starts. The only exception was the U.S. Open at Oakmont, in 1927, in which he tied for eleventh place.

His limited tournament schedule and his effectiveness in competition are underscored by the following chronological listing of his performances:

AGE	YEAR	TOURNAMENT	FINISHING POSITION
14	1916	Georgia Amateur	Winner
		U.S. Amateur	Quarter-finalist
17	1919	Yates-Gode Tournament	Winner
		Canadian Open	Tied for second
		Southern Amateur	Semifinalist
		Western Amateur	Defeated, first round
		U.S. Amateur	Runner-up
		Southern Open	Runner-up
18	1920	Georgia Amateur	Semifinalist
		Davis-Freeman Tournament	Winner
		Southern Amateur	Winner
		Western Amateur	Semifinalist
		U.S. Open	Tied for eighth
		Morris County (N.J.) Invitational	Winner
		U.S. Amateur	Semifinalist
		Southern Open	Runner-up
19	1921	British Amateur	Defeated, fourth round
		British Open	Withdrew, third round
		U.S. Open	Tied for fifth
		Western Open	Tied for fourth
		U.S. Amateur	Quarter-finalist
20	1922	Southern Amateur	Winner
		U.S. Open	Tied for second
		U.S. Amateur	Semifinalist
21	1923	U.S. Open	Winner
		U.S. Amateur	Defeated, second round

AGE	YEAR	TOURNAMENT	FINISHING POSITION
22	1924	U.S. Open	Runner-up
		U.S. Amateur	Winner
23	1925	West Coast of Florida Open	Sixteenth
		U.S. Open	Runner-up
		U.S. Amateur	Winner
24	1926	West Coast of Florida Open	Runner-up
		British Amateur	Defeated, sixth round
		British Open	Winner
		U.S. Open	Winner
		U.S. Amateur	Runner-up
25	1927	Southern Open	Winner
		U.S. Open	Tied for eleventh
		British Open	Winner
		U.S. Amateur	Winner
26	1928	U.S. Open	Runner-up
		Warren K. Wood Memorial	Winner
		U.S. Amateur	Winner
27	1929	U.S. Open	Winner
		U.S. Amateur	Defeated, first round
28	1930	Savannah Open	Runner-up
		Southeastern Open	Winner
		Golf Illustrated Gold Vase	Winner
		British Amateur	Winner
		British Open	Winner
		U.S. Open	Winner
		U.S. Amateur	Winner

18 OF JONES'S U.S. AMATEUR RECORDS STILL STAND

Jones was the outstanding performer in the U.S. Amateur Championship when it was conducted at match-play, and still holds these records:

1 The most titles: five won in 1924-25-27-28-30.
2 The most frequent finalist: seven times, in 1919-24-25-26-27-28-30.
3 The most frequent finalist in successive years: five in 1924-25-26-27-28.
4 The youngest quarter-finalist: he was only 14 at Merion in 1916.
5 The most frequent medalist: six times in 1920-23-26-27-29-30 (this record is shared with Walter J. Travis).
6 The lowest 18-hole score in the qualifying rounds at the championship proper: 67 at Minikahda in 1927. (D. Clarke Corkran set the original record at Merion in 1924, W. B. "Duff" McCullough tied it at Winged Foot in 1940, Skip Alexander at Omaha Field Club in 1941, and Skee Riegel at Baltusrol in 1946.)
7 He never failed to qualify for the championship, either sectionally or at the championship proper.
8 He won the highest percentage of matches: .843 (he won 43, lost eight).

9 He won his 43 matches by the average margin of 6.1 holes.
10 All eight of his defeats were at the hands of national champions.
11 He won the most scheduled 36-hole matches: 35.
12 He won his scheduled 36-hole matches by an average margin of seven holes.
13 He won the most double-figure victories: eight (career).
14 He won the most double-figure victories in succession: three at Brae Burn in 1928.
15 He won the most double-figure victories in one championship: three at Brae Burn in 1928.
16 He achieved the most decisive victory in a scheduled 36-hole match: 14 and 13 over John B. Beck at Brae Burn in 1928. (He shares this record with Jerome D. Travers, who set the original record at the Country Club of Detroit in 1915.)
17 He was the most holes up on opponents in one championship: 42 at Brae Burn in 1928. (In five matches, he had to play only 108 of a possible 144 holes.)
18 He was 32 up on four opponents at Oakmont in 1925, playing only 116 of a possible 144 holes.

U.S. OPEN RECORDS STILL HELD BY JONES

Most Victories—Four. (He shares this with Willie Anderson and Ben Hogan.)

Most Frequent Pacesetter at 54 Holes—Six, in 1922 (tie), 1923, 1924 (tie), 1928, 1929, 1930.

Most Playoffs in Which a Participant—Four, in 1923-25-28-29.

Most Playoffs Won—Two, in 1923-29. (He shares this with Anderson.)

Most Playoff Rounds Played—Seven.

Most Decisive Play-off Victory—23 strokes in 1929. He shot 72-69—141 to 84-80—164 for Al Espinosa, a difference of more than a half stroke per hole.

HIGHLIGHTS OF THE 1930 GRAND SLAM

The four triumphs comprising the Grand Slam required 20 calendar days spread over four months, meaning that Jones had to bring his game to a peak four different times.

The feat required 475 holes—152 in the U.S. Amateur, 143 in the British Amateur, 108 in the British Open, and 72 in the U. S. Open. He played 36 holes or was scheduled to play 36 on 10 of the 20 days—half the time.

For his 12 rounds at stroke-play (four in each Open, two in qualifying for the British Open, and two in qualifying for the U. S. Amateur), Jones averaged 72.5 strokes.

Jones won 13 matches in the two Amateur Championships. He was 32 up over nine opponents in scheduled 18-hole matches, an average margin of three and a half holes, and 30 up on four opponents in scheduled 36-hole matches, an average margin of seven and a half holes.

The key shots of the Grand Slam, in Jones's estimation, were:

- British Amateur (St. Andrews): Holing from 12 feet for a birdie 4 at the 467-yard 17th, or Road Hole, after George Voigt had rolled his 50-foot putt dead for his four. Jones won at the 18th after having been two down with five to play in their semifinal match.
- British Open (Hoylake): A bunker shot that finished two inches away from the flagstick at the 532-yard 16th in the final round, assuring a birdie four.
- U.S. Open (Interlachen): A brassie second in a strong crosswind to the long fourth in the final round. The ball stopped just short of the green, setting up a pitch close to the hole for a birdie four.
- U.S. Amateur (Merion): Holing from eight feet, then Sandy Somerville missing from seven feet at the seventh hole—a drive and pitch—in the first round. Jones was one up at the time. Had the results been turned around, the match would have been square. Jones went on to win, 5 and 4.

BEST PROFESSIONAL RECORD— JACK NICKLAUS

(Statistics compiled by Larry O'Brien and reprinted with permission.)

PERSONAL BACKGROUND

- Born Jan. 21, 1940, in Columbus, Ohio
- Height 5′ 11″; weight 180
- Married the former Barbara Bash, July 23, 1960
- Five children: Jack William II, Steven Charles, Nancy Jean, Gary Thomas, Michael Scott
- Home: North Palm Beach, Fla.
- Club: Muirfield Village G.C., Dublin, Ohio

CAREER CAPSULE
(*Professional Years: 1962 to 1978 inclusive*)

OFFICIAL TOUR VICTORIES: 66

SECOND PLACE OR TIES: 44

THIRD PLACE OR TIES: 30

TOTAL VICTORIES AROUND THE WORLD: 84

TOPS IN CAREER TOUR AVERAGE: 70.3 strokes per round

TOPS IN LOWEST SCORING AVERAGE: 8 times (1976-75-74-73-72-71-65-64); runner-up 6 times

TOP MONEY-WINNER: 8 times (1976-75-73-72-71-67-65-64); runner-up 4 times

TOPS IN CAREER OFFICIAL TOUR EARNINGS: $3,349,393

MOST "MAJOR CHAMPIONSHIPS" TITLES: 17 (Masters 5; PGA Championship 4; U.S. Open 3; British Open 3; U.S. Amateur 2)

PGA PLAYER-OF-THE-YEAR AWARD: 5 times (1976-75-73-72-67)

PLAYOFF TOUR RECORD: Won 12, Lost 8

LOWEST TOURNAMENT RECORDS: All 62's—Ohio Kings Island Open, Oct. 7, 1973 (3rd round); Sahara Invitational, Oct. 28, 1967 (3rd round); Australian Dunlop

Intl., Nov. 5, 1971 (2nd round). (Shot 59 in exhibition with three professionals March 12, 1973, at Palm Beach, Fla.)

INTERNATIONAL AND OTHER VICTORIES:

British Open (3): 1978-1970-1966 (runner-up 6 times)

Australian Open (6): 1978-76-75-71-68-64

World Series of Golf (5): 1976-70-67-63-62 (runner-up 6 times)

Ryder Cup: member of U.S. teams that defeated Britain in 1977-75-73-71 and tied Britain 1969

World Match Play Championship: 1970

World Cup: winner of individual championship a record three times (1971-64-63) and six times a partner on U.S. winning teams

MAJOR CHAMPIONSHIPS RECORDS

As a professional competing in 68 major championships, he has won 15, was second or tied for second 14 times, third or tied for third 9 times—to make it finishing 38 times in Top Three and 52 times in top ten.

YEAR	MASTERS	U.S. OPEN	BRITISH OPEN	PGA CHAMPIONSHIP
1962	15th tie	Won	32nd tie	3rd tie
1963	Won	Missed Cut	3rd	Won
1964	2nd tie	23rd tie	2nd	2nd tie
1965	Won	31st tie	12th tie	2nd tie
1966	Won	3rd	Won	22nd tie
1967	Missed Cut	Won	2nd	3rd tie
1968	5th tie	2nd	2nd tie	Missed Cut
1969	24th tie	25th tie	6th tie	11th tie
1970	8th	49th tie	Won	6th tie
1971	2nd tie	2nd	5th tie	Won
1972	Won	Won	2nd	13th tie
1973	3rd tie	4th tie	4th	Won
1974	4th tie	10th tie	3rd	2nd
1975	Won	7th tie	3rd tie	Won
1976	3rd tie	11th tie	2nd tie	4th tie
1977	2nd	10th tie	2nd	3rd
1978	7th	6th tie	Won	Missed Cut

PROFESSIONAL HIGHLIGHTS YEAR-BY-YEAR
(1962–1978 INCLUSIVE)

1962

First professional start, Los Angeles Open (January 5–8), won $33.33.

First professional victory five months later, United States Open, via 18-hole playoff with Arnold Palmer, 71–74.

Won two other tournaments (Seattle, Portland) and World Series of Golf and runner-up three times (Thunderbird, Houston, Phoenix).

Total winnings (official money): $61,868 for third place plus $50,000 for World Series of Golf victory.

Named Rookie of the Year for 1962.

1963

Won Masters and PGA Championship for the first time.

Also won three other events (Tournament of Champions, Sahara, Palm Springs Classic) and runner-up twice (Crosby, Western).

Captured World Series of Golf second straight year for another $50,000.

Second in final money standings—$100,040 "official" winnings.

Won individual honors in World Cup victory for USA at Paris.

1964

Won money title with $113,284 and four tour events (Tournament of Champions, Portland, Phoenix, Whitemarsh).

Runner-up at Masters, PGA Championship, and British Open, plus Houston, Doral, New Orleans Cajun.

Won Australian Open and individual honors in World Cup victory for USA at Hawaii.

Compiled best stroke-average on tour, with 69.9.

1965

Won Masters a second time with a record 271, breaking Ben Hogan's mark of 1953 by three strokes and winning by nine strokes.

Also took four other events (Thunderbird, Philadelphia, Memphis, Portland) and second at PGA Championship, Canadian, Pensacola, Jacksonville.

Captured money-winnings title for second straight year ($140,752).

Compiled second-straight top stroke-average, with 70.1.

1966

Won British Open to become one of only four golfers in history to take Grand Slam of major championship titles.

Won Masters for third time to become first ever to win two straight years.

Reached the half-million mark in official tour career winnings ($527,364) over a five-year period and second in 1966 with $111,419.

Also won Sahara and National Team Championship (paired with Arnold Palmer with a team record of 32 under par) and runner-up three times (Philadelphia, Thunderbird, Florida Citrus).

Teamed with Palmer to take World Cup in Tokyo.

1967

Won United States Open a second time and created a record of 275 to go along with his Masters record of 271 in 1965.

Awarded Professional Player of the Year title by PGA.

Also took four other events (Western, Westchester, Crosby, Sahara) and runner-up three times (British Open, Thunderbird, New Orleans).

Captured money-winning title for third time ($188,998) and World Series of Golf third time.

Won World Cup with Palmer fourth time, Mexico City.

1968

Won Australian Open and two tour events (Western, American Classic).

Runner-up at United States and British Opens plus Canadian, Westchester.

Runner-up in money standings ($155,285).

Won longest playoff of year, defeating Lee Elder at fifth extra hole in American Golf Classic (one week after winning Western).

1969

Won three tour events (Kaiser, Sahara, San Diego) and second (Hawaiian).

Sahara victory for a record fourth time and Kaiser win via four-man playoff extending in unprecedented period from previous night (due to darkness) to following morning.

Third in year's money standings ($140,167).

Almost reached the million mark in official winnings ($996,524).

1970

Won British Open for the second time, in 18-hole playoff with Doug Sanders (72–73).

Also overseas, won Piccadilly World Match Play Championship.

Took two tour events (Byron Nelson Classic; National Team Championship, with Palmer).

Captured World Series of Golf a record fourth time.

Runner-up three times (Westchester, Crosby, American Classic).

1971

Became first golfer ever to record a "Double" Grand Slam by winning PGA Championship, completing the cycle of major championship victories twice.

Runner-up at U.S. Open, losing 18-hole playoff to Lee Trevino, 68–71, and tied for second at Masters and at Atlanta Classic.

Established new money-winnings record in winning title ($244,490).

Other tour victories: Tournament of Champions, Disney World Open, National Team Championship (with Palmer), and Byron Nelson Classic.

Also won Australian Open, Australian Dunlop International, and World Cup individual honors (a record third time).

1972

By winning the United States Open a third time, tied the late Bobby Jones for major championship titles with his 13th major championship.

Tied the Masters victory record with his fourth win.

Became the first player ever to win over $300,000 in one year ($320,542).

Took over all-time career winnings lead $1,703,705 in 11 tour years.

Also won Doral-Eastern Open, Crosby, Westchester, Disney World, U.S. Match Play Championship, runner-up four times (British Open, Tournament of Champions, Gleason Inverrary, New Orleans).

Named PGA Player-of-the-Year for the second time.

1973

Created golf history by winning his 14th major championship—the PGA Championship, on August 12—and thereby surpassing the late Bobby Jones's career major-titles' record of 13.

Became first player ever to win over $300,000 two straight years and also first to hit the $2-million mark in career winnings (1973 total: $308,362; career official money total: $2,009,168).

Posted the lowest scoring-average of his pro career: 69.81.

Named PGA Player of the Year for the third time and second straight.

Captured seven tournaments: Crosby (for the third time), New Orleans Open, Tournament of Champions (for a record fourth), Atlanta Classic, PGA Championship (third time), Ohio Kings Island Open, Disney World Open (for the third straight time).

1974

Posted the lowest scoring-average of the year: 70.06 strokes per round.

Won the first Tournament Players Championship held and also Hawaiian Open to bring his career total of tour victories to 53.

Had three runner-up finishes (PGA Championship, World Open, and Colonial National) and ended 13 times in top 10 and 8 times in top 5 in 18 events.

Came in second in money standings, with $238,178 (in 13-year pro career, won title six times, second three times, third three times, fourth once).

Remained number one in career tour scoring-average with 70.2 and also in career tour-earnings with $2,243,623.

1975

Won six events, including Masters for a record fifth and the PGA Championship fourth time, to increase major championships total to 16.

In three straight appearances in the spring, won Doral-Eastern Open, Heritage Classic, and Masters; and later in the year, World Open and Australian Open (fourth time), in addition to PGA Championship.

Came in second twice, including playoff loss; third four times (finishing 12 times in top six and 14 times in top ten).

Posted lowest scoring of year (69.8) to win that honor a seventh time.

Captured money title for the seventh time ($298,149).

Named PGA Player of the Year for the fourth time, to tie Ben Hogan.

1976

Won the Tournament Players Championship title for the second time in its three years and the first World Series of Golf under its new format and fifth overall since its inception.

Captured Australian Open for a record fifth time.

Came second three times: British Open, Canadian Open, Doral-Eastern Open.

Won lowest scoring-average for the eighth time, with 70.17 average.

Won money title for the eighth time ($266,438).

Named PGA Player of the Year for a record fifth time (four of last 5 years).

1977

Won three events—Memorial Tournament, Jackie Gleason Inverrary Classic, and Tournament of Champions.

Came in second three times—Masters, British Open, Pleasant Valley Classic.

Finished second in lowest scoring average category and money winnings.

Became the first to go over the $3 million mark in official tour-career earnings after being the first and only player still to have broken the $2 million barrier.

In 19 appearances, including British Open, finished 11 times in top five and 15 times in top ten.

Brought his total of tour triumphs to 63, surpassing Ben Hogan's 62 and taking over second place on the all-time victories' list.

1978

Won five times: British Open, Tournament Players Championship, Gleason Inverrary Classic, IVB Philadelphia Classic, Australian Open.

Victory at British Open marked his third there and 17th major championship, and as a result, he now has won the Grand Slam events three times.

Victory at Tournament Players Championship was his third in its five years.

Victory at Inverrary was his third straight there and was highlighted by five straight birdies on final five holes.

Victory at Philadelphia was his third there and highlighted by equaling the course record of 64 and setting a new tournament record for 36 holes with 12 under-par 130.

Victory at Australian Open was a record sixth there, winning by six strokes and registering his second national championship win of the year.

In 18 appearances including foreign events, finished nine times in top six standings and 12 times in top ten.

Named Sportsman of the Year for 1978 in annual award by *Sports Illustrated*.

OTHER REFERENCES FOR SETTLING FACTUAL QUESTIONS

(See also various other books on tournaments, players, and history listed in Chapters 4 and 10.)

GOLF DIGEST ANNUAL

Golf Digest
495 Westport Avenue
Norwalk, CT 06856

The monthly magazine's February issue (on the stands in mid-January every year) contains a detailed section on current and all-time PGA and LPGA records and performances, and also on important amateur and international events. Updated annually are:

PGA Tour Records
LPGA Tour Records
Hole-in-One Records
Double Eagle Records
Age Shooting Records
Marathon Records
Most Under-Par-Holes-in-Succession
Fastest Rounds
Lowest Rounds
Fewest Putts
Longest Drives

RECORDBOOK OF USGA CHAMPIONSHIPS AND INTERNATIONAL EVENTS

U.S. Golf Association
Golf House
Far Hills, N.J. 97931

Complete results of U.S. Open, Amateur, etc., 1895–1971.

THE GOLFER'S HANDBOOK, edited by Percy Huggins.

The Golfer's Handbook
94 Hope St.
Glasgow, Scotland C.Z.

This prodigious 1,000-page-plus annual hardbound publication carries complete results of the British Open, winners of all major amateur and professional events in the world outside of the United States, brief biographies on outstanding golfers past and present, a 300-page directory of golf associations in Britain and Canada and the rest of the world (except United States), and the complete *Rules of Golf* plus clarifying decisions. In addition to its strictly service and recordkeeping role, the publication devotes 100 or so entertaining pages to a collection of unusual true events in golf history, arranged under numerous headings from "Abandoned Play for War, Rain, Lightning, Snow, Fog and Strikes" to "Youngest Champion." Below is one entry picked at random from the several pages on "Cross-Country Matches."

THE REDOUBTABLE TAIT

On a winter's day in 1898, Freddie Tait backed himself to play a gutta ball in 40 teed shots from St. George's Clubhouse, Sandwich, to the Cinque Ports Club, Deal. He was to hole out by hitting any part of the Deal clubhouse. The distance as the crow flies was three miles. The redoubtable Tait holed out with his 32nd shot, and so ef-

fectively that the ball went through a window. The stake Freddie won was considerably depleted by compensation to a serving maid, who was cleaning silver when the final shot came through the window and put her out of action and into hysterics.

—from *The Golfer's Handbook*

THE WOMAN GOLFER'S CATALOG by Jolee Edmondson. 1979, Stein & Day, $14.95 ($8.95 in paper).

Everything the woman golfer wants to know—history, records, rules, information on handicaps and course ratings, tips on fitness, beauty and equipment, surveys of the amateur, professional and international scene, essays on golf course design and the question of discrimination against women in golf. Illustrated.

THE CONCISE DICTIONARY OF GOLF by Tom Scott. 1978, 256 pages, $9.95, N.Y.: Mayflower Books.

A handy, handsome guide listing and briefly describing the game's most famous players and golf courses. Also contains a detailed lexicon on golf terms and some tournament facts and figures. A couple of the otherwise excellent color photos have been miscaptioned or flopped.

WHO'S WHO IN GOLF by Len Elliott and Barbara Kelly. 1976, 208 pages, $8.95, New Rochelle, N.Y.: Arlington House.

Short profiles on more than 600 players, teachers, architects, writers, etc.

ENCYCLOPEDIA OF GOLF, edited by Robert Scharff and the editors of *Golf Magazine*. 1970, 424 pages, N.Y.: Harper & Row.

Coverage is thorough (up to 1970) and as the following table of contents indicates, comprehensive:

1. History of Golf
2. Major Results of Tournaments & Golf Championships
3. Golfdom's Who's Who
4. Golf Equipment
5. Principles of Golf
6. Rules and Etiquette of Golf
7. Championship Golf Courses
8. Glossary of Golf Terms

GOLF HISTORY HIGHLIGHTS

(Compiled by Peter Dobereiner and reprinted with permission from *Jack Nicklaus' Golf Diary*.)

????

There is no use in pretending. Nobody knows who invented golf or where it started. From the flimsy historical evidence the most plausible theory is that golf evolved as a variation of several club-and-ball games played across country in northern Europe.

1457

The earliest written reference to golf was a royal decree by King James II of Scotland making the game illegal. The reason for the ban by the killjoy king, James of the Fiery Face, was that the Scots had become so keen on the game that they were neglecting their compulsory archery practice. Since every able bodied man was needed at a moment's notice to form a citizen's army to repel the hated English invaders, the golfing draft-dodgers had to be brought into line.

1502

Golf's new respectability was confirmed by the game claiming its first royal addict, King James IV of Scotland, known as James of the Iron Belt. That title had nothing to do with his skill at belting irons; his clubs were almost certainly all woods. The balls he used were also made of wood. The cheapness of the equipment, clubs at a penny each and balls at four pence a dozen, was the factor which enabled everyone from king to shepherd to play the game. There were no formal courses as such; you simply took your clubs to a suitable area of common land, cut some holes, and played. No greens, no tees, no bunkers other than the depressions scraped out by sheep to shelter from the wind.

1618

The feather ball came into its own. There was nothing especially new about balls made from cowhide and stuffed with boiled feathers: the Romans had made such balls for their game of *paganica* (perhaps that is when golf began) a thousand years earlier. The significance of the featherie was that it was expensive and made golf, at least in this improved form, a pastime for the wealthy.

1744

The city of Edinburgh, capital of Scotland, pioneered the first golf meeting, putting up a silver club for competition over the links of Leith (over five holes, all measuring 400 and 500 yards. Three circuits made a round and with their primitive equipment the golfers were delighted to get down in a rare five.)

1764

The first club was formed, The Honourable Company of Edinburgh Golfers. The style of these early clubs confirmed the growing element of elitism in golf. Members in ornate uniforms met once a week to dine at a local tavern, consuming prodigious quantities of food and drink and arranging matches for the morning. Wagers were recorded in the Bett Book to provide written proof of challenges rashly made after the consumption of a gallon of claret.

1779

Golf was played on American soil for the first time, by Scottish officers stationed at New York during the Revolutionary War. Earlier written references, such as the ordinance of 1659 forbidding play in the streets of Fort Orange (now Albany, New York), were almost certainly mistranslations of the Dutch game of *kolven*. Dutch colonists had brought their game with them, and also their distressing habit of playing in the town with consequent unfortunate breakage of windows. At least the Fort Orange offenders were punished only by a fine. Back in Holland, anyone playing *kolven* in the streets was liable to forfeit all the clothes he was wearing at the time and had to streak home.

1848

By a happy accident it was discovered that a ball made from gutta percha, a latex-like substance, could be made to fly much better than the featherie. This innovation had two important consequences: club-making became a refined art with a new stimulus to the evolution of iron-headed clubs; and the relative cheapness of the new ball restored golf as a recreation for the masses.

1860

Members of the Prestwick Club, on the east coast of Scotland, subscribed for a handsome red morocco Challenge Belt, richly ornamented with silver plates, at a cost of thirty guineas, as a trophy for the first professional championship. Eight players entered, completing three circuits of Prestwick's 12-hole course. The winner was Willie Park of Musselburgh with a score of 174. The following year the contest was thrown open to amateurs and became the Open Championship.

1888

A group of American golf enthusiasts joined together to form the St. Andrews Golf Club, of Yonkers, with a course laid out in an apple orchard, giving rise to the nickname of "The Apple Tree Gang."

1894

The growing popularity of golf in America resulted in the formation of the United States Golf Association to regulate the game in the New World.

1901

An American golf enthusiast from Cleveland, Coburn Haskell, perfected a method of making golf balls by winding strands of elastic under tension around a central core and covering it with a gutta percha skin. The Goodrich Rubber Company put the new ball into production and Walter Travis used one to win the U.S. Amateur Championship that year. There had been many attempts to employ rubber in the manufacture of golf balls, notably with a composition ball called the "Puttie," but none had proved superior to the old guttie. The new Haskell opened the way to a huge advance in distance and stroke-making, and led to the introduction of limits on size and weight.

At the same time, the lively Haskell eliminated a rich air of golfing mystique. The old guttie, which could be dipped in boiling water and remoulded, was available in a wide variety of sizes, weights and surface patterns to suit individual preferences, and it was quite an art to judge how long to allow a ball to mature before using it at the optimum degree of hardness.

1904

The first American victory in the British Amateur championship, by Walter Travis, was the first portent of the growing strength of American golf. The shocked administrators of the game in Britain were stung into banning the use of Schenectady (center-shaft) putters, as used by Travis.

1913

Francis Ouimet, a 20-year-old amateur, beat the seemingly invincible British champions, Harry Vardon and Ted Ray, to win the U.S. Open championship. That growing strength was turning into American golfing domination.

1922

The trend was confirmed by Walter Hagen becoming the first American-born golfer to win the British Open championship. Hagen was the prototype of the modern, globe-trotting professional who specializes exclusively in tournament play. He was also significant in the history of the game as the pioneer of the emancipation of the golf pro. Until he came along, the golf professional was basically a club servant and socially regarded as little more than a superior caddy. He was not allowed to enter the club and mix with the members. Hagen changed all that with his flamboyant lifestyle and the force of a personality, which won him the friendship of the Prince of Wales. They had to lower the social barriers for Hagen.

1930

Bobby Jones confirmed his claim to immortality by completing the Grand Slam—British and U.S. Open and Amateur championships—in the same year. Subsequently, the term Grand Slam came to mean the four professional classics, the British and U.S. Opens, PGA championship of America, and the Masters tournament. It was during the period of Jones' brilliant domination of the golfing scene that the steel shaft was pioneered and finally legalized, thus taking golf into the modern era of equipment and golfing style.

1937

American professionals scored their first victory in the Ryder Cup matches in Britain, establishing a pattern which has been broken only twice in the intervening years: a defeat in 1957 and a tie in 1969 in the biennial challenges against the professionals of Britain and Ireland.

1968

Arnold Palmer became the first professional golfer in history to earn a million dollars in prize winnings.

1975

By winning the Masters and the PGA championship, Jack Nicklaus eclipsed the record of Bobby Jones in the major championships with 16 victories and established a record as the most successful professional golfer in the history of the game.